THE COMPLETE HISTORY OF
China

THE COMPLETE HISTORY OF

China

J.A.G. ROBERTS

SUTTON PUBLISHING

This book was first published by Sutton Publishing Limited under the titles:
A History of China: Volume 1: Prehistory to c. 1800
Modern China: An Illustrated History

This new edition first published in 2003 by
Sutton Publishing Limited · Phoenix Mill
Thrupp · Stroud · Gloucestershire · GL5 2BU

Reprinted in 2003, 2004, 2005

British Library Cataloguing in Publication Data
A catalogue record for this book is available from the British Library

ISBN 0 7509 3192 2

Typeset in 11/12pt Joanna MT.
Typesetting and origination by
Sutton Publishing Limited.
Printed and bound in Great Britain by
J.H. Haynes & Co. Ltd, Sparkford.

Contents

Part One

Part Two

Introduction

The Pattern of Chinese History

Early Chinese views of human history were dominated by a belief that there had been a Golden Age in the past, an age when men lived in harmony and peace. Since that time society had degenerated, but there remained a hope that the standards of the Golden Age might be revived. This hope was nurtured by an emphasis on the cyclical pattern of nature, symbolized by the phases of the moon, and a supposition that natural laws governed the course of human affairs. The calendar was based on a sexagenary cycle and historians, relating this pattern to the rise and fall of ruling dynasties, developed the idea of a dynastic cycle. The key element in this cycle was human behaviour and the tendency of humans to stray from moral standards. It was for this reason that the Grand Historian Sima Qian, who lived between 145–90 BC, summarized the sequence of earlier dynasties as follows:

> The government of the Xia dynasty was marked by good faith, which in time deteriorated until mean men had turned it into rusticity. Therefore the men of Shang who succeeded to the Xia reformed this defect through the virtue of piety. But piety degenerated until mean men had made it a superstitious concern for the spirits. Therefore the men of Zhou who followed corrected this fault through refinement and order. But refinement again deteriorated until it became in the hands of the mean a mere hollow show. Therefore what was needed to reform this hollow show was a return to good faith, for the way of the Three Dynasties of old is like a cycle which, when it ends, must begin over again.[1]

As a consequence of this view, and because it became the practice of the scholars of each new dynasty to write the history of the previous dynasty, Chinese historians divided their country's history into dynastic periods. This contrasts with the historical tradition in the West which has perceived events as evidence of linear progression rather than of cyclical repetition. Some western historians have criticized the cyclical concept as a block to an understanding of the fundamental dynamics of Chinese history and have replaced it with linear interpretations.

Before discussing those interpretations, it should be said that some western historians have argued that the concept of a dynastic cycle has some validity if it is regarded as a superficial pattern overlying more fundamental developments. This view was put forward by E.O. Reischauer, who gave some support to the personal and moral basis of the traditional Chinese view. He pointed out that the founder of a dynasty had to be a man of great ability and force, whereas the later rulers of a dynasty, raised in a luxurious and intrigue-ridden court, were more likely to be weaklings. He added that most dynasties did later produce at least one strong ruler who revived the fortunes of the dynasty. For Reischauer this cyclical pattern of political decline might also be observed in the character of the emperor's government, which was initially efficient, but later degenerated because of the increasingly violent struggle between factions at court. However, he considered economic and administrative factors to be more significant than the human element in advancing the dynastic cycle. New dynasties eliminated most of their rivals and established peace. Under these conditions the country prospered, the frontiers were extended and the treasury was full. But as the dynasty continued, the expenses of the government increased and powerful families exerted their influence to evade taxes. The burden of taxation fell more and more heavily on the peasants. As the financial situation deteriorated, corruption became endemic and public works, particularly frontier and river defences, were allowed to fall into disrepair. The last phase of the cycle was marked by incursions across the frontiers, by the collapse of the river defences, by famine, and finally by a peasant uprising which overthrew the dynasty. This led to the emergence of a new dynasty and the inauguration of a new dynastic cycle.[2]

One reason for rejecting the use of dynastic periods to divide up Chinese history is based on the observation that some of the most important transitions have taken place in the middle of a dynastic period, or in a period of division between dynasties. An example of this occurred during the Tang dynasty (618–907), and in the period of the Five Dynasties and Ten Kingdoms (907–60). Almost exactly half-way through the Tang period the An Lushan rebellion inflicted such damage to the dynasty that it never fully recovered. However in the last years of the Tang and under the Five Dynasties – traditionally dismissed as a period of moral and political disintegration – a new type of government emerged and a new system of rule was inaugurated. These innovations were bequeathed to the new dynasty, the Northern Song.[3]

The concept of history as linear progress informs many western interpretations of Chinese history. The best-known example of this is the Marxian view, with its implicit assumption that all human societies follow the same upward path from primitive society, through slavery, feudalism, capitalism, socialism and finally to communism. It has never been easy for Marxists to apply this progression convincingly to the Chinese experience. A great deal of effort has been expended on determining when China was a slave society (supposedly in the Shang period), and when the transition from slave to feudal society took place. More time has been spent on explaining why the feudal period, the beginning of which has been traced back to the time of the Zhou (1122–256 BC) and which is deemed to have lasted until the nineteenth century, lasted so long. To accommodate China's experience of imperialism, the last stage of this feudal period, that is from the nineteenth century to the Communist victory in 1949, has been defined as 'semi-feudal, semi-colonial.'

Some western historians, notably Wolfram Eberhard, applied to China a version of the tripartite division of history into ancient, medieval and modern which has become so deeply ingrained into the western view of the development of European civilization. Eberhard not only subdivided the history of China in this way, but he also characterized each subdivision according to the dominant social class. The first age, from approximately 1600 to 250 BC, was a feudal society, an aristocratic society based on land ownership and military service. The second, the Chinese Middle Ages which lasted from 200 BC until early in the twentieth century, was a gentry society. Eberhard defined the gentry as a group of leading families whose wealth derived from the land, but who also supplied their educated sons to serve in the imperial bureaucracy. The third age commenced with the fall of the empire in 1911, by which time the gentry group was in the process of decomposition, its position challenged by an emerging urban middle class.[4]

Another approach to the periodization of Chinese history is to view the beginning of the modern period as occurring with the arrival of westerners, either with the arrival of traders and missionaries in the sixteenth century, or with the opening of China after the first Opium War. This approach was adopted in one of the most influential two-volume histories of East Asia, that by three American scholars, Edwin O. Reischauer, John K. Fairbank and Albert M. Craig, which had its origin in a lecture course which they had given at Harvard University. They entitled the first of the two volumes *East Asia: The Great Tradition* and the second *East Asia: The Modern Transformation*.[5] The chronological divide between the two volumes occurs early in the nineteenth century. A similar division has been used in this study – although, as will be argued later, an attempt is made to revise the Eurocentric view that that division implies.

Although a line between 'tradition' and 'modern' informs many studies of Chinese history, its ascription to the coming of the westerners has been challenged. The eminent Japanese historian Naito Torajiro proposed what became known as the 'Naito hypothesis.' This claimed that China's modern period really began much earlier, at the time of the Song dynasty (960–1279), for in that period aristocratic society finally disappeared. It was replaced by a society in which the despotic power of the emperor was established and at the same time there was an improvement in the position of commoners, who were no longer slaves (or rather serfs) of the aristocracy. Other important changes which, according to Naito, marked the beginning of the modern period were the selection of candidates for official appointment by examination, the development of a monetary economy and the spread of a vernacular literature.[6]

The Differentness of China

Marx's theory of history assumed that all societies shared a common experience. However, the western view of China has often started from the contrasting premiss that Chinese society is fundamentally different from the societies of the West. In the eighteenth century it was common to find travellers to China delighting in identifying Chinese 'contrarieties'. The list of ways in which Chinese custom was in direct opposition to western practice included the wearing of white to indicate mourning and the reading of books from the 'back' to the 'front'.

The perception of China as a society which is fundamentally different from the societies of the West has led to a dichotomy which has run through much subsequent western writing on China. On the one hand there is the favourable view, which casts China in the role of model for Europe. In the eighteenth century the most famous exponent of this view was Voltaire, who regarded the Chinese manner of government, with its reliance on receiving advice from learned men and its enjoinment of religious toleration, as a model to be emulated.[7] In the nineteenth century this was replaced by a hostile view, but the favourable view has re-appeared twice in the modern era, in the admiration expressed for the Chinese Communists in their wartime resistance to Japan and in the description of the communes and social changes under the Cultural Revolution in the 1960s.

The hostile view depicted Chinese society as oppressive and Chinese history as stagnant. An early expression of this view may be found in Daniel Defoe's *The Farther Adventures of Robinson Crusoe*, published in 1719, in which the Chinese were described as a 'miserable people'. J.G. von Herder castigated China as an 'embalmed mummy'. Hegel, who saw history as a process of spiritual and mental progress, identified China as the place where human progress had begun, but thereafter the consciousness of freedom born in China had moved westwards, while back in China life went on unhistorically, changing restlessly without advancing.

In the nineteenth century the most famous exponent of the negative view of China was Karl Marx. His interpretation of Asiatic society was that it was both different from and inferior to that of Europe. In Asia individual initiative played virtually no role and political activity was stifled by 'oriental despotism'. The characteristic feature of a society was its mode of production, which in the case of Asia was qualitatively different from any of the phases which had marked the development of European societies. The Asiatic mode of production was characterized by two features: at the bottom of the pyramid a multitude of tiny, isolated village communities engaging in small-scale agriculture and handicrafts; at the top a despotic state appropriated part of the surplus produced by the village communities and took charge of public works, especially irrigation.[8]

Marx's ideas were followed up by Karl Wittfogel in his once-influential book *Oriental Despotism*, published in 1957. Wittfogel classified China as a hydraulic society, a type of society not unique to Asia, for similar societies had developed in pre-Spanish America, in East Africa and on Hawaii. Such a society might be compared to, or contrasted with an 'industrial society' or a 'feudal society'. In a hydraulic society the farming economy depended on large-scale, government-managed irrigation and flood control undertakings. Because in a hydraulic society there were no constitutional, societal or cultural checks on the exercise of bureaucratic power, this form of government, as it developed in China, could be described accurately as 'oriental despotism'. According to Wittfogel, China developed the characteristics of a simple hydraulic society as early as the third century BC, and then evolved into what he termed a 'complex hydraulic society'. In such a society, private property and enterprise were tolerated, but merchants and landowners had little influence on the ruling institutions, which in the hydraulic state comprised the autocratic power of the sovereign and the hierarchy of ranking officials and underlings. So society did not change, the state remained the institution of greatest power, and China did not experience the commercial or industrial revolutions of the West.[9]

The idea that the bureaucratic state exerted a baleful influence on the development of Chinese society has been developed by a number of writers. Étienne Balazs rejected the concept of a hydraulic society as too narrow to encompass the complexities of Chinese society, but he agreed that the unlimited power of the imperial bureaucracy had stifled the development of a capitalist economy and had prevented the emergence of a western form of science. This, he said, was the price paid for the homogeneity, long duration and vitality of Chinese civilization.[10]

This view of the nature of Chinese society merges with two other wide-ranging discussions: why did China surrender her commanding lead over the West in terms of technology and why did she not develop as a capitalist society? Critics of theories of an Asiatic mode of production have pointed out that there is plenty of evidence to show that Chinese society was not static, that, for example, there was clear evidence of vigorous growth at various points in Chinese history. Investigation of these periods of growth suggested that the reason why they did not usher in full-scale capitalism was not that the imperial state was overwhelmingly powerful, but on the contrary the state was too weak and too limited to provide the infrastructure which would have enabled capitalist ventures to flourish. The truth may lie between these two extremes. A study of the state and peasant in the inland province of Hunan showed that the state was neither despotic nor laissez-faire. It did intervene in the rural economy, often in a manner that was supportive and constructive, but it did not have the capacity to check the increase in the population of the province, which between the fourteenth and nineteenth centuries rose tenfold; nor could it control the consequences of the commercialization of agriculture, which while beneficial to some were disastrous to many others.[11]

Regional Studies

It is inevitable, in a work of this size, that the emphasis of the discussion will be on national themes, and that as a consequence the history of China will be treated as if it were monolithic. In fact China is a continental country and over long periods it has been subject to political divisions. At times the country has been divided into two (for example under the Southern Song and the Jin dynasties) and at times it has been further fragmented, for example in the so-called period of division, between 316 and 589. At all times regions and provinces, the latter in many cases exceeding European states in size and population, have merited separate treatment. Some of the most interesting work on Chinese history, for example Peter Perdue's investigation of the rural economy of Hunan mentioned above, Richard von

Glahn's study of the Sichuan frontier in Song times, and Hugh R. Clark's assessment of the economic development of southern Fujian, has been set in a regional or provincial context.[12]

Nor can China, either through its long imperial history, or even today, be described as a single economic unit. One of the most influential studies of the Chinese economy was by William G. Skinner, who subdivided the country into eight macro-regions, each containing an economic core area. Each of these macroregions could be distinguished and studied in terms of its population distribution, urbanization, economic activity, etc.[13] This approach has been applied to the eighteenth century, with lively descriptions of the eight macroregions and of Taiwan and Manchuria, descriptions which bring out vividly 'the pluralism and diversity of China.'[14] But this was a pioneering study and to extend its approach across the whole span of Chinese history is well beyond the capacity of this book.

Modern China

The history of China since 1800 is the history of a country which has been racked by rebellion and revolution. It is a country in which old people alive today have witnessed extraordinary changes and in which young people may see China becoming the world's next superpower. This turbulence, and the tensions which arise from so rapid a transformation, have often affected interpretations of the country's recent past.

To write the history of a country which has changed so much in so short a time is a difficult if not an impossible task. A first and major problem is that of the 'angle of perception'. The poet Su Dongpo (1036–1101) once observed that when one looked at a mountain range from one side one saw rolling hills, but from the other side one saw rugged peaks. Chinese historians have often been under pressure to interpret the past in a manner which conforms with the political imperatives of the present. For example, the Taiping rebellion (1850–1864) was regarded with such horror by the Qing dynasty and its Confucianist supporters that not only was its character denigrated, but every effort was made to destroy all record of it, expunging it from history. On the other hand the revolutionary leader Sun Zhongshan (Sun Yatsen) used the history of the rebellion as a weapon in a propaganda war against the Manchus. A generation later the Nationalist leader Jiang Jieshi (Chiang Kaishek) rejected the Taiping revolutionary tradition. He greatly admired Zeng Guofan, the Confucian official who had played a major role in the defeat of the rebellion, and he set out to revive Zeng's memory at the expense of that of the rebels. However when the Communists came to power in 1949 they instituted a major search for surviving documents related to the rebellion and they recorded oral testimony. This material was used to present the rebellion as a class struggle which could not hope to succeed without proletarian leadership, so explaining and justifying the Communist victory. Similar political considerations have affected the perception of many other events in modern Chinese history.[15]

Western historians have also moved from one interpretation of China's past to another. A very general reason for this was supplied by Michel Foucault's power/knowledge concept. In the eighteenth century Voltaire and other French philosophes had described China as a model for Europe, but in the nineteenth century, with the rise of Europe's commercial and military power, the representation of China became increasingly negative. In the twentieth century the pendulum swung between positive and negative images, the latter dominating during the warlord era and the early years of Communist rule, the former during the Second World War, when China was the ally of Britain and the United States.[16]

There are many pitfalls set for the writer of a history of China. One very deep one concerns cultural bias, or 'ethnocentric distortion'. The two last two centuries of Chinese history are bounded by the rise and subsequent decline of western influence over China. In 1785 the first United States' ship reached Guangzhou (Canton), and in 1807 the first Protestant missionary stepped onto China's shores — two events which set the scene for a great increase in the western commercial and cultural pressures on the country. Rather too readily western historians have assumed that the most important theme in modern Chinese history is the 'response to the West', and many books — some of them very good of their sort — have been written from this perspective. Initially the assumption which informed this type of writing was that China's weakness was of her own making and that western imperialism had brought with it the benefits of modernization. From the 1960s this view was challenged, and China's 'problems' were traced to the negative effects of western imperialism. In either case the emphasis remained on western impact and Chinese response. In the 1970s a more China-centred approach became apparent, and an attempt was made - for instance in the context of nineteenth-century Chinese history - to identify the indigenous sources of China's problems and to recognize the imagination and determination which had gone into the search for solutions. This book is based on monographs and primary source material on China available in English and is thus vulnerable to the charge of ethnocentric distortion. An attempt has been made to reduce this risk by making full reference to the revisionist views contained in some more recent writings on Chinese history.[17]

Two problems for the historian relate specifically to the history of China since 1949. In a bibliographical essay written for the *Cambridge History of China*, Michael Oksenberg noted the difficulty created by the discontinuity in the availability of reliable information. This meant that

> The field has not developed in a typically cumulative fashion, with new research building upon previous findings. A major implication of our analysis is that many publications on post-1949 China become dated as new information becomes available. . . .[18]

Many books and articles have been written which contain judgements made in good faith but based on insufficient information — information which may have been withheld deliberately. The most shocking instance of this is the suppression of information on the famine caused by the mistakes of the Great Leap Forward. The restriction of information and the need to revise historical judgements in the light of fresh disclosures is neither a new problem in China, nor one which is unique to the writing of Chinese history. All states impose controls on the release of confidential papers, and when those are finally made public historical interpretations may change. Nevertheless the formidable controls of Chinese official secrecy ensure that the facts of a matter may only become available years later, if at all.

A second problem, one which has beset historians and social scientists, has been that of obtaining permission to do fieldwork. After 1949 western access to China was severely limited, and those scholars and journalists who were allowed to visit the country did so under severe restrictions. It was not until 1978 that a group of American social scientists was allowed to conduct systematic research in the countryside. Even then the problem of obtaining an accurate, objective view of conditions in China remained. As Norma Diamond observed wistfully when reviewing accounts of rural China published in the 1980s, in the wake of the dismantling of the collective economy:

> Even at their best, ethnographical accounts are never unbiased, free of the researcher's own values and judgments, and for those writing about China, the problems of maintaining objectivity seem intensified. We come to contemporary China with social values and political positions that intrude on our work more so than when we researched among the Andamans and Trobriands. . . . [T]he fear or hope of a socialist world is very much with us, and we are not neutral and balanced in our appraisal of socialist societies.[19]

Recent Writing on the History of China

The task of writing a history of China is also made difficult by various practical considerations. An obvious problem is the rapid expansion of the amount of English-language literature being published on Chinese history, and in particular on the history of China over the least two centuries. The annual bibliographic volume of the *Journal of Asian Studies* amply testifies to this. If a single-author synthesis of Chinese history has the advantage of coherence, it has the disadvantage of being based on but a fraction of the material available.

The first editions of the two volumes combined in this book appeared in 1996 and 1998. Since then the flow of works has continued unchecked – one might liken it to the flow of the Yangzi river, but that the Three Gorges dam is about to check that movement, whereas the publication of books remains unabated. It is not possible to refer to all this new literature, but the following selection will give some idea of the range and emphasis of recent historical writing.

For the prehistory and ancient history of China the most important publication of recent years has been *The Cambridge History of Ancient China*. In the 1960s, when John K.

Introduction

Fairbank and Denis Twitchett planned the *Cambridge History of China*, they felt obliged to omit a volume on ancient China because there was not yet any generally accepted synthesis of new archaeological evidence and the written record. Michael Loewe and Edward Shaughnessy have now repaired this omission and in so doing have shown how explosive an effect this new evidence has had on the traditional account. For example, the 'nuclear area hypothesis', the hypothesis that the central sector of the Yellow river, the area of north-west Henan, south-west Shanxi and the Wei river in Shaanxi was the 'cradle of Chinese civilization' is no longer tenable. The identification of other distinct cultures including that at Sanxingdui, near Chengdu, prove that Shang was but one of several contemporary communities and that Chinese civilization had not one but several origins.[20]

On the cultural history of China, one should note Edward L. Davis's study of society and the supernatural in the Song period. Davis suggested the need for a new approach to what has been described as the great transformation of Chinese culture that crystallized at this time. The traditional view is that the Song elite abandoned Buddhism and Daoism as intellectually moribund and embraced Neo-Confucianism which henceforth was to become the dominant ideology, even synonymous with Chinese culture. A revisionist view deplored this development on the grounds that the transformation led to a split between the bureaucratic class and Chinese religions which in the sixteenth century led to an unholy alliance between Confucianism and Christianity. Davis rejected both these views and argued that the Daoist and Buddhist practices of the period deserved study because they revealed a much richer religious life than might be supposed and because they indicated a more complex culture and society than the teleological views indicated.[21]

The publication of the sixth volume of the *Cambridge History of China*, which dealt with alien regimes and border states in the period 907–1368, has prompted a review of the nature of relationship between the Chinese and the peoples of Inner Asia. The term 'sinicization', which was used quite liberally in that volume, has been criticized on the grounds that it implies that 'acculturation and assimilation are unidirectional', that the barbarians were becoming civilized through their acquisition of Chinese culture.[22] This issue was the subject of a notable exchange of views between Evelyn S. Rawski and Ho Ping-ti in the pages of the *Journal of Asian Studies*. In the Presidential Address at the annual meeting of the Association for Asian Studies in 1996, Evelyn Rawski drew attention to the recent use made by scholars of Manchu-language documents and how these documents had transformed understanding of the relationship between Manchus and Chinese. When Ho Ping-ti had discussed this issue thirty years previously he had come to two conclusions: that the Manchu Qing dynasty was undoubtedly the most successful dynasty of conquest in Chinese history. It had laid the foundations of the modern Chinese nation-state - a conclusion which Qing scholars would still accept readily. Furthermore, the key to the Qing success was the adoption by early Manchu rulers of a policy of systematic sinicization. However new scholarship suggested the exact opposite to the second conclusion

the key to Qing success, at least in terms of empire building, lay in its ability to use its cultural links with the non-Han peoples of Inner Asia and to differentiate the administration of the non-Han regions from the administration of the former Ming provinces.

Recent work had shown that rather than quickly becoming sinicized the Qing had superimposed a separate conquest elite upon the Han Chinese bureaucracy and that this elite had continued to participate in the highest councils of state until the mid-nineteenth century. This arrangement was not unusual in Chinese history. For example, although the Liao, Jin, Xixia and Yuan regimes had employed Han Chinese in government service they had each resisted sinicization and had each created their own national scripts.[23]

Ho Ping-ti's responded to this argument by first pointing out that the issue of sinicization was only one of the five salient features of the Qing heritage that he had identified in his earlier paper. He challenged Rawski's argument that the Liao, Jin, Xixia and Yuan regimes had resisted sinicization as evidenced by their creation of their own national scripts – pointing out that the created scripts accelerated the absorption of Chinese culture. He then restated his view why and on what terms sinicization occurred:

long before the rise of Zhou the fundamental criterion for defining membership of the Sinitic world was the awareness of a common cultural heritage rather than rigid racial or ethnic identity.

Ho pointed out that until the tenth century AD the Chinese empire was the product of Chinese expansion and conquest and it was in this period that China became a multiethnic state and the not insubstantial non-Chinese ethnic groups were absorbed into the Chinese polity. After 960 it was the aliens who partially or wholly conquered China, but by then the Chinese had a vast numerical superiority over the invaders. Under the Qing systematic sinicization of the Manchu imperial clan took place. All the imperial princes had to undergo years of instruction in Chinese. The Kangxi emperor performed ritual kotows to Confucius's tablet – 'If this was not a ritualistic expression of the highest possible degree of "sinicization," I do not know what was.' It was the policy of systematic sinicization which enabled Manchu rulers to gain the loyal support of the overwhelming majority of their subjects. It won the Qing court Chinese support at the time of the Taiping rebellion. Only when the court dominated by the Empress Dowager had demonstrated its utter inability to strengthen the nation after defeat by Japan in 1895 did some Chinese begin to advocate the overthrow of the Manchu dynasty.[24]

Two books pursue themes related to sinicization with reference to more recent times. James A. Millward examined the motivation behind Qing policy in Central Asia in the eighteenth and nineteenth centuries. In the eighteenth century the policy had been defined by the Manchu determination to neutralize the Dzungar as a strategic threat and the Qianlong emperor's desire to enhance his reputation. But, according to Millward, in the nineteenth century the Manchu preoccupation with Central Asia also became the Chinese preoccupation.

During its last decades the Qing dynasty struck a bargain to remain in power in China and for security on the borders. The price of that security might be called "Hanization" of the empire. This was not sinicization, the idealized notion that peoples in propinquity to China spontaneously acculturated to its superior civilization, but rather a concrete and traceable process by which Han replaced Manchus and Mongols in positions of authority . . . and Han Chinese population settled frontier regions in increasing numbers.[25]

The issue of Manchu-Han relations was also taken up by Edward Rhoads, with reference to the situation in the late Qing and early Republican periods. He showed how Cixi, the Empress Dowager, realising the danger of anti-Manchu sentiment, tried to undercut the revolutionaries' appeal by reducing the difference between Manchu and Han. However other Manchu leaders, determined to reverse the decline in the authority of central government which had been apparent since the Taiping rebellion, sought not only to recentralize authority but also to 'reimperialize' it, the most notable example of this being the 'imperial kinsmen's cabinet' formed in May 1911. By highlighting these tensions, Rhoads was able to challenge Mary Wright's argument that the broad mass of Manchus had become assimilated by the early nineteenth century and that the ethnic issue was irrelevant in the 1911 revolution.[26]

Understanding of the history of the Ming dynasty has been advanced through the publication of volume 8 of the *Cambridge History of China*.[27] However for a lively discussion of a key issue; the Ming-Qing transition, one should look elsewhere. Richard Von Glahn's *Fountain of Fortune*, provides the first clear summary of monetary money and monetary policy in China between 1000 and 1700. Von Glahn challenged the application of the mid-seventeenth-century crisis argument to China, pointing out that the sharp decline in the influx of silver from abroad, said to have destabilized the Ming dynasty, actually occurred in the 1650s, after the dynasty had fallen.[28] Von Glahn's book was the first of a number of studies by a group of scholars who have been dubbed the 'California School', whose common theme is to challenge what they regard as an Eurocentric view of Chinese history. In *China Transformed* Roy Bin Wong set out to contradict the standard explanation of the 'great divergence' between the East and the West, that it derived from cultural differences between the societies of the two hemispheres. To do this he first compared the economic history of Europe and China, noting that the similarities which prevailed until the industrial revolution in the West. This raised the question, not why China failed to industrialize, but why it occurred first in the West. He then turned to the patterns of state formation in China and Europe and noted a major difference: whereas Europe experienced fierce interstate competition and social conflict between elites, China had no foreign threat and the relationship between elites was harmonious. Finally he looked at forms of conflict common to the two societies; grain seizures, tax resistance and revolutions and considered the similarities and differences in the ways these issues were handled.[29] Wong's theme was explored further by Kenneth Pomeranz in *The Great Divergence*. Pomeranz argued that until the end of the eighteenth century the most advanced Chinese regions, and parts of Japan, India and Southeast Asia, were at least as developed economically as were comparable regions in Europe. But then two fortunate factors allowed the West to industrialize: accessible coal reserves to replace exhausted supplies of wood, and the benefits of overseas colonies, which provided virtually free calories from the sugar/slave plantations and silver to buy Indian cotton and Chinese china.[30]

The Ming-Qing transition and the High Qing periods are the setting for two important studies of the role of women in Chinese society. Dorothy Ko, referring to late Ming and early Qing society, has shown how urbanization, commercialization and the print culture brought women's voices into the historical record, and how through reading and writing, elite women developed new spheres of influence, a progression which bridged, rather than was interrupted by, the change of dynasties.[31] Susan Mann, using the very large corpus of elite women's writing which has survived - mainly poetry written by women living in the lower Yangzi region - explained how in the High Qing period women expanded the domain of learning and creative expression of their Ming predecessors. She also put forward a broader thesis

> Far from being an era of unremitting female oppression, the Ming and Qing periods were dynamic and diverse centuries of social, political, and economic change with profound consequences for gender relations in China. . . .[32]

Three recent books have extended our understanding of the Qing period. Jonathan Spence has produced another fascinating case study, this one detailing the case of Zeng Jing who, inspired by the anti-Manchu writings of Lü Liuliang, in 1728 tried to raise a rebellion against the Yongzheng emperor. The emperor spared Zeng Jing's life in return for his co-operation in compiling *Awakening from Delusion*, which defended the emperor from the charge of having murdered his brothers. However Yongzheng's successor, the Qianlong emperor, reopened the case and Zeng Jing was executed by being sliced to death.[33] Jane Kate Leonard examined the Grand Canal crisis of 1824–1826, concentrating on the response of the Daoguang emperor to the breaching of the Gaojia Great Dyke, the consequent flooding and disruption of traffic along the Grand Canal. She asked was the 'emperor, indeed the whole imperial state, as tentative and faltering at this time' as scholars have tended to assume? Her answer indicated that the crisis, a geophysical problem compounded by neglect, was investigated thoroughly, and the emperor's conclusion, that there was no real solution to the problem, but it could be alleviated by greater use of sea transport, was sensible.[34] On the late Qing period, Barry Keenan's study of the last classical academies sheds an interesting light on effects of the Tongzhi Restoration. The rapid expansion of charitable public schools and local academies, particularly in the Lower Yangzi area, produced a rapidly-growing stratum of underemployed *shengyuan* who, lacking any opportunity for official employment, began to assume an increasingly important managerial role, notably in the field of education. According to Keenan, the very success of the restoration guaranteed the social restlessness of the early twentieth-century reform movement.[35]

Introduction

Two books on the Republican period stand out. In *Awakening China* John Fitzgerald explored nation-building in the 1920s. He suggested that the division between the Nationalists and Communists was not a struggle between Marxism-Leninism and nationalism, but a struggle between two phases of nationalism, 'a conflict over membership of the nation at a time when the nation was still under negotiation. Institutionally, it was a struggle between two highly competitive state-building parties. . . .'[36] A collection of papers delivered at a conference entitled 'Reappraising Republican China' looked in greater depth at some of the issues relating to the Nanjing decade, a notable contribution coming from Frederic Wakeman who coined the term 'Confucian Fascism', to describe the activities of the Lixingshe, the Society for Vigorous Practice, a powerful, secret organization connected with the Whampoa clique.[37]

How the Communists came to power, and in particular how they obtained popular support, is a question which has prompted some very interesting responses. In 1994 Odoric Wou, utilizing research done by Chinese scholars in Henan, asserted that

The Chinese revolution must be perceived as a movement deliberately and systematically fomented, organized, and built by the Chinese Communist Party. It was the outcome of purposive actions taken by the party and the party, in fact, stage-managed the revolution. External elite intervention was therefore a significant factor in the Chinese revolution.[38]

Ralph Thaxton challenged Wou by asking: did the Communists win the countryside or did the Nationalists lose it? He agreed that the Chinese Communist Party had acted as a catalyst, but did not accept that the revolution was the party's creation. He constructed a hypothesis based on his investigation into the salt industry in the Hebei-Shandong-Henan area. In the 1930s the Nationalist government, to pay its foreign debts and finance its modernization projects, put an end to the free marketing of salt and attempted to reestablish a government salt monopoly. According to Thaxton this triggered off 'a broad popular struggle to preserve the market against the aggrandizement of the Kuomintang [Guomindang] state.' The Nationalists alienated the 'marginalized peasants who marketed the salt of the earth for their existence' and thus presented the Communists with the opportunity to win their support.[39] In pursuit of a related theme Pauline Keating revisited Mark Selden's identification of the policies of the 'Yan'an Way' as the key to Communist success. She investigated villages in northern Shaanxi and concluded that the Yan'an Way was not transportable to other parts of China. If it was transported, yet not creatively shaped to suit different circumstances, the results were often disastrous.[40]

Finally, mention must be made of Peter Seybolt's biography of Wang Fucheng who from 1954 to 1984 was Communist Party branch secretary for his village in Henan. This book, which is already being described as a classic, gives a vivid insight into how a man from a humble background, who knew nothing of Confucius, who did not know the names of many of the leaders of the Communist Party and who had never seen a foreigner before Seybolt arrived in his village, played a part in the great events of his day.[41]

To summarize: much recent writing has been characterized by a revisionist turn which rejects, or at least qualifies, four characteristics of much of western writing about China - that it is Eurocentric, implying a tendency to measure China's achievement against a standard of western 'success'; that it is sinocentric, that is it has accepted uncritically the Chinese assumption of cultural authority over her neighbours; that it is too Confucianist, meaning that too much respect has been paid to Neo-Confucian orthodoxy as representing the most important aspects of China's cultural history, thereby obscuring the contribution made by other religions and the many forms of popular culture; and that it has been too willing to accept a teleological view of history, in particular to assume the inevitability of the Communist victory and the explanations for it advanced by the party.

Chronological Table

Dynasties and rulers	Events and personalities
Fuxi (?2852 BC)	
Huangdi (?2697)	
Yao	
Shun	
Xia dynasty (?2205–1776)	
Shang dynasty (?1766–1122)	Shang bronzes
Zhou dynasty (?1122–256)	Zhou feudalism
Western Zhou (?1122–771)	
Eastern Zhou (?771–221)	
Spring and Autumn (771–481)	Confucius (551–479)
Warring States (403–221)	Mencius (372–289)
	Zhuangzi (369–286)
	Xunzi (298–238)
Qin dynasty (221–207)	
Qin Shi Huangdi (221–210)	Li Si and Legalism
	Terracotta army
Former Han dynasty (206 BC–AD 9)	
Han Gaozu (206–195)	
	Mawangdui tomb (c. 168)
Wudi (141–87)	First official examinations
	Sima Qian (?145–85)
	Chinese army reaches Ferghana
	Debate on salt and iron (81)
Xin dynasty (AD 9–23)	
Wang Mang (9–23)	'Nationalisation' of land
	Red Eyebrows' rebellion
Later Han (25–220)	
Guang Wudi (25–57)	Ma Yuan suppresses rebellion in Vietnam (42–3)
	First mention of a Buddhist community in China (65)
	Rise of eunuchs at court
	Threat from Xiongnu and Xianbei
Lingdi (168–89)	Yellow Turban and Five Pecks of Rice rebellions
Three Kingdoms (220–80)	Setting for The Romance of the Three Kingdoms

Sixteen Kingdoms (316–84)
Northern Wei (386–534)

Capital transferred to Luoyang (493)
Buddhist cave temples at Longmen

Southern dynasties (304–589)
Sui dynasty (589–618)
Sui Wendi (581–604)

New capital at Chang'an
Development of examinations

Yangdi (604–18)
Tang dynasty (618–907)
Tang Gaozu (618–26)
Taizong (626–49)

Disastrous campaign against Koguryo

Reintroduction of 'equal field' system
Xuan Zang's journey to India (629–45)
Chinese victory at Issyk Kul (657)

Empress Wu (690–705)
Xuanzong (712–56)

Tang poetry: Li Bo (701–62) and Du Fu
(712–70)
Defeat at Talas river (750)
Rebellion of An Lushan (755–63)
Han Yu's Memorial on the Bone of
Buddha (803)
Ennin in China (838–47)
Official repression of Buddhism (845)
Huang Chao rebellion (874–84)

Five dynasties & Ten kingdoms (907–60)
Qidan Liao dynasty (907–1125)
Song (Northern Song) dynasty
(960–1127) Song Taizu (960–76)

Overwhelmed by Jurchen (1122)
Capital at Kaifeng

Examination system fully developed

Taizong (976–97)
Shenzong (1068–86)
Huizong (1101–25)

Reforms of Wang Anshi (1068–85)
Fang La rebellion (1120–2)
Jurchen invasion of north China (1125)

Jurchen Jin dynasty (1115–1234)

Yellow River shifts to southern course
(1194)
Jin overrun by Mongols (1211–15)
Jin defeated by Mongols (1234)

Southern Song dynasty (1127–1279)

Capital at Hangzhou
Fully convertible paper currency
Neo-Confucian synthesis of Zhu Xi
(1130–1200)

Ningzong (1194–1224)

Dictatorship of Han Tuozhou(1197–1207)
Jia Sidao chief councillor (1259–75)
Southern Song capitulate to Mongols

Chronological Table

(1279)

Yuan (Mongol) dynasty (1279–1368)
    Khubilai (1260–94)

    Yuan drama
    Marco Polo in China (1275–91)
    Construction of Grand Canal (c. 1300)
    Red Turban rebellions (1340s)
    Ming-Han war (1360–3)

Ming dynasty (1368–1644)
    Hongwu (1368–98)

    Execution of Hu Weiyong (1380)
    Yellow Registers and Fish-scale Charts
    Yongle (1403–24)
    Maritime expeditions (1405–33)
    Capital moved to Beijing
    Zhengtong (1435–49; 1457–64)
    Emperor captured at Tumu (1449)
    Construction of Ming Great Wall (1472–)
    First Portuguese reach China (1514)
    First printed version of *The Romance of the Three Kingdoms* (1522)
    Single-Whip tax reform (1531–)
    Manchus capture Fushun (1618)
    Tianqi (1621–7)
    Dominance of the eunuch dictator Wei Zhongxian
    Rebellions of Li Zicheng and Zhang Xianzhong (1640s)

Qing dynasty (1644–1912)
    Shunzhi (1644–61)

    Zheng Chenggong (Koxinga) active on Fujian coast
    Kangxi (1662–1722)
    Oboi regency (1661–9)
    Death of last Ming emperor (1662)
    Rebellion of the Three Feudatories (1673–81)
    Taiwan incorporated into the empire (1674)
    Treaty of Nerchinsk (1689)
    Ding figures frozen (1712)
    Yongzheng (1723–35)
    Reform of tax system
    Qianlong (1736–95)
    Pope issues *Ex Quo Singulari* (1742)
    Wu Jingzi writes *The Scholars* (1740s)
    Chinese occupation of Tibet (1751)
    Maritime trade restricted to Guangzhou (1760)
    Rise of Heshen (1772–99)
    Literary inquisition (1770s)
    Wang Lun uprising (1774)
    Macartney mission (1793)
    White Lotus rebellion (1796–1804)

Preface

This, the first volume of a two-volume history of China, has a specific aim and a limited purpose. It sets out to present a clear introduction to the history of China, making use of recent writings and drawing attention to areas of conflicting interpretation. This emphasis implies the omission of much of the detail which may be found in longer conventional histories. It also implies a limited treatment of important aspects of China's history, notably economic history, regional history and women's history, to name but three. Other topics, for example intellectual and cultural history, have been dealt with on an extremely selective basis.

Nevertheless it is hoped that, within these confines, this book will convey the interest and the excitement which has been aroused by the re-evaluation of Chinese history which has taken place in recent years. One reason why this has occurred is because spectacular archaeological discoveries have been made, which demand a reconsideration of some aspects of early Chinese history. A more general reason is that, in the past, few historians have been able to penetrate beyond the limitations of traditional Chinese historiography and as a consequence the long sweep of Chinese history appeared to be little more than a prolonged and repetitive catalogue of one dynasty following another. This impression of Chinese history no longer applies: detailed and exhaustive studies have been made on a number of themes, historical controversies have arisen, and new heights of scholarship and lively writing have been reached. It would be invidious to cite individual examples of this new wave, but many instances of important recent writings are referred to in the endnotes to each chapter and in the bibliography.

When writing about China, there is a perennial problem of how best to transliterate Chinese personal and geographical names and technical terms. The most substantial modern work on China, the fifteen-volume *Cambridge History of China*, has continued the use of the Wade-Giles system, and this remains the favoured system of romanisation for most monographs on China written in the West. However, since 1949, the official romanisation has been that known as *pinyin*, which is now used regularly in western newspapers and which is slowly gaining ground in academic writing. As it is intended that this book should be accessible to a broad readership, *pinyin* has been used. For the sake of consistency, direct quotations which contain spellings in the Wade-Giles system have been amended to *pinyin*.

For the most part Pinyin spelling approximates to the phonetic values of English, with the following notable exceptions:

c   is pronounced 'ts' as in Tsar

i   is pronounced 'ee', except when it follows c, ch, r, s, sh, z, and zh, in which case it is pronounced approximately 'er'

ian	is pronounced 'ien'
q	is pronounced 'ch' as in cheap
r	is similar to the English 'r' but is pronounced with the tongue behind the front teeth
x	is pronounced 'sh' as in sham
z	is pronounced 'ds' as in hands
zh	is pronounced 'j' as in jasmine

When citing Chinese names, the family name is normally given first, followed by the given name. However, in the endnotes, to maintain consistency with the citation of other names, the western practice of putting the surname last is observed. With reference to Chinese emperors, before their accession they are referred to by their personal names, but thereafter they are designated by their reign titles. For example, the first emperor of the Sui dynasty before he claimed the throne is referred to as Yang Jian, and thereafter as 'the Emperor Wendi', 'the Wendi emperor', or simply as 'Wendi'. When citing non-Chinese names or terms, for example when referring to Mongol or Manchu names, the most common form has been preferred, even if this may lead to inconsistency.

Acknowledgements

I owe a debt to the many fellow historians and librarians who have assisted me over the years and also to the many students who have attended my classes on the history of China and who have sustained my interest in the subject with their enthusiasm. In particular I would like to thank the staff of the University of Huddersfield Library Services for their patience in obtaining the range of books on which the study is based. My thanks go also to Steve Pratt of the School of Applied Sciences at the university for his meticulous work preparing the maps. I am grateful to my colleagues in the Department of History for enabling me to take a sabbatical to complete the task. Finally I must again thank my wife Jan for her forbearance over the years occupied by work on this book.

Part One

1
Prehistoric China and the Shang Dynasty

For long it had been supposed in the West that Chinese civilisation had no prehistory. However, this supposition was swept aside in the 1920s, when the field method of archaeology was introduced into China and important archaeological discoveries began to be made. Since then archaeology has produced a tremendous amount of information on the early history of China. However, much of this information is still in the process of being interpreted and there are many substantial gaps in our knowledge.

Lower Palaeolithic Cultures

The first discovery of remains of early man in China came in 1927, when the Swedish archaeologist J.G. Andersson, excavating sites at Zhoukoudian, thirty miles south-west of Beijing, found human fossil remains including five nearly complete crania. These have been ascribed to *Sinanthropus pekinensis*, otherwise known as Beijing man, who possessed hominid features: erect posture and considerable cranial capacity and the capability of making tools and implements, but who was distinguished from *Homo sapiens* by the low skull vault, the great thickness of the skull wall and by other features which made him a relation of *Homo erectus* of Java. From the associated deposits it was apparent that Beijing man hunted deer and possibly made fire and cooked his meat. He was probably a cannibal, eating the flesh, brain and marrow of his own kind. He used vein quartz to make a variety of implements and it has been suggested that the range of artefacts he made is more like the assemblages of southern and eastern Asia than those of Europe and Africa. But this suggestion and another which proposes a morphological link between Beijing man and the modern Mongoloid populations has not been generally accepted. It is not possible to apply new scientific techniques to these fossil remains because they disappeared, en route to the United States, shortly after the attack on Pearl Harbor.

In 1963, and in subsequent years, more early human remains were found in the vicinity of Lantian in eastern-central Shaanxi, about 1,000 kilometres south-west of Zhoukoudian. These remains, although closely related to Beijing man, were more primitive, the cranial capacity being considerably smaller. No habitation sites were identified in connection with these remains, although some stone implements were found which may be associated with them. Stone implements of comparable age have been found at a number of sites near Ruicheng in south-western Shanxi. There is also evidence of human occupation of about the same date at several localities in South China.

Middle and Upper Palaeolithic Cultures

Only a limited number of Middle Palaeolithic sites have been found in China, the most notable being those of the Ordos region and the Fen river valley in Shanxi. It is not clear whether the Middle Palaeolithic transitional stage also occurred in South China.

Much more is known of the Upper Palaeolithic period. In North China sites of this period have been uncovered throughout the Ordos region, that is to say the northern grasslands of the middle Yellow river, and these have become known collectively as the Ordosian culture. Not a great deal of evidence of the physical characteristics of Upper Palaeolithic man is available. The Upper Cave at Zhoukoudian contained three skeletal remains, which yielded a radiocarbon date of 16,922 BC. These remains have been described as 'pre-Chinese', 'un-specialised' Mongoloids resembling American Indians. But information on Ordos stone industries is substantial: at one site in Shanxi more than fifteen thousand pieces of stone implements and flakes were found. The blade artefacts of the culture are identical with the Perigordian and Aurignacian types of western Europe, and exhibit a clear tendency to specialise. Composite implements made of bone shafts and microlithic implements are known and regional variations have been recognised. A number of other Upper Palaeolithic sites have been discovered in south-western China.

The evidence relating to Upper Palaeolithic man in China has given rise to controversy over the origin of the Mongoloid branch of living man. In 1943 Franz Weidenreich and then in 1962 Carleton Coon argued that there was a genetic continuity from Beijing man to modern Mongoloids on the basis of common cranial and dental features, for example shovel-shaped incisors. They proposed that Beijing man was ancestral solely to the Mongoloids and that separate contemporaneous early hominids were ancestral to the other races of present-day man. The alternate view is that all modern men have a common ancestor who was later than Beijing man. Modern Chinese may have developed by direct descent from the people of the Upper Cave at Zhoukoudian, but there is as yet a lack of evidence to bridge the gap between Palaeolithic man and Neolithic man in North China, who displays physical characteristics apparently indistinguishable from the modern Chinese.

Neolithic man in China

It was long commonly believed that the Neolithic way of life – characterised by reliance on farming for food, by the use of pottery, and by the making of stone implements by grinding – had not commenced in China until the third millennium BC, and that it had been diffused to North China from western Asia.

However, from the 1950s archaeological discoveries provided evidence of an indigenous Neolithic culture in North China. In the 1960s evidence was found to indicate the existence of parallel Neolithic cultures on the south-eastern coast (the Dapenkeng culture) and the lower Yangzi and Huai river areas (the Qinglian'gang culture).

All three cultures have been the subject of a considerable amount of excavation and writing and the importance of all three has now been established. Nevertheless, the best-known Neolithic sites remain those of the Yellow river valley. The first discovery was made in 1920 by farmers of Yangshao village in northern Henan, near the great bend of the Yellow river. Subsequently, hundreds of sites identified with the Yangshao culture were found over a large area of the Yellow river valley. Typically, Yangshao culture was one practised by settled farmers, living in villages sited in the valleys of the Yellow river drainage system. They cultivated foxtail millet and, to supplement their diet, they collected wild grain and went hunting and fishing. They had domesticated dogs and pigs and a few cattle, sheep and goats, and they may have grown hemp and raised silkworms.

The best-known Yangshao site is that of Banpo near Xi'an in southern Shaanxi. It was a large village which experienced several successive periods of occupation, which has been taken to indicate that its inhabitants practised shifting cultivation, moving away from the village site when the land had been temporarily exhausted and returning when it had recovered. It was quite a large village, containing perhaps one hundred houses, and it was surrounded by a ditch. The houses were of a fairly permanent construction, with plastered floors, wattle-and-daub walls and roofs supported on wooden posts. In the latter period of occupation a longhouse was constructed in the centre of the village. At the east end of the village was a pottery centre and to the north the village cemetery. From the evidence of the longhouse and the arrangement of the cemetery, it has been suggested that the inhabitants had lineage and clan types of kinship grouping and that they had already initiated the cult of ancestors to symbolise lineage solidarity.

The best-known production of the Yangshao culture is its ceramics and in particular the painted pottery used at meals and for rituals. This pottery is handmade and moulded and there is some indication of the use of coiling techniques, but not of the wheel. The decoration is concentrated on the upper part of the vessel and usually comprises abstract designs of large joined spirals. In a few cases schematic human figures or fish are represented.

Outstanding examples of Yangshao pottery have been described as the finest artistic achievement of the Neolithic period in China – so remarkable that it has seemed difficult to explain the sudden and indigenous emergence of so sophisticated a culture. When J.G. Andersson first attempted to classify the regional variations of the pottery which had been found over a wide area of North China, he considered that the Gansu pottery of the far north-west was the oldest regional variety. This led him to suggest that Yangshao culture had come from the West and had reached China through the Gansu panhandle. This supposition was supported by apparent similarities between Yangshao pottery and the decoration of pottery of a similar age found in Turkestan. However, extensive excavation of

Yangshao sites, and in particular of Majiayao, has shown conclusively that the Gansu pottery is of a later date than that of the Zhong Yuan, or Central Plain, area of the Yellow river valley. Moreover, it is now known that the Yangshao culture, or more correctly its forerunners, is a good deal older than Andersson had supposed, and dates back to the sixth millennium BC. It seems to have originated in the nuclear area of central Shaanxi, south-western Shanxi and western Henan, and this strengthens the implication that it grew out of the terminal Palaeolithic and Mesolithic cultures of the area, although the links have yet to be established. In short, the derivation of Yangshao culture from the Middle East is no longer a tenable theory. What is now a matter of debate is the relationship between the regions in China where Neolithic cultures developed.

In 1928 the site of Chengziyai, in north-west Shandong, was first excavated. This village appeared to differ from the Yangshao culture villages, in that it was surrounded by a defensive wall of stamped earth. The design of the houses too was somewhat different and the inhabitants made greater use of polished stone implements. Most strikingly they produced a distinctively different type of pottery, which was thin, hard and burnished black, with angular shapes rather than the rounded contours of Yangshao pottery and which showed the beginnings of the use of the wheel. This culture has become known as Longshan, after another site in Shandong.

At first archaeologists recognised the Longshan culture as distinct from that of Yangshao and regarded it as localised in the east, whereas Yangshao was the Neolithic culture of the Central Plain – an interpretation which became known as the 'two-culture theory'. However, when the site of Miaodigou II was excavated, Longshan pottery was found at a level above that of the painted pottery. Consequently a second theory, the 'nuclear theory' was propounded which proposed that the Longshan culture was later than the Yangshao and that in fact it derived from it. However, this interpretation was difficult to reconcile with the evidence of the pottery: Longshan pottery is unpainted and many of the vessels are footed, unlike the Yangshao ware. This led to the view that the appearance of Longshan ware was evidence of the intrusive influence of a different and unrelated culture – a view which was confirmed when carbon-14 dating became available. It has been suggested recently that the true relationship between the two cultures is that Longshan culture was long established south of the Yellow river, that it extended into the Central Plain and that in its later development it became the dominant culture of the region.[1]

The Xia dynasty

According to early Chinese historians, and in particular to Sima Qian, who died in about 90 BC, Chinese history began with a sequence of three early rulers, followed by a succession of five emperors. The first of the three rulers was Fuxi, whose reign traditionally began in 2852 BC, and who was credited with the domestication of animals and the institution of family life. The third was Shennong, the divine farmer, who taught the people settled agriculture. These figures, who were described as half-human, half-animal, were clearly mythological. Their successors, the five emperors, were culture heroes. Huangdi, the Yellow Emperor, supposedly reigned from 2697 BC. It was he who introduced ceramics and writing. The fourth and fifth emperors of the sequence, Yao and Shun, were particularly esteemed as model rulers. Yao was said to have devised the agrarian calendar. Regarding his son as unworthy of the throne he appointed as his successor Shun, a poor peasant renowned for his devotion to his father, and he in turn became a model ruler. Shun continued Yao's practice and also chose a paragon, a man named Yu, as his successor. It is at this point that Chinese history begins to supplement the archaeological record, because Yu was believed to have founded a dynasty called the Xia, the traditional dates of which are 2205–1766 BC.

The Xia was the first of the three ancient dynasties, sometimes known as the *sandai*. The other two were the Shang and the Zhou, whose recorded dates were respectively 1766–1122 BC and 1122–256 BC. Chinese historians traditionally regarded these dynasties as sequential, each dynasty being overthrown by its successor. A recent evaluation of their relationship in the light of archaeological evidence suggests that they were only successive in terms of their relative political eminence, that Shang was already a powerful political entity prior to its subjugation of Xia, and Zhou was an important state before its overthrow of Shang. According to this interpretation the geographic dominion of the three dynasties may be accepted as having been Xia in the centre, Shang in the east and Zhou in the west. They are regarded as having shared essentially the same culture.

This re-evaluation has supported the view that the Xia dynasty, which was long regarded as belonging to legend rather than to history, did exist at approximately the times given in the early records. The late Central Plain Longshan culture has been dated to about 2000 BC, and the obvious inference is that the two are identical. In particular, the culture found at Erlitou, east of Luoyang in Henan has been identified with the Xia. Further, the evidence of pottery typology is consistent with the view that the Henan Longshan culture was the predecessor of the Erlitou culture.[2]

The Shang dynasty

According to tradition the Shang dynasty was established in 1766 BC when Cheng Tang – Tang the Completer – overthrew the tyrannical last ruler of the Xia and restored humane and virtuous government to the empire. Archaeological evidence has not confirmed this, and the dates of the Shang dynasty and the circumstances of the transition from Xia to Shang dominance are uncertain. One particular issue which remains unsolved is whether the important sites discovered in 1950, at Zhengzhou in northern Henan, belong to the early Shang or should be identified with the previous dynasty.

Despite these uncertainties there can be no doubt that the Shang dynasty, which shared a common culture with the Xia and which probably had its centre of activity somewhat to the east of the Xia sphere of activity, replaced the Xia as the most powerful political entity in north China between the dates ascribed to it by tradition. During that time the dynasty occupied a series of capitals, the most famous of which was Anyang in north Henan, the site of which was initially excavated between 1928 and 1937. It was this excavation which determined once and for all the historic existence of the dynasty, which previously had been accredited only by legends. Not only did these excavations produce extensive information relating to the physical features of the Shang capital, they also uncovered very substantial quantities of inscriptions on bone and bronze which have made it possible to build up a detailed picture of the nature of the Shang state as it existed in the middle and late Shang dynastic periods.

This state was a form of theocracy headed by a succession of kings whose main functions were probably ritual rather than political. The throne was passed from elder brother to younger brother as well as from father to son in a succession of thirty rulers. Their names were recorded by Sima Qian and their existence has been substantiated by archaeological finds. Rulers were served by officials whose titles indicate that they performed a variety of specialised functions. Although Shang culture spread over a large area of north China, it is unlikely that the control of the Shang kings extended nearly as far. What is more probable is that over much of the area authority was exercised by aristocratic leaders who accepted to some extent the leadership of the Shang kings, but who ruled in their own areas. These leaders defended the frontiers of Shang territory, supplied the manpower required for both military and construction purposes and collected tribute for the court. Surrounding the area of established and permanent Shang authority there was an outer zone ruled by tribal chieftains, friendly to the Shang, whose authority over their own people had been confirmed by investiture according to Shang political theory.[3]

At Anyang, in the enclave at Xiaotun, was situated the ceremonial and administrative focus of the Shang state. This comprised three sections, the functions of which are believed to be understood. The most northerly and perhaps the oldest section consisted of fifteen rectangular houses on stamped-earth foundations, which have been taken to be the residences of the ruling élite. The middle section contained twenty-one halls, constructed above a complex system of drainage channels and a large number of human burials. These are believed to have been the ancestral temples of the royal lineages. The most southerly section was the site of seventeen stamped-earth foundations, considered to have been the ceremonial heart of the enclave. This included a stepped structure which was almost certainly the foundation of a sacrificial altar. The scale of these structures, the evidence of elaborate planning, the extensive sacrifice of humans, the use of stamped-earth techniques and the innumerable oracle bones found on the site all point to this being the ceremonial centre of the royal house of the Shang dynasty.

About three kilometres north of Xiaotun is the site of Xibeigang, described as the royal cemetery of the Shang monarchs. The excavation of this site has revealed eleven very large cruciform graves and 1,222 small graves. It has been suggested that these are the graves of the eleven Shang kings who are recorded as having ruled from Anyang over a period of 273 years, and it has been estimated that the digging of each pit required at least seven thousand working days. The excavation of these graves has provided the most dramatic evidence of the nature of Shang kingship. The burials were accompanied by a large number of human sacrifices, the bodies, frequently with heads and torsos separated, being found around the central chamber and on the ramp leading down to it. The royal tombs contained a rich selection of Shang art. In the best known tomb, number 1001, was found an outstanding collection of stone sculptures and bronze artefacts.

Shang Bronzes

This mention of bronze artefacts leads naturally to a discussion of one of the outstanding cultural achievements of the Shang period, that is the production of ceremonial bronze vessels which are remarkably sophisticated in terms of both technology and design. Chinese collectors had long identified the Shang period with the production of these vessels, but it was only with the excavation of Anyang that this ascription could be proved correct. However, the initial response to the discoveries by western archaeologists, who were puzzled by the lack of any examples of more primitive bronze casting, was that the technology for the creation of the bronzes must have derived from outside China, that is from west Asia.

More recent studies[4] have greatly strengthened the argument that the beginning of metallurgy in China, even though it came much later than in the West, was the result of an indigenous discovery. In the case of bronze technology, the particular argument which has been put forward is concerned with the technical repertoire of the Shang craftsmen. Noel Barnard pointed out that early Chinese bronzes show that craftsmen were acquainted only with direct casting in piece-mould assemblies and the casting-on to the vessel of pre-cast members such as handles and lugs; they knew nothing of sheet metal working, annealing and other techniques and did not use many of the tools which had appeared in the West. When it came to casting, Chinese craftsmen outclassed their western counterparts, but in the more general field of metal technology they lagged far behind. This, and the indication that the forms of Shang bronzes appear to derive from pottery styles, amount to strong evidence in support of the view that the Shang bronzes were the result of independent development.

Apart from the discussion relating to the origin of bronze technology, the principal interest of the bronzes relates to their aesthetic qualities and the indications which these offer of the nature of Shang society. Much of the production of bronze items was connected with conspicuous consumption. The main categories of production were ritual vessels, luxury items sometimes to be deposited in tombs, and weapons. Various classifications of these items have been made and chronological and stylistic sequences have been suggested. The high point of sequence is seen as coming in the late Shang and early Chou period. One of the characteristic forms was that of the *jue*, a ritual vessel standing on three legs, apparently intended for the warming of wine. The surfaces of these vessels and other ritual vessels were commonly covered with stylised surface decoration, the most common motif being that of a mythical creature lacking a lower jaw, known as the *taotie* mask.

Many of the vessels carried an inscription which indicated the reason why they had been cast and the purpose to which they were to be put. Vessels were often cast for the performance of sacrifices to ancestral spirits. As time passed inscriptions tended to become longer and by the early Chou period there are many examples of inscriptions which recorded that the vessels had been cast by persons who had received gifts from their feudal superiors and were to be used in ceremonies to reinforce that relationship.

The Development of Writing

It was in the Shang period that the Chinese system of writing became fully established. Examples of incised potters' marks go back to the Banpo site and to the Yangshao culture of the fifth millennium BC. It is uncertain whether these marks should be taken as among the earliest forms of Chinese characters, as similar markings are found elsewhere on neolithic pottery. However, pottery from Jiangzhai, Lintong *xian*, for which the date 4000 BC has been proposed, is inscribed with graphs which appear to have broken away from the simple single-element structures of the inscriptions at Banpo and to be sufficiently advanced in structural form to be regarded as primitive characters.

Pottery sherds from Dawenkou culture sites, which have been dated between 3000 and 2500 BC, carry inscriptions which go beyond primitive marks or pictorial representations of objects to include composite ideographs which convey concepts such as 'morning' or 'hot'. As such composite ideographs have been found on two different sites, it has been suggested that the meaning of the graphs was widely understood by people of that time. Here, it appears, is the beginning of a form of writing which could transcend differences of dialect. Moreover, here too is important indirect evidence of the independent development of the Chinese writing system. Simple ideographs have been used at various times in various cultures worldwide, and although there is no evidence to support the suggestion, it might be supposed that the art of writing had been diffused to China from the West. However the composite ideograph, which brings together several elements to form a single graph, is the essence of the Chinese writing system. Its early appearance in the context of the development of pottery inscriptions strongly suggests an indigenous origin. Moreover, the emergence of this writing system in the nuclear area implies the subsequent centrifugal diffusion of the system throughout the Chinese sphere.[5]

In the Shang period the written record of inscriptions on pottery and bronze vessels is greatly augmented by the survival of writing on bone, turtle shells and bamboo. The bone inscriptions are often to be found on the shoulder blades of cattle or sheep, which were used for a form of divination called scapulimancy, a practice already established in the Longshan culture. The divination consisted of interpreting the cracks which appeared in the bone after it had been heated. In the

Shang period this became a sophisticated practice. The bone was treated in advance and questions were inscribed to be answered by interpreting the cracks which appeared subsequently. These oracle bones are evidence of the ceremonial practices of the time and an indication of the presence of a specialist group of augurs. To date, at least 107,000 oracle bone pieces have been assembled in more than eighty collections. Three thousand separate graphs have been identified, about half of which may be translated with varying degrees of accuracy.[6] The inscriptions which the bones bear provide much of what is known about the organisation of the Shang state.

The Shang State

Much of our knowledge of the Shang state refers to the Late Shang or Anyang period dating from approximately 1200 BC to 1040 BC. At that time the state had its main centres along the Yellow and the Huai rivers and exercised some authority up the Wei river valley in the territory to be known as the Zhou homeland.

Within this area and between these dates, the Shang rulers presided over a form of patrimonial domain. According to Paul Wheatley, who first elaborated this interpretation of the Shang state,[7] it operated through a combination of traditionalism and arbitrariness. The king regarded himself as the earthly instrument for the accomplishment of Heaven's designs. His lineage occupied a central position in the state's political, economic and ceremonial structures. The ruler treated all political administration as his personal affair and the officials, whom he had appointed on the basis of his confidence in them, performed their duties as a form of personal service to the ruler. The officials fell into three groups: the first comprised the secretariat – the councillors, including the great minister, who were in charge of agriculture (that is to say the arrangement of the agricultural calendar), the management of palace affairs, and the organisation of feasts and other matters; in this group too were the diviners and ceremonial specialists, including the court chroniclers. The second group was that of the civil officers who were appointed to various offices and who were distinguished according to rank. Finally there were military officials, who also had specified duties.

The above was the organisation of the royal domain. However, it is clear that in the Late Shang state authority was delegated by granting benefices in return for services rendered to the throne. The holders of benefices were granted titles, in return for which they performed certain duties, in particular the defence of Shang territory by the supply of manpower for military and construction purposes and by the collection of tribute for the court. It is interesting to note that a number of women were beneficed under these arrangements. In addition to these benefices, there was an outer ring of territories held by chieftains friendly to the Shang, whose authority was confirmed by investiture according to Shang political theory. This practice illustrates the process of sinicisation, the process of becoming Chinese, which was reinforced by the spread of the written language and the performance of cults related to ancestors.

Even allowing for the power of the Shang ceremonial, it is clear that the Shang state exercised only a limited control over much of the territory which lay under its influence. A recent analysis of oracle-bone inscriptions has provided fascinating, if incomplete, detail of the functioning of its authority.[8] The coercive power of the state derived from the king's armies and those of a few close supporters, and there are numerous divinations on the possible outcome of sorties made by these forces. However, the Shang diviners did not divine about expeditions which did not involve the king as well as his allies. This is taken as evidence that the military power exercised by the Shang state was dynastic: the allies of the Shang would only fight if the king fought beside them. State power was exercised in the capital and in the few places which were regularly visited by the king. Elsewhere the state might be seen as a thin network of pathways and encampments laid over a hinterland which rarely knew the king's presence.

A particular example of the nature of Shang authority, and one which is of especial interest because of subsequent developments, concerns the relationship between the Shang state and the people of Zhou who probably lived north of the Wei river. Many of the divination inscriptions refer to the Zhou in terms which imply that they were members of the Shang state: for example, they received orders from the king. On the other hand, it is clear that the Zhou were not at the heart of the Shang state, and the Shang had little direct contact with them. One reason for this was distance, the Zhou centre being 625 kilometres from Xiaotun, but the relationship also underlines the argument that the Shang state, if such a term is acceptable, exercised only a limited influence over the territory with which it is associated. Perhaps it should be described as an incipient state, a dynastic lineage, ruling in a patrimonial style over a central and perhaps shifting nucleus, and exercising intermittent influence over surrounding groups.

Shang society showed considerable class differentiation. At the top was an élite comprising the king and the royal lineages. There is evidence of an aristocratic culture in some of the burials and it is clear that military skills were valued. The Shang army comprised two main corps, one of infantry and one of chariots, and some aristocratic tombs contain chariot burials. The evidence of the use of chariots, either for hunting or for war, provides the strongest proof of direct contacts between China and the West. Although the domesticated horse had been known in Mesopotamia from the first half of the third millennium, it only became popular and was used to draw a war chariot from about 1500 BC. A mere two and a half centuries later the use of the horse chariot in China was recorded on oracle bones. Moreover, the design of the Shang horse chariot closely resembled that developed in the West.[9]

Below the aristocracy was a specialist group composed of craftsmen, and particularly those who worked in bronze. It seems probable that particular handicrafts were the prerogative of individual kinship groups. These artisan groups had a lifestyle which set them apart from the peasantry. In particular they lived in above-ground stamped-earth buildings, containing two rooms and sometimes provided with a window, altogether much superior to the dwellings of the peasants.

At the bottom of the social pyramid were the peasants. It has often been alleged that Shang society was a slave society and for Marxist historians this description has been axiomatic. There certainly was a great gulf between the aristocracy and the peasants. Peasants lived in primitive semi-subterranean dwellings. Their burials were extremely simple and contained only the most meagre display of possessions. The evidence of the great tombs, the construction of which required many thousands of man hours, and of the numerous human sacrifices – usually found in multiples of ten, offers some support for the slave society view. However, most western writers have rejected that interpretation and have argued that peasants were not slaves but serfs. In some cases, at least, those sacrificed were prisoners of war, sometimes found to be suffering from malnutrition.

2
The Zhou Dynasty

By tradition, the Zhou dynasty is dated from 1122–256 BC[1] and this immensely long period is subdivided into three parts: the Western Zhou period, 1122–771 BC, the earlier part of the Eastern Zhou period, from 771–481 BC, which is known as the Spring and Autumn period after a work of that name which records the events in the state of Lu in those years; and the Warring States period, which lasted from 403–221 BC. This era has long been regarded as the crucial formative stage in Chinese history. Of it Herrlee G. Creel once remarked, 'It would probably be generally agreed, for most practical purposes that the Chinese tradition may be said to have begun with the Zhou'.[2]

The Western Zhou

According to the tradition enshrined in the historical record, the overthrow of the Shang dynasty and its replacement by the Zhou came about because of the transfer of the mandate of heaven. The Zhou rulers were granted the mandate to enable them to rescue the suffering people from the wicked last king of the Shang. In the account given by Sima Qian, in the *Shiji*, the *Historical Records*, compiled a thousand years later, the Zhou ruler the Earl of the West, otherwise known as King Wen, was a paragon of virtue. He excited the jealousy of the last Shang monarch, who, on one occasion imprisoned him. When King Wen died his son King Wu, known for his martial qualities, attacked the Shang and overthrew them. The account of the conquest which has been handed down indicates that events took a dramatic turn. The Zhou troops numbered only 50,000 and they were met by a Shang army of 700,000 men. However, the Shang troops revolted against the cruelties of their ruler and went over to the other side. The last Shang ruler died amidst the flames of his palace.

Other scraps of evidence do not add a great deal to the traditional account. It is likely that the Zhou state was populated by people who had not completely accepted Shang culture. According to Mencius, 'King Wen was a Western barbarian'.[3] A more exact interpretation of Zhou ethnic origins was put forward by Wolfram Eberhard, who suggested that the ruling house of Zhou 'may have been related to the Turkish ethnic group'.[4] However there is no linguistic evidence to support this theory. The archaeological evidence suggests that the Zhou may have displayed some cultural differences, perhaps because they had developed their state in harsher surroundings. Nevertheless, they derived from the same Longshanoid culture which had produced the Shang. Relations had existed between Shang and Zhou over a number of generations. By the reign of King Tai, grandfather of King Wen, it is evident that a degree of sinicisation had already taken place and Zhou rulers may have accepted Shang overlordship. The reason for the Zhou attack on the Shang state may never be known, but the relative ease with which the dynasty was brought to an end suggests that its rulers were no longer able to rely on the loyalty of their leading vassals. It has been suggested recently that the Zhou victory depended less on the issue of loyalty than on military technology. At the decisive battle of Muye the Zhou army was led by three hundred chariots. Chariots were new on the battlefield; their significance was not so much as a fighting vehicle, but more as a mobile platform from which aristocratic warriors could command their troops.[5]

A variety of opinion has been expressed over the significance of the change from Shang to Zhou: should it be regarded as a major discontinuity, or were the main elements of the Shang state continued under the successor state? According to Franz Michael, the fall of the Shang and the establishment of the Zhou was more than a dynastic change, it was the end of an era. The age of magic and the belief in Shangdi, the ruler of the spirits and the ancestor of the Shang, was overturned. In its place the Zhou established a rational explanation of a moral universe. In particular two new concepts were introduced by the Zhou: the concepts of *tian* or heaven, and of *de*, human morality or man's proper conduct in harmony with the moral principles of the universe.[6]

Other writers have argued that there was continuity. Jacques Gernet wrote that

> the complex process of evolution which leads from the archaic monarchy – the main characteristics of which persist at the beginning of the Zhou period – to the centralized state and the imperial unification does not present any real break in continuity.[7]

The historical and archaeological record lends support to this view. The conquest of the Shang was followed by the enfeoffment of the son of the last Shang ruler as a vassal of the Zhou king. However, to ensure his good behaviour, two of the king's brothers were appointed to keep watch over him. Shortly after that King Wu died, and although he was succeeded by his son, real power fell into the hands of his brother, the famous Duke of Zhou. Jealousy over the duke's rule led to an uprising in which the Shang heir died. This was followed by the duke leading a military expedition to the east, on which, it was claimed, he extinguished fifty states and enfeoffed seventy-one of his followers. At this point the duke also established a new capital near Luoyang, although the old Zhou capital, near present-day Xi'an, remained the seat of the Zhou administration.

On the whole, the archaeological evidence supports the case for continuity rather than for major change. Chang Kwang-chih noted the constants relating to the construction of cities and the practices relating to burials. Even more convincing is the evidence of the bronze art of the period. The study made by Bernard Karlgren of the stylistic evolution of the ritual vessels concluded that the art of the Western Zhou was still essentially the same as the Shang, but with small innovations.[8]

A more substantial dispute has arisen over the nature of the Zhou state as established by the Duke of Zhou and developed by his successors. Traditional

Chinese historiography treated the Xia, Shang and Western Zhou states as unified empires, similar in authority to those of more modern times. However, in *La Chine antique*, published in 1927, Henri Maspero depicted China under the Zhou as a far more primitive society, 'à demi sauvage encore'. He believed that in political terms it was only a loose federation of vassal states and that the establishment of a real state in China at that time was still impossible.[9]

Maspero's view was challenged by Herrlee G. Creel, who presented a detailed argument in support of the view that the Western Zhou kings ruled an empire rather than a tribal society and that they had developed a rather tightly controlled, relatively centralised government. Creel's argument began with a consideration of the organisation of royal government. He noted that the Zhou rulers claimed to be continuing the good practices of their predecessors. Nevertheless, according to Creel, the evidence suggested that there was innovation and in particular the development of a proto-bureaucratic form of administration. He identified three types of officials, administrative, functional and military, and noted the post of chief minister, whose role was not easy to define as much remained within the personal control of the king. Officials were not true bureaucrats, for they still derived much of their living from their fiefs, but they did display bureaucratic tendencies, particularly in their addiction to the use of written records.

To control an empire, it was essential that the government should have developed certain mechanisms, and Creel went to great lengths to identify the evidence which showed that this was so. He pointed out that a unified state required a financial system. After reviewing all the evidence relating to commercial activity and finance, he concluded that it was probable that there was a considerable amount of trade in the empire, that media of exchange of various kinds – in particular cowrie shells and silk – were in use, and that extensive financial operations were carried out by the government. He also noted the probability that a system of justice had been instituted. According to Creel, even though no Zhou code of law has survived, there is no reason to doubt that laws existed, that the king was the chief dispenser of justice, that legal procedures were followed and that crimes such as theft were punished severely.

Feudalism in Early China

The debate over the character of the Western Zhou state is related to the more general issue of feudalism in early China. The suggestion that the term feudalism, a term which was coined to denote the social and economic relationships in western Europe during the mediaeval period, should be applied to the China of a thousand years earlier, was first proposed by Guo Moruo. For Guo and for other Marxist historians it formed part of an analysis of the development of Chinese society which began by identifying Shang society as slave society, and which identified the transitional point from slave to feudal society as having occurred during the Zhou period, perhaps coincidental with the shift from the Spring and Autumn stage to that of the Warring States.

The argument that Zhou society was a feudal society is based on two explanations of feudalism: the dynamic version which defines feudalism as a form of society which is liable to arise under certain conditions, and the static version which refers to the institutions and relationships within a society. In the Chinese context the dynamic version is represented by the interpretation of the Shang/Zhou change which emphasises the collapse of a powerful Shang empire, the foreignness of the Zhou and the military character of the conquest. Once the Zhou had overthrown the Shang, they found that they did not have the resources to rule the empire directly and so territory was parcelled out to Zhou leaders and allies who had participated in the conquest, and also to indigenous clan leaders who had submitted to the Zhou and were permitted to retain their lands. This led to the creation of a large number of small states, at least one hundred of which are known to have existed in the eighth century BC. Characteristically each state consisted of a walled capital, surrounded by tilled lands and separated from the next state by a 'no man's land, peopled by "barbarians"'.[10]

The descriptive version of feudalism is a more detailed interpretation, which relies on western studies of feudalism to provide a model with which the Chinese version may be compared. The model commonly adopted is that put forward by Marc Bloch in *Feudal Society*. This contained two essential elements: the institution of the fief, a delineated territory allocated to an individual who might exercise limited or unlimited control over it; and the institution of vassalage, the relationship denoted by the requirement on the holder of the fief to provide military aid to the ruler and the obligation of everlasting loyalty.

The descriptive version of feudalism begins with the concept that all land belonged to the king and he alone had the right to dispose of it. There was evidence of this in a poem in the *Shijing*, that is the *Book of Songs*:

> Everywhere under vast Heaven
> There is no land that is not the king's.
> To the borders of those lands
> There are none who are not the king's servants.[11]

It continues with reference to the existence of a fixed hierarchy of nobility of descending rank bearing specific titles. The Chinese terms *gong, hou, bo, zi* and *nan* are usually translated as duke, marquis, earl, viscount and baron. Each of these nobles was invested with a territory and the confirmation of his possession took the form of a ceremony of investiture which took place in the Zhou ancestral temple. The new vassal was presented with a jade sceptre and a tablet bearing the terms of his enfeoffment, and received other valuable gifts including bronze vessels. Rulership was hereditary and the ceremony was repeated when the son succeeded his father. In return for being granted land, nobles had to attend audiences at court, provide assistance for major construction projects and supply troops to assist the king in the event of barbarian attack. The feudal relationship was not confined to the king and nobles: nobles in turn subdivided their domains among their relatives, their officials and their courtiers, and made similar grants of land in exchange for service.

Zhou society displayed other features which made it comparable to that of feudal Europe. The aristocracy was a class clearly differentiated from the mass of the population. It did not engage in trade and it obeyed an elaborate code of ritual comparable to the code of chivalry of European knighthood. Above all it was committed to war, and the typical aristocrat went on campaigns with his four-horse chariot supported by a company of foot-soldiers. Of the commoners, the great mass of them were peasants, who were bound to the land as serfs; in times of peace they were forced to hand over a portion of their crop to their lord and to provide labour services; in times of war they had to serve their lord as foot-soldiers. The system of land tenure is imperfectly understood, because of shortage of evidence. However, it is often suggested that the 'well-field' system, later described by Mencius, was practised at this time. The Chinese character for a well resembles the pattern for a game of noughts and crosses. Under this system of land distribution, the produce of the central square, which was cultivated by the group of peasants, was reserved for the lord, whereas the produce of the surrounding eight squares was retained by individual peasant families for their own use.

This description of Zhou society has been subjected to many qualifications, which in some cases have amounted to a rejection of the application of the word 'feudal' to the Chinese situation. The most obvious point to make is that of shortage of evidence. Many of the statements contained in the description derive from sources much later than the Western Zhou period and reflect a strong tendency in such sources to describe the period as a golden age and to imply a degree of uniformity and order which most probably did not exist. Another qualification is that whereas in European feudalism the relationship between lord and vassal was a contractual one, under the Western Zhou the relationship was very often one of kinship ties and if no kinship tie existed it was usually created by marriage. This led Charles O. Hucker to say that 'all the feudal lords were expected to accept the king as head of a vast extended family and to feel themselves beholden to the Zhou ancestral spirits as its founders'.[12] As time passed, the blood ties to the Zhou became more remote and the kinship ties were loosened. As the Zhou rulers extended their area of influence, new political units were created and grants were made to vassals who were not relatives.

If the description 'feudal', is appropriate, it should used in the light of special features of China's experience. For example, Wolfram Eberhard employed the term 'superstratification' to denote the form of feudal society which had developed under the Zhou, because in that case a conquering federation had imposed itself on an already stratified society. Eberhard added that the conquering federation was a foreign one. Owen Lattimore pointed out that a special kind of feudalism developed in the frontier zone in which Chinese and nomads met. Derk Bodde argued that a fully-fledged feudal system could only have come into existence some time after the Zhou conquest, when it extended to sub-infeudation, that is it integrated not only the ruler and his vassals but the entire population into the feudal pyramid.

The most recent study of the Western Zhou period, which makes extensive use of archaeological evidence, is that of Hsu Cho-yun and Katheryn M. Linduff. They describe Zhou feudalism as 'a multilayered feudal structure that accommodated both conformity in the ruling mechanism and diversity in practice'.[13] The structure had been developed to enable the Zhou to establish its influence over the Shang and the vassal states, and subsequently over an area which spread south of the Yangzi and into the southern coastal regions. The backbone of the feudal system which was developed was the *zongfa* or kinship network. This term, which literally means 'law of kindred', referred to Zhou practice regarding patrilineal descent and exogamy, which has been seen as breaking with the Shang custom that the royal inheritance should pass to a younger brother rather than to the eldest son. Power was delegated into the hands of vassals, but the feudal relationship was strengthened either by kinship bonds or by matrimonial ties. As a consequence, the ruling class of the Zhou was tied into a 'vast extended household'. Evidence of the strength and general acceptance of these kinship bonds is to be found in cemeteries which have been excavated, which indicate that the dead were buried in an orderly fashion reflecting the ranked structure of kin groups.

Political Developments in the Western Zhou

As mentioned above, the feudal structure developed in the Western Zhou was a response to the needs created by the conquest of the Shang and subsequent expansion. It is possible to indicate how this expansion was achieved. In former Shang territory the Zhou appointed a new ruler from the Zhou royal lineage who was expected to seek the collaboration of the Shang élite. For example, in the state of Wei, the younger brother of King Wu and the Duke of Zhou was appointed as ruler, and he was urged to honour Shang traditions and to enlist the services of Shang elders. As the Zhou expanded into the areas peripheral to the Shang state, they encountered a wide variety of non-Chinese peoples. Here the Zhou could not adopt the same model of cultural fusion which they had applied to the Shang people. Nevertheless, they tried to assimilate and accommodate local people rather than to confront and suppress them. Zhou expansion proceeded in all directions from the new capital at Zhengzhou. To the north, the states of Yan and Jin were brought more firmly into the Zhou orbit through a fusion of the Shang and Zhou élites. Further extension of Zhou influence in this direction was barred by the strength of the nomadic groups from the steppes. The most significant expansion was to the east. Here the Zhou had been faced with an uprising and had had to establish their control over populations which were not ethnic Chinese. For example the state of Qi, which occupied much of present-day Shandong, had a diverse population which included non-Chinese peoples such as the Laiyi who were eventually subjugated. To manage such a diverse population, the Zhou rulers supported policies of co-existence and tolerated diverse customs and at the same time they formed coalitions with local groups. Meanwhile to the south descendants of the Zhou royal house were enfeoffed. A gradual fusion of holdings led to the emergence of the state of Chu along the Huai river valley.

While this political expansion and consolidation was taking place, two broader trends may be observed. The first was the diffusion of elements of Zhou culture throughout much of modern China. To the north-west Zhou influence reached into Gansu and to the south-west into Sichuan. It made its way south across the Yangzi, reaching as far as the Zhu river valley. In many cases the cultural diffusion was of a superficial nature. In Sichuan, for example, Zhou influence was later overwhelmed by a revival of non-Chinese culture. But elsewhere the diffusion of Zhou culture was to leave a lasting impact on local populations.

The second trend concerned the matter of identity and the use of the term *huaxia* to denote mainstream Chinese as opposed to peripheral groups. Initially the description *huaxia* applied only to the inhabitants of the Central Plain and referred to the descendants of the Neolithic traditions of Yangshao and Longshan. However the Zhou expansion extended the application of the term, through the process of cultural fusion, to those who accepted the Zhou concept of Chineseness. The Zhou, it will be remembered, had claimed that the mandate of heaven had given them the right to rule. This doctrine justified Zhou expansion and strengthened the identification of the political units created or endorsed by the Zhou with a broader political concept. Herein perhaps lies the beginning of the assumption that what is now modern China should be a single political entity rather than a collection of nation states.

The Fall of the Western Zhou, 771 BC

The Western Zhou period was one of rapid but unstable expansion. At the beginning of the period Zhou rulers, by a process of conquest, enfeoffment and the transfer of states, had spread their influence over a large part of northern China. In the middle of the period their successors conducted frequent and ambitious campaigns against non-Chinese peoples on the periphery of their territory. For example, King Mu, who reigned in the tenth century BC, made a series of expeditions into Central Asia. His chariot, it was said, was pulled by eight semi-divine stallions and his desire was to leave the track of this chariot everywhere. But after his reign Zhou authority over the regional lords began to decline and by the beginning of the eighth century BC its ability to control the non-Chinese people on the borders was in doubt.

The end came in 771 BC, when the Zhou capital Hao was overrun by non-Chinese from the north in alliance with rebel Chinese states. According to legend King You, the last king of the Western Zhou, had amused his concubine by frequently lighting beacon fires to call for assistance. On this occasion the feudal lords failed to respond to the signal and the king was defeated and killed. But the real reasons for the fall of the Western Zhou were a series of natural catastrophes, including a serious earthquake and a famine, and the decline of the royal administration. The personal failings of the last Western Zhou king may have played a part, and another factor was recurrent pressure from non-Chinese peoples. The dynasty, as originally constructed, was no longer viable. After the death of King You the capital was transferred east to Luoyang and the successors to the Zhou throne played a much more limited role.

Political, Social and Economic Developments in the Spring and Autumn Period

The Eastern Zhou period, which is traditionally divided into the Spring and Autumn period, 771–481 BC and the Warring States period 403–221 BC, will be considered first in terms of its political, social and economic developments and in a later section in terms of its philosophical and cultural aspects.

In political terms the early Spring and Autumn period saw northern China divided into perhaps fifteen major feudal states, interspersed with a large number of smaller fiefs. The Zhou dynasty itself occupied a small area around Luoyang and its influence was restricted to the performance of religious and symbolic ceremonies. The major feudal states can be divided into two: those of the Central Plain which were regarded as Chinese, and those of the periphery which were regarded by the former group as barbarian.

Typical of the Chinese feudal states was the state of Qi, which, after it had absorbed some of its smaller neighbours, occupied much of the present-day province of Shandong. After this expansion, Qi under its ruler Duke Huan began to modernise its institutions. A key figure in this was Guan Zhong, who became one of the most renowned statesmen of antiquity. A uniform tax system was introduced, a method of military recruitment enforced and steps taken to develop the commerce of the state.

Another powerful state of this early period was the state of Jin, which occupied part of modern Shanxi. The ruler of Jin had played a part in placing the first ruler of the Eastern Zhou on the throne. The geographical position of Jin allowed for expansion and the mountainous terrain it occupied may have encouraged the development of horse-breeding.

A third example of state building can be found in the southern state of Chu. This state, which was regarded as semi-Chinese, occupied the middle Yangzi region. Despite its barbaric reputation it contained substantial cities, where its leaders buried their dead in style and with the accompaniment of human sacrifices. Although the Chu leaders claimed descent from the royal house of Zhou, from the beginning they had also claimed the title of king. And although the Chu kings granted fiefs to some of their followers, they also introduced a new administrative model, that of the xian or administrative district placed under an official appointed by the ruler.

These states were powerful political entities, and they conducted themselves as sovereign bodies. Official contacts between states were frequent and in the early Spring and Autumn period were generally friendly. But the lack of any effective central authority made it difficult to co-ordinate a response to a common threat. Such a threat arose in the seventh century BC with attacks from non-Chinese tribes in the north, and grew more serious when Chu, the major state on the southern periphery, also began to encroach on the states of the Central Plain. In 651 BC, to counter this threat, the central states held a conference. In Mencius there is a record of an agreement made on that occasion.[14] The states which participated agreed to a system of collective security and chose one of their leaders to act as hegemon.

Duke Huan of Qi became the first of the 'five leaders of the feudal lords' who sought to hold this association together. His successor was Duke Wen of Jin, who was made hegemon in 632 BC. It was alleged that a regulation had been adopted which provided that interstate meetings should be held at regular intervals.[15] At its best the hegemon system was but a weak response to the failure of central authority. The ruler of Chu was not committed to the arrangement and when he became the hegemon the whole purpose of the initiative was lost and the danger of uncontrolled interstate warfare was apparent.

The change in the balance of political power was a reflection of the important social and economic changes which occurred at this time. At the beginning of the Eastern Zhou period, society had been dominated by an élite composed of rulers who for the most part were related to or appointed by the royal house. This élite in turn was served by ministers or officials drawn from the great noble families of the state and holding their position by virtue of their birth. In addition to having a position at court members of the élite were also holders of fiefs where they were feudal lords. The élite group also included those termed shi, initially a term denoting a knight or fighting gentleman. Below this group lay the great mass of society: the merchants, artisans and above all the peasants. Peasants were bound to the soil and required to do labour service for the landowner. This was also a society which had slaves. In a society organised on these lines there was very little social mobility.

This situation began to change soon after the beginning of the Spring and Autumn period. After the collapse of Zhou royal authority, a power struggle developed in several states which led to the elimination of some of the noble families. This was followed by the rise of the families of ministers and officials. In the sixth century there began what has been described as the 'crisis of aristocratic society'.[16] By this is meant the collapse of the familial system which had dominated society in the early Zhou period. As the administration of states became more complex, rulers now freed from external obligations sought to centralise their authority. They began to turn away from their reliance on the great families and to enlist the help of the shi who became increasingly important as members of a new bureaucratic group. The career of Confucius may be taken as an example of state service and of upward mobility not unusual for the time.[17]

Behind these political changes lay technological and economic advances. The most fundamental development was that of metallurgy. The use of bronze became widespread in the Spring and Autumn period and it was now used for coins, utensils and weapons and also for agricultural implements. At about the same time the use of iron began to spread. The evidence relating to the early development of iron technology in China is incomplete. Under the Shang dynasty, meteoric iron was used to make blades for bronze implements. The earliest known iron implement, a dagger with a bronze handle and an iron blade, has been dated to the early Spring and Autumn period. However, it is only in the latter part of that period that there is evidence of the widespread use of iron, which is much later than the same development in the West.[18] However, in China iron manufacturers quickly started to use the cast-iron process, a faster and cheaper method of producing iron.

20

This technology was not adopted in the West until centuries later. Once iron had begun to be manufactured in China, there was a rapid development of mining and growth of production which in turn had great influence on agriculture and warfare.

Alongside this development occurred a fundamental change in the organisation of agriculture. It will be recalled that under the Shang a form of agricultural commune, the 'well-field' system, was apparently in use. In the Spring and Autumn period, perhaps as a consequence of a rising population and the opening up of new land, any such collective system fell into disuse. In its place came a free market in land and the emergence of landlord-tenant relations. The first explicit reference to this change is to be found in the records of the state of Lu for 594 BC, which refer to the payment of taxes by peasants in place of the labour service which hitherto had been the custom.

Another important development was the growth of commerce, shown most clearly in the spread of the use of money. The earliest coins were produced in the states of Zhou and Jin in the late Spring and Autumn period and were in the form of a spade-shaped tool. There is a record that the King of Zhou in 524 BC had minted large coins, the implication being that smaller coins were already in circulation.[19] Results from the excavation of city sites dating from this period suggest an increase in urbanisation and this in turn supports the impression of a growing merchant class. There is evidence of the gradual improvement of communications both on land and on water. Another indication of the increase in commerce can be found in references to the collection of tariffs on goods crossing state boundaries and of tolls imposed on goods being brought to cities.

Transition from Spring and Autumn to Warring States

The traditional reason for dividing the Western Zhou period into two at 481 BC was that that year was the last year of the Spring and Autumn annals. Because in the Zuozhuan (a commentary on Historical Records), the record was extended to 464 BC, the latter date was also used to mark the division. Although the dates merely referred to a break in the historical record, most historians assumed that a more fundamental change occurred at about that time. The most commonly cited aspect of the difference was the increasing frequency of wars – hence the appellation Warring States for the second period. However, after Hsu Cho-yun had analysed the record he concluded that wars were equally frequent in both periods.[20] Other writers countered this conclusion by pointing out that the character of war had changed. Whereas in the earlier period wars had been the pastime of a chariot-riding aristocracy, in the latter period it was a more serious affair, dominated by professional generals commanding a massed infantry force armed with a new weapon, the crossbow.[21] The date usually adopted for the beginning of the Warring States period, 403 BC, is also connected with the increasing severity of the power struggle between the states. In that year the state of Jin fragmented between three contestants. This left seven states, sometimes known as the seven powers: Qin, the eventual victor, in the west, Qi in the east, Yan in the north-east, Chu in the south, and in the north the three successor states to Jin, namely Zhao, Han and Wei.

Marxist historians have explained the progression from Spring and Autumn to Warring States periods in a different way. They have argued that it coincided with the change from slave to feudal society. However, the evidence for widespread slavery in the early Zhou period is very limited — indeed, there are more references to slavery in the time of the Warring States. Certainly there is nothing to indicate that the economy of China up to this time had been based on slavery.[22]

The question remains: how great was the contrast between the two periods? The impression that the Warring States period was one of frequent and destructive wars was a theme dear to Mencius's heart and this may be one reason why that view has for so long been accepted. But it must be said that the figures for casualties given in the traditional accounts are too high to be credible.[23] More importantly, the evidence of population growth and economic expansion which occurred at this time does not seem compatible with the dismal reputation of the period.

Political, Social and Economic Developments in the Warring States Period

If it is accepted that the division between the Spring and Autumn and Warring States periods is little more than a historical convenience, the fact remains that there are many differences between China at the beginning and at the end of the Eastern Zhou period. The first is that of the balance of power between the states. The seven states which had dominated the political scene at the beginning of the Warring States period had, a century later, effectively been reduced to three: Qin, Chu and Qi. In the third century BC this consolidation continued with the rise of Qin. In 256 BC, Qin deposed the last Zhou ruler and absorbed the remainder of its territory. Finally, in the decade after 231 BC, Qin eliminated its rivals and for the first time established a centralised empire in China.

The common explanation for this change is the decay of Zhou feudalism and the decline of the aristocratic leadership. This was accompanied by a centralisation of power within states. In the feudal states of the early Spring and Autumn period the state resembled a large household. The closest relatives of the ruler filled the highest offices of the state. Before the end of that period the system had begun to break down and it became the practice for ministers, drawn from aristocratic families but appointed by rulers, to hold important positions. This situation in turn began to collapse because of conflicts between ministerial families. Rulers now began to appoint shi to significant positions in state politics. This was the beginning of a consolidation of state power which was one of the marked features of the Warring States period. Increasingly rulers began to rely on career experts to carry out policies which were directed at strengthening the state. These new experts needed to be trained and one of the features of states of this period was the emergence of schools in which masters taught their disciples the arts of government, strategy and diplomacy.

Interstate rivalries intensified and it was at this point that the advance in military technology changed wars from limited campaigns fought among aristocratic leaders to more extensive wars involving far larger numbers of foot soldiers. Military conscription systems became common and it was claimed that the largest states raised armies a million strong.[24] In the fifth century BC iron weapons were introduced and the crossbow began to be used. Another important change was the introduction of cavalry which by the third century BC had become the standard auxiliary arm.

Another contrast lies in the matter of social mobility. According to Hsu Cho-yun the transition of an individual from one stratum to another was easier during the Warring States period than during the Spring and Autumn period.[25] It has been demonstrated that a substantial proportion of those who became chancellors or who held other high positions in the states of the Warring States period were self-made men. Others rose from obscure origins through the profession of arms. Many of the generals of the Warring States period came of humble origins, among them Sunzi, otherwise known as Sun the Cripple, because he had had his feet cut off as a punishment. A native of the state of Wei, he became the chief of staff of the state of Qi and author of the famous treatise *The Art of War*.

Despite the intensification of war, all the evidence suggests that the Warring States period was one of substantial economic progress. Recent archaeological discoveries have produced iron objects in great numbers and variety and indicate that iron was now commonly used to make agricultural implements. In *Mencius* the following exchange was recorded:

'Does Xu Zi use an iron pot and earthenware steamer for cooking rice and iron implements for ploughing the fields?'
'Yes.'
'Does he make them himself?'
'No. He trades grain for them.'[26]

The growth of commerce is confirmed by the spread of the use of bronze coinage. In the Warring States period coinage was minted in all the seven major states and three main types have been identified: the spade coinage already referred to, a coinage in the form of a knife found in Qi and surrounding areas, and a round coin pierced by a hole, the forerunner of the copper cash, used in the southern state of Chu. A considerable interstate commerce had developed. At first this was mainly in natural products of the region, but by the Warring States period certain areas had developed specialised industrial products. The state of Han produced swords, halberds and other iron weapons and Qi was well known for a type of purple cloth.[27]

Intellectual Developments in the Eastern Zhou Period

All that has been said about the political, social and economic changes in the Eastern Zhou period may be related to the great flowering of intellectual activity which began in the sixth century BC. It has become a commonplace to see a connection between the waves of rapid change which marked that period – and the disruption which those waves caused – and the proliferation of intellectual activity, much of which concentrated on offering solutions to the problem of ordering society in such changing times.

In proposing their solutions the political theorists of the late Spring and Autumn and Warring State periods were not starting from scratch. Important philosophical concepts, which had been formulated much earlier, shaped the direction of their thinking. The idea of a supreme being, who has the power to distribute rewards and punishments, can be traced back to the Shang period. At first the deity was perceived in anthropomorphic terms, but in the Zhou period the concept changed to an abstract force signified by the use of the term *tian* or heaven. In the Shang period, as previously noted, divination was well established and the famous divination manual, the *Yijing* or the *Book of Changes* may date from the late Shang period. The practice of ancestor worship, in the context of ceremonies associated with the royal clan, can also be traced to Shang times. In the Zhou period well-established families recognised the common descent group and male descendants were expected to perform sacrifices to their ancestors and to ensure the continuity of the lineage by begetting a male heir. Another concept which goes back to the Spring and Autumn period concerns the Chinese view of the cosmos. All things in the cosmos function in accordance with the *dao* or Way and partake of two complementary forces, *yang* and *yin*. In their origin the Chinese characters for these terms may refer to a valley, one side bathed in sun and the other shrouded in darkness. By extension *yang* denotes the sun and male energy, whereas *yin* denotes the moon and the female principle.

Although these concepts remained fundamental to Chinese thought, it was in the late Spring and Autumn period and in the time of the Warring States that the key developments in political and philosophical thought occurred. First and foremost among the teachers and philosophers of that period was Kongfuzi, or Master Kong, known in the West as Confucius. Confucius, whose traditional dates are 551–479 BC, came from the small state of Lu and was of relatively humble parentage; indeed his career may be taken as an example of the rise of the *shi* to positions of influence in the state. What little is known of his personal life may be gleaned chiefly from the *Lunyu* or *Analects*, a collection of sayings and brief anecdotes relating to Confucius compiled by his followers. It appears that Confucius was orphaned at an early age and grew up in poverty. He was a scholar who aspired to public office which he eventually achieved by becoming the police commissioner of the state of Lu.[28] Perhaps because the policy which he proposed to the government was ignored, Confucius abandoned the appointment, and for the next thirteen years he travelled from state to state offering advice to the rulers and seeking employment with them. He returned to Lu in 484 BC and in the last five years of his life he was a teacher.

Confucius's teaching was primarily concerned with how a ruler should govern. He based his advice on the lessons of the past and in particular he looked back to the beginning of the Zhou dynasty as a golden age and to the founders of the dynasty, King Wen and the Duke of Zhou, as models of rectitude. He admired King Wen because he regarded him as displaying the qualities of an ideal ruler, not because of his military achievements, but because of his success as an administrator and his skill in the arts of peace, which enabled him to build up a store of moral power, a prelude to the Zhou succession to the Shang. He cited the Duke of Zhou because he was believed to have instituted the clan inheritance system known as *zongfa*, the kinship network, the form of feudalism which was reinforced either by kinship bonds or by marriage between the royal house and its vassals. It was on this system that Confucius based his ideas about the natural love and obligations which should subsist between members of a family, ideas which were to form so large a part of his teaching on the subject of morality. Nevertheless, despite this admiration and his constant citation of examples from past ages for the instruction of people of his own day, Confucius was not an arch-conservative. He was quoted as saying 'If by keeping the old warm one can provide understanding of the new, one is fit to be a teacher'.[29] For him the past was a source of examples to be applied creatively to the problems of his own day.

One particular example lay in the matter of moral conduct. Confucius referred frequently to men of virtue, using the term junzi, usually translated as 'gentleman'. The term literally meant 'prince's son', but for Confucius the qualifications required for someone to be described as a gentleman were not those of birth but those of moral qualities. The junzi would practise those qualities which have come down in history as the five constant virtues: benevolence, uprightness of mind, propriety in demeanour, knowledge or enlightenment and good faith. Of these the most important was benevolence or humanity, the supreme excellence in a man of perfect virtue. These virtues were not inherent, they were acquired through self-cultivation and this self-cultivation implied a life of study and a belief in man's perfectibility through learning. The prescription for a junzi was in the first instance offered to rulers as a model for conduct and Confucius is always associated with the idea of governing by moral virtue. By extension the qualities were also those to be sought by all who hoped to participate in government and thus Confucius established the idea that rulers should accept advice from scholars on how such government should be instituted.

Another element in Confucius's teaching was associated with the term li, usually translated as 'ritual'. He frequently stressed the importance of all those traditional forms which provided an objective standard of conduct. Once he was asked to do away with the sacrificial lamb which was offered at the announcement of each new moon. Confucius refused, saying that whereas his questioner loved the lamb, he loved the rite. By insisting on ritual, and on all those forms of behaviour which upheld traditional forms, matters which might be described as etiquette, Confucius was asserting their continued value in a time of rapid change. Among the forms of ritual, the most important was that of offering sacrifices to ancestors. Confucius certainly endorsed such practices, but he was equally firm in his teaching on the correct relationships which should subsist amongst the living. One of his most famous pronouncements was made in reply to a question from the Duke of Qi about government : 'Let the ruler be a ruler, the subject a subject, the father a father, the son a son'.[30] When Confucius was told that a man had been so upright that when his father stole a sheep, he gave evidence against him, Confucius's reply was 'In our village those who are straight are quite different. Fathers cover up for their sons, and sons cover up for their fathers. Straightness is to be found in such behaviour'.[31]

Soon after Confucius's death the philosopher Mozi challenged some of the most basic of his arguments. He criticised the concept of the gentleman as a pretext for maintaining social inequalities and came close to arguing that all men are equal before God. In place of what he termed the 'partial love' urged by Confucius, that is to say a graded love determined by a system of relationships, he argued the case for universal love, or, as it has otherwise been translated, love without discrimination. One should love every other person as much as one loves oneself and one should love another person's parents as much as one loves one's own. To sanction this belief, Mozi invoked a heaven that was much closer to a personal God than anything endorsed by Confucius. Mozi lived in troubled times. The worst calamities, he said, included the attacking of small states by large states, the plundering of the weak by the strong, and the disdain of the noble for the humble.[32] To combat this Mozi argued a strictly utilitarian role for the state. Its every effort must be directed at satisfying people's material needs, even if this meant abandoning ritual and music. Above all the state should not engage in offensive warfare. Mozi preached pacifism and was said to have intervened personally in attempts to prevent wars and to assist in the defence of states threatened with attack.

Confucius and Mozi, despite their differences, were united in their search for ways of making the world a better place to live in. The philosophy of Daoism, however, turned its back on worldly preoccupations and concerned itself with the individual and his inner life. *Dao* means literally 'the Way' and some of the concepts of Daoism, in particular the idea that man should live in harmony with nature, may date back to the Shang period. Daoism has two key texts, the first of which is the *Daodejing*, or *The Way and Power Classic*, also known as the *Laozi* after its supposed author. Laozi reputedly lived in the state of Chu and was an older contemporary of Confucius. However, there is the greatest uncertainty about his identity – the name merely means 'old man' and there is no corroborative evidence to support the biographical sketch of him which appeared in the *Shiji*. In all probability Laozi was not a historical figure at all.[33] The *Laozi* as a book is very different from the works associated with Confucius or Mozi. Whereas they were concerned with the problems of the world, the *Laozi* is preoccupied with matters of the spirit. Its opening lines proclaim that it is a work of mysticism and poetry:

The way that can be spoken of
Is not the constant way;
The name that can be named
Is not the constant name.
The nameless was the beginning of heaven and earth;
The named was the mother of the myriad creatures.
Hence always rid yourself of desires in order to observe its secrets;
But always allow yourself to have desires in order to observe its manifestations.[34]

Although much of the *Laozi* is concerned with nature and the principle of the *dao*, it also includes references to how the individual should behave and how a ruler should conduct himself. The ideal individual is the sage, and a sage is one who comprehends the Way. The ideal ruler is also the sage, who might be supposed to be able to apply his knowledge of the Way to the task of ruling. However, the question arises: how far should the ruler intervene? In the *Laozi* a key phrase is *wuwei* meaning 'without action', the implication being that the task of the ruler is to avoid doing anything which might upset the natural order. The state is a delicate thing which may be ruined by the least handling. As a consequence, 'Governing a large state is like boiling a small fish'.[35] By avoiding intervention and by setting an example, the ruler might succeed in leading his people to a state of innocence and simplicity.

The second key work of Daoism is the *Zhuangzi*, probably the work of a man of that name whose given dates are 369–286 BC. The *Zhuangzi* is also concerned with the principle of the *dao*, but the emphasis is less on how that knowledge might be put to a mundane use and more on its philosophical aspects. Zhuangzi, who probably lived as a recluse, often seems to want to distance himself from society and in an anarchic or paradoxical way to challenge its conventions. One dialogue in the book describes his behaviour after the death of his wife. He was found sitting with an inverted bowl on his knees, drumming upon it and singing a song. When he was told that his behaviour was inappropriate, he defended himself by saying:

When she died, I was in despair, as any man well might be. But soon, pondering on what had happened, I told myself that in death no strange new fate befalls us. In the beginning we lack not life only, but form. Not form only, but spirit. We are blended in the one great featureless indistinguishable mass. Then a time came when the mass evolved spirit, spirit evolved form, form evolved life. And now life in its turn has evolved death. For not nature only but man's being has its seasons, its sequence of spring and autumn, summer and winter. If someone is tired and has gone to lie down, we do not pursue him with shouting and bawling. She whom I have lost has lain down to sleep for a while in the Great Inner Room. To break in upon her rest with the noise of lamentation would but show that I knew nothing of nature's Sovereign Law. That is why I ceased to mourn.[36]

It has often been said that the doctrines of Confucianism and Daoism complement each other and that a scholar might study the Confucian texts for his career and read the texts of Daoism for relaxation. Certainly the classic texts of Daoism have continued to be read, even though before the end of the Zhou period Daoist philosophical speculation was led astray into the search for the elixir of life. Also many important elements in Daoist teaching were adopted by Confucianism and Buddhism and have lived on in that way.

The late Zhou period has been described as the time of the Hundred Schools, referring to the proliferation of philosophical ideas circulating at the time. There is not space here to refer to them all, but mention must be made of the development of Confucian teaching and of the Legalists whose ideas were adopted by the first unified empire of the Qin.

Confucius had received little recognition in his own day and his teaching had only survived because of the devotion of his followers. Subsequently they added to what he had said and it is the sum of their writings which provided the literary basis of Confucianism. First and foremost among those followers was Mengzi, known in the West as Mencius, whose probable dates were 372 to 289 BC. The main source on his teaching is the *Mencius*, which like the *Analects* is a collection of sayings compiled by his students. Mencius was a declared follower of Confucius and he considered much of what he said to be an explanation of his master's teaching. Nevertheless his reported sayings were also a reflection of his times, which were much more disturbed than those of his predecessor, and they also reflected the intellectual debates of his day. Three aspects of his teaching stand out, the first of which concerns the nature of man. For Confucius this was not an important issue, and the one direct reference he made to the topic was to say 'Men are close to one another by nature. They diverge as a result of repeated practice'.[37] But for Mencius it was fundamental, for his teaching was based on the assumption that man is by nature good, that is to say he possesses certain innate and unselfish tendencies which, if properly cultivated lead towards goodness. In a famous passage Mencius said:

> Suppose a man were, all of a sudden, to see a young child on the verge of falling into a well. He would certainly be moved to compassion, not because he wanted to get in the good graces of the parents, nor because he wished to win the praise of his fellow villagers or friends, nor yet because he disliked the cry of the child.[38]

For Mencius to be devoid of the heart of compassion was to lack that which is characteristic of a human being.

Much of what Mencius said was concerned with the application of these tendencies to the good of society. The *Mencius* begins with a famous reference to a conversation between Mencius and King Hui of Liang, on the occasion of a visit which took place in 320 BC.

> 'Sir,' said the King. 'You have come all this distance, thinking nothing of a thousand li. You must surely have some way of profiting my state?'

'Your Majesty,' answered Mencius. 'What is the point of mentioning the word "profit"? All that matters is that there should be benevolence and righteousness.'[39]

Mencius's ideal for the state was benevolent government, that is to say a government that existed for the sake of the people and which sought to provide them with peace and sufficiency. He urged the re-introduction of the 'well-field' system, the system of equal landholding which had perhaps prevailed in the early Zhou period.

The third idea forever associated with Mencius is that of the 'right to rebel'. Mencius explained the right to rule in terms of the mandate of heaven, that is to say the founders of the dynasty had won the approval of heaven by their virtue and had then been granted the right to take the throne. He stressed the obligations of the ruler to lead by example and to rule with benevolence. It was inevitable that Mencius should also address the question of what should happen if a ruler failed in his task, or if he neglected or oppressed the people. Mencius's reply was that he had forfeited the approval of heaven and this gave the people the right to rebel. At first sight this doctrine appears to be democratic – because it imposes a strong obligation on a ruler to take the interests of his people into account – and subversive, because it offers an alternative to suffering oppression. However, because according to the same argument a failed rebellion must be seen as not only treasonable but also impious, it cannot really be said to have inspired many rebellions or to have done much to counter the autocratic tendencies of imperial government in China.

Mention must also be made of the third major contributor to the establishment of the Confucian tradition, although his name is not well known outside China. Xunzi, who lived between 298 and 238 BC, was a high official in the states of Qi and Chu. His collected writings survive in the work known as the *Xunzi*. His most famous philosophical contribution was to contradict Mencius's view on the essential goodness of human nature. For Xunzi the nature of man was evil; his goodness had to be acquired. If a man's evil tendencies were not curbed, strife and injury and cruelty would result. However, goodness may be acquired under the influence of teachers, and under the discipline of laws men may be brought to follow the paths of decorum and righteousness. Xunzi's argument was associated with his rejection of Confucius's and Mencius's ideas of a golden age in the past. Although he lived in difficult times, Xunzi believed that mankind had not changed; what was needed was a commitment to good government and stern control – in other words he was an advocate of authoritarianism.

Xunzi promoted the importance of education and said that it should concentrate on the study of the classics. This was a new idea, indicative of the development and circulation of literature as well as of the establishment of authoritative texts. It is not clear which were the classics to which he referred, but it is to about this time one can trace the identification of a canon of Confucian classics. One listing of the key texts comprised the *Shijing*, the Book of Songs, an anthology of poems dating back to the early Zhou period; the *Shujing*, the Book of Documents, which reputedly derived

29

from the same date; the *Yijing* or *Book of Changes*, the famous book of divination; the *Spring and Autumn Annals* and the *Liji* or *Book of Rites*, a collection made in the Han period but incorporating earlier materials on rites and rituals. These works were known collectively as the Five Classics. Another listing became known as the Four Books. It comprised the *Analects* and *Mencius* and two extracts from the *Book of Rites*, known as the *Great Learning* and the *Doctrine of the Mean*. Of these books only the *Analects* can in a strict sense be described as the work of Confucius. Some classics entered the canon because they had been used by Confucius as a source of instruction; others, for example the *Great Learning*, were adopted because they expressed ideas which could be traced back to Confucius. Knowledge of these classics was to be deemed essential for the training of a Confucian scholar, beginning with the Four Books and then proceeding to the Five Classics.

One further school of thought must be mentioned here although fuller reference to it belongs in the next chapter. It is the set of ideas which have become known as Legalism. There is a direct link between Xunzi and Legalism, because two of his most famous students, Han Fei and Li Si, were both to become Legalists. However, it must be stressed that Xunzi was no totalitarian and the origin of those tendencies in Legalism must be sought elsewhere.

Han Fei, who died in 233 BC, was a member of the ruling family of the state of Han. It was said that it was because he suffered from a speech impediment that he turned to writing. The *Hanfeizi*, the classic text associated with him, contains a number of essays which he wrote as well as other material. This text is the most complete exposition of the ideas of Legalism. Han Fei brought together a number of disparate ideas into a coherent political philosophy. He knew of the policies of Shang Yang, the fourth-century BC minister of the state of Qin, which will be discussed later. He would also have been aware of Daoist ideas and how, in particular, the Daoist sage-ruler was not placed under any obligation to practise benevolent rule. And he certainly was familiar with the teachings of Xunzi and would have responded to his brand of Confucianism and to his conviction that human nature is evil.

The starting point for Han Fei's thought was his rejection of the Confucian idealisation of the past. He conceded that formerly men could afford to be kind and polite because they were few in number, and under such circumstances rulers might succeed by being benevolent and just. But those days were gone and more difficult times were at hand. He further provoked the Confucianists by arguing that there was no justification for continuing to honour and reward scholars as in the past:

> As long as heavy taxes are collected from the farmers while rich rewards are given to the learned gentlemen, it will be impossible to expect the people to work hard and talk little.[40]

For Han Fei the essence of good government was to strengthen the power of the state. If the ruler were to give away any element of his power he ran the risk of creating dangerous rivalries. Legalists identified three things which the ruler must use in order to govern effectively: he must strengthen his power and position; he must perfect administrative techniques, and he must promulgate a precise code of laws. The last point has been taken as the characteristic of Legalist thought. The best-known passage in the *Hanfeizi* is that which asserts that men are naturally spoiled by love, but are submissive to authority:

> That being so, rewards should be rich and certain so that people will be attracted by them; punishments should be severe and definite so that the people will fear them; and laws should be uniform and steadfast so that the people will be familiar with them.[41]

In 233 BC Han Fei travelled to the state of Qin, where his erstwhile fellow-student, Li Si, was chief adviser to the king. Perhaps because of jealousy of Han Fei's brilliance, Li Si forced him or induced him to commit suicide. Nevertheless, as will appear, Han Fei's ideas were to outlive him and to have both an immediate and a longer-term influence.

3

The Qin Empire

The span of the Qin dynasty, from 221 to 207 BC, was the shortest in China's dynastic record. Nevertheless the period is generally regarded as of great significance and three particular claims are made for it. The first is that the name 'China', the name to be adopted by the outside world to describe what the Chinese themselves have preferred to call the Middle Kingdom, probably derived from the name Qin.[1] Secondly, the dynasty has recently gained worldwide attention because of the most spectacular archaeological discovery of the late twentieth century: the uncovering of the army of terracotta soldiers guarding the entrance to the tomb of Qin Shi Huangdi, the First Emperor of the Qin. This discovery offers some confirmation of the extraordinary claims relating to the tomb to be found in the *Shiji*, or *Historical Records* compiled by Sima Qian.

Finally, and most generally, is the fact that Qin was the first national dynasty, one which swept away the feudal states of Zhou China and which created a non-feudal, non-hereditary, bureaucratic administration, a change which was described by Charles Hucker as 'a major watershed in Chinese history'.[2] Derk Bodde went even further: for him the year 221 BC, the year the dynasty was established, was 'by far the most important single date in Chinese history before the revolutionary changes of the present century'.[3]

The Rise of the State of Qin

The state of Qin grew up along the Wei river to the west of the Zhou royal domains. This was a frontier region and much of the early history of the state was connected with its struggles with the Rong, a non-Chinese group. In 770 BC Qin helped the Zhou rulers, who also suffered from attacks by the Rong, to remove their capital from Hao to Luoyang, further east. This move marks the division between the Western and Eastern Chou periods. As a reward for this assistance Qin territory was raised to the status of a full principality, and thereafter Qin shared the effective independence enjoyed by the other states of the Eastern Zhou period.

Nevertheless, until the fourth century BC, there was little to suggest that the Qin state would unify China. Qin was regarded as barbarous when compared with the Zhou and perhaps its people had been much influenced by their non-Chinese neighbours. It was said of the Qin state that it had the same customs as the Rong and Di barbarians, 'It has the heart of a tiger or a wolf. . . . It knows nothing about traditional mores, proper relationships, and virtuous conduct'.[4] But then, between 361 and 338 BC, the Qin ruler, Duke Xiao, following advice from an official named

Shang Yang, or Lord Shang, transformed the state and set in train those developments which were to lead to the triumph of Qin.

The extraordinary nature of this achievement has long been recognised. In the second century BC the scholar Jia Yi wrote of Duke Xiao:

> He cherished the idea of rolling the empire up like a mat, of lifting up the whole world in his arms and of tying up the four seas in a sack; moreover he had the intention of swallowing up the eight wild countries. At this time the Lord of Shang assisted him; in the interior he fixed models and measures, gave his attention to farming and weaving, and made the necessary preparations for defence and attack; abroad he extended the territory in an uninterrupted way from west to east and fought with the feudal lords.[5]

His minister, Shang Yang, came from the neighbouring state of Wei. It was said that the ruler of Wei once remarked of him '[he] has marvellous talents, – if he be not employed in an official post, it would be better that he were put to death, lest another kingdom obtain his services!' His particular qualification was his commitment to the ideas and policies later to be associated with the school of thought known as Legalism. The Legalists, it will be remembered, rejected the traditional virtues of humanity and righteousness, which had been advocated by the Confucianists. Instead they supported the strengthening of the state, the concentration of power into the hands of a single ruler, and the use of war as an instrument of policy.

Shang Yang's reform programme is not easy to describe accurately. The key text, the *Book of Lord Shang*, which in the past was attributed to him, is now believed to be the work of others, although it may reflect his thinking.[6] One must instead look at the record of achievements when he was the minister. These included the extension of direct state administration, as opposed to devolved administration through hereditary landholders; the abolition of the old fixed landholding system (the well-field system described above) and its replacement by a more flexible system in which the sizes of land units could vary and peasants paid taxes in kind rather than in labour services; and the development of a system of collective responsibility, under which the population was grouped into units of five or ten families, with all members of each unit collectively responsible for the wrongdoing of any individual in the unit (the forerunner of the *baojia* system). His economic reforms were seen by the Marxist historian Guo Moruo as bringing to an end the power of the declining slave-owner aristocrats and as hastening the transition from a slave society to a feudal society.[7]

Another important achievement lay in the codification of the law. Until recently, the earliest Chinese legal code known to have survived dated from the Tang dynasty (AD 618–907). In 1975 a collection of bamboo slips was found in the grave of a Qin official who had died in 217 BC. Several hundred of these slips were legal documents, referring to a legal code which had been compiled before Qin united China. It is possible that what is recorded on the slips may be the original text as established by Shang Yang.[8]

The collection also referred to a number of aspects of Qin administrative procedure. It has been suggested that any explanation of the triumph of Qin must refer to its geopolitical position on the periphery of the central area, and must emphasise its military achievement. But the explanation must also acknowledge other aspects of the Qin state which the bamboo slips illustrate: the insistence on efficiency and precision; the institution of a fixed routine in administrative procedure; the emphasis on exact quantification and data. This administrative procedure was applied to a state which was politically stable and growing economically. Another important achievement of Qin in the third century lay in the field of agriculture, where there is evidence of the improvement of agricultural production and the conserving of natural resources. Two major projects deserve mention: the canal built by Zheng Guo north of the Wei river, which irrigated nearly half a million acres of land, and the development of the irrigation system on the Chengdu plain.

The achievement of Shang Yang has received very different interpretations over the centuries. In traditional Chinese historiography he has been excoriated. He has been described as a ruthless politician who coerced the people into agriculture and warfare, who introduced a system of governmental surveillance, and who destroyed old institutions, particularly the well-field system. By permitting a free market in land he allowed the rich to become richer and the poor to become poorer. In modern times, Shang Yang's stock has risen. Early in this century he was compared to Solon and to Bismarck. In the 1970s, at the time of the anti-Confucius campaign, he was praised for having dealt blows to divisive forces within the state, for having centralised power, for having enforced ideological uniformity, and for having scorned the literati. In the language of the day Shang Yang was described as having used revolutionary violence in an attempt to suppress the old aristocracy and to introduce radical reforms. Despite his achievements, after the death of Duke Hsiao, Shang Yang became the victim of a counter-revolution, being captured and put to death by 'dismemberment by chariots'.[9] Nevertheless the reformist tendency he had initiated continued after his death.

The Triumph of Qin

From the fourth century BC Qin turned its attention away from expansion into non-Chinese areas towards achieving dominance over its rivals to the east. In an era of warring states, Qin achieved notoriety for its willingness to involve itself in war. The Shiji recorded its involvement in fifteen major battles or campaigns in the period 364–234 BC. In this contest Qin held an advantage which was to be a recurrent feature of shifts in the power balance in China. This was its situation to the west of the more settled and advanced states, which provided it with natural defences and a secure base from which to attack. The first step in Qin expansion was to undermine the position of the state of Chu to the south – this was achieved in a campaign extending into modern Sichuan.

By the middle of the third century BC the threat offered by Qin to the other states of north China was apparent. When, in 256 BC, Qin destroyed the shadowy survival of the Zhou ruling house, it seemed likely that the state would soon achieve supremacy. However the final triumph of Qin was to be delayed for a further generation of consolidation and of warfare. The key figures of this time were the Qin king, known as Zheng, meaning the Upright, who came to the throne as a youth in 246 BC, and Lü Buwei, who was the chief minister and regent of the state between the years 249 and 237 BC. According to the record Lü was a travelling merchant who became the richest man of his day. He came to power through befriending the heir to the Qin throne; a titillating story relates how Lü had surrendered his beautiful concubine – who was at the time pregnant – to the heir and how thus Lü was the putative father of the child who was to become Qin Shi Huangdi, the First Emperor of Qin. Lü's astonishing rise, at that time an unique instance of a man from a merchant background achieving political power, has been interpreted as a sign of the economic transition taken place in the last years of the Eastern Zhou period. Lü Buwei played an active role in the strengthening of the Qin state by encouraging the construction of canal systems and by patronising the literary arts. The most famous outcome of the latter activity was the work known as the *Lüshi chun jiu*, or *Spring and Autumn of Mr Lü*, an ambitious attempt by scholars working under Lü's direction to produce a compilation of current knowledge on cosmological, political and moral issues, to be used as a basis for the proper conduct of government. Lü also strengthened the military capacity of Qin and weakened the position of the other states by a policy of divide and rule. However Lü was not to live to see the outcome of his preparations. He fell from power in 237 BC after the disclosure that he was continuing his relationship with the First Emperor's mother.

His place was taken by another outstanding politician, Li Si, who was to play the foremost role in the establishment and consolidation of the Qin dynasty. Li Si came from the state of Chu and had been a fellow student of Han Fei. He came to Qin in search of employment and received patronage from Lü Buwei. After Lü's fall from power, a decree was passed expelling alien officials and this might well have led to the end of Li Si's career had he not expostulated to the king in a famous memorial. The decree was rescinded and Li Si was promoted to be Minister of Justice, thus embarking on a remarkable career which was to end only with his death in 208 BC. However, little is known of Li Si's activities in the next decade, although it is probable that he contributed to the triumph of Qin by intriguing against the other feudal states. A more significant contribution to that result – but one which is difficult to pin down – is Li Si's part in promoting the concept of empire to the ruler of Qin. According to the *Shiji*, when Li Si set out for Qin in search of employment, he had declared that 'the king of Qin desires to swallow up the world and to rule with the title of Emperor'. In Derk Bodde's opinion, few men in history have pursued this concept of empire with more rigid determination than did Li Si. Perhaps there was no Qin blueprint for conquest, but a consistency of ambition matches what is known of the character of Li Si. Whenever the opportunity arose he referred to the concept of empire and encouraged the ambitions of the ruler of Qin.[10]

In 230 BC there began the final series of campaigns which, within ten years, were to lead to the elimination of the other states and the establishment of an unified empire. Some of the factors which turned the balance in Qin's favour have already been identified: the geographical position of the state; its ability to attract outstanding figures from other states; the adoption of the ideas of Legalism; the strengthening of its economy and of its administrative institutions; its effective diplomacy preventing the other states from forming a united front to oppose Qin expansion. One other factor has been the subject of debate, namely the military prowess of Qin and in particular the significance of the use of a new weapon, the iron sword. Undoubtedly Qin did have a reputation for using war as an instrument of policy and the Book of Lord Shang contained a section on methods of warfare. The last century of the Warring States period was characterised by wars in which Qin played a prominent role both as aggressor and as beneficiary of warfare between other states. It was suggested at one point that the key to its military success lay in the spread of the use of wrought-iron swords which were superior to the bronze swords used by Qin's opponents. However, archaeological evidence has failed to support the thesis that Qin enjoyed enjoyed some kind of metallurgical superiority over its rivals.[11]

The Qin Empire, 221–210 BC

With the defeat of the feudal states, Li Si seized the opportunity to proclaim a united empire. 'This is the one moment in ten thousand ages', he wrote, 'If Your Highness allows it to slip away and does not press the advantage in haste, the feudal lords will revive their strength and organize themselves into an anti-Qin alliance'.[12] The king assumed the title of huangdi, which has been translated as 'sovereign emperor', implying that this was a political, rather than a religious title and that its assumption marked the beginning of a new political order.

What such an order might imply was soon revealed. In a famous memorial, Li Si rejected the idea that the emperor should grant fiefs to his relatives and instead urged the abolition of feudalism. He argued that the original fiefs, which had been granted by the early Zhou kings, had in time degenerated into warring states. To reinstitute a feudal nobility would not lead to peace and would not be advantageous, and the fiefs should therefore be abolished. The memorial was accepted and the rich and noble families of the states were forced to leave their ancestral land holdings and move to the capital at Xianyang, where they could be kept under the watchful eye of the emperor. According to the record, 120,000 families were forced to move. Associated with this measure was the requirement that all the weapons belonging to the feudal lords should be melted down, the metal being used to cast twelve gigantic human figures to be erected in the imperial palace.[13]

In the place of feudal fiefs, the empire was divided into commanderies and prefectures administered by appointed officials. This measure was represented as a novel departure, but there is plenty of evidence to show that this system, which was the forerunner of the modern system of provinces and prefectures, was already partly in existence. The older unit was the xian or prefecture (more accurately district), which may have existed in all the seven great states of the Warring States period. Nor was the *jun* or commandery a new administrative unit. When the order dividing the empire into thirty-six commanderies was issued, no less than eighteen of them had already existed as commanderies before the First Emperor's reign. This administrative step was not an innovation, it was the extension of a system of centralised control already introduced before the Qin conquest.

The same centralising thrust and the same move towards uniformity was reflected in other measures. In the *Shiji* it was stated that Li Si 'equalised the written characters, and made these universal throughout the empire'. By this it was meant that Li Si, or more probably a group of scholars working under his orders, carried through a series of reforms of the writing system and ensured that the new style was adopted generally. Variant forms of characters were suppressed and a standard script, known as the Small Seal, was introduced. By this means communication within the empire was facilitated and a strong weapon for cultural integration was forged.

In legal matters the same standardisation prevailed. The Qin law code was applied throughout the empire. Its two basic principles were reasserted. The first was that of mutual responsibility for law-keeping and the obligation to denounce wrongdoers. The second was the reiteration of Shang Yang's principle of making the law so severe that no one would dare to violate it. Fearful punishments, not all of them new, were prescribed, including extracting ribs and boiling in a cauldron.[14]

State intervention also occurred in economic matters. The Qin had a declared preference for agriculture over commerce. The former was seen as the basis of the state's wealth, whereas the latter was seen as non-productive. On occasion steps were taken to round up merchants and to force them to resettle in distant regions. This attitude, it has been suggested, left a prejudice against merchants which has survived in China until modern times. Nevertheless, other steps taken were of benefit to commerce. The currency was standardised, with gold and copper coins put into circulation. Clear regulations were applied to weights and measures. Examples have been found of the two main types of measure: vessels measuring capacity and weights for a balance, and these are inscribed with the imperial edict declaring that measurements should be clear and uniform.[15] Other edicts stipulated that the gauge of the wheels of carts be equal for all parts of China – the purpose being to ensure that the ruts created by the wheels would be equally far apart – and that new roads, fifty paces broad and lined with trees, should be built from the capital to the furthest reaches of the empire in the east and south.

The First Emperor has long been associated with the most ambitious of all building projects, the Great Wall. In the *Shiji* it is stated that the emperor sent a general named Meng Tian to drive the Rong and Di barbarians from the land to the south of the Yellow river. He then built a great wall, or line of fortification using convict labourers transported to the border for garrison duty. It has been generally accepted that this construction was not entirely new, but was more a matter of joining together defensive fortifications already started in the Warring States period. Nevertheless, the major part of the construction has been dated to the time of the Qin empire and the work ascribed to Meng Tian. Its length was said to have extended to ten thousand *li*. Extremely high figures have been placed on the number of persons who would have been required to build the wall and the numbers who perished in its construction. In short the Great Wall has been represented as the supreme example of the ruthless ambition and cruel operation of the First Emperor, which may in turn have contributed to the fall of the Qin empire. However, against this interpretation must be set the view of Arthur Waldron, who has treated the whole issue with great scepticism. He has pointed out that the Great Wall, as we know it today, was not constructed in the Qin period, but in the sixteenth century, under the Ming dynasty. The written records relating to wall-building under the Qin are brief and ambiguous. As a consequence it is not even clear what line the wall followed. Wall construction at this period consisted of earthen ramparts, not stone walls. They were made of local material, required far less labour than stone walls, and did not usually survive for very long.[16]

If the achievement on the northern frontiers of the empire has been exaggerated, the extension of influence to other parts of the country has perhaps been understated. Before the unification Qin had already sent an expedition south to subdue Lingnan, the area of the modern province of Guangdong. In 222 BC an even larger expedition, reputedly numbering half a million men in five armies, was dispatched to conquer the south. Engineers were sent to construct a canal to join the Xiang river in Hunan with the Xi or West river, which flows into the sea near Guangzhou, that is Canton. In 214 BC the expedition suffered a major defeat at the hands of the local population and the expansion was halted temporarily, to be resumed under the Han dynasty.[17]

Mention has already been made of the measures taken to establish a standardised script. This attempt at uniformity may be linked with the most notorious of the deeds of the First Emperor and Li Si, the burning of the books and the burial alive of the scholars. According to the account in the *Shiji*, at a banquet held in 213 BC, a scholar had the temerity to criticise the emperor for not having followed tradition by dividing the empire into feudal fiefs. Li Si responded to this in a memorial in which he inveighed against the scholars of the independent schools who sought to establish a reputation by criticising their sovereign. He accused them of praising the past in order to disparage the present and of criticising enactments of the state. He then made his famous proposal:

> Your servant suggests that all books in the imperial archives, save the memoirs of Qin, be burned. All persons in the empire, except members of the Academy of Learned Scholars, in possession of the *Book of Odes*, the *Book of History*, and discourses of the hundred philosophers should take them to the local governors and have them indiscriminately burned.[18]

Li Si's recommendation was accepted and there occurred a burning of the books which earned the undying contempt of Confucian scholars. It must be said, however, that the scale of the crime and the degree of its effectiveness are in doubt. Li Si was neither the first, nor the last bureaucrat, or ruler, in China to try to destroy literature deemed dangerous by the regime. The attack on literature was not indiscriminate. Texts on medicine, pharmacy, divination, agriculture and arboriculture were entirely spared, as were the historical records of Qin. Even in the case of the proscribed texts, copies could be retained by members of the academy. During the great recovery of books instituted under the Han dynasty, many of the prohibited books were restored, some having been committed to memory by scholars.

The second alleged great crime of the First Emperor supposedly occurred in the following year. Some scholars had complained about the emperor's excesses and as a consequence 460 scholars were executed by being buried alive. The first reference to this event was written a century later. At the very least it is unlikely that the mode of execution was as stated and it is probable that the incident was fabricated to create a legend of Confucian martyrdom.[19]

The Life and Death of the First Emperor

Zheng the Upright, later to be known as the First Emperor, was born in 259 BC and succeeded to the throne of Qin at the age of thirteen. However it was only after the fall of Lü Buwei in 237 BC that he assumed full control of the state. His relationship with Li Si is far from clear and the relative importance of the parts he and his minister played in conceiving and executing the unification of China can only be a matter for speculation. One view of the relationship between the two was that the emperor was impetuous, emotional and grossly superstitious, whereas Li Si was cold, calculating and eminently rational.[20] What does seem clear is that Li Si was careful to present his actions as the fulfilment of the will of the emperor. Certainly the emperor was an active ruler, one indication of this being the erection of at least seven inscribed stelae which record journeys he made. But, according to the Shiji, as his reign progressed, he became increasingly absorbed in metaphysics and magic. He accepted the teaching of the School of the Five Elements – earth, wood, metal, fire and water. According to this teaching each element overcomes its predecessor, flourishes for an allotted time, and then is in turn conquered by the next element in the series. As the element associated with the Zhou dynasty was fire, it followed that that of the Qin was water. The emperor also pursued a great preoccupation of Daoist philosophers or adepts: that of gaining the secret of immortality. His journeys seem to have been as much related to this preoccupation as to affairs of state and it was this hope which took him on a journey to the coast of Shandong in 210 BC. According to the tale recorded in the Shiji, the emperor on previous occasions had sent men to obtain the elixir of life which supposedly was guarded by immortals who lived on three supernatural mountains in the middle of the sea. The emperor was told that the reason for their failure to reach the immortal isles was because a great fish had prevented them. So he followed the coast for some time, armed with a large crossbow. When he saw a large fish, he killed it. But soon after that the emperor himself fell ill and died.

Many of the stories recorded about the First Emperor are of doubtful historical value and were probably invented or elaborated to emphasise his superstitious nature and megalomania. However, there is one remarkable piece of evidence which must be taken into account before delivering a final verdict on his personality and ambition. This is, of course, the evidence of the emperor's mausoleum. In the *Shiji* it was stated that work on the tomb had begun as early as 246 BC, and that after the unification of the empire more than 700,000 men had worked on it:

> The laborers dug through three subterranean streams which they sealed off with bronze in order to make the burial chamber. This they filled with models of palaces, towers, and the hundred officials, as well as precious utensils and marvelous rarities. Artisans were ordered to install mechanically triggered crossbows set to shoot any intruder. With quicksilver the various waterways of the empire, the Yangzi and Yellow Rivers, and even the great ocean itself were created and made to flow and circulate mechanically. The heavenly constellations were depicted above and the geography of the earth was laid out below. Lamps were fueled with whale oil so that they might burn forever without being extinguished.[21]

All the emperor's childless wives had been killed and were buried with him. Finally, to preserve the secrets of the tomb, those who had worked on the mausoleum were also sealed up inside it.

The location of the tomb, some thirty miles east of Xianyang, has long been known. The tomb mound rises to about 43 metres and it stands in a rectangular enclosure measuring 2,173 by 974 metres. According to records the tomb had been rifled twice and the assumption was that few of the cultural relics left in the tomb would have survived. A number of pottery figures had been found in the vicinity in recent years, but that gave no warning of the astonishing discovery, made by chance in 1974, of the terracotta army. Subsequent excavation revealed the existence of three enormous pits containing life-sized terracotta figures of soldiers. Pit No. 1 contained about six thousand figures of warriors and horses, outfitted with real weapons, chariots and chariot gear. The arrangement of the figures and their armament indicates that they represent a specific military formation. Pit No. 2 contained a force of about fourteen hundred warriors and horses. The third pit, with only sixty-eight figures, may represent a command unit. There is a fourth pit, but it is empty, and there are no pits where one might have expected to find complementary groups of soldiers to complete the army. This has been taken as indicating that the project was abandoned before it had been completed. Nevertheless the scale and accuracy of the representation is astonishing: each figure was sculptured individually and carefully painted. Even if they were not portraits of individuals, as has been suggested, the craftsmen who created them went to great lengths to differentiate each figure in terms of physical form, expression and dress. Perhaps it will never be possible to confirm Sima Qian's description of the tomb, but the evidence of the terracotta army shows that the extraordinary claims for the ambitions of the First Emperor are based on fact.

The Collapse of the Qin Empire

The empire was not to outlast the death of the First Emperor by long. Difficulties began immediately with a succession dispute, with the heir to the throne being set aside in favour of a younger son. Li Si and the new emperor's tutor, a eunuch named Zhao Gao, played a major role in this intrigue which was followed by the suicide of the original heir and of the general Meng Tian.

The new emperor, usually known as the Second Emperor, was only twenty-one at the time of his accession. He commenced ruling on the lines followed by his father, by making an imperial progression. The aged Li Si restated the principles of Legalism in a famous memorial on 'supervising and holding responsible'. But discontent was rising against heavy taxation, part of which was to pay for the work on the Ebang palace. It was focussed into what has been described as 'the first great popular revolt in Chinese history',[22] headed by a poor Henan farmer, Chen Sheng. He was killed but the rebellion was continued by others.

Meanwhile further intrigues took place at court, resulting in the rise of Zhao Gao and the imprisonment of Li Si, who, in 208 BC was condemned to be cut in two at the waist in the market place at Xianyang. According to the biography of Li Si, Zhao Gao's dominance over the Second Emperor now reached its height. It was said that he had presented a deer to the emperor, while calling it a horse. When the emperor insisted that it was a deer, he was told that he was suffering from delusions. The emperor was advised to go into retirement in a country park and was subsequently forced to commit suicide. He was succeeded by another grandson of the First Emperor, Ziying, who managed to procure the death of Zhao Gao. But by then it was too late to save the dynasty, rebellion had spread and Ziying was captured by the rebels and executed. The Qin dynasty, which was intended to last for ten thousand generations, had come to an end.

Explanations of the fall of the Qin

Traditional explanations of dynastic change relied heavily on moral factors. The outgoing dynasty was regarded as having failed to observe the dictates of heaven and therefore to have lost the mandate. The last rulers of a dynasty were inevitably portrayed as monsters or weaklings. In the case of the Qin dynasty this moral determinism was expressed even more sharply because of the Legalist outlook of the dynasty and the Confucian persuasion of its critics, which made it more acceptable to express sympathy for the cause of the rebels. The Han poet and statesman Jia Yi wrote a celebrated essay entitled 'The Faults of Qin' which became a classic exposition of this view. He condemned the First Emperor for having discarded the ways of former kings and having burned the writings of the hundred schools. He regarded Chen Sheng and his followers as having been driven to rebellion because of the severity of Qin laws and institutions. They should not have succeeded against the forces of the empire, being armed only with weapons made from hoes and the branches of trees. But Qin had a fatal flaw: it had failed to rule with humanity and righteousness and to realise that the power to attack and the power to retain what one has won are not the same.[23]

In recent times the reputation of Qin Shi Huangdi and the explanation for the collapse of the empire have given rise to controversy. After the 1911 Revolution the emperor was praised because he had rejected Confucianism, regarded at that time as a cause of China's weakness, and because he had unified the country. Later, Marxist historians explained the fall of the Qin in terms of a revolt against oppression by peasants – a revolt which undermined the dynasty, but which was bound to fail because of a compromise with 'landlord class elements'.[24] In the 1970s, in a clear reflection of the political issues of the day, Qin Shi Huangdi was portrayed as a man who had unified China after a long period of civil strife by following the progressive ideology of the time, an ideology which stressed the present and slighted the past.[25]

In the West most historians have emphasised the practical errors of the Qin dynasty rather than its moral failings or class conflicts. Derk Bodde accepted that Qin policies had created a large reservoir of desperate and resentful people who would be ready to join in a rebellion when the opportunity arose after the death of the First Emperor. But he rejected the argument that the rebellion was an indication of a class struggle or of a revolt against the institution of slavery. Instead he suggested that the transformation from Qin state to Qin empire was too much to accomplish in so short a time and so the failure of the empire was inevitable. Signs of tension, including threats to the emperor's life and price inflation, were apparent before the death of the Qin Shi Huangdi. These tensions could not be resolved by his successors in their brief reigns and so the dynasty fell, although many of its achievements, including that of uniting China, were carried over into the Han period.[26]

4
The Han Dynasty

The four centuries of Chinese history under the Han are divided into the earlier dynastic period of the Former or Western Han, dated 206 BC to AD 9, the interregnum of Wang Mang, AD 9–23, and the Later, or Eastern Han dynasty, AD 25–220. In this period some of the most characteristic features of the pattern of Chinese political, social, economic and religious life were established. Before turning to a review of the main events and developments of the Han period, two of these themes will be surveyed briefly.

Economic Development in the Han Period

It was during this period that an intensive agricultural economy became confirmed as typical of China. As Hsu Cho-yun put it:

> It appears that once the Chinese stepped upon the path of agriculture, they stayed on that course without deviation. Progress and change occurred from time to time, but agriculture remained paramount in the Chinese way of life.[1]

This concentration on agriculture has been seen as at variance with the potential for economic development, particularly in the realm of commerce, which was a noticeable feature of the Warring States period. The argument that has been put forward is that this potential was forever stifled by the rise of the imperial bureaucratic system. Whether that potential existed or not is an hypothetical question. What is clear is that the key characteristics of intensive agriculture had already been established in the Warring States period. Furthermore, the steady population growth which occurred in the Former Han period, which was not matched by a comparable increase in the area of arable land available, contributed to the development of labour-intensive agriculture.

To be more specific, in the Han period the agrarian economy acquired three characteristic features. The first was that of intensive cultivation, marked by careful field preparation, seed selection, irrigation, the use of manure, crop rotation, multi-cropping and the employment of animal power and of specialised tools. The second was the interdependency of the agrarian economy. By the Han period farm households were connected to a complex economic network which linked the agrarian economy with urban centres. Farmers not only sold their primary produce, but also engaged in a wide variety of secondary activities, which absorbed surplus or under-employed labour. Of these activities the production of textiles was perhaps the most important, and a proportion of these products was also sold. However the system was flexible, the dependence on the marketing system could be reduced and the activities of the farm household could be concentrated on home consumption. This feature linked with a third characteristic of the agrarian economy, the farmer's response to economic crisis. Governments of the Han dynasties were well aware of the importance of maintaining the security and prosperity of the farming population and in general subscribed to the idea that the tax burden should be kept at a low level. However, dynastic weakness led to the rise of landlordism and to heavy rents putting increasing burdens on the peasantry. If drought or flood or other natural catastrophe then occurred, and if self-sufficiency failed to ensure survival, the only alternative was migration. Under the Han government schemes of migration were linked with the establishment of military colonies on the north and north-west frontiers of the empire, thus solving the twin problems of overpopulation and defence. But by far the more important form of migration was free migration to the south, where peasants found a milder climate and more fertile soil. Their movement initiated a long-term trend which was to have reached its apogee in about 1290, when perhaps 90 per cent of the population lived in the area of China defined as the south.

The Nature of the Gods and the Ways to Paradise

In the chapter on the Shang dynasty brief mention was made of religious beliefs and practices. In the subsequent chapter on the Zhou reference was made to Daoism, but much more was said about the development of the schools of philosophy. This might suggest that in China interest in religion and in particular in the afterlife had been relegated to a position of unimportance. Nothing could be further from the truth. Recent archaeological finds, of artefacts interred with the dead and lost texts, have greatly increased our understanding of the religious beliefs of the inhabitants of the Han empire and have demonstrated how essential an awareness of those beliefs is for an appreciation of Han culture.

In the Han period something akin to a revolution occurred in terms of religious beliefs and practices. Michael Loewe expressed the change in the following terms:

> By AD 150, the emperors had for some time been offering services to different powers from those worshipped by their ancestors of western Han. There was a new explanation of the workings of the heavens and their wonders; a new view was taken of the miracles wrought on earth and amongst men, as the consequence of an all-embracing order of nature. Men and women saw new ways of attaining a life of eternity beyond the grave and relied on new types of talisman to achieve those ends. The emperor's authority had won new respect which derived not from the results of conquest by force, but from the legitimate power bestowed by a superior. The institutions of state now depended on a common acceptance of a series of holy books, whose texts and interpretation had passed through a lengthy process of controversy.[2]

There is not space here to summarise all the developments of Han religious thought. Instead, to convey the character of those changes, reference may first be made to one of the most important recent finds of the Han period, the excavation started in 1972 of tomb no. 1, that belonging to the countess of Dai, at Mawangdui in Hunan in central China. This tomb, which dates from about 168 BC, contained a rich collection of funerary furnishings which illustrate current ideas on life after death. It also contained the well-preserved body of the countess. At that time man was conceived as having a physical and spiritual form. The physical form might be likened to a candle, while the spiritual form resembled firstly the element which kept the body alight (known as po) and secondly the light which the flame cast (known as hun), which endowed a human being with intelligence and spiritual qualities. The careful mummification of the corpse may have been intended to provide the po with a home to which it could return. The other spiritual element, the hun required guidance on its journey to paradise. To help it to complete the journey successfully various talismans were put in the tomb, the most important of which was a painting on silk placed face downwards on top of the innermost of the four coffins. This depicted a journey which would take the hun first to the magical island of Penglai, where the soul would receive sustenance to enable it to reach the gates of paradise. The talisman would allow the hun to survive the scrutiny of the human warders and animals who guarded the gates and so enter and take up its place in the land of eternity.[3]

The change in religious belief in the Han period may be illustrated by reference to the important series of artefacts known as TLV mirrors. Mirrors had appeared in funerary furnishings from the Zhou period as evidence of wealth and as a form of protection for the deceased. However, the evolution of TLV mirrors may be dated from towards the end of the first century BC to the middle of the Eastern Han period. These mirrors bear complex symbolic features which provide a link between life on earth and life after death. The characteristic pattern is that of a square set within a circle, representing earth surrounded by the heavens. Within the square are placed the terms for the twelve divisions: the divisions of time which, by the Han period, had already been assigned animals to act as their emblems – Rat, Ox, Tiger, Hare, Dragon, Snake, Horse, Sheep, Monkey, Cock, Dog and Boar. Outside the square but inside the circle are set the animal motifs of four of the Five Elements: water, fire, wood and metal. The boss at the centre of the mirror may represent the fifth element, earth. In this part of the mirror are found the markings which resemble the letters T, L, and V, which may refer to marks on diviners' boards and which may indicate that the diviner has been consulted and has advised how the most felicitous disposal of the deceased person might be attained. Finally, the border of the mirror is frequently decorated with a scroll which represents the bank of clouds upon which the soul may mount to join the world of the immortal beings. The purpose of these mirrors was to provide the bearer, whether alive or dead, with a permanent assurance that he or she was situated in a correct relationship with the cosmos.[4]

The Founding of the Former Han Dynasty

As suggested in the previous chapter, the fall of the Qin dynasty was more the result of the errors of its rulers and chief advisers than a rejection of the principle of an unified empire. However, the transition from one dynasty to another could only come about through an armed struggle and it was inevitable that in that struggle contrasting models of the implications of unification might be discerned.

The first model was that proffered by Xiang Yu, an aristocrat and military leader from the old state of Chu, who led the attempt to overthrow the Qin dynasty and to replace the centralisation of power it represented with a return to the state system. The second model was that associated with Liu Bang, a man of peasant origins from the town of Pei in central China, who astutely offered a continuation of centralised power coupled with moderation and clemency, in contrast to the extremes practised by the Qin dynasty.

Xiang Yu made his bid for power after the defeat of the rebellion headed by Chen Sheng. He and his uncle declared the re-establishment of the state of Chu, an act which precipitated the re-formation of other states of the Warring States period. Such an action forced the dynasty to try to defeat Xiang Yu, but his capture of Julu, a city in northern China, greatly enhanced his military reputation. At this time Liu Bang, who was one of his supporters, was campaigning against the Qin in the west, in the Wei river valley which had been the strategic base from which the Qin had gained control of the country. In 207 BC he entered the Qin capital of Xianyang. Later historians were to stress the restraint of his subsequent actions. He negotiated the surrender of the city and prevented its looting. He announced the repeal of the Qin penal code and replaced it with a famous three-article code which stated simply that: he who killed anyone should suffer death; he who wounded another or stole should be punished according to the gravity of the offence; and that the rest of the Qin laws were abolished.[5] Furthermore, he was astute enough to lay claim to the city archives, which contained the information essential for the establishment of a new administration.

On the other hand, when Xiang Yu arrived, the city was looted and burned and the last king of Qin and his family put to death. Xiang Yu then revealed his preference in terms of a political settlement by announcing that the empire was to be divided into nineteen states, of which he was to be the ruler of one and from which he was to exercise the power of hegemon. This division threatened Liu Bang's position in the Wei river valley and it was at this point that the two men fell out and a civil war commenced. Although Liu Bang commanded inferior forces and by all accounts lacked the military flair of Xiang Yu, he more than made up for this with his political astuteness. When Xiang Yu had the young ruler of the state of Chu put to death, Liu Bang denounced him as a regicide. Although he could claim that right was on his side, Liu Bang's forces suffered several military defeats, and it was only through the energy of his lieutenants that his cause survived. Nevertheless Liu Bang gained allies and in 202 BC he achieved the decisive victory at Gaixia in modern Anhui. He proclaimed himself emperor (posthumous name Gaozu) and named his dynasty the Han, after the Han river and after the title of the king of Han which he had held since 206 BC, which date was taken as the official commencement of the dynasty.

The Reigns of Gaozu and His Sons, 202–141 BC

Liu Bang reigned as the Emperor Gaozu until he died in 195 BC. After his death, the throne was held by minors and real power lay in the hands of the empress dowager, the Empress Lü, until she died in 180 BC, to be succeeded first by another son of Liu Bang, and then by his grandson who ruled as the Emperor Jing or Jingdi until 141 BC.

During those years a remarkable consolidation of political power took place. This was not achieved by the harsh measures adopted by the First Emperor of the Qin, nor by the dispersed system advocated by Xiang Yu, but by pragmatic means. After Liu Bang had gained power, he had granted an amnesty and had demobilised his troops. He was not therefore in a position to coerce those who had been his allies and for this reason he had to accept a major compromise in terms of the administration of the empire. In the west, in that part of the empire encircling the capital Chang'an, direct administrative control in the form of commanderies was continued or developed. In the east, in a vast area stretching from north-east China, along the coast and down to the south, ten kingdoms were established. Initially their rulers were the *de facto* power-holders, often men who had fought on Liu Bang's side in the civil war. Within six years all but one of these men had been replaced by a member of the emperor's family. In addition to these concessions, the emperor conferred the lesser rank of *hou* or marquis on many of his principal supporters. The title was hereditary and carried a stipend derived from taxes raised within the marquisate.

Gaozu died in 195 BC, to be succeeded by his son, then a teenager. This son died in 188 BC and the succession passed to two minors. It was during this time that a classic instance occurred of a recurrent threat to the stability of the Chinese imperial institution: the domination of the empress dowager. During these years the power behind the throne was Liu Bang's widow, the Empress Lü. Confucian teaching emphasised the concept of filial piety. Since an emperor usually succeeded to the throne on the death of his father, filial piety was expressed in terms of duty to his mother. The Empress Lü was not to be the last empress dowager to take advantage of this situation and until her death in 180 BC she strenuously promoted the interests of her family. Her influence did not survive her, for after her death her family was eliminated and her memory excoriated.[6] For ever after her name was cited as evidence of the danger of female rule.

After the Empress Lü's death the empire passed peacefully through the hands of a son of Liu Bang, who reigned as Wendi, and of his son, Jingdi. During this period steps were taken to reduce the power of the kingdoms which still formed the eastern part of the empire. In 154 BC a major revolt broke out involving six of the kings in the east and south-east. After its suppression, Han direct control over the empire was extended, a process that was to be taken further as the dynastic period progressed.

The first Han emperor had also initiated two measures which were to place the imperial institution on a more stable footing. The first of these was to develop the bureaucratic form of government established by the Qin. At the highest level the emperor was assisted by three officials, known as the Three Excellencies, and they in turn were supported by nine ministers, each of whom had responsibility for a specified branch of the administration. It was a feature of Han government that senior officials were duplicated. Thus, in the most senior position, that of Chancellor, there were two chancellors, the Chancellor of the Right and the Chancellor of the Left. The bureaucracy was extended to cover the commanderies, the parts of the empire under direct imperial control. Each commandery was placed under a Commandery Administrator who was provided with subordinate staff. All officials in this bureaucracy were ranked according to their nominal salary, which was expressed in bushels of unhusked grain.[7]

The other step was more innovatory. It amounted to the discarding of Legalism as the ideological basis for government and its gradual replacement by Confucianism. Gaozu was far too suspicious of scholars to allow this to happen immediately. On one occasion he did sacrifice at the grave of Confucius, but he did not repeal the Qin decree against the ownership of proscribed Confucian books. Nevertheless the way was open for the development of a fresh justification for imperial power, one based on an ethical view of the rights and obligations of rulers and subjects. The significance of this became apparent a generation later. When Wendi was on the throne Jia Yi, the essayist whose writings on the faults of Qin have already been noticed, urged the emperor to emulate the example of the kings of Zhou, that is to care for his subjects' well-being and to listen to the criticism of his ministers.[8]

The consolidation of Han control was accompanied by the development of policies which earned the dynasty the support of the people. Mention has already been made of the rescinding of the most severe of the Qin laws. In practice the change was less apparent and much of the Qin legal code remained in force.[9] The same was true of the requirement on peasants in terms of taxation and corvée labour, which continued Qin practice. Large numbers of people were conscripted to construct the walls of the capital at Chang'an. Peasants were liable to a poll tax and a land tax, as well as to labour obligations and military service. The rate of the land tax, normally one-fifteenth of the harvest, was halved in 168 BC, and the labour and military service obligations appear to have been less onerous in the early part of the Han period than they had been under the Qin. According to the *Hanshu*, the *History of the Former Han*, these were years of prosperity:

> The government grain depots . . . were all completely filled, while the government treasury and storehouses, moreover, had surpluses of wealth of all kinds. In the capital cash had accumulated in layers of hundreds of millions, [the number of] which could not be checked because the strings [which held the coins together] were rotted.[10]

An indication of the splendour of the dynasty at this time may be found in the ruins of its capital at Chang'an, the city of Eternal Tranquillity. Its construction had been commenced under Gaozu and greatly extended by his successor. The formal layout of the city symbolised the regularity of the imperial order and the view of society as a series of interrelated groups, each placed in its own rightful position in the universe. The city was built to face south, so that when the emperor was seated in his audience chamber he occupied the favoured south-facing position. The walls, which stood 12 metres high, enclosed an area of some 26 square kilometres. Within the city were to be found imperial palaces, parks, markets and ritual structures.[11]

It was during this period of consolidation that the first steps were taken to stabilise and extend the frontiers of the empire. In this the main, indeed overriding, consideration was the relationship with the Xiongnu, inhabitants of an empire to the north of China. It was this people who were once identified with the Huns, although that is no longer accepted. In 209 BC Maodun, a dynamic new leader of the Xiongnu seized power. He rapidly brought together a new confederation of the inhabitants of the steppes and encroached on Chinese territory. This prompted Gaozu in 200 BC to mount a campaign to win the territory back, but he was defeated at the battle of Pingcheng in modern Shanxi and narrowly escaped capture. Thereupon Gaozu changed tactics from war to diplomacy. Two years later the first of a series of treaties was signed between the Han and Xiongnu empires. In each treaty a marriage alliance was arranged between a Chinese princess and a Xiongnu leader and this was accompanied by a handsome gift from the Han empire. These treaties served to reduce the risk of Xiongnu attack and gradually led to the development of a significant border trade.[12]

The Reign of Wudi, 141–87 BC

Michael Loewe, the foremost western historian of the Han dynasty, once remarked that the historical development of the Former Han period could best be understood in terms of two attitudes or convictions which characterised intellectual, religious and political change alike. He named these two attitudes 'modernist' and 'reformist'. The modernist attitude derived from Legalism, but differed from it. Modernists were concerned with the problems of the contemporary world. The reformist attitude derived from Confucian thought but was an extension of Confucianism. Reformists wished to eliminate the political and social abuses of the day by a return to conditions which they believed had existed in the remote past. According to Loewe, modernist policies dominated in the first century of the Former Han and reached their apogee in the reign of Wudi. Thereafter reformist tendencies gained strength and formed the ideological basis on which the usurper Wang Mang claimed the right to the throne.[13]

The reign of Wudi was the longest and most glorious of the Former Han. In the *Hanshu* he was the subject of a panegyric,[14] but not a great deal is known for certain of his personality. He was active in government, supervising work on the defences of the Yellow river and performing the necessary state rituals. But he never accompanied the military expeditions which were a principle source of the glorious reputation of his reign. He embodied a concept of the imperial institution which was committed inflexibly to certain basic principles of rule. An influential expression of this may be found in an essay written by the famous Confucian scholar Dong Zhongshu (c. 179–104 BC) and entitled 'The threefold obligation of the ruler'. These obligations were: to serve the basis of Heaven by making the appropriate sacrifices and setting the appropriate moral example; to serve the basis of earth by performing such symbolic acts as ploughing a furrow or feeding silkworms; and to serve the basis of man by establishing schools and enlightening the people by education.[15]

Under Wudi further steps were taken to develop the bureaucracy and important innovations were introduced. Most notable was the beginning of a career open to talent. A dramatic example of social mobility through education was the case of Gongsun Hong, who rose from being a swineherd to occupy the post of chancellor. He had studied the Confucian classics and had tendered advice to Wudi on the conduct of government. The usual way in which officials were recruited was by recommendation by provincial officials or senior ministers. If their recommendations proved unsatisfactory they were liable to punishment. In 124 BC an Imperial Academy was established with a quota of official disciples and students who studied the Confucian classics under the court scholars. After one year the students sat an examination in one of the classics and if they passed they were eligible for appointment to a government post. This has been seen as the start of the civil service examination system.[16]

Wudi's reign coincided with a great surge of intellectual activity in China. It is only possible to mention three examples of this. The first was the compilation known as the *Huainanzi*, assembled under the patronage of the prince of Huainan, who was a grandson of Gaozu. The collection had a distinctly Daoist tendency, containing, for example, a Daoist concept of the creation. But it also displayed perhaps the most characteristic feature of Han thought, its eclecticism. The essays in the book covered a variety of topics and represented a variety of views, and in the conclusion there was an attempt to synthesise what had been said:

> Casting away the foul and impure, drawing forth the pure and silent, it unifies the world, brings order to all things, responds to change and comprehends classes and categories. It does not pursue a single path, nor guard but one corner of thought, bound and led by material things and unable to change with the times. Use it in a corner of life and it will never fail; spread it over the whole world and it will never be found lacking[17]

Mention has already been made of Dong Zhongshu, the leading philosopher of the day, who may be said to have laid the foundations for orthodox Han Confucianism. His concept of the duties of the sovereign has already been noted. His writings, which included the *Chunqiu fanlu*, or *Deep Significance of the Spring and Autumn Annals*, were of great influence in at least three other areas of thought. The first was the theory of portents. Dong Zhongshu pursued the theme that if the emperor, the Son of Heaven, was failing in his duties, portents would appear which indicated Heaven's displeasure. If he failed to heed these, they would be followed by wonders, or 'Heaven's threats', which if ignored would lead to calamity. Secondly, he developed ideas relating to the order of nature, referring in particular to the Five Elements, that is water, fire, wood, metal and earth, to the yin and yang forces, and to the principle of the dao or Way. In Dong Zhongshu's writings these all formed part of one cosmic system, which in turn interlinked with political and ethical theories – heaven, earth and man all being governed by the same forces. Finally, it was Dong Zhongshu who ensured that the traditions and principles associated with Confucius would be accepted as orthodoxy by Wudi and by all succeeding emperors. This in itself was a remarkable change of fortune, after the attempt at the destruction of Confucian literature under the Qin. In Wudi's time not only were the texts restored, but they also became the basis of education and Confucius himself became the model for scholars. It was at this time that the state cult of Confucius was first established, an apotheosis transforming Confucius's thought from ethical treatise to the basis of a state religion.

Two other famous writers lived in Wudi's reign. The Grand Historian, Sima Qian, who died about 85 BC, was the author of the Shiji, the first attempt at a comprehensive survey of the history of China. He claimed merely to be completing a task started by his father, who had held the post of Grand Recorder at the court. In fact his ambition went much further, for he aimed to produce a vast and novel account of the past, based on a judicious selection from the records which had survived. In 99 BC Sima Qian spoke out in defence of a general who had been defeated by the Xiongnu, for which offence Wudi ordered that he be castrated – the sentence was carried out because the historian could not afford to redeem the punishment.[18]

The most famous poet of the day, Sima Xiangru, was rather more fortunate. He came from the province of Sichuan and married the daughter of a wealthy iron manufacturer. He became a courtier at Wudi's court and famous for his prose poems or fu. One of these contained a rhapsodic description of the Shanglin park, created by the First Emperor near Chang'an, and filled with exotic plants and strange animals. The poem's extravagant vocabulary, which was very different from the simple language of the verse in the Book of Songs, suggested that it was addressed to a minority audience of scholars and courtiers.

This was a period of active government and of state intervention in the operation of the economy. Significant changes were made in the administration of the empire. Many new commanderies were created and a system of regional inspectors established. A massive project to control the Yellow river was initiated. A free market in land was permitted and large estates were acquired, which then provided a major part of state revenue. Land was confiscated from landowners who had attempted to evade tax and then leased to peasants. In cities and towns, markets were controlled and merchants, whose status was low, were placed under various restrictions. State monopolies were established in the manufacture of salt and iron and somewhat later on the production of alcoholic liquors.

At the same time vigorous policies were pursued to prevent any significant challenge to dynastic rule. The administrative changes and the development of the bureaucracy formed part of a process of centralising power which progressively weakened the holders of kingdoms and marquisates. Several of the kingdoms suffered loss of territory and their significance was much diminished from that which they had been accorded at the beginning of the dynasty. Some 178 new marquisates were conferred in Wudi's reign, often as a means of ensuring the loyalty of former opponents, and in 112 BC over one hundred titles were also confiscated. One measure introduced by the emperor, which forced the division of an estate between all the male heirs, was to prove particularly effective against the principle of hereditary power. Coercive measures were also used against merchants who had profited greatly from the laissez-faire policies of the early Han emperors. Their position had improved even further as trade routes to Central Asia were opened up, and there were many instances quoted of merchants rapidly acquiring vast fortunes. Increased economic activity also gave a great boost to manufacturing, especially the production of iron and salt. Entrepreneurs amassed fortunes and then invested their profits in land. When, in 119 BC, the state set up monopolies in iron and salt the intention was not only to take a share of the profits, but also to challenge the accumulation of wealth and power in merchant hands. A similar profit motive may be detected in the introduction of a system of government purchase of surplus products in times of plenty and their sale in times of shortage.

The most dramatic indication of the growing power of the state was the policy of expansion with the effort first directed against the Xiongnu. In 138 BC Wudi despatched Zhang Qian as an envoy to the Yuezhi, a central Asian people known to be enemies of the Xiongnu, with whom he hoped to conclude an alliance. When Zhang Qian returned thirteen years later, having been held captive by the Xiongnu, he brought back invaluable information on Central Asia. He was also said to have introduced alfalfa and the grape to China. In the meantime military expeditions had been launched against the Xiongnu and the leading general of the day, Huo Qubing, achieved major victories over them in 121 and 119 BC. Later in the reign Chinese armies even reached Ferghana and the Pamirs. In the wake of these victories came colonisation of the Gansu panhandle and the development of trade along the Silk Road. At the same time Chinese expansion occurred in other directions. In 108 BC an expedition was sent to Korea which resulted in the establishment of four commanderies in the north of the peninsula. In the south victories were achieved over the people of Nanyue and commanderies were established in present-day Yunnan and Sichuan.

Without doubt the reign of Wudi was, from the Chinese point of view, a period of great progress. A sense of achievement was revealed in 104 BC when the emperor sanctioned the performance of ceremonies at which the dynasty's patron element of water, which had not been changed at the fall of the Qin dynasty, was now altered to that of earth, and the favoured colour became yellow in place of black. At the same time a new expression, Grand Beginning, was adopted for the counting of years.

Nevertheless, serious strains had already become evident and were to increase before the reign was over. Expeditions against the Xiongnu were extremely costly and so too was the effort required to maintain Chinese influence in the far-flung outposts of the empire. In 103 BC an expedition to obtain the 'heavenly horses' of Ferghana had failed and soon after that Xiongnu raiding started again. Trouble was not only apparent on the periphery of the empire, for in 99 BC serious outbreaks of banditry in eastern China forced the government to send special armed commissioners to restore order. In 91 BC the court itself was convulsed by a dynastic crisis which derived from a perennial problem suffered by dynasties, that of the power of the family of the empress. This was exacerbated by another frequent cause of dissension, the issue of the succession. For much of Wudi's reign the family of the Empress Wei had been in the ascendant and members of the family had occupied senior military and bureaucratic positions. The accumulation of problems encouraged the Li family, that is to say the family of Lady Li, one of the emperor's principal consorts, to challenge the dominance of the Wei. Accusations of witchcraft and embezzlement were traded. Open fighting broke out in which, it was said, ten thousand people died, and the Empress Wei and the heir apparent were both forced to commit suicide. At the same time the Li family was virtually eliminated. The one man who did improve his position as a result of the infighting was Huo Guang, a relative of the Empress Wei and half-brother of general Huo Qubing whose successes against the Xiongnu have already been noted. When Wudi fell terminally ill in 87 BC it was Huo Guang who headed the triumvirate which secured the succession of the eight-year-old boy who was to reign as Zhaodi.[19]

Later Rulers of the Former Han Dynasty

Almost immediately after the death of Wudi, the underlying discontents of his reign came to the surface. In 81 BC a conference was held to discuss the cause of the hardship which the population was suffering. The record of this conference has survived in the *Yan tie lun* or *Discourses on Salt and Iron*. The protagonists in the debate were the modernists and reformists referred to above. The apologists for the government represented the modernist view and their critics that of the reformists. The fundamental issue was defining the aims of a government. The reformists argued that these should be based on principles while the modernists replied that a government must respond to practical and material considerations. The debate then moved on to specific concerns and especially to criticism of foreign policy and state monopolies. Spokesmen for the modernist view replied that the Xiongnu threat had made it necessary to fight a defensive war and that monopolies had been established to protect the people from exploitation. Furthermore, the opening of trade with Central Asia had led to the introduction of many new and exotic products. In return, the critics of government questioned the need to venture so far to the west and described the operation of the monopolies as inefficient and corrupt. The most successful part of the reformists' argument related to contemporary living conditions, which they compared unfavourably with those which had prevailed in the early years of the dynasty. Perhaps this earned them a moral victory in the debate and it is true that, after Wudi's death, state intervention declined and the monopolies fell into disuse.

Among the complexities of the last seventy years of Former Han rule three themes stand out: court politics, foreign policy and the economy. Michael Loewe once remarked that 'the development of Han politics can only be understood in the context of the rivalries and scandals within the palace'.[20] However, the record of court intrigue quickly degenerates into a catalogue of names and does not make for easy reading. Perhaps one incident stands out sufficiently to demand notice and to illustrate the character of these intrigues. This concerned the fate of Huo Guang, the leader of the triumvirate which had arranged the succession to Wudi. As sole survivor of that triumvirate he played a similar role in securing the succession of Xuandi in 74 BC and until his death eight years later Huo Guang dominated the court. However, Xuandi's succession inevitably raised the question of who should be empress. The emperor insisted that his consort, who had already borne him a son, should be elevated to that rank, and her son thus be recognised as heir to the throne. Huo Guang was unable to prevent this, but shortly afterwards his wife secretly procured the death of the empress by poisoning. In 68 BC Huo Guang himself died and as a mark of the great esteem he was held in he was buried in a style hitherto reserved for emperors. His body was dressed in a suit of jade and a settlement of 300 families was established to maintain his tomb. But within two years a power struggle at court led to the elimination of almost every one of Huo Guang's descendants. Moreover, after his death the range of policies for which he stood – the modernist policies of expansion, control of the population and exploitation of resources, were gradually replaced by reformist policies of retrenchment and laissez-faire.[21]

In foreign policy, likewise, the reign of Xuandi has been identified as a turning point. Until then expansion into central Asia had continued, helped by internal quarrels among the Xiongnu and other tribes, notably the Qiang, ancestors of the modern Tibetans. From about 60 BC a new phase of consolidation began, associated with the advice tendered to the emperor by Zhao Chongguo, an experienced general. He drew attention to the danger and expense of relying on military force to sustain the Chinese position, and the difficulty of securing any decisive victory. He suggested instead that the correct policy in the frontier areas was the permanent establishment of sponsored farming settlements. This proposal was adopted and shortly afterwards the office of Protector-General of the Western Regions was created with the task of co-ordinating Chinese initiatives in the region.

Finally there was the matter of the economy, which despite the growth of industry and commerce was still overwhelmingly based on agriculture. A fundamental problem was the growth of large landholdings and the impoverishment of the peasantry. In about 100 BC Dong Zhongshu had submitted a memorial to Wudi advising the limitation of land and slave ownership and recalling the merits of the 'well-field' system. His advice went unheeded and the problem continued to grow with the increase in population reducing the average size of peasant lots.

Dynastic Decline and the Usurpation of Wang Mang

The last years of the Former Han dynasty illustrated many of the characteristics of what was later recognised as the downward phase of the dynastic cycle. These included extravagance at court followed by an unsuccessful attempt at retrenchment, one measure being a sharp reduction in the budget of the office of music. Another recurrent problem was the deepening conflict between court factions, often representing the family of the empress and the eunuchs. The latter, whose task was to ensure the well-being of the emperor and his women, only occasionally exerted influence in the former Han period, unlike the situation which was to prevail under the Later Han. Other factors which weakened the dynasty were succession disputes and regencies on behalf of child emperors. In the last decades of the Former Han the imperial line of succession from Xuandi failed, and the last three emperors of the dynasty were either invalids or minors.

Other problems added to the sense of crisis. One was the difficulty and expense of maintaining distant frontiers. Before the dynasty fell there was a partial withdrawal from Korea, but the suppression of rebellion in southwest China had imposed a severe strain on the empire's military capacity. There were also strains relating to raising tax revenues with a shift of the tax burden from large landowners to those least able to pay. The concentration of landownership was itself a recurrent difficulty. At the very end of the Han period, in 7 BC, a desperate and unsuccessful attempt was made to rectify this by the forcible redistribution of landholdings. Yet another problem was the neglect of river defences, which led to the disastrous flooding of the Yellow river in 30–29 BC.

The collapse of the dynasty was associated with the dominance of the Empress Wang, the mother of Chengdi, the emperor who reigned from 33 to 7 BC. Although the empress did not wield power herself, her influence was felt through members of her family who held the office of regent. Her nephew Wang Mang was regent while Pingdi was on the throne from AD 1 to 6. Shortly afterwards he claimed the throne, formally declaring himself as the first emperor of the Xin or New dynasty in AD 9.

Few characters in Chinese history have aroused more controversy than Wang Mang. For centuries, in China's traditional historiography, he was denounced as a tyrant, as a hypocrite and as an usurper. Yet earlier in this century the famous scholar Hu Shi hailed him as a pioneer of state socialism, who followed policies similar to those pursued in Russia in the 1920s.[22] More recently he has been classed as a reformist who tried to put into practice a genuine form of Confucianism,[23] or described as a pragmatist who governed China very much as the Han emperors had done before him.[24]

The basis on which these judgments have been formed are the factors which contributed to Wang Mang's rise to power, the measures which he took as emperor and the circumstances which led to his fall. In every case this evidence is limited and is heavily imbued with the horror of usurpers expressed in traditional historiography. As for Wang Mang's rise to power, the allegation was that he achieved this through a combination of ambition and guile, although that might be countered by a justification for his actions. The office of regent had been monopolised by the Wang family for twenty-five years and he had been preceded by three of his uncles. Moreover, Wang Mang had a reputation as a scholar, as a model of filial piety and as a man of modest personal needs. His decision to seize the throne was supported by a claim that twelve auspicious omens had appeared, which showed that heaven had awarded its mandate to him. The court nobility and officials had urged him to accept the offer.[25] Much of this case was astute propaganda and his motives may have been a combination of ambition and an awareness of the probable danger to himself and to his family if he did not seize power.

When in power Wang Mang pursued a range of policies which amounted to a programme of reform, although at times he appeared to be engaged in crisis management. His actions may be summarised under five headings, the first of which was the promulgation of an edict ordering the introduction of an equal landholding system based on the ancient 'well-field' principle. This measure, which has been described as the 'nationalisation' of the land, involved the abolition of private landownership and the prohibition of the sale of land or of slaves. In the edict it was made clear that this was an attack on large landholders and on their exploitation of peasants and that it was intended to return to the practices of the days of the Emperors Yao and Shun. The edict was issued in AD 9 and rescinded three years later, having proved entirely impractical.

A second major step was the reinstatement of the monopolies in salt, iron and alcohol which had been instituted under Wudi and which had been allowed to pass into disuse. At the same time a controlled market was introduced in grain, cloth and silk, with the government purchasing goods when they were cheap and selling them when the prices were high. It is not clear whether this was meant as a relief programme or to raise finance, but what is apparent is the anti-mercantile nature of the measure.

Thirdly, Wang Mang enacted a series of laws relating to taxation and the currency. A tax of ten per cent of income was levied on merchants and craftsmen. Several changes were made to the coinage system, with a large number of new denominations being introduced and an effective devaluation being carried out by allowing a discrepancy between face value and actual weight of the currency. A prohibition on the possession of gold and a requirement that it be exchanged for coinage, a measure probably intended to impoverish the nobility, was also passed.

It was perhaps inevitable that Wang Mang's disputed accession to the throne would be followed by trouble on the frontiers. The most serious danger arose from the alleged demotion of the tribal leader of the Xiongnu, but the threat of trouble was effectively countered by a show of force and a policy of divide and rule. Another area of difficulty was in the Western Regions, where in AD 13 a rebellion resulted in the death of the Chinese protector-general. Once again Wang Mang was able to deal with this, by dispatching a force large enough to re-establish the Chinese position.

Finally, Wang Mang sponsored scholarly research on the Confucian classics. He was patron to the historian Liu Xin and through him encouraged a revival of interest in ancient texts. Wang Mang himself was deeply interested in the record of

China's antiquity. He assumed titles from the Zhou period and on occasions claimed to be recreating the ideal Confucian state. In a more practical vein, Wang Mang also encouraged scientific research, permitting a medical dissection to take place; and in AD 19 he encouraged an early attempt at manned flight.

If at least some of these actions might be regarded as achievements, why did Wang Mang's reign come to a premature end? Ban Gu, the historian of the Former Han, was in no doubt: it was because the measures he took were so ill-conceived that he antagonised all classes of society:

> The people could not turn a hand without violating some prohibition. . . . The rich had no means to protect themselves and the poor no way to stay alive. They rose up and became thieves and bandits, infesting the hills and marshes, and the officials, being unable to seize them, contrived on the contrary to hide their presence so that they grew more prevalent day by day. . . . Famine and pestilence raged and people ate each other so that before Wang Mang was finally punished half the population of the empire had perished. . . .[26]

Many writers have echoed Ban Gu and have found fault with the measures taken by Wang Mang. These have been decried as impractical in the case of the land reform, and a cause of confusion, distress and loss of confidence in the case of the currency innovations.[27] The attempt to re-introduce monopolies has been criticised as certain to antagonise the merchants without leading to any financial advantage to the population as a whole. The conduct of foreign relations has been decried as inept. At best Wang Mang has been portrayed as an idealistic intellectual, with many genuine humanitarian impulses, who became corrupted by power.[28] Less charitably, he has been referred to as an over-ambitious ruler whose attempt to bring about change led to abject failure accompanied by ridicule and farce.[29]

In these opinions the common explanation for the collapse of the short-lived Xin dynasty was the innovatory, if not to say revolutionary, domestic policy espoused by Wang Mang. Hans Bielenstein, however, argued that there was nothing new about these measures, for they all derived from past example and in particular from practices dating from the reign of Wudi. Wang Mang was 'a pragmatist who governed China very much as the Han emperors had done before him'.[30] For Bielenstein the essential reason for Wang Mang's fall was a natural disaster, the shifting of the Yellow river to a southern course debouching just north of the Shandong peninsula. This caused a massive loss of life, widespread famine and many people became refugees. It also gave rise to peasant rebellion, the most famous manifestation of which was the rebel group who became known as the Red Eyebrows because they painted their foreheads red to distinguish themselves from the government troops. Wang Mang's forces had several unsuccessful encounters with the rebels, and he then found his position challenged by a gentry-led group, centred on Nanyang in present-day Henan, and led by a descendant of the founder of the Former Han dynasty. In AD 23 this group inflicted a decisive defeat on Wang Mang, who retreated to Chang'an where he was killed. It took another two years of civil war between rival claimants before Liu Xiu claimed the throne as the first emperor of the Later Han dynasty.

Restoration and Recovery in the Later Han

Liu Xiu, later to be known by his posthumous name, Guang Wudi, occupied the throne until AD 57. During that period, and during the reigns of his successors Mingdi and Zhangdi, the Han dynasty was restored and China achieved a level of prosperity and security comparable to that of the Former Han.

Guang Wudi's first task was to suppress peasant rebellion and to overcome rivals to the throne. The Red Eyebrows had already been weakened by internal division and through clashes with other contenders. In communist historiography the reason for their defeat has been described as the seizure of the fruits of the peasant class struggle by representatives of the landlord class.[31] Liu Xiu, the future emperor, who came from Henan, was a landowner and his most dangerous rival for the throne, Gongsun Shu, was the leader of a powerful family based in present-day Sichuan. Liu Xiu had declared himself emperor in AD 23, but it was not until AD 36 that Gongsun Shu was killed and his capital Chengdu captured.

It was one thing to achieve a military victory, but the more difficult task was to fashion a political settlement that would last. Although Guang Wudi claimed to have restored the Han dynasty, the restoration was only partial. Many of the fiefs of the Former Han were not revived and only a limited return was made to the Former Han practice of nominating the emperor's sons as rulers of kingdoms. Another break with the past was the decision to move the imperial capital from Chang'an to Luoyang, some 200 miles to the east (hence the alternative name of the dynasty, the Eastern Han). Luoyang was to become the most populous city in the world at that time. The most marked discontinuity was in the matter of the national élite. The Former Han had seen the rise of great families to positions of power and influence. Some of these had been displaced under Wang Mang. The restoration, however, 'was not a restoration of the old social order'.[32] Guang Wudi's support had not derived from the great families of the former dynasty but for the most part came from the lesser gentry. Initially this gave him freedom of action in determining how to reward his allies. In the longer term this did not amount to absolute power and all emperors of the Later Han had to look for additional sources of support to remain in power. The political history of Guang Wudi's reign and that of his successors was dominated by attempts to manipulate the rivalry between various factions at court and in the bureaucracy.

In administrative terms, much of Later Han practice derived from the previous dynasty, although there were some changes in terms of the location of power and of cost. The most important development was the rise in influence of the secretariat, which although of lesser formal importance than the three great offices of state, was increasingly relied upon by the emperor. In terms of expense, Guang Wudi, like some other founders of dynasties, was able to make economies by cutting superfluous offices, for example in the palace guard and in the stable and coachhouse establishment. A much larger economy was achieved by reducing the number of counties by 400, a change made possible because of population decline and migration from the north-west.

The Han Dynasty

There is evidence to suggest that the turbulent years of dynastic change accompanied by natural disasters had led to a substantial reduction in population. Two sets of figures have survived, the annual registrations of the population for the purpose of taxation for AD 2 and for AD 140. The first showed the population to number 57.7 million individuals and the latter indicated slightly over 48 million individuals. In the same period there had been a dramatic shift in the regional distribution of the population. At the earlier date 76 per cent of the population lived in North China, but by the later date this proportion had fallen to 54 per cent.

These figures belie a pattern of improvements in agriculture, with the greater use of iron farming implements, the repair and extension of irrigation projects and the increased use of draft animals. The significance of the last-named change was shown in AD 76 when a serious cattle epidemic occurred and this caused large areas of land to be taken out of cultivation. The benefits of agricultural improvement were not shared out evenly, for powerful landowners extended their holdings and grew rich at the expense of their labourers. Much of the migration from the north-west and the Central Plain southwards may have been due to the impoverishment of peasants who could not keep up with technological change or who had fallen into debt. Some confirmation of this situation is to be found in measures taken by the government to assist poor peasants. These included taxing agriculture lightly, helping peasants who had lost their land to resettle elsewhere, and providing direct grants of assistance. It is testimony to the efficiency of Later Han government in the first century AD that it contained the effects of natural disaster while remaining solvent.

In towns and cities too there was evidence of economic improvement. It was in this period that a money economy became fully accepted, with wages commonly being paid in cash and labour services being partially commuted into a monetary tax. Communications were improved and it has been suggested that land transportation in North China was probably as good during the Later Han as it was in any period before modern times.[33] This advance encouraged commercial activity which was subject to less government interference than in the past. Interregional trade flourished and new and improved products such as paper and lacquerware were distributed widely.

In foreign relations, Guang Wudi and his successors achieved short-term glory at the expense of creating disastrous long-term problems. In terms of relations with the Xiongnu, the policy was one of divide and rule. A southern branch of the Xiongnu was allowed to settle in the Ordos region, but sporadic campaigns were fought against the northern branch, culminating in a major victory in AD 89. This permitted the restoration of Chinese influence in the Western Regions, the key figure in this venture being Ban Chao, brother of the historian Ban Gu. He led an army across the Pamirs, reached the Caspian Sea and sent an envoy to make contact with the Roman Empire. In the meantime, in the north-east, the Han dynasty was involved in dealings with two other important tribal groupings who had been brought into contact with China through the campaigns against the Xiongnu. The Wuhuan lived beyond the Great Wall in modern Hebei and Liaoning. They had formerly been in a tributary relationship with the Xiongnu, but from AD 49 they were drawn into the Han tributary system, their leaders being offered titles and gifts in return for guarding the frontier against their former overlords. As a result they began to settle in the northern commanderies. The Xianbei lived beyond the Wuhuan. They too became clients of the Han with the duty of fighting the Xiongnu, a task which they fulfilled only too successfully. In AD 91 they defeated the northern Xiongnu and occupied their lands, only then to turn against the Chinese. For the next century the Xianbei were to be the main threat on China's northern frontier. Meanwhile throughout the south the Han empire continued to expand. Another famous name in Chinese military history, Ma Yuan, is remembered for his heroic campaign which in AD 43 ended the attempt by two Vietnamese sisters to shake off the Chinese yoke.

The Beginnings of Decline and the Crisis of AD 168

A century before it came to an end, the Later Han dynasty was already showing signs of disorder, which were to culminate in the crisis of AD 168. The problems besetting the dynasty may be divided into three, of which the first appeared at court. For a century, starting from 88, a succession of minors had occupied the throne. Effective power was in the hands of a regent, or more often in the hands of the empress dowager. There were frequent examples of contested succession and of violent deaths at court. The most notorious exponent of the latter practices was Liang Ji, brother of the empress of Shundi, who allegedly procured the murder of one infant emperor and made his sister regent for his successor. Over a period of twenty years, until his murder in 159, he accumulated every conceivable post of importance and amassed a fortune estimated at 3,000 million cash. At court at this time the influence of the family of the 'external clans', as the family of the empress was termed, was challenged by the eunuchs, castrated men employed in the imperial palace. Eunuchs, who were often of plebeian origins, owed their influence to their relationship to the emperor whose harem they guarded. In return the emperor looked to them for support against the 'external clans'. Under the Later Han the number of eunuchs at court increased greatly, reaching 2,000, and they began to exercise political influence. Their position improved in 114 when the adopted son of an eunuch was permitted to inherit his fief, and again in 135 when eunuchs were granted the right to hand down noble titles to their adopted heirs. It was a group of five eunuchs who murdered Liang Ji and throughout the reign of Huandi the eunuchs played a prominent role. When Huandi died in 169, a major crisis occurred at the Han court, the outcome of which was a triumph for the eunuchs. For the next fifteen years eunuchs controlled the government and pursued a vendetta against those whom they regarded as having acted against their interests in the past.

The second problem was the growing unevenness in the distribution of wealth. The celebrated scholar Wang Fu lived between AD 90 and 165. A man who never obtained official preferment, he expressed his views on the age in a work called

Qianfu lun or *Criticisms of a Hidden Man*. In one chapter of the book, entitled 'On excessive luxury', he railed against the social conditions and morals of his day. He noted how agriculture was being abandoned in favour of trade, how people, even the servants and slaves of the aristocracy, ate and dressed extravagantly, and how the administration of justice had become too expensive for the poor to use.[34] Some of this accumulation of wealth derived from large estates and the wealth of some landowners outstripped that of officials. Evidence of this wealth has been found in the thousands of tombs of Han date which have been identified. Many tombs contain pottery models, representing the various possessions of the deceased and sometimes drawing attention to his position as a landowner.[35] But alongside this wealthy minority the great mass of the agricultural population lived in abject poverty, oppressed by taxes and labour services and often in danger of losing the plot of land which represented to them some degree of independence, and without which they would become landless labourers.[36]

Finally there was the problem of the frontier. In the second century AD the dynasty had to face the consequences of previous policies of compromise. One difficulty was that of expense. When the dynasty had restored tributary relations with the Western Regions in AD 73, it had become the established practice for the Chinese to make regular payments amounting to a total of 74,800,000 cash a year to leaders of the tribes in the area and this was a tremendous burden on state finances. An even larger sum was spent on maintaining the southern Xiongnu, now settled within Han territory. Although the Xiongnu presence alongside Chinese settlers was expected to stabilise this section of the frontier, in fact it created a complicated and often dangerous racial situation, the full implications of which became apparent a century later. However it was from the Xianbei in the north that the most pressing threat emerged. In the middle of the century a leader named Tanshihuai created a great steppe confederation of his peoples and between 168 and his death in 180 he inflicted a series of defeats on the Chinese, so destabilising the whole of the northern frontier.

Similarities have been noted between the problems of the Chinese and Roman empires in coping with the threat of uncivilised or nomadic peoples on their borders. It has been pointed out that effective control meant a combination of two factors: adequate military power to dominate such peoples and acceptance of their position by the peoples so dominated. In the Former Han period this combination had been achieved and control maintained. However in the Later Han, with the appearance of Xianbei, who initially lacked a coherent political system with which the Chinese could deal, there was no acceptance of Chinese authority. At the same time the loss of Chinese population in the north, and the weakening of government finances and commitment, undermined the principle of adequate military power. The fact that until the year 177, when an expedition against Tanshihuai ended in disaster, Chinese armies were successful in their campaigns, disguised the extent of the erosion of the Chinese position. By the end of the dynasty, Chinese authority had been driven well to the south and the frontier lands had fallen out of Chinese control. In this region, a century later, were to emerge the barbarian states which dominated North China in the centuries of division.[37]

The Fall of the Later Han

Although the Han dynasty did not come to an end until 220, its effective collapse as a dynasty occurred in 189. A discussion of the reasons for its decline and fall must therefore concentrate on the reign of Lingdi, that is on the period from 168 to 189. Some of the reasons for dynastic decline had already become established by the start of his reign: factional fighting at court, great disparities in wealth, and threats on the frontier. Under Lingdi the situation worsened: the sale of high office became established, and Xianbei raiding on the frontier became increasingly frequent. These were later to be recognised as typical features of dynastic decline. So too was a third factor, peasant rebellion, which Marxist writers attributed to the struggle of peasants against the landlord class. However, even Marxist writers would have to admit that the rebellion which challenged the dynasty in 184 was a rebellion of a new type, although it was to have many repetitions, for it was a rebellion which derived its inspiration from religion. Adherents of popular Daoism, perhaps responding to the fact that the year 184 marked the beginning of a new sexagenary cycle in the calendar, rose in a number of movements. There were two main rebellions, the Yellow Turbans, headed by Zhang Jue in the east, and the Five Pecks of Rice (so named after the subscription paid by each follower), headed by Zhang Lu in the west. The inspiration of these millenarian sects was a book dating from the end of the former Han entitled Taiping jing, or The Book of the Great Peace, which announced the coming of a new golden age of prosperity and equality. This promise attracted a following of many thousands of peasants, who attacked government officials. This provoked savage reprisals, said to have cost the lives of half a million people in the first year alone.[38]

The Yellow Turban and Five Pecks of Rice rebellions, which undoubtedly brought widespread devastation, are often cited as the cause of the downfall of the Han dynasty. However, it must be remembered that the direct threat from these rebellions had been countered by 189 and that there is some doubt whether the rebellions aimed to overthrow the dynasty. To what then should the collapse of the dynasty be attributed? One could say that a dynasty which was already severely weakened suffered a series of hammer blows which ensured its fall. The first blow came on the death of Lingdi when the eunuchs, who throughout the reign had been the emperor's main support, were massacred.[39] The second came in the following year when Luoyang was sacked and the emperor removed to the old capital of Chang'an. By now effective power lay in the hands of the generals, the most famous of whom, Cao Cao was dominant in the north, Liu Bei in Sichuan and Sun Quan in the south. The dynasty survived in name, but only because Cao Cao declined to usurp it. When he died in 220 his son formally ended the Han period by declaring the establishment of a new dynasty, the Wei.

5
The Period of Division

Although the Han dynasty did not officially end until 220, its power collapsed in 189. For over three hundred years from that date no single dynasty had effective control over the whole of China. Between 189 and 220 there was a three-way division of power between three Later Han generals. When Cao Cao, the most famous of these, died in 220, the empire was divided into three kingdoms: the Wei dynasty under Cao Pei, the son of Cao Cao at Luoyang; the Wu dynasty under Sun Quan at Jiankang; and the Shu Han dynasty under Liu Bei at Chengdu. The era of the Three Kingdoms ended in 280 when the successors to the Wei dynasty defeated their rivals and as the Western Jin reunited China, at least in name. But in 311 the dynasty's capital at Luoyang was sacked by the Xiongnu and in 316 the state was destroyed.

From 316 to 589 China was divided politically between dynasties of the south which sought to revive the tradition of the Han, and dynasties of the north, generally established by non-Chinese peoples. To describe the political succession in the south, the term the Six Dynasties is used, referring to the dynasties which had their capital at Jiankang, or modern Nanjing. In the north the fragmentation of authority was even more extreme and the period between 316 and 384 is known as that of the Sixteen Kingdoms. But from that time onwards a new power began to emerge, headed by a branch of the Xianbei known as the Toba, who had originally settled in northern Shanxi. In 386 the Toba adopted the dynastic name of the Northern Wei and from then on they became increasingly sinicised. In 493 the Toba emperor established his capital at Luoyang and inaugurated a period of peace and prosperity. In 534, however, the dynasty split and the north again experienced division under dynasties known collectively as the northern dynasties. From one of these emerged a general named Yang Jian, who not only gained control of the north, but also defeated the last of the southern dynasties. In 589 the Sui dynasty reunited China.

The Fall of the Roman and Chinese Empires Compared

The idea that there might be a connection between the fall of the Roman and the early Chinese empires has been current since at least 1788, when Edward Gibbon completed *The History of the Decline and Fall of the Roman Empire*. In that work Gibbon emphasised the role of what he called the barbarian tribes in undermining the two empires and explained this by stressing the contrast between the civilised but effete values of the Romans and Chinese and the rude vigour of the barbarians.

More recently the collapse has been explained as the consequence of systemic weaknesses in the two empires. The key weaknesses which have been identified are first those to do with the economy, with reference to the growth of great and privileged estates run by large landowning families, and the alleged effect of the institution of slavery. Secondly, there are the factors which undermined the culture or ideology which had informed the empire at the time of its rise, which might be defined as a combination of degeneracy and intrusive religion. For Rome, Gibbon had identified the enemies as the increase in luxury and the adoption of Christianity. For Han China, the same allegations have been made about the effects of luxury, the spread of Buddhism, and the attraction of Daoist escapism. Finally there is the matter of the relationship with 'barbarian' tribes on the frontiers. For some writers[1] the fall of the two empires derived from a common event, the rise of a Mongol people called the Avars who, throughout the fifth century, maintained an empire which extended from the boundary of Korea to Lake Balkhash. The repercussions of their expansion were to bring both empires to their knees at virtually the same time. In both empires a fatal weakness had been created by permitting nomadic peoples to settle within the boundaries of the empire and allowing the defences of the frontier to fall into the hands of auxiliary soldiers recruited among the settlers. Financial weakness made it difficult for either empire to sustain an active defence and this ensured that the policy was one of diplomacy and compromise. And so, as the empires also weakened from within, it was only a matter of time until they collapsed.[2]

With the disappearance of central government, China and western Europe entered a prolonged period of division described as a dark age. In each case one half of the former empire experienced political disintegration, while in the other half, either in form of the Byzantine empire or in the succession of empires centred on Jiankang and known as the Six Dynasties, there was an attempt to preserve the traditions of a glorious past and the hope of recovering that which had been lost.

But there the parallels cease because the Chinese empire recovered. The consensus as to why this occurred is that it had qualities superior to those of the Roman empire. These included a stronger ethnic and cultural unity, with special reference to the Chinese writing system, and a greater geographic unity, with China the more compact empire, not divided by major natural barriers like the Alps. It has been suggested that the Han imperial concept was superior to that of Rome: that the ideal of a just and ethical rule by an emperor who held the mandate of heaven, and who ruled through a bureaucracy composed of educated men, had a greater appeal than the personal rule of the Roman emperors implemented through an impartial code of law. Finally, in practical terms, the weight of population and the age and persistence of Chinese culture in the north of the country, where China was at its weakest, proved a decisive factor. The barbarians who invaded China were unable to change this. The majority absorbed the invaders and converted them into Chinese.[3]

The Era of the Three Kingdoms and of the Western Jin

Between 220 and 280 China was divided into three states. Wolfram Eberhard described the two southern ones as 'condottiere states', that is to say states conquered by generals from the north and for a time ruled by those generals and their northern troops.[4] In the south-west, occupying present-day Sichuan, an area which in Chinese history has often become a regional power base, was the kingdom of Shu Han. Its first ruler, Liu Bei, claimed descent from the Han royal family, and his pretensions to be the legitimate successor were later upheld. In its first years Shu Han achieved some success in extending its influence among the non-Chinese peoples of modern Yunnan and after Liu Bei's death in 226, his chief minister Zhuge Liang gained a reputation as a wily strategist. But after Zhuge Liang died in 234 Shu Han, which had the smallest population of the Three Kingdoms, went into decline and was absorbed by Wei in 263.

In the south-east, occupying the Yangzi valley and a vast area to the south, was the Kingdom of Wu. This area had only become sinicised under the Han and the political control of its rulers was tenuous. Some attempt was made to establish foreign relations, and there is a record of Wu making overtures to the state of Yan in southern Manchuria and to Yamato in the south of Japan. In both cases the motive seems to have been to seek allies against Wei in the north. In this the Wu rulers were not successful and the kingdom fell to Wei in 280.

The kingdom of Wei had been established by Cao Pei, son of Cao Cao, that most famous of the generals of the late Han period. From the start the condition of the state was insecure. It retained the style, and the expense, of an imperial court at Luoyang and it tried to protect its trade routes to the north-west. However, it was forced to make heavy payments to the nineteen Xiongnu tribes which had been allowed to settle in the north and its attempts to subjugate the kingdoms of the south entailed further military expenses.

In the meantime, a more subtle change was taking place in the kingdom's political organisation. Under the Later Han a few powerful families had risen to national importance. Large estates had been established and their owners had come to dominate local affairs. With the decline of central authority these magnates had established enclaves of local power. Some of them had also adopted the ideas of a moralistic revival group whose members called themselves qingliu, that is the 'pures'. They railed against the dominance of the imperial throne by the eunuchs and by the family of the empress dowager. They argued that this malign influence should be replaced by the appointment of men who were known locally for maintaining traditional moral standards. This view reinforced a tendency to give increased respect to pedigree and to promote to high office those whose ancestors had formerly achieved eminence.

From these changes there evolved a new system of recruiting men to office, known as the arbiter system, which was to be used by new rulers to gain legitimacy and to obtain the cooperation of powerful local families. Under this system an arbiter, a man chosen from the local upper class, was appointed to each commandery, and later also to each prefecture. His task was to classify candidates for office into nine ranks of character and ability: the higher the rank a man received from the arbiter, the higher the office for which he was eligible. This system precipitated a major change in social stratification, leading to the emergence of aristocratic families, whose status depended partly on their local wealth and influence, and partly on their access to office.[5]

Long before this system was properly established, events in the state of Wei demonstrated the fragility of the political situation. Having conquered Shu Han in 263, the ruler of Wei was deposed by Sima Yan, one of his generals and a member of one of the leading families. Sima Yan established a dynasty called the Western Jin and entitled himself Jin Wudi, the 'martial emperor'. During his reign the state of Wu was subjugated and China reunited. Thereafter some attempt was made to rehabilitate a country which had been ravaged by war by disbanding soldiers and attempting to settle them on the land. The need for such a measure was indicated by the sharp decline in the official census of the taxable population, which by 280 had fallen to 16 million from 56 million under the Later Han. But the dynasty was too weak to coerce the great landowners and generals. After the emperor's death in 290 the country lapsed into the civil war known as the Revolt of the Eight Kings. With the disintegration of imperial government, Xiongnu incursions form the north increased, and in 311 they sacked the capital Luoyang.

While historians have often dismissed the period of the Three Kingdoms and the Northern Wei as a period of dreary disorder, in popular culture it has acquired a romantic reputation. This is largely because it is the period depicted in the seventeenth-century novel *The Romance of the Three Kingdoms*, attributed to Luo Guanzhong. In its pages appear fictionalised representations of Cao Cao, Liu Bei and Zhuge Liang. An even more assured place in popular memory was achieved by Guan Yu, a confederate of Liu Bei, who in the sixteenth century was raised to the rank of Guandi, the God of War.

The Southern Dynasties

After the collapse of the Western Jin dynasty in the north, for two centuries China was effectively divided into two. It is convenient to describe first the developments to the south of the Yangzi. The record began with the establishment in 317, by a survivor of the Western Jin, of a new dynasty known as the Eastern Jin, with its capital at Jiankang. To the capital came many refugees from the north, while at the same time the Chinese population was increasing rapidly, causing tension between old and new settlers and between the Chinese and non-Chinese populations. The dynasty maintained its claim to be the true heir to the Han and sought to reconquer the north, but it was hampered by intrigues at court and rivalry among generals. In 399 the dynasty was faced with a different sort of threat, a popular rising along the southern coast, perhaps triggered off by tension between new and old settlers. Its leaders claimed a connection with the Yellow Turbans of the last years of the Later Han period. The rising was suppressed by an army commander named Liu Yu, who in 420 usurped the throne and established what became known as the Liu-Song dynasty.

Under Liu Yu and his successor a period of political stability ensued, but after the fall of the Liu Song in 479 three more undistinguished dynasties were to rise and fall in quick succession. Despite the failure of any of the southern dynasties to recover political authority, this period was one of population growth and the rise of what has been called a manorial system.

The Northern Dynasties

Meanwhile, in the north, there occurred the long period of anarchy known as the time of the Sixteen Kingdoms. During this era, the settled population of north China was invaded and overrun by various tribal groupings coming from the west and the north. Among these, three major ethnic conglomerations have been distinguished. To the west, in the area of modern Gansu, Shaanxi, Sichuan and Qinghai, were the Tibetan Di and Qiang, peoples who were essentially sheep herders rather than horse breeders and whose states were based on a military rather than on a tribal structure. In the north-west were the Xiongnu, traditionally divided into nineteen tribes, and the Jie, both ethnically described as Turkic. Finally, to the north were the Xianbei, whose ethnic origins were variously described as proto-Mongol or Tungus. These ethnic labels must be treated with caution. At most they only refer to the language and culture of the leading tribe within a group or confederation. Tribes with different ethnic characteristics could and did join together in confederations.[6]

The first major incursion into north China in this period came from the Xiongnu and resulted in the capture of Luoyang and Chang'an and the destruction of the Western Jin dynasty. The leading figure in this train of events was Liu Yuan, descendant of Maodun, whose dynamic leadership of the Xiongnu in the early years of the Former Han dynasty, five hundred years previously, has already been noted. Liu Yuan came from a new mould of Xiongnu leadership, one who had acquired a Chinese education and whose concept of empire was not the nomadic empire of the past, but one which laid claim to settled territory and to the imperial throne of China. To support this claim Liu Yuan could point to the intermarriage between the Xiongnu and the Han dynasty, to the fact that his surname was the same as that of the Han, and that at his capital, Pingcheng, Chinese court ceremonial had been adopted and to it he had already attracted educated Chinese. Liu Yuan died in 310, the year before the capture of Luoyang, though his successors established the short-lived dynasty known as the Earlier Zhao (304–20). But Liu Yuan's vision of empire was not shared by other tribal leaders. A new tribal confederation formed under Shi Luo, who rejected the Chinese model in favour of a return to the Xiongnu nomadic state, but who also broke with tradition by usurping the rightful succession and declaring himself ruler of the Later Zhao dynasty.

The second main challenge came from the Tibetan peoples in the west. When the Later Zhao dynasty collapsed, the leader of a Tibetan tribal confederation declared himself emperor of the Earlier Qin dynasty. In 357 he was succeeded on the dynastic throne by a man named Fu Jian, who built up a formidable fighting force, consisting not only of cavalry, but also of infantry, recruited among the Chinese. With this force he was able to conquer much of North China. In 383 he turned his attention to the conquest of the south and to the destruction of the Eastern Jin. This campaign was the most famous of the period. Fu Jian is supposed to have mustered one million men when he descended the Yangzi to capture Jiankang. But his forces were accustomed to open terrain and were unable to adapt to the conditions of the Yangzi valley. They were defeated by the Jin troops at a decisive battle, which led not only to the failure of the expedition, but also to the rapid disintegration of the Earlier Qin empire.

The third instance of the rise of a non-Chinese dynasty, to be called the Northern Wei, was that of the tribal federation known as the Toba. The original Toba state had been destroyed by Fu Jian, but in about 385 it was re-formed in the north of the present province of Shanxi. Its leadership group may have been of Turkic origin, although the federation incorporated Xiongnu and Xianbei tribes and, as the state prospered, an increasing number of Chinese were employed as officials. Towards the end of the fourth century the Toba state extended its control over much of the North China Plain. It then began a process of adaptation and change, including progressive sinicisation, which gave it a strength and permanency which exceeded that of all previous non-Chinese dynasties.

This process had several components. The first was that the Toba developed sufficient military power to ward off rivals, which was achieved initially by the gradual subversion of the tribal system and its replacement by a military administration. This enabled the Toba to extend their influence in two directions. To the north, the settled Toba attacked and defeated yet another confederation of nomadic tribes, known as the Ruanruan, sometimes identified with the Avars who were later to settle on the Danube. There followed a series of successful expeditions which extended Toba influence into Gansu and gave access to the commerce of Central Asia. By 440 the Toba empire was the most powerful state in East Asia, ruling the whole of north China.[7]

Another factor was the increasing participation of Chinese in the government of the Toba state. From 440, Pingcheng was developed as a capital city. Although still a barbarous place in the eyes of Chinese visitors, it had a huge palace complex, residential wards and religious buildings. Such a city required the service of Chinese officials accustomed to urban life. From 476, when the Empress Dowager Feng, herself from an aristocratic Chinese family, gained paramount power, the advancement of Chinese to high office gathered pace. Between 472 and 499 a series of decrees was issued, known as the Taihe reforms, which were 'a conscious and deliberate attempt to bring the country closer to the . . . ideal of a Han-Chinese, Confucian, bureaucratic monarchy ruling an ordered aristocratic state'.[8] The reforms included the development of a Confucianised bureaucracy and the promotion of Confucian morality, control of Toba religious and social customs, and the introduction of more sophisticated systems of taxation and forced labour. They were accompanied by a change in frontier policy, with a switch away from the aggressive policy of sending powerful forces on raids against the Ruanruan, to one of wall-building, static defence and appeasement. Policies such as these, aimed at sinicisation and undermining tribal customs, inevitably excited the hostility of traditionalist Toba aristocratic families.

An important economic reform had a more complicated purpose. In 477 a plan was accepted for a 'land equalisation scheme', (juntian). All land was decreed to belong to the state. Every free man and woman had the right to receive a certain amount of land for their lifetime, but after their death the land would be redistributed. In addition to this allocation, which was defined as 'personal land', people could also hold a small area known as 'mulberry land', to be planted with mulberries and other crops, which land could be inherited. The introduction of this reform has been associated with the impoverishment of the Toba tribespeople who, as they became more settled, could no longer obtain the plunder on which they had previously relied. It may also have been occasioned by the desire to curtail the growing prosperity of the Chinese gentry.[9] Another view of the reform is that it was intended to extend the land under cultivation and to increase grain production, while at the same time curbing the influence of powerful landlords.[10] It has also been described as a return to the policy attempted by Wang Mang in AD 9 to preserve a free peasantry, essential for the maintenance of the tax revenue of the state.[11] The reform was put into practice from 485 and there is some fragmentary evidence relating to its implementation. It was accompanied by the revival of a collective guarantee system, whereby the population was divided into groups whose members were individually responsible for the conduct and payment of tax within the group, a system later to be refined and known as the baojia.

Early in 493 the young Emperor Xiao had said of Pingcheng 'This is a place from which to wage war, not one from which civilized rule can come'.[12] Before the end of that year the emperor announced his decision that the Northern Wei capital would be transferred five hundred miles south, to the site of the historic city of Luoyang. The move was probably intended as a further blow to the declining influence of the Toba aristocratic leadership. Luoyang was chosen because of its cultural associations – it was at the very centre of Chinese civilisation – and because it was at the heart of the most populous and wealthy agricultural region of north China. The move itself took time, two years to move the court and the bureaucracy to Luoyang and a further seven years to build the new capital. But then the city grew rapidly, achieving a population in excess of 500,000 and becoming one of the great cities of the ancient world. The inner city measured about 9.5 square kilometres and was surrounded by massive walls, the remains of which measure 25–30 metres thick. The roads were set out on a grid system and the city was furnished with a sophisticated water supply. Beyond the inner city lay an outer city, which contained the residential wards and over five hundred magnificent Buddhist monasteries and nunneries. One such, the Jingming, was an imperial foundation and it served not only a religious function but it also contributed to the revenues of the state. Within its walls the most advanced water-powered grain-processing machinery of the day was in use. This technology may have been developed by captives or émigrés from the south, and its use may have been monopolised by the imperial house.[13] Another part of the outer city was set aside for the large community of foreign traders. Beyond the city lay the imperial domain and an intensively farmed countryside which supplied the city's food requirements. In 534, when the dynasty collapsed, this great city was to be abandoned in three days.

Intellectual and Religious Developments: the Transformation of Daoism

Before concluding the discussion of the period of division, the important issue of the intellectual and religious trends which had set in at the end of the Han dynasty must be considered. These include the transformation of Daoism and the introduction and rise of Buddhism.

Confucianism derived its strength from its importance as a state cult and because of its role in the training of bureaucrats. With the decline of the Han dynasty, the way was opened for the development of more speculative and individualistic philosophies. In the third century a number of writers developed the ideas of what has sometimes been described as neo-Daoism or philosophical Daoism. One aspect of the movement was known as *xuanxue* or 'dark learning', whose proponents set out to harmonise the Daoist spirit with Confucian social and moral doctrines. Guo Xiang, who died in 312, conceived the sage to be a person who moved between the realm of human affairs and the transcendental world. He wrote a famous commentary on the *Zhuangzi* in which he developed the Daoist theme of non-action, saying:

In the cutting of a tree the workman does not take any action; the only action he takes is in plying the ax. In the actual managing of affairs, the ruler does not take any action; the only action he takes is in employing his ministers. If the minister can manage affairs, the ruler can employ ministers, the ax can cut the tree, and the woodman can use the ax, each corresponding to his capacity, then the laws of nature will operate of themselves, not because someone takes action.[14]

Other groups engaged in *qingtan* or 'pure conversation', which often implied metaphysical discussion. The most famous of these groups was the Seven Immortals of the Bamboo Grove, a group of men of letters who met near Luoyang to hold discussions, to write poetry and play music, and to drink heavily. An important element in Daoist thought was the search for immortality, which led investigators to the study of medicine and inner hygiene and which also encouraged an interest in alchemy. Daoism also became a popular religion, with temples and a priesthood and a pantheon of gods. It was also at this time that the close connection between Daoism and art was established. In his *Introduction to Landscape Painting* Zong Bing (375–443) summed up many of the points of this relationship when he wrote:

And so I live in leisure and nourish my vital power. I drain clean the wine-cup, play the lute, lay down the picture of scenery, face it in silence, and, while seated, travel beyond the four borders of the land, never leaving the realm where nature exerts her influence, and alone responding to the call of wilderness. Here the cliffs and peaks seem to rise to soaring heights, and groves in the midst of clouds are dense and extend to the vanishing point. Sages and virtuous men of far antiquity come back to live in my imagination and all interesting things come together in my spirit and in my thoughts. What else need I do? I gratify my spirit, that is all. What is there that is more important than gratifying the spirit?[15]

The Introduction and Rise of Buddhism

The origins of Buddhism are traced back to Gautama Sakyamuni, an Indian prince who lived during the sixth and fifth centuries BC. Extravagant claims were later made about the earliness of the coming of Buddhism to China. It was alleged that Confucius had known about the existence of Buddha, or that the explorer Zhang Qian had brought back information on Buddhism gleaned on his travels in central Asia in the second century BC. Another story told how Mingdi, the emperor of the Later Han dynasty who reigned between AD 57 and 75, had in a dream seen a golden deity fly in front of his palace. He was told that his dream was of the Buddha and he thereupon sent an envoy to India who returned with the *Sutra in Forty Sections*, thus introducing Buddhism to China.

Less fanciful accounts suggest that some knowledge of Buddhism may have reached China from the kingdom of Scythia in the reign of the Emperor Ai (6 BC–AD 1) and that a Buddhist community may have already been in existence in northern Jiangsu by the time of Mingdi's dream. This community was probably composed of foreign monks and it is likely that most early adherents of Buddhism in China were traders or missionaries, with the conversion of ethnic Chinese coming at a later stage in the establishment of the religion.

Over the next two centuries Buddhism made only slow progress in China, a fact which has been explained on various grounds. Elsewhere in Asia, Buddhism was perceived as the religion of a more advanced culture and its arrival also introduced a written language to an illiterate community. However China already had a highly developed written language and Buddhism was likely to be received with indifference or hostility by the educated classes. Although the political disintegration of China may have been advantageous to the introduction of Buddhism, Chinese culture remained as a powerful obstacle to the adoption of a new religion. Once Buddhism had arrived in China, other obstacles to its spread became apparent. With its doctrine of renunciation of worldly concerns, including those of family ties, Buddhist values were directly opposed to those of Confucianism which emphasised the importance of the family. Another obstacle derived from the translation of Buddhist texts. The Chinese language had a developed vocabulary of religious and metaphysical terms and so, when the concepts of Buddhism were translated into Chinese, endless confusion was created because the words used in translation already had philosophical connotations. No Chinese scholars at this time knew Sanskrit, the original language of the Buddhist texts, and all translations had to be made indirectly. Because Buddhism came to China by two main routes, overland from central Asia and by sea, and because each route conveyed different versions of Buddhism, further confusion was created. Finally, when Buddhist ideas did become available in China, there was a strong tendency on the Chinese part to treat them eclectically, to select, for example, from the range of Buddhist thought only those techniques which could add to the intuitive faculties, which could provide knowledge of elixirs and practices that might contribute to longevity, or which might perhaps coincide with some of the interests of the neo-Daoist movement referred to above.

Nevertheless, probably before the fall of the Later Han dynasty, the *Sutra in Forty Sections* had been translated into Chinese and in the third and fourth centuries other key texts were translated, albeit crudely. The stage was set for that epoch in Chinese history, extending from the mid-fourth to the end of the eighth centuries, which has been called the Buddhist Age.

In the south of China, in the time of the Eastern Jin, Buddhism found its first adherents among those educated Chinese who had been attracted to neo-Daoism. As a representative of what has been described as gentry Buddhism one might refer to Zhi Dun, who lived between 314 and 366. He was a gentleman scholar who moved among the prominent laymen of his day, engaging in 'pure conversation', in which he introduced ideas derived from Buddhism. Alternatively, as an example of an early Chinese convert to Buddhism one could mention Huiyuan, who lived between 334 and 417. He founded a centre at Lushan, in northern Jiangxi, where monks and laymen practised a devotional creed which was clearly Buddhist, that is to say it was derived from Buddhist thought, and it was not superimposed on existing Chinese practices. In the fifth and early sixth centuries Buddhism continued to progress among literary figures and the aristocracy. Its most famous patron was the Emperor Wu of the Liang dynasty, who ruled from 502 to 549 and who became a convert to Buddhism. During his reign Daoists were persecuted, the emperor calling for the abolition of all Daoist temples and the return of Daoist priests to the laity. He sought to rule in the manner of a Buddhist monarch, taking as his model the Indian emperor Asoka. He built many Buddhist temples, renounced the eating of meat and on occasions served as a menial in a temple. Although the emperor's support of Buddhism remained undiminished throughout his reign, he found himself criticised by Buddhists who thought he was too concerned with earthly matters. He was also taken to task by the opponents of Buddhism who were alarmed by the excessive number of monks and nuns.[16]

In the north the progress of Buddhism was more rapid. Buddhism reached this area more directly, across inner Asia. The rulers of the region were non-Chinese who had none of the cultural reservations which had impeded and influenced the reception of Buddhism in the south. An early example of how under these circumstances Buddhism might easily gain acceptance was demonstrated by the case of Fotudeng, a monk of central Asiatic origin who arrived at the court of the Later Zhao dynasty in about the year 310. He gave a display of occult powers – he produced a lotus out of a bowl of water and, using toothpicks, drew water from dried-up wells – and thus gained the confidence of the emperor. Other rulers were drawn to Buddhism because it provided an alternative to the Confucianism urged upon them by their Chinese advisers. The most dramatic example of this was the adoption of Buddhism by the rulers of the Toba state who were to found the Northern Wei dynasty. Under the second emperor the

Buddhist community of monks had already become a significant presence. A government office was charged with their supervision and a monk named Faguo was appointed Chief of Monks. At first this relationship ensured imperial support, but under the Emperor Wu, who reigned from 424–51, Buddhism in China suffered its first major persecution in which several leading Buddhists and many of their followers were killed. The fundamental situation behind this attack was the tension caused by the sinicisation of the Toba state and the hostility felt by Chinese Confucianists towards Buddhism, which was still regarded as a foreign religion.

This proved to be only a temporary setback. An indication that enthusiasm for Buddhism was undiminished was shown in 460 when work commenced on the cliffs at Yungang, about ten miles west of Pingcheng. A half-mile stretch of the rock-face was honeycombed with caves and decorated with carvings of the Buddha, the largest of which measured seventeen metres in height. When, in 493, the Northern Wei dynasty transferred its capital to Luoyang, Buddhism received yet further encouragement. Numerous temples and monasteries were established in the city, many on a lavish scale. Among them was the Yongning monastery which had a nine-storeyed pagoda which reputedly rose 900 feet and was surmounted by a golden pole which added a further one hundred feet to its height. From the pole were suspended golden dishes and bells.[17] The whole building was so extravagantly finished that its cost exhausted the imperial treasury. In the capital, rival translation schools competed in producing Chinese versions of Buddhist texts, including the *Lotus Sutra* and the *Diamond Sutra*. In the surrounding countryside, Buddhist communities supervised agricultural settlements. Seven miles south of the city, at a site on the Yi river, the Longmen cave complex was carved and decorated to create a permanent symbol of Buddhist devotion.

By the middle of the sixth century Buddhism was firmly established in China, and it had gone far along the road towards acquiring distinctive Chinese features. This was evident in Buddhist art. The figures carved in the cliffs at Yungang, and indeed the whole idea of cave temples, indicated Indian influence. But at Longmen the Chinese tradition of linear, as opposed to plastic, pictorial expression re-asserted itself. This tendency to sinicise Buddhism was also apparent in the development of Chinese sects of Buddhism. The Tiantai school, which had a strongly scholastic and philosophical emphasis, emerged in the south in the sixth century. It called upon its followers to practise meditation and to study Buddhist texts, particularly the *Lotus Sutra*. By contrast the adherents of the Jingtu or Pure Land school, which traced its origin back to Huiyuan and to the fourth century, believed that the single act of calling on the Buddha's name was sufficient to obtain salvation. It was this school which was to popularise the worship of Guanyin, the Goddess of Mercy. In some respects these two sects stood in sharp contrast, but they had one feature in common: they both derived from the adaptation of Buddhism to suit the spiritual and political assumptions of China.

The Fall of the Northern Wei and the Final Years of Division

Despite its achievements, the Northern Wei dynasty was built on shaky foundations and its collapse was to be even more rapid than its rise. Two main fault lines ran under its structure. One was the perennial difficulty of any dynasty of conquest: how to retain its identity after assuming a Chinese form of government. The Toba solution had been for the emperor, his court and the aristocracy to adopt fully the Chinese style and to rule through Chinese officials. On the other hand the Toba people, and their allies in the tribal confederation, retained many aspects of their traditional life style. Because they were separated from their land and herds, the Toba people grew increasingly impoverished and alienated. The other problem was that of the northern frontier which, after the removal of the capital to Luoyang, was distant and difficult to garrison. The armed forces had been weakened by corruption and when, in 524, the Ruanruan crossed the frontier in force, the Toba garrisons mutinied rather than support the dynasty. Even at this point the dynasty might have survived, because the invading tribal groups entirely lacked leadership and a common purpose. But factionalism at court destroyed that chance. In 528 a tribal group known as the Erzhu, who may formerly have come from the state of Sogdiana, perpetrated a massacre of the aristocratic inhabitants of Luoyang. Out of the confusion which followed there rose to prominence a soldier named Gao Huan, who completed the destruction of Luoyang and removed the capital westwards to Ye, taking with him the child-emperor of the Wei. When Gao Huan died in 547 his son usurped the throne and established the Northern Qi dynasty. This brought about a split in the Toba empire, for in the west a separate regime, known as the Northern Zhou dynasty, was established. Once again northern China had lapsed into disunity and the dream of a revival of the Han dynasty seemed more remote than ever.

6

The Sui and Tang Dynasties

The period of division came to an end when a general named Yang Jian, who had usurped the throne of the Northern Zhou, defeated the last of the southern dynasties and in 589 reunified China. The Sui dynasty, which only lasted until 618 when it collapsed, has often been likened to the first empire of the Qin. Both dynasties established a new national unity after a long period of division. In both cases the dynasties were headed by rulers of enormous ambition: the Qin by the First Emperor, the Sui by Sui Wendi and his son Yangdi, all of whom combined a capacity for firm government and constructive design with an inability to foresee the degree of resentment that their actions would elicit. Finally, under both dynasties patterns of rule were established and initiatives taken which were to lead, under the successor dynasty, to a period of prosperity and cultural achievement.

The Establishment of the Sui Dynasty

In the middle of the sixth century much of China was under the control of one of four dynasties or ruling houses. The springboard for the establishment of the Sui dynasty was the Northern Zhou empire which sprawled over north-western and western China. Its main rival for the control of the north was the Northern Qi. These two states, both of which suffered from sharp racial and economic tensions, were deadly competitors until the Northern Zhou destroyed its eastern counterpart in 577. In central China, along the banks of the Yangzi river, was the much smaller state of Liang ruled by the Emperor Wu, whose conversion to Buddhism has already been noted. In the earlier part of his reign he had some success in centralising power within the state and even showed some aspirations to reunite China. But by the time of his death in 549 the state had collapsed and it was only a cipher when it was overrun by the Northern Zhou in 587. The fourth component was the state of Chen in the south-east, which had been carved out of Liang territory. Chen had ill-advisedly assisted the Northern Zhou in the defeat of the Northern Qi. In 589 the Northern Zhou ruler launched a combined naval and military operation which overwhelmed the Chen troops, while the Chen élite was won over by promises of leniency.

In these operations the prime mover was Yang Jian. He came from an aristocratic family of the Northern Wei, which was probably of Xianbei extraction. His family had been involved in the founding of the Northern Zhou and he was connected by marriage with the leading families of North China, including that of the emperor,

75

for his daughter had married the heir apparent. However in 580, incensed by the misdeeds of his son-in-law, he usurped the throne. There followed a civil war in which Yang Jian owed his success to assistance from a man named Gao Jiong, who was to be his chief minister through much of his reign. In 581 Yang Jian claimed that the mandate of heaven had passed to him and he founded the Sui dynasty with himself being given the posthumous title of Wendi.[1]

Up to this point what had happened was no more than a dynastic coup. But Wendi's ambitions went far beyond this, for he aimed to recreate the imperial tradition of the Han and to have himself recognised as the Son of Heaven. To ensure that his newly- founded dynasty was accepted as legitimate he had forged an edict, purportedly signed by the last Northern Zhou emperor on his deathbed, ordering Yang Jian to take command of the armed forces and to assist the child emperor in carrying on the government. This was followed by other edicts and rituals intended to simulate the mode of succession allegedly followed by the first kings, and to advertise that the new dynasty embodied the continuation of Han tradition. The claim of legitimacy was only the first step in Wendi's campaign to establish his position. The new dynasty also needed to be furnished with an ideology which would sustain its authority and this meant establishing a proper relationship with Confucianism and Buddhism. To assert his support for Confucian morality, Wendi arranged the offering of incentives to those whose conduct exemplified the Confucian virtues and in particular that of filial piety. With regard to Buddhism, which had been under attack under the Northern Zhou, Wendi went out of his way to present himself as an ideal monarch in the Buddhist sense, giving generously to Buddhist foundations, improving the condition of Buddhist clergy and promoting the acceptance of Buddhism as the common faith of the people. Taken together these actions have been described as imperial Buddhism and seen as giving the Sui dynasty an unique character in the annals of the Chinese empire.

Wendi's reign was also memorable for the vigorous practical steps he took to establish a unified state. One of his first decisions, and again a decision heavy in symbolism, was to build a new capital on a new site near the old city of Chang'an. In the edict recommending its construction he wrote 'a capital city is the administrative seat of the myriad officials and the place to which all those within the four seas will turn'.[2] He now had to fulfil that description by reforming central government. Under the Northern Zhou power had been held by a small group of military aristocrats, the majority of whom were non-Chinese origin. Wendi set out to recruit a new élite which would more nearly represent the diverse regions of the new empire, and which would therefore include a higher proportion of Chinese. This he achieved, although the new bureaucracy still retained a preponderance from the north and from the families associated with the imperial line in its senior posts. This élite staffed a central government which bore titles reminiscent of the Han, but that was its only archaic element, for Wendi was indefatigable in maintaining his control of appointments and in demanding a new level of efficiency of his officials.

It was in this context that the essential features of the examination system and the nomination of degrees emerged. In 587 Wendi ordered that all prefectures should send three men annually to the capital as candidates for official appointment. These men were to be examined and ranked in two groups. Eight years later, in 595, the provision of a written examination for the degree of *xiucai*, 'cultivated talent', was mentioned for the first time. This examination tested a candidate's broad general learning; other examinations were devised to test a candidate on a single classical text, and on his general literary ability. It is in the Sui period that the use of examinations to select officials, a system which had been attempted under the Han, became an established practice, although it is uncertain what proportion of officials were chosen by this means.

Whether they were holders of degrees or not, officials after appointment remained subject to regular supervision. One method of checking them was to summon representative officials from each prefecture and call upon them to give, in open court, a report on how their colleagues had discharged their duties. Another means was the appointment of censors who had the task of making tours and investigating the conduct of local officials. The emperor himself made tours and inquired of the local people how well his officials had discharged their duties. Another means of maintaining control of the bureaucracy was the application of the so-called 'law of avoidance', whereby an official was not allowed to serve in his own district of origin.

Alongside these administrative reforms, Wendi also sponsored a major revision of the law, which resulted in the promulgation of the Kaihuang Code, which has been described as 'a remarkable synthesis of the legal traditions of the age of disunity', which proved to be the model for the Tang legal code and thereafter of the successive legal codes of imperial China.[3] At the same time a rationalisation and simplification of the system of local government was carried through. By such means did Wendi assert the power of the ruler, and in so doing established many of the practices which were to be elaborated under the Tang and by later dynasties.

These administrative and legal reforms did not exhaust the list of activities of the first Sui emperor. To finance the costs of government he was forced to improve the system of taxation, which meant an overhaul of the 'land equalisation' or 'equal field' system established under the Northern Wei and a revision of the tax registers. The common people were required to pay taxes of three kinds: a land tax at the rate of three bushels of grain per family per annum, a payment in kind of silk or linen, and a labour service of twenty days labour per annum from each adult male. In order to combat tax evasion the *baojia* system, the system of surveillance, was also revived.

The Sui dynasty derived its power from its conquest of rival dynasties, and it was inevitable that, in the first instance, the maintenance of its military capacity was given great emphasis. But after 590 it became policy to demilitarise the population of the North China Plain. This was achieved in part by an overhaul of the system of recruiting soldiers, and in part by the confiscation of weapons and the prohibition of their future manufacture. Within the empire a system of regional military commands was established which placed the surviving armed forces under central government control. On the frontier military colonies were settled and a programme of wall building was pursued.

Having ensured its internal security, the Sui, like other powerful dynasties, turned to expansion. This involved completing the subjugation of the state of Chen and the destruction of Jiankang, the capital of the Six Dynasties. This was followed by the reassertion of Chinese influence in Vietnam and an abortive attempt to force the state of Champa, in modern times known as Annam, to accept Chinese rule. In the north the main danger was from the people known as the Tujue, ancestral to the Turks. Here Sui success owed more to intrigue and dissension among the frontier tribes than to conquest. The Sui empire had now achieved an extent as great as that of the Han, and was probably more firmly administered, because Wendi supported his conquests with improved communications, the most famous example of this being the construction of a canal linking Chang'an to the Yellow river, thus improving the supply of grain to the capital.

What sort of man was it who engaged in so ambitious a scheme of empire-building? Coming from a northern aristocratic family Wendi retained the preferences of his class for a life on horseback and a disdain for intellectualism. He had been brought up in a Buddhist temple and throughout his life he favoured Buddhism over Confucianism, although he approved the support the latter gave for the harshly authoritarian attitude he adopted towards his sons. Of his conduct of business it was said:

> He labored diligently and concentrated on good government. Every time he held an audience, it could last until late afternoon. He would invite officials of the fifth rank and above to sit and discuss affairs of state, and he would allow the palace guards to eat their evening meal while on duty. Though by nature he was neither benevolent nor enlightened, he was nonetheless a hard-working and perspicacious ruler.[4]

The family culture of the northern aristocrats permitted women a much more active role than that available to Chinese women of a comparable background. Wendi's consort, the Wenxian empress, came from a sinicised Xiongnu clan, that is to say her background was similar to that of the emperor, and this enabled them to form a close working relationship, perhaps unique in the annals of the emperors and empresses of China. In the early years of his reign the empress gave Wendi powerful support and tempered his immoderate rages. However, later in his reign she became increasingly jealous and vengeful, falling out with the emperor's adviser Gao Jiong and contributing to the crisis which ended in the emperor's death.

The Second Emperor

One way in which the empress exerted her influence was through the preference she showed for her second son, Yang Guang, who later, as the Emperor Yang, was to earn an infamous reputation. He had been born in 569 and in his early life he had developed a strong interest in the south of the empire, where he had cultivated an acquaintance with both Buddhist and Confucian scholars. In 600 he was party with his mother to an intrigue against the heir apparent which led to his being nominated heir. Two years later the empress died and two years after that the emperor also deceased, in suspicious circumstances. The crime of parricide is held in horror in Chinese history, and because Yangdi was not only the second but also the last emperor of the Sui dynasty, these suspicions, for which there is some documentary evidence, were magnified into a certainty.

The hostile view of Yangdi was based partly on his character, which was depicted as licentious, and partly on his actions, which were represented as the deeds of a spendthrift and a megalomaniac. This view has been challenged by Arthur Wright, who has pointed to his devotion to his wife and to the sensitive landscape poetry which came from his brush. He has shown that, when he became emperor, he followed similar policies to those of his father in terms of appointment to office and performance of rituals and, despite the allegations, he had no great liking for extravagance. However, in other respects he replaced the cautious miserliness of the first emperor with a more ambitious concept of his role as 'supreme autocrat, wise ruler, and cosmic pivot'.[5] Within a year of his accession he had ordered the building, or, along some stretches, the reconstruction, of a canal to link Luoyang to the Huai river. It was said that for this task a million or more workers were mobilised. In 608 work began on another vast project, the construction of a canal from Luoyang to the vicinity of present-day Beijing. Once again vast numbers of men, and for the first time women, were conscripted. These canals were built to perform an important economic function, the shipment of grain and military supplies, and much of the prosperity of the Tang has been attributed to their construction. But at the time the cost, the enforced labour and the extravagant expenditure dominated the accounts.

Although Arthur Wright challenged some aspects of the criticism of Yangdi, he accepted the opinion of the famous Song historian Sima Guang, that an important turning point occurred in the reign in the year 609. It was from that date that Yangdi became increasingly preoccupied with foreign expansion at the expense of dealing with domestic problems. In Wright's opinion his objectives in pursuing this expansion were little different from those of his father, and still conformed with the idea of emulating the achievement of the Han. However, Yangdi and his senior advisers made two basic errors: that of attempting a conquest without first obtaining adequate intelligence and that of refusing to accept defeat.

The campaign which proved a disaster was conducted against the state of Koguryo which occupied what is now north Korea and eastern Manchuria. This area had been under Chinese control during the Han dynasty; it was regarded as a civilised state and also as a potential danger because of the threat of an alliance between Koguryo and the eastern Tujue or Turks, who remained the most potent threat to the dynasty from the north. Early in Wendi's reign an official named Pei Ju had been responsible for foreign and barbarian affairs. He had been relatively successful in controlling the eastern Turks by using a combination of military and diplomatic means. When Yangdi succeeded to the throne, Pei Ju was dispatched to Inner Asia on fact-finding tours, and these were followed by an imperial progress which took the emperor to the far west of his territories. On this tour the emperor discovered that the western Turks had received an embassy from Koguryo. The

Koguryo ambassador was instructed to return home and to tell his ruler to send a tributary mission to China immediately, which he failed to do. Pei Ju thereupon advised Yangdi to send an expedition against Koguryo, informing him that Turkish mercenaries were available to support the attack and that Koguryo would quickly submit. Yangdi accepted this advice and in 612, after extensive preparations, a massive force was launched. But the Turkish mercenaries were not available and Pei Ju had seriously underestimated Koguryo determination to resist. Yangdi was forced to withdraw, having suffered heavy losses. In the following year the emperor launched a second attack, which likewise failed. By this time serious rebellions had arisen in China, in one instance headed by a senior official. Nevertheless in 614 a third expedition was launched which also ended in disaster. From that time onwards Yangdi seems to have lost control of events, for he took no effective measures to restore order at home. In 618 he was murdered in his bathhouse by the son of his most trusted general.

It would be an oversimplification to say that it was the failure of the Korean expeditions which brought about Yangdi's downfall, for there were other causes of discontent. The programme of canal-building had been accompanied by other large-scale construction works, including the building of a new capital at Luoyang, and these had been carried out by conscripted labour. Disastrous flooding in the Yellow river valley in 611 was followed by the outbreak of several rebellions in the area. Nevertheless Yangdi's attempt to conquer Koguryo did become a dangerous obsession. Having accepted unsound advice from Pei Ju and having allowed himself to be surrounded with sycophants, he appeared unable to stop the campaigns before they had caused the dynasty irreparable damage. It seemed that in a single reign much of the Sui achievement had been lost, but this was an illusion, for it was on the foundations dug by the two Sui emperors that the Tang dynasty was to reconstitute the empire.

The Founding of the Tang Dynasty

By 617 the Sui dynasty was in deep trouble. The heavy demands of the Korean expeditions had led to extensive rebellions in the north of China. There was also a real danger that the eastern Turks, who had already made several deep incursions into Shanxi, and who had obtained promises of allegiance from a number of the leaders of rebellion, might invade the country.

It was under these circumstances that a new contender for power emerged. Li Yuan came from an aristocratic family which had become influential under the Northern Zhou, his grandfather having been created the Duke of Tang. When the Tang dynastic history came to be written, his family was supplied with an ancestry which could be traced back to the Han, but it is likely that its origins were less august and that Li Yuan's ethnic background was a mixture of Chinese, Xianbei and Turkish. Early in his career Li Yuan had occupied a series of important military posts, and in 617 he was appointed garrison commander at Taiyuan, a key strategic position in present-day Shanxi, a place which was traditionally regarded as impregnable and from which previously successful assaults had been made on the capital Chang'an.

An answer to the question why Li Yuan became a rebel and ultimately founder of a new dynasty is inextricably mixed with the assessment made of his personality and that of his son Li Shimin, who was to reign as Taizong, the famous second emperor of the Tang dynasty. Most traditional accounts presented Li Yuan as a cautious, plodding figure, who was tricked into heading a rebellion by his ambitious son. In the subsequent events Li Shimin has been credited with the military skills and leadership which gained the throne for his father. However, modern historians, relying on the eye-witness account of Wen Daya in *Diary of the Founding of the Great Tang Dynasty*, have rejected that view and have reinstated Li Yuan as chiefly responsible for his own success.[6] He is said to have conceived the idea of making a bid for the throne before the Taiyuan revolt, being encouraged by a popular ballad which predicted that the next ruler would have the surname Li. It was on his initiative that the next step was taken, which was to neutralise the threat from the eastern Turks by hinting at a willingness to become a Turkish vassal. This obtained Li Yuan Turkish military support and enabled him to start a military campaign which before the end of the year resulted in the capture of the capital. In the following year Li Yuan declared himself the founder of a new dynasty, the Tang. He adopted the reign title of Wude, but is usually known by his posthumous temple name Gaozu.

The transfer of power from Sui to Tang dynasties did not imply any major change in the nature of government. Both royal houses had similar origins in the north-western aristocracy. Both dynasties relied heavily on the aristocracy to supply them with officials. Already under the Sui an attempt had been made to broaden the basis of support by employing more Chinese officials and this was continued in the early Tang period. The state examination system, which had been introduced by the Sui, became the established means of selection. So at first the structure of government was little altered and the emphasis was on continuity rather than on a break with the past.

One reason for the absence of dramatic change was the slow pace of the dynastic succession, which from the outbreak of rebellion in 617 took seven years to complete. Although a number of important military engagements took place, Gaozu's victory depended substantially on the moderation he exercised in dealing with his rivals. Amnesties were granted to those who surrendered to him. Defeated aristocrats were often confirmed in their territories and Sui officials allowed to remain in their posts. The basic structure of central government under the Sui, the three ministries – the Secretariat which drafted edicts, the Chancellery which reviewed and commented on them, and the Department of State Affairs, which put the decisions into effect – was retained and rationalised. There was a general continuity in local administration and in the maintenance of law and order. The Sui system of taxation was largely revived and the equal-field system re-established.[7]

But it would do Gaozu less than justice to imply that the measures he took merely replicated the Sui system. In several aspects of his administration he laid the foundations for the future success of the dynasty. Thus he introduced a new coinage, which was to become the standard currency through the Tang period. He set up a legal commission which, building on the Sui achievement, codified the law and administrative statutes in the form which was not only to remain in force until the fourteenth century, but which was became the basis of the first legal codes in Vietnam, Korea and Japan. He took the first steps on the path which was to lead to the revival of Confucianism and to the attack on the influence of Buddhism. Finally, although he was forced to bribe the eastern Turks to dissuade them from invading the empire, it was while he was on the throne that a start was made to construct an effective defence of the northern border.

Gaozu, however, did not remain long on the throne. A bitter rivalry had developed between two of his sons, Li Jiancheng, the heir apparent, and Li Shimin, his younger brother. The former had his main power base at court and at the capital, where he maintained his own fighting force. The latter, who had a notable record of success as a military commander entrusted with the task of suppressing rivals to the throne, had his power base among the military and civil officials of the Luoyang region. In 626 Li Shimin, suspecting that his brother was plotting against him and believing that his father would take the side of the heir apparent, engineered a coup. In rapid succession Li Jiancheng was murdered, Li Shimin declared heir apparent, and Gaozu himself forced to abdicate to allow Li Shimin to become emperor.

The Reign of Taizong

Li Shimin, who is better known as Taizong, his posthumous title, was to remain on the throne until 649. His reign has been described as 'unsurpassed in brilliancy and glory in the entire annals of China'.[8] Despite the fact that he had secured the murder of his brother and the enforced retirement of his father, he was presented as a paragon of virtue and his achievements regarded as a model for all subsequent emperors to emulate.

Modern historians have been unwilling to accept an unblemished portrait. Arthur Wright suggested that a more truthful representation would be to divide the emperor's reign into two halves. In the first decade Taizong adopted the role of 'humble learner of the arts of government'. His attitude to his responsibility was illustrated by a remark which he made in 629:

> Recently the number of memorials submitted to us has greatly increased. We have pasted them on the walls of our room so that as We come in or go out We can't fail to notice them. The reason that We are so tirelessly diligent is that We want to understand fully our ministers' sentiments. When we reflect on the principles of government, it is often the third watch of the night (11.00 p.m.–1.00 a.m.) before we fall asleep. We expect our ministers also to use their minds and energies tirelessly to help us realize our hopes.[9]

But after the death of his father and then of the empress, that is to say from 636, Taizong began to behave like the 'supreme autocrat of a rich and powerful empire, increasingly self-confident, self-indulgent and impatient of criticism',[10] a condition which Wright described as 'the pathology of supreme power' and as a pattern of behaviour which had already been demonstrated in the second century BC by Wudi. Whereas in the first decade Taizong had been frugal and cautious, he now became extravagant and capricious, although still occasionally displaying the positive qualities of the earlier half of the reign, those of 'a gifted administrator, a master strategist, a shrewd politician and a loyal friend'.[11]

What did Taizong achieve which has earned him such praise? His reputation undoubtedly rests on his role as consolidator rather than of innovator. It is generally accepted that Taizong built on the foundations laid by the Sui dynasty and restored by his father. Nevertheless this was a formidable part to play and it deserves elaboration.

One aspect of Taizong's brilliant reputation derives from his ability to surround himself with capable ministers, thus establishing a model of the appropriate relationship which should exist between the emperor and those who served him. Taizong carefully cultivated his reputation in this respect, once writing:

> The enlightened ruler employs men in the manner of a skilled carpenter. If the wood is straight, he uses it as a shaft for a cart; if it is crooked, he uses it as a wheel. If it is long, he uses it as a roof-beam; if it is short, he uses it as a rafter. No matter whether crooked or straight, long or short, each has something that can be utilized. The enlightened ruler's employment of men is also like this.[12]

The men he employed were indeed different in character and ability. Throughout the reign the emperor's chief confidant was his brother-in-law, Zhangsun Wuji. A second great minister was Fang Xuanling, who had taken the examinations and who became the architect of the system of executive administration and a model of honesty and efficiency. A third important figure was Wei Zheng, who earned the reputation of being an 'unbending moralist and fearless remonstrator', who was to gain the admiration of successive generations of Confucian scholars, not only for his probity, but also for his tireless advocacy of the pre-eminence of civil officials at court.[13]

Under Taizong the principal components of government, which had been created or revived by his father, received further refinement and were to achieve the character of 'ideal institutions' for future generations. At the capital, Chang'an, the central administration was to be found. This comprised the three central ministries: the Department of State Affairs, which in turn comprised the six ministries of public administration, finance, rites, army, justice and public works; the Chancellery and the Secretariat. There were also other government offices, the most notable being the Censorate, whose officials were charged with the investigation of abuses and complaints from the public; and the Supreme Court of Justice, which reviewed the evidence relating to serious crimes and made recommendations to the emperor on the appropriate sentences. Outside the capital the country was divided into administrative regions and these in turn were subdivided into prefectures. Taizong's reforms included a determined effort to reduce the size of the bureaucracy and to strengthen control over the prefectures. The value of service in the provincial bureaucracy, which hitherto had been despised, was affirmed and the emperor made the selection of prefects his personal responsibility. The legal code, which had been compiled first in 624, and which was based on the code of the Northern Zhou, was subject to further revisions to remove anomalies in the prescription of punishment and in some cases to reduce the severity of the penalty.

The same emphasis on consolidation of existing practice can be seen in the financial administration of the empire. In 624 Taizong's father had issued a series of Land Statutes which set out in detail the *juntian* or 'equal field' system which went back to the fifth century and to the time of the Northern Wei. This system, which had been devised in the simpler times of the northern dynasties, with its precise provisions for distribution and redistribution of land, would seem to have been quite inappropriate for the more complex society of the Tang. Nevertheless it remained in force and there are fragmentary records of attempts to apply it and to deal with the problems which were created by the increase in population and the strength of the aristocratic families and monastic foundations. Likewise the provisions for direct taxation remained unchanged, with taxpayers who, it was assumed, had equal landholdings, having equal tax liabilities: a tax in grain, a tax in cloth, and two types of labour service.[14]

What has been said so far of Taizong's reign suggests that it contained little of originality. Its true claim to fame lies not in its innovation, but in its consolidation, which enabled the imperial institution and the Chinese Empire itself to achieve new levels of power and influence. The Tang imperial line had at first merely been a very successful example of a northern aristocratic family. There were other great aristocratic clans, many of which came from the north-east of China. They still regarded status as having been fixed in the fifth century by the Northern Wei under a system known as the *sixing*, or the Four Categories of Clans. In 632 Taizong called for a new compilation of the national genealogy, but when it had been completed and presented to him he was infuriated to discover that the Li clan, that is the imperial line, had been placed in the third class, below several of the north-eastern families. A revised version was prepared, which placed the imperial line in the premier class. This was a clear statement of the superiority of office and ability over lineage. The new compilation did not immediately destroy the prestige of the aristocratic families, but it marked a stage in the decline of their influence.[15]

Another means of enhancing the position of the dynasty was through the development of the examination system. Under Taizong the number and frequency of examinations increased. A system of state schools intended to prepare candidates for the examinations was established, and this led to a marked increase in the number of candidates, some of whom came from the aristocratic families. When Taizong saw a group of successful candidates for the *jinshi* or 'presented scholar' degree leaving the government building in a triumphant column, it is said that he declared, 'The heroes of the empire are all in my pocket!'[16] Undoubtedly he exaggerated, but it is true to say that, in the early Tang period, the expansion of the examination system and the new emphasis on scholarly activity promoted the status of the Tang scholarly élite and enhanced the attraction of an official career.

At the beginning of the Tang period Buddhism enjoyed enormous popularity in China. Numerous monasteries had been established which amassed great wealth and claimed exemption from taxation. Eminent monks declared that the Buddhist clergy owed obedience neither to the state nor to the family. Not surprisingly these pretensions concerned rulers and twice, under the Northern Wei between the years 446 and 452, and under the Northern Zhou between the years 574 and 578, attempts were made to suppress Buddhism. But because of the strength of the popular reaction the repressive legislation was soon repealed. The early Tang emperors were in a stronger position to challenge Buddhism. Gaozu favoured Daoism over Buddhism and even claimed that the royal line was descended from Laozi. His views were encouraged by the sharp criticism of Buddhism expressed by Fu Yi, a Daoist priest who had been appointed chief astrologer. At first it seemed that Taizong was going to reverse that policy, for immediately after his succession he rescinded his father's order for a purge of the Buddhist clergy and a reduction in the number of monasteries. But his true feelings were revealed when he honoured Fu Yi and listened with approval as he delivered a familiar diatribe against Buddhism:

> The Buddha was nothing more than a crafty barbarian who succeeded in deluding his own countrymen. Ill-intentioned men in China subsequently perverted the teachings of Zhuangzi and Laozi to serve the ends of Buddhism and dressed up its doctrines in bizarre and mysterious language in order to mislead the uneducated masses. Buddhism offers no benefits to our people; on the contrary it is injurious to the state. It is not that I do not understand Buddhism, but rather that I despise it and refuse to study it.[17]

Taizong was too shrewd to make a direct attack and in 629 he even ordered the erection of seven monasteries to commemorate the battles fought at the founding of the dynasty. But his true sentiments were revealed in 637 when he ordered that henceforth at all ceremonies Daoist monks and nuns would take precedence over their Buddhist counterparts. At about the same time he approved the *Daoseng ge*, the *Regulations Regarding the Daoist and Buddhist Clergies*, which provided harsh punishments for clergy committing various offences. His objective was to reduce the participation of Buddhist clergy in secular life and to confine monks and nuns to their monasteries where they would be occupied with religious observances. By so doing he sought to establish control over the Buddhist church.

Nevertheless towards the end of his life his views altered. This was perhaps because of the admiration which he felt for the monk-translator Xuan Zang, whose epic travels to India in search of Buddhist scriptures had impressed him deeply, if only because of the knowledge Xuan Zang had gained of foreign affairs. Before he died Taizong revised his views on Buddhism and accepted Xuan Zang as his spiritual mentor. He authorised the ordination of 18,500 Buddhist clergy, regretting that he had met Xuan Zang too late to have helped him in the dissemination of Buddhism.

In Taizong's closing years a succession dispute embroiled the emperor and split the court. Initially the heir apparent was the emperor's eldest son, Li Chengqian. His position was undermined by complaints of bizarre behaviour and homosexuality, and because he displayed pro-Turkish proclivities. The emperor was persuaded to shift his favour to a younger son, Li Tai. Li Chengqian attempted a revolt which failed and he was sent into exile. Li Tai in turn was accused of plotting and the emperor was persuaded by his senior ministers to appoint as his heir yet another son, Li Zhi, Prince of Jin. In 649 he succeeded to the throne as the Emperor Gaozong.

Gaozong and the Empress Wu

Gaozong was only twenty when he succeeded to the throne. Inevitably the senior officials of his father's court, in particular his uncle Zhangsun Wuji, retained great influence. Another powerful force was the family of the Empress Wang. To add to the emperor's insecurity the early years of his reign were troubled by persistent plotting, which may have been a continuation of the factional conflict of the later years of his father's life.[18]

This situation was to be transformed by the rise of one of the most notorious characters in Chinese history: Wu Zhao, later to become the Empress Wu. She was born in 627 and was brought to the court at Chang'an as a concubine in 640. After Taizong's death she may have become a Buddhist nun. Gaozong, who perhaps knew her before his father's death, flouted convention and started a liaison with her and in 652 she bore him a son. Wu Zhao began an intrigue against the Empress Wang, which culminated in the alleged smothering of the empress's new-born daughter, an atrocious act intended to incriminate the empress. By 655 Wu Zhao had secured the demotion of the empress, her own enthronement, and the recognition of her son as heir apparent.

How can this extraordinary rise be explained? Undoubtedly the Empress Wu was a formidable character, as her subsequent career amply demonstrated. Her ascendancy, however, has also been attributed to rivalry between regional aristocratic groups. Early in the dynastic period the great aristocratic families of north-western China had been dominant, and the Empress Wang had been a representative of their influence. Her downfall, it has been claimed, marked an important shift in the location of influence, for the Empress Wu's support came from families from the north-eastern plain and it was for this reason that she later transferred the capital from Chang'an to Luoyang in the east. Another explanation of her rise attributes it to a class struggle: Wu Zhao, it is said, came from a humble background, and she represented the interests of the newly risen merchant class in a struggle for power with the entrenched aristocratic ruling class. Confirmation for this view is sought in her support for progressive ideas and the preference she showed for the selection of officials by examination, that is to say by merit rather than by birth. It has to be said that both explanations have their weaknesses. The factions at court supporting and opposing the Empress Wang were never as homogeneous as the theory of a power struggle suggests, and other explanations have been put forward for the change of capital.[19] The argument that it was a class struggle is weakened by the fact that the evidence of the Empress Wu's origins do not support the theory, nor is it true that she made greater use of the examination system. Perhaps both theories contain some elements of truth, but a more probable general explanation lies in personal and political alignments at court, which were ably exploited by a strong-minded and ambitious individual.[20]

At first the empress exercised her influence through Gaozong. After 660, when his health deteriorated for long periods of time, she became *de facto* ruler. When Gaozong died in 683 he was succeeded in turn by two of his sons, but power remained in the hands of the empress. In 690 she forsook pretence and usurped the throne, establishing the Zhou dynasty. This lasted until 705, when a restoration of the former emperor took place, the formidable empress dying a few months later at the age of eighty.

A discussion of this period can best be divided by the death of Gaozong. While the emperor lived, much of the empress's efforts were directed at consolidating her position, often, according to hostile accounts, by the most unscrupulous and violent means. Shortly after her enthronement in 655 she heard that the emperor was showing signs of remorse for his treatment of former Empress Wang and a favourite concubine. She thereupon ordered that their hands and feet should be cut off and that they should be thrown into a brewing vat, saying, 'Now these two witches can get drunk to their bones'.[21] Through intrigues she disposed of other court rivals and the group of elder statesmen who had served Taizong.

At the same time she promoted the career of Xu Jingzong, who until 670 was in effect her chief minister. With his help she pursued other policies which also served to advance her interests. Mention has already been made of the transfer of the capital from Chang'an to Luoyang, a move commenced in 657. In 666 she arranged for the performance of the *feng* and *shan* sacrifices on Taishan, the holy mountain in Shandong province. These ceremonies, which had not been performed for over six hundred years, symbolised the complete pacification of the empire and its contented submission to the sovereign. In defiance of all precedent, the empress herself participated in the rites. She also arranged for a revision of the register of prominent clans in the empire, thereby ensuring the inclusion of her clan, the Wu. Another, and more extensive exercise of her influence came through her patronage of Buddhism. From about 660 the emperor had started to take an increasing interest in Daoism and as a consequence several Daoist adepts had achieved powerful positions at court. To counter this the empress advanced the interests of Buddhists. She commissioned the carving of a 56-foot high Vairocana Buddha at the cave temple complex at Longmen, near Luoyang. It was alleged that the features of the statue were those of the empress herself. She also secured the rescinding of an edict which gave Daoists precedence over Buddhists at court ceremonies.

A recital of these developments would suggest that the ascendancy of the empress was a triumph for a vengeful, arbitrary and personal rule which set aside all the principles on which the imperial system was based. However, at a deeper level, the case can be made out that her rise saw not only the continuance, but even the strengthening of those principles. Undoubtedly Gaozong was the beneficiary of the achievements of his predecessors:

[He] inherited a stable state with a smoothly functioning set of institutions, and with a system of administration governed by a centralized system of statute law, in which the authority and responsibility of each office was carefully restricted and defined by law. The military and financial systems had been so devised that direct intervention of the central administration was kept to a minimum. Active government policy was kept within strictly drawn limits: the maintenance of order, military matters, and the administration of the land and tax systems.[22]

The empress made no attempt to interfere with these arrangements, indeed she sought to improve on them – for example, during her ascendancy, an extensive revision of codified law took place.

Perhaps more significantly the examination system for the selection of officials was refined, and a reform credited to the empress was the introduction of a method of concealing from the examiners the names of candidates, so that their identity and social origins could not affect the outcome. It has been alleged that because the empress was not part of the earlier Tang ruling class, she strove to replace that class with a new one, and to achieve this she placed unusual emphasis on the literary examinations as a means of recruiting civil servants. However, such an interpretation oversimplifies a situation in which the composition of the ruling class was more fluid, and the examination system less clearly the source of promotion of a meritocracy, than has been suggested.[23]

Gaozong's reign saw the boundaries of the Chinese state expand to a point previously unsurpassed and never to be exceeded. In 659 the western Turks, having been weakened by internal strife, were placed under Chinese protectorates and the sway of the Tang empire extended westwards to the borders of Persia. At the other extremity, Gaozong capitalised on his father's activities in Korea. In 668 Pyongyang, capital of the north Korean state of Koguryo was captured and the country turned into a Chinese protectorate. However these early successes were not to be sustained, and before the end of Gaozong's reign the central Asian protectorates and the state of Koguryo were slipping away from Chinese control. In the south-west the expansion of Tibet was threatening Gansu and Sichuan, and in the north the revival of the eastern Turks presented a fresh danger.

Frontier defence was a great drain on resources and securing an adequate revenue was an underlying problem of the dynasty. Already in Taizong's reign many households had evaded registration for taxation purposes. Under Gaozong, expensive foreign campaigns and a series of bad harvests aggravated the situation. At the same time prices for basic commodities rose and this was interpreted by officials as signifying that there was too much coin in circulation. The response was to suspend minting coins and to take severe steps against counterfeiting. The years 679 to 683 were a period of serious financial crisis.[24]

The Reign of the Empress Wu

After Gaozong's death, it became apparent that the Empress Wu was determined on power for herself. She ordered the deposition of the first heir to the throne, who had reigned for six weeks as the Zhongzong emperor, and replaced him with his brother. She then took steps indicating her intention to retain control, even to the point of herself claiming the throne. These actions prompted a revolt headed by Li Jingye, which broke out in 684. He and other leading rebels came from prominent families that had fallen into disgrace and had been exiled to the Yangzi region. They had plotted with leading officials at court and when their intrigues were exposed the empress took a terrible revenge and instituted what has been described as a reign of terror. Allegedly deliberately favouring the use men of humble origin as spies and informers, she created a secret police, headed by Zhou Xing and Lai Junchen, who 'earned the same sombre notoriety as Himmler and his aides have gained in modern times'.[25] Many of their victims were members of the upper aristocracy. As a consequence of the terror no official would henceforth dare to challenge openly the actions of the empress. It ensured that when she became scandalously involved with a former pedlar of cosmetics, Xue Huaiyi, and even made him abbot of a Buddhist monastery, none dared accuse her of impropriety.

Nevertheless the empress still hesitated before usurping the throne. Her decision to act may have been prompted partly by another uprising, partly by promptings from her supporters who claimed to have discovered a white stone predicting her future role. She was encouraged by the Buddhist clergy, who hailed her as an incarnation of the Maitreya Buddha. It was also significant that she had assured herself of at least some measure of popular support by making generous gestures towards the common people through a series of Acts of Grace. In 690 three petitions, the last said to contain sixty thousand signatures, were presented to the empress, each urging her to ascend the throne. She consented to the last of these, the emperor abdicated and she became the first ruler of a new dynasty, the Zhou, with the title of 'Holy and Divine Emperor'.

In many ways the Zhou dynasty was a continuation of the Tang, for the empress pursued the policies and practices of her earlier years. Nevertheless her assumption of imperial power did result in important changes of emphasis. For example, she exercised to the full her powers of appointment and dismissal, and as a result the position of chief minister, the title given to the heads of the three central ministries, was substantially undermined. At first she continued to show favour to the Buddhist community and as a demonstration of this she commissioned the construction of a remarkable symbolic building, the Mingtang, or Hall of Light, which was to serve as an audience hall on great occasions. Behind it stood a pagoda of great height containing an enormous wooden Buddha. The construction was supervised by Xue Huaiyi. In the pagoda wild religious rites were performed with the abbot acting as master of ceremonies. But at this point he fell out of favour with the empress and in revenge he burnt down the Mingtang. This event resulted in a distinct shift in the empress's patronage towards Confucianism.

These vast projects undoubtedly put a strain on the exchequer, but the real crisis of the reign began in 695, when a massive uprising occurred among the Qidan to the north-east. They seized the area around modern Beijing and their success encouraged the northern Turks and Tibetans to raid Chinese territory. The empress was forced to buy off the Turks by offering an imperial marriage, thus outflanking the Qidan rebellion. However the problems of the dynasty were not over. In 697 the empress became besotted with two brothers surnamed Zhang who, it was said, dressed in gaily coloured silks and, with powdered and rouged faces, frequented the palace and became so arrogant that they even treated senior officials with disdain.[26] The hostility aroused by their influence forced the empress to declare her wishes on the key issue of the succession, which was that the throne should revert to the deposed Emperor Zhongzong. Even this was not enough to stem criticism and charges of corruption were brought against one of the brothers. When the empress sought to overrule the legal process a plot among senior officials led to the murder of the brothers and the forced abdication of the empress.

What judgments have been passed on the Empress Wu and on this unique period in Chinese history? Because she had defied the principle of male descent and because she had treated harshly those officials who displeased her, the judgment of her in traditional historiography was inevitably condemnatory. Modern historians have taken a different view. C.P. Fitzgerald likened her to Elizabeth I of England, because under her prolonged rule 'China was stronger, more united and richer than ever before in her history'. Through her firm leadership she saved China from another century of civil war and confusion. Her legacy was such that, under her grandson, the Emperor Xuanzong, China was to experience a famous age of poets and artists, a real golden age.[27] A more recent assessment, while not disregarding some of the unsavoury aspects of her reign, emphasises its positive achievements: the development of the examination system as a means of upward mobility and the evidence of improvement in the condition of the mass of the population. Against this however should be set the costs of her ambitious policy of expansion and her failure to provide for a settled succession.[28]

The Reign of Xuanzong, 712–56

For the record of Xuanzong's reign one must rely almost exclusively on the National History compiled by the contemporary historian Liu Fang. He divided the reign into three sections: an early period of consolidation, a central period increasingly marred by court tensions, and a final period in which the emperor withdrew from an active political role, with dire consequences.[29]

The Emperor Xuanzong came to the throne after a period of intrigue. He was young, only twenty-seven years old, a man of attractive personality and considerable firmness of mind. At the beginning of his reign he acted decisively to free himself from the influence of members of the court, to instal ministers of his choice and to pursue his own policies. His first choice of minister was Yao Chong, who, like many of his early appointments, had served under the Empress Wu. Yao Chong's selection, and that of others who were also successful examination candidates, indicates that by now the place of aristocratic families at court was being taken by literati recruited through the examination system.[30]

On Yao Chong's suggestion a ten-point programme of reform of government was instituted – a programme which attempted to revive and stabilise the fortunes of the dynasty. Under these reforms the authority of the chief minister was strengthened and the practice of the open conduct of business was resumed. The operation of the bureaucracy was overhauled to ensure the proper staffing of provincial posts. Legal reforms developed a centrally codified administrative law and the application of uniform administrative rules. Another group of reforms attempted to improve the finances of the dynasty. One problem was the difficulty of supplying the capital Chang'an with grain and this required an improvement in the transport system. Behind this problem lay a chronic situation of recurrent famine and oppressive taxation. To relieve the former, 'price-regulating granaries' were established widely; to combat the latter, some attempt was made to restrict the grant of noble titles which carried with them tax exemptions and at the same time the emperor himself tried to practise austerity.

Finally there was the matter of military reform. Xuanzong had inherited an empire which stretched far beyond the confines of China Proper. Its defence required a very large standing army, estimated at about 600,000 men. Apart from the cost of maintaining so large a military force, the other difficulty lay in delegating command so that a rapid and effective response could be made to any threat to Chinese interests. The solution adopted for this was the establishment of nine major command zones, each headed by a military governor who commanded a large headquarters army, while at the same time administering the military colonies which supported the command zones. This system initially succeeded in stabilising the frontiers, but at the expense of allowing a great accumulation of power in a few hands.

In the middle period of the reign, from 720 to 736, the consolidation continued, but two new issues became important. The first related to the making of senior appointments. Under the Empress Wu many scholar officials had been appointed, perhaps as part of a move to counteract the power of the aristocracy. This practice had been continued under Xuanzong, but from the 720s a struggle began which was to lead to the aristocratic element re-establishing itself in senior positions. Why this shift took place is uncertain, and it should be accepted that the division between the aristocracy and the scholar officials was by no means clear cut. Nevertheless this apparent shift in the balance of power may explain the court rivalries of the time.

The second issue related to the financing of the government. One problem concerned the so-called 'runaway households'. Since the beginning of the dynasty, with greater economic security prevailing, a great agricultural expansion had occurred in the south. This had led to large-scale migration from the north, resulting in peasant families disappearing from the household registers. The first serious attempt to deal with this problem was made by Yuwen Rong. In 724 he proposed a scheme for the general registration of all vagrant unregistered households, which achieved considerable success and which resulted in 800,000 households being registered. However the policy also excited criticism, probably because Yuwen Rong was an aristocrat and his scheme, which was to be carried out by special commissioners directly responsible to the throne, bypassed the regular officials.[31] Another task was to resolve the persistent difficulty of supplying grain to the court when the capital was situated at Chang'an. In 734 Pei Yaoqing was made a minister to implement his own proposal to deal with this problem. His plan involved the establishment of a new commission for transportation and the definition of a new route for the movement of grain to Chang'an which was to be almost entirely by water. It appears that this new route was extremely successful, the amount of grain supplied being more than doubled. This enabled the emperor to confirm Chang'an as the effective capital of the empire and to continue his policies of a greater centralisation of power.[32]

The beginning of the third stage of Xuanzong's reign was marked by the advent to power of Li Linfu who, from 736 until his death in 752, was virtually a dictator.[33] Li was the man to be execrated in history as the source of the misfortunes which were to befall the emperor. He was an aristocrat and a member of the imperial clan and had entered public life through hereditary privilege rather than by examination, though his shortcomings as a scholar were exaggerated. His rise led to the dismissal of Zhang Jiuling, the austere exemplary scholar-official who was said, on the occasion of the emperor's birthday, to have offered his sovereign a compilation of pieces of moral advice instead of an expensive gift.[34]

Li had shown himself to be an efficient administrator and his promotion reflected the emperor's desire to create a strong, centralised and financially sound government.[35] Some of the measures he took have a very modern ring. For example, he discovered that the annual returns relating to taxation, conscription etc., consumed half a million sheets of paper. He devised a more practicable and efficient system, his reform being set out in a compilation known as the Permanently Applicable Directives.[36]

Until the early 740s the measures Li took to improve efficiency were generally acceptable and resulted in a period of prosperity, but from 746 onwards the situation deteriorated. Li became increasingly determined to assert his authority and carried out a purge of his opponents. The emperor, by now sixty years old, had begun to turn his attention from current affairs to personal enlightenment through Daoism and Tantric Buddhism. He had also become infatuated with Yang Guifei, the most bewitching of all favourites in Chinese history, and he had allowed members of the Yang clan to take up powerful positions at court. Meanwhile important changes had been taking place on the borders of the empire. As mentioned earlier, the frontier had been divided into command zones under military governors. In the past its defence had been in the hands of a mixture of troops – some professional soldiers, others convicts and militiamen. In the early eighth century, in response to the demand for more effective defence, these were replaced by much larger contingents of professional soldiers, often of non-Chinese origin whose commanders too were frequently non-Chinese.[37] Among them was a general named An Lushan, himself half-Sogdian and half-Turkish, whose headquarters were at Fanyang, that is present-day Beijing. In addition to commanding a large body of troops and occupying a key position, An Lushan enjoyed the patronage of Yang Guifen.

After a period of relative calm and security, in the middle years of the reign the empire had to respond to threats from the Qidan and the Tibetans. From 750 China suffered a series of military reverses, in the long run the most serious being a defeat at the hands of the Arabs on the Talas river, near Ferghana, the beginning of a collapse of Chinese power in Central Asia.

The Rebellion of An Lushan

When Li Linfu died in 752, the implication of these developments became apparent. He was succeeded by Yang Guozhong, second cousin of Yang Guifei, who proceeded to consolidate his position at court and to obtain support from some of the military governors. This brought him into conflict with An Lushan. Yang Guozhong did all that he could to warn the emperor of the danger presented by the general. But An Lushan had the continued support of Yang Guifei, who had supposedly adopted him as her son and may also have been his mistress, and so Xuanzong ignored the warning. Nevertheless it was clear to the general that he was in danger and in late 755, on the pretext that he had been summoned to court to subdue the 'bandit' Yang Guozhong, he led his troops south.

An Lushan's rebellion exposed the weakness at the heart of the Tang empire, for the forces loyal to the throne were no match for An Lushan's mounted cavalry. Within thirty-three days of commencing his march he had captured Luoyang and had declared the establishment of a new dynasty. He would probably have taken Chang'an as well had he not paused, so allowing his opponents to regroup and to win a major victory. The emperor's supporters began to hope that the rebellion might yet be crushed and Yang Guozhong tried to recapture Luoyang, which was a serious miscalculation for it resulted in a disastrous defeat which forced the emperor to abandon Chang'an.

It was at this point that the most poignant of episodes in Chinese history occurred. The emperor's escort held Yang Guozhong responsible for what had happened and they killed him and his family. The commander of the escort then demanded that the emperor himself should order that Yang Guifei be put to death, which sadly he did. The event was celebrated in one of China's most famous poems, *Changhen ge*, the 'Song of Unending Sorrow', by Bo Juyi:

> The Emperor could not save her, he could only cover his face.
> And later when he turned to look, the place of blood and tears
> Was hidden in a yellow dust blown by a cold wind.[38]

The end of the reign came swiftly. The emperor fled to Chengdu in the south-west where he established a court in exile. The heir apparent went north-west and began to rally opposition to the rebels. Realising that his father was no longer capable of ruling effectively, he usurped the throne. To defeat the rebels was a greater task, although it was made easier by the assassination of An Lushan in 757. However it was not until 763 that the rebellion was crushed.

An Lushan's rebellion has commonly been regarded as the turning point in the history of the Tang dynasty, even a turning point in Chinese history. Edwin G. Pulleyblank, in the classic study of the origins of the rebellion, commented:

Before [An Lushan] China was a vast, unified empire, extending its power far beyond its frontiers. After he raised rebellion it was a shattered and bruised remnant, confined to its own borders, pressed by invaders without, and harassed within by parasitic and lawless armies over which a eunuch-ridden central government exerted a precarious suzerainty. The Tang dynasty never recovered from the blow. . . . Never again did a native Chinese dynasty reach the summit of glory from which An Lushan rudely pushed the Emperor Xuanzong and his brilliant court in 755–6.[39]

It is clear from Pulleyblank's study, and from those studies which have been published since, that the rebellion was the catalyst but not the cause of this decisive change. Pulleyblank rejected the suggestion that the rebellion was an agrarian revolt or that it was triggered by a series of calamities. However he did accept that the changed economic situation was an essential part of the background to the rebellion: an economic revolution which had led to a great increase in trade and the creation of new wealth, had begun 'to crack the seams of the nation's social structure'.[40] Referring to the political background he stressed the conflict of interest within the governing class which has already been identified. Finally, with reference to the military background, he set the rise of An Lushan within the general context of a centrifugal tendency which drew authority away from the centre of the empire to the military commands on its periphery.

More recently C.A. Peterson has sought to distinguish between the background and the origins of the rebellion, which he did not regard as inevitable. He noted the historical tradition which asserted that An Lushan's non-Chinese background and his supposedly barbarous temperament made it likely that he would turn against the throne. He pointed out that the emperor failed to act to counter the potential threat that he posed. He then discussed theories which sought to explain the rebellion by referring to its specific regional features, that is to say why it arose in Hebei. One view was that Hebei, by this time, had received such an influx of non-Chinese that the Tang court had concluded that it could only be held by a 'barbarian', hence the toleration of An Lushan. Another was that Hebei still nourished a separate consciousness from the government at Chang'an. Peterson, however, suggested that neither explanation was supported by adequate evidence and concluded that Hebei itself was not significant in the origin of the rebellion. What was important was the social and cultural gap between the court and its frontier commanders, a situation which could be exploited by a powerful commander concerned about his own position, for example in the case of An Lushan.[41]

The Late Tang period

Although the rebellion was defeated, it has been seen as having profound consequences. A summary account of these mentions: large scale militarisation with perhaps 750,000 men under arms; the development of autonomous or semi-autonomous governments at provincial level; the rise of men of military background to roles in the official hierarchy; the collapse of the state's financial structure; the final disappearance of the land allocation system; large scale shifts of population; effective loss of control of Hebei and parts of Henan; increased importance to the empire of the Yangzi and Huai valleys and finally the loss of control in Central Asia.[42]

None of this can be gainsaid, but before dismissing the late Tang period as a mere shadow of former glory, reference should be made to important innovations in the matter of financial administration introduced in the decades after the rebellion. Two of these were attributed, at least in part, to an official named Liu Yan, who served under the Daizong emperor (reigned 762–9). It was he who developed the monopoly on salt which by 780 was to provide more than half of the cash revenue at the disposal of the central authorities. He also improved the system of grain transport instituted by Pei Yaoqing, placing it under a Transport Commission and greatly reducing the cost of transport. His reforms, which were seen as encouraging the development of independent agencies, were to be challenged by another innovative official, Yang Yan. To him has been credited an even more important measure: the *liangshuifa* or two-tax system. Put simply this reform consolidated various taxes on property and land and provided that they should be collected twice annually. It enabled the state to derive revenue not only from the peasants, but from all productive classes, a reform even more necessary because of the growth of great estates. The arrangement introduced by this reform was to serve as the basic system of taxation for the next seven centuries.[43]

Two further points may be made to support the view that the late Tang period cannot be dismissed as merely a period of dynastic decline. The first concerns the so-called restoration under the Xianzong emperor, who ruled from 805 to 820. Half a century after the rebellion central government still did not control the provinces effectively. Some of them, particularly in the north and east, were entirely autonomous; others, although administered by court-appointed officials, were only partially controlled from the centre. Xianzong's task was to try to extend his government's effective control and to a certain extent he succeeded. On seven occasions during his reign he used military force against recalcitrant provinces. Such campaigns were expensive and another of Xianzong's achievements was to increase greatly the contribution of the Yangzi valley to government finances. Meanwhile the emperor took steps to restore the morale of the bureaucracy, with some success, although the end of his reign was marred by a dispute with Pei Du, a celebrated official of the period, who questioned the emperor's decision on the appointment of officials. This incident, and claims that towards the end of his reign the emperor grew intolerant and avaricious, have damaged the reputation of a man who was an able ruler, and who, but for his premature death – he may have been poisoned – might have gone further in restoring imperial control.[44]

The other piece of evidence which can be used to adjust the view of the late Tang period is a remarkable document, the diary of a Japanese Buddhist monk known in the west as Ennin. Ennin spent nine years in China, including some five years in Chang'an, and his diary contained detailed descriptions of many aspects of the country, including much information on religion and commerce. He also made many references to the working of government, and this led E.O. Reischauer to remark:

> there emerges a picture of government in operation which is amazing for the ninth century, even in China. The remarkable degree of centralized control still existing, the meticulous attention to written instructions from higher

authorities, and the tremendous amount of paper work involved in even the smallest matters of administration are all the more striking just because this was a period of dynastic decline.

This led Reischauer to suggest that this, in a more fundamental sense, was a period of significant political maturation, for the Chinese government had now achieved such a high level of administrative efficiency that the country was never again to undergo the general collapse which ensued after the downfall of the Han.[45]

The Decline and Fall of the Tang Dynasty

Despite the efforts of Xianzong to curb provincial autonomy, the key problem of the power and independence of the military commands remained. After 820, young emperors were unable to assert their authority, their courts being the scene of factional intrigue and of eunuch influence. In the middle of the century, under an outstanding minister, Li Deyu, effective government was briefly restored and at the same time an attack was made on Buddhism, state support for the religion being a heavy drain on finance. But Li Deyu was dismissed by the next emperor Xuanzong[46] who also restrained the persecution of Buddhism.

Before the end of his reign armed revolts and mutinies had broken out which presaged the fall of the dynasty. These threats were to be eclipsed by the disastrous surge of rebellion headed by Wang Xianzhi and Huang Chao which began in 874. This had its origin in the growth of banditry, particularly in the area between the Yellow and Huai rivers, an area hit by a combination of natural disasters and government exploitation. The two leaders who headed bandit gangs were men of some education, Huang Chao being a failed examination candidate. Their banditry turned into a revolt after government suppression had proved ineffective. The rebellion devastated large areas as far south as the Yangzi. The government, having failed to defeat the rebel bands, tried in vain to buy off its leaders and to encourage resistance by permitting the raising of militia. In 878 more effective commanders of government forces were appointed and they gained a series of victories in which Wang Xianzhi was killed. Huang Chao was forced to move south and in 879 he seized Guangzhou, which he sacked with tremendous loss of life among the foreign community. He then turned north, encountering ill-organised opposition from government forces, and was able to ensconce himself in the lower Yangzi region. At this point he should have been defeated by superior government forces, but inexplicably he was allowed to break through their lines and late in 880 he captured Chang'an, the emperor and the court fleeing westwards to Chengdu. Huang Chao established a new dynasty, but he had little control over his followers, who pillaged Chang'an, and his attempt to win over officials to his side failed. Government forces rallied and besieged the capital. Foreign troops under the command of Li Keyong from the Shatuo, a Turkish tribe, inflicted a series of major defeats on the rebels, Huang Chao being killed in 884.

The emperor returned to the devastated capital, but was quite unable to restore the authority of the dynasty. He died in 888 and neither of his two successors was any more capable of recovering power. In 907 Zhu Wen, a former lieutenant of Huang Chao, declared that that part of north China which he controlled was an independent state under the newly established Liang dynasty. This act confirmed the demise of the Tang.[47]

How has the collapse of the Tang been explained? A recurrent theme is the instability of the Tang court and, particularly in the ninth century, the excessive power of the eunuchs, who were implicated in the deaths of several emperors. A series of minorities and an apparent dearth of capable ministers contributed to a lack of leadership at the centre.

Another explanation relates to the financial position of the government. Despite the introduction of the two-tax system, government revenues remained inadequate to maintain the armed forces it needed to reassert its authority, and had to be supplemented by additional levies which typically fell most severely on the hard-pressed peasantry. The pattern of peasants deserting their lands to take refuge with powerful landowners was repeated. In the key lower Yangzi region, where the tax burden fell most heavily, this pressure led to the growth of social unrest and banditry.

A more fundamental problem, and one which has already been discussed in the context of the rebellion of An Lushan, was the government's loss of power to the military commands on the periphery of the empire. By the early ninth century much of the country was divided into semi-autonomous provinces which had developed their own forms of government and in which the military forces played a major role. Some provinces in the north-east were in effect independent. The independent provinces still recognised Tang sovereignty and the semi-autonomous ones still accepted appointments made by central government. But even this degree of central government influence was to be lost with the disorder which culminated in the great Huang Chao rebellion. Now even the sovereignty of the Tang could no longer command respect and effective control passed to regional states formed from the independent provinces. When one of these, the Liang, usurped the throne, the dynasty came to an end.

7

China and the World in the Early Imperial Period

In the Sui and Tang periods, China's foreign relations underwent a complete transformation. At the beginning of the period only one neighbouring state, Koguryo on the Korean peninsula, could claim to be a stable political entity. Elsewhere China was surrounded by mainly nomadic tribal peoples, who could occasionally form powerful confederations, but who, for the most part, were markedly inferior to China in terms of cultural and political achievement. However, by the end of the period much had changed. In the north-east, in the south, and in the south-west, stable agrarian societies had been formed, the 'Chinese-dominated east Asian cultural sphere had taken shape'. Only to the north did China still share a frontier with nomadic societies, but even these were much more stable and advanced than they had been in the past. This important change was to have a major effect on the development of China's relationship with the outside world.[1]

In this changing political setting, the Chinese empire, ruled for over a century by a powerful dynasty, consolidated Chinese dominance within China proper and extended its influence through much of eastern and central Asia. From the eighth century, particularly after the An Lushan rebellion, Chinese influence declined and by the end of the tenth century part of north China had fallen under foreign rule. A review of these developments may start at the centre and then continue with reference to each of the main zones on the periphery.

Chang'an

Chang'an, the Sui and later the Tang capital, was carefully sited near the spot which had been the capital of the Han empire. The modern city of Xi'an occupies the same site. Under the Tang, Chang'an

> was perhaps the world's greatest city – the political hub of a vast empire, the epicentre of Chinese civilization in an age of brilliant creativity, a cosmopolis which attracted merchants and travellers from distant lands, a model for the city-builders of neighbouring states.[2]

The outer walls of this great city enclosed an area of about 30 square miles. The imperial palace stood in front of the northern city gate and in front of this in turn was the administrative centre. The city itself was laid out like a chessboard with the streets running from north to south and from east to west.

Chang'an was indeed the hub of the empire. To the north and east and south it was linked to the rest of China by a canal system, supplemented by a network of imperial roads. Along these roads were post stations for official travellers and inns for merchants. To the west lay the route which in modern times has been called the Silk Road. This took the traveller through the Gansu corridor to the oasis of Dunhuang. There it divided with one route going to the north and the other to the south of the notorious Taklamakan desert. The northern route led, via Samarkand and Bokhara, to the Mediterranean coast; the latter through Yarkand and Srinagar, to India.

By the eighth century Chang'an had a population of about one million, with perhaps another million living in its metropolitan area. Not only was this a vast population, but it was also a cosmopolitan one. In the vicinity of the West Market were to be found Zoroastrian and Manichaean temples, a Christian church and houses of foreign merchants. To the West Market came camel trains from central and western Asia, bringing exotic goods. For example, in 647, after the conquest of the Tarim Basin, a Turkish ruler sent specimens of a new wine-making grape to the emperor. This was the 'mare-teat' grape, an elongated form of grape which was planted in the imperial park in Chang'an.[3] From the south came other exotic fruits, famously the lichee, for which Yang Guifei, Xuanzong's consort, had a craving. They were brought by special courier from Guangzhou.

Chang'an was not alone in having strong links with the outside world. In the eighth century Guangzhou had a population of about 200,000, which included a large merchant class, chiefly Indo-Chinese, Indonesians, Indians, Singhalese, Persians and Arabs.[4] The foreigners lived in a prescribed quarter of the city, were ruled over by specially designated elders, and enjoyed some extraterritorial privileges. Most of China's maritime trade passed through Guangzhou, though not much of it was in Chinese hands. The largest of the ships employed were built in Ceylon and had Persian-speaking crews. Among the goods imported were pearls from India and rhinoceros horn from Indo-China.

Travellers and Pilgrims

While China under the Tang received many foreign visitors, in the same period Chinese awareness of the outside world was greatly enhanced by travellers who crossed central Asia or who ventured over the Southern Ocean. Those who left records of their journeys were in many cases Buddhist pilgrims, who had set out for India to obtain copies of Buddhist scriptures, to visit holy places, or to study at the great Buddhist monasteries. One of the earliest records was kept by a pilgrim named Fa Xian, who left China in 399, taking an overland route to India and then returning by sea. He spent two years in Ceylon and also visited what was probably Java, before finally landing in Shandong after a voyage of two hundred days.

The most famous Buddhist pilgrim of the Tang period was Xuan Zang, who travelled to India between 629 and 645.[5] It was this journey which was the inspiration of the sixteenth-century novel by Wu Cheng'en entitled *Record of a Journey to the West*, or, in Arthur Waley's translation, *Monkey*. Xuan Zang made a full record of his experiences: how he had left Chang'an by stealth, how he had nearly been murdered by his guide, how he had almost died of thirst in the desert. After he reached India his adventures continued. When travelling down the Ganges he was captured by pirates who planned to use him as a human sacrifice. To this proposal Xuan Zang replied:

> As far as my own miserable body is concerned, I have no objection at all to your using it for your sacrifice. But I think I ought to tell you that I came all the way from a far country in order to worship the image of Buddha under the Bodhi-tree and visit the Vulture Park where he preached. I have come for instruction in his scriptures and his Law, and none of these purposes have I yet fulfilled. So that I fear that if you were now to sacrifice me it would be more likely to bring you bad luck than good.[6]

The pirates appeared unmoved by his words, but a great storm arose which terrified his captors who hastened to release him. Xuan Zang continued his pilgrimage to the holy places of Buddhism and assembled his collection of manuscripts. When he returned to Chang'an in 645, he took with him 657 items packed in 520 cases, works which in his remaining years he laboured to translate.

A third famous pilgrim who went to India in search of the law was Yi Jing. He departed from Yangzhou on a Persian ship in 671 and called at the important Buddhist centre of Srivijaya on Sumatra and the Nicobar Islands before landing in Bengal. He visited the holy sites of Buddhism and carried away from India some ten thousand Sanskrit texts. For nine years he remained at Srivijaya, engaged in the task of translation, and then returned to China in 695 to be greeted personally by the Empress Wu when he reached Luoyang.[7]

The efforts of Xuan Zang and Yi Jing, and those of other Chinese Buddhist pilgrims, played an invaluable part in the preservation of early Buddhist culture. Buddhism in India was already under challenge from Hinduism, and many of the texts collected by Xuan Zang were to survive only in Chinese. Before Buddhism in China had come under attack and had suffered a similar decline, Japanese monks in turn had come to Chang'an and had borne home the texts from which Japanese Buddhism was to develop.

Southern Expansion

The southern expansion of the Han people was brought about by two main means, one being the determined thrust under a strong dynasty, using soldiers and establishing bases or military colonies. Alternatively, and possibly associated with periods of confusion in the empire, it came about through the migration of displaced people fleeing from the north and through the establishment of separate regimes in the southern provinces.[8] Underlying these developments was the much less perceptible process of the sinicisation of non-Chinese societies. These movements can be traced in three main theatres: in the extreme south, in the area which is today northern Vietnam, and in the south-west of China, particularly in the province of Yunnan.

In the extreme south, after the early expeditions sent by the First Emperor, the region known as Nan Yue or southern Yue was conquered by the soldiers of the Emperor Wu of the Han dynasty, and a Chinese administration was established in the region. After the fall of the Han the Yue people recovered their independence, but under the Tang Chinese control was reasserted. The present area of Guangdong, Guangxi and part of north Vietnam was designated Lingnan province and large-scale 'development' begun. One means of extending Chinese control was though the system later known as *tusi*, that is to say the appointment of tribal chiefs as officials, which applied a system of indirect rule to ethnic minorities. Another method used was the widespread establishment of *tuntian* or military agricultural colonies. Under the Empress Wu, Lingnan was a favoured place to which to exile opponents and this led to the diffusion of Tang culture in the region. Exceptionally, men from the south achieved distinction under the Tang and this led to a gradual amendment of northern attitudes, from believing Lingnan to be a strange and frightening land to recognising it as part of China. An outstanding example of a southerner who achieved distinction was Zhang Jiuling, who rose to become chief minister under Xuanzong.[9]

Prior to the Tang period Lingnan had been badly affected by malaria, and this and the hostile environment had discouraged settlement. By the end of the Tang period the malarial threat may have declined and southward migration, which had already led to an enormous surge in the proportion of Chinese living south of the Yangzi, now reached the extreme south. Between 606 and 742 the population of the Guangzhou delta rose by over 100 per cent and that of the eastern part of Lingnan by up to 100 per cent. Further massive increases in population occurred in the centuries which followed.[10] This movement is reflected in the linguistic legacy, with Cantonese, the dialect spoken in the region around Guangzhou, most closely resembling the standard spoken language of the Tang period. Following behind the first migratory waves, and forced to take up poorer land, came the dialect group known as the Hakka or *kejia* ('guest people') who to this day call themselves Tang rather than Han Chinese. Although the Yue language, and Yue customs almost entirely disappeared, the Yue population was not displaced and through intermarriage and sinicisation it became virtually indistinguishable from the Chinese immigrants.[11]

As an example of how Chinese settlement of the south evolved one could refer to the case of Fujian province. Chinese migrants first reached Fujian in the late second century AD and formed a settlement on the banks of the Jin river. Over the next four centuries this colony of agriculturalists was enlarged by the arrival of several distinct groups: a group with some claim to membership of the élite society of post-Han China; the possible descendants of an intermediate warrior class of similar origin, and a small artisan class of unknown provenance. On the fringes of the settlement were Han Chinese Buddhist communities and 'boat people' of Chinese origin. The early records contain references to conflict with an indigenous group, but the territory occupied by the colony, between the mountains and the coastal region, was sparsely populated. The main obstacle to growth was the marshy condition of the land near the coast, an ideal breeding ground for malaria-bearing mosquitoes and for parasitic diseases such as schistosomiasis. But by the eighth century a combination of acquired resistance to malaria and gradual progress in the draining of marshes enabled settlement to extend onto the coastal plains, which were ideally suited to wet rice farming, and so it became possible to use the excellent harbour of Quanzhou bay. Further immigration from the north raised the Chinese population to perhaps 200,000, urban settlements were formed and a commercial economy developed. But the most significant change, and the one which was to have a decisive impact in transforming the region into one of the most prosperous in China, came in the ninth century with the start of Quanzhou's trade with the South Seas.[12]

The western part of Lingnan included the Red river basin in present day northern Vietnam. By the time of the Han dynasty, when the region was conquered by the Chinese, this area was already heavily populated and there was no need to bring in Chinese settlers. Instead a few Chinese administrators introduced a Chinese-style administration and the Yue people, in particular the native chiefs, accepted elements of Chinese culture and co-operated with Chinese rule. The peasants, however, were less sinicised and it was they who lent their support to the uprising led by the Trung sisters in AD 39. Chinese rule was restored under the Later Han, was lost again in the period of division and recovered once more under the Sui. Under the Tang the country was named Annan, meaning 'the pacified south', and for two hundred and fifty years it remained under Chinese government. In fact the pacification was never complete and, after a major revolt in 722, China had to maintain a large force in the country to ensure control. In 934, after the fall of the Tang, another rebellion led to the establishment of an independent state. Although the Song attempted to reconquer the former province, the invasion was repelled, and never again was the country to be governed by China.

Nanzhao

For C.P. FitzGerald, the history of Vietnam seemed to illustrate one aspect of the southern expansion of the Chinese people – that it had a natural limit and would be halted when the Chinese reached an area where people of an advanced civilisation had already installed themselves. In Yunnan, as in the case of Lingnan already discussed, he found an example of the opposite process:

> Yunnan thus presents . . . a history of Chinese expansion from its early beginnings with relations between a distant Court and local barbarian rulers, through a period of cultural infusion contemporary with political rejection, and then through the successive stages of conquest, occupation and assimilation.[13]

The first stage of this process had occurred under the Han, when the ruler of the area around Kunming acknowledged the suzerainty of Emperor Wu. Adventurous traders opened an indirect trade route with India and local chiefs became involved in this trade. But then came the period of division and a long hiatus in the process of absorption. In that period what is now Yunnan came under Buddhist influence deriving from Burma, the local tribes adopting Hinayana Buddhism. Under the Tang, west and central Yunnan was for a time divided among six kings. Of these the southern king was to become the dominant ruler, with a capital situated at modern Dali. He, and the ruling class which supported him, were probably of Tai origin, that is to say of the same ethnic background as the people of Thailand, but the Tai were only one of a number of ethnic groups which made up the population of the region. At first the Chinese encouraged these developments and tolerated the rise of the Nanzhao, that is to say the southern king, even though in 731 he had burned his fellow kings alive. In 742 a grandson of the king of Nanzhao married an imperial princess at Chang'an.

This was the high point of Nanzhao's history as a client state. In 751, in the declining years of Xuanzong's reign, Tang forces were sent to punish the kingdom for raiding Chinese settlements in eastern Yunnan. However, the Nanzhao troops won a signal victory which, together with the outbreak of An Lushan's rebellion, ensured that any hope of speedy retribution disappeared. Over the next century Nanzhao grew to become a significant power on China's borders, its territory incorporating northern Burma and western Sichuan.

Only in 879, when a further invasion of Sichuan was repulsed, did this expansion stop and thereafter Nanzhao began to contract. Various reasons have been suggested for why this happened: Burma was a difficult territory to defend and Sichuan, with a dense population, a difficult region to absorb; the Nanzhao state was built on shaky foundations for it had neither ethnic nor cultural homogeneity; Nanzhao political independence was not easy to maintain and when, in the tenth century, the Nanzhao ruling house was deposed and power taken by rulers of Chinese ancestry, the process of sinicisation accelerated. Nevertheless, Nanzhao remained an independent kingdom until the final years of the Song dynasty, and when it was conquered in 1252, it was not by the Chinese but by the Mongols, who incorporated it into their empire. Only in 1382 did the Ming in turn conquer the territory and incorporate Yunnan fully as a province of the Chinese empire.[14]

The Turkish Empires of the Steppe

Referring now to Central Asia and to the relationship between China and the nomadic nations of the steppes, a preliminary observation should be made. In the past it was a commonplace to describe the nomads of the central steppe as prowling like wolves, waiting for China to weaken, so that they could rush in and devour it. More recently the metaphor of a mirror has been used to describe the relationship, with the settled society of China and the nomadic society of the steppe reflecting the changes which had occurred in the other society. To develop the metaphor, a comparison has been made between developments in the Tang period and those which occurred earlier, under the Qin and Han dynasties. In the earlier period the unified Chinese state had been matched by the unified steppe state of the Xiongnu. Thereafter the period of division had been matched by disunity on the steppe. Three hundred years later a newly united China under the Sui and Tang was again matched by a succession of unified Turkish empires. This, it has been argued, was no coincidence: 'the state organization of the steppe needed a stable China to exploit'. Periods of division in China were mirrored by periods of division on the steppe, but the unification of China was followed within a generation by a unification of the steppe.[15]

The steppe people who first achieved this unification were the Tujue or Turks. Until the middle of the sixth century they were vassals of the Mongol Ruanruan, their traditional trade being metal-working and their totem, perhaps appropriately, was the wolf. An incident in which the Tujue chief was refused the hand of a Ruanruan princess led to a revolt, with the Tujue allying themselves with the sinicised Western Wei state. While Yang Jian was engaged in establishing the Sui dynasty, the Turks were creating a massive empire which was to extend from Manchuria to the Caspian Sea. The empire owed its existence to its military power and the Turks utilised their strength to extort wealth from China. They traded horses in return for silk, and also demanded lavish gifts for their support. The Northern Zhou made them an annual gift of 100,000 rolls of silk and entertained many Turkish visitors at court. This silk was then traded on to Iran and Byzantium, making the Turks extremely wealthy.

So uneven an arrangement could not endure for long, but some time was to elapse before it was revised in China's favour. Succession disputes made the Turkish empire inherently unstable. In 581 it was divided into two khaghanates, that of the eastern Turks centred on the future Karakorum in Mongolia, and the khaghanate of the western Turks centred on Ili and western Turkestan. At this point the newly established Sui dynasty risked deporting the Turks living at court and refused to continue the silk payments. In retaliation, and in the hope of healing divisions in their ranks, the Turks carried out a major raid on China. Such actions benefited neither side and a compromise was reached. The essence of this was that the Turkish khaghan, in return for receiving aid against rival tribal leaders, formally submitted to China. For the Sui this carried the considerable advantage that their new dynasty was seen as truly holding the mandate of heaven. The relationship was strengthened by the dispatch of a Chinese princess to marry the khaghan and by fomenting rivalry between various Turkish tribes. By the early seventh century the eastern Turks were important allies of the dynasty, used by them as mercenaries against the Qidan to the east. But when Yangdi invaded Korea he discovered that the new khaghan was not prepared to give the expected support. The disastrous campaigns which followed contributed largely to the collapse of the dynasty.

The Turks, however, did not try to capitalise on the dynastic collapse with an invasion. Instead they bided their time until the Tang dynasty was established and then profited from what has been described as the 'outer frontier strategy', under which the Turks raided deep into Chinese territory, yet refused to occupy Chinese land even after great victories. By this means the Tang dynasty, like the Northern Zhou before it, was forced to appease the Turks with lavish gifts and trade privileges.[16]

Then Li Shimin, who was to reign as Taizong, the second emperor of the Tang and effective leader of a strong dynasty, significantly altered the relationship. He came from the north-western aristocratic stock which was only partly Chinese. He was a soldier and an excellent horseman, and in these qualities he was closer to the Turks than to the southern Chinese. On one occasion before he became emperor he had challenged a khaghan to personal combat, such conduct being most untypical of a Chinese ruler. In 626, when the Turks under Xieli invaded the Chang'an region, Li Shimin showed great personal bravery, and through brotherhood ceremonies established personal links with the Turkish leaders. In the following year Xieli found himself facing a rebellion, with the Chinese supporting the rebels. A Chinese army inflicted a disastrous defeat and almost all the Turkish tribes in the east went over to the Tang. New tribal leaders were chosen from among the Turkish élite, the Turkish tribal structure was incorporated into Tang government and Turkish leaders became Tang officials. Li Shimin himself became the 'heavenly khaghan'.[17]

There followed an extraordinary period of Chinese expansion. With the eastern Turks as their faithful allies, the frontiers of Chinese influence were extended even beyond the limits of the Han empire. In a series of campaigns the western Turks were defeated. Before one memorable engagement the Chinese general Su Dingfang said to his troops: 'The fog sheds darkness everywhere. The wind is icy. The barbarians do not believe that we can campaign at this season. Let us hasten to surprise them!'[18] This battle, fought near Issyk Kul in 657, reduced the western Turks to vassals of the Chinese. The Chinese empire now stretched to the borders of Persia.

Yet as the Tang dynasty advanced its frontiers the problems of maintaining its control increased. None of Taizong's successors possessed his skills in manipulating Turkish leaders. Even the eastern Turks grew dissatisfied and revolted. A memorial inscription recorded their grievances:

Those chieftains who were in China adopted Chinese titles and obeyed the Chinese emperor. They gave their services and their strength to him for fifty years. . . . They surrendered to the Chinese emperor their empire and their own law. Then the Turks and all the common people said as follows: "I used to be of a people who had an empire. Where is my empire now? For whose benefit am I conquering realms?" They said "I used to be of a polity that had an emperor. Where is my emperor now? To which emperor do I give my services and strength?" they said. By saying so they became the foes of the Chinese emperor.[19]

The western Turks resumed the 'outer frontier strategy' and carried out a series of raids into Chinese territory, seizing many captives and extorting vast sums of money. However, by the early eighth century, the age of the great Turkish khaghanates had passed and new situations had developed on China's frontiers.

The Rise of Tibet

Before considering the rise of the Uighur, or second Turkish empire, it is appropriate to look at another dramatic development, the rise of Tibet. Little is known of Tibetan history before the seventh century, because of the absence of written records. The early inhabitants of Tibet were known to the Chinese as the Qiang. They were a Mongoloid people who in the north were nomadic but in the south had settled on agricultural land. They followed the Bon religion, a shamanist faith formerly widely prevalent over Central Asia. Early in the seventh century two major developments occurred affecting the Qiang: tribal society gave way to a centralised monarchy, and Buddhism was introduced, which in turn encouraged the development of a writing system. Buddhism at first challenged the Bon religion, but later a synthesis occurred which produced Lamaism.

Between about 620 and 649 the ruler of Tibet was Song-tsen Gampo and it was he who initiated a period of rapid expansion, his possible motive being to placate the aristocracy for their loss of independence by offering them opportunities for plunder. His primary target was the Tuyuhun nomads who used the pastures around Lake Kokonor. In 634, for the first time, the Tibetans sent envoys and tribute to the Tang court. A few years later the Tibetan king, having heard that a Chinese princess had been given in marriage to a ruler of the Tuyuhun, demanded similar treatment. When he was refused he launched an attack into Sichuan which, although repulsed, persuaded the Chinese of the value of a marriage alliance and a Chinese princess was duly sent to Tibet.

There now began a period of intensive sinicisation. Song-tsen Gampo had also asked that men who could read and write Chinese be sent to Tibet, and that members of the Tibetan royal family be permitted to study at the State University. The Chinese princess was a devout Buddhist, and she brought Buddhist monks and Buddhist sacred writings with her to Tibet. Soon afterwards the Tibetans asked for technicians who could teach sericulture, wine-brewing and paper-making, and who could construct grain mills.[20]

In the 660s the Tibetans recommenced their expansion and expelled the Tuyuhun from around the Kokonor. By so doing they 'destroyed the only buffer state between Tibet and Chinese territory'.[21] They twice seized control of the Tarim Basin only to be repulsed by Chinese troops, but still the Tibetan drive continued and by 680 they had gained control of parts of Sichuan. In 696, with the Empress Wu now on the throne, a Tibetan army defeated a large Chinese force less than two hundred miles from Chang'an. The empress, by adroit diplomacy, sowed dissension in the Tibetan ranks, and the immediate danger was averted. Nevertheless the Tibetans posed a very serious danger to the Chinese position in Central Asia. In order to maintain their influence in the Tarim Basin, the Chinese were forced onto the defensive and had to maintain a chain of garrisons and military colonies to safeguard communications.

In 722 Tibetan raiding started once again, but the hostilities culminated in a series of Chinese victories and the Tibetans were forced to sue for peace. In the resultant treaty, negotiated in 730, the Tibetan king acknowledged Chinese suzerainty, embassies were exchanged and a border demarcated. The settlement did not last, and large-scale hostilities occurred again in the 740s and 750s, principally in the Gansu corridor, where the Chinese were defending the approaches to Chang'an from the threat of Tibetan attack. Tibetan expansion was also occurring in the far west, in the Pamirs, but their progress in that region was halted by a spectacular Chinese victory at Gilgit. However, in 755 the Tibetan king died, his successor accepted investiture with Chinese titles and it seemed as if the Tibetan threat had again receded.

Then came An Lushan's rebellion, which forced the withdrawal of Chinese forces – or rather the forces of the military commands which had been set up on the frontiers – and this in turn led to the collapse of the defensive strategy. The Tibetan king decided to take advantage of China's problems by first encroaching on present-day Gansu and Qinghai and then moving on into Shaanxi. In so doing he deprived the Chinese of the horse-breeding and pasture lands essential for the maintenance of cavalry forces. From there, in 763, Tibetan forces attacked and captured Chang'an, which they proceeded to loot. Although they soon withdrew, this was the first of thirteen years of annual Tibetan attacks which gravely weakened the restored dynasty. In 784, the two sides being exhausted, a peace treaty was signed which contained a definition of the border between the contestants, and which conceded vast tracts of territory to the Tibetans. Within a few years it became clear that this was not a solution to the conflict and China was forced to employ a new strategy, seeking as allies the recently emerged Uighur empire. Shortly afterwards China succeeded in detaching the state of Nanzhao from its habitual support of the Tibetans.

In 821 Tibet and China negotiated a second treaty, which this time was to last. The terms of the agreement were carved in Tibetan and Chinese on a stone pillar which was erected in Lhasa. It was an agreement between 'nephew and uncle', as the rulers of Tibet and China were described, which called for an end to the fighting and established a boundary between the two countries. Even while the treaty was being negotiated dissension had broken out in Tibet. It arose from the attempt of the Tibetan monarchy to use Buddhism as an instrument to establish its authority over the aristocracy, which continued to support the Bon religion. In the 840s a bitter religious strife destroyed the Tibetan monarchy and with it the military power which had for so long threatened China. As a consequence the Tibetan kingdom 'played no significant role in east Asian interstate relations thereafter'.[22]

The Uighur Empire

The long periods of warfare with the Tibetans had destroyed one of the main means used by China to protect her western frontiers, that is to say by the establishment of military colonies. As a consequence a new strategy had to be found to protect China. The means for this was found in the support of the Uighur, a Turkish group closely related to the eastern Turks, who established an empire which lasted from 744 to 840 in the area which is now Mongolia. The relationship which developed between the Uighur and the Chinese was one of mutual benefit:

to a weak Chinese dynasty the Uighur provided invaluable military support; while the Uighur received from China an immense revenue and a privileged position in trade. This was a symbiotic relationship, for the Uighur were trusty allies who recognised that it was not in their interest to allow the Tang dynasty to be overthrown.

The Uighur empire was established after a revolt among the vassal tribes had precipitated the collapse of the royal clan of the eastern Turks. The leader of the Uighur, one of those vassal tribes, became khaghan, and to demonstrate that he was in control he sent the severed head of the last Turkish khaghan to the Tang court. At first the Uighur pursued the traditional outer frontier strategy of exploiting China from a distance, but then the rebellion of An Lushan offered them a marvellous opportunity to capitalise on the situation. In exchange for an alliance, and the marriage of the khaghan's daughter to a Tang prince, the Uighur sent a force of 4,000 horsemen to China. This force played a key role in the recapture of Luoyang, but the price to be paid for assistance was heavy, for the Uighur were allowed to loot the city and in addition were promised an annual payment of 20,000 rolls of silk. When the Uighur had returned home they demanded and obtained a marriage alliance with a Tang princess.

Until the 780s the Uighur periodically campaigned in China, demanding a heavy payment for their services. Thereafter the pattern was more for the Uighur to extort payment from a distance. Some of this revenue came from charging an exorbitant price for horses, which were exchanged for silk. An Arab traveller who visited the Uighur capital reported that the khaghan received annual payments of half a million pieces of silk from China. This immense wealth gave the Uighur leaders extensive patronage, and they were able to establish a much more stable state than any of their predecessors. To the capital at Karabalghasun came Sogdians who provided literate administrators, enabling the running of 'a true city on the steppe'.[23] The sack of Luoyang had led to the khaghan meeting Manichaean missionaries, who converted him. A trilingual inscription on a monument at Karabalghasun recorded that this 'country of barbarous customs, full of the fumes of blood, was changed into a land where the people live on vegetables; from a land of killing to where good deeds are fostered.'[24] Thereafter the Uighur were recognised as the official protectors of Manichaean missions in China. Their claim to be a civilised people was further advanced with the development of a Uighur script and the translation of Manichaean and Buddhist scripts into the Uighur language.

Perhaps this cultural advance and the adoption of a more sedentary existence weakened the Uighur empire. In 840, after the empire had been split by a succession dispute, the Kirghiz tribe from the north seized and looted the capital. The Uighur empire fell and with it went the most dependable support of the Tang dynasty.

The Qidan

Meanwhile, in the north-east, another type of tribal confederation had taken shape which was to pose a quite different set of demands on China. The people involved were the Qidan, from whose name the word Cathay was derived. They spoke a language ancestral to Mongolian, though the term Mongol was not yet in use. They were pastoral nomads who came from what in modern times has been named Manchuria and from the area around Rehe. This area was in the marginal zone, that is to say between the open steppe and settled areas. It has long been noted that dynasties of conquest have come from such areas and more recently it has been pointed out that the vast majority of the dynasties of conquest came from the Manchurian marginal zone.[25]

The Qidan first appeared in Chinese annals at the beginning of the fifth century. By the early seventh century they were trying to create an autonomous state on China's frontier, an objective which was not tolerable to a powerful dynasty, and in the early Tang period the Qidan were forced to accept Chinese rule. When in 696 the Qidan revolted, the Chinese, with the assistance of the eastern Turks, suppressed them with such ferocity that their expansion was halted until the beginning of the tenth century.

In the meantime the Qidan began to profit from their proximity to China and Qidan society started to change. They adopted farming, began to produce cloth and commenced living in urban settlements. Traditionally the leadership of the tribal organisation of the eight Qidan tribes was rotated. However, early in the tenth century, Abaoji, the leader of the Yila tribe, broke away from the system. After having completed his term of office he refused to step down and declared himself to be emperor of the Qidan. He thereupon massacred other Qidan leaders and moved to make himself the ruler of a Chinese-style dynasty. Chinese advisers were brought in, and in 916 he adopted a Chinese reign title. He reorganised the military forces, replacing the tribal units with a force personally loyal to him. An imperial bodyguard of mounted archers was formed, its men being drawn from different tribes. At first this was an élite force, but later it became the model for the *ordo* or 'horde', the military formation into which the Qidan people were mobilised.

The Qidan expansion then began. One aspect of this was directed against tribal peoples to the west, first against the Kirghiz in Mongolia, the successors of the Uighur, who were displaced in 924. Two years later the kingdom of Pohai, which extended over northern Korea and part of Manchuria, was overthrown. After Abaoji's death, his son Deguang turned his attention to the south. Following the final collapse of the Tang dynasty in 907, north China had been ruled by the Five Dynasties, a series of ephemeral regimes. In 936 Deguang intervened in the region, supporting Shi Jingtang, a rebellious general, in a bid for power. Shi became the emperor of the Later Jin dynasty and a client of the Qidan, ceding to them territory within the Great Wall in northern Hebei and Shanxi. Such a surrender was a dramatic departure from the practice when dealing with the Uighur, and the humiliating outcome was further stressed by the demand for an annual tribute. When Shi's successor tried to stop the payment of the tribute, he was overthrown, and the Qidan seemed poised to establish themselves as rulers in north China. However, a series of setbacks, including succession disputes and the establishment of the Song dynasty in 960, curbed those ambitions. Nevertheless, despite the efforts of the new dynasty, the Qidan could not be driven out of north China. In 1004, in an agreement known as the treaty of Shanyuan, the Chinese dynasty and the Qidan agreed to a compromise, which left the Qidan, now known as the Liao dynasty, as rulers of part of north China and of territories beyond. A further indication of the limited power of the Song dynasty, was that the Tangut, a Tibetan people, were able to establish the Xi Xia kingdom in modern Gansu.

The Liao empire, which in its first form lasted from 947 until 1125, was a refinement of a type of administration which had been pioneered by the Xianbei in the fourth century and further developed by the Toba in the Northern Wei dynasty. Its essential feature was a form of dualism initiated by Deguang:

> he divided the government into North and South. The Qidan were governed according to their own national system, while the Chinese were governed according to their own system. The national system was plain and simple. In the Chinese system the usage of traditional terminology was preserved.[26]

Under this dual system, features of both Qidan and Chinese society were maintained. On the Qidan side, the survival of the semi-nomadic tradition was evident in the use of no less than five capitals, including modern-day Beijing. The tribal organisation was retained, and the development of it, the ordo was improved. The Qidan language was preserved and a codified Qidan law applied. In the areas of China under Qidan rule the Tang system of government remained in force and the Liao emperor performed the functions of a Confucian ruler. The examination system continued in use for the selection of officials. This dual system, which made it possible to rule parts of the steppe and parts of China at the same time, was to provide a model for the later Jurchen Jin empire, and most notably for the Manchu Qing dynasty.

Relations with Korea

To the north-east of China, during the Sui and Tang periods, a unified Korea had emerged. Chinese influence, which had spread into the Korean peninsula in the Han period, had subsequently declined. With the reunification of China the desire to secure this quarter revived and Yangdi, the second emperor of the Sui, three times attempted to conquer Koguryo, the northern of the three kingdoms which then composed Korea. He failed, with disastrous consequences. However, in 663, during Gaozong's reign, Paekche in the southwest was defeated. Five years later, with the assistance of Silla, the third Korean kingdom, Koguryo was also subdued and a Chinese protectorate established at Pyongyang. The country was divided into administrative districts and Chinese officials put in charge of them. When Silla started a movement of resistance against the Chinese presence, this arrangement proved untenable and in 676 the Chinese were forced to withdraw. Silla then created a unified Korean state covering most of the Korean peninsula.

Although independent, the state of Silla, which lasted until 935, was heavily indebted to influence from Tang China. A bureaucratic form of government was introduced, the country was divided into provinces, and a landholding system derived from China was inaugurated. There were also strong cultural links, with the spread of Buddhism, the encouragement of Confucian scholarship and the introduction of competitive examinations. Another indication of the closeness of the relationship which subsisted between Silla and China was that between 703 and 738 no less than forty-five embassies were sent to China. Officials of Korean origin were to be found at the Tang court and many Korean monks settled in China. Large numbers of Koreans lived along the coast from the mouth of the Huai river to the coast of Shandong, many of them being traders and sailors, but others were settlers who formed autonomous colonies.

However, other features of Korean society were antipathetic to a total acceptance of the Chinese model. Korea had an aristocratic order, and the idea of a competitive examination system, which in China had undermined the position of the great aristocratic families, was bound to induce resistance. Confucianism never gained dominance as a state ideology and the concept of the Confucian ruler never took root in Korea.

Pohai

When Koguryo was defeated, a large number of Koguryo captives, including many from the aristocracy, were transported to the north. In time they settled near Jilin in northern Manchuria, in territory inhabited by Tungusic people, and there they founded a state which from 713 became known to the Chinese as Pohai. This state, which at one time extended from the Sungari and Amur rivers into north Korea was, like Silla, organised on the Chinese model. Its administration was based on the Tang bureaucracy, Buddhist influence was strong, and commercial and tributary links were maintained with China. The state survived until it was conquered by the Qidan in 927.

Japan

The Tang period was also the high-water mark of Chinese influence on the development of Japan. The use of Chinese writing and the knowledge of Chinese Confucian texts had reached Japan early in the fifth century, and at about the same time technology derived from China, for example improved irrigation techniques, was also introduced. In 538 Buddhism reached Japan via Korea. But it was not until the sixth and seventh centuries, after the reunification of China under the Sui, that the most sustained period of Chinese influence occurred. Two themes predominated in this influence: 'the institutions of government, particularly as perfected under the Tang dynasty, and the doctrines of Buddhism, as institutionalized under the power of the Chinese emperors and the Sinified sectarian orders'.[27] The person most associated with this development was Prince Shōtoku, regent from 593 until his death in 622. In 604 he promulgated a document, known as the Seventeen-Article Constitution, which expressed Confucian ethical and political doctrines and endorsed Buddhism as contributing to the ideal of social harmony.[28] In 702 a compendium of penal laws and administrative practice, known as the Taiho Code, was produced, and once again the model was Tang China. Two other striking examples of borrowing were the introduction of provisions for equal landholding and the practice of choosing officials by means of examinations.[29] Yet in Japan, as in Korea, borrowing from China could only go so far before it met with resistance from indigenous sources. As the power of the Tang empire waned, cultural borrowing declined and these peripheral states increasingly established an independent cultural identity.

China's Relationship With the Outside World

During the Sui and Tang dynasties embassies from various countries were sent to the Chinese imperial court and students and monks went to China to study religion and culture. The Japanese monk Ennin was a member of the last official Japanese embassy to the Tang court. He arrived in China in 838 and remained there for nine years, studying esoteric Buddhism. His diary provides the first example, and an outstanding one, of a description of China by a foreign visitor. In it he gives details of the preparations made for the dispatch of a tribute mission and the hazards of a voyage to China. Ennin was not at the imperial audience when the tribute was presented, but he recorded that embassies from no less than five countries were received on that day. His diary is packed with details of what he had seen of life in China and it is a major source on Buddhism and its persecution.[30]

The tributary mission to which Ennin belonged represented one form of relationship between China and the outside world. This unequal partnership had its foundation in a myth of Chinese superiority which can be traced back to the formative period of the Chinese empire. At that time the empire was expanding, either through military victories or through the assimilation of surrounding peoples, in a manner which seemed to confirm that Chinese civilisation was indeed superior. In the Han period the language used to describe the relationship between China and those surrounding states, which had accepted Chinese culture and which recognised Chinese superiority, was formalised. Foreign missions to the Chinese court were described as tribute missions. Although tributary missions took gifts to the Chinese court and were rewarded with trade privileges, their essential purpose was perceived as political, as a visible recognition of Chinese superiority. In the Tang period, when Chinese influence was at a high point, the claim for superiority was reinforced by the actuality of power. However, in terms of rhetoric, the justification for superiority was not based on the power balance but on the superiority of China's Confucian culture.[31]

The relationship which developed in the Tang period between China and the nomadic peoples of the steppe had rather different characteristics. For a start, it was a dynamic relationship which altered according to the relative strength of steppe confederations and the Chinese state. Secondly, the relationship was based on economic factors, and in particular on the need of nomadic societies, particularly ones which had achieved a degree of sophistication, to secure grain and quality goods from China. Finally it was a relationship based on the equality, or even on the superiority, in military terms, of the nomadic peoples over the Chinese. The relationship took the form of frontier markets, tributary exchange and intermarriage arrangements, mechanisms first used under the Han and then developed by the Tang. When these mechanisms worked effectively, the northern frontiers were relatively peaceful, but when they broke down the nomadic peoples resumed their alternative relationship, the outer frontier strategy of periodically raiding China and seizing or extorting what they required.[32]

8

Thought, Religion and Culture under the Sui and Tang Dynasties

The Rise and Decline of Buddhism

In the sixth century, the whole of northern Chinese society was suffused with Buddhism:

> it penetrated economic life and affected customs at all levels of society. Its monasteries and shrines dotted the landscape; its clergy assumed many social roles; that of preacher and teacher, medical doctor and chanter of magic spells, performers of masses for the dead and guardians of temples that also served as family shrines. Elite families were for the most part Buddhist in belief. They made gifts to monasteries and shrines, used clergy for family and seasonal observances, had the lay vows administered to their sons. . . .[1]

The reasons for this extraordinary growth are by no means certain. In a number of respects Buddhism appeared to be opposed to important aspects of Chinese culture. Whereas the Chinese view of life was that it was to be enjoyed, Buddhist teaching stressed that life was full of suffering and that one should seek release from its repetitive cycle. The Chinese traditionally emphasised the family and in particular its perpetuation through the birth of a son, whereas Buddhists practised celibacy. The Chinese valued productive labour and harmonious social relationships whereas for the Buddhist the objective was enlightenment, which came through a disregard for worldly goods and the abandonment of the household. Furthermore, for the Confucianist it was a requirement to uphold the laws of the state, whereas members of a Buddhist monastic community deemed themselves to be outside the law.[2]

However, from the fourth century onwards Buddhism was to make rapid progress in China. It achieved this at a time of disunity within the state and of uncertainty in men's minds:

> There was no central dynasty motivated by Confucian concepts of government to oppose the Indian religion. Thoughtful Chinese . . . were looking about for a substitute; they were groping for a new way of life, a new standard of conduct, to take the place of the Confucian ideology which had been found

114

wanting. In this quest they turned to Buddhism to see whether or not this religion could offer some satisfactory solutions to the problems they faced.[3]

An important additional reason for the success of Buddhism in China was that it was not a monolithic faith but a religion which was capable of wide variation and was adaptable to Chinese circumstances. Through the establishment of schools, Chinese forms of Buddhism were developed and characteristic Chinese features incorporated. A common Chinese saying describing the four most influential schools declared, 'The Tiantai and Huayan schools for doctrine, and the Meditation and Pure Land schools for practice'.[4] Of these four schools, the Tiantai did not even exist in India, while the other three, which did have their antecedents in India, developed Chinese characteristics. A brief review of their main features will convey the essentials of Chinese Buddhist thought in this period.

The Tiantai school, which was named after the sacred mountain in Zhejiang, was established by Zhiyi late in the sixth century. His teachings were based on a minute examination of the *Lotus Sutra*, which he regarded as the most complete doctrine among all Buddhist teachings – all other doctrines, although each containing something of value, he considered to be preparatory to it. The sutra taught that the historical Gautama Sakyamuni, who lived in the sixth and fifth centuries BC, was but an earthly manifestation of the eternal Buddha. The Tiantai school offered a doctrine of universal salvation, to be achieved both through intellectual enquiry and meditative practice. The second school, the Huayan or Flower Garden school, had many similarities to the Tiantai school. It was in effect founded by Fazang, the Great Master of Xianshou, and he too was concerned with the universal principle and the nature of matter. It also classified the various Buddhist sects into vehicles, with the perfect doctrine of the Huayan combining what was valuable in all the other vehicles. In this way both the Tiantai and Huayan schools displayed a typical Chinese preference for syncretism. Their philosophical teachings tended to attract an intellectual following rather than popular support.

The Meditation school, known as Chan in China and Zen in Japan and in the West, was by tradition brought to the Northern Wei kingdom by the Indian master Bodhidharma in about the year 520. There, it was said, he practised wall contemplation – sitting in front of a wall – for nine years, before engaging in teaching. In fact Chan Buddhism appears to be a Chinese development, perhaps fusing elements of the Buddhist concept of enlightenment with philosophical ideas derived from Daoism. Chan taught that the Buddha-nature is inherent in all human beings and that nature may be perceived through meditation. In the eighth century Chan Buddhism split into northern and southern schools, the former believing in gradual enlightenment, the latter in sudden enlightenment. The southern school, which rejected all scriptures and which stressed intuition rather than intellect, became extremely popular and has survived to this day.

Also popular was the Jingtu or Pure Land school which emphasised salvation through faith rather than through good works, and thus attracted many simple worshippers. It took its name from the Pure Land or Western Paradise, presided over by Amitabha, the Amita Buddha. According to the shorter version of the *Pure Land*

Sutra, the believer can gain access to that land through the repetition of the name of the Amitabha, that is Amituofo in Chinese. In the Pure Land the Amita Buddha has as his chief minister the always compassionate bodhisattva Avalokitesvara, known in Chinese as Guanyin. Through the Tang and into the Song period this figure was depicted as male, but thereafter Guanyin came to be the Goddess of Mercy, clad in white.

The spread of Buddhism represented a major challenge to the authority of the Chinese state. Monasteries were endowed with large parcels of land which were tax exempt. Buddhist clergy, particularly in the south, claimed that they did not owe obedience to the civil authority. The popular support on which the Buddhist church could rely made it difficult, if not dangerous, for emperors to take effective action against it. It was for this reason that Yang Jian, the first Sui emperor, deliberately used Buddhism 'as an ideological force capable of bringing together the country which had been divided for two and a half centuries'.[5]

The early Tang rulers did not display the same enthusiasm for Buddhism. However, because they recognised its influence, they took care to use patronage to conciliate Buddhists by constructing monasteries in key places and by holding services for the dead. At the same time they increasingly applied curbs to the spread of Buddhism. From the beginning of the dynasty Tang emperors had given favours to the Daoist church, and in 637 Taizong challenged the pre-eminent position which Buddhism had come to occupy by issuing an edict that in future Daoist monks and nuns would take precedence over their Buddhist counterparts. Through other measures he confined monks and nuns to their monasteries and restricted them to their religious duties. However, before the end of his reign, and perhaps because of his admiration for Xuan Zang, the Buddhist monk who had brought the scriptures back from India, Taizong withdrew his opposition to Buddhism and authorised the ordination of some 18,500 new monks.[6]

Under the Empress Wu the Buddhist church regained favour. She herself came from a devoutly Buddhist family. The threat of her usurpation of the throne had outraged the Confucianists and alienated the Daoist church, and so it was only natural that she should look to Buddhism for support. Buddhist priests claimed that oracles had identified her as the Maitreya Buddha and had asserted that the mandate of heaven had passed to her. When enthroned she repaid her obligation by reversing Taizong's edict and giving Buddhist priests precedence over the Daoist clergy. During her reign she gave particular favour to the Chan and Huayan schools.

After the empress's death Buddhism again fell from favour. Xuanzong took a harder line than his predecessors, enacting a series of measures to restrict the wealth of the Buddhist church. At the same time he commissioned translations of Buddhist scriptures and offered favours to Chinese and Indian monks, but these were practitioners of esoteric Buddhism, which, like Daoism, used ritual practices to avert disasters.

The An Lushan rebellion, which convulsed north China between 755 and 763, had a major effect on the relationship between Buddhism and the state. On the one hand the dynasty, desperately weakened by the rebellion, was forced to relax its policies towards Buddhism. For example, for a fee it allowed the unrestricted ordination of Buddhist clergy, thus raising short-term revenue while decreasing the number of people liable to taxation. This practice, euphemistically known as 'money for the purchase of scented rice', rebounded on Buddhism – a Buddhist historian later observed: 'The corrupt practice of selling ordination certificates has destroyed our religion'.[7] On the other hand the ravages of war had a destructive effect on the monastic communities near Luoyang and Chang'an. The damage was greater to the philosophical schools than to the popular sects. In the years after the rebellion Pure Land Buddhism not only grew in popularity, but was also introduced at court, where hitherto it had been treated with disdain.

Imperial patronage of Buddhism increased in the years after the rebellion. Daizong (reigned 762–79) authorised vast expenditure on the construction of monasteries and he himself paid reverence to Buddhist relics and encouraged the mass ordination of monks and nuns. His son was less enthusiastic, but was unable to take decisive steps to reduce the heavy cost that the support of Buddhism was placing on the state. Nevertheless he encouraged large translation projects of Buddhist texts. Xianzong (reigned 805–20), took an interest in Chan Buddhism, and gave demonstrations of his own personal piety, most notably in 819 when he had a famous relic, the supposed fingerbone of Buddha, brought to Chang'an so that he could worship it.

It was this event which provoked the celebrated protest by Han Yu, which has sometimes been seen as having initiated the later suppression of Buddhism. In fact, his criticism was neither the first, nor the decisive contribution to that decision. From the beginning of the Tang period voices had been raised against Buddhism. In 621 the grand astrologer and Daoist priest Fu Yi had summarised the commonly-expressed view that the Buddhist monastic communities were a burden on the state. He had urged the emperor to disband the Buddhist clergy and put the monasteries to a better use. Taizong's extravagant expenditure on monasteries had been sharply criticised by a scholar named Gao Ying, who argued that in the past wise rulers had sought merit through good deeds and not by depleting the treasury.[8] An official who served Dezong had estimated that the cost of supplying food and clothing to a single monk was greater than the tax paid by five adult males.[9]

Nevertheless Han Yu's response was significant. He was a famous Confucian scholar, and his 'Memorial on the Bone of Buddha' was an outstandingly vehement criticism of the display of the relic in the imperial palace. He wrote scathingly that 'Buddha was a man of the barbarians who did not speak the language of China and wore clothes of a different fashion'. He understood 'neither the duties that bind a sovereign and subject, nor the affections of father and son'. If the Buddha were still alive he might merely have been granted an audience in an outer hall. Why then, asked Han Yu, after he had long been dead, 'could his rotten bones, the foul and unlucky remains of his body, be rightly admitted to the palace?'[10] For this outburst Han Yu was sentenced to death, his sentence later being commuted to one of exile to the south.

However in 842 the opponents of Buddhism found, in the emperor Wuzong, a ruler willing to take decisive action. In that year decrees were published which called for the expulsion of unregistered monks from monasteries, the laicisation of undesirable monks and the seizure of property belonging to individual members of the Buddhist clergy. Further decrees followed, culminating in 845 with two edicts. One of these prohibited Buddhist monasteries from holding estates and ordered that all monastic wealth be handed over to pay government salaries; the other called for the laicisation of all Buddhist monks and nuns under the age of forty. The Japanese monk Ennin, who witnessed these events, noted that 'the monks and nuns are being exterminated. The scheme is generally the same throughout the land'.[11]

Why did Wuzong act thus? In the Edict on the Suppression of Buddhism he referred to the foreignness of the religion and how recently it had grown in numbers and wealth. He repeated other commonly voiced criticisms:

It wears out the strength of the people with constructions of earth and wood, pilfers their wealth for ornaments of gold and precious objects, causes men to abandon their lords and parents for the company of teachers, and severs man and wife with its monastic decrees.[12]

According to Ennin's account there was a link between the suppression and the Wuzong emperor's preoccupation with Daoism. A major Daoist project, the construction of 'a terrace for viewing the immortals', was being completed when the edict of suppression was promulgated. Nevertheless it is difficult to accept that the suppression was mainly a response to the demands of the Daoist clergy. There is perhaps a stronger case for arguing that it was Confucian officials who led the attack. Buddhist historians have often claimed that Li Deyu, the chief minister, incited the emperor to act. If this was true, and there is some evidence of his involvement, it seems likely that his motivation was political rather than ideological. Even if some stirrings of a Confucian revival had become apparent, this did not amount to a serious challenge to the philosophical aspects of Buddhism.

There remains the question of the importance of the economic motive. All the critics of Buddhism emphasised the cost of state support of Buddhism, and the economic implications of a substantial proportion of the population withdrawing from economic activity and escaping from the burden of taxation. The temptation to confiscate the wealth of Buddhist establishments was clearly there, in particular because the Buddhist church was alleged to have converted much of the nation's precious metal into statues and bells. Nevertheless, it has been pointed out that the actual accumulation of wealth and diversion of human resources by the Buddhist church was much less than might be expected: only one per cent of the population dwelt in Buddhist establishments and these establishments worked no more than four per cent of the cultivated land.[13]

The great suppression was said to have resulted in the destruction of 4,600 monasteries and 40,000 temples and shrines, the laicisation of 260,500 monks and nuns and the confiscation of millions of acres of tax-exempt farmland.[14] Nevertheless it did not destroy Buddhism in China, for under Wuzong's successor something like a restoration of Buddhism took place. However Huang Chao's rebellion was to add greatly to the process of destruction. Buddhist monasteries in almost every part of China were affected, major centres of learning were sacked and the clergy scattered. The schools of Buddhist scholarship fell into disuse, key texts were lost and the transmission of knowledge discontinued.

Other Religions Introduced into China

During the Tang period several new religions reached China, including Zoroastrianism, Manichaeism, Christianity, Judaism and Islam. Zoroastrianism reached China from Persia during the reign of the Taizong emperor. The Persian Sassanian dynasty had been overthrown by an Arab invasion and the Persian king sent his son on an embassy to China to ask for assistance against the Arabs. A Persian court in exile was established at Chang'an and permission was given for the building of a Zoroastrian temple. Manichaeism was brought to Chang'an by Uighur merchants in the eighth century and they established a number of temples there and in other cities to serve their fellow countrymen. Manichaeans made no attempt to convert the Chinese population, but this did not protect them from persecution at the time of the suppression of Buddhism. Before the full weight of Wuzong's prejudice had fallen upon the Buddhists, the Manichaeans had their property confiscated and Manichaean priests may have been executed. Similar harsh treatment was meted out to the Zoroastrians.

The Nestorians were a Syrian Christian sect. This form of Christianity (which believed that Jesus had a human as well as a divine identity) had reached China in 635. Its first representative, a monk possibly named Reuben, had presented the Nestorian scriptures to the Taizong emperor, who, it was recorded, 'thoroughly understood their propriety and truth and specially ordered their preaching and transmission'.[15] The first church was built in 638 and the Nestorians received marks of favour from subsequent emperors. An account of Nestorian teachings was inscribed on a monument in 781 and the stone was buried soon after the suppression edict of 845 was promulgated. It was rediscovered in 1625 and may now be seen in the Shaanxi Provincial Museum in Xi'an.

Islam came to China during the Tang period by both the land and the sea routes. A mission from Caliph Othman is recorded as having reached China in 651, and an Arab community, made up of soldiers who had assisted in the suppression of the rebellion of An Lushan, existed in Gansu and Shaanxi from the eighth century. It was from the descendants of these Arabs that the present Muslim population of China derived. In the south Arab traders resided in several ports, where they enjoyed extraterritoriality and the freedom to practise their own religion. However, many of them were to die in the disastrous rebellion led by Huang Chao.[16]

Confucianism

Of Confucian scholarship during the Tang period it has been said that its main function was to serve the bureaucracy and that learned men devoted themselves to textual exegesis to provide authoritative versions of Confucian texts for use in the examinations. This work was important, 'yet we find in it evidence only of painstaking study and not of creative thought'.[17] More recently a somewhat different view has been expressed. Although much of Tang Confucian scholarship was concerned with the classical and ritual texts and with the compilation of dynastic history, and Confucian scholars displayed an overriding preoccupation with success in the examination system and the pursuit of an official career, there was another side to their activity. This was concerned with the policies to be adopted to deal with contemporary issues, issues which ranged from matters of ritual to defence against the barbarians and economic and financial management. In the first part of the dynasty, before An Lushan's rebellion, much of this activity was state-sponsored, and Confucian scholars participated actively in debates over policy issues. In the later part of the dynasty private scholarship and informal writing became more important and this in turn contributed to the later development of Confucianism.[18]

The best-remembered Confucian scholar of the age was Han Yu (768–824), whose famous attack on Buddhism has already been noted. It has been said of the Tang that 'at no other time in Chinese history did the Confucian tradition come closer to extinction.' It has been claimed that it survived because Han Yu self-consciously took upon himself the task of redefining Confucian values, thus earning the title of the first of the great Neo-Confucians.[19] In his 'Discourse on Teachers' he wrote:

Alas, the teaching of the Way has long been neglected! Hard it is, then, to expect men to be without doubts. The sages of antiquity far excelled ordinary men, and yet they sought teachers and questioned them. But the common people of today, though they are equally far from the level of the sages, count it a shame to study with a teacher. Thus do sages become even wiser, and the stupid more stupid.[20]

According to this view Han Yu was 'a man involved in a life-long attempt to restore political, cultural and religious unity to the Tang world'. He was an innovator, one who represented the dynamic spirit of a new age. However this opinion has been challenged and the essentially conservative quality of Han Yu's thought has been stressed. For example, he had participated in the contemporary debate on whether the heir to the throne should be selected from the imperial sons or on the basis of merit. Han Yu had supported the conservative line which endorsed hereditary succession. With reference to the official educational system, Han Yu had at first appeared to be a reformer, but later, after he had had experience of office, the career values which prevailed in the bureaucracy gained precedence in his mind over the teaching ideals he had developed earlier. Even his stridently anti-Buddhist views did not represent a radical new attitude, nor did they derive from his development as an introspective thinker – the criticism was based on the social and political effects of the spread of Buddhism and echoed the commonly expressed view of officials of his day.[21]

Tang Literature: Poetry

'The splendour and the subsequent decline of the Tang period are reflected in its poetry. Tang China, like Elizabethan England, was virtually a nation of singing birds'. Of this outpouring some 50,000 poems, from the brushes of 2,300 poets, have survived.[22] Later generations have regarded the poetry written during the reign of Xuanzong (712–56) as the apogee of all Chinese poetry, a model which later poets could imitate but could never hope to surpass. The most popular anthology of Chinese verse, the eighteenth-century compilation *Three Hundred Tang Poems*, has ensured that these poems remain familiar to educated Chinese to this day.

This poetic flowering did not come out of the blue. During the period of division poetry had become associated with the life of the recluse. The outstanding example of such a person was Tao Qian (376–427), who had abandoned an official post to take up the life of a farmer. His poems celebrated the joys of the simple country life, and his enjoyment of drinking wine:

> No dust and confusion
>> within my doors and courtyard;
> In the empty rooms,
>> more than sufficient leisure.
> Too long I was held
>> within the barred cage.
> Now I am able
>> to return again to Nature.[23]

After the reunification of China under the Sui, the need for poets to distance themselves from the life of politics and the city grew less and many of the most famous poets of the Tang period served as officials and were familiar with life in the capital Chang'an. It has been said of Tang poets that their motivation to write was quite different from that of their western counterparts. For them, the writing of poetry was not an exclusive vocation, but something which they did under particular circumstances or on a special occasion. In the early Tang period much of the poetry written was court poetry, a response to events at court, composed by that small minority who attended there. By the late eighth century, poetry had been transformed from a minor diversion into an art form. It had become a vehicle for the expression of the feelings of the individual, feelings often related to the poet's moral values, doubts, suffering – feelings often aroused by the experience of absence or exile.[24]

Of the poets of the age, one of the most remarkable was Wang Wei (699–759), for he was equally well-known as a painter. Although he had passed the imperial examinations and had been appointed to office, he was then demoted and required to serve in a lowly position in Shandong. There he wrote in the style of an exile and expressed in simple language his close relationship with nature, a relationship often defined by reference to Buddhist sentiments. He was later reinstated and held a variety of offices until he was captured by An Lushan's rebel army. It was typical of Wang Wei that he did not mention that traumatic experience in his verse. He became famous for his mastery of the brief poem known as *jueju*, the 'cut-short' quatrain, poems which have been described as 'visually complete but intellectually incomplete', which invite the reader to deipher some hidden truth. A poem from the *Wang Stream Collection* illustrates this style:

> The moaning of wind in autumn rain,
> Swift water trickling over stones.
> Leaping waves strike one another –
> A white egret startles up, comes down again.[25]
>
> 'Rapids by the Luan Trees'

Li Bo (701–62), often described as China's best-loved poet, was a close contemporary of Wang Wei. He was a precocious poet, always at pains to cultivate his poetic identity – he was 'an immortal, different from ordinary men and privileged to act differently'.[26] His social background is unclear – he came from Sichuan and his family may have been Turkish. It is a testimony to the force of his personality that he was able to impress the emperor and obtain a post in the Hanlin Academy and so become a court poet. There he cultivated his reputation for eccentricity and for wild drinking. Many of his poems refer to this habit. He wrote:

> Once I am drunk
>   losing Heaven and Earth,
> Unsteadily
>   I go to my lonely pillow.
> Not to know
>   that my self exists –
> Of all my joys
>   This is the highest.[27]

But after a few years he fell out of favour at court and spent much of the rest of his life in the Yangzi valley. It was fitting that his most famous poem, and perhaps the best-known poem in the Chinese language, should be written on the subject of absence from home:

> Before my bed
>   there is bright moonlight
> So that it seems
>   like frost on the ground:
>
> Lifting my head
>   I watch the bright moon,
> Lowering my head
>   I dream that I'm home.[28]
>
> 'Quiet night thoughts'

The name of Li Bo is forever coupled with that of Du Fu (712–70). The two men are seen as representing the opposed but complementary forces of nature, the yin and the yang:

> Li Bo is the Daoist in this pair of poets, and his constantly recurring symbol is the reflected light of the Moon at night; whilst Du Fu is the Confucian who from early childhood made the Phoenix his symbol, the Fire Bird symbolizing the Yang.[29]

This contrast may be traced to their backgrounds and life experience. Du Fu was born near Xi'an of a family in modest circumstances. He studied hard and took the examinations – and failed, for reasons which have never been fully explained. He met Li Bo and was much influenced by him. He too obtained a post at court, and might have succeeded in gaining official preferment, but for An Lushan's rebellion. The hardship this brought to him and his family darkened the rest of his life. He spent his last eleven years in the north-west, and it was there that his most powerful poetry was written.

It is difficult to do justice to the range and depth of Du Fu's poetry in a few lines. Some sense of it might be conveyed by an extract from a poem called 'Song of Pengya', which in graphic terms described the journey he and his family had made at the time of the rebellion:

> The whole family had been traveling long on foot –
> Most whom we met seemed to have no shame.
> Here and there birds of the valley sang,
> We saw no travelers going the other way.
> My baby girl gnawed at me in her hunger,
> And I feared wild beasts would hear her cries:
> I held her to my chest, covered her mouth,
> But she twisted and turned crying louder in rage.
> My little son did his best to take care of things,
> With purpose went off and got sour plums to eat.
> It had thundered and rained half the past week,
> We clung together, pulling through mud and mire,
> And having made no provision against the rain,
> The paths were slippery, our clothes were cold.[30]

There has been a tendency to regard the Tang period as dominated by these two poets and to see the antithesis between their characters and poetry as defining the two extremes of the poetical achievement of the age. In fact neither poet can be stereotyped so easily, nor can they be regarded as representative of their time. This point can be illustrated by reference to two other poets, both born more than two generations later.

The first of these, Bo Juyi (772–846), has already been encountered, for it was he who wrote the celebrated poem 'Song of Unending Sorrow' which commemorated the death of Yang Guifei, the mistress of the Xuanzong emperor. Bo

Juyi had a long and relatively successful career as an official. In 825 he was appointed governor of Suzhou, a post which he found to be no sinecure:

> At break of day I confront a pile of papers,
> Dusk has come before I get away.
> The beauty of the morning, the beauty of the afternoon
> Pass while I sit clamped to an office desk.[31]

Nevertheless Bo Juyi found time to be a prolific poet and his poems, written in a simple style and treating of popular sentiments, earned him great contemporary fame. He once wrote to his great friend Yuan Zhen 'from Chang'an to Jiangxi I found my poems publicly written everywhere: in village schools, Buddhist temples, inns, and ships; they were often chanted by scholars, monks, widows, and young girls.'[32] His appeal is illustrated by a short poem which refers to the trade in tropical birds and to the fate of outspoken intellectuals:

> Sent as a present from Annam –
> A red cockatoo.
> Coloured like the peach-tree blossom,
> Speaking with the speech of men.
> And they did to it what is always done
> To the learned and the eloquent.
> They took a cage with stout bars
> And shut it up inside.[33]
>
> 'The Red Cockatoo'

The range of Tang poetry, and the danger of generalising about it, is illustrated by reference to one more poet, Li He (790–816). An old aphorism declared that Du Fu's genius was that of a Confucian sage, Li Bo's that of a Daoist immortal, that Bo Juyi's was human and Li He's ghostly or demonic. Although famous in the ninth century, his taste for morbidity and violence led to him being long neglected. He is now recognised as one of the great poets of the period, an innovator who has been compared with Baudelaire. Some idea of his tone is conveyed by a few lines from 'Don't Go out of the Door':

> Heaven is inscrutable,
> Earth keeps its secrets.
> The nine-headed monster eats our souls,
> Frosts and snows snap our bones.
> Dogs are set on us, snarl and sniff around us,
> And lick their paws, partial to the orchid-girdled,
> Till the end of all afflictions, when God sends us his chariot,
> And the sword starred with jewels and the yoke of yellow gold.[34]

Prose and Drama

In the Tang period the distinction between the poet and the writer of prose was not an absolute one, a point illustrated by reference to Han Yu, whose poems appear in the poetry anthologies, but who achieved his enduring influence through his prose. This rejected the existing style known as 'parallel prose' in favour of a simpler, but more archaic form called the 'ancient prose', which took as its model the style of the classics.

As well as his famous memorial on the bone of Buddha, Han Yu wrote dynamic and eloquent essays. When he was exiled to Chaozhou in 819, he found that his district was plagued by crocodiles. This led him to compose his imaginary 'Proclamation to the Crocodile'. In it he described how he had caused an officer to throw a sheep and a pig into the waters where the crocodile lived. He declared that crocodiles had been expelled by the Han, but had returned in the age of division. Their presence was no longer tolerable under the Tang. He, the governor, had been instructed to look after the people of his area, 'but you, crocodile, goggle-eyed, are not content with the deep waters of the creek, but seize your advantage to devour the people and their stock'. He therefore gave the animal an ultimatum – he must either remove to the great sea or be killed with poisoned arrows. Thus, in a short essay, Han Yu demonstrated the effectiveness of his style which combined simplicity with dry humour.

Liu Zongyuan (773–819), a friend and close contemporary of Han Yu is remembered for his satirical fables and biographical sketches. A sketch entitled 'Camel Guo the Gardener' told of a hunchback nicknamed 'Camel', who had an extraordinary ability to make plants grow. When questioned about this he had replied in terms which revealed his Daoist sympathies:

I cannot make a tree live for ever or flourish. What I can do is comply with the nature of the tree so that it takes the way of its kind . . . all I do is to avoid harming its growth – I have no power to make it grow.

His questioner then asked whether his philosophy also applied to government. Camel Guo replied cautiously that there might be some resemblance between the art of government and the art of growing trees. 'Wonderful', replied his questioner, 'The art I sought was of cultivating trees; the art I found was of cultivating men. Let this be passed on to all in office!'.[35]

Liu Zongyuan had reason to be critical of how those in office cultivated men. In 805 he was exiled for ten years to southern Hunan, and then from 815 until his early death he was posted as governor to Liuzhou in Guangxi. In his prose he described vividly the scenery of those remote areas, such as the limestone karst features of Liuzhou. Of the curiously-named Mountain of the Transcendents Go-game he wrote:

This mountain can be ascended from the west. There is a cavern at its top, and this cavern has screens, chambers, and eaves. Under these eaves there are figures formed from flowing stone, like lungs and livers, and like eggplants – sometimes heaped up below – and like men, like birds, like utensils and other objects, in great abundance.[36]

It was in the Tang period that a colloquial literature developed which was the beginnings of fiction and drama. This literary activity was centred on Chang'an and it took as its subject matter the activities of city-dwellers, dealing with them in realistic human terms. One pioneer in this genre was Bo Xingjian, the brother of Bo Juyi. Having passed the imperial examinations, he served in the capital as an officer in charge of foreign tributes. He wrote 'The Story of Miss Li', the tale of a rich young man who fell hopelessly in love with a young courtesan. Her mother, with her daughter's collusion, ruthlessly exploited the situation and relieved the young man of his fortune. Left penniless, he was forced to earn a living by singing dirges for an undertaker and then his father horsewhipped him for disgracing the family name. At that point Miss Li had a change of heart and encouraged the young man to return to his studies. He eventually achieved the highest success and was reconciled to his father, bringing the tale to a happy conclusion.

The origins of Chinese drama can be traced back to the Han dynasty, but it was only in the Tang period that dances, songs, sketches and acrobatics were combined into drama. An early dramatic form, widely performed from the ninth century, is known as the 'adjutant play'. It had as its recurrent theme the humiliation of an official for accepting bribes. The performance involved both actors and actresses, and included dialogue, singing, costume and make-up.[37]

Architecture, Sculpture and Painting

Although Chang'an was the greatest city of its age, it did not leave an architectural legacy comparable with that of Rome. Chang'an's buildings were of ephemeral construction, usually built of wood and hence vulnerable to fire. Other reasons explain why more durable buildings were not erected:

Chinese anthropocentrism did not encourage building for the ages or for eternity, and Buddhism – with its illusionist strain – perhaps reinforced this disposition. One should also note that no buildings in Chang'an were built from what we call 'civic pride'.[38]

Nevertheless a few remains of Tang architecture have survived; for example, the foundations of Taizong's palace in Chang'an have been excavated. Little is left of Tang Buddhist temples, but some idea of their scale and character may be obtained from the Great Buddha Hall of the Todaiji at Nara in Japan, built in the Tang style and in the Tang period, which today is the largest wooden building in the world. Some masonry pagodas have survived, for example the much-altered Great Wild Goose Pagoda at Chang'an, which was climbed by the Japanese monk Ennin in 841. The pagoda derived from the Indian stupa, a Buddhist reliquary tower. In China most pagodas were constructed in wood, to a design resembling the Han timber towers known as *lou*. During the Tang period, the practice of building roofs with uplifted corners, derived from south-east Asia, gradually spread to north China. Applied to pagodas it produced elegant buildings, such as the pagoda at the Yakushiji at Nara which dates from the eighth century, and which was based on a Chinese model.

Both architecture and sculpture were heavily influenced by Buddhism and in both art forms ideas derived from India were to become sinicised. Mention has already been made of the sixth-century cave temples at Longmen, near Luoyang, and of the way in which the carvings there provide examples of how the Chinese tradition of linear pictorial expressions re-asserted itself. Under the Tang a more sophisticated cultural fusion was achieved. An example of this can be found in the sculptured figures of cave-shrines at Tianlongshan in southern Shanxi, carved in the reign of the Empress Wu. Of them it was said:

In these figures the Indian feeling for solid, swelling form and the Chinese genius for expression in terms of linear rhythm are at last successfully fused and reconciled, to produce a style which was to become the basis of all later Buddhist sculpture in China.[39]

Painters of the Tang period are usually divided into figure painters and landscape painters. Of the former the first important figure is Yan Liben (c. 600–73), who was not only a painter but also a prominent official. The best surviving example of his work is a famous scroll depicting thirteen emperors, now in the Boston Museum of Fine Arts. Yan Liben's name is also associated with a series of murals on the walls of the tomb of Princess Yongtai, which was discovered in 1960 near Chang'an. The princess, the daughter of the Zhongzong emperor, was put to death by her grandmother, the Empress Wu. The tomb was built by her grieving father after the empress's death. The paintings, which depict serving girls, are now in poor condition, but of them it has been said that they 'bring us probably as close as we shall ever get to Tang courtly wall-painting as it approached its climax in the eighth century'.[40]

Wu Daozi (c. 700–60), who has been described as the Michelangelo of Tang China, is credited with having had the 'power to transform the essentially sculptured ideals of India into the linear, painterly, terms of the Chinese tradition'.[41] He painted with such whirlwind energy that crowds gathered to watch him as he worked. It was said of him:

Wu Daozi's figures remind one of sculpture. One can see them sideways and all round. His line-work consists of minute curves like rolled copper wire; however thickly his red or white paint is laid on, the structure of the forms and modelling of the flesh are never obscured.[42]

No original work by Wu Daozi has survived. However a stone engraving, *The Spirit of Hengyue*, the sacred mountain of the north, to be seen at a Daoist temple at Quyang in Hebei, may be taken as a faithful representation of a design by him. It shows a figure with long billowing hair and scarves and brandishing a spear, which is all energy and movement.[43]

Some court painters specialised in painting horses. The most famous of these in the Tang period was Han Gan (c. 715–81), who was summoned by the Xuanzong emperor to paint the imperial horse. Much of this painting, *Shining White of the Night*, which is in the Metropolitan Museum of Art, New York, is the work of a later restorer, who omitted to restore the tail. However, enough remains of the painting to enable the viewer to appreciate the energetic movement and to allow a comparison with Tang pottery figurines.

The Ming artist and art critic Dong Qichang (1555–1636), referring to landscape painting, made a celebrated division between landscape painters of the 'Northern' and 'Southern' Schools. Artists ascribed to the former school were largely professionals and court painters, and those to the latter school were amateurs and scholars. He traced this division back to the Tang period and identified as the founder of the second school the poet Wang Wei, who was said to have been the first painter to have painted landscapes in monochrome ink. No original painting of his has survived, but copies of a handscroll entitled *Clearing after a Snowfall along the River* may provide some idea of his technique. Of the 'Northern' school, Li Sixun (651–716) and his son Li Zhaodao (died about 735) are two of the best-known names. Their paintings were characterised by the use of malachite green and azurite blue. A famous example of this palette, *Minghuang's journey to Shu* attributed to Li Zhaodao, is said to depict the flight of the emperor from An Lushan's rebels in 756.

A notable development in the art of this period can be found in the work of painters such as Zhang Zao and Wang Mo, whose work anticipated that of twentieth-century action painters. The former was said to have painted with worn, blunt brushes, or to have used his fingers, and has therefore been described as the inventor of 'finger-painting'. Wang Mo spattered and splashed his ink onto silk. Such a technique accorded with Chan Buddhist ideas that enlightenment was an irrational experience arrived at through spontaneity and not by careful preparation. Another remarkable style was developed by the monk-painter Guanxiu (832–912), who painted a series of grotesque portraits of Buddhist saints.

Decorative Arts and Ceramics

Whereas Tang painting remained largely committed to Chinese subject matter and style, the decorative arts and ceramics showed clearly the strength of the links between China and the outside world. Chinese silk filled the bazaars of the Middle East, while at the same time Iranian craftsmen brought new weaving techniques to Chang'an. Remarkable examples of these fabrics have been preserved in the caves at Dunhuang on the Silk Road. A wide variety of gold and silver work was produced which likewise showed Middle-eastern influences. A major hoard discovered at Hejiacun near Xi'an included many foreign shapes. One gold bowl had its sides pressed out as lotus leaves; the traced ornament on it showed deer and birds in the Chinese tradition, but the beaded rim on the foot replicated a design used on Iranian silverware.[44]

During the Tang period a wide variety of ceramics was produced and polychrome glazes were developed. From the seventh century, in Hebei province, a high-quality white ware was made out of kaolinitic clay. At about the same time a development in the use of lead glazes led to the production of *sancai*, three-coloured pottery and figurines. Other advances included the production of ceramics decorated with underglaze painting and the perfection of the greenwares known in the West as celadon. The finest examples of this type of ceramics, called Yue ware, was manufactured in Zhejiang. The most coveted examples of it were those vessels which displayed the 'secret colour', that is a particular shade achieved in the glaze.[45]

An important category of Tang pottery was that of figurines and models made to be placed in tombs. These represented the wealth and status of the deceased and were intended to provide for his or her needs in the next world. In the first half of the eighth century enormous quantities of these were produced for tombs around Chang'an and Luoyang. The figurines were made in moulds and glazed with coloured glazes. A general who died at Luoyang in 728 was buried with figurines representing two earth spirits, two Buddhist guardian figures and two civil officials. At the entrance to his tomb were two horses, two camels and three grooms.[46] Other figurines represented foreigners, caricaturing their clothes, large noses and beards.

Porcelain may be defined as a type of ceramic where the clay has become completely fused, which transmits light, and which emits a ringing tone when struck. Several different types of ceramic produced during the Tang period may be described as porcelain. One of the earliest examples was Xing ware, developed in kilns in Hebei from the late sixth century. Another high-quality early porcelain came from Dingzhou likewise in Hebei, the forerunner of the famous Ding ware of the Song dynasty.

9
The Song Dynasty

The political developments of the three hundred years after the fall of the Tang are complex, but the main events may be summarised as follows. The period from the fall of the Tang in 907 to the establishment of the Song in 960 is known as the period of the Five Dynasties and Ten Kingdoms. During that time part of northern China was ruled by the Qidan Liao dynasty. The rest of the country was divided into two, the northern part being ruled by a succession of five dynasties and the southern part being fragmented into ten regional states. In 960 a general from the fifth of the northern dynasties seized power and established the Song empire (also known as the Northern Song), which lasted until 1127. Initially Song rule extended over much of China Proper, with the exception of the territory of the Liao empire in the north and the Nanzhao kingdom in the south-west. From about 1038 the area of modern Gansu came under the control of the Tangut Xi Xia kingdom. By the early twelfth century the Liao empire was in decline and in 1122 it was overwhelmed by the Jurchen who established the Jin dynasty. The Jin expansion continued into the rest of northern China, finally stabilising north of the Huai river. The south of China remained under the control of the Song dynasty, now usually known as the Southern Song, with dates 1127 to 1279. Meanwhile, Qidan survivors of the Jurchen invasion had fled west to central Asia, and as the 'Black Qidan' had established the Western Liao dynasty, which lasted until 1211.

The Significance of the Song Period

The Tang period, at least until the rebellion of An Lushan, has commonly been regarded as a high point in the history of China. The Song period, however, has been the subject of conflicting verdicts. The traditional view of the period was that the arts of civilisation progressed, but the dynasty suffered from severe political and military weaknesses, for which China was to pay dearly, first with the loss of north China to the Jin and then, in the thirteenth century, with the loss of the entire country to the Mongols.

Some recent analyses have modified or rejected that view. The achievements of the period have been stressed and the age has been compared with the European Renaissance, emphasising the breadth of the changes taking place and their enduring quality. It has been claimed that it was under the Song that the features of Chinese society which were to last until modern times were established. An extensive debate has arisen over the reforms initiated by Wang Anshi in the middle of the eleventh century. This in turn has encouraged research into other aspects of Song society: the evolution of the civil service and the operation of the examination system; social changes and in particular the rise of the gentry; and the economic advances made in this period. At the same time the appreciation of the Song intellectual and cultural achievement has continued.

The Five Dynasties and Ten Kingdoms

Many historians have noted that whereas after the fall of the Later Han dynasty China experienced nearly four centuries of division, after the fall of the Tang the division only lasted for half a century. This difference has been attributed to the strengthening of the traditions and techniques of centralised rule under the Tang. China would never again be divided into competing political units for even so long as half a century.[1]

In political terms the disintegration of China did not imply a sharp break with the past. The northern dynasties all aspired to reunite China and by 959 the Later Zhou had already brought much of north China back under a single ruler. Moreover the changes of dynasty amounted only to changes in the ruling family. The ruling élite remained unaltered and the civil service continued the routine tasks of government without serious disruption. In the south, in several of the Ten Kingdoms, the same continuity was evident, with the examination system still operating.[2]

Nevertheless the traditional assumption that the Song dynasty merely re-established the Tang system with a few modifications has been firmly rejected. According to an important study by Wang Gungwu key changes took place during the Five Dynasties period which amounted to the creation of a new structure of power. A new central government was formed which incorporated the basic features of the system of military governors, which had emerged in the latter part of the Tang period. The emperors of the Five Dynasties were themselves former military governors. They modelled their courts on their provincial governments, using their retainers as palace commissioners. The governor's private army was transformed into the Emperor's Army and a palace corps created to counter any threat from that army. It was on this platform that the early Northern Song emperors were able to assert control over the central institutions of the state preparatory to conquering the independent states of the south.[3]

The period of division was also one of economic growth and technical innovation, particularly in the south. Perhaps even as a consequence of the relaxation of central control, the small states of the south made rapid progress in terms of commerce. There was an expansion of the trade in tea and the production of ceramics. The shortage of copper, the standard metallic currency, led to the use of other metals including lead and iron and the introduction of 'flying money', the forerunner of a paper currency.

The Establishment of the Song Dynasty

Zhao Kuangyin, a military leader under the Later Zhou dynasty, seized power through a coup in 960. He is known as Taizu, the founder of the Song dynasty. In a restrained and methodical manner, he proceeded to consolidate and extend his control. After half a century of warlordism, his first task was prevent any further military coups. He achieved this by persuading his commanders to retire or to accept minor posts, by creating a professional army loyal to the dynasty and by asserting central government authority over the regional commanders. For the rest of his reign he concentrated on winning over the independent states of the south, with such success that when he died in 976 China Proper, apart from Zhejiang, Shanxi, Nanzhao and the area ruled by the Qidan, had come under Song control. Ever cautious, Taizu did not attempt to challenge the Qidan and even less was he interested in recovering the Tang empire in central Asia. He was succeeded by his brother, the Taizong emperor, who obtained the submission of the regimes in Zhejiang and Shanxi, and received tribute from the Xi Xia kingdom. He then attempted to expel the Qidan, but after two unsuccessful campaigns was forced to make peace and to promise to hand over large quantities of silk and silver in annual payments. So ended the expansive stage of the Song empire, which henceforth relied on a defensive strategy in its dealings with the outside world. Unlike the Tang, the Song empire could never claim to be an universal empire, for even in its dealings with the Qidan, relations were conducted on a basis of equality.

In the meantime the first two Song rulers had taken important steps to strengthen the administration. As rulers of a new dynasty they had the opportunity to innovate and their actions have been seen as having led to an unprecedented accumulation of power in the emperor's own hands. For their capital they chose Kaifeng on the Grand Canal and there they established the organs of government. In many respects these continued the practices of the Tang, but there were some significant changes. As mentioned previously Taizu had managed to assert control over the military, and this was institutionalised by putting military affairs into the hands of the privy council. The chief administrative body was the secretariat-chancellery, which combined two bodies which had been separate under the Tang. Both privy council and secretariat-chancellery were under the personal control of the emperor and his autocratic position was further strengthened by the development of the Censorate, the officers of which kept him informed of complaints. There was considerable overlap between the powers and responsibilities of the various administrative bodies. This arose in part from the emperor's reluctance to carry out too sweeping a rationalisation, but it also served as another means of increasing his personal power.

Supporting these developments were important changes in the recruitment to the bureaucracy and the operation of the examination system. These are connected with what have been seen as key transformations occurring in the late Tang and early Song periods: the subordination of the military to the civil authority and the replacement of aristocratic power with something akin to a meritocracy. Both these aspects of the Song state have been subject to considerable study and more should be said about them.

The development of the bureaucracy was of course based on earlier achievements. Under the Han dynasty a civil service had existed, which had been selected through the use of examinations and which had developed fixed procedures. Under the Tang these processes had been much developed and the system of selection through examinations greatly expanded. Officials were ranked in grades which determined their salaries, and their efficiency in office was subject to regular assessment. Nevertheless it was only under the Song dynasty that these developments reached maturity. Methods of recruitment, appointment and control of civil servants were refined and scholar-officials (*dushu ren*, literally 'persons who read books'), who owed their position entirely to the operation of this system rather than to any hereditary claim to status, administered the country. Through this development 'Confucian China evolved much that has entered the common heritage of personnel administration in the modern state'.[4]

The most important method of recruitment to the civil service lay through the examination system. Under the Song, examinations were held at two levels, the prefectural examination and the metropolitan examination, the latter being followed by a palace examination under the personal supervision of the emperor. At the beginning of the Song period a variety of degrees was awarded to successful candidates, but later the only degree awarded at the scheduled examinations was that of jinshi, the doctorate of letters. A number of other significant innovations were made in the early Song period. Under Taizong there was a sharp increase in the number of degrees awarded and this in turn led to an increase in the number of candidates. To cope with this expansion the examination arrangements were overhauled: rules relating to the eligibility of candidates were introduced, certain occupations – for example having been previously a Buddhist or Daoist priest, or having been an artisan, merchant or clerk – were defined as a bar to candidature; residency requirements were enforced to ensure that candidates only took the examinations in their home prefectures; candidates were required to provide evidence of satisfactory character; quotas were established for the number of successful candidates at the prefectural level; and in the examinations measures were taken to ensure the anonymity of candidates' scripts.[5]

Accompanying the expansion of the examination system there was a major growth in the educational provision. Although officially-supported government schools had existed under the Tang, the decline of the dynasty had led to education at local level being much neglected. Early in the eleventh century local officials began to establish new schools. Taking advantage of the spread of printing, these schools were provided with a set of the classics and endowed with a Confucian temple and a piece of land. The Imperial University at Kaifeng continued and expanded the opportunities for higher education which had been available under the Tang. The requirement that it should only provide education for the sons of officials was relaxed. Students of the university received free board and lodging and were exempted from having to take the preliminary prefectural examinations.[6]

The examination system, and the education system which underpinned it, served to provide candidates for the civil service. However, it was not the only source of supply of candidates, for in the Song period it was balanced by the yin privilege, or protection system. This allowed certain high officials to nominate members of their family for entry into the civil service. Candidates who availed themselves of this opportunity had to take a placement examination, but this was nevertheless a relatively easy way of entering the service. The protection system supplied over half the successful candidates.

These channels of recruitment produced far more men qualified for office than there were posts available. To deal with this situation, and to ensure control over the bureaucracy, various strategies were adopted. The most important of these was the commission system under which officials were assigned to particular posts for a set period, usually three or four years. As reassignment to the same post was not permitted, this system ensured that an official could not build up a local following. A further check was the 'law of avoidance', which prohibited an official from service in his home prefecture. Yet another control was exercised through sponsorship, a term used to denote the privilege granted to senior officials of sponsoring persons known to them to particular appointments. As these officials were held responsible for the performance of their nominee in office, this has been regarded as an effective way of raising the standards of public service.[7]

The most disputed issue in relation to the examination system and the operation of the bureaucracy is how far it offered a career open to talent. The case for the existence of a meritocracy is perhaps best supported by reference to the early Song period. According to John W. Chaffee, 'By expanding degree numbers, adding a formal prefectural examination, introducing such procedures as covered names and copied examinations, and, under Renzong, promoting education, the early emperors were really trying to create a meritocratic state.'[8]

To what extent did they succeed? Before answering that question one must first note the conflict between the Confucian stress on human virtue and the state's practical need to recruit men of ability. Under the Song there was an attempt to recruit a civil service which had both these qualities. Genuine attempts were made to ensure the impartiality of the examinations, which certainly tested ability, albeit within a restricted range of skills. The importance of virtue was recognised in the sponsorship system and it was not entirely vitiated by the protection system. The latter arrangement, which allowed officials to enable their sons to follow them into the bureaucracy, thus preserving a hereditary practice, also provided officials with a powerful incentive to commit themselves unreservedly to the emperor's service.

There is some evidence to show that candidates from poor backgrounds did have a chance of succeeding in the examination system and of obtaining official appointment. One study of the family background of prominent officials shows that between 998 and 1126 47.3 per cent of these officials came from families categorised as poor. The very existence of the system promoted the idea of equal opportunity, but it has been pointed out that 'To have about 7,905 (47.3 per cent of a bureaucracy of about 15,000 civil bureaucrats) prominent officials coming from a commoner background in a nation of about one hundred million people is not a specially remarkable achievement'.[9]

Reform in Song China

Far from being complacent about the state of the empire, a number of Song scholars and officials were acutely aware that the previous dynasty had collapsed and that their own dynasty had failed to incorporate the whole of China under its rule. Moreover, in their eyes, the country seemed plagued by certain chronic weaknesses: the concentration of landholding in the hands of people who avoided taxation; the suspect quality of the bureaucracy; the ineffectiveness and expense of the military forces. These concerns led them to make proposals on how the empire might be preserved. For example, in 1039 the writer and teacher Li Gou produced a work entitled 'Thirty plans for enriching the country, strengthening military power, and satisfying the needs of the people'.[10] In 1043–4 Fan Zhongyan, a celebrated scholar and statesman, proposed a ten-point programme of reform which aimed at eliminating entrenched bureaucrats, official favouritism and nepotism, and which proposed examination reform, the establishment of a national school system, land reclamation and the creation of a local militia. Fan was ousted before most of this programme could be attempted, but his proposal for a national school system was followed up and his suggestion for preserving the anonymity of candidates' scripts in examinations was acted upon.

For a reform programme to succeed, it needed an organised body to promote it. However the tradition of Confucian government did not allow officials to form factions or parties. This dilemma led Ouyang Xiu (1007–72), a leading official and one of China's best-known literary figures, to present a famous memorial On Factions in which he wrote:

> Your servant is aware that from ancient times there have been discussions of the worth of parties. It is only to be hoped that a ruler will distinguish between those of gentlemen and those of inferior men. In general, gentlemen join with other gentlemen in parties because of common principles, while inferior men join with other inferior men for reasons of common profit.

However Ouyang Xiu's defence of factions, which may have owed more to a desire to encourage reform than to a belief in the right to dissent, did not gain acceptance, either in his day or subsequently. Under a system of government in which the emperor had absolute power, political opposition remained indistinguishable from disloyalty.[11]

The reform proposals which have attracted by far the most attention, and which have excited by far the most controversy, were those put forward by Wang Anshi during the reign of the Shenzong emperor, who reigned from 1068 to 1085. Wang Anshi (1021–86), who came from the same part of Jiangxi as did Li Gou, and who was a former protégé of Fan Zhongyan, had occupied several official positions and had experience of practical affairs. In 1058, in a document known as the Ten Thousand Word Memorial, he first praised the diligence, humanity and judgment of the emperor. He continued:

We should expect, therefore, that the needs of every household and man would be filled and that the empire would enjoy a state of perfect order. And yet this result has not been attained. Within the empire the security of the state is a cause for some anxiety, and on our borders there is the constant threat of the barbarians. Day by day the resources of the nation become more depleted and exhausted, while the moral tone and habits of life among the people daily deteriorate.[12]

For Wang Anshi, the way to remedy this situation was a truism of Confucian thought: it was to secure capable men, to assess what should be done and to change the laws to bring them back in line with the ideas of the ancient kings. In a manner typical of radical reformers, he cited Mencius as his authority, yet he broke with precedent by suggesting that the emperor should adopt a proactive role and that officials should have special qualifications rather than be generalists.

In 1068 Wang Anshi was summoned to take over the post of chief minister, which he occupied until 1076 when he was ousted by the conservatives, and which he re-occupied from 1078 until 1085. It was in the early years of his first period of office that he promoted his famous reform programme known as the New Laws or New Policies. These reforms can be summarised under three headings: taxation and the economy, security and military affairs, and the administration.

On taxation Wang's views sounded remarkably modern:

The deficit of the government nowadays is not due to excessive expenditures alone, but also to the lack of ways to increase incomes. Those who wish to enrich their families merely take from the state; those who wish to enrich the state merely take from the country; and those who wish to enrich the country merely take from natural resources.[13]

Wang's solution was to rationalise taxation, and to try to help the people become more productive. He sought to reduce the concentration of land in the hands of landlords by offering state farming loans to enable farmers to avoid falling into debt. He introduced other innovative measures to improve the state finances, including a tribute and distribution scheme, under which a procurement office was established at Yangzhou. This office replaced the system of collecting tribute in kind, instead buying such goods as the court required in the cheapest market. Another measure, the hired services system, replaced labour services, which had often been evaded by wealthy families, with a graduated tax.

With reference to security and military affairs, Wang's aim was to provide for the state's defence while at the same time reducing the cost to the state of an army of over a million men. His name is associated with the introduction, or rather the revival and improvement, of the system of collective security known as the *baojia*. Able-bodied men from groups of ten households (the *bao*) were to enforce law and order in the neighbourhood and also were eligible to be trained as a militia. At the same time a horse-breeding scheme was set up to enable militia families in the frontier regions to be provided with a horse and fodder.

In his memorial Wang Anshi had stressed the importance of securing capable men for the service of the state. A key objective was to raise the moral status of candidates, and several of his reforms were intended to achieve this. He reorganised the Imperial University, introducing the Three-Hall system, which required students to go through classes before gaining exemptions in the examinations. The apparent purpose of this was to encourage the promotion of candidates of good character rather than those who merely showed cleverness in the examinations. He introduced reforms in the examinations themselves, replacing traditional tests of memory and of formal composition with an essay on the 'general meaning' of the Confucian classics, and with exercises connected to the practical tasks of government. In support of this, he himself wrote commentaries on the classics. In addition he passed regulations placing government clerks on fixed salaries and under strict supervision.

Wang's New Policies were immediately criticised and his reputation ever since has been the subject of controversy. Before his reform programme had even been implemented a member of the censorate attempted to impeach Wang on counts of being overbearing and exceeding his authority. The famous poet and painter Su Dongpo, who at first had been a supporter of reform, later criticised the fiscal reforms and in particular the introduction of state crop loans. He was particularly alarmed by the commission set up by Wang:

> Six or seven young men are made to discuss fiscal policies day and night within the bureau, while more than forty aides are sent out to explore the situation. The vast scale of their initial operations has made people frightened and suspicious; the strangeness of the new laws adopted has made officials fearful and puzzled.[14]

Even more damaging was the opposition from the distinguished scholar and statesman Sima Guang. In 1070 he left office because of his disagreement with the New Policies and later wrote memorials calling for their abolition. He was particularly incensed by the hired services system, the *baojia* arrangement, and the establishment of general commanderies which excluded civilian control over army administration. But the emphasis of his criticism, which has echoed down the centuries, was on Wang's character:

> He was self-satisfied and self-opinionated, considering himself without equal among the men of the past and present. He did not know how to select what was best in the laws and institutions of the imperial ancestors and to bring together the happiest proposals put forth throughout the empire. . . . All he wanted was to satisfy his own ambitions, without regard to the best interests of the nation.[15]

Sima Guang was instrumental in bringing about the repeal of many of the New Policies, and the apparent rejection of the proactive style of government which they implied. In fact a number of the proposals – for example the *baojia*, the militia system and the changes in the examinations – were later to be revived and implemented. Wang's reputation was partly restored in the following century by the famous philosopher Zhu Xi. He argued that the need for reform had been widely accepted and that it was only when the reforms provoked criticism that Wang Anshi had become obdurate, rejecting advice and forcing his policies through. Nevertheless it was Sima Guang's condemnation of Wang's character and motives which set the tone for Confucian scholars for generations to come.

In modern times the debate over Wang Anshi has centred on the motivation for and practicality of his reforms. The re-evaluation began in the nineteenth century and was developed early this century by John C. Ferguson who described Wang as a utilitarian, but one who had the interests of the people at heart.[16] Wang's relevance to modern times was picked up by the famous scholar Liang Qichao, who emphasised Wang's far-sightedness and the resemblance of his New Policies to modern ideals.[17] The practicality of his reforms was investigated in the 1930s by H.R. Williamson. He argued that the need for reform was pressing and that the measures conceived by Wang Anshi were intended to relieve the poorer classes and to share the tax burden more equitably. The criticism which greeted the reforms was not because they were inappropriate, but because they attacked the interests of the better off. This line was pursued in Marxist interpretations of Wang, who was described as a man of the bureaucrat-landlord class, whereas his opponents, such as Sima Guang, came from the powerful gentry and big landlord class. His reforms were supported by the dynasty because they offered a solution to two problems: the foreign threat and the danger of a peasant uprising. The remedy he proposed was to implement policies which would contain peasant discontent by winning the support of the middle and small landlord class. His reforms were seen by the powerful gentry and big landlords as an attack on their interests and were consequently frustrated by them.[18]

More recent interpretations have discussed other issues. For the Japanese scholar Ichisada Miyazaki, Wang Anshi's reforms fell into two categories. Some, for example the crop loans, were first-aid measures dealing with social and economic changes; others, especially the *baojia* and the hired-services system, sought to make fundamental social changes. For Miyazaki these reforms related to the major social transition occurring at this time, that is the evolution from an aristocratic to an autocratic society. The reforms were progressive, and may have served to prolong the existence of the Northern Song until 1126 rather than to have advanced its fall.[19] For James T.C. Liu, Wang Anshi was 'a bureaucratic idealist who upheld the ideal of a professionally well-trained and administratively well-controlled bureaucracy as the principal instrument for the realization of a Confucian moral society'. His reforms were not intended to further the interests of a social class, but to improve the performance of the bureaucratic state; they failed because he did not have the support of the bureaucrats themselves and because the system of bureaucratic government was being undermined by the growth of absolutism.[20] Recently Ray Huang has returned to the question of the practicability of the reforms and has concluded that they were premature, in that the attempt to institutionalise monetary management of state affairs was bound to run into insuperable difficulties, because the nation's economic organisation had not yet reached that level of integration which would make such management possible.[21]

The Decline of the Northern Song and the Rise of the Jin Dynasty

The reform period extended until the death of the Shenzong emperor in 1086, whereupon a reaction ensued, initially led by Sima Guang. In 1093 the Zhezong emperor came to the throne, and appointed to office Cai Jing, brother of Wang Anshi's son-in-law. He revived the New Policies and extended them to fresh areas and at the same time carried out a witch-hunt against the conservatives. This alternation between reform and conservatism weakened the dynasty. Blame for that decline has also been heaped personally on Cai Jing, who remained in power until 1125. He was said to have pursued his political opponents vindictively, to have tolerated the growth of corruption, and to have encouraged the Huizong emperor to neglect his duties in favour of artistic pursuits.

A further indication of dynastic decline was the rise of peasant rebellion, which may be attributed to various factors, including the increasing concentration of landownership, the mounting burden of tax and the effect of oppressive government measures. The best-known of the rebellions was that headed by Fang La which broke out in Fujian and Zhejiang in 1120. In these revolts the leaders were often men of some wealth who appeared to be supporting the cause of social justice. Fang La was the owner of a plantation of lacquer trees, who turned against the government because of the heaviness of the levies he was required to pay. It is for this reason that the revolts became the basis of the most famous of Chinese novels, *Shuihu zhuan*, known in the West under the titles *Water Margin* and *All Men Are Brothers*. The Fang La rebellion also had a connection with Manichaeism which had survived in this area. It caused great loss of life, said in one source to have amounted to one million dead.[22]

The most important threat to the dynasty was the rise of the Jurchen in the north. When the dynasty had been founded, the Qidan Liao empire extended to include sixteen prefectures in north China. Despite the efforts of the second Song emperor to dislodge them, the Qidan had retained their position, receiving annual tribute from China and developing a dualistic form of government.[23] As time passed the Qidan ceased to present a danger to the Song dynasty. Their population was very small and in the Chinese part of their empire they were in a minority. Moreover as time went on they became increasingly sinicised.

In turn the Liao dynasty fell under threat. The danger came from the Jurchen,[24] a semi-nomadic Tungusic people ancestral to the Manchus, who appeared in eastern Manchuria in the tenth century. Like the Qidan they came from the marginal zone, between the open steppe and the settled areas. Although their favourite pursuit was hunting and they were all skilled horsemen, they also practised agriculture, raised pigs and had small walled towns. Their social organisation was tribal, the basic organisational unit being the lineage, occupying a lineage village. Every adult male was a potential soldier and a body of Jurchen cavalry was a formidable force.[25]

In the tenth century the Jurchen had been subdued by the Qidan and subsequently they had paid tribute to both the Liao and Northern Song dynasties. Part of that tribute had been paid in horses and the development of the horse trade was to have a major role in the rise of the Jurchen. By the twelfth century the Jurchen had adopted metal weapons and had developed the use of horses in warfare. A political struggle among the Jurchen clans resulted in the supremacy of the Wanyan clan. After a period of fighting against Koryo, the dynasty ruling Korea, the Jurchen turned their attention to the Qidan. In 1112 the Liao emperor visited northern Manchuria and gave a feast for the Jurchen at which Aguda, leader of the Wanyan clan refused to perform a tribal dance. This refusal led to the breakdown of relations between Jurchen and Qidan. In 1114 Aguda proclaimed himself emperor of the Jin state and began a campaign against the Liao empire, which had already been weakened by internal dissension. Ill-advisedly the Northern Song added its support to the Qidan, yet within six years the Liao empire collapsed.

In a treaty agreed in 1120, Liao territories were divided between the Jurchen Jin dynasty and the Northern Song. However, the Song court persisted in trying to recover the lost Sixteen Prefectures and various acts of bad faith led to the Jurchen invading China in 1125. By now they had developed formidable military skills. Their mounted horsemen wore heavy armour and sometimes several horses were chained together to form a horse team. They had developed war machines for attacking walled cities and later they pioneered the use of firearms. They also made astute use of collaborators who joined them in the hope of securing a share of the booty. Against this power the Northern Song was outmatched. In 1126, after a protracted siege, the Jurchen captured the capital Kaifeng, and the Huizong emperor and his son were carried off to Manchuria, so ending the Northen Song dynasty. In the years that followed the Jurchen continued to press southwards and it seemed as if only the Yangzi river would block their further advance, for at first the Jurchen had no capability for fighting on water and they were repulsed by the Southern Song fleet. Later the Yangzi was crossed and the Jurchen penetrated as far south as Hangzhou and Ningbo, but a combination of factors – the death of the Jin emperor and the unsuitability of the terrain for the Jurchen cavalry – led to a withdrawal. In 1141 peace was agreed between the Jin and Southern Song, leaving the Jurchen as rulers of most of China north of the Yangzi and the Song as rulers of the south. In addition the Southern Song agreed to pay an annual tribute of 200,000 taels of silver and 200,000 bolts of silk.

The Jin Dynasty, 1115–1234

The Jurchen Jin dynasty ruled over much of northern China until it was destroyed by the Mongols in 1234. Its record is a striking example of the problems of non-Chinese rule. It may be compared with that of the Qidan before them and that of the Mongols and Manchus who were to follow in their footsteps. The history of the dynasty may be divided into three stages: a period of dualism from 1115 to 1142, a period of increasing sinicisation until 1215, and a final period of decline.

In the first period the dynasty sought ways of ruling a Chinese population numbering perhaps forty million. Its first stratagem was a form of dualism reminiscent of that used by the Qidan. In Jurchen territory north of the Great Wall tribal administration was retained. In the south Jurchen tribal units were stationed at strategic points, where they cultivated the land and kept a watch over the conquered peoples. There was little benevolence towards either the surviving Qidan or the indigenous population at this early stage. Many Chinese were killed when uprisings were suppressed and perhaps 100,000 Chinese were forcibly resettled in Manchuria. Nevertheless Qidan and Chinese were employed in administrative and military capacities. At the Jin southern capital, Chinese scholars were employed to write proclamations and in 1126 the Chinese bureaucratic system was adopted. Yet further south, in the regions bordering the territory of the Southern Song, the Jurchen tried to set up puppet regimes. In one such state, situated between the Yangzi and Huai rivers, Jurchen generals briefly attempted a Jurchenising movement, forbidding the Chinese to wear native dress and ordering them to cut their hair in the Jurchen style.[26]

From 1142 there was a twenty-year period of peaceful co-existence between the north and the south. During that time many Jurchen moved into China, and were given grants of land and a privileged tax position. Jurchen continued to monopolise military authority and to retain a majority of senior political positions. Nevertheless it was in this period that the Jurchen increasingly adopted Chinese institutions and customs. Hailing, the emperor who ruled from 1150 to 1161, established his central capital at what is now Beijing. He was proud of his knowledge of the Chinese classics and had ambitions to establish a legitimate Confucian dynasty extending over the whole of China. At the same time he ordered the brutal murder of Jurchen nobles who might challenge his claim to the throne which he had usurped, and he planned to conquer the south. He launched the attack in 1161, suffered a reverse, and was assassinated.

His successor Shizong, who reigned 1161–90, ostensibly rejected the sinicisation policies of his predecessor and in some respects attempted to restore the old Jurchen way of life. He made hunting an annual royal activity and encouraged all forms of military exercises. He took several steps to promote Jurchen learning and in 1188 prohibited the Jurchen from wearing Chinese dress. However this nativistic movement did not succeed, in part because it was poorly planned and inconsistent. Shizong's concern for hunting ran contrary to his encouragement to Jurchen to take up farming. The Jurchen language was already dying out when he ordered that the Chinese classics be translated into Jurchen. The policy of centralisation which he continued accelerated rather than fended off sinicisation, and the adoption of the Chinese practice relating to succession was a rejection of Jurchen tribal custom.

So it was not surprising that under his successor Zhangzong further sinicising changes took place. A legal code based on that of the Tang was adopted. In 1191 the ban on intermarriage between Jurchen and Chinese, which had been flouted by both rulers and officials, was rescinded. A final indication of the sinicisation of the dynasty was the prolonged discussion of the appropriate dynastic element, the choice placing the Jin in the line of the legitimate dynasties of China.

A number of events combined to weaken the dynasty. In 1194 the Yellow river shifted to its southern course, causing immense damage. In 1206 the Southern Song minister Han Tuozhou, in an attempt to divert attention from his difficulties at court, declared war on the Jin. The campaign was unsuccessful and Han Tuozhou paid for his rashness with his life. Nevertheless the campaign hampered the Jin efforts against the Mongol threat in Manchuria. At the very moment that the Mongols made their first attacks on China, a succession dispute further weakened the dynasty. By 1215 the Jin had lost Manchuria and much of China north of the Yellow river. There was a pause in the Mongol attacks and a further respite followed the death of Genghis khan in 1227. But in 1230 the new khan Ögödei launched a full-scale attack against the remnants of the Jin empire. Kaifeng, the capital since 1214, was captured by the Mongols after a year-long siege in which both sides used firearms, and in 1234 the dynasty was finally extinguished.[27]

Whatever one might conclude about the reasons for the fall of the Jin dynasty, that of rejection by the majority Chinese population should not be included. Both Chinese and Jurchen defended Kaifeng and it was Chinese who provided the expertise to devise a rocket or flamethrower to use against the invaders. The Jin state was destroyed by the Mongols, with the misguided assistance of the Southern Song. Nevertheless internal weaknesses played their part in this defeat. The sinicisation process had gravely weakened the military capacity of the Jurchen. Paradoxically it could be said that this sinicisation had not gone far enough, for the Jurchen remained an alien minority which had failed to employ to the full the abilities of Chinese scholar-officials to create a durable state.[28]

The Southern Song, 1127–1279

Political developments

Resistance in south China rallied around a younger son of the Huizong emperor, known by his posthumous title Gaozong. He chose to make his capital at Hangzhou, a defensible site which was also at the commercial centre of the new empire. He carried out an internal pacification which eventually brought the whole of southern China, including Sichuan, under Song control. The tactic that he adopted was that of *zhaoan*, meaning 'summoning to pacification'. Leaders of rebel bands were offered the opportunity to come over to the Song side and their soldiers were allowed to join the imperial army. If they did not take up the offer they were liable to be attacked by the pro-government forces. This tactic was employed very effectively by Yue Fei, a young soldier from a humble background, who outwitted the largest of the armed bands which operated around the Dongting lake in Hunan.

However, to achieve a permanent peace it was necessary to come to agreement with the Jurchen. The peace settlement of 1141 was a humiliating affair, for not only did it require the payment of tribute, but also the admission that the Song was a vassal state. It is also remembered for a celebrated confrontation between the advocates of patriotic resistance and those who endorsed a settlement with the invaders. The patriotic cause was represented by Yue Fei who had led several successful campaigns against the Jurchen and who in 1140 had fought his way north to near Kaifeng. He now proposed another attack on Jurchen-held territory. The proposal was rejected by the emperor's chief councillor, Qin Gui, who was already in negotiation with the Jurchen. Yue Fei was arrested on a trumped-up charge and put to death in prison. For this act Qin Gui became one of the most celebrated villains in Chinese history, while Yue Fei came to personify the patriot who puts loyalty to his country before his duty of obedience to his ruler. A poem entitled *Redness All Across the River* was engraved on his tomb. Its words were used in a song which was popular during the Second World War:

> My fierce ambition is to feed upon the flesh of the Huns,
> And, laughing, I thirst for the blood of the Barbarians.
> Oh, let everything begin afresh.
> Let all the rivers and mountains be recovered,
> Before we pay our respect once more to the Emperor.[29]

Gaozong's use of Qin Gui in the peace negotiations was indicative of a pattern of relations between ruler and bureaucracy that was to become typical under the Southern Song. The emperor did not supervise the bureaucracy personally - that was the task of his ministers, and in particular of those who served as his chief councillors. Early in his reign there were often two councillors, who served for short terms in office. From 1139, with the appointment of Qin Gui, the more common arrangement was for there to be a single chief councillor who wielded autocratic power for and on behalf of the emperor. It was Qin Gui who conducted the peace negotiations and who then began to tighten his grip on the government. He dealt with any criticism by arranging for his opponents to be denounced by the *yanguan* or 'opinion officials.[30] At the same time he built up his own power base through nepotism. Such a record suggests a selfish pursuit of power, but it must be added that in the twenty years that followed making peace with the Jurchen, the Southern Song enjoyed political stability and economic growth. Some of this at least should be credited to Qin Gui, although after his death in 1155 Gaozong was quick to blame his minister for any shortcomings that had occurred.

In 1162 Gaozong abdicated in favour of his son Xiaozong although he remained the power behind the throne until his death. In the previous year war had been renewed with the Jurchen. The campaign ended in a stalemate without any recovery of lost territory, but under the peace treaty of 1165 the obnoxious reference to the Southern Song as a vassal state was removed. Until his father's death in 1187 Xiaozong performed his duties conscientiously, but he then he fell into a deep depression and decided to abdicate. That moment marked the beginning of a decisive decline in imperial leadership, for all subsequent emperors showed signs of mental illness or of an inability to perform their duties effectively. As a consequence, in the later years of the dynasty, chief councillors played a key role in government .

The epithet of the Ningzong emperor, who reigned 1194–1224, was 'the tranquil' and of him it has been said that he 'may well represent the most unopinionated and passive emperor of the entire dynasty'.[31] Throughout his long reign two ministers controlled the emperor and the court. The first of these was Han Tuozhou, the nephew of Gaozong's empress, a man without an examination degree, who had first served as supervisor of the Palace Postern, a post which gave him control over access to the throne. Han Tuozhou had close ties with the eunuchs and poor relations with the civil service, who regarded him as unworthy of high office. From 1197 'he reigned as undisputed decision maker at court, the sole formulator of government policy, arbiter of bureaucratic disputes, and shepherd of official advancement'.[32] Such an accumulation of power was bound to lead to his over-reaching himself. He carried out a highly controversial purge of scholar-officials associated with Neo-Confucianist teaching. It may have been the hostility which this evoked which in 1206 prompted him to make his next rash move, an attack on the Jurchen. His plans went badly wrong, for one of his military commanders changed sides and a series of military defeats followed. In November 1207, after recriminations at court, Han Tuozhou was bludgeoned to death by palace guardsmen just outside the walls of the imperial palace. Nobody in authority admitted responsibility for this deed which was probably done on orders from the empress and with the tacit assent of the emperor. Han Tuozhou's end was unprecedented. Confucian propriety recognised the right to express an opinion. A discredited minister might be dismissed, or sent into exile, but not murdered, and it was for this reason that there was no admission of the court's involvement.

The second long-serving councillor was Shi Miyuan, who dominated the court for twenty-five years from 1208. The Shi family came from Ningbo, rising from comparative obscurity under the Northern Song to remarkable prominence under the Southern Song, when it provided three successive generations of chief councillors, only to return to obscurity after the dynasty's collapse. Shi Miyuan was the second of these councillors. He began his tenure of office by reversing the war policy of Han Tuozhou, making a humiliating peace with the Jurchen, the conditions of which included the sending of Han Tuozhou's head to the enemy as a war trophy. He also rescinded the ban on Neo-Confucian teaching. He then took steps to eliminate rivals and consolidate his position, steps which might be criticised as overbearing, but which fell within the expected pattern of behaviour of a chief councillor. However, in 1224, the Ningzong emperor died and Shi Miyuan set aside Zhao Hong, the elder adopted prince, in favour of the younger one who took the throne as the Lizong emperor. Subsequently Zhao Hong was implicated in a rebellion and forced to commit suicide. For this Shi Miyuan was accused of having procured an usurpation followed by a political murder. The subsequent controversy polarised the court and inhibited the development of a policy towards the alarming encroachment of the Mongols on the Jin empire. Nevertheless Shi Miyuan remained in office until his death in 1233, exercising his skill in political manipulation and his caution in handling foreign affairs.

The fourth, and by far the most notorious, of the long-serving chief councillors of the Southern Song period was Jia Sidao. He has been execrated as the archetypal 'bad last minister', the person chiefly responsible for the fall of the Song dynasty. This view, which is that of traditional historiography, has been challenged in modern times.

Jia Sidao (1213–75), who came from a family of medium-grade military officials, first gained office after his sister had entered the Lizong emperor's harem. He earned a reputation for being licentious and also for having a fascination for fighting crickets, a subject on which he wrote a treatise. However he was by no means a mere dilettante. Before appointment to high office in 1259 he had spent twenty years in various provincial and metropolitan posts, where he had gained financial and administrative experience. As chief councillor he carried out several reforms suggestive of a desire to improve standards of government: he took steps to curb the influence of the eunuchs and instituted a system of public letter-boxes where people could place complaints.[33]

However, it was not for his domestic actions that he was to be excoriated, but for his conduct of foreign affairs. In 1234 the Jin dynasty had been crushed by the Mongols, with the assistance of the Southern Song. Soon afterwards the Song found itself defending the rest of China with increasing desperation. In 1251 the Mongol hordes swept through Yunnan as far as the borders of Vietnam. In short, the threat to the dynasty was already very serious when Jia Sidao was appointed chief councillor. The accusation levelled against him was that in 1259, after he had falsely claimed to have gained victories against the Mongols, he negotiated a secret agreement with them in which, in return for a Mongol withdrawal, he promised to make the Yangzi the frontier and for the Song to pay them an annual tribute. This particular accusation has been convincingly refuted – Jia Sidao may have attempted to negotiate, but no agreement was reached. The subsequent decision of the Mongols to retire had nothing to do with the negotiation but was a consequence of the death of the Great Khan Möngke and the need to convoke an assembly to choose his successor.[34] To blame Jia Sidao for the Mongol overthrow of the empire would seem unreasonable, indeed it might be argued that his efforts contributed to the prolonged resistance to the Mongol threat, a resistance more protracted in South China than elsewhere in Asia.

Jia Sidao was also attacked for his promotion of radical agrarian and economic policies. His intention was to increase revenue by taxing large landowners effectively, a policy certain to alienate vested interests. While still a financial commissioner he had taken steps to collect overdue taxes and in 1261 he had proposed measures to prevent the rich hoarding grain. In 1263 he went further by putting forward his infamous 'public field laws'. Under these laws the maximum size of a landed property was restricted according to the rank held by the owner. Holdings of land exceeding these limits were to be bought by the state and converted into public fields, the revenue from which would be used to support the armed forces. The laws were in effect from 1263 to 1275, by which time the revenues from state lands were sufficient to supply the army. However, the cost in loss of support for the dynasty was high, large landowners and government officials were alienated and as a consequence responsive to the overtures of the Mongols. Within four days of Jia Sidao's fall the suggestion was made that the public fields be returned to their owners. By then it was too late, the Mongol armies were approaching and the Song gentry went over to the invaders in large numbers. Jia Sidao was blamed for having promoted a measure which caused this loss of confidence, although in the longer term it might have enabled the dynasty to resist the invasion.

Economic changes

In the Tang-Song era, and in particular in the Southern Song period, China experienced remarkable economic growth. Such was the pace and magnitude of change that writers such as Mark Elvin have referred to it as a 'mediaeval economic revolution'.[35] He described it as having five dimensions. The first was a revolution in farming, particularly in the development of wet-rice cultivation. This was brought about by the systematic application of organic manure; by the introduction of drought-resistant and fast-ripening strains of rice from Vietnam which enabled double-cropping; by improvements in water management and by the development of commercial agriculture. Secondly there was a revolution in water transport: for sea voyages junks, built with watertight bulkheads, used the magnetic compass; even greater progress was made in river and canal transportation, with the development of a national network of waterways. This in turn stimulated a growing interdependence of China's regional economies. At the same time there occurred a revolution in systems of money and credit. 'Flying money', government certificates of credit entitling the bearer to draw an equivalent sum at provincial treasuries, had appeared in the Tang period. This was supplemented by credit instruments and promissory notes. By the twelfth century the Southern Song government was issuing a fully-convertible paper currency and credit systems were well established. Accompanying this were revolutionary changes in marketing structure and urbanisation. Elvin noted that the Chinese rural economy was becoming linked with the market mechanism, that economic advances were bringing about an urban revolution, and that a rising proportion of the population was residing in cities. Finally he argued that in this period China 'advanced to the threshold of a systematic experimental investigation of nature, and created the world's earliest mechanized industry'.[36] To justify this last claim he stressed the spread of printing, the investigation of disease, the advances in mathematics and the appearance of a silk-reeling machine which almost anticipated the technology of the early industrial revolution in the West.

Elvin's argument, which was based on research carried out by Japanese historians, is related to a general interpretation of Chinese history concerning the emergence of capitalism. According to the Japanese historian Naito Torajiro the important economic and social changes which occurred in the Tang-Song era indicated that it was at this point that the 'modern' period in Chinese history began. The implication of this claim is that capitalism, or at least its beginnings, emerged in the Song period. If that was the case, then a reason must be given for why it failed to develop further. One of the most persuasive explanations for this was put forward by Etienne Balazs who argued that the rise of a Chinese bourgeoisie in the Tang-Song period occurred at a time when national sovereignty was divided, and as a consequence the power of the state and that of the ruling scholar-officials was weakened. He admitted that the superabundance of cheap labour in China inhibited the development of time-saving devices, but he argued that this was not the key to why a further development of capitalism did not occur. The real reason was that

> what was chiefly lacking in China for the further development of capitalism was not mechanical skill or scientific aptitude, nor a sufficient accumulation of wealth, but scope for individual enterprise. There was no individual freedom and no security for private enterprise, no legal foundation for rights other than those of the state, no alternative investment other than landed property, no guarantee against being penalized by arbitrary exactions from officials or against intervention by the state. But perhaps the supreme inhibiting factor was the overwhelming prestige of the state bureaucracy, which maimed from the start any attempt of the bourgeoisie to be different, to become aware of themselves as a class and fight for an autonomous position in society.[37]

Nevertheless the changes which did take place left an ineradicable mark on the Chinese economy. In the Tang-Song period the population may have doubled, with spectacular growth in the south and east contrasting with limited growth or even decrease in the north.[38] There had been a marked trend towards urbanisation, a massive growth of commerce and the widespread adoption of a monetary economy. Moreover important technological advances had occurred, for example in the production of iron. Iron output increased twelve-fold between 850 and 1050. This occasioned a demand for charcoal which so reduced timber supplies that a precocious development of the coal industry occurred. Coal became a major source of energy for both industrial and domestic use, a development which only occurred in Britain in the period 1540–1640.[39]

Social changes

Mention has already been made of some social changes which occurred in the Northern Song. These changes appear to have completed a process already well under way in the later Tang period, namely the elimination of aristocratic families from positions of power. In their place a new élite had emerged, a professional body of scholar officials, defined by achievement in examinations and by appointment to government office.

The traditional interpretation of this development measured social standing through bureaucratic success and concluded that there was a good deal of social mobility in Song society. More recently it has been argued that beyond the nationally prominent political élite (which might indeed be mobile) there was a locally influential social élite which could dominate a locality for centuries. This revisionary view has been challenged by Richard L. Davies, in a study of the Shi clan of Ningpo, the clan which produced the chief councillor Shi Miyuan. Davies noted that in the early imperial period politically mobile kin groups had usually required at least ten generations to reach the height of their influence, and another ten generations passed before decline set in. However in the Song period, in a society which was more complex and competitive, the entire cycle, of rise, prominence and obscurity, might be completed within ten generations. In the case of the Shi the rise was indeed the product of examination success, reinforced by a family tendency to longevity. There was nothing in this to support the idea of a hereditary élite founded on regional prominence[40] – rather the rise and unimpeded decline of the Shi suggested that 'turbulence within a highly competitive bureaucracy' made it difficult for any kinship group to maintain a position of power for long.[41]

Another important change had occurred in rural society. During the Tang-Song period the tradition that government should control the distribution of land, through the equitable or 'equal field' system, was finally abandoned. It has been estimated that by the end of the eleventh century official and first to third rank households, which constituted a mere 14 per cent of the population of the empire, held 77½ per cent of the land under cultivation. The remainder of the population held only 22½ per cent of the land. However, it is debatable whether the manor was the dominant institution in the Chinese countryside, or whether the small-scale farm worked under a system of private ownership was more typical. It may be that manorial development became more marked as the southern Song period progressed and that it was only a notable feature of certain areas, for example in the prefectures around Lake Tai.[42]

Accompanying rural change was the great increase in urbanisation. Constraints on the growth of towns had broken down in the Tang period and under the Northern and Southern Song towns overflowed their traditional layout into suburbs. Of Southern Song cities, by far the best known was Hangzhou, the 'temporary residence' of the dynasty, known to Marco Polo as Quinsai. In the thirteenth century Hangzhou grew to be the largest and richest city in the world, with a population perhaps numbering two million. The city proper was surrounded by a wall eleven miles in length, it was intersected by canals which in turn were criss-crossed by bridges – Marco Polo claimed that there were 'twelve thousand bridges of stone', in fact they numbered 367. The city was home to the Imperial Palace, to the organs of central government and to the officials who ran them. Hangzhou was also a great commercial city and its population included large numbers of merchants, artisans, workmen and members of the 'low-class professions', for example entertainers and prostitutes. The extensive commercial activities of the city population indicate that another significant social change had occurred in the Southern Song period.[43]

The growth of cities and the spread of printing has ensured that the historical materials describing Song society are plentiful. Consequently more is known of the position of women in Song society than in any previous period in Chinese history. This is an issue which has given rise to disagreement. Until recently the dominant view was that a contrast existed between the position of women under the Tang and that which they occupied under the Song. Under the former dynasty, it was claimed, women from élite backgrounds participated in society with considerable freedom. Some Tang women – the example of the Empress Wu is perhaps not the most fortunate – could be taken as role models. However under the Song the position of women deteriorated: there was the spread of foot-binding and the strong condemnation of the remarriage of widows. It was true that women during the period seemed to enjoy particularly strong property rights, but this was more than matched by the ideological pressure for women to conform to the submissive role endorsed by Neo-Confucian writers.[44]

However Patricia Buckley Ebrey, in her study of marriage and the lives of women in the Song period, emphasised continuity as well as change, for women's lives remained centred on the home throughout the period. Nevertheless important changes did take place which reflected the broader social and economic developments of the time. The commercialisation of cloth production, which involved a good deal of female labour, set a monetary value on women's work; the spread of printing encouraged an increase in literacy among women from scholarly families – literacy seems to have enhanced marriageability; the increased importance for the educated class of making advantageous marriages led to a spectacular increase in the size of dowries, and it was in this context that Song law provided some protection for orphaned girls, allocating to them half a son's share of the estate; more generally, greater affluence encouraged the employment of women as concubines, maids and prostitutes; and in a male society which admired languid women there was the gradual extension of footbinding from the palace and entertainment quarters to the homes of officials. These changes in the role of women may have encouraged Confucian scholars, anxious to fix people in well-defined roles, to emphasise notions of female modesty and widow fidelity, and to condemn women's literary creativity, their claims to property, and their involvement in affairs outside the home.[45]

Intellectual developments: Neo-Confucianism

Under the Southern Song there occurred a Confucian revival which was to have a long-lasting effect on Chinese culture. The antecedents of this movement lay in the Tang period and the writings of Han Yu, in which he had rejected Buddhism as a foreign doctrine and had called for a reassertion of Confucian ethics as a basis for government. During the Northern Song Han Yu's ideas and literary style were revived by Ouyang Xiu who called for a renovation of Chinese society. His call came at the time when the activist Confucianism of Wang Anshi had divided Confucians. His opponents, who have been labelled moralistic conservatives[46] had likened his reforms to Legalism, and their rejection of Wang, made in an atmosphere of dynastic decline, had led to bitter controversy.

At the same time philosophical speculation extended the range of Confucianism. Zhou Tunyi (1017–73) looked back to the *Book of Changes* and also borrowed ideas from Buddhism and Daoism. From these ingredients he constructed a cosmology, a science of the universe, which combined reference to the workings of *yin* and *yang* and the five agents, to explain what he termed the Great Ultimate, the first principle from which all is derived. The heavenly principle, the male element, and the earthly principle, the female element, the two material forces, interacted to engender and transform all. Man received these material forces in their highest excellence, which made him the most intelligent being, capable of developing consciousness. Zhang Zai (1020–77) suggested that a single primal substance, defined as qi, and translated as 'material-force' or 'vital energy' composed the entire universe. The world was not illusory, as Buddhists maintained, but composed of this primal material.[47]

These ideas were developed in contrasting ways by the brothers Cheng. Cheng Hao (1032–85), in an essay entitled "Understanding the Nature of Humanity", was concerned with the unity of the human mind and the mind of the universe. His ideas later became the foundation of the Neo-Confucian school of the Mind. The writings of his younger brother Cheng Yi (1033–1107) had the more immediate impact. He adopted Zhang Zai's idea of material-force, but then added a second concept, that of li or 'principle', the immutable, immaterial principle in all things that gives them their form. Human nature comprised both principle and material-force. According to Mencius, man was by his nature good. This was the principle, but man's material endowment – his material-force – varied and hence men's character differed. However, Cheng Yi was not a fatalist: he believed that man could cultivate a moral attitude and overcome his shortcomings. This self-cultivation involved the investigation of the principle of things, which sequence of ideas led to the Neo-Confucian School of Principle.

These ideas were later synthesised by Zhu Xi (1130–1200), who brought the concepts of the Great Ultimate, material-force and principle into a single doctrine which was to have an enormous influence. Zhu Xi also established the sequence of the Confucian classics – the Four Books – and wrote commentaries on them. These in time became the central texts for primary education and the examination system. He defined the process of the 'investigation of things' to enable one to acquire moral understanding and to cultivate the inner self. 'Book reading, quiet sitting, ritual practice, physical exercise, calligraphy, arithmetic, and empirical observation all have a place in his pedagogical program'.[48] He taught his ideas at his academy, the White Deer Grotto in Jiangxi, where he acquired an extensive following. In his day his ideas were by no means universally accepted. At a philosophical level he was challenged by Lu Xiangshan (1139–93), who emphasised meditation and intuition, elaborating on the ideas of Cheng Hao. In 1175 a famous confrontation took place between the two at the Goose Lake Temple. Zhu Xi also fell foul of the chief councillor, Han Tuozhou, who found his teaching, which implied an ideological superiority over the current practices of government, to be subversive, and had his followers banned from the court.

James T.C. Liu, in a striking phrase, described the intellectual and political changes which reached a crisis point in the early twelfth century as 'China turning inward'. After the fall of Wang Anshi the path of reform, which perhaps offered a solution to the crisis of empire, had been blocked. Under the Southern Song the rise of chief councillors, and increasingly autocratic rule, had progressively alienated scholar-officials. Foreign invasion compounded by profound social and economic change provoked a deep uncertainty. This was translated by Zhu Xi and his predecessors into a need to transform Confucianism by incorporating metaphysical concepts: the true Confucian examined himself inwardly, while statecraft became a secondary concern. This redirection of concern affected not only the individual, but also society, for Neo-Confucianism did not extend its empirical approach to scientific investigation. When the Mongol threat became imminent and when they in turn laid claim to Confucian orthodoxy, the Southern Song responded by adopting Zhu Xi's teaching, arrogating true Confucianism to themselves. Of course this did not save the dynasty, but it left the way open for Neo-Confucianism to become the state ideology.

The arts in the Song period: landscape painting and ceramics

The period of the Five Dynasties and the Song dynasty was one of high achievement in a range of arts, but above all one of excellence in landscape painting and ceramics.

It was in this period that landscape painting achieved the maturity which led to its recognition as the dominant form of artistic expression. Under the Tang, the landscape painter Jing Hao (c. 855–915) had written a treatise in which he set out the six essentials of painting which were: spirit, harmony, thought, scenery, the brush and ink. In this sequence he proceeded from thought to execution, the underlying implication being that the painter sought not only to represent the true forms of nature but also to reveal their deeper significance.

These principles were followed by Fan Kuan (c. 960–1030), whose painting *Travelling amid mountains and gorges*, is a very rare example of a Song painting which has survived. It has been said that:

> It perfectly fulfils the ideal of the Northern Song that a landscape-painting should be of such compelling realism that the viewer will feel that he has been actually transported to the place depicted.[49]

Among the many important artists of the period one should mention the statesman Su Dongpo (1036–1101), who combined painting with calligraphy, poetry and art criticism, and Mi Fu (1051–1107), also known as a calligrapher. They belonged to a group of artists who were literati, who found their means of self-expression in painting. They subscribed to the amateur ideal, Mi Fu once writing 'In matters of calligraphy and painting, one is not to discuss price. The gentleman is hard to capture by money'.[50]

Some idea of the importance attached to painting in the Song period may be gauged by reference to Huizong, the Northern Song emperor who reigned from 1101 to 1125. He was an accomplished painter of birds and flowers and also supported an academy of painting which rigorously controlled the artists who attended the court. However, the emperor was not able to prevent the development of new styles and unconventional approaches to painting. Among the later members of the academy was Ma Yuan (fl. 1190–1225), who rejected the monumental style of the Northern landscape painters and instead painted evocative scenes of individuals dwarfed by the landscape. Xia Gui (fl. 1180–1224), his younger contemporary at the Southern Song court at Hangzhou, went even further in using expressive brushwork to convey emotion. In this intent, his paintings were not dissimilar to those of Chan Buddhist painters, of whom Mu Qi (c. 1200–1270) is best known in the West for his painting *Six Persimmons*.

With reference to ceramics, in the past it was supposed that the outstanding wares of the time were the product of a few centres which specialised in the small-scale production of particular types of ceramic. Recent excavations at Northern Song ceramic centres have revealed this to be untrue: factories produced a variety of wares, often imitating those made by other centres, and production was on a large scale and governed by economic considerations. The state-sponsored kiln centre at Jingdezhen in Jiangxi province, which began production at the beginning of the eleventh century, became an outstanding example of a centre which combined mass production with high quality.

For connoisseurs, however, the ceramics of the period remain known by their specific names or by their supposed places of manufacture. These included Ding ware, more refined than the Tang product – the bodies of the vessels were so thin that the rims were often bound with metal; *qingbai*, meaning 'blue-white', a type of fine white porcelain, often with incised decoration; Cizhou ware, named after a site in Hebei, but produced right across north China, which featured a slip-painted decoration beneath a transparent glaze; Jun ware, a rather heavy ware characteristically glazed in lavender blue with purple splashes; the black or dark brown Jian ware, produced in Fujian and exported in large quantities to Japan, where it was known as *temmoku*; Guan or 'official' ware, from Hangzhou and Longquan, with a distinctive crackle glaze; and the highly-prized Ru ware, a finer crackleware produced for the Song court for a few years early in the twelfth century. The porcelain of this period has been described as 'both technically and artistically the finest the world has produced'.[51]

10
The Yuan Dynasty

The Mongol conquest of China came in a series of stages. The Xi Xia kingdom in the north-west was attacked between 1205 and 1209 and the Jin empire of North China was first overrun between 1211 and 1215. The Mongols then turned westwards and seized the Western Liao empire, the state founded by the remnants of the Qidan. After a pause the Mongol attack was resumed, the Jin empire was destroyed in 1234, the remains of the Nanzhao kingdom in the south-west fell in 1253 and Korea was conquered by 1258. The Yuan dynasty was established in 1271 and the Southern Song capitulated in 1279. However, Mongol rule of the whole of China was to last less than a century. By 1351 major rebellions had broken out and in 1368 the Yuan court gave up the unequal struggle and retreated to the steppes.

The Significance of the Yuan Dynasty

In traditional Chinese historiography the Mongol conquest was treated as a disaster, and this pejorative view of the Yuan dynasty has been accepted by many western writers. Jacques Gernet, for example, emphasised that this was a Mongol occupation of China. He described how the Mongols had devised a system of economic exploitation and practised racial discrimination, and concluded that their harsh regime and unjust policies had provoked the hatred of the Chinese and had led to their inevitable expulsion.[1] Another charge which has been laid at the Mongols' door is that they caused a major setback to the development of Chinese society, terminating the progress of the Song period, including the economic and technological changes which have been seen as verging on the birth of capitalism, and thus ensuring that the successor Ming dynasty would be an introverted and non-competitive state.[2] It has also been claimed that Mongol rule led to a brutalisation of Chinese politics and that this bore tragic fruit in Ming times, the evidence quoted including the practice instituted by the first Ming emperor of ordering the public flogging of ministers with whom he was displeased.[3]

These views, which are to an extent justifiable, conceal important features of the Yuan dynasty. Many Chinese supported the dynasty because it brought about a reunification of the country. The claim that the Han Chinese despised being ruled by Mongols, and that throughout the Yuan period they wanted to drive them out, ignores the fact that many Mongols remained in China after the Yuan court had left. It is more likely that the Chinese came to accept the Mongol emperors as the legitimate holders of the mandate of heaven. There is evidence to show that Han

Chinese culture, far from having been despoiled by the Mongols, as the founder of the Ming dynasty alleged, actually flourished in the Yuan period. A positive view of Mongol rule has claimed that it was more humane than that of the Song, that less use was made of capital punishment and of irregular taxation, that there were no 'literary inquisitions', and that classical scholarship flourished. This revisionary view points out that the verdict on the Yuan of the early Ming period was initially highly favourable, but was reversed after an incident which occurred in 1449 when the Ming emperor was captured by the Oirat Mongols.[4]

The impression which remains is that there is still much to be discovered about the Yuan period. One unresolved mystery concerns population. According to fiscal records the combined population of Song and Jin China amounted to well over 100,000,000, whereas the records of the 1290s indicate a population of roughly 70,000,000. How far that reduction was the product of inadequate recording, how far the result of a demographic disaster, remains unclear.[5] It must also be said that Mongol rule was essentially superficial and that for the great majority of the Chinese population it probably had only a slight impact.

Genghis Khan and the Conquest of North China

In the twelfth century the people known to history as the Mongols lived in separate tribes on the steppes of central Asia. Each tribe claimed a common ancestry and the nobles of the tribe regarded themselves as the direct descendants of the tribe's founder. Rulership of a tribe was awarded to an individual by a convocation of the nobles of that tribe. The Mongol economy was based on cattle herding, supplemented by hunting, the Mongols being accomplished horsemen. The Mongols were frequently in conflict with the Tatars, their neighbours to the west, an animosity which was encouraged by the Jurchen Jin dynasty as a means of promoting dissension on the steppe.

The early history of Temujin, the man who was to become Genghis khan, was recorded in the *Secret History of the Mongols*. He was born in about 1167. His father, known as Yesugei the Brave, was a tribal leader who had participated in the struggle against the Tatars. According to the *Secret History* he was poisoned by the Tatars while Temujin was still a child. This grievance, and the ties of friendship and alliance which he developed with other tribal groupings, formed the background of Temujin's claim, made in about 1187, to be the khan of the Mongols. However, it was not until a decade later that with the assistance of the Jin he was able to take revenge on the Tatars. Yet another decade of tribal fighting was to pass until Temujin's position was so strong that at a convocation of tribes held in 1206 he was acclaimed Genghis khan, universal sovereign, ruler of the steppe peoples.

Genghis khan then carried out an extensive reform of the religious, legal, political and above all military organisation of the Mongols. He claimed to be heaven's chosen instrument and assumed that all who stood in his way did so in defiance of heaven's will. It was on this assertion that the Mongol objective of universal rule was based. His wishes took the form of decrees, now for the first time set down in a written form of Mongolian and intended to serve as precedents. He distributed titles and responsibilities and regulated the tribal structure. With reference to military organisation, he elaborated on the decimal system which dated back to the Xiongnu. According to the *Secret History* he created ninety-five tribal units each of a thousand men and each divided into units of tens and hundreds. Together with his own élite corps, the Mongol forces numbered rather more than one hundred thousand men. They fought under their tribal chieftains, operated under strict discipline and were capable of remarkable feats of endurance. This Mongol fighting machine was to create the largest land empire the world has ever seen.

Genghis khan then set in train a series of campaigns which were to take the Mongol forces from Korea to the Black Sea. Between 1211 and 1215, in a series of annual raids, increasingly penetrative attacks were made on Jin territory in north China and the Jurchen homeland in Manchuria was overrun. However, at the very moment that it seemed that the Jin empire was about to collapse, Genghis khan turned his attention westwards and destroyed the Western Liao empire and captured Samarkand and Bokhara. In the meantime Mongol encroachment on China continued and increasingly the Mongols began to take into their service Qidan and Chinese officials, among them Yelüchucai, a Qidan of royal descent, who became a court official and chief astrologer. In 1226 Genghis khan attacked and destroyed the Xi Xia kingdom, himself dying the following year in the course of the campaign.[6]

Genghis khan was succeeded by his third son Ögödei, who took the title of khaghan or emperor, indicating his elevation above his brothers, between whom the rest of the Mongol empire was divided. Under Ögödei a further burst of expansion took place, with Mongol forces invading Korea and reaching Vienna in the west. In 1230 he recommenced the campaign against the Jin, captured Kaifeng in 1233 and destroyed the Jin dynasty in the following year.

Having conquered North China, the Mongols now had to devise a means of ruling it. Up to this point the Mongol practice in China had been that of a nomadic society, exploiting the economy by the imposition of heavy exactions and the enslavement of sections of the population. Large tracts of land were commandeered for grazing and one Mongol nobleman even went as far as to suggest the complete annihilation of the native population and the use of the entire occupied territory as pasture. It was at this point that Yelüchucai made his famous proposal on how the country might be exploited in a more rational way. He suggested, as a first step towards establishing a relationship with the population, the granting of an amnesty to the Chinese who had unwittingly broken Mongolian law. He advised the establishment of a strong central government, the delineation of new administrative districts, and the creation of tax collection bureaux which would supervise the receipt of regular tax payments.

The success of these initial measures encouraged Ögödei to promote Yelüchucai and to allow him to go further in adopting Chinese administrative methods. The next step was the conduct of a national census between 1234 and 1236. For

Yelüchucai this was a preliminary to improving the administration, however Ögödei used the information provided to divide North China into appanages for the Mongol princes. This working at cross purposes continued in other respects. Yelüchucai brought Chinese officials into the Mongol service, encouraged the study of the Chinese classics and attempted to re-introduce the examination system. However Ögödei awarded the privilege of farming the taxes of North China to a Muslim businessman and promoted other Muslims to influential positions. By the time of Ögödei's death in 1241, and that of Yelüchucai two years later, the stratagem for ruling China the latter had tried to introduce had been seriously undermined.[7]

The Conquest of the Southern Song

In 1251 Möngke became khaghan and the encroachment on China resumed. His brother Khubilai conducted an ambitious campaign to subdue the kingdom of Nanzhao. In 1254 raiding of Southern Song territory commenced and Möngke invaded Sichuan in 1258, only to die in the following year. The succession dispute which followed delayed the Mongol assault on the Southern Song for a further twenty years.

Nevertheless it was inevitable that Khubilai, prompted both by the Mongolian concept of universal rule and by the expectation that an emperor who ruled North China should rule the totality of China, would aim to incorporate the Southern Song territory into his domains. However, to achieve this meant overcoming the problems which had restricted the Jurchen to the north: the unsuitable terrain for cavalry, the need to capture walled cities and the threat of Song naval power.

The principal invasion route to the Yangzi valley was along the Han river on which lay the important fortress-town of Xiangyang. The siege of Xiangyang, which lasted from 1268 to 1273, was a decisive contest. With the help of two Muslim engineers, and the use of a vast mangonel to hurl rocks at the fortifications, the walls of the town were finally breached. The conquest of the south was carried out by Bayan, an outstanding general. In 1275 he defeated Jia Sidao, the last chief councillor of the Southern Song and in the following year occupied Hangzhou and received the formal surrender of the Song. However Song loyalists continued their resistance until 1279. They retreated to Guangzhou and were finally forced to put to sea, where Liu Xiufu, the last devoted servant of the dynasty, leapt into the sea with the boy-emperor in his arms and drowned them both.

The Reign of Khubilai Khan

In the meantime Khubilai khan, as ruler of North China, took steps to transform his position from that of Mongol invader to that of Chinese emperor. The process began at his acclamation as khaghan in 1260 at which he promulgated an edict in Chinese, written by his Confucian advisor, which contained a Chinese reign-name. It continued with the construction of capitals, the first at Kaiping in Inner

Mongolia, later to be known as Shangdu, the Supreme Capital, and to Coleridge as Xanadu, which was a new town modelled on the Tang capital at Chang'an. Later, on the site of modern Beijing, he had laid out Dadu, the Great Capital, otherwise known as Khanbalik, the city of the khan. Each capital had 'strong historical associations fitting well into the architectural symbolism of a new dynasty.'[8] Despite these claims to Chinese legitimacy, the Mongol court continued to follow nomad practices and moved between the two capitals, spending the summer at Shangdu and the winter at Dadu.

This tension between the assertion of distinctiveness and the danger – in Mongol eyes – of assimilation, remained throughout the Yuan period. Under Khubilai khan the Mongol dream of universal empire began to disintegrate and it became clear that he was the ruler of an east Asian state. The extent of this was determined by the failure of his attempts, made in 1274 and 1281, to subdue the Japanese. The second of these attacks, in which Mongol troops landed on Japanese soil, was frustrated by a storm, the *kamikaze* or 'divine wind' which destroyed the Mongol fleet. Further disastrous failures occurred late in Khubilai's reign when he attempted to coerce the rulers of Champa (in modern Vietnam) and Java.

From 1260 Khubilai had begun to utilise the bureaucratic tradition of the Chinese state. His adviser on this was a former Buddhist monk, Liu Bingzhong, who gave him the famous advice that 'although the empire had been conquered on horseback, it could not be administered on horseback'.[9] He re-established the secretariat and the traditional six ministries. The division between civil, military and censorial branches of government was retained. A system of territorial administration divided China and Korea into twelve provinces. The arrangements resembled those previously in use, although it appears that the delegation of authority was far more extensive. Further steps were taken to confirm the legitimacy of Khubilai as a Chinese emperor. Chinese court ceremonial and Confucian rites were revived and in the early 1260s a national history office was established to collect the historical records of the preceding dynasties.[10] In 1271 Khubilai decided to adopt a Chinese dynastic title, that of *Da Yuan* or 'Great Origin'.

Nevertheless these changes fell well short of sinicisation. In several respects Khubilai himself showed an unwillingness to accept fundamental characteristics of the Chinese state as it had developed. The first was the examination system, which Khubilai rejected as a means of selecting men for appointment to the bureaucracy. For forty years, until the system of examinations was partly revived in 1315, recruits to the bureaucracy came from those who were qualified by status, that it to say because of their family background, or because a member of the family, already a member of the bureaucracy, could exercise the *yin* privilege. Some of these were Chinese, but many came from non-Chinese backgrounds and included many Uighur and Turks. A second essential difference concerned the status and recruitment of the military establishment. Mongol society was highly militarised whereas Chinese society, both in practice and in sentiment, held military values and military men in low esteem. Under Khubilai and his successors the hereditary principle of recruitment was maintained and Chinese forces were recruited in a similar fashion. However, the two elements were never fused and the Mongols never surrendered their military claims to superiority even when the Mongol military machine had ceased to exist.[11] Finally there was the matter of the codification of the law. For centuries China had had a unified legal code and the Jin dynasty, despite being a dynasty of conquest, had adopted a version of the Tang code. The Mongols had brought with them the *jasagh*, the collection of rules and instructions promulgated by Genghis khan, but Chinese society was too complex to be administered through Mongol customary law. Undoubtedly there were great legal difficulties in the way of drafting a code which could be applied to the multicultural society of Yuan China, and this may explain why it was not until 1323 that a compilation of legal documents was promulgated which attempted to strike a balance between Chinese tradition, Mongolian practice, and new social conditions.[12] The fact remained that the Mongols did not accept previous Chinese legal codes, nor could the Chinese accept Mongol customary law.

The Successors of Khubilai Khan

The last years of Khubilai's reign were clouded by the failure of his foreign adventures, by his ill-health and above all by the problem of succession. In contrast to the Chinese practice of the ruler nominating his successor, the Mongols retained the custom of public acclamation of a ruler from among those eligible to succeed. This gave rise to a recurrent difficulty throughout the Yuan period which weakened the dynasty. Khubilai's original choice of successor was his son Zhenjin but he died in 1285. After Khubilai's death Zhenjin's son Temür was acclaimed khaghan and reigned as the emperor Chengzong from 1294 to 1307. His reign in many respects saw the continuation of policies initiated by Khubilai, and he achieved nominal suzerainty over the whole of the Mongol world. However it was also marked by the onset of administrative inefficiency and corruption. He was followed on the throne by Khaishan (the Wuzong emperor), who rejected much of Khubilai's programme, plunged recklessly into debt and adopted a variety of unsound financial practices to try to recover the situation.

A more settled period of government ensued under Khaishan's brother Ayurbarwada, the emperor Renzong (reigned 1311–20). More than any of his predecessors, Ayurbarwada had absorbed Chinese culture. He employed Confucian scholar-officials in his bureaucracy and in 1315 he partly revived the civil service examinations using a curriculum based on Neo-Confucian texts. However, Mongolian and other non-Chinese groups were given easier tests and a racial quota system was employed. Although the examinations conducted under Ayurbarwada and until the end of the dynasty only recruited four percent of the official appointments, the reform alarmed the Mongol élite.

In the years following his death a prolonged struggle broke out between factions at court, who were divided partly by the stand they took towards sinicisation and partly by the rival claims of the descendants of the two lines from Khubilai. In 1323 a coup took place which put Yesün Temür on the throne, a man whose steppe background made him unsympathetic to Chinese scholar-officials and led him to appoint Muslims to senior positions. When he died in 1328 an even more bloody succession struggle followed which ended with Tugh Temür being enthroned twice. He has been represented as the 'Yuan candidate', that is to say as a Mongol whose commitment was to China rather than to the steppe. He certainly went out of his way to honour Confucius and to promote Chinese culture. Finally, in 1333 Toghön Temür was placed on the throne at the age of thirteen, his reign lasting until 1368 when the Mongol court fled from China.[13]

Discriminatory Policies

One of the most notorious aspects of Mongol rule over China was the application of a 'four-class' system. The population was divided into four ethnic groups in order of descending privilege: Mongols; semu ren, that is 'miscellaneous aliens', referring mainly to Western and Central Asians; Han ren, the inhabitants of northern China, conquered in 1234, comprising not only Chinese but also including Qidan, Jurchen etc.; and finally and lowest in the order, the nan ren, the population of the Southern Song territories acquired in 1279. It is true that the division between the classes was not as rigid as has sometimes been suggested. Nevertheless, discrimination on the grounds of ethnic and political background was an important element in the Yuan social order and it had connotations in terms of bureaucratic appointment, legal treatment and taxation.

With regard to appointments the Mongols certainly practised discrimination in the sense that they never relied on Chinese scholar officials as a class to support their rule. Obstacles were placed in the way of Chinese, even Chinese who had succeeded in the Mongolian version of the examination system, to bar them from high office. Some Chinese literati refused to participate in public life. Nevertheless there were many individual exceptions to this discrimination. Chinese collaborated with the Mongols against the Jurchen and so facilitated the establishment of the Yuan dynasty. Khubilai employed a number of Chinese advisers, including Xu Heng who was appointed chancellor of the Imperial College in 1274, and Wang E who had recommended to Khubilai that he, like Chinese emperors before him, should order the compilation of the records of previous dynasties. After the conquest of the Southern Song, Chinese advisers continued to play a significant role. Ayurbarwada surrounded himself with Chinese scholars and appointed Chinese to senior posts in the secretariat, and his reintroduction of the examinations gave southern Chinese a chance of obtaining office. Tugh Temür also was a patron of Chinese scholarship and he supported a number of Chinese in office, among them the eminent scholar Yu Ji. This is not to suggest that there was no discrimination, but it is possible to argue that Chinese participation in Mongol rule has been underestimated.

With reference to legal treatment the evidence of discrimination is even less convincing. In the past China had permitted ethnic minorities to punish offenders within their own communities according to their own customary law. In the Yuan period Mongols and semu ren were tried according to their own Mongolian or Central Asian laws, and Chinese were tried according to Chinese law. This led to some difference in punishment, for example a Chinese offender (but not a

Mongol or a Central Asian) in addition to the imposition of the principal punishment was tattooed – a practice which has led writers to assert that legal discrimination was carried out against the Chinese, although such tattooing had in fact been prescribed under Song law. Special courts were established to deal with cases involving two ethnic groups. Mongols did have some legal advantages: in the case of an offence within a mixed marriage the dispute would be adjudicated according to the law of the husband unless the wife happened to be Mongolian, in which case she would have the benefit. In the *Yuan History* it is stated that if a Mongol beat a Chinese, the latter could not fight back, and this has been taken as clear evidence of discrimination. However it has been shown that the Chinese victim was instead provided with a legal remedy for the assault.[14]

On the matter of taxation, the Mongols certainly began with the intention of exploiting the Chinese. Under Ögödei harsh requisitions were replaced with the more orderly form of taxation proposed by Yelüchucai. However his reforms were later abandoned in favour of tax-farming by Muslim entrepreneurs. As north China had already suffered from the disruption of previous conquests and the ravages of natural disasters, the burden of taxation may well have appeared excessive and, under Khubilai and his successors, sporadic attempts were made to moderate it. In the south, although Mongols enjoyed favoured status with regard to taxation, the tax burden on the Chinese population does not appear to have been excessive and the landowners of south China may have benefited considerably from Yuan economic policies.[15] Although excessive taxation was to figure among the reasons given for the fall of the dynasty, the evidence to prove impoverishment of Chinese society and to show that it should be attributed to the exploitation by the Mongols must be regarded as inconclusive.

The Economy

One view of the consequences of Mongol rule on China is that it inhibited economic growth and even caused regression. This view emphasises that after the Mongol invasion of north China great quantities of arable land were confiscated from Chinese owners and turned into pasture. Much state and private land was given to the Mongol aristocracy and to Buddhist establishments. These actions and heavy taxation ruined many peasants and there was a second wave of migration to the south. The Mongols were ignorant of the need to maintain river defences and as a consequence dikes broke and the Yellow river shifted its course, causing great loss of life. Artisans lost their freedom and became dependents of the Mongols. Even the incorporation of China into the Mongol empire brought no marked benefit as almost all the trade was in the hands of foreigners. The profits of trade were taken out of China and there was a drain on metallic currency, which led to the use of paper money and subsequently to inflation. The Mongol government permitted corruption on a vast scale and the impoverishment that this caused was exacerbated by the Mongol love of splendour epitomised by the building of Dadu and the demands made for its supply.[16]

The evidence that the Mongol invasion had a catastrophic effect on north China appears to be strong, and the calculation that in the Yuan period there was a sharp population decline seems well founded. However, to conclude that the economic impact was purely negative would appear to be too sweeping. Under Khubilai steps were taken to promote economic recovery. In the north he sought to foster agriculture, encouraging the formation of groups of fifty households to open up barren land, improve flood control and irrigation, and to increase silk production. He promoted the interests of both merchants and artisans, who under previous dynasties had held low status and suffered numerous restrictions. He supported the *ortogh*, the associations of merchants, mainly Muslims, who handled the trade along the Silk Road. He made wider use of paper currency than ever before and, as this was adequately backed by a silver reserve, it acted as an encouragement to commerce. He also constructed roads, improved canals and developed the postal system. The division of China had been an impediment to trade and its reunification served to encourage economic activity.

However, towards the end of Khubilai's reign economic problems began to multiply. His foreign expeditions and his massive public works programmes, including the extension of the Grand Canal, imposed a heavy burden on state finances which Khubilai dealt with by employing a series of *semu* ministers whose methods of raising revenue earned them a hateful reputation. Khubilai's successors continued to face fiscal problems which were dealt with by raising revenue from monopolies, by currency manipulation and by profiting from the growth of maritime trade. Under Ayurbarwada an attempt was made to carry out a land survey preparatory to revising the land registers to include landholdings that had been omitted fraudulently from the tax schedules. The opposition provoked by this move led to the survey being stopped and thereafter south China's landlords were left to prosper.[17]

These contradictory indicators make it impossible to deliver a confident assessment of the economic effects of Mongol occupation. The economic decline of the north continued, but the prosperity of cities such as Hangzhou indicates that commerce was thriving. The role of the *ortogh* in terms of benefiting or harming the Chinese economy is likewise unclear, although a recent study has suggested that the Mongols' dealings with the *ortogh* did stimulate foreign trade and enrich the treasury.[18] Even less is known for certain about the situation of the rural population. In the north, and to a lesser extent in the south, the Mongols rulers rewarded their followers with appanages, grants of territory which gave them rights over the resident population which became households in bondage. After the conquest the government sought to prevent the excessive exploitation of these households, but the scale of internal migration suggests that they were not very successful. As noted above, the Mongols did encourage agricultural improvement, but the proliferation of peasant uprisings at the end of the Yuan period is an indicator the harshness of rural life. This may have been exacerbated by poor climatic conditions. In the fourteenth century China experienced thirty-five severe winters and in 1332 extraordinarily great rains and river floods are alleged to have brought about the loss of seven million lives and possibly to have a connection with the origin of the Black Death.[19]

Religion and Culture

The Mongols practised a form of shamanism, but they made no attempt to impose this on their subjects. Instead the Yuan period was notable for religious freedom, although the Mongols did favour some religions at the expense of others. Their reliance on divination before settling on a course of action led them to make use of Daoist adepts, for example the Daoist patriarch known as Changchun, who had a famous interview with Genghis khan in 1219 and gained a privileged position for Daoists over Buddhists under Mongol rule.[20] The growth in the numbers of clergy led Ögödei in 1229 to issue an edict that all Daoist and Buddhist clergy below the age of fifty should pass an examination on the scriptures of their religion, or lose their tax exemption. Rivalry between Daoists and Buddhists continued under Möngke and between 1255 and 1258 a series of public debates took place between the two sides. The Buddhists claimed that their religion had been slandered by the Daoists' 'conversion of the barbarians' theory, which alleged that Laozi had travelled to India, there transforming himself into the Buddha and adapting his teachings to suit his audience. A more substantive issue was the Buddhist claim for restitution of monastic properties occupied by the Daoists. Khubilai, who presided at the last of these debates, decided in the Buddhists' favour.[21]

At that debate a key role was played by a Tibetan lama named 'Phags-pa. The Tibetan form of Buddhism had a strong appeal for the Mongols, who preferred its colourful ceremonial and emphasis on magic to the more subtle philosophy of Chan Buddhism. In 1260 'Phags-pa was appointed State Preceptor and it was through his actions that Tibetan Buddhism established a firm hold in China and the Mongol emperors received Buddhist legitimation. 'Phags-pa had another claim to fame, for he had invented the most effective alphabet for writing pre-classical Mongolian.[22]

The Mongol attitude towards Confucianism was originally one of contempt, but as the Mongol conquest of China proceeded first Khubilai, and then to a greater extent Ayurbarwada, recognised the value of Confucian officials in government. After the reunification of China Neo-Confucianism, which up to this point had been restricted to the south, made rapid progress in the north and confirmed its claim to be the new orthodoxy.

For Confucian scholars the Mongol conquest presented a dilemma which could never be resolved. Should they accept foreign conquest and utilise their skills to moderate the effect of Mongol rule? Or should they withdraw from government and retreat into the world of scholarly activity? Two famous examples illustrate these opposing responses. On the one hand Xu Heng (1209–81), Khubilai's chancellor at the Imperial College, and a leading intellectual figure in his day, chose to play an active role. His main intellectual contribution was to promote the Neo-Confucian text known as the Xiaoxue, the Elementary Learning, which was concerned with the moral education of the young, which he said should start with the performance of simple tasks like cleaning the floor. He served the Mongols because this accorded with his sense of Confucian duty which overrode any loyalist claim that the Mongols did not have the mandate of heaven.[23] The figure cited to represent the opposite reaction was Liu Yin (1249–83), who refused to take office under Mongol rule. Liu Yin was also a distinguished scholar who, in 1291, had been invited to become an academician of the Imperial College. He refused, alleging ill-health, and as he died only two years later this may have been the true reason. However the motive for his refusal has become a matter of dispute. An apocryphal story relates how in 1260 Xu Heng visited the 11-year old Liu Yin and was criticised by him for his decision to serve the Mongols. Defending himself, Xu Heng said that if Confucian scholars were not prepared to serve the invaders, the Confucian way 'could not prevail'. When, twenty years later, Liu Yin refused office, he supposedly said that if Confucian scholars did not decline to serve the way 'would not be respected'. Liu Yin's response has been seen as a veiled protest against Mongol rule and has been described as an outstanding example of 'Confucian eremitism', a withdrawal of the scholar from the world of affairs to that of self-realisation.[24]

Another matter of dispute relating to the attitude towards Mongol rule has arisen in the field of drama. In this period the play became firmly established as a literary form. At least 700 plays – or 'mixed entertainment', because they included singing, music and dancing – were written under the Yuan, and of these at least 150 have survived. They are known collectively as the 'Yuan northern drama' as many were written for performance in Beijing, although drama also flourished in Hangzhou and in other cities. Dramatic performances were very popular and a number of cities had theatrical districts which might contain a score of theatres. The plays have remained in performance in China, and Beijing opera is descended from them. Many of the plays have been translated into western languages, and one of them, translated under the title 'The Orphan of Chao' was adapted by Voltaire and performed at his theatre at Ferney.

The dispute concerns the significance of this development. In the past the argument has been put forward that the plays were the product of the frustrated energies of Chinese scholars. Being deprived under the Mongols of access to their natural environment, that of government service, some abandoned the world, turned to scholarly pursuits and became recluses. Others abandoned the world in a different sense, plunging into an unfamiliar environment, that of city life, where they exercised their talents to raise a limited folk art to the status of literature. However, their motives were not entirely escapist, for the argument continues by identifying in the new drama expressions of resentment of Mongol rule. If such political criticism was being expressed, this was ironic, for it was Mongol patronage which sustained the new theatre and it was allegedly for the Mongols' benefit that the new drama was written in the vernacular, they being unable to understand classical Chinese.

This interpretation has not stood up well to recent investigation. It is now clear that Yuan drama did not emerge as a response to the effects of the Mongol invasion, but was the outcome of a long theatrical development. There is some evidence to show that literati interest in writing for the theatre increased under the Yuan and that there was a degree of collaboration between actors and playwrights in the production of new plays. This development, however, was related to the changing role of the writer. The Yuan period saw not only an efflorescence of dramatic literature, but also a notable advance in fiction, the common element being that both forms of literature were written in the vernacular. The suggestion that Yuan drama 'was to be the weapon of the conquered'[25] is even harder to sustain. The texts themselves rarely contain any direct political allusions and these may have been added in later editions. Moreover, in the past the literati had found in the standard poetic forms ample opportunity to express their feelings.[26]

China's Contact with the Outside World in the Yuan Period

During the thirteenth century the *pax mongolica* permitted travellers for the first time to move safely between China, western Asia and Europe. At the same time the Mongol rulers encouraged the settlement in China of foreigners, in particular western Asians. Their heavy reliance on foreign advisers diverted some of the Chinese animosity away from the Mongols and towards the incomers.

All Muslims in China were grouped as *semu*, and treated as a separate class with special privileges. Many were merchants and those who assisted the government did so mainly because of their financial abilities. Others were experts in fields as diverse as astronomy, medicine, armaments and architecture. The financial experts in particular incurred the odium of the Chinese. Khubilai employed as his finance minister Ahmad, later denounced as the first of three villainous ministers of the dynasty for his oppressive taxation and nepotism. Under Khubilai the merchant associations known as *ortogh* were established in China. They financed the caravans which crossed the deserts to the West carrying Chinese silks and ceramics. In return they were given tax-farming privileges, which again excited Chinese hostility. Until the end of the Yuan dynasty Muslims continued to hold positions of importance at the Mongol court, though as the court became more sinicised greater trust was placed in Chinese advisers.[27]

Another dramatic consequence of the freedom of travel was the arrival of the first Europeans in China and the journeying of Chinese and others to the West. Three motives for these travels may be distinguished. Probably the most common, though the least recorded, was the desire for trade. A political motive can be discerned in the response to the rise of Islam and to the crusades, with both East and West looking for allies. Associated with this hope there was a third motive, that of proselytism. The first of these dramatic journeys was made by the famous Daoist priest Changchun who had an audience with Genghis khan at Kabul in 1222 and gained a privileged position for Daoism under Mongolian rule. The first European to reach the Mongol court at Karakorum was a Franciscan monk, John of Plano Carpini. He had been sent by Pope Innocent IV on a diplomatic mission to the Mongols and was present at the enthronement of Güyüg khan in 1246. He was followed by William of Rubruck, who reached Karakorum in 1253 and made an important record of the Mongol way of life.

It was at this point that the Polo family made its enterprising journeys. The brothers Maffeo and Niccolo, both Venetian merchants, reached Khanbalik in 1262 and were received by Khubilai khan. When they went back to Europe four years later it was with a request from Khubilai that they returned with 'up to a hundred men learned in the Christian religion, well versed in the seven arts, and skilled to argue and demonstrate plainly to idolaters . . . that their religion is utterly mistaken'.[28] They returned to China in 1271, without the scholars, but with Niccolo's son Marco, and remained for the next twenty years in the East. Marco Polo's *Travels* gave a lively impression of Cathay, as north China was known to Europeans at the time, and of Khubilai's court. He described Hangzhou, or as he termed it 'the splendid city of Kinsai' in words which indicated that it far surpassed his native Venice. His accounts are full of superlatives and doubts have been raised about their reliability, there even being speculation whether he actually reached China. It is certainly surprising that he did not remark upon Chinese writing, nor upon the habit of drinking tea. Nevertheless there is sufficient independent evidence to show that he was in China during the reign of Khubilai, although he may not have visited all the places he described.[29] In the meantime the first recorded journey to Europe of a person born in China took place. In 1287 Rabban Sauma, a Turk born in China, reached Naples and then travelled to Paris where he was greeted by the French king Philip IV and went on to Bordeaux where he met Edward I, King of England.[30]

The Franciscan mission to China was continued by Friar John of Montecorvino, who reached China by sea and arrived at Khanbalik in 1295. There he established a mission and made some converts, although he found himself competing with the Nestorians for the court's favour. After twelve years he was made archbishop of Khanbalik and his mission survived into the second half of the fourteenth century. Another Franciscan, Friar Odoric of Pordenone, spent time in Guangzhou and in Khanbalik and left a travel narrative which described those features of Chinese life which later became the stereotype of western concepts of China. Another interesting record was left by Ibn Batuta, who had been born in Tangier and travelled widely, reaching China near the end of the Yuan period.

The Decline and Expulsion of the Yuan Dynasty

Explanations of why the Yuan dynasty came to an end have most commonly been expressed from the perspective of China and have tended to emphasise the dynastic decline of the Yuan and the strength of Chinese resentment of the Mongol presence, culminating in the expulsion of the invaders. From what has already been said it will be clear that the degree of sinicisation of the Mongols and the strength of Chinese resentment of their presence are matters difficult to quantify. Nevertheless, despite the efforts of Khubilai and Ayurbarwada to claim legitimacy as Chinese emperors, despite the substantial adoption of Chinese bureaucratic traditions, despite the co-operation, at least to a degree, of Chinese in government, the Mongol court and the Mongol nobility remained alien to the Chinese and were bound to fail as rulers. Behind that failure other changes were taking place, of which three in particular will be discussed.

The first is the undeniable evidence of the declining ability of the Mongol rulers. The murderous intrigues which beset the court were matched by a fragmented and increasingly ineffective administration. Toghon Temür, the last Yuan emperor, showed little aptitude for rule. He relied heavily on chief councillors and the last effective Mongol administrator, Toghto, was dismissed in 1354, an action which precipitated the disintegration of the government.

A second important reason for the Mongol withdrawal was their loss of military advantage. The Mongol position had been achieved by military conquest and, notwithstanding the efforts made to present themselves as legitimate Chinese rulers, had been maintained by military power. After the conquest a complex process took place involving the reorganisation of the Mongol forces and the absorption of the Chinese armies. Out of this emerged four main military formations: the Mongol army; the Mongol forces of the five clans used to garrison conquered areas; the Han army composed of Chinese and non-Chinese, including Qidan, from north China; and the Newly-adhered armies composed of Chinese from the south. Although the Mongols did make use of conscription, for the most part the rank and file of these units were drawn from hereditary military households. These households (apart from the Newly-adhered forces) were given grants of land and were supposedly self-sustaining. Many military households had the services of slaves, sometimes former war captives, and received tax exemptions. In return Chinese military households were expected to provide one soldier for service, whereas in Mongol households there was nearly universal conscription of males. The officer class was treated separately and has been described as a 'self-perpetuating salaried aristocracy'. Officers were members of the Chinese imperial bureaucracy and were paid a salary according to their rank. This position they could pass on to their sons.[31]

It is clear that the Mongol military system deteriorated fairly quickly. A fundamental weakness lay in the inadequate funding of the military households. The Mongol military households, which should have been the core of the Mongol system, were ill-equipped to sustain themselves by farming. The sons of the households were conscripted and their labour force, that is to say their slaves, frequently fled. By the 1290s there were many records of impoverishment, including an extraordinary decree of 1291 which forbade the exportation of Mongolian men and women as slaves to India and Islamic countries. Military standards fell and evidence suggests that intermarriage with Chinese was common. By the end of the dynasty Mongol military families were probably 'not much different from poor Chinese peasants'. Moreover, the garrison system, which had been created to repress internal disturbances had been allowed to decay. In Kublai's reign it had been effective in quelling frequent disturbances, but by the 1340s this capacity had completely disappeared.[32]

A third significant issue concerns the character of the rebellions which became increasingly frequent from the 1330s and which were eventually to overwhelm the dynasty. The most important of these are known as the Red Turban rebellions, after the characteristic headdress of the adherents. These rebellions had a common origin in religious sectarianism and the Red Turban movement was supposedly founded by Peng Yingyu who had transformed the Maitreya cult of the White Lotus sect into an ideology of rebellion.

In the 1340s manifestations of the Red Turban movement sprang up in several places in the Huai region and subsequently elsewhere. By the 1350s two main wings of the movement had appeared, one on the middle Yangzi and the other in the Huai valley. In 1351 the latter wing profited from the unrest caused by the massive conscription of labour to re-route the Yellow river. Some of these uprisings were clearly messianic, following the White Lotus tradition and announcing the imminent coming of the Maitreya Buddha. Others were more obviously class-based and were directed against landlords and officials. The rebels themselves were referred to as 'shiftless elements', and included bandits, idlers, salt smugglers and of course peasants, who were described as deluded. Although this was a great popular rebellion it lacked effective leadership and clear political objectives. These weaknesses enabled the Yuan government to follow the traditional pattern and to allow the gentry to raise peasant militia forces, a stratagem which by 1354 had largely pacified the region.[33] But then a second round of disturbances began, in which various surviving rebel leaders contended for power, and sought allies among local gentry militia leaders. The most successful exponent of this stratagem was Zhu Yuanzhang, who in 1368 was to ascend the throne as first emperor of the Ming dynasty.

This complex sequence of events has been subject to Marxist interpretations and rebuttals. The earlier rebellions have been described as class wars directed against the landlord class, but the later rebellions have been identified as a national struggle against the Mongols with the rebels, in particular Zhu Yuanzhang, deserting their class and siding with the landlords to expel the foreigners. The claim that the rebellions were motivated by ethnic or nationalist feeling is difficult to sustain. Rebel ideology made little if any reference to it, and it has been pointed out that Zhu Yuanzhang made use of defecting Mongols and even ennobled Mongols who gave him meritorious service.[34]

The Impact of the Mongol Occupation of China

Before concluding this discussion of the Mongol dynasty a further word should be said on the impact that this event had on the development of China. As indicated earlier, the traditional emphasis has been to speak dismissively of the whole episode and to define its impact in entirely negative terms. It is clear however that this was a period in which important developments took place, among them being the rise of literature and drama using the colloquial language.

This point may be supported by citing two other changes which were of importance for China's future development. The first of these concerns the military establishment. Up to the Yuan period, for much of the previous one thousand years, the military system considered as the norm was the conscript army, this conforming to the classical ideal expressed in the phrase 'the union of the soldiery and the peasantry'. This system, which could only work effectively under a strong and efficient government, had been abandoned by the Tang, and the late Tang and Song governments had relied instead on mercenaries. This had imposed an immense financial burden on the state. The arrival of the dynasties of conquest introduced a new principle of military organisation, that of hereditary military families. This principle was to be adopted by both the Ming and the Qing and played a part in ensuring dynastic strength and encouraging despotic tendencies.[35]

Another example of a long-standing influence can be found in the development of the Chinese legal tradition under the Mongols. Later Chinese scholars were inclined to speak contemptuously of the legal codes drawn up under the Yuan. A Qing scholar wrote of the Institutions of the Yuan Dynasty that it was 'minute, rustic and confusing'. Nevertheless it can be shown that under the influence of Mongol customary law, important legal innovations occurred which were retained by later dynasties. One example of this is the use of supplemental penalties, that is to say penalties additional to, or alternative to, the substantive punishment prescribed for the offence. These penalties might be financial, for example the requirement to pay 'nourishment expenses' while the injured person was being treated, or they might be physical, the imposition of retaliatory punishment on certain classes of wrongdoers.[36]

11
The Ming Dynasty

The Ming dynasty extended from 1368 to 1644. Its founder, Zhu Yuanzhang, reigned as the Hongwu emperor until 1398. He was succeeded by his grandson, but in 1403 the throne was usurped by his fourth son, who ruled as the Yongle emperor from 1403 to 1424. These two reigns are seen as the period of the dynasty's greatest vigour, for this was the age of the oceanic voyages and of achievement in various fields. There followed a long period of slow decline in terms of effective government. In the latter half of the sixteenth century there was a period of reform, but under the Wanli emperor and subsequent rulers the pace of decline quickened. The dynasty proved incapable of meeting challenges from within and without and in 1644 was overthrown by peasant rebellion and replaced by the Manchu Qing dynasty. In the south the Southern Ming survived until 1662, when the last emperor of the dynasty, who had fled to Burma, was captured and put to death.

The Founding of the Dynasty

Edward Dreyer traced the origins of the Ming dynasty back to the 1350s and to 'an obscure band of dislocated soldiers'.[1] The founder of the dynasty, Zhu Yuanzhang, had been born of a very poor family near Fengyang in modern Anhui. Both his parents died in a famine and Zhu entered a Buddhist monastery as a novice. Later he resorted to begging. In 1352, when he was twenty-five, he joined the Red Turban rebels led by Guo Zixing. Zhu showed military ability and also became connected to Guo by marriage. Zhu began to gather his own circle of advisers and administrators and this support, in addition to his military following, enabled him to achieve a degree of independence. From 1355 he offered allegiance to the rebellion headed by Han Liner, the leader of a rebel group, who had declared himself emperor of a restored Song dynasty. In the meantime Zhu developed his own base at Nanjing which he had captured in 1356. A key feature of his strategy was to fuse together his military machine and the support of local gentry.[2] He also fostered a reputation for having a concern for the condition of the people and went out of his way to establish good relations with eminent scholars.[3]

By 1360 the key struggle for power was centred on the Yangzi valley, which was divided between three regimes, the Ming,[4] the Han and the Wu. Zhu Yuanzhang's main rival Chen Youliang, another former Red Turban rebel, had proclaimed himself emperor of the Han dynasty. The principal battles of what has become known as the Ming-Han war took place between 1360 and 1363. The sequence began with the Han, who had a strong naval force, sailing down the Yangzi and seizing the important city of Taiping. They then moved on to attack Nanjing, the Ming capital, but suffered a serious defeat, with the loss of a considerable number of ships. It was now the Ming leaders' turn to go on the offensive and in September 1361 the Ming fleet sailed upriver, achieved a naval victory and obtained the surrender of Jiujiang. Chen Youliang retreated upriver, and Zhu Yuanzhang, aware of the danger of being absent from Nanjing for a long time, was forced to return to his base. In 1363 the final, famous battle took place on Lake Poyang. By this time the Han had built a new fleet, their ships were large three-decked galleasses with iron-sheathed turrets for archers and sterns high enough to overtower city walls. The Ming fleet was composed of smaller, but more numerous ships. A four-day battle on the lake, in which the Ming used fireships effectively, weakened but did not destroy the Han fleet. However, it was now trapped in the lake and when it tried to break out it was annihilated and in that same action Chen Youliang was killed.[5]

The way was now open for Zhu Yuanzhang to exploit the situation he had created. Between 1365 and 1367 he defeated the Wu regime, the key campaign being the siege and capture of Suzhou. There now remained the final settlement with the Yuan government, which by this time had influence only in the area around Beijing. Late in 1367 Zhu Yuanzhang dispatched expeditions to the north and to the south. So confident was he of their success that in January 1368 he formally ascended to the imperial throne. Such confidence was not misplaced, for the southern expedition quickly brought the south under Ming rule and the northern expedition captured Beijing, the Yuan court fleeing to Inner Mongolia.

The Establishment of the Dynasty: the Reign of Hongwu, 1368–98

The new emperor, who took the reign name of Hongwu, had a choice of three traditions on which to model his empire. The first was implicit in the name chosen for the dynasty, *ming*, signifying 'bright' or 'brightening', which might be taken as a reference to Manichaeism, or to Maitreyan Buddhism, with which the successful rebellion had previously been associated. However it was soon clear that the emperor no longer had any sympathy for sectarian religion. The second choice was to aspire to recreate the Confucian empire of previous Chinese dynasties. Although Hongwu was prepared to play that role, he was always to treat Confucian officials with deep suspicion. The third choice was the obvious one, but it was also the one which traditional historiography has denied to be the one Hongwu pursued. It was to rule according to the precedent set by the Yuan dynasty. It has been argued that in virtually every essential field, in government institutions and in social and military organisation, the first emperor of the Ming followed practices employed by and often initiated by the Mongols.[6]

His first task was to obtain the military security of the empire and this meant striking at the Mongol court which he did successfully in 1370. The next target was the Yuan loyalist Kökö Temür, who, in the final years of the Yuan dynasty, had been a regional powerholder in the area around Taiyuan, but with Hongwu's victory had been forced to move north. In 1372 a large expeditionary force was sent across the Gobi desert to Karakorum to deal with him. After an initial victory it suffered a disastrous reverse. Kökö Temür died in 1375, but the threat from the Mongols continued until 1388, when Lan Yu crossed the Gobi and achieved a major victory which fragmented the Mongol leadership and ended the Mongol threat for a generation. Meanwhile campaigns were conducted against independent regimes in the south-west and by 1390 the modern provinces of Sichuan and Yunnan had been brought firmly under Ming control.

Such extensive military operations demanded an effective military establishment. Hongwu recognised the need to develop a system which did not ruin the economy, which provided for the demobilisation of troops and which offered adequate rewards to his generals. The solution he arrived at was clearly derived from the precedent set by the Yuan. Known as the *weiso* system, literally 'guards' and 'battalions', it evolved from the military units which had surrendered to the Ming on the establishment of the dynasty. Their leaders had been assured that their commands would be made permanent and that their units would be kept intact. The consequence was the hereditary succession of military commanders. As their soldiers could not be disbanded, it was necessary to provide for their upkeep, and this was achieved by making the armies self-sufficient through the military colony system. The first generals included the 'dislocated soldiers' who had joined Zhu Yuanzhang before 1355. Later generals were awarded noble titles and stipends. Important though this military establishment was, it was clearly subject to imperial control, and from about 1372 its influence was overtaken by that of the civil government.[7]

In its early stages the Ming system of government also owed much to the Yuan precedent. At central government level the emperor retained the secretariat, with its two chief councillors or prime ministers, and the subordinate six ministries which carried out routine administration. At what was to become the provincial level he retained the branch secretariats, although in 1376 he added military and surveillance agencies alongside them to ensure control. A civil service was created to staff these positions, although initially only in 1373 was the examination system used to select candidates.

The period of consolidation came to an abrupt end in 1380 when Hu Weiyong, the senior chief councillor, was put on trial for plotting to assassinate the emperor and to overthrow the dynasty. The charges were almost certainly fabricated, but they illustrate Hongwu's fear of any challenge to his authority. For his supposed crimes Hu Weiyong was executed and perhaps 15,000 others put to death. The secretariat and the office of chief councillor were abolished and henceforth Hongwu resorted to direct rule. In his attempt to keep all affairs of state under his personal supervision, he undertook an immense administrative burden. It was recorded that in one ten-day period towards the end of his reign he received 1,660 documents relating to 3,391 matters which required an imperial decision.[8] At the same time he maintained a punishing schedule of audiences, which kept him in touch with his officials although he did not leave the capital Nanjing.

In the latter part of his reign Hongwu introduced measures which were to have a marked influence on the developing character of the imperial system of government. On his orders a comprehensive overhaul of the land and tax system was inaugurated. Population statistics were entered in the Yellow Registers and the ownership of land was recorded on the Fish-scale Charts and Registers (so called because the topographical charts resembled fish skin in appearance).[9] Alongside these registers, two other systems were introduced to allocate responsibility for tax payment: under the 'tax-captain system' wealthy families were made responsible for the collection of taxes in their area, and under the lijia system peasant households were organised into groups of ten families which were mutually responsible for the payment of taxes and the performance of labour services. The compilation of these registers required an immense effort and provided an unprecedentedly detailed set of statistics, but the records were not updated accurately after Hongwu's death. It may be that the effort was misplaced for another reason. The level of land tax was relatively low, which limited the government's potential revenue and its ability to promote economic improvement.[10]

The second example of Hongwu's intervention concerned the examination system. In 1384 the examinations were revived and thereafter were held at regular intervals. At the same time, throughout the empire, there was an expansion of the government schools which enabled talented young men to compete for office. The curriculum they studied was based on the Confucian classics. In this way a Confucian civil bureaucracy, which was to remain a feature of the empire for the next six hundred years, was created. It must not be supposed, however, that Hongwu intended that these measures should encourage any challenge to his autocracy. This bureaucracy was created to carry out his instructions, not to initiate policy.

Hongwu died in 1398 after a short illness. His personality and the achievements of his reign have long been the subject of debate. There can be few comparable cases of a person of so humble a background and so lacking in prepossessiveness – he had a high forehead, thick nose and protruding jaw – achieving so exalted a position and leaving so distinctive a legacy. On the negative side he has been denounced for having betrayed his social class by relying on the support of the landlords and gentry. He has been accused of paranoia for his distrust of any person he thought opposed to him. On occasions he sank to depths of vindictiveness and cruelty, none worse than the purge he ordered in 1393 after he had executed Lan Yu, one of his foremost generals. On the positive side, he established the most durable dynasty in Chinese history and laid the foundations for what was later to be defined as the requirements of good government.

The Reign of Yongle, 1402–24

Hongwu was succeeded by his grandson, who in a short reign as the Jianwen emperor tried to rule with the support of Confucian officials and attempted to break the power of the princes who had been granted fiefs by his grandfather. In this he achieved some degree of success, but he was finally defeated by one of those princes, his uncle the Prince of Yen, and reportedly died in a fire at the imperial palace. His uncle thereupon took the throne and was subsequently given the reign name of Yongle.

Yongle proved to be the epitome of the strong second emperor of a dynasty. He began his reign by reducing the bodyguards of the surviving princes and transferring the princes themselves to strategically less important regions. This averted the danger of a challenge to the throne from a member of the imperial clan. He reorganised the machinery of central government, ostensibly to restore the practices of his father which he declared had been disregarded by his predecessor. In fact he introduced a grand secretariat, a revised version of the body which his father had angrily dismissed in 1380. To this secretariat were appointed seven grand secretaries, all with impeccable Confucian backgrounds. A feature of his reign was the long tenure of office enjoyed by his senior officials and this ensured a degree of political stability. A more sinister method of protecting his position was achieved through using the the imperial bodyguard to investigate suspected cases of opposition, a role which was also performed by the palace eunuchs.

Through these reforms he ensured the safety of the throne, and this permitted him to concentrate on military security and expansion, with particular reference to the northern frontier, his own main power base. It was this concern which lay behind the decision to transfer the capital from Nanjing to Beijing, a process commenced in 1402 but only completed in 1421. It involved a massive movement of workmen to the site of the new capital and a major task of constructing new buildings. The Forbidden City of today retains the layout as determined by Yongle, and the Hall of Supreme Harmony stands where the emperor sat enthroned on important state occasions, at the symbolic centre of the capital and of the empire. To supply Beijing it was necessary to accomplish another major task, the restoration of the Grand Canal, which was completed by 1415.[11]

In the meantime Yongle had turned his attention to frontier affairs. At the beginning of his reign the imminent threat came from the Mongol ruler known in the West as Tamerlane, who in the late fourteenth century had established a mighty empire in central Asia and who, in 1404, advanced on China only to die before he had effected an invasion. To the north-east, in what is now Jilin and Inner Mongolia, the Jurchen and Urianghad were persuaded to accept Chinese overlordship by the award of titles and the presentation of gifts. Further west along the frontier were the Mongol tribes now known as the Oirat and the Tatar, the latter including the remnants of the Yuan forces. It was against these that Yongle decided to make a demonstration of China's military power. Five times, between 1410 and 1424, he personally led expeditions across the desert to chastise them. Each expedition required an extraordinary commitment of men and material and involved considerable hardship: the emperor himself died when he returned from the fifth expedition. No major victory was achieved despite this massive expenditure of effort, but the campaigns did ensure that the Mongols would remain divided and unable to threaten China for a generation.[12] Such an outcome was more beneficial than the result of the intervention in

Annam in 1407. A Chinese force, sent to there to restore the person believed to be the true claimant to the Annamese throne, was ambushed and the pretender killed. In retaliation Yongle sent two large armies which overran Annam, but he then rashly decided to make the country a province of China. Rebellion against the Chinese presence broke out in 1418 and China was forced to withdraw in 1427–8.

The most spectacular of Yongle's foreign initiatives was the dispatch of the famous oceanic expeditions. The motives behind these have never been entirely clear. A legend ascribes them to a search for his predecessor the Jianwen emperor, who, it was said, had not died in Nanjing but, disguised as a monk, had fled overseas. A more plausible reason was Yongle's desire to enhance his reputation and his claim to legitimacy – for it could not be forgotten that he was an usurper – by securing tributary relations with a large number of states. Another possible motive was that of commercial advantage, prompted in particular by the conquests of Tamerlane which had cut the continental silk route. From 1405 onwards seven maritime expeditions were sent out, six of them in the Yongle period. Most of these were headed by the grand eunuch Zheng He and they were very substantial affairs, the first expedition, according to the record, comprising 317 ships and 27,870 men.[13] In the course of these voyages Zheng He himself reached Hormuz and detachments from the fleets followed the African coast as far south as Malindi and also reached Jidda. The account of the voyages was written by Ma Huan, his interpreter, who was a Muslim and was probably among the group which visited Mecca. Ma Huan made a careful record of the products of the countries visited and the customs of the peoples who lived in them, noting for example the practice of *suttee* on Java and the skill of the jewellers of Aden.

As there is some doubt about why the expeditions were sent, so too is there debate about why they were suspended. One probable reason is that the voyages were closely connected with Yongle's political agenda, and after his death the motivation of seeking recognition no longer applied. The issue of cost and economic benefit is difficult to determine, for the expeditions were financed by eunuch agencies and no record was made of profit and loss. However, Yongle's construction of a new capital, his campaigns in Mongolia, and other costly projects did draw criticism from officials and did lead to retrenchment immediately after his death.[14] The discontinuation of these voyages was to have a significant long-term effect. In the Yongle reign China held an unrivalled position as the leading commercial power throughout Asia and as the leading naval power in the Indian Ocean as far as the African coast. This advantage was to be surrendered on the eve of the western penetration of the Indian Ocean and China was to retire into semi-isolation.

The Middle Years of the Ming Dynasty: Foreign Relations

A striking feature of the Ming period is the contrast between the aggressive, expansionist policies pursued by the early emperors and the passive, defensive policies followed by their successors. An indication, and perhaps an explanation, of this change can be found in the events of the reign of Zhengtong emperor, who came to the throne as a minor in 1436. At that time the dominant group among the Mongols were the Oirat, who had developed an important trade with China by providing horses in exchange for tea. In the 1440s a new Oirat leader, Esen, had unified the Mongol tribes and had begun to encroach on Chinese territory. Early in Zhengtong's reign the most powerful influence at the Ming court was the chief eunuch Wang Zhen and his self-seeking influence is suspected in what was to follow. In 1448 an Oirat tribute mission to the Ming court was treated discourteously. Esen's response was to launch a major attack on the important market town of Datong to the north-east of Beijing. This prompted Zhengtong, perhaps on the advice of Wang Zhen, to take the extraordinarily risky step of placing himself at the head of the army which was to advance against Esen. Commanding a force of perhaps half a million men, he set out on what was intended to be a short and glorious campaign. Instead his forces were first ambushed and then surrounded by the Mongols at Tumu, some seventy miles north-west of Beijing. The army was destroyed, the senior officers and officials were killed, vast quantities of booty were seized, and the emperor was led off into captivity. In Beijing opposing views were put forward on what to do, with one suggestion being that the capital should be abandoned. To this Yu Qian, the vice-minister of war, reportedly replied:

> Those talking about moving south should be beheaded. The capital is the foundation of the empire. Once you move it the empire is lost.
> Don't you know what happened to the Song after it moved south?[15]

For his determined response, which ensured that Beijing did not fall, Yu Qian was to become a symbol of national resistance and popular hero of opera. His stand has been seen as marking the end of a characteristic feature of the early Ming period, the dominance of an élite of hereditary military officers. This dominance had already been eroded, but the disgrace of the fiasco at Tumu allowed Yu Qian to assume leadership. Through the rest of the imperial period the civil bureaucracy was to retain this superiority over the military command.[16]

The Tumu incident had other important consequences. In Beijing the decision was taken not to await the outcome of the attempt to ransom the emperor, but instead, in defiance of tradition, to place the emperor's half-brother on the throne. The new emperor, who assumed the reign name of Jingtai, took vigorous steps to stabilise the government and to deal with the Mongol threat. The deposed emperor was released, but kept away from all political power. For a time, the recent disaster united the court and encouraged a mood of reform. But then factional struggles resumed, often connected with the former emperor. In 1457, at a time when Jingtai was ill, a swift coup d'état placed the former emperor back on the throne. There followed a period of violent settlement of scores. Yu Qian, held largely responsible for the deposition, was condemned to death for treason. The purge weakened the government and left the restored emperor and later Ming emperors very much in the hands of factions of eunuchs and officials.

Another consequence of the Tumu disaster related to frontier defence. Although the fiasco had occurred because of one foolish decision, the danger from the Oirat derived from a deeper cause. A crucial element in the balance of power between the settled territory of China and the society of the steppe was the control of the steppe transition zone. Hongwu, recognising this, had not only campaigned against the Mongols, but had also established a defence line comprising eight outer garrisons to maintain control of the Ordos region. For reasons which are not clear, Yongle abandoned these garrisons and thus relinquished Chinese control of the steppe transition zone. At about the same time the shortcomings of the *weiso* system, which could not produce enough trained and mounted soldiers for defence, had started to emerge. The Tumu disaster, which destroyed the dynasty's military prestige, also forced the adoption of a defensive strategy.[17] In the next twenty years many suggestions were put forward on how the Ordos region, now increasingly occupied by Mongols, might be recovered. It was conceded that to mount a major campaign against them would be enormously expensive and would impose an unacceptable burden on the local population. In 1472 Wang Yue, one of the ablest generals of the day, gained an important victory over the Mongols near Red Salt Lake. Two years later, using the respite so gained, Yu Zijun, an official with long experience of working in the area, commenced the project he had long recommended, the construction of a wall which ran for 566 miles from north-eastern Shaanxi to north-western Ningxia. Together with a shorter wall constructed by Wang Yue these fortifications created a barrier which cut the Ordos off from the south. This was the beginning of the Great Wall as it is known today. Although not recognised at the time, its construction marked a decisive shift in strategy towards the nomadic societies of the steppe. The wall was a defensive construction. Its building implied a policy of exclusion, which repudiated previous attempts to establish working relations with the nomads through the promotion of trade and diplomacy.[18]

Ming Absolutism

The phrases 'Ming absolutism' and 'Ming despotism' are used to refer to the unchecked growth of imperial power from the late fourteenth century. Absolutism refers to the development of institutions which enhanced imperial power, whereas despotism may also imply the abuse of power by an individual ruler. Monarchical absolutism was implicit in the doctrine of the mandate of heaven, but early emperors had had any absolutist tendencies limited by the presence of an aristocracy. With the decline of the aristocracy and the increased reliance on a civil bureaucracy, the potential for absolutism increased, but it was moderated by the Confucian concept of an ideal ruler who emphasised benevolence and righteousness. Under the Song, absolutist tendencies had been encouraged by two developments: on the one hand reformers like Wang Anshi promoted the idea that, to meet the crisis which they believed threatened the state, the legal and fiscal powers of central government should be increased; on the other hand the opponents of the reformers, like Sima Guang, rejected practical reform but promoted the exaltation of the ruler.[19]

Dynasties of conquest, which derived from the tribal society of the steppe, continued to rely on tribal chieftains for their support, and as a consequence were not in themselves absolute. However, it is commonly alleged that the Yuan dynasty, because of its indifference to Chinese values and to Chinese standards of government, and because of its neglect of the civil bureaucracy, encouraged the tendency towards absolutism. Hongwu's decision in 1380 to abolish the secretariat and the office of chief councillor has been regarded as an important step along that same road. The emperor was also a despot, carrying out pogroms, operating a secret police organisation, known as the Brocade Uniform Guard, and instituting a literary inquisition to search out any written slights cast on the ruler.

A discussion of Ming absolutism is not complete without reference to the role of the eunuchs, often seen as the sinister agents of imperial despotism. Eunuchs had been employed at court from as early as the eighth century BC. As no uncastrated male was permitted to enter the imperial palace, eunuchs had exceptional opportunities to ingratiate themselves with emperors, or even more commonly to ally themselves with empresses and consorts, in a common front against the bureaucrats, who despised the eunuchs for lack of breeding and education. Eunuchs had played an important role in court politics in the late Tang period, but their influence had declined under the Song. Although many eunuchs served at the Yuan court they exerted little influence on the emperor. When Hongwu came to the throne, being aware that eunuchs in the past had meddled in politics, he issued an edict restricting them to household tasks. In 1384 he had an iron tablet engraved with the inscription 'Eunuchs are forbidden to interfere with government affairs. Those who attempt to do so will be subjected to capital punishment.'[20] However Yongle, who had gained the throne with the assistance of the eunuchs, used them in important and confidential posts. Mention has already been made of the eunuch Zheng He's leadership of the maritime expeditions. A more sinister role was played by the Eastern Depot, the headquarters of the secret police in Beijing, which was controlled by the eunuchs and which reported solely to the emperor. Under Xuande (reigned 1426–35) another means of keeping the eunuchs under control was removed, in that the prohibition on eunuchs receiving a literary education was relaxed.[21]

The consequences of these changes was felt later in the dynasty, with the emergence of eunuch dictators. The first of these was Wang Zhen, whose disastrous encouragement of Zhengtong to attack the Oirat has already been noted. He had been one of the first eunuchs to attend the palace school for eunuchs and had been the emperor's first tutor. This enabled him to establish an ascendancy over the emperor. His appointment as head of the palace eunuch establishment, and hence of the Eastern Depot, gave him control of the Brocade Uniform Guard. Against such a system of influence senior bureaucrats could do little. This concentration of power recurred in later reigns when the emperor, either through incompetence, or through indifference to the duties of his office, allowed a eunuch dictator to emerge. In the middle years of the dynasty the most notorious instance of this occurred in the reign of Zhengde (r. 1506–21). The eunuch Liu Jin dominated the court and used the emperor's authority to extort money to cover the emperor's extravagances. He instituted a reign of terror against any officials who dared to oppose him and eventually incited a revolt. In 1510 he was charged with plotting to kill the emperor and to seize the throne, and for this he was put to death. An even more notorious case, indeed the most notorious case of eunuch dominance in Chinese history, occurred in the Tianqi reign (1621–7). The eunuch dictator Wei Zhongxian gained total control of the emperor and the government: the abuses which he encouraged and the brutal suppression of opposition which he practised were subsequently regarded as having played an important part in the decline and fall of the dynasty.

Absolutism implies the failure of the checks on the arbitrary use of power. In imperial China the formal agency for maintaining such checks was the censorial system, the functions of which were to maintain surveillance of government activities, to impeach or censure officials whose conduct had been exposed as unsatisfactory, and to make recommendations for change, which could include remonstrances directed against the conduct of emperor. This system was of great antiquity for it can be traced back to the Qin. It was strengthened during the Yuan period, although the duty of remonstrance was neglected, and it continued to be a standard and important branch of early Ming government. The censorate might be expected to challenge absolutism, if absolutism implied a departure from the principles of Confucian government. It has been shown that in the period 1424–34 the censorate was reformed, and that in routine matters it appeared to operate efficiently, although it failed to remonstrate with the emperor on matters of personal conduct and neglected to challenge the increase in eunuch power. However a century later, in the time of Wei Zhongxian, although the censorate was ostensibly still active, it appeared incapable of making an effective protest against the excesses of the eunuch dictator.[22]

A discussion of Ming absolutism, with its reference to abuses of power, emphasises negative aspects of Ming government. This is not a balanced judgment to make on the dynasty before its final decline. Despite occasional aberrations, imperial absolutism provided great stability and a quality of administration which was probably not matched by any other state in the world at that time. Moreover absolutism did not imply that there was no consultation in the decision-making process. One study of how Ming foreign policy decisions relating to war and peace were made concluded that, far from being taken in an arbitrary fashion by the emperor or by his favourite, decisions were only arrived at after many people had been consulted, and after long deliberations and careful calculations of the chances of success had taken place.[23]

Demographic, Economic and Fiscal Developments Under the Ming

As a result of Hongwu's policy of requiring the compilation of the Yellow Registers, the population statistics of the early Ming period are very full and probably fairly accurate. Allowing for under-registration, the population of China towards the end of the fourteenth century was probably somewhat over 65,000,000. Subsequently, because of various practices, including deliberate under-reporting and avoidance of registration, the system of population registration became obsolete. The official record showed the population in the late Ming as amounting to only 60,000,000 people. In fact by about 1600, after two centuries of comparative peace, the population had reached approximately 150,000,000. Although the data does not allow any close analysis of population distribution, it seems likely that in that period growth rates were higher in the south than in the north, although the population of the north, which had been decimated at the time of the Mongol invasions, had made a recovery.[24]

The main reasons why this linear growth of population had been possible were prolonged peace and an increase in the food supply. In the eleventh century early-ripening rice, which permitted double-cropping, was introduced from Champa and subsequently underwent further improvement. Under the Ming the sixty-day variety was gradually disseminated to Guangdong and Guangxi and then to other provinces. New crops, for example sorghum, known as the millet of the Sichuan basin, which had been introduced in or before the Yuan period, was now grown more extensively. In the sixteenth century sweet potato, maize and peanuts, all of which came from America, crops which could be grown in dry conditions, were brought to China. Accompanying these improvements in planting materials there were significant advances in farming methods including the extension of irrigation and the increased use of fertiliser.[25]

This reference to the dynamic changes in cropping patterns occurring over the centuries of Ming rule hints at the problem of making generalisations about economic change over so large an area and over so long a period. A recent study of Hunan has shown that at the beginning of the Ming period that province, which was to become a major rice-producing area, was only populated with any degree of density in the counties around the Dongting Lake. By 1582 the proportion of cultivated land had increased considerably and land clearance had spread along the tributaries which fed into the lake. Hunan was now known as a grain-exporting province, but it was still referred to as a place where 'grain is cheap, land is abundant, there are no people to cultivate it, and people do not set a high value on land.'[26] The experience of Hunan was repeated in other parts of the country. In the Ming period migration on a large scale took place to frontier regions, particularly to the west and south-west, to the north-west, and overseas to Taiwan. Much of this migration was the voluntary movement of families in search of better land, and is therefore unrecorded and difficult to estimate. However some migration was state sponsored. Hongwu, for example, had 150,000 families moved to the Huai region, his own birthplace. Yongle moved large numbers of artisans to Beijing to work on his new imperial capital.

The great majority of the population depended on agriculture and lived in the countryside. Nevertheless in the Ming period important industrial and commercial changes took place. One of these was the development of the cotton textile industry. Cotton had been introduced into China during the Tang dynasty and by the Ming period cotton production had spread over a very wide area. However it was only in Songjiang prefecture in the Yangzi delta that a cotton industry developed. This area was economically advanced and some technological transfer may have taken place from the silk industry of Suzhou. It has been suggested that the high level of land tax imposed on the region may have played a part in encouraging the switch away from agriculture to industrial production, although this is disputed. Cotton textile production had first developed as a means of supplementing household income and the whole process of production had been carried out in the household. By the fifteenth century a division of labour was being practised and a wide variety of cotton cloth was being produced. Spinning remained largely a rural activity, but weaving became a professionalised urban industry. Alvaro Semedo, a Portuguese Jesuit missionary living in Shanghai, estimated that in 1621 there were 200,000 looms operating in Shanghai and its administrative area. Gradual advances in the technology in use, increases in the supply of raw cotton and improvements in distribution enabled the increase in demand to be met and the price of cotton cloth to remain relatively stable. These factors, together with the continued availability of cheap labour, may explain why this important industry continued to grow in size but did not pass beyond the stage of handicraft-style production.[27]

In the Ming period the trend towards large-scale urbanisation, which had been noticeable in the Song and Yuan periods, may have slowed or even stopped. Instead, from the sixteenth century, the trend was the proliferation of smaller market towns. This type of development was very noticeable in the more advanced regions, for example around Shanghai. An important function of these towns was to provide a market close enough for spinners and weavers to make daily trips to obtain their raw materials and to trade their finished products. More generally the increase in market towns was a symptom of increasing trade, and the growth in the numbers and wealth of merchants.[28]

It is against this background that one should consider Ming policies relating to currency and taxation. Despite the overall growth of the economy, in many respects these policies were a continuation of the past. The Ming administration has been described as committed to preserving a 'village commodity economy', an outlook which made it reluctant to promote the advanced sectors of the economy, that is to say industrial development and foreign trade, and thus widen the economic gap between different parts of the empire. An example of this outlook can be found in the dynasty's failure to work out an effective monetary policy. The paper currency, which had been introduced under the Yuan with some degree of success, was under the Ming to cause long-term damage to government finances. Hongwu circulated paper currency in large quantities which provoked a serious monetary inflation and eventually the currency lost all commercial value. Copper cash, which for a time had been proscribed, returned to use, but the quantity minted was quite inadequate. Gradually bulk silver came to be used as a form of currency, the unit being the tael or ounce of silver, but this never became a proper coinage.

The main source of government revenue under the Ming, as under previous dynasties, was the land tax. The system under which it was levied was modified by Hongwu, who established tax quotas for each province and prefecture and who, in 1393, declared that the total quotas, amounting to 32,789,000 piculs of grain (a picul equalled 107.4 litres), should be regarded as fixed permanently. In addition the dynasty levied various requisitions on labour and basic commodities, most importantly on salt. It has long been supposed that these levies, even at the beginning of the dynasty, amounted to a heavy burden of taxation, and that by the end of the period they had become so oppressive that they played an important part in the Ming collapse. More recently it has been argued that the value of the taxes which actually reached the government, amounting to perhaps ten per cent of agrarian output, was in fact rather low. It was sufficient to pay the costs of a government which ran a self-sufficient army and which maintained only a thin veneer of administration, but it was quite inadequate to allow the government to play an active role in developing the economy, although no such policy would have been given serious consideration. However, although the official levels of taxation were relatively light, a whole array of additional impositions and forms of unauthorised taxation were added to the total tax bill and this burden fell disproportionately on those least able to pay. As a consequence tax evasion and tax arrears were serious problems.[29]

In the sixteenth century, beginning from 1531, a protracted attempt was made to revise the system of taxation. The measures taken became known as the Single-Whip reform, the term implying the combination of various levies into a single payment. In fact the reform covered four separate measures: the elimination of the service levy, that is to say the labour service imposed on adult males between the ages of sixteen and sixty, including services relating to the lijia system, which in effect became defunct; the simplification and amalgamation of land tax rates; the payment of the taxes in silver; and changes in the arrangements for the collection of taxes. The implications of these reforms are not easy to assess. They have been regarded as an extremely important turning point and as the beginning of the modern land tax system.[30] The requirement that taxes be paid in silver has been seen as accelerating the process of the monetisation of the economy and as sounding the death knell of whatever remained of the natural economy.[31] At one time Marxist historians maintained that the reforms had been beneficial to the poor, because they had relieved them of labour services. More recently the stress has been on the limitations of the reforms. These were never consolidated or applied consistently. Taxation was non-progressive and made no provision for destitution. It failed to take advantage of the growth of the economy and did not provide the government with a surplus which might have allowed it to invest. In fact, Ming financial administration was more concerned with maintaining political stability than with allowing the state to act as an agent of change and improvement. Its legacy was an attitude of complacency which prevented government in China from taking an active role in the economy until modern times.[32]

Social and Literary Changes in the Ming Period

The founder of the Ming dynasty set out to restore social stability and to that end he introduced a form of village government which was intended to promote harmony and to suppress disorder. Under the lijia system the entire population was divided into groups of one hundred and ten families. The ten most wealthy families represented the community to the local magistrate and carried out duties on his behalf. Community chiefs settled disputes and also relayed the moral exhortations of the emperor to the population. The remaining one hundred families were divided into ten groups of ten, and each group supplied a headman who organised the group in carrying out a variety of labour duties.[33]

In the Ming period there emerged fully the status group most commonly known in the west as the gentry. The term is used to translate the Chinese term *shenshi*, literally 'officials and scholars' and in its narrow definition it refers to those individuals who had obtained the formal educational qualifications to make them eligible for office. A broader definition of the gentry presents them as a class which owed its position to the possession of large landed estates, their wealth giving them access to education and thence to influence. The gentry was not a large group. One estimate put their numbers at the end of the Ming period at perhaps 2 per cent of population and at rather less than a quarter of a million families.[34]

A detailed survey of Tongcheng county in Anhui has provided an insight into the character of this élite. Tongcheng was a county of academic distinction, but the total number of persons with degrees of any kind amounted to only 1,800 out of a population of over 200,000. However these degree-holders belonged to the important families and lineage organisations of the county. Their families saw the obtaining of degrees not as an end in itself, but as a means of achieving office and exercising influence. In fact obtaining degrees and holding office were not the only means whereby lineages could exert influence. Some notable lineages owed their social position to organisation and corporate wealth and to systematic intermarriage with other powerful lineages. In these operations the ownership of land was a factor of considerable importance. It has been shown that the fortunes of the great families of Tongcheng county were originally based on land and that subsequently they went to great pains to protect and increase their estates. It has been suggested that the insecurity of basing a lineage's fortunes on examinations and office was an important factor in promoting lineage organisation and in particular the administration of a charitable estate for the support of the lineage. Tongcheng's important lineages were established by the middle or late Ming period and there was little evidence of subsequent upward, or indeed of subsequent downward movement.[35]

The evidence of Tongcheng county leads to a reappraisal of two views on gentry status and social mobility. The first is the argument put forward by Chang Chung-li that gentry income came largely from gentry status rather than from the ownership of land. He suggested that, in the nineteenth century, 'The gentry's control of Chinese society, including its economic aspects, was not dependent on landowning. . . . A gentry member was not necessarily a landlord, nor was a landlord necessarily a member of the gentry.'[36]

The second view concerns social mobility into the élite. Ho Ping-ti, who wrote the best-known study on this topic, noted how Confucian ideology asserted that there should be equal educational opportunity for all. China's competitive civil service examination system seemed to be the perfect embodiment of that principle. He analysed the social composition of the 14,562 men who obtained the *jinshi* 'advanced scholar' degree between 1371 and 1904, placing them into three categories: candidates whose families during the three preceding generations had failed to produce a single holder of the *shengyuan*, the elementary degree; those who in the same period had produced a holder of the elementary degree, but no holder of a higher degree or of office; and those whose families had produced one or more holders of a higher degree or office. He found that in the Ming period 49.5 per cent of *jinshi* fell into the first two categories and 50.5 per cent into the third, whereas the figures for the same categories under the Qing were 37.6 per cent and 62.4 per cent. The most marked evidence of upward mobility came in the early Ming period, that is between 1371 and 1496, when 57.6 per cent of *jinshi* came from the first category. This he took as evidence of an unparalleled instance of upward social mobility in a major society prior to the industrial revolution.[37] However the case of Tongcheng suggests that in the early Ming, and indeed throughout the Ming-Qing period, class structure in the county was much more stable and less mobile than has been argued, and that the stability of the élite was based on the ownership of land.

A statistical analysis can give one a view of Ming society. A more vivid, if more subjective, impression may be obtained from contemporary literature. The Ming period was the time when colloquial fiction, in the form of short stories and novels, came into its own. These had their origin in the plot books used by storytellers and they give a vivid picture of life, particularly as it was lived by the inhabitants of the cities of the lower Yangzi. In the late Ming period collected editions of these stories were made, for example by Feng Menglong (1574–1646), a scholar and failed examination candidate who lived in Suzhou. One such story, entitled 'The Pearl-sewn Shirt', was typical of the genre in that it told of an illicit passion which nevertheless served as a moral tale. It concerned a woman named Fortune, whose husband was a travelling vendor. While he was absent on a journey she was seduced by a merchant who used the services of an old dame as a go-between. The affair was revealed when the pearl-sewn shirt of the title, which Fortune had given to her lover, was recognised by her husband. The story concluded rather improbably with a reconciliation between husband and wife. A notable feature of the story is its lively depiction of the female characters, above all that of the go-between, who like the Wife of Bath in Chaucer's *Canterbury Tales*, used confessions of her own youthful indiscretions to prompt a response from her audience.[38] Such tales may be contrasted with many other Ming stories and accounts which deal with female virtue, but which place the emphasis on a heroine dedicated to the Confucian virtues, who is prepared to undergo horrific ordeals in their defence. Ming local histories all contain biographies of virtuous women, and of the thirty-six thousand women so described, a third of them are recorded as having committed suicide, or being murdered, while resisting rape.[39]

Alongside the development of the short story came the emergence of the full-length novel. Of the four famous novels of the Ming period three evolved from earlier oral versions. The earliest extant printed version of *The Romance of the Three Kingdoms* was published in 1522, but handwritten copies of the novel, set in the turbulent last years of the Later Han dynasty, had been circulating long before this. The same was true of *Water Margin*, the tale of 108 outlaws in the days of the Northern Song, which had been in circulation for almost a century and a half before it was published in 1540 and then went through ten editions in the next century. The *Journey to the West*, known also as *Monkey*, was written down by Wu Cheng'en and published in 1592, but was based on earlier versions. It gave a highly fictionalised version of the travels to India of the Buddhist monk Xuan Zang. The fourth novel, an original work, the notorious *Jin Ping Mei*, was both pornographic and also the world's first realistic social novel.[40] Taken together these works have been described as the only great heritage of novels found in a premodern civilisation outside Europe.[41]

Foreign Contacts in the Later Ming Period

After the discontinuation of the oceanic voyages in 1436, the Ming dynasty had presented a defensive attitude towards the outside world. One aspect of this had been the restriction of foreign commerce to trade carried out by tribute missions; another had been the adoption of conciliatory policies in relations with the steppe nomads. However, these policies were to be subverted by developments in the middle of the sixteenth century.

To the north, the key development came in the early 1540s with the unification of the Mongols under Altan khan. He established his capital at Hohhot in what is now Inner Mongolia and began to employ Chinese in his administration. When his requests for the resumption of trade, which had been cut off in about 1500, were refused, he made a series of raids into China. This provoked an important clash at the Jiajing (r. 1522–66) emperor's court between the grand secretary Xia Yan, a reputedly upright official and Yan Song, his main rival, later to be castigated as a villain. In 1547 Xia Yan obtained the emperor's support for an ambitious plan to recover the Ordos area. However the following year the plan was suddenly abandoned and Xia Yan executed. The dispute left the court paralysed, which allowed Altan to make further successful raids, culminating in 1550 with a sortie to the walls of Beijing. Raiding continued for the next twenty years, and the Chinese response was a second major programme of wall construction. Finally, in 1571, an agreement was made with Altan which for the time being quietened the situation.[42]

A second border threat was eventually dealt with more effectively, although this was not to the credit of the court. From early in the sixteenth century raiders, often described as pirates although their objective was as much smuggling as piracy, had been making raids on the south-eastern coast of China. The official reaction to this was to prohibit overseas trade. From the 1540s Japanese smugglers began to trade with China, exchanging silver for Chinese silk. As the trade grew in importance, so did the disorder associated with it and in 1548 a piratical attack on Ningbo caused extensive damage. This was the first of a series of major raids in which cities were captured and looted and officials put to death. The marauders were commonly described as *wokou* or Japanese pirates. The situation only improved when a number of able commanders, the best-remembered being Qi Jiguang, developed new methods of combating the raiders. Rather than use soldiers from hereditary military families Qi Jiguang raised a volunteer force from Zhejiang, trained them in the proper use of weapons, instilled a harsh discipline and above all encouraged teamwork. He made a limited use of firearms, observing that as muskets had a tendency to explode, soldiers did not dare hold them in both hands and that consequently their aim was poor. More through persistence than any other factor, Qi Jiguang demonstrated to the raiders that their activities were no longer profitable. But the real reason why piracy stopped was that in 1567 the ban on foreign trade was rescinded.[43]

One other foreign contact initially went almost unnoticed. The first Portuguese reached China in 1514, and three years later Tomé Pires, who bore a letter from the king of Portugal, landed at Guangzhou and was allowed to proceed to Beijing although he was later expelled. Thereafter Portuguese traders arrived with increasing frequency and having failed to settle at Ningbo began to congregate at Macao. In the 1550s they were given permission to reside there and in 1574 a wall was erected to seal off the settlement and the Portuguese were permitted to administer it as a self-governing enclave. In the meantime the Jesuit mission to Japan had been established and in 1577 Alessandro Valignano, the Jesuit Visitor to the Indies, arrived at Macao. He was followed in 1582 by Matteo Ricci, who eventually obtained permission to reside permanently in Beijing and from there to extend the Jesuit mission to the court. Ricci's strategy for obtaining conversions was to make a cultural accommodation with the Chinese. He studied the Chinese classics and offered to the Chinese his knowledge of western mathematics and science. He described his approach in his journal:

> In order that the appearance of a new religion might not arouse suspicion among the Chinese people, the Fathers did not speak openly about religious matters when they began to appear in public. What time was left to them, after paying their respects and civil compliments and courteously receiving their visitors, was spent in studying the language of the country, the methods of writing and the customs of the people. They did, however, endeavor to teach this pagan people in a more direct way, namely, by virtue of their example and by the sanctity of their lives.[44]

Decline and Fall of the Ming Dynasty

The events which culminated in the fall of the Ming dynasty may be summarised briefly. Two long-reigning emperors, Jiajing (r. 1522–66) and Wanli (r. 1573–1620) both withdrew for long periods of time from active participation in government. During the reign of Jiajing there had been the Mongol raids headed by Altan and the attacks of the Japanese pirates. The emperor did not concern himself with these matters, but instead became increasingly concerned with Daoist practices for achieving immortality and this led to his consumption of elixirs which made him ill. For many years he left Yan Song in charge of affairs, a man who enjoyed a reputation for corruption and treachery and for avoiding the real problems of government. Jiajing's grandson Wanli started his reign more promisingly. Between 1573 and 1582 he had the benefit of the services of Zhang Juzheng, whose administration has been described as 'a last radiant glow in the twilight of the Ming dynasty.'[45] It was notable principally for an austerity programme which restored government finances, but it did not introduce any new measures to deal with the deep-seated problems which beset the dynasty. But after Zhang Juzheng's death the emperor increasingly handed over administrative tasks to eunuchs. The Wanli emperor was credited with having conducted three successful campaigns in the latter part of his reign. The most significant of these was the response to the Japanese invasion of Korea in 1592, which involved the dispatch of major and costly expeditions and was only concluded in 1598 by a Japanese withdrawal after the death of Hideyoshi. In the last years of the reign a political crisis associated with the Donglin academy divided the court into factions and paralysed government.

The Tianqi emperor who came to the throne in 1620 has been described as 'a dim-wit interested mainly in carpentry'[46] His reign was marked by the ascendancy of Wei Zhongxian, the most notorious of the eunuch dictators. His successor Chongzhen was more capable, but was unable to combat the succession of crises which now hit the dynasty. The growing threat from the Manchus was made explicit in 1629 by a raid south of the Great Wall which undermined confidence in the armed forces. In the years that followed a series of droughts and famines led to the rise of rebellion, initially in Shaanxi but later spreading across the North China Plain. By the early 1640s two rebel leaders were prominent. Li Zicheng, whose father had been a rich peasant and who had served in the government postal service, emerged as a contender for the throne. He represented himself as a friend of the poor and ordered that in places which he had captured the people should be exempt from taxes for three years. The other rebel leader, Zhang Xianzhong, known as the 'Yellow Tiger' was notorious for his cruelty. By 1643 Li had occupied Henan and the dynasty's control was crumbling. In the following year he declared the establishment of a new dynasty and entered Beijing. The emperor, deserted by his supporters, hanged himself. Meanwhile Zhang Xianzhong had established his own regime in the south-west with its capital at Chengdu.

The most frequently cited explanation for this dramatic sequence of events has been to invoke the process of the dynastic cycle. In its traditional form this emphasised personal factors, the weakness of the later emperors and the machinations of their ministers and the eunuchs, most notably Yan Song and Wei Zhongxian. To this may be added the record of court extravagance and the consequent oppressive taxation, giving rise to the great peasant rebellions which toppled the dynasty. A more impersonal version of this cycle would note how the first rulers of a dynasty were able to command and to innovate, whereas later rulers became captives of their advisers and of the policies which could only be reformed by attacking vested interests.

A more complex political explanation of the fall of the dynasty has derived from a discussion of the Donglin movement. This movement took its name from the Donglin academy, near Wuxi in the Yangzi delta. The academy provided a focus for scholars and officials who were alarmed by what they saw as a deterioration in standards in public life and who argued for a moral revival and a return to Confucian education and values. Sympathisers with these ideas were dominant in government in the early part of Tianqi's reign, but the tide turned when Wei Zhongxian gained power and carried out a purge of Donglin supporters. The significance the movement had for the decline of the dynasty has been defined variously. Donglin leaders have been described as representing a landowning class reacting against Ming absolutism. Their protest against what they saw as arbitrary and unacceptable actions on the part of the monarch – in particular his attempt to change the order of succession – was part of a move aimed at transforming government from an autocracy to a form which reflected their interests. Other suggestions are that the confrontation arose over political issues or because the factions had a regional alignment. In fact, there was only one issue which united the Donglin supporters and that was opposition to Wei Zhongxian. Analyses of Donglin supporters and their opponents has not revealed any clear regional attachment. Charles Hucker argued that the differences between the factions were essentially moral and that the Donglin supporters represented traditional Confucian morality, which demanded resoluteness and integrity, pitted against the Ming power structure, which at that stage in the dynasty did not permit success to any but the unprincipled. Whatever its origins, the Donglin movement divided the court and encouraged factionalism. Even after the death of Wei Zhongxian, during the reign of Tianqi, 'partisan bickering had become a habit', detaching scholars and officials from the dynasty and paving the way for the switch of allegiance which occurred in 1644.[47]

A different type of explanation for the fall of the dynasty begins with reference to the population rise and then draws attention to the evidence of deteriorating climate and catastrophic epidemics which swept the country in the late Ming period. It includes reference to the effects of China's early involvement in world trade, which brought an influx of silver and which stimulated commercial regions along the south-east coast. At first this had a beneficial effect on government which enjoyed increased revenues. However, economic growth slowed in the early seventeenth century and government expenditure rose with the costs of the Korean campaigns and the gross extravagance of the Wanli emperor. These factors may have amounted to a form of seventeenth-century crisis, comparable in some ways with developments in Europe at the same time.[48]

Why did popular rebellions arise and topple the dynasty? Economic hardship certainly played a part in this process. The rebellions had their origin in northern Shaanxi, an impoverished area which had experienced none of the economic growth which had benefited some other regions, notably the lower Yangzi valley. Another underlying cause was the decline of standards of local administration, with many official posts left unfilled. In 1628 a drought in the area was followed by a famine which might have been averted if local officials had done their duty. Disorder broke out involving peasants, bandits, and soldiers who had deserted their units. The senior official sent to deal with the rebellion initially extended an offer of peaceful surrender towards the rebels, with some degree of success. But in 1629 the first Manchu raid into north China wrecked the pacification programme. The government now switched its policy to that of total suppression but this resulted in the rebel bands moving out of their base area and becoming mobile raiders, often mounted on horseback. Government forces had no answer to this situation and a combination of bad planning, institutional weakness and personal failures allowed the rebellions to survive. At first there was no immediate risk of the rebellions overthrowing the dynasty. However in 1641 Li Zicheng, by now the most prominent rebel leader, captured Luoyang and began to attract gentry members to his cause, who suggested that to gain popular support he should improve his image. Li then set himself the task of capturing Kaifeng, which he did after a protracted siege and at the cost of a major disaster, for during the campaign the Yellow river defences were breached and many thousands of lives were lost. Later the same year he also captured Xi'an. By now the Ming government was incapable a putting an effective force into the field and the fall of Beijing in the following year was a foregone conclusion.[49]

A final reason for the fall of the dynasty, albeit an indirect one, was the rise of Manchu power. In 1619 the Wanli emperor had been persuaded to launch an attack against the Manchu leader Nurhaci. At the time China's state finances were in crisis and the emperor was unwilling to contribute from his own substantial reserves to the cost of the campaign. As a consequence a silver surcharge was added to the land tax, which was unpopular if not exhorbitant. The campaign itself was a disaster and it encouraged the Manchus to attack Chinese territory. In 1629, as mentioned above, they made the deep raid which interrupted the attempt to suppress rebellion in Shaanxi. The continued threat from the Manchus necessitated maintaining a large part of the dynasty's military strength along the northern frontier, rather than deploying it against the rebels. This was of crucial importance in the final days of the dynasty. One of the last effective forces on the imperial side was that commanded by Wu Sangui and stationed near Shanhaiguan. In April 1644, Wu was reportedly about to submit to Li Zicheng, who was holding his father hostage. Instead, in a famous act of treachery, he cast his lot in with the Manchu leader Dorgon. In the following month Manchu troops, with the assistance of Wu Sangui's soldiers, inflicted a crushing defeat on the rebels. The way was now open for the Manchu invasion of China.

12
The Qing Dynasty

The events which culminated in the Manchu conquest of China occupied only twelve years, from 1640 to 1652. However, the establishment and consolidation of the Qing dynasty, the 'great enterprise' as Frederic Wakeman described it,[1] occupied a much longer time, from the Manchu capture of Fushun in 1618 to the defeat of the Three Feudatories and of Zheng Chenggong on Taiwan in the 1680s.

By then the Kangxi emperor was on the throne. His reign, from 1662 to 1722, established the character of Manchu rule in China. He was succeeded by his fourth son, who reigned as the Yongzheng emperor between 1723 and 1735. After him came the Qianlong emperor who, after ruling for sixty years, abdicated in 1795 rather than exceed the record of his grandfather, although he, or rather his favourite Heshen, retained power until the emperor's death in 1799. In these three reigns the Chinese empire reached its greatest extent, its population attained its massive quality, and its culture acquired those characteristics which were to determine its modern transformation.

Some writers regarded the Manchu conquest as a victory of barbarism over culture, as an opportunistic victory achieved with great cruelty which established a foreign despotism over a subjugated people. This view became popular at the end of the nineteenth century, when anti-Manchuism became an important component of nationalism. In the manifesto of the Revolutionary Alliance promulgated in 1905 Sun Zhongshan (Sun Yat-sen) declared:

The Manchus of today were originally the eastern barbarians beyond the Great Wall. They frequently caused border troubles during the Ming dynasty; then when China was in a disturbed state they came inside [the Great Wall], conquered China, and enslaved our Chinese people. Those who opposed them were killed by the hundreds of thousands, and our Chinese have been a people without a nation for two hundred and sixty years.[2]

Modern western interpretations have tended to play down the subjugation, if not the cruelty, of the conquest. Emphasis has been placed on the continuities between Ming and Qing and on the collaboration between the Chinese élite and the conquerors. Certainly there were acts of heroic resistance and examples of irreconcilable hostility, but there were also many examples of Chinese submitting to the Manchus and serving them faithfully.

189

The Rise of the Manchus

The Manchus were originally a Jurchen people, that is to say near relatives of the peoples that had founded the Jin dynasty in 1122. Although skilled in mounted archery, the Jurchen were not steppe nomads. They practised agriculture, traded extensively with China and sent tributary missions to Beijing. The Jianzhou Jurchen, the group directly ancestral to the Manchus, emerged in the late sixteenth century in Jilin, in the region known as the Changbaishan, the Long White Mountains. Its people formed an administrative unit, a commandery, within the Ming framework for the control of this region, which was based essentially on the principle of divide and rule.

The fortunes of this group were to be determined largely by the efforts of one man, Nurhaci (1559–1626), the creator of the Manchu state and founder of the Qing dynasty. In his early life he struggled to avenge the murder of his father and grandfather by a neighbouring tribal leader and through his efforts became recognised as the leader of the Jianzhou Jurchen. His success in defeating a bandit group and releasing some Chinese captives led in 1590 to his heading a tribute mission to Beijing. In the following years he grew rich from the trade in ginseng and his ambition led him to attack the tribes to the north. His rapid rise to power, his establishment of a capital, the development of his military capacity, all alarmed the Chinese and ensured that a confrontation would take place. In 1618 Nurhaci listed 'Seven Great Vexations' against the Ming, a list of supposed insults and grievances. He called upon the commander of Fushun, the key garrison town and horse-trading centre of Liaodong, to surrender, which he did. Nurhaci treated him with respect and offered him one of his granddaughters in marriage. Within two years Nurhaci had defeated the Chinese force sent to chastise him and had brought most of Liaodong under his control.[3]

In his later years Nurhaci transformed his confederation of Jianzhou Jurchen tribes and their supporters into a Manchu state (although the name Manchu was only adopted in 1635). In 1601 Nurhaci ordered a registration of the people and then divided the population into niru, meaning 'arrows', each composed of 300 households of warriors, this being the first step towards the creation of a new military organisation. Five niru formed a battalion and ten battalions formed a banner. At first the Manchu people as a whole were divided into four banners, with four more created in 1615. It has been suggested that the banner organisation was an adaptation of the Chinese weisuo system. Both systems were civil as well as military organisations, both embodied a military bureaucracy, both were intended to be self-regulating and self-supporting. However the systems had an important difference: unlike the Chinese weisuo the Manchu banners did not have a fixed regional base. The introduction of the banners was part of a more general policy of adopting bureaucratic and imperial features derived from the Chinese state. In 1616 offices of government were created and Nurhaci assumed the title of emperor and founder of a dynasty. Increasingly Chinese were brought into the Manchu administration, a tendency which accelerated after the capture of Fushun. With Liaodong under his control, Nurhaci began to organise the Chinese population as well into banners and the same process was applied to the Mongol tribes that had joined him. At first Nurhaci offered a policy of equality towards the Chinese, but frequent cases of poisoning and a Chinese revolt in 1625 caused him to revert to a policy of racial discrimination. Nurhaci died in 1626, but the process of adopting Chinese methods of government continued under his son Abahai. In 1631 he introduced the six ministries modelled on the Ming administration and in 1636 he formally announced the establishment of the Qing or 'pure' dynasty. In short, before the conquest of China Proper began, the Manchu rulers had already moved away from their traditional clan system of government towards the adoption of Chinese administrative methods. They had also gained valuable experience of ruling a sedentary Chinese population with the help of Chinese collaborators. This debt to Chinese practice led Franz Michael to declare, 'It was the Chinese system, Chinese officials and Chinese ideas that enabled the Manchus to conquer China.'[4] However this view has been challenged as overemphasising the sinicisation of the Manchus both before and after the conquest.[5]

The Manchu Conquest of China

Although a Manchu conquest of China had long been anticipated, and major raids into northern China had taken place from early in Abahai's reign, the opportunity for conquest derived from the situation which presented itself in the last years of the Ming dynasty. In 1643 Abahai died. Because his heir was a child, Dorgon, another son of Nurhaci, became regent. The capture of Beijing by Li Zicheng and the death of the Ming emperor forced Dorgon to decide whether the time was ripe for the abandonment of the traditional policy of profitable raiding and instead to risk an invasion. His decision to do the latter was perhaps based on Wu Sangui's offer of an alliance against Li Zicheng, for it has been argued that the Manchu forces were not strong enough to defeat both Wu Sangui and Li Zicheng.[6]

The combined armies inflicted a crushing defeat on Li Zicheng's troops and Dorgon immediately pressed on to Beijing. The rapid sequence of events had left officials quite uncertain how to respond to the Manchu advance. Dorgon seized this opportunity to bring the Chinese élite over to his side. His first proclamation in part read:

> The empire is not an individual's private empire. Whosoever possesses virtue holds it. The army and people are not an individual's private army and people. Whosoever possesses virtue commands them. We now hold it. We took revenge upon the enemy of your ruler-father in place of your dynasty. We burned our bridges behind us, and we have pledged not to return until every bandit is destroyed. In the counties, districts, and locales we pass through, all those who are able to shave their heads and surrender, opening their gates to welcome us, will be given rank and reward, retaining their wealth and nobility for generations. But if there are those who resist us disobediently, then when our Grand Army arrives, the stones themselves will be set ablaze and everyone will be massacred.[7]

The response of the rest of the country to the Qing conquest was a complex mixture of resistance and of compliance. Once the Manchu forces had routed Li Zicheng's troops, their next objective was the occupation of the Yangzi valley, the Ming court having fled, in the first instance, to Nanjing. In May 1645 Manchu forces commanded by Dodo besieged Yangzhou, the defence of which was led by the famous Ming loyalist general Shi Kefa. Although the defenders had a new Portuguese type of cannon, such was the ferocity of the Manchu assault that the siege only lasted a week. Shi Kefa was captured but, unlike many other generals, he refused to change sides. He was thereupon executed and Yangzhou delivered over to an infamous ten-day massacre, intended to deter further resistance.[8] This certainly worked in the case of many cities, where the inhabitants were quick to post notices signifying 'surrendering people' on the city gates. Nevertheless instances of resistance occurred, notably at Jiangyin and Jiading.

The famous outburst of resistance at Jiangyin, which is a hundred miles upriver from Shanghai, was apparently sparked off by the Manchu hair-cutting order. After Nanjing had fallen, the Qing authorities had ordered other administrative centres in the region to hand over their tax and population registers, this being the first step towards obtaining the co-operation of the local élite in the orderly transfer of power. The Jiangnan authorities appeared to have no problem with complying with this instruction. But shortly afterwards, in July 1645, the news arrived that the Qing government had also issued a proclamation stating that the regulation requiring men to wear their hair in the Manchu style – that is to say to shave their head at the front and grow a pig-tailed queue at the back – was to be enforced immediately. Anyone found not to have complied with the regulation was to be treated as a bandit. Opposition to this order led to the formation of a resistance movement in Jiangyin. Qing troops were dispatched to subdue the city and this was done ruthlessly with the alleged loss of up to 100,000 lives. Much has been written about the tragedy of Jiangyin, but it has been shown that the resistance was not a clear example of collective loyalism against a foreign invader. Divisions existed among the local élite of Jiangnan and the slaughter was actually perpetrated by Chinese troops.[9]

After the capture of Nanjing, Ming successor regimes fled south. In 1650 Qing forces commanded by Shang Kexi, a Chinese military commander who had switched to the Manchu side in 1634, captured Guangzhou after a prolonged siege and massacred the inhabitants. Ming resistance continued but was now confined to the fringes of the empire. The last Ming emperor was pursued to Burma and captured and executed there in 1662. In the meantime another form of resistance to the Qing had appeared in the person of Zheng Chenggong, known in the West as Koxinga. From about 1646 he led a resistance movement along the coast of Fujian, his long survival depending considerably on his use of sea-power, a form of warfare with which the Manchus were not familiar. In 1659 a large naval force under his command sailed up the Yangzi and besieged Nanjing, but he received little encouragement from the local gentry and had to abandon the attack. Before his death in 1662 he captured the Dutch fort of Zeelandia on Taiwan. His son continued the resistance and in retaliation the Qing resorted to the draconian policy of forcing the coastal population of the area to abandon their settlements and to remove ten miles inland. Koxinga is remembered to this day as the hero of a puppet play by the Japanese dramatist Chikamatsu (Koxinga's mother was Japanese). He has also been celebrated in modern times by both Nationalists and Communists. The former have identified him as an early anti-Manchu nationalist, while the latter have claimed him as an early anti-imperialist. One might suggest that his real intentions were not to expel the Manchus but to carve out an independent kingdom for himself.[10]

The Consolidation of Manchu Rule: 1644–89

From the moment that the Manchus entered Beijing, and Abahai's son was proclaimed emperor, using the reign title of Shunzhi, the Manchu leaders had to decide how they would rule China. The responsibility for making this decision fell on the regent Dorgon. It was under his direction that the conquest of China and the destruction of Ming resistance was pursued. At the same time he established the general line that was to be taken towards the conquered. The central feature of this was that the Manchus would retain all essential elements of Ming rule, and it was this which has led to the conquest being described as 'the least disruptive transition from one major dynasty to another in the whole of Chinese history.'[11] Dorgon immediately made it clear that he would welcome the services of former Ming officials and a very substantial number of officials, particularly from the north and especially from Shandong, became 'twice-serving ministers'. The examination system was continued and in the palace examinations of 1646 the dominance of the north was apparent, although this was later to shift to the south.[12] From the beginning of the Manchu period the principle of a Manchu-Chinese diarchy, that is to say the duplication of senior appointments by the appointment of a Manchu and a Chinese, was adopted. The main administrative arrangements and the system of checks and balances were retained. An extensive programme of reform derived from suggestions made by former Ming officials was initiated.[13] Finally the Shunzhi emperor was carefully instructed in the performance of his role as a Confucian emperor, a part which he played willingly.

Nevertheless Dorgon was a Manchu and he was determined to maintain the ethnic distinction and dominance of the Manchus. In the early years of his regency, the requirement that Chinese wear the queue was extended and enforced throughout the country, the popular saying being 'off with your hair, or off with your head'. Extensive tracts of land in north China were confiscated from Chinese owners and distributed among Manchu princes and generals. Although the diarchic system appeared to offer the Chinese a substantial role in government, the top metropolitan positions, the positions of power, were kept in Manchu hands.[14] Moreover, the impression that the Manchus accepted the return of a large number of Chinese into positions of responsibility is misleading. Most of the Chinese who supported the new dynasty were Chinese bannermen, that is to say members of the eight Chinese banners formed in 1642, which had fought alongside the Manchus in the conquest and which had then supplied military and civil personnel to the conquerors. Chinese bannermen, because of their reliance on the Manchus, were more trustworthy than Chinese officials who had changed sides.

Dorgon died on the last day of 1650, while on a hunting expedition. His ambitious manoeuvring, followed by his sudden death, precipitated a sharp factional struggle among the Manchu élite, which was temporarily resolved by the success of the faction which had coalesced around Shunzhi. In 1651 the young emperor – he was then thirteen years old – gave his support to a public denunciation of Dorgon, who allegedly had tried to make himself emperor. Shunzhi began to take an active part in government and between 1652 and 1655 a series of important institutional reforms were introduced, many of which, as previously under Dorgon, were suggested by 'twice-serving ministers'.[15] These reforms concerned such practical matters as water conservancy and grain tribute transportation, as well as the improvement of the tax registers and tax collection and the suppression of corruption. Of these the land tax reforms were the most significant, for they increased the number of ding, that is adult males liable to labour service, by 60 per cent and nearly doubled the registered acreage of land liable to tax. At the same time Shunzhi initiated measures to curb the activities of the Manchu aristocracy and took the controversial step of re-introducing the eunuch directorates in the Forbidden City.[16]

Shunzhi is also remembered on a more personal note for his love for his consort, the Empress Xiaoxian. This romance has been supposed, probably incorrectly, to have been the subject of the famous Qing novel The Dream of the Red Chamber. Xiaoxian died in 1660 and the extravagance of her funeral aroused the resentment of Shunzhi's mother.

Shunzhi died, probably of smallpox, in February 1661. His will named as his heir his seven-year-old son, who was to reign as the celebrated Kangxi emperor. This was one of the few true statements in the document, which was based on the emperor's testament, but which had been mendaciously embroidered by the four regents and his mother, the Grand Empress Dowager. In the will the Shunzhi emperor reproached himself for having rejected his Manchu heritage, for unfilial conduct towards his mother and for excessive interest in Chinese matters. This abject self-criticism may be contrasted with the flattering portrait of the emperor presented by the Jesuit missionary Adam Schall, who held a privileged position at court because of his knowledge of astronomy. At one time an intimacy had sprung up between the emperor and the elderly missionary. The emperor had called Schall 'grandfather' and Schall had entertained hopes that the emperor, of whom he approved strongly, might convert to Christianity. This was not to be and later the emperor became more interested in Chan Buddhism.[17]

Between 1661 and 1669, while the new emperor was a minor, power was held by the four regents known collectively as the Oboi regency after one of their number. This period was marked by a sharp policy shift, away from accommodation with the Chinese system and towards a greater emphasis on Manchu dominance. The first step was to abolish the eunuch directorates, which allegedly threatened to restore one of the worst features of the Ming dynasty, although Shunzhi's true purpose in establishing them may have been to create an organisation that was independent of the Manchu élite. Steps were also taken to reduce the influence of the Jesuits, and Buddhist advisers were also dismissed. This was only the beginning of the promotion of a Manchu 'reign of virtue'. At the metropolitan level of government a determined effort was made to increase the importance of Manchu representation at the expense of Chinese institutions. The most notable example of this was the reform of the Council of Deliberative Officials to make it a forum where senior Manchu military and civil leaders could discuss issues and formulate policy. At the same time steps were taken to reverse changes made by Shunzhi and to reduce the power of key elements retained from Ming metropolitan government. In particular the Grand Secretariat and the Hanlin Academy were abolished, and the Censorate was greatly reduced in influence. Two other reforms carried the Manchu emphasis even further. In Ming China a system of evaluation of officials had operated, which covered a wide variety of criteria and which permitted self-assessment. After 1662 the criteria for performance were restricted to the fulfilment of tax quotas and the completion of criminal cases, and evaluation was placed solely in the hands of senior officials. Another reform concerned the examination system, where the syllabus was amended by the abolition of the formal 'eight-legged essay', and a sharp reduction was made in the quotas for the *jinshi* degree.[18]

Alongside these metropolitan policies the Oboi regents sought to affirm Manchu superiority in the provinces. As few Manchus had the administrative experience and linguistic skills to enable them to occupy senior provincial posts, there was no alternative to relying on Chinese bannermen as governors-general and governors. Under Dorgon there had been an assumption that their loyalty was beyond question, but by the time of the Oboi regency, their intermediate position led to their being treated with a degree of mistrust. At the start of the regency almost all senior provincial officials were replaced, and their successors were kept under close supervision and expected to enforce policies strictly. The demand for the prompt payment of taxes had alienated the Chinese élite in several places and provoked a particularly sharp reaction in Zhejiang and Jiangnan, leading to many individuals being punished with the loss of their degrees.[19] Another example of the severity of Manchu rule was the previously-mentioned adoption in 1661–2 of the policy of removing the coastal population some ten miles inland to prevent Ming loyalists, and in particular Zheng Chenggong, from obtaining supplies.[20]

By the late 1660s the Oboi regency had been replaced by a faction grouped around Oboi, whose pursuit of his private ambitions had alienated both Chinese and Manchus. In 1667 the Grand Empress Dowager secured an agreement that the emperor should assume personal command while continuing to be advised by the regents. Two years later the emperor ordered the arrest of Oboi and a purge of his supporters. It was at this point that the Kangxi emperor began to rule in his own right.

The final stage in the consolidation of Manchu rule was accomplished in the first fifteen years of Kangxi's reign and it involved military, political and cultural initiatives. The military action derived from a situation which dated back to the pacification of the south. At that time the Manchus had relied on Chinese collaborators to gain control. Of these Shang Kexi, Kong Youde and Geng Zhongming had all come from Shandong and had joined forces with the Manchus in the 1630s. To their number should be added Wu Sangui who had changed sides in 1644. All four men had played a key role in the conquest of north China and all had been rewarded with the title of prince. In 1649 they were sent to the south with broad discretionary powers to eliminate Ming resistance and to establish Manchu control. Kong Youde was surrounded by Ming forces at Guilin and committed suicide, but the other three not only subdued resistance but also carved themselves out semi-independent fiefdoms: Wu Sangui in Yunnan and Guizhou, Shang Kexi in Guangdong, and Geng Jingzhong, the grandson of Geng Zhongming, in Fujian. Each commanded his own forces and was allowed to raise taxes through monopolies and to administer his territory very much as he saw fit.

Concern over the independence of the three feudatories was expressed from the early 1660s, one cause of complaint being the very high cost of their military expenditure. However it was only in 1673 that an opportunity to take action arose. Shang Kexi requested permission to retire because of old age, his intention being to hand his position over to his son. His example prompted an offer of retirement from the other feudatories. Wu Sangui assumed that he would be reinstated, but Kangxi, largely on his own initiative, refused to comply, thus forcing the issue and precipitating a rebellion.[21]

The rebellion of the Three Feudatories lasted eight years and was the most serious threat to the survival of the dynasty. Wu Sangui commanded a large army and he could hope to capitalise on anti-Manchu feeling. He declared the establishment of a new dynasty, the Zhou, gained widespread support in Yunnan and Guizhou, and his armies marched unopposed into Hunan. Before the end of 1674 much of south and west China was in rebellion. The initial threat was met with indecision at court and rumours circulated that the Manchus were about to abandon Beijing. However Kangxi responded by taking personal control of military strategy, and the crisis was relieved when Shang Kexi declared his continued loyalty to the Manchus, so denying the rebels control of Guangdong. Moreover Wu Sangui failed signally to win over anti-Manchu Ming loyalist scholars.[22] In the prolonged struggle which followed a key factor in favour of the Qing dynasty was that Jiangnan, the economic heartland of the empire, remained loyal. This gave the government the resources to pay more troops and to equip them with artillery, designed by Father Verbiest, the Jesuit missionary who was also President of the Tribunal of Mathematics.[23] Military campaigns were supplemented by propaganda which offered an amnesty to the population of the provinces that had been drawn into the rebellion. By the time of Wu Sangui's death in 1678 the rebellion was in effect defeated.

The consolidation of the Qing empire required success in two further campaigns. The first was the subjugation of Taiwan, now held by Zheng Jing, son of the famous Zheng Chenggong, who had allied himself with Geng Jingzhong, one of the three feudatories. This was achieved in 1683, by negotiation rather than by conquest. As the island no longer represented a threat the intention at first was to abandon it. However it was claimed that if it was abandoned it might be re-occupied by the Dutch, who for some years after 1624 had maintained a trading colony on its south-western coast. So in 1684 Taiwan was incorporated into the empire as a prefecture of Fujian province and the policy of removing the coastal population was rescinded.

The second campaign was directed against a relatively new threat. In 1643 Cossacks engaged in the fur trade had reached the Amur river. Taking advantage of Manchu preoccupation elsewhere they established a trading post at Nerchinsk and then a fortress at Albazin. The Kangxi emperor took a personal interest in the situation and resolved to halt Russian encroachment either by diplomatic means or by force. The indigenous population was enrolled in new Manchu banners and the Russian settlers were warned that they must either accept Chinese suzerainty of the area or withdraw. Having concluded that negotiation had failed, the emperor ordered the capture of Albazin. Aware of a growing threat from the Dzungar in the west, Kangxi quickly authorised the negotiation of the Treaty of Nerchinsk. This agreement, which was negotiated in 1689, was China's first treaty with a western state and her first treaty concluded on terms of diplomatic equality with another power. Under it Russia recognised the Amur basin as Qing territory and the two countries made arrangements for trade.[24]

The Later Years of Kangxi's Reign, 1689–1722

The Kangxi emperor has been described as 'probably the most admirable ruler of the entire later imperial age.'[25] His commitment to his responsibilities was prodigious. The early Qing emperors dealt personally with many aspects of government business. The Kangxi emperor claimed that on some days during the rebellion of the Three Feudatories he had handled five hundred items of business. Even in normal times he read and corrected some fifty memorials a day.[26] At the same time he carried out numerous regular duties, including receiving officials and envoys from foreign states, performing religious ceremonies, reviewing judicial decisions and supervising the highest stages of the examination system. In addition he travelled widely, claiming to have travelled two thousand li in each of the four cardinal directions. His tours involved hunting expeditions and military exercises, and he made a point of meeting the people and expressing an interest in their welfare, farming methods, tax burden and similar matters.

Being a Manchu ruler, it was inevitable that Kangxi would be concerned about military affairs and at the time of the rebellion of the Three Feudatories he had taken his role as commander-in-chief very seriously. As a consequence of those campaigns important changes occurred in the size and relative importance of the two main military organisations. At first Kangxi relied heavily on the banner formations and by 1684 the number of banner troops had risen to about 315,000. But as the campaign continued greater use was made of Chinese forces, known as the army of the Green Standard, which at one point reached a total of 900,000 men, though this was later reduced by a third. After the suppression of the rebellion the roles of the two formations stabilised. Banner forces for the most part were stationed in the north, around Beijing and in Manchuria, but seven cities in central and southern China were also garrisoned by banner troops. The army of the Green Standard was more widely scattered and its units placed under the command of both civil and military officials. Apart from garrison duties, its men took on a variety of responsibilities including postal functions and guarding buildings. These changes demonstrate that in the latter part of his reign Kangxi was sufficiently confident of the loyalty of his Chinese subjects to entrust the security of the south largely to their keeping.[27]

The reason why Kangxi's envoys had been quick to negotiate the Treaty of Nerchinsk with the Tsar was the fear of Russian support for the Dzungar, the western Mongols who, under the leadership of Galdan, threatened to unite the other Mongol tribes under their control. However the Dzungar failed in their efforts to win over the Khalkha or eastern Mongols, and moreover they were divided among themselves and this gave Kangxi an opportunity to settle the issue. In 1696, and again in the following year, he personally led campaigns against Galdan which resulted in the latter's defeat and later suicide. Afterwards he wrote:

Now Galdan is dead, and his followers have come back to their allegiance. My great task is done. In two years I made three journeys, across deserts combed by wind and bathed with rain, eating every other day, in the barren and uninhabitable deserts – one could have called it a hardship but I never called it that; people all shun such things but I didn't shun them. The constant journeying and hardship has led to this great achievement. I would never have said such a thing had it not been for Galdan.[28]

The Dzungar were the last major threat to Qing China out of Inner Asia.[29] Because they had made an alliance with Tibet the Qing court then found it necessary to send expeditions against the Tibetans and eventually, in 1728, to establish a permanent garrison in Lhasa and to appoint an imperial resident there. These were the first expansionist moves which, during the eighteenth century, were to double the area of the Chinese empire.

In many respects the practice of government under Kangxi continued on the lines established under the Ming. However some features were novel and have been the subject of scholarly interest. One such feature, which sheds light on the relationship between Manchus and Chinese, was the role of the *baoyi* or bondservant.

Bondservants were originally household slaves of diverse ethnic origin. However after the Manchu expansion in the 1620s their numbers came to include many Chinese and they were incorporated into the banner system. After the Manchu conquest, and particularly after the death of the Shunzhi emperor, there was a reaction against a revival of eunuch influence at court. Bondservants now took over the main tasks which had been carried out by eunuchs under the Ming, although eunuchs remained an essential part of court personnel.[30] Because of the past danger from eunuch power, this change may have improved the dynasty's chances of survival, but it also strengthened the trend towards autocracy.

Bondservants came to play a key role in the Imperial Household Department, the department which handled the emperor's personal affairs. Most of those who served in the department were bondservants from the upper three, or imperial banners. This was a large and complex department which by the end of Kangxi's reign employed nearly one thousand officials. It was an informal and private institution and members of its staff owed everything to their master who was also the emperor. It might be described as a microcosm of the Manchu-Chinese state, for in organisation it reflected the Chinese bureaucratic administrative apparatus, whereas in personnel it derived from the banner system. In the eighteenth century the department assumed a wider role, and bondservants were appointed to important financial positions often in the provinces. There they acted as the emperor's trusted agents and remitted funds back to his personal treasury. A famous example of this type of appointment was the Cao family, who were bondservants of the Plain White Banner. For much of the time between 1663 and 1728 members of the family held the post of textile commissioner in Nanjing, in charge of the management of government silk factories, until the family then fell into disgrace. Its days of prosperity and decline were to be the background for Cao Xueqin's famous novel, The Dream of the Red Chamber, known also as The Story of the Stone.[31]

The use of bondservants was connected with a significant development in government practice concerning communications. The official system used by the Ming and continued under the Qing was one of open communication through regular bureaucratic channels. This system was inevitably cumbersome and confined by precedent; it belonged to what has been denominated as the 'outer-court', and was centred on the operations of the bureaucracy. As under previous dynasties, there was also an 'inner court' centred on the emperor and including the Imperial Household Department. To circumvent the procedures of the outer court, Kangxi began to use what became known as the 'palace memorial', the emperor's private mode of communication with correspondents. The first of these correspondents were bondservants serving the emperor in provincial appointments in the south, among them Cao Yin, the textile commissioner at Suzhou. Initially the correspondents reported on the weather, and in particular sent information on droughts and floods – which may seem surprising until it is recalled that Kangxi, like previous emperors, believed in the significance of omens and was fond of repeating that 'if our administration is at fault on earth, Heaven will respond with calamities above'. Later some correspondents were provincial officials and their reports contained a wider range of information, including informal comments on fellow officials. Such a system was a valuable aid to the development of autocratic government which was to progress further in the following reign.[32]

The Manchu willingness to make use of the services of foreigners was illustrated by their response to the Jesuit mission to China. Mention has already been made of Adam Schall, tutor to the Shunzhi emperor and director of the Bureau of Astronomy. After Shunzhi's death Schall was attacked by Chinese astronomers and accused of high treason. He was found guilty, although the punishment was stayed. His successor, Ferdinand Verbiest, challenged Chinese astronomers to a demonstration of skills and having defeated them, was himself appointed director of the astronomical bureau, a post he held until 1687. Kangxi employed other Jesuits who had skills in mathematics, architecture and painting. In return for their assistance, the emperor allowed Christianity to be promoted and in 1692 promulgated an 'edict of tolerance'. On the vexed question of whether Christian converts should continue to perform Confucian rites and practise ancestor worship, a formulation drawn up by the Jesuits in Beijing and agreed by the emperor read:

that Confucius was honored by the Chinese as a master, but his name was not invoked in prayer for the purpose of gaining happiness, rank, or wealth; that worship of ancestors was an expression of love and filial remembrance, not intended to bring protection to the worshiper; and that there was no idea, when an ancestral tablet was erected, that the soul of the ancestor dwelt in that tablet. And when sacrifices were offered to Heaven it was not the blue existent sky that was addressed, but the lord and creator of all things. If the ruler Shangdi was sometimes called Heaven, Tian, that had no more significance than giving honorific names to the emperor.[33]

Although the transmission of ideas between East and West was not as smooth as depicted by either side, for each had its own agenda, these years marked the closest point yet achieved to a mutual understanding.

This understanding was not to last. Dominican and Franciscan missionaries criticised the Jesuit strategy of accommodation to the Chinese way of life and commitment to the service of the Manchu emperor. By the beginning of the eighteenth century the Jesuits had lost influence in Rome and their willingness to compromise with the Chinese practice of ancestor worship was condemned by the Inquisition. In an attempt to settle the controversy the Pope sent a special legate, Charles Maillard de Tournon, to the Qing court. He was received in audience by Kangxi but it soon became clear that no agreement was possible. The legate rejected the formulation which had been agreed regarding rites. The emperor would not countenance any claim of equality between the Pope and himself, nor that the Pope should assert any authority over Christian missionaries in China. In 1706 Kangxi ordered that all missionaries must accept the agreed formulation and undertake to remain in China for life. If they did not agree they should leave. Maillard de Tournon countered by forbidding missionaries to accept. This disagreement precipitated what became known as the Rites Controversy, which culminated in 1742 with the Pope issuing the bull Ex Quo Singulari, which condemned all forms of accommodation with Chinese rites.

An important underlying issue during the reign concerned government revenue and in particular the level of the land and labour-service taxes. One of Kangxi's best-known measures was the decision taken in 1712 to use the previous year's ding figures, that is the number of adult males paying tax, as the permanent basis for computing the labour-service tax. As increases in land and labour taxes were regarded as a major cause of dynastic instability, such a measure would appear to be enlightened and a gesture of confidence in the willingness of the state to curb its fiscal demands. However, the truth of the matter was somewhat different, for Kangxi had inherited, and then left to his successors, a legacy of chronic fiscal shortage. The fundamental reason for this was the difficulty of wresting an adequate revenue from an impoverished peasant economy. Chinese governments lacked an income sufficient to administer the country effectively, let alone enough to provide a surplus to invest in economic improvement. At the beginning of the Ming period Hongwu had recognised this in part, when he overhauled the tax system and fixed the land tax at a relatively low level. In the late sixteenth century the fiscal measures known as the Single-Whip reforms improved things a little, by consolidating some taxes and requiring their payment in silver. But this still left many anomalies and had one unexpected result: because revenues were now collected in silver rather than in kind, it became much easier for central government to appropriate resources which had in the past been used to maintain the local administration. Local officials were forced to find new sources of revenue to run their offices and this they did through the collection of a variety of surcharges. When the Manchus came to power they had continued Ming fiscal practices, but the costs of pacification, the maintenance of the Three Feudatories and then the suppression of their rebellion, all had imposed heavy burdens on the treasury. Kangxi had commanded frugality in government expenditure and efforts had been made to encourage land reclamation and settlement. These measures had enabled the government to remain solvent, but the dramatic declaration of 1712 flew in the face of the reality of the tax situation and exacerbated the constraints on the fiscal system at a time when the population was climbing steadily.[34]

Another recurrent problem, one which clouded Kangxi's final years, was the settlement of the succession. Emperors tended to have a large progeny: Kangxi had thirty-five sons, of whom twenty lived beyond the age of eleven, and twenty daughters, of whom only eight reached maturity.[35] According to Manchu custom a successor was elected by the elders of a tribe from all the sons of the previous ruler, but by Chinese tradition only sons born of the empress, the sole legitimate wife of the emperor, were eligible to succeed, with the firstborn enjoying priority.[36] Following the latter principle the emperor's heir apparent was his second son Yinreng, born in 1674, whose mother was the empress Xiaocheng, who had died at his birth. Yinreng was given an indulgent upbringing but after he had reached adulthood tensions arose between him and his father. Nevertheless Kangxi appointed Yinreng regent when he was away campaigning against Galdan. However the incessant factional struggles at court ensured that no opportunity would be lost in informing the emperor of any shortcoming in the heir apparent. In 1697 Yinreng was accused of some serious but unspecified misconduct and later he came under suspicion of involvement in a plot on his father's life. More damaging complaints were made after the emperor's southern tour of 1707, alleging that Yinreng was engaged in a frenzied search for 'pretty girls' and 'fair-looking boys'.[37] In the following year Kangxi publicly denounced Yinreng for his immorality, extravagance and usurpation of imperial privileges, and ordered him to be put in chains and imprisoned. He was later reinstated, on the grounds that he must have been possessed by evil spirits, but he was finally deposed in 1712. For a quarter of a century the issue of the succession fuelled factional struggles at Kangxi's court, and for the last ten years of his reign the emperor had no acknowledged heir apparent, which created an atmosphere of uncertainty about the future.

In 1717 Kangxi issued a valedictory edict in which he wrote:

I am already old, and have reigned long, and I cannot foretell what posterity will think of me. Besides which, because of what is going on now, I cannot hold back my tears of bitterness; and so I have prepared these notes to make my own record, for I still fear that the country may not know the depth of my sorrow.[38]

He died a disillusioned old man, yet his official reputation maintained that he was an outstanding emperor. Undoubtedly his conscientiousness, his attempt to be impartial between Manchus and Chinese, his efforts to fulfil the obligations of a Confucian emperor, all justify this high reputation. But if a broader view is taken of the achievements of his reign it must be said that the glory of it concealed serious and unresolved problems.

The Reign of the Yongzheng Emperor, 1722–35

Kangxi's successor was his fourth son, Yinzhen, who reigned as the Yongzheng emperor. His reign was much shorter than that of his father, and was also more controversial. He was alleged to have usurped the throne and then to have disposed of his brothers and rivals ruthlessly. Thereafter he pursued his objectives single-mindedly, strengthening the autocratic character of the imperial institution. This negative verdict may be contrasted with the claim that he was 'the greatest centralizer and stabilizer' of the Qing dynasty, and that he 'revitalized the state administration, and fostered a time of economic prosperity'.[39]

The question of his succession and treatment of his brothers may be dealt with first. The argument that Yongzheng usurped the throne is based on suggestions that the intended successor was Yinti, Kangxi's fourteenth son, who was unable to enforce his claim because he was absent from Beijing at the crucial moment of his father's final illness. According to some accounts Kangxi's death was sudden and even accelerated by Yinzhen, who then seized the throne and fabricated evidence to prove that the late emperor had named him as his successor in the presence of several of his sons. The usurpation thesis has been challenged, one view being that Yinzhen succeeded because his actions were more astute than those of his rivals, another that there is evidence to show that he was indeed Kangxi's chosen successor. The allegations of usurpation are discredited as the work of southern intellectuals who had found favour under Kangxi but who were to be set aside by Yongzheng.[40] As for the accusation of ruthlessness, there was certainly some truth in that. Eight of his brothers died during his reign and Yinti was kept in confinement for most of that time. The most notorious incident was Yongzheng's imprisonment of Kangxi's eighth and ninth sons who both died in captivity under suspicious circumstances. However, an autocratic emperor could not tolerate any challenge to his position and his ruthless actions can be matched by the trust and affection he bestowed on Yinxiang, Kangxi's thirteenth son, until he died in 1730.

The more important estimate of Yongzheng concerns his achievements as a ruler. Undoubtedly in his reign a number of valuable reforms were introduced. In 1723 he started a new system for nominating the heir apparent. Under this the ruler selected his heir from among his eligible sons and then, without revealing his choice, placed the name in a sealed box which was only to be opened upon the emperor's death. Such a method might prevent the growth of factions centred on those Manchu princes who had a claim to the throne. A similar objective lay behind a reform of the banner system under which command of the five inferior

202

banners, the banners loyal to the imperial princes, was taken out of their hands and put under bureaucratic control.

Two other areas of reform were more complex and more difficult to assess. One of these concerned the effective operation of the offices of central government. It has been noted earlier how in the later years of Kangxi's reign the system of palace memorials was introduced, and how this enabled the emperor to receive confidential information. Under Yongzheng, in response to the increasing volume of work and the need to deal rapidly with military emergencies, a form of response to such memorials was introduced. Known as a 'court letter' this was an informal and secret communication. In an early surviving example Yongzheng wrote to Yue Zhongqi, the governor-general of Sichuan:

> Because I have so many edicts, there is no time personally to write on the memorials. [I just] orally tell the grand secretaries [that is, those on duty in the inner court] what to send in a court letter.[41]

The next development was the creation of a consolidated agency to handle the business of the inner court, the institution to be known as the Grand Council. It has often been claimed that the Grand Council was the creation of Yongzheng and that it came into being in 1729, with the establishment of the Military Finance Section set up in the inner court to deal with matters relating to the campaign against the Dzungar. Recent research suggests a more complex and evolutionary origin. Under Yongzheng several informal, and in the first instance temporary, bodies were created to handle the Dzungar campaign, the reason being that this was an ambitious and costly venture, liable to be undermined by embezzlement. However it was only in the early years of Qianlong's reign that these separate groups were consolidated into what is recognisably the Grand Council.

Another fundamental reform initiated in Yongzheng's reign concerned taxation. He had inherited a fiscal system which impoverished peasants, enriched wealthy landowners and left both central and local government inadequately supplied with funds to carry out their responsibilities. Two particular problems may be identified: the imposition on peasants of substantial surcharges on top of the regular taxes, and the apportionment of tax revenue between central and local government, with perhaps only 21 per cent of the land and head taxes being retained to support local administration, and much of this being used for purposes properly described as the responsibilities of central government.[42]

The key measure promoted by Yongzheng concerned what was known as the meltage fee. In theory this was the surcharge levied to cover the losses caused by melting down the broken silver used for the payment of tax and casting it into ingots to be remitted to central government. This surcharge, which in some provinces was a heavy burden on those least able to pay, was a tolerated abuse and much of it went on customary gifts to officials to supplement their entirely inadequate salaries. The reforms sponsored by Yongzheng legalised the meltage fee at a lower rate and prohibited or reduced the customary gifts. The legalised meltage fee was to be retained locally and used for public welfare projects and to supplement officials' salary, the additional payment being described as *yanglian*, that is to 'nourish incorruptibility'.

How effective were these reforms? It has been claimed that they consolidated Yongzheng's power, improved state finances and enhanced the common people's well-being.[43] They have been described as marking an important step in the development of the modern state in which the concept of government responsibility went beyond the collection of taxes and the maintenance of public order, to include an element of social responsibility. Certainly until the last decades of the eighteenth century public finances were much improved, the treasury was in surplus and it was possible to grant tax remission to areas hit by famine. But it has also been admitted that the effect of the reforms did not last and that the problems which had prompted them returned before the end of the century. Moreover it has been suggested that these problems were in fact insoluble: China was an agrarian society, with only a limited overseas trade. Almost to the end of the dynasty the yield of its agrarian taxes exceeded that of commercial taxes.[44] This tax base was too narrow and incapable of bearing a high level of taxation. It yielded less than 5 per cent of the gross national product – insufficient to finance a modern government or to promote industrialisation.[45]

It would be unfair to judge Yongzheng's reign solely on these grounds, for his achievement in several other spheres should also be taken into account. The common theme in these activities, as in the case of his administrative and fiscal reforms, was the extension of imperial power. He pursued a vigorous policy towards the ethnic minorities in the south. The traditional means of controlling these minorities, for example the Miao, Yao and Lolo peoples, whose main centres of population were in Guangxi, Guizhou, Yunnan and Sichuan, was the *tusi* or tribal headman system, under which a senior member of the community was given an official rank and title, which was usually hereditary.[46] The headman was expected to maintain peace, but otherwise the community was allowed to remain undisturbed. Such a policy might allow sufficient control in the early stages of Chinese expansion, but by the Qing period this was no longer the case. The loyalty of some tribes had come under suspicion at the time of the rebellion of the Three Feudatories. In addition economic motives, for example the demand for copper from Yunnan, may in part explain the forward move. But the underlying reason was the undesirability of allowing tribal chiefs to exercise feudal power within the confines of a centralised empire. Under Yongzheng, Oertai, a Manchu who had unusually passed the *juren* examination, was promoted to acting governor-general of Yunnan and Guizhou with the specific task of 'pacifying' the Miao, abolishing the hereditary headmen and bringing the ethnic minorities into the provincial administrative system. His responsibilites were later extended to Guangxi and over a period of six years he forcibly expanded the power of central government in the region.

Yongzheng was very aware of the importance of asserting ideological conformity. In 1670 Kangxi had circulated the famous Sacred Edict which contained sixteen maxims defining appropriate behaviour. Early in his reign Yongzheng went further, issuing the *Amplified Instructions on the Sacred Edict*, which included his own commentaries on his father's work, with an additional emphasis on the importance of loyalty to the sovereign. These precepts were to be recited aloud publicly and memorised by scholars. Yongzheng was sensitive to any sign of residual anti-Manchu sentiment as well as any accusation that he had usurped the throne, and certain vindictive acts may be attributed to this. One such occurred in the case of the seventeenth-century scholar Lu Liuliang, who had included some anti-Manchu comments in his essays and who had famously stipulated in his will that he should not be buried in any clothes of Manchu design. His writings inspired a Hunanese scholar named Zeng Jing to plot a rebellion against Yongzheng. In 1729 he tried to involve Yue Zhongqi, governor-general of Sichuan and Shaanxi, in his plans. Yue betrayed the plot and Yongzheng wreaked a dreadful revenge not on Zeng Jing but on Lu Liuliang, ordering the destruction of his writings, the dismemberment of his corpse and the punishment of his descendants. But he dealt leniently with Zeng Jing, using him as an example in an ideological campaign intended to forestall any further criticism of Yongzheng himself or of the Manchus. After the Lu Liuliang affair Yongzheng produced a book justifying Manchu rule of China on orthodox Confucian grounds, claiming that it was the virtue of their rulers which had led to the mandate of heaven being transferred to them.

Qing China at its Height: the Reign of Qianlong, 1736–95

If Yongzheng may be said to have consolidated the Manchu position on the Chinese throne, it was his fourth son, who ruled as the Qianlong emperor, who profited from his endeavours. Qianlong's reign was the longest, and in some ways the most glorious, in Chinese history. During those years China's boundaries reached their widest extent, her population attained a new high point, a prolonged period of internal peace occurred, and feats of scholarly and artistic achievement were recorded. On the other hand, and with hindsight, it has been argued that it was under Qianlong that the evidence of dynastic decline can first be detected, and even more serious threats to the imperial system and China's traditional society began to emerge.

What sort of person was this occupant of the Chinese throne? Because the identity of the heir to the throne was a secret, the future Qianlong emperor had been given the same education as his half-brother. This was an education designed to produce a monarch who had learnt the Chinese classics and who had studied the orthodox Zhu Xi commentaries, who was familiar with history and the arts as well as adept in the military skills expected of a Manchu ruler. It was an education which stressed historical precedents and the ethical basis of imperial role. From it Qianlong learned of the importance of the emperor's personal example and the necessity of his using ministers of high talent. In the first decade of his reign these lessons appeared to have been well learned, for he relied on experienced statesmen, such as Oertai, and he pursued modest objectives. But in the middle years his principal minister, Yu Minzhong, never dared to disagree with him, and Qianlong assumed a large personal role in making policy decisions. His energy was extraordinary, for apart from dealing with the massive quantities of paperwork which reached him, he emulated his grandfather in making six major tours and in directing military campaigns. These were expensive operations and were accompanied by increasing extravagance at court. In his final years Qianlong fell under the influence of his favourite, Heshen, and all semblance of practising what he had been taught seemed to be lost.[47] However his abdication in 1796, a gesture of piety towards his grandfather, the length of whose reign he did not wish to outstrip, was a remarkable assertion of the continued strength of the concept of a Confucian monarch.

In terms of the practice of government Qianlong's reign saw a consolidation of the centralising tendencies which had been a marked feature of his father's rule. The most obvious example of this was the development of the Grand Council from the inner-court groups developed under Yongzheng. The council, which acted in secret and was frequently presided over by the emperor himself, handled all the most important business of the day, from the conduct of military campaigns to the promotion of literary enterprises. It was a relatively small body, usually having five or six members, which made it practicable for it to accompany the emperor on tour. Although Manchus remained the dominant ethnic group on the council, through it Chinese officials gained new influence on policy-making. Ironically, as the council increased its effectiveness during the course of the reign, it reduced the need for the emperor's personal intervention, a factor which was to become significant under the less capable successors of Qianlong.[48]

Under Qianlong the operation of the bureaucracy remained largely unchanged. At the centre routine business was handled by the six boards or ministries, which had limited authority because senior provincial officials were answerable directly to the emperor. Qianlong continued the established policy of making these appointments without distinction between Chinese and Manchus. Nevertheless, an important change in the ethnic composition of this essential group was taking place. Chinese bannermen, who at the beginning of the dynasty had occupied the majority of the appointments as governors-general and governors now lost their dominance. New appointees were for the most part Manchu or Han Chinese. This alteration epitomised the changing relationship between the Manchu ruling class and its Chinese subjects: Manchus were now sufficiently sinicised and sufficiently administratively skilled to take on these posts and at the same time the dynasty no longer feared sharing key provincial appointments with Han Chinese.[49]

During Qianlong's reign, and under his patronage, the arts and literature flourished. The emperor himself practised painting and calligraphy. He claimed to be an arbiter of taste, calling for paintings in the imperial collection to be displayed before him so that he could endorse them with his own inscriptions and seals. Among the artists he approved was the Italian Jesuit Giuseppe Castiglione, who became a court painter.[50] For the same reason he wrote prose and verse, leaving some 42,000 verses attributed to him. He commissioned major scholarly enterprises, the largest being the Siku quanshu, the Complete Library of the Four Branches of Literature, compiled between 1773 and 1782. This was a collection of 3,500 literary works representing the best in the Chinese literary tradition. Collecting and editing these works and transcribing them to make seven copies provided work, often of a routine kind, for an army of scholars.

The making of this collection preserved many rare works, but it also had a more sinister purpose, for its compilation was used to carry out a literary inquisition. Books were searched for any hint of disrespectful comments about the Manchus. These were either expunged or the destruction of the book itself was ordered: in this way over two thousand works of literature were suppressed. In addition punishment was meted out to all held responsible for the offensive publication.

This aspect of the enterprise has led to a conflict of views. Writing in the 1930s, L. Carrington Goodrich saw the literary inquisition as the major reason for the compilation of the *Complete Library*, and identified Qianlong as the instigator of this censorship, his purpose being to establish greater control over the lives and thoughts of his subjects. Goodrich concluded that its effects were to further estrange the Manchus and the Chinese, to cause a great gap in Chinese literature and to intimidate a generation of Chinese writers. He suggested that it played a part in bringing about a spirit of revolt which became manifest in the nineteenth century.[51] More recently, R. Kent Guy has pointed out that the scholars who undertook the compilation were not doing so for self-seeking or craven motives, and that the suppression of material offensive to the Manchus was only a small part of the project. They co-operated with enthusiasm because the work gave them an opportunity to review texts on a larger scale than it would be possible for them to do as individuals, and in the course of their review they could select among the ancient texts those which most closely supported their opinions.[52]

How powerful were the intellectual currents during these years? In the early Qing period much scholarly activity had been expended on what were known as *kaozheng*, literally 'search for evidence', studies – careful textual studies of the Confucian classics. It has been argued that this type of work, exemplified by the compilation of the *Complete Library*, coupled with the effects of the examination system and the rising competition for scholarly employment, had by the eighteenth century led to the dominance of an inward-looking conservatism and a sterile quest for minute and often trivial knowledge. On the other hand a more positive view has been taken of *kaozheng* studies. It has been suggested that textual studies required empirical methods and exact scholarship, qualities quite foreign to the tradition of Confucian scholarly enquiry. Although only a minority of students became involved in these studies, in Jiangnan an academic community developed and scholarly research and teaching were promoted. Among the subjects studied were mathematics and astronomy; information from Jesuit sources was incorporated and a sense of progress was asserted.[53]

Under Qianlong the Qing empire in Inner Asia achieved its greatest extent. By 1800 Chinese Inner Asia comprised four main areas: Manchuria, Mongolia, Xinjiang and Tibet. Manchuria was treated as a Manchu homeland and restraints were imposed on Han Chinese immigration, although settlers had already arrived in Fengtian in considerable numbers. Mongolia was garrisoned by Qing forces, but there was no longer any danger from Mongol warriors. Mongol society was now divided into banners and Mongol nobles held ranks in the Qing aristocracy. Another means of control lay through Qing patronage of Lamaism or Tibetan Buddhism. The opulent Lama Temple in Beijing, which has recently been restored, provides a vivid glimpse of how effectively this was done. Further to the west Qianlong consolidated his father's success, waging further campaigns which established China as the dominant power in Central Asia. Between 1755 and 1757 the Dzungar were finally subdued and subsequently an administrative centre was established at Ili and military units stationed in that region. Further campaigns confirmed Chinese dominance in Eastern Turkestan. This newly acquired territory, which amounted to approximately six million square miles, was named Xinjiang, the 'new frontier'. Finally there was the question of Tibet. In 1750 the Chinese position of influence achieved under Kangxi was threatened by a civil war. Qianlong's response was to have the Dalai Lama installed as both civil and spiritual leader of his country while at the same time keeping him firmly under Chinese control.[54]

The Qing continued the Ming procedures for the conduct of relations with foreigners and under Qianlong these reached a new level of formality. Foreign relations were conducted through the tributary system, an expression of Chinese cultural superiority over barbarians, which was modified to suit the needs of the Manchus. Under this system, states in a tributary relationship with China sent embassies to the Qing court at fixed intervals, the most frequent embassies being those of Korea which sent an annual tribute mission. The ceremony for the presentation of tribute was prescribed in minute detail, indicative of the moral value of the transaction for the rulers of China. Nevertheless it was also true that the granting of permission to trade was an important economic benefit to tributary states and of course to China as well.[55]

In the eighteenth century western commercial contacts with China increased, particularly because of the rising demand for tea. On the British side the monopoly of the trade was held by the British East India Company, which was also the effective government of large parts of India. The Chinese government confined the trade to southern ports and required foreign merchants to observe protocol when dealing with officials. The latter requirement infuriated Admiral George Anson, commanding a British squadron preying on Spanish shipping, who was kept waiting at Macao in 1743 after he had requested permission to refit his ship. The account of his voyage, which became a best-seller, included a hostile view of the Chinese which marks the beginning of a significant deterioration in western attitudes towards China. In 1759 a British trader named James Flint, sent to China by the East India Company to request an expansion of trade, reached Tianjin, only to be imprisoned and expelled. From 1760 foreign maritime trade was restricted to Guangzhou and had to be conducted with the Chinese merchant monopoly, known as the Cohong or Hong merchants, who operated under official supervision.

These measures indicated that the Qing government was determined to preserve the tributary system as the method of dealing with the barbarians from the Western Ocean, even though it had previous treated Russian envoys on a basis of equality. It was this which guaranteed the failure of the Macartney mission which reached Qianlong's court at Rehe in 1793. The mission had been sent by the British government to request better trading facilities. The barge which carried the mission sailed up the Bei river displaying flags bearing the inscription 'The English Ambassador bringing Tribute to the Emperor of China'. Considerable pressure was brought to bear on Macartney to observe the ceremonial required of a tributary mission and that in particular he should perform the *kotow*, the ritual three prostrations and nine head knockings. Macartney refused to do this and was only willing to treat the Qianlong emperor as he would his own sovereign, which was by going down before him on one knee. In the end the emperor agreed to this modification and Macartney was received at an audience. But in all other respects the visit was treated as a tribute mission, and all Macartney's requests were rejected.[56]

The key economic development of the eighteenth century was the massive increase in population. Between the end of the seventeenth century and the end of the eighteenth, the population of China approximately doubled from about 150 million to over 300 million. It continued to grow at a somewhat slower rate until the middle of the nineteenth century. This growth derived mainly from a decline in the mortality rate, although the reason for this is not entirely clear. It may be connected with the diffusion of new crops from America and with the prolonged peace of the eighteenth century. Such growth imposed an increasing strain on resources which was partly relieved by internal migration, the most important movements in the Qianlong period being to less developed parts of China, particularly to the upper Yangzi region, Taiwan and southern Manchuria. The clearing of new land in these areas provided good opportunities for pioneering farming families, though in time their activities were to cause disastrous erosion and flooding.[57] The increase in the area of land under cultivation and increases in output per acre produced a growth in food supply which, well into the eighteenth century, outstripped population growth. The evidence from various parts of the country suggests a rising standard of living and a general increase of wealth. But it has been calculated that at some point between 1750 and 1775, the optimum point was passed and the law of diminishing returns ensured that a slow decline in the amount of food available per head of population began to occur.[58]

Nevertheless an observer might be forgiven for regarding the economy of China under Qianlong as thriving. Commerce flourished, and a banking system had appeared which advanced loans and remitted funds, so encouraging long-distance trade. It was true that the monetary system in other respects remained poorly developed and that transportation depended heavily on the river and canal system. At the same time several important industries were flourishing, notably porcelain and iron and most importantly textiles. This evidence has encouraged a further debate on why China did not experience an industrial revolution, this time referring to the eighteenth century. The Marxist interpretation, as represented in China, has been to assert that the 'sprouts of capitalism' were emerging in China at this time, but they failed to develop because of the combined repressive effects of Qing feudalism and foreign capitalism. Western economic historians have been less willing to identify such 'sprouts of capitalism' and have tended to point out that it is more surprising that Europe did experience an industrial revolution than that China did not. Nevertheless they have identified a number of obstacles to industrialisation. One of these allegedly was the Chinese character: that although the Chinese had the capacity to invent new machinery, they lacked the entrepreneurial instinct to capitalise on their inventions. Another was the social system and the cultural values which it endorsed, in other words blame was laid on Confucianism and on the attitudes of officials. The third obstacle was government, the accusation being that the government failed to create the infrastructure necessary to foster industrialisation. Perhaps the most convincing argument is that put forward by Mark Elvin referring to the 'high-level equilibrium trap.' He suggested that the fundamental obstacle to China's industrialisation at this time was a positive, not a negative feature. It was the ability of the Chinese economy to respond effectively to any bottlenecks in production. For example, food output was increased by a constant series of small improvements which utilised the potential of traditional technology without resorting to the possibilities of modern science. In a similar manner, textile production was expanded not by importing cotton or by introducing machinery, but by using beancake fertiliser to increase the cotton crop, and by using moist underground cellars to enable cotton spinning to be carried out in the dry north. By these means the economy could continue to expand without going through a fundamental change. Such a process could continue, albeit with declining living standards, until either a Malthusian check reduced the population, or an exogenous shock forced the introduction of new technology.[59]

So far the description of Qianlong's reign has emphasised the successful extension of the imperial power and the prevalence of the dominant culture, an emphasis which reflects the assertions of official history. Over recent years a number of studies have appeared which explore the extent and character of dissent and of opposition during this period. One such study considered social criticism, taking as its starting point the famous novel *Rulin waishi*, *The Scholars*, written by Wu Jingzi in the 1740s. The book's main target was the civil service examination system and the appointment to office of those who had succeeded in it. Wu Jingzi himself was a failed examination candidate and his father, who had passed, made no progress in his career. The ironic description of a character in *The Scholars* may be based on Wu Jingzi's perception of his father:

When he was an official he showed no respect at all for his superiors, but instead just schemed to please the common people. And every day he spouted that nonsense about "fostering filiality and brotherhood" and "encouraging agriculture." These phrases are merely educational topics and flowery terms for use in essays, but he took them seriously. Since his superiors didn't approve, they dismissed him from office.[60]

Wu Jingzi satirised the operation of the examination system and in particular how it rewarded incompetence, but his criticism went deeper than merely protesting against the faults of a system of selection. The novel has been interpreted as a covert attack on Manchu rule, or on feudal exploitation, but perhaps it is better described as an expression of social criticism and as evidence of an intellectual unease which contrasted sharply with the complacent and conservative attitudes of the dominant culture.

Two other themes are prominent in the novel and may be related to tensions in Chinese society in the eighteenth century. The first was that of the position of women. It has been argued that while the subordination of women can be traced far back in Chinese history, that subordination was never stronger than under the Qing. Under the Manchus foot-binding became more popular, increased restrictions were placed on women mixing with men in public, and the pressure on widows to remain faithful to their husband's memory, even if this meant preferring suicide to dishonour, became increasingly strong.[61] In *The Scholars* Wu Jingzi attacked widow suicide and portrayed women as capable of intelligence and cultural refinement, often at the expense of boorish men. His contemporary, the poet and essayist Yuan Mei, wrote in the same vein, attacking the traditional view that 'absence of talent in women is synonymous with virtue'.[62] In the eighteenth century an increasing number of women received some education, although it was assumed that this would confirm their subordinate position in the society. However, before the end of the century, a debate had arisen over the content of women's learning which has been seen as marking a significant stage in the development of a female consciousness in China.[63]

The second issue related to popular religion. In *The Scholars*, Wu Jingzi had made satirical comments about supernatural religious beliefs, for example fortune-telling and geomancy. In so doing he echoed the scepticism publicly expressed by Confucian intellectuals, although in private they often followed the same practices. His scepticism was based on evidence of the inefficacy of such procedures rather than on any increase in scientific knowledge or rationalism. Popular religion continued to be strongly supported and incipient social strains – what has been called a 'premonitory shiver' on the eve of China's tragic modern age[64] – were revealed not by a rejection of popular religion, but by a manifestation of the strength of its hold on the population. The reference is to the sorcery scare of 1768, when a rumour began to circulate in the lower Yangzi region alleging that sorcerers were roaming the land and stealing men's souls by clipping off the ends of their queues. As the rumour spread, and as supposed instances of soul-stealing multiplied, the emperor himself, believing that soul-stealing masked sedition, urged provincial officials to apprehend suspected sorcerers. They complied in a routine fashion and by the autumn the scare had died down. Nevertheless the scare may be interpreted as having a wider significance, a response to 'danger from persons unknown and forces unseen'. It might be seen as a reflection of a changing economy, population pressure, increased migration and the growth of an underclass of displaced persons.[65]

The same factors may have been relevant to the rebellion, known as the Wang Lun uprising, which broke out in Shandong in 1774. This was the precursor of the much larger White Lotus Rebellion of 1796–1804, with which it shared a common ideology. The White Lotus religion had first appeared in the sixteenth century, mainly in the north of China. In normal times members of White Lotus sects practised various life-prolonging and salvation-inducing arts. At other times sects became the nuclei of millenarian movements which might also become anti-dynastic rebellions. Because of this danger the state suppressed such cults when discovered, and the action taken in the years preceding the Wang Lun uprising against two other White Lotus groups may have alarmed the sectarians. However, the reason for their actions given by those involved in the uprising was their belief in the imminence of the millennium. With this inspiration, in the summer of 1774

Wang Lun's followers seized three local towns, killing officials, releasing prisoners and appropriating grain and silver reserves. Their apparent goal was to seize Beijing, but they failed to achieve their first major target, the capture of the important city of Linqing. The account of the attack on Linqing reveals what importance both sides placed on ritual and magic in these affairs. Wang Lun had recruited women to his sect and the attackers made conspicuous use of magical arts. To negate their use of magical power the defenders likewise used women and Wang Lun himself noted that 'on the city wall there were women wearing red clothing but naked from the waist down, bleeding and urinating in order to destroy our power.'[66] Eventually the Qing government managed to concentrate sufficient well-armed forces against the rebels to defeat them. Wang Lun and many of his followers died in the fighting, but other rebels were captured and punished with methodical severity.

This uprising has been described as the 'first crack in the smooth facade' of the high Qing. Perhaps that is to put it too dramatically: the military ineffectiveness displayed by banner and army of the Green Standard troops was nothing new; the uprising was eventually quelled and it was not followed by a wave of popular movements.[67]

However the facade was damaged by a different type of threat, that occasioned by the rise to power of Heshen, the emperor's favourite. Heshen, who had been born in 1750, was a Manchu bannerman. He attracted Qianlong's attention in 1772 and was quickly promoted to be a member of the Grand Council. It has often been claimed that his relationship with the emperor was a homosexual one, although this has never been proved. Once he had established himself as the emperor's favourite, he wielded a tremendous amount of influence, being able to secure the appointment of his nominees to key positions and being able to demand lavish bribes from all who needed his support in matters requiring Qianlong's attention. He has been accused of having brought about a disastrous fall in the standards of government by his demands on officials for bribes. As these demands were passed on to the people, this was said to have aroused discontent leading to rebellion, the reference being to the outbreak of the White Lotus rebellion. It was further alleged that the reason why it took so long to suppress that rebellion was because Heshen and his friends were embezzling vast sums from the military appropriations. The situation became even worse after Qianlong's abdication, when Heshen was effectively regent, profiting from the retired emperor's increased senility. Immediately after Qianlong's death in 1799 Heshen was forced to commit suicide, leaving a fortune estimated at 80,000,000 taels.

Heshen's career poses a conundrum: was he the cause or a symptom of the dynastic decline that began to manifest itself in the last year's of Qianlong's reign? It has been argued that there are too many other explanations for the beginning of dynastic decline to justify heaping much of the blame onto one man – that being the verdict of traditional Chinese historiography which has tended to lay blame on the moral shortcomings of the individual. Certainly the emperor himself should share the responsibility because he failed to respect the principle of taking advice from loyal ministers. But that was a principle to which the Manchu emperors only paid lip service. If they chose to ignore it and exercise their autocratic powers there was little that could be done by officials to stop them.[68] To blame Heshen for a disastrous increase in official corruption is to ignore evidence of earlier evidence of embezzlement of funds intended for military purposes, for example for the suppression of uprisings of aboriginal tribes in western Sichuan in 1747–9 and 1771–6. It is also to misunderstand the reason why corruption existed, which was not necessarily because officials and their assistants were venal, or because the standards of government had declined. It arose from the system itself, which did not recognise the tension between a bureaucratic imperial state which operated on detailed and impersonal regulations, and the individual interests of those affected by its operation. What was condemned as corruption might be described as the use of inducements to make this system work, and for this reason the suggestion that the Qing government collapsed because it became increasingly corrupt has been rejected.[69]

But even blaming the autocracy and citing corruption as evidence of the beginnings of dynastic decline would not be enough to explain the deep crisis which was now beginning to emerge, albeit largely unnoticed. In the eighteenth century the Qing empire had been in its glory. In the nineteenth century the same empire was to experience internal humiliation and external defeat. The point of change between those two conditions had now been reached.

Part Two

Preface

The purpose of this book is to provide an introduction to the history of China since 1800, which draws on recent scholarship and highlights areas of historical controversy. To achieve this in a single volume much detail has been omitted in favour of a discussion of some broad themes. This implies a process of selection, which is necessarily arbitrary and subjective. As the poet Ziya Pasha wrote:

> The things I've chosen are a drop, no more;
> The undiminished sea still crowds the shore.

In the companion volume to this publication, *A History of China: Prehistory to c. 1800*, reference was made to the excitement aroused by recent archaeological discoveries in China, and the fresh light which these had shed on the country's early history. In the period studied in this volume no discoveries of like importance have been made. However, a different sort of excitement has been engendered by the dramatic events which crowd into this period and by the sharp controversies sparked off by them. It is hoped that this book will convey some of this excitement to the reader and encourage him or her to read further, exploring the scholarly literature which is now appearing in ever-increasing quantity and, for the most part, increasing sophistication.

This book is intended to appeal to readers and students for whom the study of Chinese history is a relatively new experience. To avoid making that experience too frustrating an effort has been made to present the information and interpretation in a clear and acceptable form. Each chapter begins with a brief summary of the main events covered and the Chronological Table (see p. xiii) sets out the sequence of incidents. It is recognized that Chinese names and Chinese terms can cause confusion, so the references have been kept within the bounds of moderation. The use of place names has also been restricted. Very often a location is indicated by the name of a province or a major city, and it is assumed that the reader will become familiar with these names. The maps provided are intended to illustrate historical situations where the spatial context is of particular importance.

In the transliteration of Chinese personal and geographical names, and technical terms, the form used is *pinyin*, the official system of romanization, rather than the traditional Wade-Giles system. *Pinyin* is the form which is now used in newspapers and which is being adopted generally in scholarly works, although Wade-Giles is still used in the ongoing fifteen-volume *Cambridge History of China*. All Chinese personal and place names have been transliterated into *pinyin*. Thus Mao Tse-tung is rendered as Mao Zedong and, rather less familiarly, Chiang Kai-shek is referred to as Jiang Jieshi. Likewise, Peking is transliterated as Beijing, Canton as Guangzhou and Hong Kong as Xianggang. Direct quotations which contain spellings in the Wade-Giles system have been amended to *pinyin*. When familiar names first appear in unfamiliar forms, the familiar form is also quoted and this practice is also followed in the index.

For the most part Pinyin spelling approximates to the phonetic values of English, with the following notable exceptions:

c   is pronounced 'ts' as in Tsar

i   is pronounced 'ee', except when it follows c, ch, r, s, sh, z and zh, in which case it is pronounced approximately 'er'

ian is pronounced 'ien'

q   is pronounced 'ch' as in cheap

r   is similar to the English 'r' but is pronounced with the tongue behind the front teeth

x   is pronounced 'sh' as in sham

z   is pronounced 'ds' as in hands

zh   is pronounced 'j' as in jasmine

When citing Chinese names the family name is given first, followed by the given name. However, in the endnotes, to maintain consistency with the citation of other names, the Western practice of putting the surname last is observed.

The emperors of the Qing dynasty are not designated by their personal names, but by their reign titles as follows:

Shunzhi	1644–61
Kangxi	1662–1722
Yongzheng	1723–35
Qianlong	1736–95
Jiaqing	1796–1820
Daoguang	1821–50
Xianfeng	1851–61
Tongzhi	1862–74
Guangxu	1875–1908
Xuantong	1909–12

When citing non-Chinese names or terms, for example when referring to Mongol or Manchu names, the form in which they are best known in Western writing has been preferred.

Acknowledgements

I would like to thank my colleagues at the University of Huddersfield for their support and encouragement, and for the allowance of time which has enabled me to write this book. Over the years I have discussed many of the issues with my students and their lively responses and insights have contributed significantly to the development of the views expressed here.

Modern China: An Illustrated History is intended to offer a distillation of recent scholarship on the modern history of China. My most substantial debt is therefore to the many other historians of China whose work has provided the substance and inspiration for this book. I have endeavoured to acknowledge my debt fully by references in the endnotes. My access to the literature has been greatly helped by the friendly assistance which I have received from the University of Huddersfield Library Services. My thanks should also go to Steve Pratt of the School of Applied Sciences at the University for his many hours of work on the maps. Last, but not least, I must thank my wife Jan for her constant support and assistance in bringing this work to a conclusion.

Chronological Table

	1644	Manchu conquest of China
	1689	China and Russia conclude the Treaty of Nerchinsk
	1712	The Kangxi emperor fixes in perpetuity the number of adult males liable to pay tax
	1720	Formation of the Cohong
	1725	Treaty of Kiakhta defines Sino–Russian border
	1742	The Pope condemns accommodation with Chinese rites
	1760	Foreign maritime trade confined to Guangzhou
	1774	Wang Lun uprising
	1784	*Lady Hughes* incident
Sept	1793	The Qianlong emperor receives Lord Macartney
	1796	Outbreak of White Lotus rebellion
	1813	Eight Trigrams uprising in Shandong and Zhili
	1816	Lord Amherst's embassy to China
	1834	British East India Company's monopoly of trade with China ends
Dec	1838	Lin Zexu appointed Imperial Commissioner
Mar	1839	Lin Zexu forces British traders to hand over opium stocks
Jan	1841	Convention of Chuanbi
May	1841	Sanyuanli incident
Aug	1842	Treaty of Nanjing
	1843	Hong Xiuquan experiences his visions
		Supplementary Treaty of the Bogue
Jan	1851	Establishment of the Taiping Heavenly Kingdom
	1852	Yellow river begins to shift to its northern course
Mar	1853	Taiping rebels capture Nanjing
Sept	1853	Small Sword society captures Shanghai
Oct	1856	*Arrow* incident
Dec	1857	British and French forces capture Guangzhou
June	1858	Treaty of Tianjin
June	1859	British and French forces defeated at Dagu forts
Oct	1860	Convention of Beijing
Mar	1861	Establishment of the Zongli Yamen
	1861	Publication of *A Record of Facts to Ward Off Heterodoxy*
July	1864	Nanjing recaptured from Taiping rebels
Sept	1865	Establishment of the Jiangnan arsenal
	1867	Woren's *Objection to Western Learning*
	1868	Nian rebels defeated
Aug	1868	Yangzhou anti-missionary incident

	June	1870	Tianjin massacre
		1872	China Merchants' Steam Navigation Company proposed
		1873	North-west Muslim rebellion defeated
		1875	Guo Songtao appointed to head an apology mission to Great Britain
		1876	Zhefu Convention
			Start of three-year drought and famine in North China
		1877	*Wei Yuan*, China's first iron-framed ship launched
		1878	Drilling begins at the Kaiping mines
		1879	Liuqiu (Ryukyu) islands annexed by Japan
		1883	France and China contest control of Tongking
	Aug	1884	France destroys the Fuzhou shipyard
	June	1885	Treaty of Tianjin concludes Sino-French War
		1891	Kang Youwei publishes *An Enquiry into the Classics Forged during the Xin Period*
	Aug	1894	Outbreak of the Sino-Japanese War
	Sept	1894	Beiyang fleet defeated at the Battle of the Yalu river
	Nov	1894	Sun Zhongshan founds Society to Restore China's Prosperity
17	Apr	1895	Treaty of Shimonoseki concludes the Sino-Japanese War
23	Apr	1895	Triple intervention leads to Japan retroceding the Liaodong peninsula to China
	June	1896	Secret Sino-Russian treaty signed
	Nov	1897	Germany obtains a ninety-nine year lease on Jiaozhou bay
	May	1898	Zhang Zhidong publishes *An Exhortation to Study*
	June	1898	Great Britain obtains a ninety-nine year lease on the Xianggang (Hong Kong) New Territories
11	June	1898	Edict issued committing the dynasty to reform
21	Sept	1898	The Empress Dowager resumes the regency and orders the arrest of Kang Youwei and other reformers
	Sept	1899	Boxers begin attacks on Christian converts
20	June	1900	Start of siege of foreign legations in Beijing
21	June	1900	Court edict referring to a 'declaration of war' against foreigners
	Jan	1901	Reform edict promulgated
	Sept	1901	Boxer protocol signed
	July	1905	Empress Dowager announces her commitment to constitutional change
			Formation of the Revolutionary Alliance
2	Sept	1905	Edict announcing the abolition of the examination system
	Dec	1906	Pingliuli uprising suppressed
14	Nov	1908	Death of the Guangxu emperor
15	Nov	1908	Death of the Empress Dowager
		1909	First elections for provincial assemblies
	Oct	1910	First National Assembly convened
10	Oct	1911	'Double Tenth' uprising at Wuchang
1	Jan	1912	Chinese Republic established

	Feb	1912	Abdication of the Xuantong emperor
	Sept	1913	'Second Revolution' defeated
	Jan	1915	Japan presents the Twenty-one Demands
	Sept	1915	*New Youth* magazine founded
	June	1916	Death of Yuan Shikai
	July	1917	Zhang Xun briefly restores the Manchu emperor
	Aug	1917	China declares war on Germany
4	May	1919	News that the Paris Peace Conference has awarded former German interests in Shandong to Japan reaches Beijing
	July	1921	First Congress of the Chinese Communist Party
	Jan	1922	Chinese Seamen's Union strike starts in Xianggang
	Oct	1923	Borodin begins reorganization of the Guomindang
	May	1924	Jiang Jieshi appointed Commandant of the Huangpu (Whampoa) Military Academy
12	Mar	1925	Death of Sun Zhongshan
30	May	1925	Twelve Chinese demonstrators killed in Shanghai
	July	1926	Northern Expedition launched
	Jan	1927	Mao Zedong investigates the peasant movement in Hunan
	Apr	1927	Jiang Jieshi purges left-wing organizations in Shanghai
	July	1927	Communists expelled from the Guomindang
1	Aug	1927	CCP attempts uprising at Nanchang
	Sept	1927	Autumn Harvest insurrection
	Dec	1927	Guangzhou Commune established and suppressed
	May	1928	Guomindang and Japanese troops clash at Jinan
10	Oct	1928	Nationalist government inaugurated at Nanjing
	Feb	1929	Mao Zedong establishes a rural base at Ruijin, Jiangxi
	Sept	1931	Shenyang (Mukden) incident
7	Nov	1931	Chinese Soviet Republic established at Ruijin
	Oct	1933	Fifth 'bandit-suppression campaign' launched by Jiang Jieshi
	Oct	1934	Start of Long March
	Jan	1935	Zunyi conference
9	Dec	1935	Student-led protest against the Guomindang's failure to oppose Japanese encroachment
	Dec	1936	Xi'an incident
7	July	1937	Marco Polo Bridge incident and start of the Sino-Japanese War
	Dec	1937	Rape of Nanjing
	Dec	1938	Defection of Wang Jingwei
	Aug	1940	Communists launch the Hundred Regiments campaign
	Jan	1941	Communist New Fourth Army attacked by Nationalist forces
7	Dec	1941	Japanese attack on Pearl Harbor
	Feb	1942	CCP 'rectification campaign' launched at Yan'an
	Apr	1944	Japan launches Operation Ichigo
14	Aug	1945	Surrender of Japan
	July	1946	Start of civil war
10	Oct	1947	Outline Agrarian Law promulgated

Chronological Table

	Nov	1948	Shenyang captured by the Communists
			Start of the Battle of Huai-Hai
1	Oct	1949	Proclamation of the People's Republic of China
	Feb	1950	China and the Soviet Union sign the Treaty of Alliance and Mutual Assistance
	Nov	1950	China intervenes in the Korean War
30	June	1953	Census of population
	Sept	1953	First Five-Year Plan initiated
	May	1956	Mao Zedong declares 'Let a hundred flowers bloom'
	June	1957	Anti-Rightist campaign directed against intellectuals
	Apr	1958	First commune formed
	May	1958	Beginning of the Great Leap Forward
	Mar	1959	Outbreak of Tibetan revolt
	July	1959	Lushan conference
	July	1960	Soviet experts withdrawn from China
	Oct	1962	Start of war with India
	Oct	1964	China's first atomic bomb exploded
5	Aug	1966	Mao Zedong's 'big-character poster' 'Bombard the Headquarters' published
18	Aug	1966	Mao Zedong reviews Red Guards in Tiananmen Square
	Jan	1967	The 'Shanghai storm'
	Mar	1969	Sino-Soviet clash on Zhenbao (Damansky) island
	Apr	1969	New CCP leadership established
	Sept	1971	Lin Biao killed in a plane crash
	Feb	1972	President Nixon visits China
	Jan	1976	Death of Zhou Enlai
	Apr	1976	Demonstration in memory of Zhou Enlai suppressed
	July	1976	Tangshan earthquake
9	Sept	1976	Death of Mao Zedong
	July	1977	Deng Xiaoping returns to office
	Aug	1977	Four Modernizations policy adopted
		1979	Responsibility system introduced
			First 'Special Economic Zones' opened
			'One-child family' campaign started
	Nov	1980	Start of the trial of the Gang of Four
	Apr	1981	Arrest of leading dissidents
	Dec	1986	Student demonstrations start at the Chinese University of Science and Technology, Hefei
		1987	Zhao Ziyang becomes Secretary-General of the CCP
	Apr	1989	Death of Hu Yaobang
3	June	1989	Tiananmen Square massacre
	Jan	1992	Deng Xiaoping makes a southern tour and visits Shenzhen
	Feb	1997	Death of Deng Xiaoping
30	June	1997	Xianggang (Hong Kong) returned to China

13
China at the Beginning of the Nineteenth Century

China in Decline?

Lord Macartney, sent by Britain to China in 1792 to open diplomatic relations and to seek commercial advantages, wrote in his journal:

> The Empire of China is an old, crazy, First rate man-of-war, which a fortunate succession of able and vigilant officers has contrived to keep afloat for these one hundred and fifty years past, and to overawe their neighbours merely by her bulk and appearance, but whenever an insufficient man happens to have the command upon deck, adieu to the discipline and safety of the ship. She may perhaps not sink outright; she may drift some time as a wreck, and will then be dashed to pieces on the shore; but she can never be rebuilt on the old bottom.[1]

This view, that by the end of the eighteenth century imperial China had reached an irreversible stage in its decline, is commonly expressed in many Western and Chinese histories of the country. It is a view which suggests that it was internal decay rather than external aggression which initially undermined the empire. In Western accounts particular stress has been put on the growth of bureaucratic corruption, on the failure to achieve technological progress, and on the effects of the growth of the Chinese population, which approximately doubled in the eighteenth century. The outbreak of peasant rebellion, in the form of the White Lotus rebellion which began in 1796, has been seen as a symptom of the downward phase of the dynastic cycle which would inevitably have led to the overthrow of the Qing, or Manchu, dynasty. This decline encouraged, perhaps even justified, the aggression of the West, which after securing the imperialist privileges it desired, then found it in its interest to prop up the dynasty until it fell in 1911. As Macartney predicted, the Chinese empire did not sink outright, it drifted some time as a wreck, but it could not be rebuilt on the old bottom. The imperial system of government and the economy and culture which had developed under its aegis had come to the end of its effective life.

For rather different reasons, a similarly pessimistic view of China's situation at the end of the eighteenth century has been taken by both Chinese nationalists and

Chinese Marxists. For Liang Qichao, the leading nationalist thinker of the late imperial period, the evidence of decline could be found in the sterility of eighteenth-century Qing scholarship. For Marxists there was evidence that the Chinese economy had once had the capacity to develop. Under the Ming it had produced 'sprouts of capitalism', but these had shrivelled, partly because of the disastrous impact of the Manchu invasion. A second burgeoning occurred in the eighteenth century, but the effects of oppressive bureaucracy and the onset of Western imperialism prevented China from initiating an indigenous industrial revolution.[2]

Such a picture of irreversible decay has not been fully discredited, but recent scholarship has stressed some positive aspects of eighteenth-century China. Under the Qianlong emperor (r. 1736–95) the Chinese empire had reached its greatest extent. The massive population rise was the result of prolonged peace and security and for much of the century was accompanied by rising living standards. Overpopulation was eased by extensive migration to underpopulated areas. The operation of government became increasingly centralized and more sophisticated. There was bureaucratic corruption, but this was an endemic problem and one common to bureaucracies in all parts of the world rather than a peculiar weakness of China's bureaucratic system. As for intellectual stagnation, the textual studies of the Confucian scholar, which have been regarded as evidence of an inward-looking conservatism, have been re-interpreted as achieving new standards of exact scholarship and empirical method. Accompanying this scholarly activity, the eighteenth century also saw the development of a lively urban culture, its most characteristic product being the novel.

Of course the debate does not end there. For those who argue that imperial China had reached the limits of its achievement, one particular failure of government is seen as having special significance. In the early part of the century the Yongzheng emperor had tried to solve an intractable problem: how could an empire, based on an agrarian economy, extract from its peasants sufficient income to operate effectively at both central and provincial government level? The failure of his attempt to improve the finances of local government and to raise the salaries of local officials ensured that the imperial system of government lacked the resources to meet the demands created by the growth in population and the increasing complexity of government.[3]

The Emperor and the Court

Since 1644 China had been ruled by the Manchu or Qing dynasty. The Manchus are a non-Chinese people who originated in what is now Heilongjiang and Jilin in north-east China. The previous dynasty, the Ming, had collapsed under the weight of peasant rebellions, and this had enabled the Manchu forces, aided by Chinese collaborators, to sweep into China, to occupy Beijing and then to carry out a systematic conquest of the rest of the country. In some places, for example at Jiangyin, there was a heroic Chinese resistance, but for the most part the

China Proper, *c*.1800

population acquiesced to the Manchu presence. It was only a generation later, in the rebellion known as the Revolt of the Three Feudatories, that a serious challenge to the Manchus arose. This was headed by Wu Sangui, the most notorious of those Chinese who had collaborated in the Manchu invasion. It was a testimony to the success already achieved by the Manchus in allaying Chinese hostility that he failed to arouse Chinese resentment of foreign conquest.

In many respects the Manchus adopted the principles and practices of the government of their predecessors the Ming. Manchu emperors conscientiously set out to fill the role of a Confucian ruler. The emperor was the Son of Heaven, the mediator between earth and heaven. The uniqueness of his position and person was emphasized in every aspect of his existence, for example the court robes which he wore on state occasions were embroidered with the 'Twelve Symbols', motifs which had a hierarchical and political significance.[4] The sacred quality of his personage was emphasized when he performed the sequence of essential annual rituals, for example conducting the sacrifices at the Tiantan, the Temple of Heaven. The Forbidden City, the imperial palace, was built on a north–south axis and in each audience hall the emperor's throne faced south. In the three outer halls the emperor performed his public duties; behind them, in the inner palace, he lived a segregated existence, accompanied only by the empress and members of the imperial harem and by the eunuchs who staffed the palace.

Nevertheless, the emperor was far more than a symbol of autocratic power, for he was also deeply involved in the day-to-day running of the empire. His routine work involved summoning ministers for consultation and giving audiences to officials. Every day he read the memorials, the official communications from senior officials, and indicated his response to them in vermilion ink, the colour reserved for his use alone. He presided over the Grand Council, an innovation of the Yongzheng emperor, which advised the emperor and executed his orders.

The emperor was the current head of the Manchu Aisin Gioro clan from which the ruling line had sprung. It was essential that the emperor should preserve elements of this Manchu identity. Thus the Jiaqing emperor, who occupied the throne from 1796 to 1820, cultivated the skills of hunting and archery and made regular visits to Manchuria. It was also essential that the emperor should be able to demonstrate his knowledge of and commitment to Chinese culture. Manchu emperors went through an extended programme of education in the Confucian classics; they were expected to acquire skills in writing Chinese prose and poetry and in calligraphy. They regarded themselves as connoisseurs of Chinese art and its foremost patrons. Thus Jiaqing thought it appropriate that he should commission a complete collection of prose from the Tang period (618–907), the golden age of Chinese literature.

The Manchu-Chinese Diarchy

Even after a century and a half on the throne, the Manchus remained very conscious of their ethnic differences and they continued to promote measures to prevent their assimilation into the majority population. These included the reservation of what is now Manchuria as their homeland, the use of Manchu as an official language, the retention of the Manchu military forces known as the Eight Banners, the prohibition of marriage between Manchus and Chinese and the interdiction on Manchu women on following the Chinese practice of foot-binding. For the most part the administration of Manchu affairs was kept separate from the normal administration of China and handled by agencies such as the Imperial Clan Court.

The most important problem was how to maintain the Manchu position in the government of China. Early in the dynastic period, when few Manchus had acquired the linguistic or administrative skills to fill senior positions effectively, many important positions were held by Chinese bannermen, who had joined the Manchus before the invasion of China and whose particular duty of allegiance to the Manchus made them trustworthy. As the dynasty progressed a system of duplication of offices was developed. Each of the Six Boards of government had both a Manchu and a Chinese officer at its head and the same principle applied to the senior presidents of the censorate and to the chancellors of the Hanlin Academy. The senior provincial appointments were similarly balanced. If a Manchu was appointed governor-general of a group of provinces, his provincial governors were usually Chinese. Over the whole Qing period, 57 per cent of those appointed governor-general were Manchus, Mongols or Chinese bannermen and 43 per cent of the appointments were Han Chinese; of those appointed governor 48 per cent were Manchu, Mongol and Chinese bannermen and 52 per cent were Han Chinese. Below this level of administration almost all the official positions were held by Chinese.[5]

Administration

The administration of the empire closely followed the pattern set by the Ming. In Beijing the offices of central government comprised the Six Boards, that is the Boards of Civil Appointments, Revenue, Rites, War, Punishments and Works. Each of these boards was responsible for the routine administration of one aspect of government activity. Thus the Board of Civil Appointments dealt with all matters relating to appointment, transfer and promotion in the civil bureaucracy and the Board of Revenue was responsible for land registration and the collection of revenue. Standing apart from the Six Boards, and empowered to investigate their activities, was the organization known as the Censorate. The officials appointed to this body were known as the 'eyes and ears' of the emperor. They could investigate or impeach any official whose actions aroused their suspicions and they presented themselves as guardians of Confucian ethics in government.[6]

China Proper was divided into eighteen provinces, each of which had its own administration. Each provincial administration was headed by a governor and in most cases provinces were grouped in twos and threes and placed under a governor-general. Senior provincial officials included the director of studies, responsible for aspects of education in the province, a provincial treasurer and a provincial judge. Provinces in turn were divided into circuits, prefectures and districts. The district magistrate was the most junior official within the formal administration. District magistrates were described as 'officials close to the people' and addressed by the people under their jurisdiction as 'father and mother officials'.[7] There were about 1,200 or 1,300 districts, which meant that on average each magistrate had responsibility for the well-being of a quarter of a million people.

The officials who filled the bureaucratic appointments within the administration were for the most part selected through the examination system. A parallel system existed for the selection of military officials. Examinations were held at district, provincial and metropolitan levels, successful candidates receiving the degrees known as shengyuan, 'government student' (colloquially referred to as xiucai, 'cultivated talent'), juren, 'recommended man' and jinshi, 'presented scholar'. The syllabus was based on the Confucian classics and candidates were expected to write formal compositions, including the so-called 'eight-legged essay'. The examinations at district level were held twice every three years, with very large numbers of candidates present – in some large districts as many as two thousand candidates competed for the civil examinations and two hundred for the military examinations. However, examination quotas severely restricted the numbers allowed to pass, the national quota for *shengyuan* being fixed at 25,089. Provincial examinations were held triennially and again a very large number of candidates competed, but only 1,400 candidates, or about 1 or 2 per cent of those who entered, were successful in obtaining the *juren* degree. The metropolitan examinations followed a similar pattern, with the emperor himself presiding over the final stages. In the metropolitan examinations held in 1799, 220 candidates were awarded the *jinshi* degree. The most promising of these were appointed to the Hanlin Academy in Beijing.[8]

It was from this pool of degree holders by examination that about half the official appointments were made. Almost all those who had obtained the *jinshi* degree became officials and about one-third of those who had become *juren* received appointments. The total number of civil officials was approximately 20,000 and of military officials approximately 7,000. About half of the civil officials were court officials, the other half served in the provinces.[9]

The bureaucracy was subject to a variety of checks and balances, one of these being the role of the Censorate, which has already been mentioned. Another important control was the balancing of the 'regular' members of the bureaucracy, that is to say officials who had been appointed after succeeding in the examinations, with an 'irregular' component of men who had purchased an academic title, usually that of *jiansheng*, which in turn enabled them to purchase either an official title or an official position. The 'irregular' members of the bureaucracy were usually appointed to posts at a lower level than 'regular' degree holders. The Yongzheng emperor justified the use of the purchase system in an edict of 1727:

> If the official career should be left completely to those who rise through examinations, they would just firmly join together and work for their private interest against the public interest. This is of great harm to the public welfare and to the livelihood of the people. The purchase system should be appropriately expanded.[10]

Two additional checks were applied. One, known as the 'law of avoidance', prohibited a magistrate from serving in his native province or within 165 miles of his native district. The other measure, which applied to all officials, limited the initial term of appointment to office to three years.

The Population

The Manchus ruled a population which had grown from about 150 million in 1700 to approximately 313 million in 1794.[11] Although in absolute numbers this was an enormous expansion, it is unlikely that in the eighteenth century the rate of increase rose as high as 1 per cent per annum for any sustained period – well below the population growth rate of over 2 per cent per annum recorded in China in the 1950s.[12] The vast majority of this population was Chinese or, as they chose to describe themselves, Han Chinese, identifying with the Han dynasty which ruled China from 206 BC to AD 220. The population also included substantial non-Chinese groups, although it is impossible to estimate accurately their numbers at the beginning of the nineteenth century. Modern estimates of China's national minorities suggest they amount to 4 to 6 per cent of the population. Among the largest groups are the Zhuang in western Guangxi and the Uighur living mainly in Xinjiang. All minority groups in modern times have been forced to compete for resources and to accept or resist assimilation. Some important minority groups have clearly suffered in this respect. The Yao and Miao, who occupy hilly regions in south-west China, were vigorously suppressed in the eighteenth century as the Chinese began to exploit the resources of their areas. The Hui, Chinese converts to Islam, paid dearly for their participation in rebellion in the mid-nineteenth century.[13]

The most heavily populated regions of China at the beginning of the nineteenth century were the lower Yangzi valley and delta regions in southern China. Major movements of population took place during the Qing period. A large-scale peasant rebellion in Sichuan at the time of the Manchu conquest led to serious depopulation. The government responded by encouraging migration into the province, leading to a continuous influx of migrants from all over China for more than two hundred years. Another important destination for migrants was the Yangzi highlands, in particular the hilly districts of the provinces of Jiangxi and Hunan. Much of this area was still under forest in the early Qing period. The settlers, who became known as *pengmin* or 'shack people', cleared the forests and planted maize and sweet potatoes, crops introduced from America in the sixteenth century. As early as 1745 this practice threatened to cause an ecological disaster.

> The shack people usually dig the mountain soil five or six inches deep. The loosened soil at first yielded ten times as large a crop. But from time to time there were torrential rains which washed down the soil and choked rivers and streams. After consecutive planting for more than ten years none of the fertile topsoil was left and the soil was utterly exhausted.[14]

A similar movement of population occurred north of the Yangzi, into the area of the Han river drainage. The province of Hubei almost doubled its population between 1786 and 1850 and one district in southern Shaanxi recorded that 90 per cent of the population were immigrants.[15]

China annexed Taiwan in 1683, by which time the island already had a population of about 100,000 Chinese. In order to reduce friction with the aboriginal peoples, the Kangxi emperor prohibited further Chinese settlement and the purchase or rental of aboriginal land. It is an indication of the strength of the pressure to emigrate, in particular from the mainland province of

Fujian, that the response was widespread illegal settlement, which forced a relaxation of the ban. The 1811 census showed Taiwan had a Chinese population of almost two million.[16]

The Economy

Until nearly the end of the eighteenth century the growth of agricultural output probably continued to exceed the growth of population. About half of this increase was achieved by opening up new land for cultivation, the other half coming from a rise in yields which in turn derived from a combination of factors including the spread of double-cropping, improved planting material and increased inputs in terms of labour and capital. However, it has been calculated that at some point between 1750 and 1775 the optimum point was passed and the law of diminishing returns from inputs ensured that a slow decline in the amount of food available per capita commenced.[17]

China was not a country of large landed estates, one reason for this being the absence of primogeniture and the practice of sharing out the estate among all surviving sons. The evidence relating to landownership is very defective and only the roughest idea of how land was distributed can be obtained. Perhaps one million landowners formed an elite, owning on average 100 to 150 mou of land.[18] Below them in economic terms were the owner-farmers who in north China might cultivate 20 to 30 mou and in the south 12 to 15 mou. Tenancy was much more widespread in the south than in the north, but taking the country as a whole perhaps 30 per cent of farm families were tenants and another 20 per cent both owned land and worked rented land. Rents were usually paid in kind. In the north the landlord usually took 50 per cent of the principal crop, while in the south it was more common for there to be a fixed rent in kind.[19]

Many peasant households, particularly the poorer ones, supplemented their income from agriculture by engaging in handicraft enterprises. In the lower Yangzi valley, the principal cotton-producing area, spinning and weaving was commonly carried out in the peasant household, and the unfinished cloth was worn by the common people. Surplus produce was sold and the finishing processes, such as calendering and dyeing, were more frequently performed in the towns and the better quality cloth sold to the wealthier urban classes, or even exported. A similar division occurred in the production of silk, although rather more households took the risk of specializing in a single product.

Tea production was concentrated in Zhejiang, Fujian and Guangdong. Peasants grew tea alongside their subsistence crops and after harvesting it they carried out the preparatory processes of drying, sifting and packing. They then carried the tea to markets where it was sold to brokers, who in turn sold it to wealthy tea merchants. Already by the eighteenth century, a considerable quantity of tea was being exported and this tea was specially prepared for foreign consumption. Noting foreign preference for coloured green teas, suppliers adulterated the tea with a mixture of Prussian blue and gypsum.[20]

Among the most advanced industries were those producing iron and ceramics.

Ironworks on the Hubei–Shaanxi–Sichuan border were described as having furnaces 17 to 18 feet high and employing up to two or three thousand men. The output compared favourably with that of English ironworks in the seventeenth century. The most famous ceramic centre was at Jingdezhen in Jiangxi, where, according to a Jesuit missionary's account of the early eighteenth century, a town of a million people had grown up. Very high quality porcelain was produced and this was traded throughout the empire and a considerable quantity was shipped overseas.

Obstacles to Industrialization

The evidence above supports the claim that China in the eighteenth century was on the verge of an industrial revolution. However, the majority of Western economic historians have stressed that various obstacles prevented China's industrialization at this stage. An influential exposition of this view was put forward by Mark Elvin. He pointed out that China was not obviously short of resources or capital and Chinese inventiveness was at least equal to that of the West. In any case the availability of technology did not determine whether a country would be able to industrialize. He considered the suggestion that the problem lay in bureaucratic disdain for mercantile activity, and the prevalence of monopolistic practices which prevented the development of free enterprise, but concluded that there was 'a symbiosis between bureaucrats and businessmen'. Another explanation identified a variety of factors, including the absence of commercial law to provide protection for businesses, which made it difficult for large private economic organizations to develop or to remain in existence over a long period of time. But Elvin noted that large organizations had developed in China and did survive for long periods.

What then was the obstacle? Mark Elvin argued the case for the 'high-level equilibrium trap', an explanation which embraced many of the factors determining the Chinese economy, and which is therefore worth explaining in some detail. Elvin pointed out that China did not suffer from 'technological stagnation', for small but significant improvements were being made in a wide variety of techniques. Similar improvements were occurring in economic organizations and there was no lack of entrepreneurial talent in a variety of fields. However, the limited development of transportation restricted the development of commerce, and shortages of many resources were growing more severe. This last factor was a consequence of population growth and its significance was most obvious in the context of the availability of land. Elvin summarized the Chinese dilemma as follows:

> Yields per acre were very nearly as high as was possible without the use of advanced industrial-scientific inputs such as selected seeds, chemical fertilizers and pesticides, machinery and pumps powered by the internal combustion engine or electricity, concrete and so on. Furthermore, there was not enough suitable land to raise the yields per worker for the Chinese farm labour force as a whole by using either eighteenth-century British techniques, which depended

critically on the interdependence of crop-raising and animal husbandry, or nineteenth-century American techniques of extensive, low per-acre yield, mechanized cultivation.[21]

Agriculture by the end of the eighteenth century combined high-level farming with low per capita income. In the sixteenth and seventeenth centuries China had suffered major epidemics, which may have led to a population reduction of between 35 and 45 per cent. But under the Qing the population first recovered and then continued to rise. In the eighteenth century diminishing returns from inputs ensured that output began to fall behind population growth. The one abundantly available resource was labour and its very abundance was a deterrent to innovation. The only solution to the 'high-level equilibrium trap' was an exogenous shock, initiated by Western contact, and as far as agriculture was concerned taking the form of mechanization, electrification and scientific inputs, a process which is only now taking place.

Although Elvin's argument has been well received, it has not brought the discussion to a conclusion. Ramon Myers approached the issue from a different angle. He pointed out that the economic history of China and Europe had followed quite different paths. China's period of pre-modern economic development, most clearly from the late seventeenth century, was accompanied by a small but significant redistribution of wealth in favour of the poorer sections of society. In this the state played a limited but important part, for Myers argued that its role went beyond tax collection and the administration of justice to include provisions such as state-managed granaries and water conservancy projects. As a consequence China, unlike continental Europe, did not experience great fluctuations in population growth. Nor did it experience any sharp changes in the relative prices of goods or services. By contrast Europe in the Middle Ages had already begun to make substantial use of water power and animal power. In the seventeenth century a long-term decline in interest rates began, and the influx of precious metals from the New World brought about a price revolution. This led to a shift in terms of trade between agriculture and industry, to the advantage of the latter, so creating the setting for the onset of the industrial revolution.[22]

In a more recent synthesis, Lloyd E. Eastman accepted the validity of some of the arguments already put forward, for example that the insecurity of private wealth and entrepreneurial investments from government exactions acted as a deterrent to entrepreneurship. He agreed also that because, by about 1800, per capita income was probably stagnating, there was little inducement for manufacturers to introduce new technology to increase productivity. He emphasized the status attached to the scholar-official class and to the literary and intellectual interests which they pursued rather than to technical and scientific concerns. However, he rejected one often-repeated argument: that Confucianism lay at the root of China's inability to industrialize, on the grounds that the parameters of Confucianism were extremely elastic and that the recent economic success of Japan and of other nations on the Pacific rim, all of which have a Confucian tradition, suggested that Confucianism might be capable of playing a role comparable to that of

Protestantism in supplying an ethic justifying change rather than stasis. Obviously dissatisfied with the answers previously given, Eastman emphasized one particular cultural characteristic: the contrasting Western and Chinese attitudes towards nature. Whereas Europeans possessed an irrepressible urge to dominate the natural world, the Chinese tended to view the universe as an organism, in which all elements existed in harmony. To justify this claim Eastman referred to the portrayal of man's relations with nature in European still-life painting, where man dominates nature, and Chinese landscape painting where nature dominates man. The urge to dominate led Europeans to apply inventions, the Chinese to absorb them within the traditional system. In short they placed a higher value on stability and harmony than on change and domination.[23]

The Social Elite

China had no hereditary aristocracy which might be compared with that of Europe. Such a class had disappeared in the ninth and tenth centuries, at the time of the change from the Tang to the Song dynasties. Nevertheless, under the Qing there was an hereditary elite which enjoyed economic and social privileges, even though it exerted little political influence. This comprised firstly the imperial Manchu clansmen, the direct male descendants of Nurhaci, the effective founder of the dynasty. A larger group, the bannermen, were the descendants of the Manchus (and Chinese and Mongols) who had been organized by Nurhaci into military-civil units known as banners. Finally, there was a titular nobility, divided into five classes, mainly composed of meritorious civil and military officials.

However, the true social elite was the group known in Chinese as the shenshi[24] and in English as the 'literati' or 'gentry'. This was a non-hereditary group, membership of which was acquired by either passing at least the lowest level of the examinations described above, or by purchasing an educational title. It has been estimated that in the first half of the nineteenth century the gentry numbered about 1.1 million. Taking into account the members of their families, this social elite numbered about 5.5 million or approximately 1.3 per cent of the population. The gentry have been described as a distinct social group in Chinese society, one which enjoyed political, economic and social privileges and which led a special mode of life. The gentry stood above the mass of commoners and dominated the social and economic life of the communities from whence they came.[25] Local officials regarded the gentry as their social equals and they shared with them formal distinctions in the way of modes of address and distinctive costume, both officials and gentry wearing buttons on their hats indicating the status of the wearer. The gentry also had economic privileges, being exempted from the official labour service tax. They were subject to the land tax, but they were sometimes allowed to delay payment and there were many examples of gentry abusing their position by gaining illegal economic advantages over tax payment.

The gentry performed, or were expected to perform, a variety of functions. Because of their training they were prominent in the promotion of education and in all matters connected with the dissemination of Confucian ideas. Their close relationship with the bureaucracy led to them acting as intermediaries between officials and the people. Because in China there were no formal institutions of local government and consequently no bodies responsible for tasks associated with public welfare, it fell to the gentry to initiate such activities. Local gazetteers, compiled by the gentry, recorded numerous examples of gentry active in the repair of roads, the construction of bridges and the promotion of irrigation projects. Gentry also took the lead in the promotion of charitable projects, for example the management of homes for orphans.

The relationship between the central government and the local elite was a symbiotic one, both parties depending upon the other. The gentry performed a vital role in maintaining local control, assisting local officials and supporting ideological conformity. Twice a month officials were required to expound the Sacred Edict, a collection of maxims written by the emperor to exhort the people to good behaviour. Gentry assisted officials in this duty and carried out other tasks supportive of the orthodox line, for example keeping the examination halls in good repair. However, the gentry also had to be kept under control. This was achieved partly by the same emphasis on ideological conformity, achieved through the gentry pursuing what has been called 'a life of examination'.[26] Gentry spent many years preparing for examinations, and if successful took further examinations to retain status. It was also achieved by the close regulation of the quotas set for examination success, which determined the size of the gentry group. A further important check came from the exclusion of gentry from participation in certain activities. Gentry were not permitted to organize the baojia, the system of mutual responsibility applied to village communities; nor were they allowed to collect taxes or to infringe on the judicial authority of the government. Most importantly they were not allowed to engage in any form of military activity unless they received express permission to raise a militia or local corps to deal with banditry or other forms of disorder.[27]

The social position of the gentry did not derive from their ownership of land. In theory the examination system offered the prospect of social mobility to all except the 'mean people', defined as the families of slaves, servants, prostitutes, entertainers and some other identified groups. In practice preparation for the examinations was such a long and arduous process that only those candidates whose families could support them over a period of time could hope to succeed. As landownership was so commonly the basis of a family's wealth the connection between belonging to a family which owned land and becoming a member of the gentry was usually close.

The Family

So much has been written about the traditional Chinese family that it is not easy to summarize its main characteristics in a few lines. It was the common practice that daughters married out of the family group, whereas sons and their wives shared their residence with their father. In wealthier families brides brought a dowry with them, but in poorer families this situation might be reversed, with the daughter's family receiving compensation in the form of bride-price. It was the general rule that property was regarded as belonging not to the individual but to the family and that on the death of the male head of the family it should be divided equally among his sons.

According to Confucian tradition, the ideal family situation was one which saw five generations residing under one roof. The traditional Chinese house, built to accommodate an extended family, comprised a series of courtyards around which was ranged accommodation for members of the family and for servants. The compound was surrounded by high walls, pierced only by the main entrance and by a narrow opening from which charity was dispensed. Even the main entrance was shielded from the outside world by a screen intended to bar the way to malign spirits.[28] This pattern of living was only available to wealthier sections of the population and was most common in the Yangzi delta and in the south. There prosperous and long-established families had created clan or lineage organizations which encompassed both rich and poor families who shared a common ancestor. In some villages the entire population belonged to a single lineage and some lineages might have as many as ten thousand members.

Lineage organizations might own substantial corporate property and this enabled them to carry out a number of functions. They took on social responsibilities, for example the construction of orphanages and granaries, which enhanced their social standing. They established charitable schools, which demonstrated their commitment to learning but which also provided the opportunity for promising young men from the lineage to prepare themselves for the imperial examinations. This ensured that the lineage contained members of the gentry and from time to time could share in the benefits of a member of the lineage obtaining office.

Successful lineages produced compilations of clan rules which contained exhortations relating to moral behaviour and social action. They also played a major role in promoting what is referred to in the West as 'ancestor worship'. Wealthy lineages maintained ancestral halls which housed the spirit tablets of ancestors. On the anniversary of the deaths of important members of the family, on major festivals and on occasions such as weddings and funerals, offerings were made to these spirit tablets. In Confucian parlance these rites were not worship of spirits but the 'expression of human feelings', conveying respect for the dead and cultivating the virtues of filial piety, loyalty and faithfulness.[29]

Women

The family and the lineage were patrilineal organizations, that is to say descent was through the male line and only sons could perform the rites associated with ancestor worship, which were essential to the family's well-being. By excluding women from these vital roles, the family and lineage reinforced the subordinate position of women in Chinese society which was already sanctioned by Confucianism. Other aspects of the life of women appeared to confirm that subordination. The birth of a boy child was greeted with joy, that of a girl with dismay and allegedly female infanticide was common. Whereas women were expected to be monogamous, it was considered entirely acceptable for a man, who could afford to do so and who perhaps had not yet obtained a male heir, to introduce a concubine into the family home. Women were excluded from the examination system and had no access to public positions. Although wealthy women might have a private income and women from poor families might have an economic value, generally women enjoyed no economic freedom. Severe injunctions controlled a woman's behaviour in public, in particular with reference to the opposite sex, and the remarriage of widows was regarded as reprehensible. Most obviously women were repressed by their own sex through the wide support given to the practice of foot-binding. Girls from about the age of six had their feet bound in a manner which made them effectively cripples.

The view that women were oppressed was endorsed by many Western observers in the nineteenth century. Writing in the 1850s, the Catholic missionary Évariste Huc commented:

> The condition of the Chinese woman is most pitiable; suffering, privation, contempt, all kinds of misery and degradation, seize on her in the cradle, and accompany her pitilessly to the tomb. Her very birth is commonly regarded as a humiliation and a disgrace to the family – an evident sign of the malediction of Heaven. If she be not immediately suffocated . . . she is regarded and treated as a creature radically despicable, and scarcely belonging to the human race.[30]

Recently it has been suggested that 'Chinese women are too easily seen as passive victims of the traditional society'.[31] There is evidence of rising female literacy rates and expanding female economic roles after the sixteenth century. In the late eighteenth century a debate arose not about whether women should be educated but about what they should learn, and in that debate a distinctive female voice had begun to express itself.[32]

Culture

In mid-Qing China, as under previous dynasties, the dominant culture was associated with Confucianism. All who aspired to education had to be familiar with the Confucian classics, commonly listed as the Four Books: the *Analects of Confucius*, the *Great Learning*, the *Doctrine of the Mean* and *Mencius*, the last-named being a record of the conversations of Confucius's most famous follower. These were not only works of literature, but also the canon of texts for the imperial examinations and the repository of moral teaching.

Confucius had spoken of the attributes of the *junzi*, the gentleman, describing him as one who should pursue self-cultivation in order to serve humanity.

> Zilu asked about the gentleman. The Master said: 'He cultivates himself in order to show reverence.' 'Is that all?' asked Zilu. The Master said: 'He cultivates himself

so as to bring tranquillity to others.' 'Is that all?', Zilu again asked. The Master said: 'He cultivates himself so as to bring tranquillity to all the people. Even Yao and Shun would have found this a difficult task.'[33]

In the seventeenth and eighteenth centuries scholarly activity was very much in evidence. As mentioned earlier, textual studies flourished. In an attempt to reverse what was regarded as a misguided literary pursuit of sageness and a propensity to become involved in factional disputes – errors believed to have contributed to the fall of the Ming – Confucian scholars developed 'evidential scholarship' as a means of reconstructing the original Confucian texts. Many scholars were involved in the compilation of the Complete Library of the Four Treasuries, a collection of what were regarded as the most important books and manuscripts, carefully edited and reproduced in a sequence of thirty-six thousand volumes. At the same time works regarded as offensive to the Manchus were destroyed, thus combining scholarship and censorship in a single operation.[34]

Some scholars concentrated on geographical writing, which reached a high standard under the Qing. A major publication was the Comprehensive Gazetteer of the Great Qing Dynasty, an expanded version of which was published in 1790 to include reference to the territories acquired during the reign of the Qianlong emperor. Another example of careful scholarship was the dictionary of Chinese place-names compiled by Li Zhaoluo (1769–1841). Li was also involved in a favourite occupation of scholars, the compilation of local gazetteers, which proliferated during this period.[35]

Much literature fell outside the bounds of Confucian scholarship. In the eighteenth century great advances took place in vernacular writing, the most famous example being Honglou meng, The Dream of the Red Chamber, also known as The Story of the Stone. The novel had a complex authorship, the first eighty chapters of the work being attributed to Cao Xueqin (c. 1715–63) and the last forty chapters Gao E (either as author or editor), and first appeared in 1792. The novel is both a realistic description of the life of a great family in decline and a complex allegory on the nature of reality and illusion.[36]

Another writer who broke with tradition was Yuan Mei (1716–98), who after a brief official career retired to Nanjing to a house and garden which he believed to have a connection with The Dream of the Red Chamber. He devoted himself to literature and achieved a wide reputation as a poet. Whereas some of the leading poets of the day, for example Shen Deqian, believed that poetry should have a moral purpose and should adhere to standard forms, Yuan Mei had a light touch and an unconventional mind. His self-deprecating style is illustrated in poems he wrote about growing old, one of which read:

> If at seventy I still plant trees,
> Lookers-on, do not laugh at my folly.
> It is true of course that no one lives forever;
> But nothing is gained by knowing so in advance.[37]

Yuan Mei also gained notoriety by associating with young married women poets and by asserting that the best poetry was intuitive and spontaneous and that women were more likely than men to produce it.[38]

It is not possible to do credit in a few lines to the achievement of the mid-Qing period in terms of the arts and applied arts. However, a few notable pieces may be mentioned. Landscape painting remained highly esteemed and attracted many thousands of practitioners, both professional and amateur. While much of what was produced was traditional a number of outstandingly individual painters emerged, among them Daoji, also known as Shitao (c. 1642–1707), who summed up his philosophy by saying 'The method which consists of following no method is the best method'.[39] Calligraphy developed strongly during this period. It was often used to adorn paintings, but also flourished independently. Among the best-remembered calligraphers of the time was Deng Shiru (c. 1740–1805), who made rubbings from inscriptions on seals on stone and bronze. A man described as large-minded and unconventional, irregular in his habits and a heavy drinker, he became particularly skilled in using the archaic styles of writing known as large and small seal and clerical script.[40]

With reference to the applied arts, it is also appropriate to remark on the extraordinary variety and high level of sophistication of the best products of the time. From the wide range of examples one might select three for comment. With the conquest of Xinjiang the supply of jade and nephrite increased and large numbers of carved objects were produced.[41] Whereas ordinary people smoked tobacco, which had been introduced into China in the Ming period, the elite took tobacco in the form of snuff. A new type of decorative artefact appeared in the form of the snuff bottle, made out of a variety of materials. The production of high quality porcelain continued and the range of styles was augmented by European influence, both in terms of design and glaze and also by demand for the European market. Very large quantities of porcelain were exported – some idea of the scale of the trade can be illustrated by reference to the cargo recovered from the Dutch East India Company ship the *Geldermalsen*, which sank in 1752.[42] A particular item in the export trade was what was known as armorial porcelain. European aristocratic families sent orders for porcelain services to China accompanied by requests that they be decorated with the families' armorial bearings, illustrations of which were provided.

China's Place in the World

The Qing dynasty had inherited from the Ming well-defined principles and practices governing the conduct of foreign relations. China was the Middle Kingdom and the neighbouring states of Asia were perceived as occupying an inferior position on her periphery. The Manchu rulers adopted the Chinese world view and continued Ming practices, as if they themselves were Chinese.

This assumption of superiority worked best when dealing with those states which had adopted features of Chinese culture, in particular Korea, the Liuqiu islands, Annam, Laos, Thailand, Burma and other peripheral states. These states participated in what has been described as the tributary system, a reciprocal arrangement which offered certain benefits to tributary states, which in return confirmed China's pre-eminent position. The size, frequency and procedure for tribute missions were minutely prescribed by the Board of Rites. Korea sent an annual tribute, Liuqiu and Annam sent tribute every other year, whereas Burma and Laos only sent missions every ten years.

The procedure relating to the dispatch of a tribute mission can be illustrated by reference to Korea, the 'model tributary'. The dispatch of such a mission was a major undertaking, for it was composed of some 30 members and a large number of retainers, in all 200 to 300 persons. The journey took between forty and sixty days and the party stayed in Beijing for up to two months. The mission brought with it tribute mainly in the form of paper and textiles which was valued at well over 100,000 copper taels. The tribute was formally presented to the emperor in a ceremony in which the envoys had to perform the kotow, the ritual three prostrations and nine head knockings. In response the mission was presented with gifts and the merchants who had accompanied the mission were allowed to trade. Nevertheless, the exchange left Korea at a net financial disadvantage.[43]

An even more elaborate procedure was provided for when a tributary king requested investiture by the Chinese emperor. When a new Liuqiu king required investiture he had to send up to four missions to China and had to receive a large Chinese mission which might stay for up to five months. The cost of investiture for a poor state like Liuqiu was so great that the ceremony was often delayed for several years.[44]

Different procedures applied to relations with Mongolia, Central Asia, Tibet and Russia. In 1638, before the conquest, the Manchus had established the Lifan yuan, the Court of Colonial Affairs. This ranked immediately below the Six Boards of Government and was staffed exclusively by Manchus and Mongols. The Lifan yuan used a variety of strategies to retain influence in the areas within its purview. An important element was trade, for there was a symbiotic relationship between the economies of the nomadic societies of the steppe and settled population of much of China Proper. As a consequence the regulation of trade could be used as a method of control. The Qing dynasty also used its military power to assert its authority. Mongolia was secured by garrisons of Chinese military forces and Xinjiang, or 'new frontier', the name applied from 1768 to Eastern Turkestan and Dzungaria, was held by an expensive garrison. It was not the intention to absorb these regions into China and the policy was that of jimi or 'loose rein', whereby tribal leaders who accepted China's position in the area were permitted to remain in power. Nevertheless, with the establishment of administrative and military settlements, the Han Chinese population of Xinjiang began to increase and the process of assimilation began.

The position of Tibet was ambiguous. At the beginning of the Qing period Tibet had the appearance of an independent state, albeit one which had close religious ties with China. It was only in the eighteenth century, when Tibet was invaded first by forces from Dzungaria and then from Nepal, that China intervened directly in Tibetan affairs and established a protectorate, under which the Dalai Lama acted as both spiritual leader and temporal ruler, backed by a Chinese resident official and a small Chinese garrison. Chinese influence in Tibet reached its height in 1792 when a Chinese army marched on Nepal to protect Tibet. But from that time onwards China's increasing military weakness and the rise of British power in India ensured that Tibet was a Chinese protectorate in name only.[45]

In 1643 the first Russians reached the Amur, the only Siberian river which flows into the Pacific. In 1665 a Russian fort was built at Albazin. Concerns over Russian expansion and the fear that the Dzungar leaders might make common cause with them prompted the Qing to negotiate the Treaty of Nerchinsk in 1689. This was the first treaty that China had concluded with a neighbouring state on the basis of equality. It was nevertheless an agreement in China's favour, for the Qing profited from Russian military weakness in the area to exclude Russia from the Amur valley. Otherwise Russia was permitted to send trade caravans to Beijing, under strict conditions, with the leader of the trade mission being required to perform the kotow. A second settlement was agreed in 1727 by the Treaty of Kiakhta, which defined the boundary between Russia and China. Under the terms of the treaty a Russian Orthodox mission and a language school to enable Russians to learn Chinese and Manchu were established in Beijing. Neither establishment was a great success. The clergy of the Orthodox mission, required to spend ten years in China, became demoralized and the language students, with a few notable exceptions, drank too much, learnt little and often died in China. Despite some novelties in the Chinese manner of dealing with Russia, for the most part the Lifan yuan accommodated the relationship within the principles it had applied to control other peoples along China's land frontier.[46]

From early times the Chinese had referred to those people who did not recognize the superiority of Chinese culture as barbarians. Barbarians who occupied adjacent territories to China were described as 'inner barbarians', whereas those who lived in remote regions, or who arrived in China from across the sea, were described as 'outer barbarians'. The latter term was applied to the Europeans who reached China by the sea route from early in the sixteenth century. Most of the early arrivals were Portuguese traders who were allowed to establish a settlement at Aomen (Macao) in the 1550s. In the meantime the Jesuits had established a mission in Japan and in 1577 Alessandro Valignano, the Jesuit Visitor to the Indies, arrived in Aomen. He was followed by Matteo Ricci, who in 1601, after twenty years of negotiation, was allowed to reside in Beijing.

The Jesuit mission achieved considerable success in the closing years of the Ming dynasty, and under the Manchus Jesuit fathers continued to serve at court as astronomers and mathematicians, and to assist in the manufacture of arms and the production of arts and crafts. The Jesuit willingness to serve the Manchus, and to permit Chinese converts to perform Confucian rites and make sacrifices to their ancestors, provoked hostile comment from the Dominican and Franciscan missionaries who had also made their way to China. In 1692 the Kangxi emperor promulgated an edict of tolerance accepting the Jesuit policy on the rites. This agreement was condemned in Rome, where the Jesuits had lost influence, and a papal legate was sent to China to regulate the affair. The idea that foreign missionaries on Chinese soil should be subject to foreign jurisdiction was quite unacceptable to the emperor and Christian missionaries were ordered either to accept the edict of tolerance and to remain in China for life, or to leave immediately. This precipitated what has become known as the Rites Controversy, which culminated in 1742 when the Pope promulgated the bull *Ex Quo Singulari*, which condemned all forms of accommodation with Chinese rites.

In the meantime the Portuguese traders operating in south China had been largely supplanted first by the Dutch, who had established the trading station known as Zeelandia on Taiwan in 1624, and later by the British. British trade with China began in 1637 with the arrival of Captain Weddell at Guangzhou. However, it was only in 1699 that the *Macclesfield*, a ship belonging to the East India Company, reached Guangzhou and established there a 'factory', a trading post operated by a factor or agent of the Honourable Company, that regular trade began. The most important export commodity from China to the European market was tea. Shipments of tea into Britain quadrupled between the 1720s and the 1760s, although only about one-third of this was carried by Company ships, the rest being carried by the ships of other European states and then smuggled into Britain to avoid heavy duties. In 1784, under the Commutation Act, the British government cut the duty on tea from 119 per cent to 12½ per cent. The smuggling trade collapsed and the East India Company's demand for tea increased dramatically.

From a Western perspective the religious mission, the intellectual contacts and the growth of trade were dynamic changes, deriving from the enterprise, improved technological skills and religious convictions which had developed in Europe. Accompanying them had come a revision of the European perception of China. It had been in the interest of the Jesuits to present Chinese culture in a positive light and this portrayal had been used by Voltaire and other *philosophes* of the Enlightenment to promote China, a country which practised religious toleration and where scholars became officials, as a model for Europe. However, the growth of commercial contacts, and the negative impression of Chinese bureaucracy gained by Admiral Anson, who had visited China twice in the course of his circumnavigation of the globe between 1742 and 1744, had led to a more critical perception.

The Qing dynasty's response to these new circumstances was not to alter its method of dealing with the outer barbarians, but to accommodate the new contacts within the framework of its traditional foreign relations. The Jesuit missionaries had brought with them new knowledge, and their Christian gospel had not been entirely ignored. Nevertheless, the missionaries' willingness to adopt Chinese dress, to learn the Chinese language and to compromise with Confucianism, ensured that at first they could be received without yielding any ground on the Chinese assumption of superiority. The tributary system had usually made provision for foreign trade, but it was not the case that foreign traders had always presented tribute. The Chinese government assumed the right to control foreign traders. Arab traders who had arrived in south China in the Tang period had been permitted to establish carefully regulated, self-governing communities. The same principle was to be applied to European traders. At the time of the Manchu conquest internal disorder and the presence of a rebel regime on Taiwan had led the government to impose draconian restrictions on foreign trade. However, when these threats had been defeated, the economic value of trade was accepted and it was permitted under close regulation. A superintendent of maritime customs, the official to be known to Europeans as the Hoppo, was stationed at Guangzhou, with responsibility to regulate trade and to collect customs duties. He followed the tradition of authorizing a group of merchants, heads of business firms known as 'hongs', to conduct the trade from the Chinese side. In 1720 the Hong merchants formed themselves into a monopolistic group known to Europeans as the Cohong and later devised a security system whereby individual hongs took responsibility for the behaviour and debts of foreign traders. From 1760, as a further means of control, foreign trade was confined to Guangzhou and members of the foreign community were required to observe the restrictions on activities known as the Eight Regulations. Compliance with these restrictions and regulations gave the impression that Westerners understood and accepted the Chinese view of inequality. As far as interstate relations were concerned, the Chinese assumption remained that the outer barbarians could be controlled by the traditional methods of using trade as a reward for good behaviour.[47]

This chapter began with a reference to the dispatch of Lord Macartney to China in 1792, in an attempt to gain for Britain improved commercial access to what were believed to be important markets. Macartney was permitted to go to Beijing and from there to proceed to the summer palace at Rehe. A prolonged negotiation took place over whether Macartney should comply with the protocol for receiving a tributary mission and perform the kotow. Macartney had brought with him a letter from George III to the emperor which had contained a number of requests, including the proposal that a British envoy should reside at Beijing, implying that the intercourse between the two countries should be established on a basis of equality. After receiving Macartney at an audience the Qianlong emperor wrote a poem which contained the lines 'formerly Portugal paid tribute: now Britain is paying homage'. In fact Macartney did not perform the kotow, but knelt before the emperor on one knee.[48]

The emperor's two edicts to George III in response to Macartney's mission are, for Westerners, among the best-known documents of Chinese history. He began:

> You, O King, live beyond the confines of many seas, nevertheless, impelled by your humble desire to partake of the benefits of our civilization, you have dispatched a mission respectfully bearing your memorial. Your Envoy has crossed the seas and paid respects at my Court on the anniversary of my birthday. To show your devotion, you have also sent offerings of your country's produce.

He then responded to the various requests which Macartney had made, in each case refusing them: there was no question of allowing foreign trade at ports other than Guangzhou or of providing a site near there where foreign merchants might reside; dynastic regulations would not permit the accrediting of a foreign national at court; it was not acceptable to allow the propagation of Christianity in China; as for the gifts which Macartney had sent, the emperor replied 'I set no value on objects strange or ingenious, and have no use for your country's manufactures.'[49]

These edicts have been quoted to support the view that at the end of the eighteenth century the key characteristics of China's view of the outside world were a sense of superiority and a deep ignorance. The former was evinced by Qianlong's assumption that Macartney had come as an envoy bearing tribute, not as a representative of a modern state seeking to improve mutual trade relations; the latter was revealed by the emperor's inability to appreciate the significance of the technological achievement revealed in some of the gifts. However, it has been suggested that one reason for Qianlong's negative response to the embassy was a well-justified suspicion of the motive for Macartney's mission. As for the gifts which Macartney had presented, the emperor's response had nothing to do with a failure to appreciate them as evidence of the advanced state of Britain's technology – in fact he had previously been given similar examples of 'strange or ingenious objects'. From the emperor's point of view the significance of the presentation of gifts, and importantly his bestowals in return, was that they were part of a ceremonial which confirmed the imperial hegemony, and so were essential to maintaining the Manchu position – an implication which Macartney failed to appreciate.[50]

14
The Opium Wars

Between 1839 and 1842 China fought the first Opium War with Britain. The war was concluded by the Treaty of Nanjing, the first of what were to be described as the unequal treaties. A second conflict occurred between 1856 and 1860, this time also involving France. As the incident which precipitated the war concerned the treatment of a ship called the *Arrow*, this war is known as the *Arrow* or Anglo-French War. A first attempt at a settlement was made by the Treaty of Tianjin, 1858. When the British and French delegates were prevented from ratifying the treaty, a second round of hostilities occurred which resulted in a Chinese capitulation and the signing of the Convention of Beijing, 1860. These treaties, and others signed at this time, provided the framework for Western imperialist penetration of China.

On the Origins of the Opium War

Western perspectives on modern Chinese history have emphasized the significance of these conflicts and have often treated the first Opium War and the Treaty of Nanjing as the starting point of modern Chinese history. More recently attempts have been made to discard this Eurocentric approach and to set the Opium War in the continuum of Chinese relations with the outside world.

The overriding concern of the Qing dynasty in its foreign relations was the security of its Inner Asian frontier. Having achieved that security, in the eighteenth century the dynasty had expanded westwards, into Central Asia, a further confirmation of the continental direction of the dynasty's priorities.

The Manchu attitude to maritime relations was influenced by the memory of having encountered the strongest opposition to the conquest in the south. A feature of this period had been the resistance offered by Zheng Chenggong, known to Westerners as Koxinga, on the island of Taiwan. In 1656, in an attempt to deny him resources, the Qing had carried out the draconian step of forcing the coastal population to move ten miles inland, a policy which was only formally rescinded in 1687.

The Qing government's attitude to the south remained suspicious, but it recognized that the best means of gaining support in the region lay in promoting its prosperity. One step towards achieving this was to legalize the junk trade which had grown up between China and south-east Asia. As much of the trade was in the hands of Chinese merchants, or at least of merchants who sailed in Chinese junks, this did not involve direct dealings with foreign states.

The same policy was applied to the growing trade with Great Britain, which likewise did not involve direct dealing with a foreign power because the trade was handled on the British side by the East India Company. Nevertheless, this trade did entail some security risks, such as the growth of piracy and the intrusion of Western missionaries.

Maritime trade had developed outside the tributary relationship and was subject to separate regulation. All foreign trade, including the junk trade and trade with Europe, was placed under the restrictions of what became known as the Guangzhou system. When the British government sent Macartney to China in 1792, he came as the representative of his country, but his instructions were to seek to improve commercial access. In Chinese eyes this confused two issues. He was received as an envoy leading a tributary mission, although his refusal to kotow was a challenge to the symbolism involved in that relationship. His main request, however, concerned the restriction of foreign trade, a matter which the Qing government regarded as non-negotiable as it impinged on its policies for security in the south.[1]

From the end of the eighteenth century a number of developments threatened the continuation of Qing policy towards maritime trade. Piracy, often connected with secret society activity, had become a serious problem, and the suppression of piracy became a major concern for both the court and provincial officials. A new concern related to the smuggling of opium into China. The value of opium as a medicine had been known in China for a long time, but it was only in the reign of Yongzheng (1723–35) that the danger of its use as an addictive drug was recognized and its sale and consumption made illegal. Nevertheless, small quantities of opium continued to be brought to China by Westerners. From 1773 the East India Company became involved in the growth of the opium poppy on its territory in India. After processing, the drug was shipped to China, not on board Company ships, but on ships operated by private merchants operating between India and China, who became known as 'country traders'. By the 1790s some 4,000 chests of opium were being shipped to China each year. There it was used as a drug, the usual method of ingestion being by smoking a pipe and drawing in the vapour produced by the opium. The danger of this drug abuse was recognized by the court and in 1796 the importation of opium was made illegal. Until this point much of the imported opium had been handled by the Cohong, but its distribution now became the business of professional smugglers operating along the China coast.

A third problem concerned the position of the Hong merchants. To facilitate trade they had to be willing to advance credit for the purchase of tea. In order to retain the favour of the Hoppo, the superintendent of maritime customs, and of the emperor, they were expected to mark important occasions by offering them expensive gifts. The merchants sought to protect themselves by contributing 10 per cent of their profits to the Consoo fund, a reserve to be used against the threat of bankruptcy. From 1780 the fund was supplemented by a 3 per cent levy on imports. Such a fund was unlikely to remain intact and between 1807 and 1813 forced contributions were made from it to the emperor, amounting to at least 5,000,000 taels.[2]

By then Westerners were becoming increasingly dissatisfied with the Guangzhou system of trade and the way they were treated in China. In 1784 two events occurred that were to have important implications for the future. The first ship from the United States arrived in Guangzhou, heralding a challenge to the quasi-monopolistic position of British traders. Then an unfortunate incident happened: a British ship, the *Lady Hughes*, fired a ceremonial salute and accidentally killed two Chinese officials. Chinese law required the identification of a culprit and on the threat of a suspension of trade, one of the ship's gunners was handed over to the Chinese authorities, whereupon he was strangled. This event exposed the differences between the Western and Chinese concepts of responsibility and due process of law.

After the end of the Napoleonic Wars British commercial interest in Asia quickened and the principle of free trade gained support. In 1813 the British East India Company's monopoly in India came to an end and its monopoly in China was scheduled to expire in 1834. In 1816 the British government made a further attempt to negotiate improvements in the commercial arrangements by sending Lord Amherst to China. Amherst was treated peremptorily and his refusal to perform the kotow ensured that the mission was a total failure.

It was at this point that the trade in opium began to assume a major significance for both Britain and China. One reason for this was the imbalance of direct trade between the two countries. In 1800 tea exports were valued at £3,655,000 but imports of British goods only amounted to about one-third of that sum. The balance was made up in silver and increasingly through credits derived from the country trade, the main commodity being Indian cotton. A second reason was a sharp fall in the price of opium and a consequent rise in opium sales. When the opium trade was first established, most of the opium came from East India Company estates in Bengal and was rather expensive. From 1817 the production of cheaper Malwa opium produced in the Indian native states began to rise and this forced a cut in the price of Bengal opium. Another reason for a heightened interest in opium was the vigorous action taken by Ruan Yuan, the governor-general of Guangdong and Guangxi. His investigation into the trade exposed the complicity of Chinese officials and forced the removal of the main opium distribution centre from Aomen to the island of Lintin in the Zhu (Pearl) river estuary.

Between 1822 and 1830 up to 18,766 chests of opium were being imported in a year.[3] The illegal trade encouraged increased involvement of Triad gangs in the distribution of the drug. It also reversed the favourable balance of trade which China had hitherto enjoyed and from the mid-1820s China became a net exporter of silver to cover the cost of opium. This caused a silver shortage in China and an increase in the price of silver against that of copper, which affected the payment of taxes which were paid in silver. The situation worsened in 1832 when William Jardine, head of the firm of Jardine, Matheson, extended the sale of opium along the China coast to Fuzhou and Xiamen and then assembled a fleet of opium clippers to exploit the new markets.[4]

The Road to War

The first crisis arising out of these developments occurred in 1834–5. With the ending of the East India Company monopoly, it became necessary for Britain to appoint a superintendent of trade in China, the first nominee to the post being Lord Napier. Lord Palmerston, the British Secretary of State for Foreign Affairs, gave instructions to Napier that on his arrival in China he should proceed immediately to Guangzhou and open direct communication with the senior Chinese official on the spot, that is to say the Governor-General of Guangdong and Guangxi, to ascertain whether it might be practicable to extend trade to other parts of China. Napier was told that it would be desirable to establish direct communications with the court at Beijing, but was warned to be very circumspect on this point for fear of causing offence and bringing about a stoppage of trade.[5] Such an instruction implied flouting Chinese protocol which required all foreigners to remain in Aomen until given permission to go upriver to Guangzhou. Napier went to Guangzhou without permission, but his attempt to open negotiations was firmly rejected, trade was suspended and he was held as a hostage. He ordered two frigates to make their way upriver and they destroyed the forts at the Bogue or Bocca Tigris, the names given by Westerners to the narrow entrance to the Zhu river. But the ships were then blockaded in the river and Napier was forced to accept humiliating terms before he was allowed to leave Guangzhou. He died on the return passage to Aomen.[6]

The Napier affair, or the 'Napier Fizzle', as it was rudely described, forced a reconsideration of British policy in China. At first, with the fall of the Whig government, there was a return to the policy of accepting Chinese restrictions on trade. But by now the free traders were more vociferous. In February 1836 the Manchester Chamber of Commerce, following the promptings of William Jardine, wrote to the Foreign Secretary to stress the importance of the trade with China, which provided employment for British shipping, a market for British manufactures and an outlet for the products of India, which in turn enabled India to afford British manufactures. The failure of Napier's mission had exposed the uncertain and unprotected state of that trade. This influential memorial brought the weight of Manchester merchants behind the country traders. The implication was that the trade was vital to British interests and it must be protected, if necessary by the use of force.

In the meantime the failure to stem the growth in the importation and use of opium had provoked a high-level debate in China. In 1836 an official named Xu Naiji proposed that the most practical way of curbing the drain of silver would be to legalize the importation of Indian opium and to permit the production of opium in China. This provoked a powerful response from other officials who deplored the abandonment of the moral high ground. The memorial submitted in October 1836 by Zhu Zun, a member of the Board of Rites, put this argument forcefully:

It has been represented, that advantage is taken of the laws against opium, by extortionate underlings, and worthless vagrants to benefit themselves. . . . But none surely would contend that the law, because in such instances rendered ineffectual, should therefore be abrogated!

It is said that opium should be admitted, subject to a duty, the importers being required to give it into the hands of the Hong merchants, in barter only for merchandise, without being allowed to sell it for money. And this is proposed as a means of preventing money secretly oozing out of the country. . . . As to the proposition to give tea in exchange, and entirely to prohibit the exportation of even foreign silver, I apprehend that, if the tea should not be found sufficient, money will still be given in exchange for the drug. . . .

Now the English are of the race of foreigners called [Red Hairs]. In introducing opium into this country, their purpose has been to weaken and enfeeble the Central Empire. If not early aroused to a sense of our danger, we shall find ourselves, ere long, on the last step towards ruin. . . .[7]

The Daoguang emperor, who had reigned since 1821, had already voiced his concern over the growth of opium addiction and he now supported those who argued that the existing laws should be enforced. Throughout 1837 a vigorous anti-opium campaign was waged against smugglers and dealers in the area around Guangzhou, but this was not enough to suppress the trade or to deter foreigners from promoting it. It was at this point that Lin Zexu, the Governor-General of Hubei and Hunan, suggested that the campaign should be extended to include sanctions against consumers, the hope being that the collapse of the market would persuade the British to sacrifice the drug trade to salvage the profits of legal commerce.[8] His suggestion gained the emperor's approval and in December 1838 Lin was appointed imperial commissioner with instructions to proceed to Guangzhou and carry out a comprehensive suppression of the opium trade – in the words of the emperor to 'radically sever the trunk from the roots'.[9]

Lin's journey from Beijing to Guangzhou, carried out partly on land and partly by river, and pursued with all due speed, took two months. Even before he reached his destination he had ordered the arrest of some sixty notorious opium dealers and throughout the next few months he was to continue a vigorous campaign against all Chinese aspects of the trade. But he was also convinced of the need to tackle the foreign suppliers and when he reached Guangzhou he addressed a remonstrance to Queen Victoria, describing the growth of the trade in opium, which he understood was prohibited in her country, and calling upon her to exert her influence to prevent the manufacture of opium by her subjects or on her territory. The letter was never received.[10] Lin then turned to more direct measures. On 18 March he told the foreign merchants that within three days they must hand over their stocks of opium to the Hong merchants and sign a bond stating that they would never again trade in opium, on penalty of death. He also attempted to arrest Lancelot Dent, head of one of the main opium-smuggling firms. At this point Charles Elliot, the British Superintendent of Trade, arrived from Aomen. To increase the pressure on the foreign community, Lin then ordered a stoppage of trade and the confinement of the foreign traders to the area of the Thirteen Factories. On 27 March Elliot responded by ordering British subjects to hand over their stocks. Some

21,000 chests of opium were surrendered to Lin, who had their contents solemnly destroyed. Most of the foreign community then departed for Aomen. Later that year two further incidents added to the tension. In early July, in a village on the mainland opposite Xianggang, a party of drunken British sailors beat and killed a Chinese farmer named Lin Weixi. Recalling the *Lady Hughes* case, Elliot refused to hand over the culprits. In response Lin exerted such pressure on the Portuguese authorities in Aomen that the English community transferred to Xianggang. In November 1839, in an incident to be known as the Battle of Chuanbi, two British warships engaged a Chinese fleet and sank three war junks.

Even at that point war did not appear inevitable. Neither Lin nor the Chinese government considered that what had happened amounted to more than a justifiable campaign to deal with the opium problem. The foreign community certainly believed that it was time that the Chinese were taught a lesson and that section of the community which dealt in opium was determined to take action. However, Elliot himself was a known opponent of the opium trade and several merchants, including some Americans, were quite prepared to sign the bonds prepared by Lin so that they could continue trading on the terms available.

The decision for war was taken in London in the light of the information received from China and in response to the political pressure from firms which had an interest in China. Elliot's dispatch of 27 March 1839, in which he described the situation in Guangzhou after Lin's ultimatum to the foreign traders, reached Palmerston, once again Foreign Secretary, on 21 September. From it Palmerston could infer that British citizens had been imprisoned and maltreated, and that Elliot, the British representative, had been coerced into committing the British government to compensate the traders who had surrendered their stocks of opium. At the same time Palmerston was urged to intervene in China by William Jardine, on behalf of the opium interest, and by firms from London, Manchester and Liverpool, on behalf of the legitimate trade with China, principally in cotton textiles. Although Palmerston himself had previously acknowledged the right of the Chinese government to stop the import of opium, the Whig government of which he was a member was vulnerable to the charge of failing to protect British commercial interests and he was aware that the only way the opium losses could be compensated was by forcing the Chinese government to pay. So in October Palmerston authorized the dispatch to China of an expeditionary force to China under the command of Charles Elliot and his cousin Admiral George Elliot. The force had instructions to compel the Chinese government to abolish the Cohong, to cede an island base where British traders could operate, and to recompense Britain for the opium losses and other expenses.

The First Opium War and its Immediate Outcome

The first Opium War fell into two phases. In the first phase the expeditionary force blockaded the approaches to Guangzhou, seized the island of Zhoushan near the port of Ningbo, and then moved north to the mouth of the Bei river, threatening Tianjin and Beijing. At this point the emperor abandoned Lin Zexu and authorized Qishan, the Manchu Governor-General of Zhili, to start negotiations. Qishan, adopting a variation on the traditional policy of jimi, 'controlling the barbarian with a loose rein', offered concessions to create a sense of personal obligation. He persuaded the British to withdraw to the south and followed them there to negotiate. When negotiations faltered, a British amphibious force attacked and destroyed the outermost of the Bogue forts, an action which was notable for two reasons. Among the British ships involved was the *Nemesis*, the first iron steam vessel to reach China. She displaced about 700 tons and was armed with two 32-pounder guns. As she drew only about 6 feet of water she was the ideal vessel for service in the shallow waters around Guangzhou. From the moment that the *Nemesis* arrived in Chinese waters, there was no doubt that Britain had an absolute naval superiority over China. The second point worthy of note is the heroic defence of the Bogue forts put up by the Manchu garrison, which preferred to die rather than to surrender.

The outcome of this renewed pressure was the Convention of Chuanbi, agreed in January 1841, in which Qishan, on China's behalf, conceded to the British demands, including the cession of Xianggang. Now that the immediate threat to Beijing had been withdrawn, the emperor castigated Qishan for secret dealings with the enemy and in particular for agreeing to cede Xianggang. He was stripped of all his honours, his fortune was confiscated and he was led out of Guangzhou in chains. On the British side Palmerston concluded that in view of the military force which he had at his disposal Elliot had accepted the lowest possible terms. He was replaced by a new British plenipotentiary, Sir Henry Pottinger. In the meantime, in response to an attempt by the Chinese to use fire-ships to destroy the British fleet, at the end of May Elliot landed troops and captured the forts which commanded Guangzhou from the north. However, rather than risk an assault and then have the problem of controlling a city with a population of at least half a million, he accepted a ransom of six million dollars and withdrew.[11]

Before the siege of Guangzhou had been broken off an incident occurred which in British eyes was a minor skirmish, but to the Chinese was to acquire the reputation of a great popular victory. The incident occurred on 29 May 1841 near the village of Sanyuanli, a few miles north of Guangzhou. After British and Indian troops had landed there were several instances of rape of Chinese women and the desecration of Chinese tombs. In response local gentry leaders raised a militia of about twenty thousand men, and threatened the British camp, only to be driven off. However, a British patrol which had become separated from the main force was trapped by militia. Heavy rain was falling and the British troops were unable to use their flintlock muskets. They were in real danger until a relief force reached them and they escaped with one man killed and fifteen casualties. In subsequent Chinese accounts this incident acquired a legendary significance: Guangzhou peasant troops, supported by their wives, had smashed the British invasion force. Their heroic action had exposed the cowardice of the Qing officials who had preferred to ransom Guangzhou rather than fight.[12]

The second phase of the war began in August 1841, with the arrival of Pottinger at Xianggang. He had at his disposal a much larger expeditionary force and before the end of the year British troops had occupied Xiamen, Zhoushan and Ningbo. The following spring Yijing, the emperor's cousin, attempted a counter-attack on Ningbo and Zhoushan, but his lack of military experience, coupled with the inadequate training and equipment of his troops, merely led to a disaster. By now further British reinforcements had arrived from India and this enabled Pottinger to move north. He first captured Zhapu, where once again the Manchu garrison troops fought heroically and their wives committed suicide rather than be captured. He then took Shanghai and finally the important city of Zhenjiang, which commanded both the Yangzi and the Grand Canal. At this point, with British ships poised to capture Nanjing, the emperor authorized negotiations and Qiying, an imperial clansman and senior diplomat, was empowered to act.

The outcome was the Treaty of Nanjing, which was signed on board Pottinger's ship, the *Cornwallis*, on 29 August 1842. The main provisions of the treaty were: that China would pay Britain an indemnity of $21,000,000 to cover the cost of the war and of the opium which had been confiscated; that the Cohong would be abolished; that five ports would be opened to British trade and residence, namely Guangzhou, Xiamen, Fuzhou, Ningbo and Shanghai; that the island of Xianggang would be ceded to Great Britain; that there would be equality in official correspondence; and that a fixed tariff would be agreed in the near future.

The Debate on the Origins of the First Opium War

The decision of the British government to support the merchants detained in Guangzhou and to demand compensation for their losses was immediately challenged in the British parliament. In a debate on 7–8 April 1840 censuring Palmerston's actions, T.B. Macaulay, the Secretary at War, did not try to defend the opium trade, but claimed that criticism of it could not excuse the mistreatment of British subjects. In response W.E. Gladstone declared:

> I do not know how it can be urged as a crime against the Chinese that they refused provisions to those who refused obedience to their laws whilst residing within their territory. I am not competent to judge how long this war may last ... but this I can say, that a war more unjust in its origin, a war more calculated in its progress to cover this country with disgrace, I do not know and I have not read of.[13]

On the other hand, John Quincy Adams, former President of the United States, speaking to the Massachusetts Historical Society in December 1841, argued that the chests of opium which had been confiscated were no more the cause of the war in China than were the chests of tea, which had been thrown overboard in Boston harbour, the cause of the American revolution. In his opinion:

The cause of war is the *kotow!* – the arrogant and insupportable pretensions of China, that she will hold commercial intercourse with the rest of mankind, not upon terms of equal reciprocity, but upon the insulting and degrading forms of relation between lord and vassal.[14]

Karl Marx regarded the growth of the opium trade as a central issue in the origin of the war, although he argued that its sale to China so absorbed China's purchasing capacity that the market for British manufactured goods was effectively blocked. This for him was ironic for it had led to a deadly duel

> in which the representative of the antiquated world appears prompted by ethical motives, while the representative of overwhelming modern society fights for the privilege of buying in the cheapest and selling in the dearest markets – this, indeed, is a sort of tragical couplet stranger than any poet would ever have dared to fancy.[15]

In the last century several variations on these themes were developed. P.C. Kuo, writing in 1935, argued that the definition of the war as an opium war revealed only part of the truth:

> The remote causes antedate the opium question. At the root of the intercourse between Europe and China there was an incompatibility of points of view. The theory of the Chinese empire was marked by a predominant spirit of aloofness and self-sufficiency.

This, he said, had led to a belief that China was superior to the rest of the world in civilization – a self-sufficient and condescending attitude which proved unacceptable to Great Britain.[16]

This view was later to be supported by the influential Harvard scholar John K. Fairbank. In *Trade and Diplomacy on the China Coast* he wrote:

> Historians generally agree that opium provided the occasion rather than the sole cause of war. One leading Chinese historian has concluded that the Opium War was essentially a conflict between Eastern and Western cultures.[17]

He added that the conflict stemmed from three causes: a clash between two conceptions of international order – the Western system of national states and the universal ethico-political order of the Son of Heaven; conflicting economic conceptions – Chinese self-sufficiency and Western belief in free trade; and a dispute over legal institutions – British ideas on codes of law, rules of evidence and legal responsibility clashing with the Chinese view that the emperor's administration operated on an ethical basis, above the mere letter of legal regulations.

The significance of the opium issue was restated by Michael Greenberg. In *British Trade and the Opening of China*, based on the papers of Jardine, Matheson and Company, he argued that the causes of the conflict were different according to the perspective of the two contestants:

> To the Chinese the war was fought over the opium question; but for the British merchants the issues were wider. 'The grand cardinal point of the expedition' was to Matheson 'the future mode of conducting the foreign trade in China.'[18]

In recent years the tide has turned against what may be termed the 'cultural' view in favour of the economic significance of the opium trade. In *Commissioner Lin and the Opium War*, Chang Hsin-pao conceded that the cultural argument was not invalid from a long-term point of view. However, it was no coincidence that the war broke out in 1839–40, after the phenomenal growth of the opium trade had alarmed the Chinese authorities into strictly enforcing the prohibition laws. He noted how William Jardine, the senior British trader in opium, had almost single-handedly drawn up the plans for the expedition of 1839. He concluded:

> The close and concrete connection between the opium trade and the war of 1839–1842 cannot be denied, and there is nothing unfitting about the term 'Opium War', which has been disavowed by many as being unjustifiably pejorative.[19]

The wider economic significance of the opium trade was put forward by D.K. Fieldhouse. He remarked that,

> The special feature of the British interest in the China trade was that it formed an integral part of the pattern of British economic activity in India and was in some ways fundamental to it.[20]

He argued that the East India Company had found it impossible to import sufficient goods from India to Britain to provide dividends for its shareholders and to enable its employees to repatriate their private capital. For a time this imbalance had been offset by selling raw cotton to China and using the proceeds to purchase tea. Later the sale of opium to China more than balanced the cost of tea and in addition it defrayed the cost of the administration of India. In this way a triangular trade was established between Britain, British India and China. This trade, in which opium was an essential commodity, was of immense importance to British interests, and when it was threatened it was inevitable that the British government would take steps to protect it. Moreover, by the 1840s Britain was an industrial power and her cotton textile industry was producing cloth and yarn which could undersell Asian products. It was imperative to secure markets for British products and, as China was deemed to have an enormous commercial potential, the opening of the Chinese market became a prime objective for the British government.

For James Polachek the origins of the Opium War lay in part in the factional politics of the Qing court. He argued that the showdown over the drug question in 1840 was not precipitated by the British side but by the Qing government.

Furthermore, the Qing government was responding to internal political pressures and not to foreign economic or military threats. The political pressure came from a group of degree-holders known as the Spring Purification circle which had emerged in the 1830s. This loosely knit group, which modelled itself on the Donglin academy of the late Ming period, was part political network and part exponent of a form of literary criticism. Like the Donglin academy it occupied the high moral ground and campaigned for Confucian philosophical rectification. In so doing it was following a tradition that non-officials had the right of qingyi, that is of moral censure. In the early 1830s censure took the form of criticism of provincial officials who had failed to respond effectively to natural catastrophes. In 1836 the Spring Purification circle played a role in persuading the Daoguang emperor to reject the proposal to legalize the opium trade. It now had to propose its own solution to the problem and this turned out to be a moral crusade directed primarily against the Chinese opium consumer, a moral crusade which called for the active involvement of the local gentry of Guangdong. To achieve this Lin Zexu, an active supporter of the Spring Purification circle, was appointed as imperial commissioner. Lin was committed to leading a moral crusade, but he also hoped thereby to gain promotion. In short the Spring Purification party led the way to a war for reasons which were based on the internal processes of Qing politics.[21]

The Unequal Treaties

The Treaty of Nanjing was the first of a series of agreements made between China and Western states and it foreshadowed similar agreements concluded by the Western powers with Japan, Korea, Vietnam and Thailand. These agreements are known collectively as the 'unequal treaties' on the grounds that they conveyed benefits to the West, without affording reciprocal benefits to the Asiatic states which were forced to sign them. These treaties had four characteristic features: the opening of treaty ports to foreign trade and residence; the provision of extraterritoriality, which removed foreigners from the jurisdiction of Chinese courts; the fixing of external tariffs by treaty; and what became known as the 'most-favoured-nation clause', a provision guaranteeing that if after the signing of the treaty the Asiatic power should confer additional privileges on another state, those privileges would automatically accrue to the Western state which had obtained the earlier agreement. The last provision had the effect of tying the agreements together into what has been referred to as the 'unequal treaty system'.

The first treaty settlement was completed between 1842 and 1844. At the Supplementary Treaty of the Bogue, 1843, import duties on foreign goods were fixed at an average of 5 per cent, much the same level as previously applied but no longer to be increased by special fees. Other articles in the treaty provided for the restriction of foreign trade to treaty limits, for extraterritoriality and the extradition of criminals, and for most-favoured nation status. Early in the following year Caleb Cushing, the first American commissioner to China, negotiated the Treaty of Wangxia, which largely replicated the terms obtained by Britain. Later that year the French representative, Lagrené, negotiated the Treaty of Huangpu, which in turn

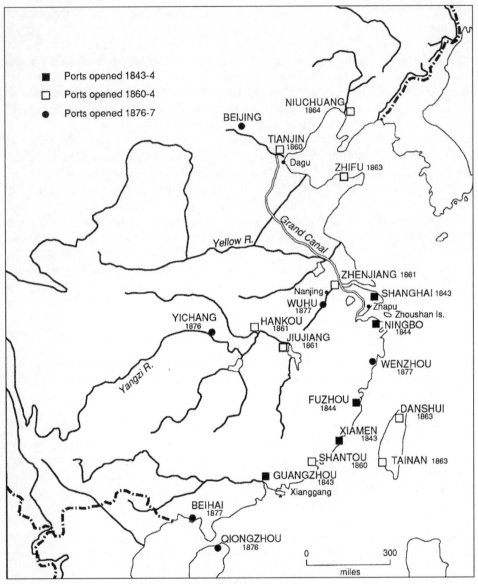

The opening of the treaty ports.

was copied from the American treaty. However, Lagrené also obtained an imperial edict which granted toleration to Roman Catholicism, a toleration extended in the following year to other Christian sects. By entering into these treaties voluntarily the Chinese government was applying the principle of equal treatment to all barbarians as a means of controlling them.

The issue which was not settled in these negotiations was that of opium. The indemnity required under the Treaty of Nanjing had in part been to defray the cost of the confiscated opium, but nothing was said in the treaties about the future of the opium trade. As a consequence the trade remained illegal, and British consuls were instructed not to permit it in the treaty ports. However, the illegal trade flourished at receiving stations along the south-east coast and Xianggang became an important opium distribution centre.[22]

Two views have been taken of the significance of the Treaty of Nanjing and of the unequal treaty system which it initiated. One is that the treaties represented a sharp break with the past, with China being forced to abandon its traditional method of dealing with the outside world and having imposed in its place a treaty structure designed to serve the imperialist interests of the foreign powers.[23] A second view, proposed by J.K. Fairbank, was that there was no sharp break, but merely a modification of the practice of permitting foreign participation in the government of China. Dynasties of conquest, such as the Manchu dynasty, had accepted many features of the traditional Chinese state and could be said to have participated in the government of China at the highest level. To describe the situation created by the unequal treaties Fairbank used the term 'synarchy', which he defined as the 'joint Sino-foreign administration of the government of China under a foreign dynasty'. To support this view he argued that several features of the treaties, for example extraterritoriality, were 'new versions of the conquerors' traditional prerogatives'. To illustrate the practice of joint administration he cited the Imperial Maritime Customs Service, which was administered by a British inspector-general but which worked in partnership with the Chinese superintendents of customs.[24]

From the Opium War to the Anglo-French War of 1856—60

Both sides were soon to express their dissatisfaction with the first treaty settlement, and the second conflict and the second treaty settlement can be interpreted as the inevitable outcome of this dissatisfaction.

On the British side two grievances were most prominent. The first was one of disappointed expectations. When Sir Henry Pottinger returned to England in 1842 he assured an audience in Manchester that victory in China

> opened up a new world to their trade so vast that all the mills in Lancashire could not make stocking stuff sufficient for one of its provinces.[25]

Immediately after the conclusion of the war British trade did increase substantially but thereafter it fell back. British merchant interests, in particular the Manchester Chamber of Commerce, maintained that the reasons for the failure of trade to expand as anticipated were obstruction by Chinese officials, the levying of internal transit duties and the continued use of licensed merchants and trade monopolies. In fact, although official obstruction and other restrictions may have played a part in limiting the sale of British textiles in China, the fundamental reason was lack of demand in the Chinese market, a situation which had already been made plain in a select committee report to the House of Commons in 1847.[26]

The second grievance centred on the British claim to a right of entry into the city of Guangzhou. The origin of the dispute lay in the discrepancy between the English and Chinese versions of Article II of the Treaty of Nanjing. In the English version British subjects had the right to reside at 'the Cities and Towns of Canton', but in the Chinese version this was rendered as the temporary residence of British subjects at the 'harbours' or 'anchorages' of the five port cities and the residence of the British consuls at the corresponding 'walled cities'.[27] After the signature of the treaty, the British plenipotentiary, Sir Henry Pottinger, was persuaded by Qiying, the Imperial Commissioner, with whom he was on good terms, to defer enforcing the right of entry to Guangzhou. However, in 1844 Pottinger was succeeded by Sir John Davis, who believed that the right of entry should be enforced, despite the increase in anti-foreign incidents and the repeated assertion of local Chinese officials that they would not be able to restrain the hostility of the people of Guangzhou if entry were granted. In March 1847, after Qiying had failed to deal with an anti-foreign incident to his satisfaction, Davis ordered an attack on the forts defending the Bogue and Guangzhou itself was threatened. Qiying was forced to promise that the British might enter the city in April 1849.

In March 1848 Sir John Davis was replaced by George Bonham. Davis had believed that the Guangzhou entry issue was the key to Chinese intransigence: only if Guangzhou resistance was crushed would the empire's arrogant policy towards Britain change. However, Bonham considered that a lasting settlement could only be achieved by putting pressure on Beijing, and as a consequence he was less concerned about entry into Guangzhou.[28] In February 1848 Qiying was succeeded as Governor-General of Guangdong and Guangxi by Xu Guangjin, and at the same time Ye Mingchen was appointed Governor of Guangdong. Both these Chinese officials were much less willing to co-operate with the foreigners than Qiying, who was a Manchu, had been. Xu gave encouragement to local gentry leaders organizing a militia to oppose entry, and when April 1849 arrived he boldly fabricated an edict, supposedly addressed to himself, in which the emperor ordered him to refuse the British entry to the city. Concerned about the threat to trade and aware of his limited military support, Bonham accepted the situation. On the Chinese side the outcome was regarded as a great triumph and both Xu and Ye were heaped with honours. In 1850 the Daoguang emperor died, to be succeeded by his son, the Xianfeng emperor, who was perhaps even more anti-foreign than his father. One of the first acts of his reign was to degrade Qiying for having oppressed the people to please foreigners.

A number of other issues added to British dissatisfaction, most notably the lack of direct representation in Beijing, a desire for which can be traced back to the Macartney mission. Taken in combination with the pressure to improve commercial access and the frustration over the Guangzhou entry crisis, the accumulated grievances became the agenda for treaty revision. In the American Treaty of Wangxia it had been agreed that the treaty would be revised after an interval of

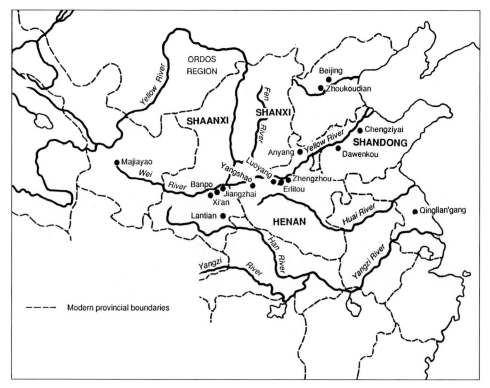

Prehistoric and early historic sites in north China

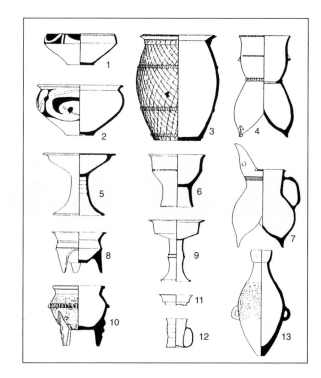

Neolithic pottery types of north China, first half of the second millennium BC; types 1–4 are Yangshao and types 5–12 are Longshan

Bronze sacrificial vessels of the late Shang dynasty; type 1 is a jue

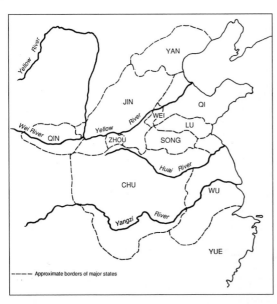

China at the time of Confucius (*c.* 551–479 BC)

Zhuangzi drumming on a bowl and singing after his wife's death; nineteenth-century woodblock (O/C 15331.e.12)

Bronze figure of Laozi riding on a buffalo

Kneeling archer from the terracotta army

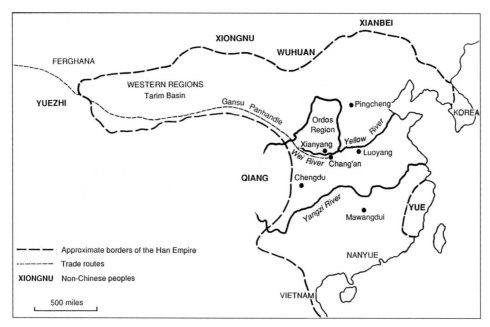

The Han Empire

Bronze figure of a flying horse, excavated from a tomb at Wuwei, Gansu; Eastern Han dynasty

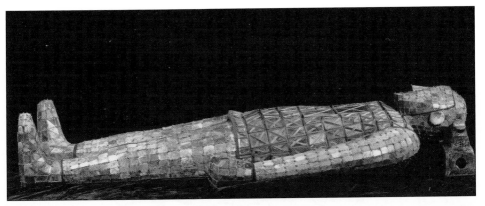

The jade funeral suit of Princess Dou Wan, Western Han dynasty. It was believed that jade would prevent the decay of the corpse

The Empress Wei in procession with court ladies; restored relief panel from Longmen, late Northern Wei dynasty

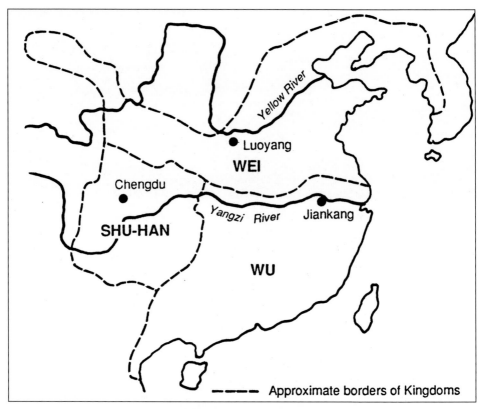

The Three Kingdoms, AD 220–80

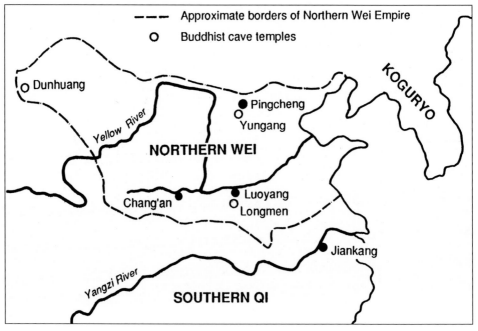

The Toba (Northern Wei) empire, c. AD 500

China Proper on the eve of the
rebellion of An Lushan, AD 755

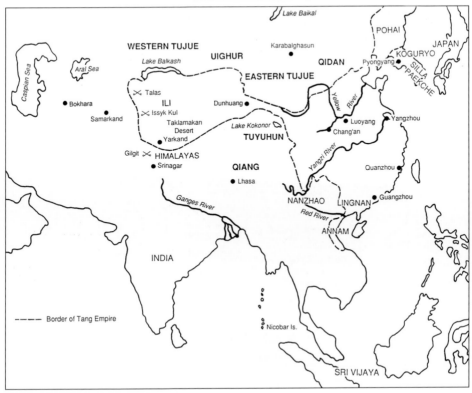

China and the world in the Tang period

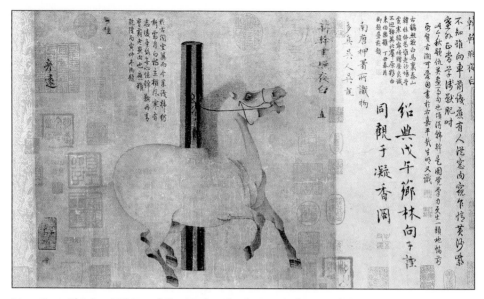

古錦脞粼白馬東茶山
韓佳徐喬涂沙塚学
衰東駿髦髦焦学
志凌辜錦毛髦寒省
髦龍焦夏固也雖
乾隆丙申何伯本於題

南唐押署所識物
多其吳人毀

新幹書照沒台 至

斉造

卓遠

韓幹照夜白
不知雖向車前後庄有人沈怠肉窝作惜黃沙梁
家敎岳咨琴溥獸肥耐
峰入秋駭仇吳童一子白困覺摹力先生一頭地掲雄
而冀吉澗可愛因音扑右嘉平臥生旳又識

紹典戊午鄭林向子謹
同覿于凝香洞
御題聲伯覦丁酉月
御劉繼壹月

Han Gan, Shining White of the Night, the favourite horse of the Emperor Xuanzong,
from a handscroll (1977.78)

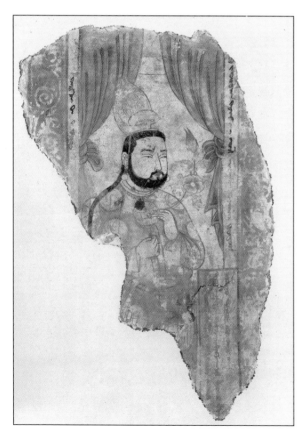

Uighur prince, from
Bauzäklik, Xinjiang, ninth-
century fresco

China under the Song, c. 1050

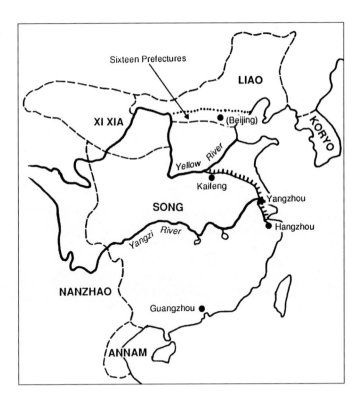

China under the Southern Song and the Jin, c. 1140

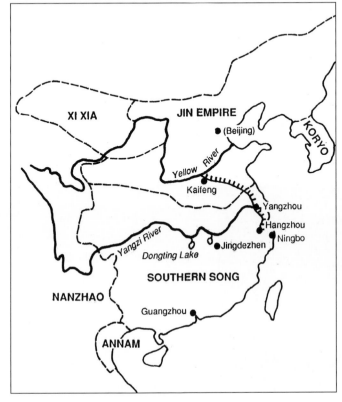

The Emperor Huizong (reigned 1101–25), The Five-Colored Parakeet on Blossoming Apricot Tree; handscroll, Northern Song dynasty

Confucian temple at Suzhou

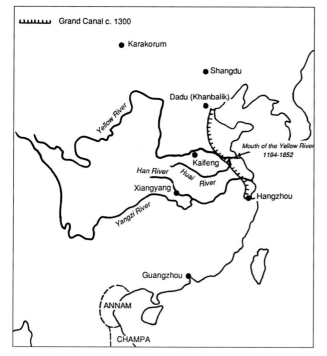

China under the Yuan (Mongol) dynasty, 1279–1368

Ivory figure of a seated official from the Ming dynasty

China in the early Ming period

The Humble Administrator's Garden, Suzhou; early sixteenth century

拘鸞肘出步顛剁搬

下掌擦打其心拿鷹

捉兔硬開弓手腳必

須相應

當頭砲勢衝人怕

步虎直攔兩夸他退

閃我又顛端不跌倒

他也忙然

Soldiers drilling in the martial arts; Qi
Jiguang's *New Treatise on Tactics* (O/C
15291.a.18)

Restored section of the Great Wall near
Badaling, north-west of Beijing

The Journey to the West, showing Pigsy being trapped into accepting food, while Monkey and Tripitaka (Xuan Zang) look on; eighteenth century (O/C 15271.c.13)

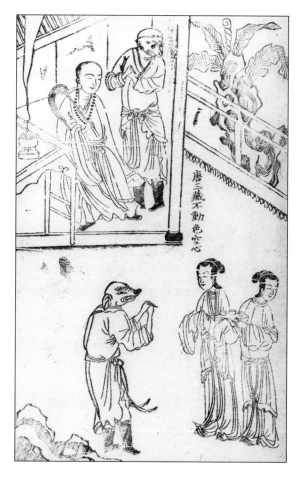

The Hall of the Supreme Harmony, Forbidden City, Beijing

The Temple of Heaven, Beijing

Porcelain production at Jingdezhen, Jiangxi province, late Ming dynasty; woodblock prints (O/C 15226.b.19)

China in the seventeenth century: the Manchu
invasion and the revolt of the three feudatories

Statue of Li Zicheng, in the
outskirts of Beijing

Mu Lan, who disguised herself as a soldier to relieve her father from doing military
service; woodblock print from *Biographies of Exemplary Women*, 1779
(O/C 15291.a.18)

tsè watering
tcha tea

茶　瀬

Watering tea-plants

Péé

To us th order. head of Imperia...

府廣品四

y ping tà Gin
first rank great Woman

人夫品　一

Kĕ

a guest at Canton new...

商　客

Chinese export watercolours, c. 1795. Clockwise from top left: Watering tea-plants;
Official of the Top Rank; Merchant; Lady of the First Rank.

The examination cells, Guangzhou, c. 1873.

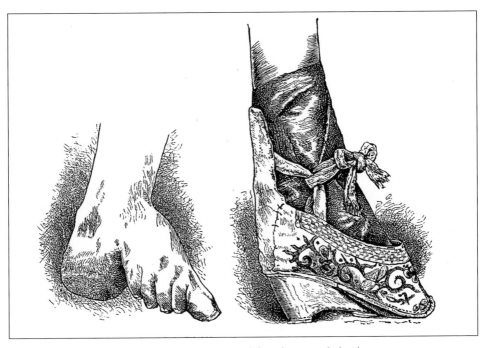

'Golden Lilies' – bound feet bare and shod.

Barbarian envoys presenting tribute.

Ye Mingchen, Governor-General
of Guangdong and Guangxi.

Interior of one of the Dagu forts after the explosion of the magazine, August 1860.

Ruins of the Far Sea View Building, the Summer Palace, August 1860.

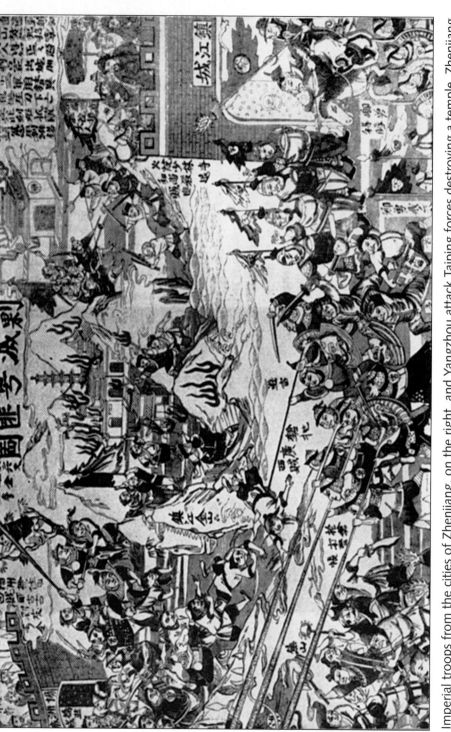

Imperial troops from the cities of Zhenjiang, on the right, and Yangzhou attack Taiping forces destroying a temple. Zhenjiang had been recaptured by the imperialists in December 1857.

Prince Gong.

Zuo Zongtang.

The Nanjing arsenal.

Chinese schoolboys on their way to the USA, 1872.

An anonymous painting showing the the stages of tea production,
mid-nineteenth century.

Missionaries in Chinese costume.

Engine works at Hanyang, *c.* 1894.

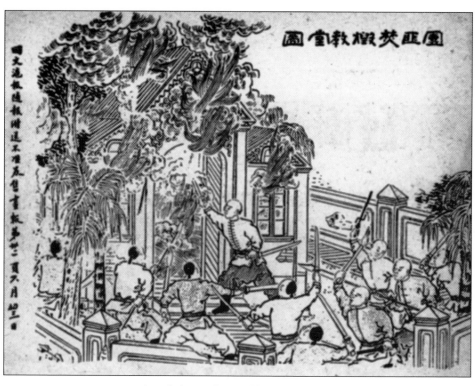

Church being burned by the Boxers.

The 'Holy Mother', Her Majesty Cixi.

His Majesty Xuantong, Emperor of China.

Jiang Jieshi and Sun Zhongshan.

Wu Peifu, the Philosopher Marshal.

Li Dazhao.

Site of the first Party Congress, Shanghai, July 1921.

Immigrant farm workers from Shandong province awaiting transport at Dalian, Manzhouguo, 1932.

The tomb of Sun Zhongshan, Nanjing.

The Shanghai Bund, 1930s. The building with the dome is the Hongkong and Shanghai Bank, that with the clock tower is the custom house, and that with the pyramid roof is the Cathay Hotel.

A rural school in Zhejiang province. The posters refer to the New Life Movement.

Mao Zedong at Yan'an.

Mao Zedong proclaiming the establishment of the People's Republic of China, 1 October 1949.

People working on the Ming Tombs dam, near Beijing, 1958.

Distribution of *Quotations* from Chairman Mao Zedong, 1967.

Hua Guofeng.

Zhao Ziyang, Deng Xiaoping and Hu Yaobang stand to commemorate the centenary
of the death of Karl Marx, March 1983.

twelve years. The British argued that by analogy the Treaty of Nanjing should be revised in 1854, but when representatives of Britain, France and the United States jointly attempted to initiate discussions on revision, first at Guangzhou with Ye Mingchen and later in Beijing, they were told that all their major demands were refused. In 1850 Palmerston had noted

> the Time is fast coming when we shall be obliged to strike another Blow in China. . . . These half-civilized Governments such as those of China Portugal Spanish America all require a Dressing every eight or Ten years to keep them in order.[29]

With the rejection of treaty revision there was a widespread feeling, particularly among the British in China, that the time had now come to strike that other blow.

The Chinese governmental response to the first treaty settlement may be discussed in two stages. Until 1848 its main characteristic was a conciliatory approach to the management of 'barbarian affairs'. The most influential figures promoting this line were Muchanga, the Chief Grand Councillor, and Qiying, who for much of this period was imperial commissioner entrusted with the conduct of foreign affairs. It has long been noted that both were Manchus and that the appeasement policy was advocated by Manchus who allegedly were more concerned about the survival of the dynasty than about the fate of China.[30] It was Muchanga who had recommended acceptance of the terms of the Treaty of Nanjing and it was he who thereafter was held responsible for not advocating resistance. Qiying dealt directly with foreigners and attempted to establish a personal relationship with Pottinger, on one occasion, at a banquet in Nanjing, popping sugar plums into the British envoy's mouth. During the negotiations for the Treaty of Huangpu, Qiying visited Xianggang where he was fêted and expressed the wish to adopt Pottinger's eldest son. Such actions did enable the negotiations to be concluded swiftly and amicably, but they exposed Qiying to bitter attacks from those opposed to any concessions to foreigners.

Qiying's position depended on Muchanga's influence at court. In the years after the war Muchanga had been extremely successful in displacing officials who had supported the radical measures advocated by Lin Zexu which had led to war, and in securing the promotion of his own supporters. In the words of one of his critics, 'those who warmed their hands over his brazier felt no cold'.[31] Nevertheless, in the 1840s there was the gradual emergence of an opposition to Muchanga, centred on the 'Southern City', the southern, Chinese part of Beijing, where lower-grade officials who had excelled in the examinations usually resided.[32]

Far to the south, in and around Guangzhou, a more overt rejection of the appeasement policy was apparent. The agitation which had arisen at Sanyuanli in September 1841 was kept alive by the issue of the British entry into the city. Qiying carefully avoided offering any encouragement to the gentry leaders of the movement. However, the appointments in 1848 of Xu Guangjin and Ye Mingchen altered the situation. Xu realized that if he kept the promise to open the city in April 1849 he would be excoriated by the local population. In February 1849 he made a vital concession to the local gentry, permitting them to raise a militia to prevent the barbarians entering the city.[33]

The refusal to admit foreigners to Guangzhou, the 'victory' of 1849, marked the beginning of a second stage in foreign policy. When Daoguang died in 1850 and was succeeded by the eighteen-year-old Xianfeng emperor this change accelerated. Muchanga and Qiying were dismissed and in 1852 Ye Mingchen, whose obdurate attitude to foreigners was already well known, was made acting Governor-General of Guangdong and Guangxi and Imperial Commissioner in charge of foreign affairs. His refusal to discuss how anti-foreign incidents might be resolved and his reluctance to deal directly with representatives of the foreign powers was matched by an unwillingness on the part of the government in Beijing to enter into any communication with Britain.

Under these circumstances a further conflict between China and the Western powers was likely. That it did not occur in the early 1850s can perhaps be explained by a variety of fortuitous circumstances. In December 1851 Palmerston was dismissed as British Foreign Secretary and his successors were less inclined to take vigorous action in China. Also, Dr John Bowring, who had been appointed British consul at Guangzhou, was initially an advocate of a negotiated settlement. More significant were two important events which distracted attention from the confrontation. The first was the rise of rebellion in China – the Taiping rebellion began in July 1850 and Nanjing was captured by the rebels in March 1853. In the same period disorder spread through Guangdong culminating in the Red Turban revolt which began in July 1854. Between March 1854 and February 1856 the Crimean War, involving Britain, France and Russia as adversaries, preoccupied the Western powers.

The deadlock was ended in October 1856 by a dispute arising from the arrest by the Chinese authorities of the crew of a ship called the *Arrow*. The *Arrow* had been registered in Xianggang (although its registration had expired) and its crew was accused of piracy. Nevertheless Harry Parkes, the acting British consul at Guangzhou and Bowring, now Sir John Bowring, the Governor of Xianggang, seized upon the incident as an insult to the British flag. Bowring authorized a naval attack on Guangzhou which breached the city walls and entered Ye Mingchen's official residence. However, Ye had departed and the force had to retire. In December of 1856 the level of bitterness was increased with the burning of the foreign factories outside the walls of Guangzhou and the offer of 30 taels in silver in head-money for every Englishman killed or captured.

The Arrow War and the Treaties of 1858 and 1860

By the time that news of these events reached London, Palmerston had become Prime Minister and he was forced to defend Bowring's actions which were regarded as the consequence of Palmerston's aggressive policy in China. Palmerston was defeated in a vote of censure, but won a resounding victory in the ensuing general election. He then sent the Earl of Elgin with an expeditionary force to China with instructions to enforce the right of entry into Guangzhou and to obtain agreement to the appointment of a minister to Beijing. In the meantime the murder of a missionary, Auguste Chapdelaine, prompted the French government to join with Britain in the venture. The assembling of the British expeditionary force was delayed by the outbreak of the Indian Mutiny and it was not until December 1857 that hostilities commenced with an attack on Guangzhou. This resulted in the capture of Ye Mingchen, who, still obdurate, was sent to India, where he died the following year. His stubborn but passive response was remembered in a popular ditty of the time:

> He did not treat, nor make defence,
> Nor yielded, nor showed fight;
> He did not die a soldier's death,
> And did not take to flight.
> A statesman of such policy,
> A general of such might
> Was never seen in yesteryear
> And seldom comes to light.[34]

Elgin then installed an allied government which ruled Guangzhou until the end of the war.

In the next phase of the war the allies went north, capturing the Dagu forts which guarded the river access to Tianjin and thence to Beijing. At this point the court decided to negotiate and nominated as one of its negotiators the aged Qiying. He tried to revive the cordial relations he had established with Pottinger sixteen years previously, but he was comprehensively shamed by revelations of his double-dealing contained in memorials seized in the capture of Guangzhou. He was later sentenced to death, but was permitted by the emperor to commit suicide. In the meantime treaties were negotiated with Britain and France and similar agreements were made with Russia and the United States.

The most important terms of the Treaty of Tianjin, signed by Britain and China in June 1858, were: the opening of ten further treaty ports, including ports on the Yangzi; permission for foreign travel in China; freedom of movement for missionaries; an agreement relating to the liability of foreign goods to the payment of inland transit dues; the legalization of the opium trade; and, most importantly, the right of a British minister to reside in Beijing.

These terms, and in particular that of foreign representation in Beijing, were odious to the emperor. They were agreed in poor faith and because of the threat from internal rebellion. However, the subsequent rupture was more probably the outcome of British highhandedness and of poor communications between the two sides, rather than of a decision by the court to reject the treaty. In June 1859 the allied representatives returned to Dagu, *en route* for Beijing, where they expected to ratify the treaty. They found the river blocked and when the British forces attempted to remove the obstructions they became dangerously exposed. British ships began to bombard the forts, but when the guns of the Dagu forts responded the British force suffered heavy casualties. In a notable example of co-operation between the Western nations, the commander of the United States' ship carrying the American minister as observer abandoned his neutral status and, declaring 'blood is thicker than water', went to the rescue of the British.[35] Nevertheless, this was a humiliating defeat for Britain and a cause of great encouragement to anti-foreign elements at court.

Retribution soon followed. In August 1860 British and French representatives returned to the north of China supported by a large force. Harry Parkes was sent ahead to make arrangements for the ratification of the treaty in Beijing. In an incident which was to be regarded on the British side as the darkest treachery Parkes was arrested by the sixth Prince Yi and sent to Beijing in chains, where he was kept prisoner and several members of his escort were killed. In revenge Elgin ordered the burning of the Summer Palace. As a consequence of these events China was forced to accept a further unequal treaty, the Convention of Beijing, which increased the indemnity payable, opened Tianjin as a treaty port, and ceded Jiulong (Kowloon) peninsula opposite Xianggang to Britain.

In these negotiations the Russian ambassador Count Ignatiev played an astute role as mediator between the British and French representatives and Prince Gong, a son of the Daoguang emperor, who had been given the invidious task of making peace. In return for his good offices Ignatiev obtained confirmation that territory to the north of the Amur river had been ceded to Russia, and in addition he obtained the transfer to Russia of another vast tract of territory to the east of the Ussuri river, later to be known as the Maritime Province. This confirmed Russia's access to the newly opened port of Vladivostok.

15
Rebellion and Restoration

Between 1796 and the 1870s China experienced a series of rebellions which came close to overthrowing the Qing dynasty. The first of these, the White Lotus rebellion (1796–1804) arose in the mountainous region between the Yangzi and the Yellow rivers, in the provinces of Shandong, Henan and Zhili. In the following years further White Lotus uprisings took place in the Henan–Anhui border region. After a period of relative calm, in the mid-century a major cycle of rebellions arose. The most devastating of these, the Taiping rebellion (1850–64), started in the southern province of Guangxi, but for most of its course was centred on Nanjing. To the north a group of rebels known as the Nian had its base area in northern Anhui. In north-west and south-west China, in Yunnan (1855–73) and in Gansu (1862–73), major Muslim revolts threatened the secession of these areas from China. This period also witnessed a burst of secret society activity leading to the capture in 1853 of Shanghai and Xiamen by the Small Sword society, a Triad society, and the near capture of Guangzhou by the Red Turbans in the following year. If this was not enough, the middle decades of the century saw sharp outbursts of ethnic fighting between the Chinese dialect groups in western Guangdong and uprisings by the Miao in Guizhou.

On Peasant Rebellions

In an essay entitled 'The Chinese revolution and the Communist Party', published in 1940, Mao Zedong declared:

> The ruthless economic exploitation and political oppression of the peasantry by the landlord class could not fail to force the peasants to rise repeatedly in revolt against its rule. From . . . the Qin dynasty . . . down to the Taiping Heavenly Kingdom in the Qing dynasty, there have been several hundred uprisings, all of them peasant movements of resistance, that is, peasant revolutionary wars. The gigantic scale of such peasant uprisings and peasant wars in Chinese history is without parallel in world history. These peasant uprisings and peasant wars alone formed the real motive force of China's historical evolution.[1]

Mao Zedong's identification of peasant revolt as a symptom of the class struggle, and his stress on the importance of peasant rebellions in Chinese history, ensured that during his lifetime the subject was given extensive coverage in Chinese Communist historiography. Even after Mao's death, the revolutionary nature of peasant wars and the class consciousness of the peasants remained central to historical debate. However, the emphasis shifted to why peasant rebellions failed, either through defeat or because their leaders turned into anti-egalitarian 'feudal' rulers. The conclusion was that peasants could oppose feudal oppression, but they were unable to rid themselves of a 'feudal' world view.

Marxist historians have emphasized the economic foundations of peasant rebellion and have characterized them as a response to the economic oppression of a landlord class. Other writers have been more impressed by the recurrent themes of sectarian religion and millenarian expectations, which they have interpreted as a form of opposition to the Confucian political order. Many rebellions through Chinese history began as sectarian movements, but having been persecuted as a threat to the state then turned against the government. Some such movements were led by a charismatic leader, for example Zhu Yuanzhang, the founder of the Ming dynasty, and were inspired by a belief in an imminent millennium. However, on gaining power the utopian dream was quickly replaced by a preoccupation with mundane matters.[2]

On the Rise of Rebellion

The traditional explanation for the rise of rebellion was to connect it with the decline of the dynasty. Confucian historians interpreted history in terms of a dynastic cycle. Founders of dynasties epitomized personal virtue and their rule was sanctioned by the mandate of heaven. But their successors were unable to maintain those standards of conduct, the quality of government declined and rebellions arose which in time overthrew the dynasty and started the cycle again. Some modern historians have developed this interpretation by explaining the cycle in administrative rather than in moral terms: early in a dynasty a vigorous ruler with an efficient bureaucracy and an effective military force expanded the empire. However, at a later stage the costs of government rose, bureaucratic corruption increased, the military was unable to protect distant frontiers, and the tax burden increasingly shifted towards those least able to pay and aroused peasant discontent, the prelude to the rise of rebellion. There is undoubtedly some evidence to support the case that dynastic decline occurred in the late eighteenth century. The reign of the Qianlong emperor, although in many respects the pinnacle of Qing power, was marred by the corruption associated with the emperor's favourite Heshen. However, the argument that an historical cycle was repeating itself is neither complete nor entirely convincing. Qianlong's successor, the Jiaqing emperor, made commendable efforts to stamp out corruption and other examples of attempts at reform cast doubt on any assumption that the dynasty was already doomed by the beginning of the nineteenth century.

The factor most liable to destabilize the dynasty was a new one, that of unprecedented population growth. In the late seventeenth century China's population was about 150 million. A hundred years later this population had doubled. Between 1779 and 1850, the population grew by an estimated 56 per cent. The population rise depended on the steady expansion of the food supply and this was achieved largely through the application of labour-intensive methods of farming and the spread of the cultivation of maize, sweet potatoes and peanuts, all crops introduced from America. Until the middle of the eighteenth century the growth in the food supply outstripped the growth in the population, but from then onwards the law of diminishing returns ensured that a slow decline in the availability of food per capita set in.[3]

Accompanying this population growth there was extensive migration. In the seventeenth century, at the time of the dynastic transfer from Ming to Qing, some parts of China, for example Sichuan, were seriously depopulated. After the Manchu conquest had been completed, government-sponsored migration was directed at the repopulation of these areas. But, as the population continued to grow and as these areas became saturated, further waves of migrants penetrated to more inhospitable and more remote regions, for example the mountainous area between the Yellow and Yangzi rivers. Elsewhere migrants moved into settled regions, for example in Guangxi, where they took up poor hilly land and competed for resources with earlier migrants who cultivated the valley bottoms. The connection between migration and civil disorder is brought out clearly in the following description of the settlers who moved into the Yangzi uplands, to the upper waters of the Han river and to the borders of Shaanxi, Sichuan and Hubei:

> The new communities, unruly and disorganized, had but weak kinship bonds and scanty education. There was much moving about, as settlers scratched a bare living from unfruitful soil, and some were known to have several abodes in the course of a year as they pursued the growing season up the mountainsides. Traditional control mechanisms like *baojia*, which could only be imposed on a settled population, were thus virtually useless, save within market towns and cities. Disorder was aggravated by the existence of a growing pool of outlaws, who lived in the deep forests and were entirely cut off from normal society.[4]

Population growth undermined the operation of government in a variety of ways. The most prestigious occupation for educated men was within the bureaucracy, but the size of the civil bureaucracy remained fixed at about 20,000 appointments. The competition in the examination system became intense and many of those who qualified were unable to obtain substantive appointments and formed a stratum of supernumerary personnel. In some cases they supplied a form of assistance to officials such as district magistrates, whose administrative resources were quite inadequate to deal effectively with the problems of a vastly increased population. But such men had to live and their needs were met by the taxpayer. In the words of Susan Mann Jones and Philip Kuhn, 'Government at all levels was becoming the host organism of an expanding occupational group, which used the empire's administrative machinery as a weapon in its own economic struggle'.[5] A vivid example of how the accumulation of superfluous personnel could paralyse government operations has been found in the case of the grain transport administration, the task of which was to arrange the collection and transportation of a rice tax from the Yangzi delta to Beijing.[6]

The Manchus had gained power by conquest and their position was supported by

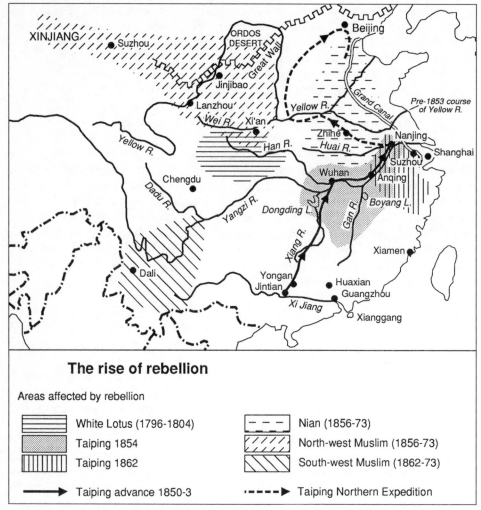

The rise of rebellion.

military force in reserve. Their most reliable forces were the banner troops, hereditary military formations of Manchus, Mongols and Chinese which had been raised at the time of the conquest. These were supplemented by the predominantly Chinese Army of the Green Standard, units of which were placed under the command of provincial governors-general and governors and provincial military commanders, a divided responsibility which was likely to make these forces ineffective. Moreover, military standards had declined, officers used soldiers as their servants, soldiers were often not paid and desertions were frequent. This situation led Franz Michael to comment 'From the beginning of the nineteenth century onward, the larger part of the army existed on paper only'.[7]

The White Lotus Rebellion

The White Lotus religion, which had spread widely in north China, derived from Buddhism, popular Daoism and Manichaeism. Its principal deity was the Eternal Venerable Mother, whose concern for her children led her to send the Maitreya, the future Buddha, to earth to usher in the millennium. It was the White Lotus religion which had been the inspiration of much anti-Mongol agitation which culminated in the rebellion led by Zhu Yuanzhang.

In normal times White Lotus adherents lived peacefully in small communities. The religion had no central organization and the only connection between different sects was intermittent relations between sect leaders. However, if the sect leaders predicted that the coming of the millennium was imminent, or if the sects were subject to persecution, adherents might be transformed into rebels and the sects could become the basis of a rebel movement.[8] Such a transformation had occurred in the Wang Lun uprising of 1774. It was to occur again on a more devastating scale in the White Lotus rebellion.

In the late eighteenth century White Lotus sects became particularly active in the Hubei–Sichuan–Shaanxi region, an area already noted as having received many recent immigrants. Various happenings: the appearance of a charismatic sect leader, the announcement of the imminent millennium and a call for a Ming restoration, led to government intervention, which proved a catalyst for open rebellion. The White Lotus sectarians were only a minority of the rebels. Others who joined included members of martial arts groups, salt smugglers and bandits living in militarized bands in remote border areas. Against a rebellious movement of this kind, which was both part of and separate from settled communities, the imperial forces were largely ineffective. The systematic suppression of the movement was only achieved by establishing strategic hamlets where the peaceful population could be kept separate from the rebels, and by implementing a programme of 'strengthening the walls and clearing the countryside'. In addition local gentry raised militia forces and these were strengthened by the dangerous expedient of hiring local mercenaries. By these means the rebellion was defeated, though this had been achieved at heavy cost in terms of the government's finances and its military prestige.[9]

The danger of White Lotus activism was not, however, ended. In 1813 White Lotus sects calling themselves the Eight Trigrams rose in Shandong and Zhili in anticipation of the millennium. With the connivance of palace eunuchs, the rebels even entered the Forbidden City, but were easily defeated. The effective suppression of the rebellion, although rather laboured, has been seen as an indication that the Qing government retained a certain vigour.[10]

Secret Societies

Whereas in north China religious sects associated with the White Lotus religion were the most common form of clandestine and heterodox activity, in the south that role was more commonly played by the secret societies known in the West as the Triad and in Chinese as the Heaven and Earth Society and many other names. It is probable that the Triad secret societies originated in Taiwan in the late seventeenth century. There was no central organization but each society shared a common ideology and similar ritual. Their declared political objective was to overthrow the Qing and restore the Ming. Those who joined Triad lodges underwent complex initiation rituals and became members of a brotherhood which in its benign aspect provided a system of mutual support for many whose social background, as labourers and boatmen and unemployed urban workers, did not provide the security of the extended family. It was a sisterhood too, as women were often recruited into Triad lodges.[11] In times of peace secret societies were deeply involved in criminal activity, whether it be smuggling or piracy, or more generally racketeering. In times of unrest every minor rebellion stimulated secret society activity. In the 1840s a distinct shift occurred in the secret societies' social base. Whereas until this time they had subsisted largely on the fringes of settled society, they now began to make progress among the settled peasantry of the Zhu river delta and to infiltrate local government offices. Their blatant activity forced loyal gentry (and not all gentry were loyal) to raise militia to suppress them. However, in 1853, after two years of economic recession, secret society activity reached a new peak. In September 1853 the Small Sword society, whose members came from Guangdong and Fujian, seized Shanghai and held the city for eighteen months, and members of the same society also captured Xiamen. The gravest threat came in the districts around Guangzhou where in 1854 a major uprising, known as the Red Turban revolt, seized the important city of Foshan and nearly captured Guangzhou. The threat was only averted by the efforts of the gentry who organized militia forces, and later by the ferocious purge of secret society adherents conducted by Ye Mingchen, the Governor-General of Guangdong and Guangxi, who boasted that he had personally ordered the execution of 100,000 rebels.[12]

The Taiping Rebellion

As with many other rebellions, the inspiration and leadership of the Taiping rebellion came from a disaffected member of the elite, an unsuccessful examination candidate named Hong Xiuquan. Hong (1814–64) was a Hakka Chinese, who came from the village of Huaxian, north-west of Guangzhou. In 1836, when taking the provincial examinations, he heard a Protestant missionary preaching in the streets of Guangzhou and was given a collection of Christian tracts entitled *Good Words to Admonish the Age*, although he did not read them at this stage. The following year, after another examination failure, he experienced a nervous breakdown and had a series of visions. In these visions he was carried into a beautiful palace, where he was bathed and his heart and other organs were replaced by new, red ones. He was then brought before an old man with a golden beard who said to him:

> All human beings in the whole world are produced and sustained by me; they eat my food and wear my clothing, but not a single one among them has a heart to remember and venerate me; what is however still worse than that, they take of

my gifts, and therewith worship demons; they purposely rebel against me, and arouse my anger. Do thou not imitate them.

The old man then gave Hong a sword with which to exterminate demons, a seal with which to overcome evil spirits and a sweet fruit to eat. In another vision Hong encountered a middle-aged man, whom he called elder brother, who gave him advice. He also heard the old man reproach Confucius for not having preached the true doctrine.[13]

After Hong had recovered from his illness it was noted that his physical appearance had changed. In 1843 he made another attempt at the examinations and once more failed. He then happened to pick up the tracts which he had been given seven years previously. He interpreted their contents in the light of his visions and concluded that the old man was the Christian God, that the middle-aged person who had advised him was Jesus Christ, and that he himself was the younger brother of Jesus who had been given a divine commission to restore the true faith to China.

Hong's first action was to impart his vision to his cousin, Hong Ren'gan and to a friend and fellow schoolteacher, Feng Yunshan. They caused offence to their neighbours by removing statues from the schoolroom and this may have been the reason why Hong and Feng Yunshan decided to go to southern Guangxi to make converts among the Hakka living there. Hong himself did not stay long with the mission. In 1847 he was back in Guangzhou and together with his cousin he attended the church run by a fundamentalist Southern Baptist missionary, Issachar J. Roberts.

Later that year Hong returned to Guangxi and found that Feng Yunshan had established a religious community known as the God Worshippers' society which had attracted a congregation of some two thousand peasants and miners. This movement was soon in conflict with the local community and Feng Yunshan was arrested on a charge of planning a rebellion. Hong Xiuquan's efforts to secure his release left the God Worshippers' society without its founders at a key moment. To fill the vacuum new leaders emerged who were to transform the society into a millennial movement. Yang Xiuqing, later to be known as the Eastern king, was the leader of the miners and charcoal burners who had joined the movement. He claimed to be able to cure illnesses by himself taking on the suffering of those afflicted. He had trances and declared himself to be possessed by the Holy Ghost. Xiao Chaogui, a poor hill farmer, to be known as the Western king, also had trances in which he professed to speak as the voice of Jesus Christ. Both of the new leaders incorporated local popular religious beliefs and practices into the revelation experienced by Hong Xiuquan. From the summer of 1850 the movement entered a millenarian phase. Families of God Worshippers began to assemble at the village of Jintian, having abandoned, and in some cases having burned, their crops and their houses. They handed their valuables in to a sacred treasury and accepted a camp discipline which required the strict segregation of the sexes.[15]

The sectarian movement turned into a rebellion in January 1851 after a period of increasingly severe clashes between the God Worshippers and the local militia. Hong declared the establishment of the *Taiping Tianguo*, the Heavenly Kingdom of Great Peace, and himself assumed the title of the *Tian wang*, the Heavenly king.

Those who had joined the movement were organized into a complex military organization and subjected to severe military discipline.[16] After a series of clashes with government troops, in September 1851 the Taipings captured the small walled town of Yongan. There the movement was reorganized. A collective leadership was established, with each of the principal leaders receiving the rank of *wang*, or king, of one of the cardinal points of the compass. Printing presses were used and the rebels began to produce the remarkable set of publications which proclaimed and justified their cause. Among those publications was the Taiping calendar, which combined elements of the Chinese lunar and the Western solar calendar.[17]

By April 1852 government troops were besieging Yongan and the Taiping supplies were exhausted. Two days before breaking out from the siege, Hong issued a proclamation in which he stressed the imminence of the millennium:

> Let men and women officers all grasp the sword.
> As for your present clothing needs, one change will be sufficient.
> With united hearts rouse your courage and together slay the demons.
> Gold, valuables, and baggage shall be put aside.
> Divest yourselves of worldly affections and uphold high Heaven;
> Golden bricks and golden houses await you, all brilliant and flashing;
> In high heaven shall you enjoy happiness, majesty in the highest.
> The smallest and the lowest shall all wear silks and satins.
> Men shall wear dragon robes and women shall be garlanded in flowers.
> Let each be a faithful minister and exert his utmost energies.[18]

The Taipings moved north, traversing Hunan and gathering a following estimated at over one million people. They asserted their divine mission, denounced the Manchus, attacked rapacious officials and reassured scholars that they would retain the examinations. In March 1853 they captured Nanjing and then made what was probably a serious strategic error by deciding to make it their Heavenly City. Expeditions were sent north, to capture Beijing, and west, to control the middle Yangzi valley. Both were defeated and the rebellion became centred on Nanjing and lost its first impetus.

Nevertheless, at Nanjing the Taipings were able to introduce elements of a new order which contained striking features. For the time being the millennial aspects of the movement – the segregation of the sexes, the sacred treasury, the restrictions on trade, the prohibitions of alcohol and opium – were enforced. Other more practical measures, for example examinations which followed the established pattern but which were based on Taiping, not Confucian texts, were introduced.

Perhaps the most ambitious of all the Taiping proposals was the one contained in the document entitled *The Land System of the Heavenly Dynasty*. This document prescribed a classification of land into various grades and its division among families according to their size, with women being granted a share equal to that given to men. The document did not restrict itself to matters directly connected with the land. In the new society the population would be divided into units of twenty-five families. Each unit would be placed under a sergeant whose duties would include the religious education of children and the settlement of disputes. The land system was related to the Taiping military organization. The two systems envisioned a society in which every individual would have security provided that he or she accepted the Taiping dispensation. It was notable that, in a movement which is commonly described as a peasant rebellion, the punishment prescribed for officials who neglected their religious duties was reduction to the status of a peasant.[19]

An important issue which has arisen in the assessment of the rebellion concerns the extent to which the Taiping programme, and in particular the land system, was implemented. In the surviving Taiping records there is some evidence that a start was made in establishing the twenty-five family system and a civil administration.[20] In areas under Taiping control no attempt was made to alter the existing distribution of land, but there is some evidence to suggest that the land tax levied by the Taiping government was significantly less than that collected previously by the imperial government.[21] There is also some indication that until 1860 the Taipings refrained from coercing tenants into paying rent to landlords, but that after that date they actually helped landlords to collect rents.[22]

The first phase of the rebellion came to an abrupt end in 1856 when a violent internecine struggle resulted in the death of the Eastern king and a large number of Taiping adherents. The following year Shi Dakai, perhaps the best educated of the Taiping leaders, who had in effect been head of the Taiping government in Nanjing, departed on an independent campaign in south-west China from which he and his troops were never to return. The situation deteriorated further as the opponents of the rebellion began to organize resistance. The most significant development centred on the actions of the famous Hunanese scholar-official Zeng Guofan. When the Taipings were crossing Hunan, Zeng was at home observing the mourning period for his mother. When the government at last appreciated the magnitude of the Taiping threat it appointed a number of officials, including Zeng, to supervise the raising of local corps to oppose the rebels. Zeng was well aware that local corps, raised only to protect their locality, were incapable of defeating the rebels. Without the knowledge of the government he began to expand the small mercenary force which had already been raised. This force became the Hunan or Xiang Army, the first of the regional armies. The characteristics of these armies, compared with previous gentry-led forces, were summarized by Mary Wright:

The new armies were larger, stronger, more cohesive, and more independent. The commander-in-chief personally selected the officers, 83 per cent of whom were Hunanese . . . and each officer recruited his soldiers from his own native district, sometimes from his own clan. With the battalion of 500 or less as the unit, close attachments were formed. The army and the groups within it were handled somewhat like a Confucian family, with much emphasis on moral instruction and guidance. Moreover, the new armies were supported by local revenues, independently of central government. Pay and rations were generous – triple the normal standards of the time.[23]

The reference to local revenues is significant. When the Hunan Army was first raised, Zeng adopted various expedients, including the sale of ranks and titles, to defray the costs. However, in 1853 a new source of revenue became available. This was the lijin (likin) tax, literally the tax of a thousandth, levied on goods in transit, which was collected to support the Hunan army.

The other source of opposition derived from the attitude of the Western powers. When the Taiping rebellion broke out, some Protestant missionaries hailed it as presaging the general conversion of China to Christianity. British officials were more cautious and after the first contacts had been made with the rebel leaders in 1853, the policy decided upon was one of strict neutrality between the two sides in the conflict. This policy was maintained until the outbreak of the *Arrow* War and for a time thereafter, even when Britain and France and the rebels shared a common enemy. The situation only changed when China signed the Treaty of Tianjin in 1858, for that treaty provided for the opening of three additional ports on the Yangzi river 'So soon as Peace shall have been restored'.[24] Thereafter, British policy was to contain the rebellion and after 1860 to support the imperial side in its suppression.

The Later Stages of the Taiping Rebellion and its Suppression

After the 1856 massacre new military leaders emerged, the best known of whom was Li Xiucheng, the Loyal king. He co-operated with the Nian rebels and in 1858 inflicted a devastating defeat on the Hunan army. In the following year Hong Xiuquan's cousin Hong Ren'gan, who had been an adherent of the movement since its very beginning, but who had been forced to remain in Xianggang, arrived in Nanjing. He gave the rebellion a fresh political impetus, for he created a new administration and also published *A New Treatise on Aids to Administration*, which contained a remarkable, if impracticable, reform programme. In it he urged the introduction of various institutions derived from the West, including modern communications and a form of elections.[25]

Under this new leadership the rebellion enjoyed a short revival. Hong Ren'gan devised a strategy to relieve Nanjing and to extend Taiping territory in the lower Yangzi provinces and then to swing back and strike at the Hunan army besieging the important city of Anqing. The first part of this plan succeeded and between 1860 and 1864 the Taipings occupied a large part of the Jiangnan area of the lower Yangzi, thus securing an economic base. The impact on the rural population of this phase of the rebellion has been the subject of a recent study by Kathryn Bernhardt. She investigated the Taiping system of local government, and in particular the appointment of rural officials, and found that this group contained both representatives of the pre-rebellion elite and others from humble backgrounds. She connected this finding with the Chinese historians' debate about the class character of the Taiping rebellion: whether the movement remained true to its peasant origins or whether it allowed power to remain in the hands of the landlord class. She noted that the Taipings made no attempt to introduce the land redistribution programme of the Land System of the Heavenly Dynasty. However, in two important ways (albeit in a sporadic and inconsistent manner) the Taipings did interfere in landlord-tenant relations. The first was by introducing tenant (rather than landlord) payment of taxes, a measure brought about because many landlords had fled, but which did carry some implication that the ownership of the land had passed to the tenant. The second was the introduction, in some areas under Taiping control, of mandatory reductions in rent. In the 1840s and 1850s the Jiangnan area had witnessed a sharp burst of popular resistance to the payment of increased rents, and Taiping policies may have been determined by this as much as any commitment to peasant interests. Taking into account all these factors, Kathryn Bernhardt rejected the view that the Taiping occupation resulted in a complete restructuring of power and property relations, but she suggested that 'while the world was not turned upside down in Jiangnan, it was certainly knocked askew'.[26]

On the military front Li Xiucheng did not carry out his part of the plan and the campaign failed to achieve its main objective. When Anqing fell in late 1861 the Taiping capital at Nanjing could no longer be supplied and was bound to fall.[27] However, before that happened a final round was to be fought in the hinterland of Shanghai. Li Xiucheng's main base was at Suzhou and his main opponent in that area was the Anhui or Huai army, the regional army raised by Zeng Guofan's former protégé Li Hongzhang. In addition two other forms of opposition emerged. In Shaoxing prefecture, Zhejiang, a peasant named Bao Lisheng, who was reputed to possess supernatural powers, raised a force known as the 'Righteous Army of Dongan' to protect his village. That a peasant should lead a form of popular resistance to the Taipings shows that the gentry did not monopolize the defence of the established order. Bao Lisheng died in 1862 with many of his followers after a prolonged siege of the village.[28] In Shanghai the foreign community raised a mercenary force to be known as the 'Ever-Victorious Army', which was for a time led by Captain Charles Gordon, a British army officer on secondment. This force played a significant role in denying Shanghai to the Taipings and Britain also assisted the enemies of the rebellion by supplying arms and lending steamships for the conveyance of troops. But undoubtedly the Taiping defeat owed more to the dissensions within the rebel ranks, and to the opposition of the regional armies, which denied the rebels the middle Yangzi valley, than it did to foreign intervention.

Meanwhile in Nanjing the rebellion was entering its final stages. In June 1864 Hong Xiuquan either died or committed suicide and in the following month Nanjing was captured with a tremendous loss of life. Hong Xiuquan's son and Hong Ren'gan escaped and fled south but were soon caught and executed. The Qing government then began a systematic destruction of all traces of the rebellion.

The Nian Rebellion

The Nian rebellion arose in northern Anhui, in the area north of the Huai river, an exceptionally harsh habitat which was repeatedly ravaged by flood and drought. Peasants frequently supplemented their meagre incomes by engaging in various predatory activities, including salt smuggling and banditry. In the struggle for survival villagers were forced to adopt protective strategies which included raising militia and fortifying their settlements.[29]

Two main explanations have been put forward for the origin of the rebellion. The older of the two, which suggested that the Nian (the name simply means 'group')[30] was a transformation of the White Lotus society, has been discredited, for it has been shown that the connection between the two organizations was at most tenuous.[31] More recently it has been suggested that the origin of the Nian rebellion lay in the extension of the predatory activities which had already become common in the first half of the nineteenth century. At this stage the Nian bands were independent, dispersed and often involved in feuding between themselves. An important factor behind their rise was the tacit or even active support that they obtained from some government officials, who found it advantageous to conceal Nian activities and even to profit from them.[32]

Nian predatory activity turned to rebellion in the early 1850s. An underlying cause of this was a major ecological disaster: in 1851 the neglected Yellow river flood defences collapsed, leading to disastrous flooding and the beginning of the river's shift to its northern course. By this time a process of evolution had led to the emergence of larger Nian bands and these bands were in contact with the Taipings, which may have encouraged the Nian to adopt the language of rebellion. After the fall of Anqing, the provincial capital of Anhui, the imperial government ordered that throughout the province the people should erect earthwall forts and train garrison forces. This policy was subverted by the Nian leaders, who occupied the forts and extended them, creating an articulated defence. As one writer put it, 'They are linked in such an organic way that when you touch the head, the tail will react'.[33]

In 1856 a group of Nian chieftains chose one of their number, Zhang Luoxing, as their commander and adopted a political programme: they had risen up 'to rescue the impoverished, eliminate treachery, punish wrongdoing, and appease the public indignation'. Their soldiers would be punished severely for plunder or rape and nothing would be taken from the poor.[34] Early in 1857 the Nian and the Taiping concluded a form of military alliance and between 1857 and 1859 they jointly occupied some cities in the Huai valley.[35] Some Nian leaders, including Zhang Luoxing, were given titles as Taiping kings. Nevertheless, the main occupation of the Nian rebels at this stage remained plunder, although they were mindful of the Chinese proverb which declares 'A rabbit never eats the grass around its own hole'. In the early 1860s Nian activity extended into Shandong and this kindled outbreaks of White Lotus activity. The court responded by dispatching the Mongol Prince Senggelinqin to lead the campaign against the Nian. By 1863 he had captured and executed Zhang Luoxing and persuaded other Nian chiefs to change their allegiance.

In 1864 the Nian rebellion entered a new and more expansive phase. It has been suggested that this began when a Taiping force which had been cut off from Nanjing joined the Nian and provided a more professional military element and superior cavalry techniques. A more probable explanation is that by this date the 'nest area' of the Nian, centred on the town of Zhihe, had been captured by the imperial forces and the area subjected to a major programme of pacification.[36] The Nian now became roving bandits, their cavalry ranging over the North China plain. The most notable incident of this stage was the ambush and death of Senggelinqin in 1865.

This change in tactics prompted an important shift in the imperial government's policy. In 1864, after the Taiping had been defeated and Nanjing recaptured, it had become clear that the court had reservations about the power which had accumulated in the hands of Zeng Guofan, creator of the Hunan army and Governor-General of Jiangsu, Jiangxi and Anhui.[37] It now concluded reluctantly that it would have to turn again to Zeng Guofan, who was placed in charge of the campaign to suppress the Nian. He proceeded cautiously, conducting a systematic investigation of the 'nest area' and blockading the area to prevent the return of the Nian mobile forces. Against the Nian cavalry he deployed units of Li Hongzhang's Anhui army, which had firearms and had adopted Western-style drill. It was Li who completed the campaign by forcing the Nian to split and then blockading them in eastern Shandong, their final defeat coming in 1868.[38]

The Muslim Rebellions

The two great Muslim rebellions of the mid-nineteenth century, in Yunnan (1856–73) and Shaanxi and Gansu (1862–73) shared a common background of the increasingly severe discrimination against Muslims which had been practised from the mid-eighteenth century. In Yunnan in the 1840s a sharp conflict arose between Han Chinese and Muslims over the control of a silver mine. In 1856 two Muslim leaders emerged, Du Wenxiu, who has been described as the political leader, and Ma Dexin, who was the religious leader. Du Wenxiu established what was known in the West as the Panthay kingdom, with its capital at Dali. His administration, although nominally Muslim, relied heavily on the use of Chinese officials, and he also attempted to obtain British recognition. Chinese resistance was organized by Cen Yuying, who had begun his career fighting the Taipings. He managed to divide the Muslims and he eventually captured Dali in 1872 and had Du Wenxiu executed.[39]

In Shaanxi and Gansu Islam was well established and its influence had been strengthened by the New Teaching, a term used to denote a Sufi (Muslim mystic) practice known as 'vocal recollection' which had appeared in Shaanxi in the 1760s. This innovation led to incessant conflict between adherents of the New Teaching and other Muslims, with the Chinese authorities generally siding with the latter. In 1862–3 a Taiping detachment traversed the area and its appearance may have contributed to changing the endemic conflict into a rebellion in which Chinese Muslims – known as Dongan in this area – were in conflict with Han Chinese. A mystic named Ma Hualong, the most prominent of the Muslim leaders, by 1864 controlled much of Gansu.

The loss of Gansu implied the collapse of the Qing position in Central Asia and the likelihood of this was only too apparent when separate Muslim rebellions broke out in Xinjiang and a leader known in the West as Yakub Beg first became prominent. However, there was little that the court could do about this until the Taiping and Nian rebellions had been suppressed. In 1866 Zuo Zongtang, who had distinguished himself in the mopping-up of the Taiping remnants, was appointed Governor-General of Shaanxi and Gansu. After completing the suppression of the Nian in his area he was given the task of dealing with the Muslim rebellion in Gansu. He recognized that this required a political as well as a military campaign and announced 'Do not distinguish between Chinese and Muslim; distinguish only between good and evil'.[40] Zuo demonstrated a remarkable capacity for organization and a willingness to play the long game – he anticipated that the recovery of Shaanxi and Gansu would take five years. His most reliable troops came from units of the Hunan regional army, initially raised by Zeng Guofan. He promised rebels – other than active adherents of the New Teaching, for whom no mercy was available – the chance to turn in their weapons and to accept resettlement. Zuo's campaign was handicapped by the harsh terrain, the shortage of supplies, mutinies among his own troops and the fanatical commitment of the rebels. Eventually Ma Hualong was trapped in Jinjibao, known as 'the Medina of Chinese Islam' and the fortress there was bombarded with Krupp siege guns. After its surrender Ma Hualong was executed and his troops massacred. The population was transported and the city was turned over for settlement by Han Chinese. Two years later Zuo Zongtang captured Suzhou, the last main Muslim stronghold in Gansu.[41]

There remained the problem of Yakub Beg. This danger was compounded in 1871 when Russia, alarmed by the situation in Xinjiang and determined to protect her interests in that area, occupied the fertile Ili valley in the north-west of the region. In 1874, when Zuo Zongtang was about to extend his campaign into this area, a Japanese force landed on Taiwan as a reprisal for the murder of shipwrecked sailors from the Liuqiu islands.

This combination of events provoked an important policy debate at the Zongli Yamen, the prototype foreign office, and among senior provincial officials. It concerned the relative importance of inland defence or coastal defence, or to put it in other terms, whether the Qing dynasty should concentrate its resources on becoming a land power or a naval power. Li Hongzhang, anticipating the threat from Japan, emerged as the main proponent of coastal defence. Zuo Zongtang argued that the coastal threat came from the Western maritime nations which only sought commercial advantages, whereas the inland threat came from Russia, which sought both commercial and territorial gains. The Manchu court, recalling that in the past failure to control Inner Asia indicated dynastic weakness, chose inland defence.[42] In 1875 Zuo Zongtang was placed in charge of military affairs in Xinjiang and by 1878, through a supreme effort, he had re-established imperial authority in the area. There remained the matter of the Ili region, which Russia had undertaken to restore to China once the region had been pacified. The first attempt at a diplomatic settlement resulted in only part of Ili being returned. The Zongli Yamen rejected the settlement and in return Russia threatened war. The Ili crisis was settled by the Treaty of St Petersburg in 1881, with almost all China's territorial claims being agreed. In 1884 Xinjiang became a province of China.[43]

The Consequences of the Rebellions

The rebellions and their suppression had important consequences for the Chinese state. These included demographic and economic effects, and consequences in terms of the power balance between the central government and the provinces. In the longer term the rebellions were to serve both as a warning and as an inspiration for future generations.

There is no doubt that the rebellions caused a very large number of deaths. Some of these came in combat, many from starvation, and many too from the willingness of both the rebels and perhaps even more the imperialists and their supporters to execute any they thought might oppose them. Zeng Guofan, early in his career, earned the nickname of 'head-shaver Zeng' for his propensity for having the heads of rebels removed.[44]

The lack of accurate post-rebellion statistics makes it impossible to arrive at a complete reckoning of the population loss caused by the mid-nineteenth-century rebellions. However, the demographic impact on some areas can be calculated with some accuracy. In Anhui, Zeng Guofan ordered a population count as a preliminary to instituting a programme of land rehabilitation. According to the figures which he collected the population of Guangde county, an area representative of much of southern Anhui, experienced a population decline from 309,000 in 1865 to a little over 5,000 in 1865. Thereafter, sponsored immigration brought a slow recovery, but even a century later, in 1953, the recorded population of Anhui was 19.3 per cent below that of the 1850 figure. Estimates of the loss of life caused by the north-west Muslim rebellion in Gansu alone run to several million. In the opinion of Ho Ping-ti the estimate of contemporary Western residents that the population loss caused by the Taiping wars was in the order of twenty to thirty million, was 'too low'. The effect of the rebellions was to offer some relief from population pressure, particularly in the lower Yangzi region. However, this was a brief respite, for China's population probably surpassed its 1850 peak at some time in the last quarter of the nineteenth century.[45]

The most important social effect attributed to the mid-nineteenth century concerned the position of the gentry. Gentry support was vital for the defeat of the rebellions and of course essential in the raising of the regional armies. To obtain this support the Qing government was forced to make important concessions to the gentry which have been seen as bringing about a fundamental readjustment in the relationship between the two parties. The size of the regular gentry group (that is, those who had obtained admission by examination) was determined by the frequency of the examinations and the quota of successful candidates; that of the irregular gentry group (that is, those who had obtained titles or offices by purchase) was determined by the number of sales. In the first half of the nineteenth century the number of those who had gentry status amounted to approximately 1.1 million. During the period of the rebellions the government rewarded provinces and districts where local people had contributed to the military fund raised to support the imperial forces, by increasing the quotas for juren and shengyuan in proportion to the level of the contributions. Later this concession was also given for contributions to the support of local corps raised by the gentry. With reference to the purchase of titles, this was encouraged by a sharp reduction in the price, one estimate being that the cost of purchasing a jiansheng title fell from 1,000 taels of silver to about 200 taels.

As a consequence of these measures the total number of gentry rose to approximately 1.45 million, with the increase in the number of irregular gentry being proportionately greater and the rise in numbers being most marked in the more wealthy provinces. According to Chang Chung-li, who compiled the statistics, the rise in gentry numbers, and the change in the composition of the group, was an indication of a weakening of the government. The gentry escaped government control and became more difficult to manage. Their traditional role in the community and the standing which they had enjoyed in society were also affected and this contributed to the disintegration of a society which had been dominated by this group.[46]

An influential interpretation of the change in the role of the gentry was put forward by Philip Kuhn in *Rebellion and Its Enemies in Late Imperial China*. He showed how the rise of disorder, and subsequently of rebellion, forced the rural elite to organize its own defence. Gentry leaders formed local self-defence associations and raised militia, following the system known as *tuanlian* or 'grouping and drilling'. These associations took on a wider role, raising taxes and later organizing the collection of the lijin tax, and supporting the development of the regional armies discussed above. Kuhn suggested that when the rebellions had been suppressed the local militarization which had occurred was to continue to shape the relationship between the district administration and the local elite. The *tuanlian* associations assumed a semi-official administrative role, organizing the baojia and intervening in tax collection. The result was an increase in the power of the local elite and the consequent diminution of the power of central government.[47]

Another broad interpretation of the effects of the rebellions concerns the growth of 'regionalism'. Regionalism has been defined as 'the emergence in key areas of China of military and political power centers that assumed some of the important functions of the state but still remained within its framework'.[48] Such regional power centres emerged at times of dynastic crisis, for example that provoked by the mid-nineteenth-century rebellions. Before the rebellions the Qing dynasty had exercised three important powers: a monopoly of military force, an exclusive control over taxation and the sole right to make official appointments. When the Taiping rebels swept across Hunan in 1852 the dynasty had been forced to make a crucial concession: it had allowed Zeng Guofan, although he held an appointment as a senior official, to resign from government service and organize a gentry-led militia in his home province. Zeng had done more than that, for he had transformed the militia forces into a regional army. Its finances had come largely from the lijin tax, a tax neither collected nor disbursed by the central government. When in 1860 the dynasty had faced an even more severe crisis it had surrendered another cardinal principle, the separation of military and civil power, for in that year Zeng had been appointed Governor-General of Jiangsu, Jiangxi and Anhui. Moreover, he had then secured the appointment of his protégé Li Hongzhang as Governor of Jiangsu province. Li in turn raised the Anhui army and as part of the Self-strengthening programme was to establish a formidable industrial empire. In 1870 he was transferred to the governor-generalship of the metropolitan province of Zhili, a post which he occupied for an unprecedented term of twenty-five years in disregard of the usual practice of limited appointment.

The three themes mentioned here – the changing position of the gentry, militarization and regionalism – all support the argument that the dynasty never fully recovered from the effects of the rebellions. Such an interpretation inevitably colours one's view of the last half century of the dynasty's course. It is an interpretation which is difficult to dismiss entirely, but it is also one which must be treated with a degree of caution. Mary Wright once commented:

> Zeng Guofan is often referred to as the prototype of later independent provincial leaders, and there can be no question of his enormous regional power. The critical point is this: On whose behalf did he exercise that power and to what end? On the evidence – and it is voluminous – Zeng saw no conflict between his national and regional loyalties, and used his talents, powers, and prestige toward the restoration of a central Confucian state firmly grounded in local Confucian society.[49]

Other arguments which have been set against the regionalism thesis are that the lijin tax was later brought under central government control, the appointment of officials remained firmly in imperial hands and the case of Li Hongzhang's long tenure of office was exceptional, with senior provincial officials usually serving shorter rather than longer periods in office.[50] With reference to the expansion of gentry influence, the point has been well made that in war-torn areas, such as the lower Yangzi valley, officials realized that reconstruction lay beyond the resources at their disposal.

> Just as the state had encouraged gentry activism in the 1840's and 1850's to cope with popular unrest and the Taiping threat, so it would now rely on the elite's assistance to reestablish the Qing order. To that end the government permitted the gentry in the post-rebellion years an even greater hand in the administration of local affairs than it had enjoyed in the decades immediately preceding the Taiping occupation.[51]

16
Restoration and Self-strengthening

To some observers by 1860 the Manchu dynasty appeared to be on the verge of collapse. In May Taiping armies broke out of Nanjing and inflicted a major defeat on the government forces besieging the rebel capital. In August a British and French expeditionary force landed near the Dagu forts with the intention of advancing on Beijing to force the court to ratify the Treaty of Tianjin. In September Harry Parkes, the most aggressive of the British diplomats, was seized and imprisoned, together with other British and French members of the expedition. The Western forces won the Battle of Baliqiao and the Xianfeng emperor and the court fled to Rehe. In retaliation for the attack on the diplomats Lord Elgin, the British plenipotentiary, ordered the destruction of the Summer Palace.

However, at this point the situation began to stabilize. Prince Gong, the emperor's half-brother, negotiated the settlement known as the Convention of Beijing, which was to usher in a decade of co-operation between China and the Western powers. Before the end of the year the Taiping expansion had faltered and the regional armies, as previously described, had begun the protracted task of countering and eventually subduing the rebellions. Under the Tongzhi emperor what was described as a restoration took place and constructive measures to repair the ravages of the rebellions were initiated. In response to the evidence of the grave disparity between China and the West in terms of military technology, the policy to be known as 'self-strengthening' was defined and some steps were taken to rectify that imbalance.

Court Politics: the Coup of 1861 and the Rise of Cixi

The Xianfeng emperor died in August 1861 and was succeeded by his only son, who reigned as the Tongzhi emperor. As the new emperor was only five years old at his father's death an eight-man council was formed to advise the emperor. This included Sushun, a Manchu prince whose attempt to stamp out corruption in government banks had earned him a reputation for severity. He had also played a prominent role in the negotiations with the Western powers. While preparations were being made for the funeral, the new emperor was taken to Beijing by his mother, a concubine named Yehonala, who had now been given the title of the Empress Dowager Cixi. Having confirmed the support of Prince Gong, she issued an edict accusing the eight-man council of having precipitated war with Britain and France in

1860, of having contributed to the Xianfeng emperor's premature death, and of having plotted to usurp the government. The men were arrested and some were allowed to commit suicide, but Sushun was executed.

For the time being Prince Gong appeared to be the most powerful figure at court. He was only twenty-eight years old at the time of the coup but he was advised by Wenxiang, a senior Manchu official whose common-sense advice was to play an important part in shaping government policy until his death in 1876. Nevertheless, the Empress Dowager was already an important power behind the throne. In 1865 Prince Gong was deprived of his offices although later permitted to resume his direction of foreign affairs. From this time onwards the dominant influence of Cixi was unmistakable. When the Tongzhi emperor reached his majority in 1873, her authority over him as his mother remained undiminished. Tongzhi died of smallpox in 1875 and Cixi then violated the rules of succession and obtained the appointment of her three-year-old nephew. He reigned as the Guangxu emperor until his death in 1908. He reached his majority in 1887, but Cixi retained the power to rule for a further two years, and subsequently her influence was exercised through the empress, whom she had nominated. In the 1890s the emperor managed to achieve a degree of independence, but his support of the Hundred Days' reforms in 1898 led the Empress Dowager to re-assume her power as regent, which she retained until her death, one day after that of the Guangxu emperor.

What was the significance of Cixi's dominance during these forty-seven years? Most writers have not hesitated to blame her for the misfortunes that China suffered during that period. As an usurper, as a female ruler and as a Manchu she has had few admirers. She has been blamed for her extravagance, her capriciousness and her abuse of power. Her role in the restoration of the 1860s was described as 'more distinguished for political maneuvring than for the true statesmanship of reconstruction'.[1] This concern for her own position was to persist throughout her lifetime. Her long exercise of power provided some political stability and she did accept the initiatives of the great provincial officials of the day, most apparently in the case of Li Hongzhang. But even in this context she has been seen as playing a malign role. Because her position was never entirely secure, she had to manipulate sections of the bureaucracy. In the context of the day this meant playing off the provincial bureaucracy against the central bureaucracy and the conservatives against those who supported the pragmatic policies of self-strengthening. In so doing she ensured that there was no consistency of aim and as a consequence the throne failed to provide effective leadership.

The Tongzhi Restoration

The term 'restoration', applied to the reign of the Tongzhi emperor, implied that the decline of the dynasty had been arrested and even temporarily reversed. Such an event was deemed extremely rare in Chinese history, the precedent most commonly cited being that of the recovery of the Tang dynasty after the rebellion of An Lushan in the eighth century. The assumption behind the concept of restoration was that in the properly regulated Confucian state harmony prevailed because each member of society had clearly defined rights and obligations. The calamities which had overwhelmed China were symptomatic of a failure to maintain Confucian ideology. The remedy was therefore to restore orthodox doctrine and the instrument to achieve this was the upright official. It will be noted that the concept of a restoration made no reference to reform. At the most it accepted that there might be a change in methods, but the goal of sustaining Confucian values and institutions remained unchanged.[2]

If this was the theory, what did the men of the restoration achieve in practice? The suppression of rebellion has already been considered. This was an immense task, but it was only a beginning. To achieve a general restoration of the Confucian order it was essential to re-establish a satisfactory relationship with the gentry and the common people. With regard to the former the schedule of examinations, which in some provinces had been suspended for ten years, was resumed. It was estimated that during the restoration period two million candidates were taking examinations at the various levels each year. Although the form of the examinations did not change, great effort was made to prevent corruption and to ensure that candidates demonstrated their awareness of moral truths and their ability to discuss issues relating to good government.[3] In another initiative, schools and academies were revived and libraries, many of which had been looted, were restocked. With regard to the common people, the *baojia*, the system of collective responsibility, was revived and a variety of social welfare projects, including famine relief, were sponsored.

Another major task was economic rehabilitation. Vast areas of the country had been ravaged by the rebellions and in some places had become completely depopulated. Government revenue, much of which was collected through the land tax and the grain tribute, had fallen alarmingly, and monetary inflation had set in. To deal with these problems, the leading officials of the restoration period did not contemplate a programme of economic reform, let alone one of economic development. Their objective was to restore the economy to its former condition of stability by rehabilitating the agricultural sector. Areas of abandoned land were resettled by sponsored migration, new lands were opened up and irrigation schemes were repaired and extended. A most important issue was the lightening of the burden of the land tax and its more even distribution. In the first instance land taxes were remitted in areas suffering from the effects of war or natural disaster. It was to be one of the proudest boasts of the restoration that the land tax was permanently reduced in a number of provinces and most famously the grain tribute quota, payable in the Susongtai circuit of Jiangsu province, an area which had suffered severely during the Taiping rebellion, was cut by one third.[4]

Mary Wright, who wrote the classic study of the Tongzhi restoration, claimed that in the short term the restoration was a success,

> not only a dynasty but also a civilization which appeared to have collapsed was revived to last for another sixty years by the extraordinary efforts of extraordinary men in the 1860's.[5]

However, this claim has been subject to criticism and modification. James Polachek began by distinguishing between the paternalism of restoration officials such as Zeng Guofan and Hu Linyi, who came from Hunan, and the 'Machiavellian maneuvering' of Li Hongzhang and Feng Guifen. He argued that the latter pair were far more representative of the character of the restoration. Li Hongzhang, who had formerly been a member of Zeng Guofan's secretariat, had organized the Anhui army and in 1861 was appointed acting Governor of Jiangsu. Feng Guifen,

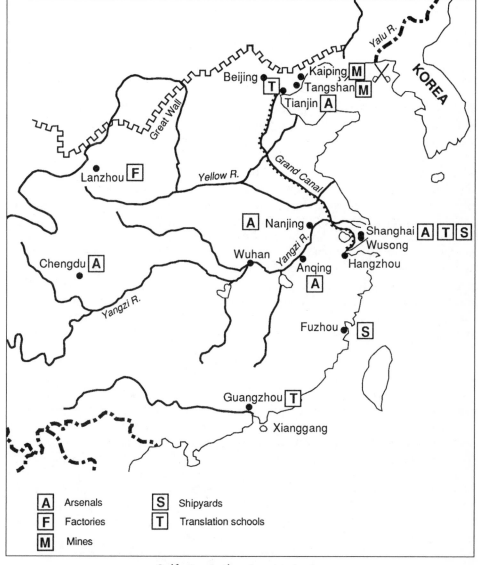

Self-strengthening projects.

283

who came from Suzhou and was a celebrated scholar and essayist, became an adviser to Li. Both played a leading role in securing the Susongtai tax reduction. However, according to Polachek, their true objective was neither to relieve peasants of an unfair burden of tax, nor to reduce the excessive demands of yamen officials for surcharges, but to secure an effective accommodation between the bureaucracy and gentry leaders in Jiangsu, an accommodation which would create a 'gentry oligarchy within a framework of superficial bureaucratic control'.[6]

In another study of Jiangsu, Jonathan Ocko concentrated on the career of Ding Richang, who was governor of the province from 1867 to 1870. Jiangsu, Ocko pointed out, was the area most devastated by the Taiping rebellion and its suppression. Ding Richang was reputed to be one of the ablest provincial officials of his time, so the question of whether the Qing dynasty not only survived but actually revived might be answered by looking at his achievement. The key issues were the re-establishment of local control, the rehabilitation of the economy, the reform of local government and the restoration of government by superior civil officials. Ding Richang acted vigorously on many of these matters, for example he revived what was regarded as an important element of ideological control, the teaching of Confucian principles to the masses through the lecture system. Salaried lecturers were appointed, the Sacred Edicts, the series of maxims composed by the emperor, were reprinted, and education officials were given special responsibility to ensure the system worked. But most officials dismissed the lectures as irrelevant, and it is hard to show that his other measures had much effect. In a more fundamental way the labours of Ding Richang and of other restoration officials were frustrated. The increased power of the local elite blocked any attempt by the bureaucracy to re-establish its relationship with the ordinary people. This augmentation of power might be regarded as a factor in the dynasty's survival for half a century, but for Ocko it also prevented the dynasty from achieving a genuine revival – not a restoration of the pre-Taiping status quo, which already showed the signs of dynastic decline – but the truly vital Confucian order of an earlier age. And so the restoration was not revival but survival, and the support of the rural elite for the dynasty was to last only as long as it remained in its interest to offer it.[7]

Self-strengthening

Feng Guifen, whose role in tax reform has just been discussed, is best remembered for his contribution to the debate which was triggered off by the recognition of the superiority of the West in terms of science and technology, particularly in the context of military technology. In an essay dated 1860 entitled On the Adoption of Western Knowledge, Feng Guifen noted that Western books on mathematics, chemistry and other subjects contained the best principles of the natural sciences, and that Western books on geography contained full descriptions of the countries of the world, information which was beyond the reach of the Chinese. He proposed the establishment of translation offices and the training of brilliant students in a syllabus which included Western languages and mathematics as well as the Chinese classics. The most successful of the students would be eligible for the juren degree. This led him to formulate his famous stratagem:

If we let Chinese ethics and famous [Confucian] teachings serve as an original foundation, and let them be supplemented by the methods used by the various nations for the attainment of prosperity and strength, would it not be the best of all procedures?[8]

It was this proposal which the late Qing official Zhang Zhidong rendered as 'Chinese learning as the base, Western studies for use'. It became the slogan for the policy known as *ziqiang*, 'self-strengthening', which was to gain momentum in the 1860s.

It is important to recognize that self-strengthening was never a national policy endorsed by a national government. The nearest it achieved to receiving the support of the court was through the role played by the Zongli Yamen, the 'office for general management', the prototype foreign office which had been established in March 1861 to handle relations with the Western powers. In time this body became the main agency handling what were referred to as *yangwu*, that is Western affairs. The Zongli Yamen, which was presided over by Prince Gong, was in effect a committee of the Grand Council. When first constituted it was described as a temporary arrangement and its actions were always liable to being curbed by the Empress Dowager. Nevertheless, in the 1860s it did play a significant role in establishing a co-operative policy towards the Western powers and sponsoring various initiatives connected with self-strengthening.[9]

One of its first initiatives was the establishment in Beijing of a school for the teaching of foreign languages. This institution, known as the Tongwenguan, began to operate in 1862 and shortly afterwards similar institutions were started in Shanghai, Guangzhou and Fuzhou. As no Chinese staff could be found who were competent to teach Western languages, the first appointments to these colleges were European missionaries who were strictly forbidden to proselytize. In 1864 W.A.P. Martin, an American missionary, was appointed Professor of English at the Beijing Tongwenguan. He later became Principal of the college, a post that he was to occupy for over a quarter of a century.[10] Martin also played an important role as translator of key Western-language works into Chinese, his translations including Henry Wheaton's *Elements of International Law*.

The true exponents of the principles of self-strengthening were a group of senior provincial officials, most notably Zeng Guofan, Li Hongzhang and Zuo Zongtang, who have already been identified as the architects of the defeat of the mid-nineteenth-century rebellions. In the 1860s they pioneered the introduction of Western technology and established arsenals and shipyards to enable China to produce armaments to emulate those produced by the Western powers.

In 1862 Zeng Guofan recaptured from the Taipings the city of Anqing on the middle Yangzi. When there, he recalled,

I established a factory to try to make foreign weapons, I used Chinese exclusively and did not employ any foreign mechanics. Although a small steamboat was built its speed was very slow. The knack of building it was not completely acquired.[11]

In addition attempts were made to produce shrapnel and copper percussion caps as well as traditional weapons such as gingalls and matchlocks.[12] The following year Zeng Guofan arranged that Rong Hong (Yung Wing) should go to the United States to purchase machinery. Rong Hong (1828–1912), who had attended a mission school at Aomen, was the first Chinese to graduate from an American university. While he was a student at Yale he had supported himself by managing a boarding house and acting as a librarian. He returned to China and had dealings with the Taipings before he was commissioned by Zeng Guofan.[13]

The purchase of machinery from Western sources was one method, albeit an expensive one, whereby China could hope to acquire Western technology. It was a method which was not without risk, as the case of the Lay-Osborn flotilla indicated. In 1861 Robert Hart, who later became Inspector-General of the Imperial Maritime Customs, proposed to Prince Gong that China should purchase a steam flotilla from England. Prince Gong authorized H.N. Lay, the current Inspector-General of Customs then on leave in England, to buy the ships. Lay purchased eight ships and engaged Captain Sherard Osborn to command the flotilla. Lay also made a secret agreement with Osborn, promising him command of the flotilla and telling him that it would be subject only to the orders of the emperor, which would be transmitted to Osborn by Lay himself, and only if he considered those orders to be reasonable. However, when Osborn arrived in China with the ships he was placed under the orders of Zeng Guofan. As neither party would compromise, Osborn and the crews were paid off and the ships sent back to England. One view of the consequences of this incident is that 'The modernization of China's navy was delayed, but greater foreign influence in China's military and financial affairs was avoided.'[14]

The next steps in the development of the self-strengthening programme were taken by Li Hongzhang. In 1863 he began to manufacture shells at the Shanghai and Suzhou arsenals, at the latter arsenal employing Halliday Macartney, a British doctor, as a technical adviser. The following year he memorialized the court of the need to acquire capital equipment and to train technical personnel and then instructed Ding Richang, at that time the Shanghai *taotai*, to purchase the content of a foreign machine shop already operating in Shanghai. A year later the Jiangnan General Manufacturing Bureau, known to Westerners as the Jiangnan Arsenal, began operating. Its machinery was augmented by the purchases made in America by Rong Hong, and Chinese managers and Western technicians were employed. Its first commission was to produce small arms and ammunition to supply Li's Anhui army in its campaign against the Nian rebels. However, it proved difficult to adapt the machinery to produce armaments, and Li was forced to purchase foreign small arms. In 1866 Zeng Guofan returned to his post as Governor-General at Nanjing, thereby taking over responsibility for the arsenal from Li. Zeng now concentrated the arsenal's effort on the production of steamships, and by 1875 (Zeng had died in 1872), the arsenal had launched seven naval vessels, including one which was an ironclad. But although the vessels incorporated substantial new technology they were extremely expensive. In 1875 a change in defence policy led to a halt in the shipbuilding programme and the arsenal now concentrated on the production of ordnance and small arms. By that time the arsenal was producing a dozen breech-loading Remington rifles a day, but these had iron rather than steel barrels and the parts were not interchangeable. Western observers estimated that with the manpower and machinery employed the output should have reached at least fifty rifles a day. By 1881 the Jiangnan Remington was obsolescent and a new model was introduced. Nevertheless, technical problems and high costs still ensured that imported rifles were both cheaper and better.[15]

One other example may be given of self-strengthening projects to produce armaments. In 1865 Zuo Zongtang, the Governor-General of Fujian and Zhejiang, who had previously campaigned against the Taipings and who had experimented with steamships on the west lake at Hangzhou, submitted a memorial in which he proposed that China should build her own ships and train Chinese to operate them. In it he identified the main objections to the establishment of a shipyard,

> . . . first, the difficulty of selecting a place for the shipyard; second, the difficulty of finding and buying steamship machinery; third, the difficulty of engaging head mechanics; fourth, the difficulty of raising and accumulating a huge amount of funds; fifth, the difficulty that the Chinese are unaccustomed to navigation and that after the completion of the ships we would still have to engage foreigners; sixth, the difficulties of the numerous requirements of expenditures for coal, salaries, and wages after the ships have been completed. . . . Seventh, in this unusual enterprise it is easy for slander and criticism to arise. . . .[16]

Zuo's first and last points concern the political implications of his proposal and may refer to rivalry between himself and Zeng Guofan, a rivalry which the court may have been happy to encourage. The establishment of the shipyard at Fuzhou gave Zuo a manufacturing base to balance the bases developed by Zeng and Li Hongzhang. The other difficulties were all taken into consideration in his detailed recommendations. Before the shipyard was in operation a school had been established and its instructors were teaching students English, French, mathematics and the techniques of shipbuilding and ship operation. As soon as the court had given its approval Zuo contracted two Frenchmen, Prosper Giquel and Paul d'Aiguebelle, to establish the shipyard, obtain the machinery required, supervise the school of navigation and complete sixteen steamships.[17] The costs of the scheme, estimated at 40,000 taels a month, were to be borne by the Fujian customs revenues. By February 1874 fifteen steamships had been launched (a 250 h.p. corvette named the Yang Wu, the flagship of the Fuzhou fleet, was counted as two ships) and the naval school and the courses in engineering and navigation had started successfully. From 1874 onwards the yard was operated solely by Chinese officials and workmen and in 1877 they registered an important achievement, the launching of the Wei Yuan, China's first iron-framed ship. But thereafter financial problems and poor management led to a decline in output. In August 1884, when China and France were at war over Annam, a French naval squadron attacked the dockyard and destroyed and sank eleven ships, including the Yang Wu. The dockyard was repaired and production continued but at a lower level.

In 1872, in an important memorial, Li Hongzhang defended the building of steamships, but then observed:

> Furthermore, the building of ships, cannon, and machinery will be impossible without iron, and then we shall be helpless without coal. The reason for England's power and influence over the Western lands is only her possession of these two items [iron and coal]. The various arsenals in Fuzhou and Shanghai daily need a huge amount of imported coal and iron, because the Chinese product is most unsuitable.[18]

Li's recognition that military industry had to be underpinned by heavy industry marked a broadening of the self-strengthening programme both in scope and in financing. In the next phase projects were initiated to improve transportation and to establish profit-oriented enterprises.

The China Merchants' Steam Navigation Company, which Li established in 1872, was the first of a dozen large projects organized as *guandu shangban*, that is 'official-supervision merchant-management' enterprises. The company was intended to compete with foreign shipping, mainly British, which had penetrated China's coastal trade, and to encourage Chinese merchants to risk investing in modern undertakings. Its key features became the prototype of all future *guandu shangban* enterprises: Chinese merchants would organize and finance the company, an official manager would direct them, and it would receive some form of monopoly, in this case a concession for the carriage of tribute rice from the Yangzi to Tianjin, to ensure the company's profitable operations.[19] Such enterprises incorporated both traditional and modern features. The tribute rice concession harked back to state monopolies such as that on salt, and the role of officials and bureaucratic methods of management were also indications of continuity rather than of change. However, the organization of the enterprise as a joint-stock company rather than as a partnership or state-owned enterprise was a departure from previous practice and intended to enable it to compete with foreign firms.[20]

Until the 1890s the China Merchants' company made uneven but generally encouraging progress. Some of its original capital came from Chinese merchants, but for the most part they were unwilling to accept the risk and additional finance came from government loans, in the first instance from Tianjin military funds, and from Li Hongzhang's private investment. In 1873 its management was taken over by Tang Tingshu, known to foreigners as Tong Kingsing, previously the compradore (Chinese agent) of the British firm Jardine, Matheson and Company, and Xu Jun, who had held a similar position with the firm of Dent and Company. They brought valuable commercial experience and a knowledge of Western business methods to the operation of the new company. By 1876 the China Merchants' had acquired eleven ships, and in the following year, with the help of a loan of one million taels, it bought the merchant fleet of the American firm Russell and Company. Despite intense competition with the firm Butterfield and Swire over freight rates, it managed to pay its shareholders an annual dividend of 10 per cent. However, in 1885 the company was placed under the control of Sheng Xuanhuai, who although an able entrepreneur came from an official background, and thereafter bureaucratic control of the company increased and its expansion was curtailed.[21]

Tang Tingshu left the China Merchants' to head a new venture initiated by Li Hongzhang, to be known as the Kaiping mines. In 1872 Li had stressed the importance of coal in the development of industry. His remarks had been occasioned by foreign requests to open coal mines in China to provide steamer fuel, but the matter was equally important from the Chinese viewpoint, for almost all the coal used in the early self-strengthening industries was imported from Japan, Germany and Britain. Between 1871 and 1880 the average annual import exceeded 150,000 tons, and this was regarded as a major loss to the country's wealth.[22] To reduce this loss, and to develop his own industrial interests, in 1874 Li Hongzhang requested permission to open a modern mining enterprise at Cizhou in southern Zhili. He had chosen a site distant from Beijing because he anticipated opposition from the court to the use of foreign machinery near the capital. The opposition partly arose from fears that mining would injure the fengshui, the spirits of wind and water, that is the geomantic principles applied to the siting of buildings and tombs, and partly from suspicion of miners as an unruly group in society. However, the problem of transporting coal and iron ore from that site was so great that the proposal was switched to Tangshan, 60 miles north-east of Tianjin, a traditional mining area but one which could not be exploited further without the application of modern technology. The development of the mine was placed in the hands of Tang Tingshu. Drilling began at the site in 1878 and revealed the presence of high-quality bituminous coal. By 1882 such good progress had been made that the North China Herald was reporting that the lay-out, construction and materials of the 'the Tang colliery will compare very favourably with the best of the kind in England and elsewhere'.[23] In 1883 coal production reached 75,000 tons and was rising rapidly. However, the problem of transportation remained acute. From the beginning Tang Tingshu had recommended the construction of a railway, but imperial approval was not available and at first the coal was transported by canal and by horse-drawn tramway. However, the tramway had been constructed with bridges strong enough to carry a locomotive, and in 1882 the Rocket of China, a locomotive built surreptitiously and from scrap, pulled a train carrying a party of officials at 20 miles per hour. This was China's first permanent railway.

Brief mention should be made of some other self-strengthening enterprises. In 1877 Zuo Zongtang had established a woollen mill at Lanzhou in Gansu province as part of a scheme for economic improvement in the region. German technicians were engaged and foreign machinery bought, including two steam engines, the first application of steam power to industry in China. The mill started production of woollen cloth, but suffered from many technical problems and had closed down by 1883, after the contracts with foreign employees had ended.[24]

The Imperial Telegraph Administration began in 1880 as a governmental operation supported by public funds and was mainly concerned with transmitting military messages. In 1882, on the initiative of Sheng Xuanhuai, it was converted to a guandu shangban enterprise. The technical expertise was at first supplied by the Danish Great Northern Telegraph Company, Denmark's involvement being preferred to reliance on Britain. By 1897 the company had established about 10,000 miles of telegraph lines.[25]

The Shanghai Cotton Cloth Mill was yet another venture credited to Li Hongzhang. After the opening of the Yangzi to foreign trade under the treaties of 1858–60, foreign imports of cotton yarn and cloth had risen significantly and by 1871 cotton goods comprised one-third of China's imports by value.[26] Various suggestions were made on how this flow might be countered and in 1878 Li received a proposal for the establishment of a spinning and weaving factory in Shanghai relying on merchant capital and management. This plan failed to materialize, but in 1882 Li revived the idea and suggested using the *guandu shangban* method of organization. The company was given a ten-year monopoly in the use of foreign machinery to manufacture cotton cloth and granted exemption from taxes. However, because of inadequacy of capital and the cupidity and inexperience of the management, progress in setting up the mill was very slow. In 1887 Li intervened and persuaded Sheng Xuanhuai to take over as director. More capital was raised, a loan was received from the China Merchants' Steam Navigation Company and at last the mill was constructed. It was described as 'the largest industrial enterprise in Shanghai'. It employed 4,000 workers and in 1892 produced 4,000,000 yards of cloth. But, on the morning of 19 October 1893 the mill was totally destroyed by fire. The company was not adequately insured and it was forced out of existence, but during its short history it had demonstrated that textile manufacture using modern machinery was potentially a profitable business.[27]

The Assessment of Self-Strengthening Projects

In the Sino-Japanese War of 1894–5 China suffered severe defeats on land and at sea. In these conflicts it appeared that the shortcomings of China's military self-strengthening had been exposed. In the years that followed, the acceleration of Western economic penetration revealed the limitations of the 'wealth and power' projects. Many writers, noting these developments, have concluded that self-strengthening was a mistaken strategy which, at a crucial stage in China's history, failed to provide the impetus for industrialization. In passing this judgement unflattering comparisons were often made with Japan's success in achieving industrial take-off in the same decades.

Having assumed, perhaps prematurely, that the self-strengthening programme failed, a number of writers then offered reasons for that failure. The most far-reaching explanation was that there was a fundamental incompatibility between the requirements of the Confucian order and the needs of a modern state. In *The Last Stand of Chinese Conservatism*, Mary Wright remarked that:

> conservatism has been tried in modern China under extraordinarily favorable conditions; that the performance was brilliant but the final result dismal failure; that the obstacles to successful adaptation to the modern world were not imperialist aggression, Manchu rule, mandarin stupidity, or the accidents of history, but nothing less than the constituent elements of the Confucian system itself.[28]

An elegant intellectual explanation of this incompatibility was put forward by Joseph Levenson. He noted how the self-strengthening formula: 'Chinese learning as the base, Western studies for use', had been promoted to allow Western culture a place without rejecting Chinese learning. The latter was *ti* ('substance', 'essence'), whereas the former was *yong* ('function', 'utility'). But, Levenson argued, this rationalization could not be sustained, for it was not possible to occupy the middle ground between 'perfect loyalty to the basic Chinese values' and indiscriminate acceptance of Western culture. The distinction between *ti* and *yong* was artificial: Chinese learning was both substance and useful for a career; Western studies were not only useful, they also contained their own substance, and the list of 'superior techniques' was endless.[29]

The most incisive intellectual opponent of self-strengthening, and the man who according to Levenson exposed the weakness of the *ti-yong* rationalization, was the Mongol Grand Secretary, Woren. In late 1866 Prince Gong, on behalf of the Zongli Yamen, had proposed that the Beijing language school, the Tongwenguan, should open a new department of mathematics and astronomy and that young men who had demonstrated their ability in the examination system should be persuaded to take up these new subjects by promising them large stipends and rapid promotion.[30] Woren responded to this in a famous outburst:

Mathematics, one of the six arts, should indeed be learned by scholars as indicated in the Imperial decree, and it should not be considered an unworthy subject. But according to the viewpoint of your slave,[31] astronomy and mathematics are of very little use. If these subjects are going to be taught by Westerners as regular studies, the damage will be great. . . . Your slave has learned that the way to establish a nation is to lay emphasis on propriety and righteousness, not on power and plotting.[32]

Woren's objection was overruled, but it was nevertheless effective, for no young official was prepared to risk his career by entering the Tongwenguan.

Another cultural explanation for the failure of self-strengthening stresses the irrationality and superstition which characterized Chinese response to Western science and technology. For example, in 1863 a Western mining engineer conducted a group of officials from the Zongli Yamen to inspect some coal mines to the west of Beijing, in response to a request for permission to develop the mines using Western technology. The engineer reported that one of the officials' objections to the proposal was that they understood that coal grew in abandoned mines, but its rate of growth was uncertain, and to extract it rapidly might deprive future generations of a supply.[33]

The case of the Wusong railway is a much-quoted example of this alleged obscurantism. In 1876 a British consortium led by Jardine, Matheson and Company completed a 9 mile length of railway between Shanghai and Wusong and began to operate a rail service, the first in China. However, within months the consortium was bought out by Chinese officials and the line subsequently destroyed. Their action was condemned as irrational and superstitious and Shen

Baozhen, the governor-general who opposed the construction, was described as stupid and childish. However, Shen's objections were entirely rational. Shen was well aware of the potential value of railway development for China. He had previously directed the Fuzhou shipyard and had introduced the first Chinese-run telegraph line on Taiwan.[34] But the construction of this railway had taken place on Chinese soil without Chinese permission. Soon after it started operating a Chinese had been killed by a train and this had increased popular agitation, which had already been aroused by the threat to the *fengshui* and to the livelihood of the common people – matters which no official could ignore. David Pong described Shen's response as 'Confucian patriotism', a concept which embraced,

> first, a strong reaction against foreign encroachment on Chinese territorial and administrative integrity; second, a strong distaste for the corrupting elements, both at the official and the popular levels, brought about by the introduction and the presence of the railway; third, a genuine concern for the well-being of the poorer sections of the Chinese society; and lastly, a concern for the development and independence of Chinese economic interests.[35]

A second line of explanation for the failure of self-strengthening refers to the political factors which are regarded as having obstructed progress. These included the role of government, the part played by the Empress Dowager, the effect of regionalism and the contribution of the provincial officials who played the major role in the initiation of self-strengthening projects.

The importance of the role of government in the promotion of industrialization is a well-rehearsed theme. Alexander Gershenkron's theory, that in nations which industrialize late the state's role must be proportionately larger than that of private enterprise, would seem to apply particularly well to China. Furthermore, many of the criticisms of China's economic performance in the nineteenth century contain an implied comparison with Japan, where the government played a crucial role not only through state entrepreneurship, but also through 'its moulding of society to conform to its military and therefore its economic objectives'.[36]

The role played by the Chinese government in self-strengthening and, by extension, in the promotion of economic development has usually been regarded as inadequate, if not obstructive. The political system has been castigated for permitting 'excessive and capricious taxation, omnipresent corruption, and a general disdain for commerce and the merchant'. The Empress Dowager, the dominant force at court throughout this period, has been depicted as preoccupied with her own position and the gratification of her own expensive pleasures. A more moderate view has largely acquitted the government of deliberate obstruction or culpable neglect. Its supposed hostility to commerce and industry contained an element of truth, but this must be set against the overwhelming evidence of China's commercial development and the blurring of the social distinctions between merchant and official. Fiscal policies were not designed to encourage economic activity, but the burden of taxation was light, not heavy. There was corruption in China, as in other countries, but the supposition that corruption was widespread derived in part from foreigners' perception of the informal but institutionalized 'customary exactions' added to taxes.[37]

Government policy towards industrialization has been described as 'not so much wrong as inadequate'.[38] In the Tongzhi restoration the government's objective had been the rehabilitation of an agrarian economy, which was a traditional ideal. It would have required a remarkable change in that role for the government to have embarked on interventionist policies directed at promoting economic development. Moreover, it was not able to do so for two connected reasons. The first was that, through a combination of deliberate policy and weakness, central government had only a limited control over its tax revenue. In 1712 the Kangxi emperor had fixed in perpetuity the number of adult males liable to pay tax, in effect capping the land tax. From that date until the third quarter of the nineteenth century the statutory receipts recorded by the central government remained static. As a result of the mid-nineteenth-century rebellions government control over taxes levied to support provincial governments disappeared, and its access to the new lijin tax on internal commerce was very limited. The only major new source of revenue, customs duty on foreign trade, was fixed by treaty. As a result central government revenue only sufficed to cover regular expenditure and to defray the non-profit-making costs of the military establishment needed for internal security and external defence. In short, the government did not have surplus capital for investment in the economy. Inadequate government revenue was a symptom of a more fundamental problem: a massive population, much of it living close to subsistence with only limited resources in terms of land.

Of course the capriciousness of the Empress Dowager and the regional rivalries of some leading officials did not help the cause of self-strengthening. Both of these handicaps can be illustrated by reference to the fate of China's first modern navy. Western naval supremacy had soon been recognized as a formidable coercive threat and it was for this reason that the acquisition of naval vessels was given a high priority. The early efforts at shipbuilding and the fiasco of the Lay-Osborn flotilla have already been described. Nevertheless, the construction and purchase of ships continued and by 1894 the Chinese navy comprised some sixty-five large ships and some forty-three torpedo boats. These were organized as four fleets, the largest being the Beiyang fleet under the control of Li Hongzhang. On 17 September 1894, twelve ships from this fleet fought an engagement with twelve Japanese warships off the mouth of the Yalu river. By the end of the battle four Chinese ships had been sunk and four others had broken off the engagement, whereas the Japanese fleet was still intact. In one day the most substantial achievement of the self-strengthening endeavours had been destroyed, and the reputation of Li Hongzhang, who was thereupon deprived of his three-eyed peacock feather and Yellow Jacket, had been damaged irreparably.[39] One reason given for the defeat is that the Empress Dowager, with the encouragement of Li Lianying, the chief eunuch, and in preparation for the celebrations for her sixtieth birthday, spent a substantial part of the funds supplied for the navy on refurbishing the Summer Palace. The only connection between naval building and the palace was the construction of a pavilion in the form of a marble barge.[40] The second allegation concerns the division of the navy into four fleets, which has been ascribed to the growth of regionalism. It has been claimed that the Empress Dowager's misuse of naval funding prevented Li from buying any more ships after 1888, and that the division of the naval forces meant that the other fleets would not be available to support the Beiyang fleet. However, it has been shown that much of the expenditure on the Summer Palace was incurred after the Sino-Japanese War and that the reason for China's defeat was not the size of her fleet but the inadequate training of her sailors.[41]

In the discussion of self-strengthening details were given of *guandu shangban*, 'official supervision and merchant management' enterprises. Albert Feuerwerker regarded the adoption of this form of organization as an important reason for the failure of the policy. He suggested that the *guandu shangban* enterprises reflected and reinforced the tendency to regionalism. The most marked example of this was Li Hongzhang's creation of a military-industrial empire, based on Shanghai and Tianjin and incorporating his interests in the China Merchants' Steam Navigation Company and the Kaiping coal mines. Feuerwerker regarded Li as more concerned with building up his own power base than committed to self-strengthening in the national interest, and he supported this view by referring to the famous controversy which arose in 1888–9 over a proposal to extend the railway line, which connected the Kaiping mines at Tangshan to Tianjin, to Beijing. The suggested intrusion of a railway into the environs of the capital aroused fierce opposition, which served to mask Li's real objective, which was to use the revenue generated by the Beijing extension to continue the railway northwards, thereby bringing Manchuria under his control.[42] The *guandu shangban* pattern had other shortcomings. It was intended to attract capital for investment in the enterprises from treaty port merchants, but Chinese merchants were neither willing nor able to support a full-scale industrialization effort. Those who were persuaded to invest looked for short-term profits. As a consequence the enterprises were commonly under-capitalized and forced to borrow to pay dividends. Another problem was bureaucratic management. Official appointees were not qualified to operate business enterprises; they expected to make money from their appointments and they lacked any entrepreneurial drive. The enterprises they headed were always open to demands for funds from other officials, and even the court was prepared to lay claim to a share of the profits of some enterprises. The monopolistic privileges, which were often part of the original constitution of these projects, were intended to give an advantage against foreign competition. For example, the grant to the China Merchants' Steam Navigation Company of monopoly rights to ship tribute rice to Beijing was intended to give it a competitive edge against foreign shipping. But in practice such monopolies were used to secure the interests of the shareholders in the enterprise against all competition, whether foreign or Chinese.

These criticisms carry weight, but it must be added that a version of state entrepreneurship was used effectively in Japan. However, there was an important difference in the sequence of events in the two countries. In China, in the early years, the managers of these enterprises were former compradores who had good commercial experience, but later the role of officials increased. Tang Tingshu, a former compradore, achieved considerable success as the first manager of the

Kaiping mines. But, after his death in 1892, the manager's position was given to a Chinese bannerman and bureaucrat, who was unable to obtain merchant investment. His period in office, it was said, 'marked the beginning of gross corruption and creeping bureaucratization'.[43] In Japan the progression from a contribution from private enterprise to full bureaucratic control was reversed. Initially the Meiji government was directly involved in the running of state enterprises, but in 1881, in the interests of financial retrenchment, it sold all its industrial and commercial interests apart from those of military significance.

In all discussions about the failure of self-strengthening, reference is made to the inhibiting role of Western imperialism. While leaving the general issue of the impact of imperialism on China in the nineteenth century to the following chapter, the question may be asked whether the actions of the Western powers in China aided or impeded the development of the self-strengthening enterprises.

In several instances Westerners played a significant role in the advancement of self-strengthening projects. The parts played by W.A.P. Martin in the development of the Tongwenguan and that of Prosper Giquel in the establishment of the Fuzhou arsenal have already been mentioned. Halliday Macartney, formerly a surgeon in the British army, who organized the Nanjing arsenal, was one of a number of foreign experts employed by Li Hongzhang. Another missionary, John Fryer, translated at least 108 technical and scientific texts for the Jiangnan arsenal.[44] Fryer was also the editor of the periodical the *Chinese Scientific Magazine*, which appeared between 1876 and 1892 and diffused knowledge of Western science among the literati and merchants in the treaty ports.[45] A different example of Sino-Western co-operation was the dispatch of the Chinese Educational Mission to the United States. Between 1872 and 1875, at the instigation of Rong Hong, 120 Chinese boys were sent to Hartford, Connecticut, where they lived with American families and attended American schools. However, after reports had reached Li Hongzhang that the boys were becoming Americanized the mission was recalled.[46]

Some writers have argued that an important reason for the failure of self-strengthening was the oppressive presence of the Western powers. Frances Moulder identified shortage of capital as a major reason for the failure of self-strengthening projects and identified the cost of the Opium Wars and the indemnities levied as a cause of that shortage. Another impediment was the effects of the unequal treaties, which made it difficult for China to protect domestic industries. In the case of the China Merchants' Steam Navigation Company, which had been set up to counter the Western penetration of China's coastal trade, the government was unable to force Chinese merchants to ship with the company because the Western powers would have objected to this as a violation of the unequal treaties. Instead the company was given various financial advantages, including the monopoly on tribute rice, which it carried at double the rate charged by Western shipping lines. More generally, Moulder argued that the reason why China's attempt at national industrialization appeared feeble in comparison with that of Japan, was not because of the heavy weight of Chinese culture – she suggested that in cultural terms there was not much to choose between the two countries – but because the burden of Western intervention was much heavier in China.[47]

The preceding discussion is based on the assumption that self-strengthening endeavours failed and that it is therefore legitimate to discuss why that failure occurred. In recent years a more sympathetic consideration has been given to the efforts of the Qing government and the magnitude of the task which it faced has been given fuller recognition, and this has led to a number of reflections on China's experience. Mary Wright's confident assertion that 'even in the most favorable circumstances there is no way in which an effective modern state can be grafted onto a Confucian society'[48] has been called into question by the extraordinary success in recent years of the Pacific-rim economies, which share a Confucian background. The unflattering comparisons drawn between China and Japan in terms of state entrepreneurship need to be revised to take account of evidence that the Japanese government's initiatives were by no means uniformly successful.[49]

Furthermore, some recent studies of self-strengthening enterprises have modified the dismissive tone formerly directed at them. Thomas L. Kennedy, discussing the Jiangnan arsenal, pointed out that although the arsenals did not achieve their primary aim – to rid China of foreign influence – they were important in China's economic development.

> The introduction of steam-powered production machinery in the arsenals opened the era of mass production. . . . The use of machine tools and precision measurement and the production of interchangeable components. . . provided the technological infrastructure upon which China's light industry would develop. Other fundamental technology essential to industrial modernization, such as the production of electrical equipment and the industrial processing of chemicals, was first introduced in the Chinese arsenals.[50]

Some writers have given the *guandu shangban* enterprises a positive endorsement. According to Stephen T. Thomas, the six largest enterprises 'showed promise of being the basis of China's eventual industrialization'. The China Merchants' Steam Navigation Company, in the period up to 1897, thrived in the face of foreign competition, its rate of growth was impressive and it managed to pay attractive dividends to its investors. Western technology, including electric lighting, was introduced successfully in the Kaiping mines. Even the Imperial Chinese Railway Administration, approved in 1876 and hampered by geomantic considerations and shortage of capital, had managed to complete 270 miles of railway lines by 1897 'under Chinese control and for Chinese benefit'. For Thomas the period 1860–97, that is until the Sino-Japanese War and its aftermath, was a trial-and-error period in which China's record in many ways equalled that of Japan.[51]

The relationship between the Qing state and the economy was a complex one, liable to be misunderstood if judged by Western assumptions. The ultimate goal of the state was not economic development, but 'the achievement of a more perfect moral-political order'. The state pursued economic policies to ensure the people's livelihood, an essential part of that order. State involvement in the development of modern enterprises was always peripheral, and as such may be faulted. The initiative was taken by senior provincial officials and this in itself has been seen as a shortcoming, for their activities were weakly co-ordinated and were condemned as being motivated by self-interest, particularly in the case of Li Hongzhang. Yet even Li's role in self-strengthening has been defended recently. His promotion of the China Merchants' Steam Navigation Company has been described as 'a kind of commercial nationalism'. In the early years of the company Li's arrangements provided an appropriate balance between official and merchant interests. But the Sino-French War of 1883–5 weakened Li's political position and imposed fresh demands on the government's limited resources, with the consequence that bureaucratic management of the company increased and its growth slowed down.[52]

17
Imperialism in the Late Qing Period

In this chapter the emphasis is on the evaluation of the various forms of imperial activity which affected China in the late Qing period. The discussion will first consider the increase in Western political influence and the significance of the Sino-French and Sino-Japanese Wars. It will then review the debate which has arisen over the economic impact of imperialism and consider the significance of missionary activity.

The Unequal Treaty Framework

With the conclusion of the Treaty of Tianjin and the Convention of Beijing in 1858–60, the Western powers, that is to say Great Britain, France, the United States and Russia, had obtained a series of important political and economic advantages in China. These included the opening of some fourteen treaty ports for trade and residence, the ports being situated along the south-east coast, up the Yangzi river as far as Hankou, and as far north as Tianjin and Niuchuang. They had also acquired territorial concessions and settlements in Shanghai and other treaty ports.[1] In addition to the establishment of a fixed tariff on imports and exports, which had been agreed in the Supplementary Treaty of the Bogue in 1843, two other important economic concessions had been obtained in the Tianjin treaty: a restriction on the level of interior transit taxes payable on foreign goods, and a fixed duty for opium imports (even though the importation of opium was prohibited under Chinese law). The Western powers had also obtained the right to appoint an ambassador to reside in Beijing and for their missionaries to preach Christianity and to travel freely throughout the country.

In the 1860s the Zongli Yamen, anxious to avoid offering further pretexts for Western intervention, pursued a policy of co-operation with the foreign powers. The vexed problem of the collection of customs duties was in part solved by the development of the Imperial Maritime Customs service, a hybrid organization, staffed by Chinese, officered by Europeans and for many years headed by Robert Hart, which collected and handed over a growing and important part of the government's revenue. In response to the stationing of foreign embassies in Beijing, the court took the first tentative steps towards accepting the Western view of a world order composed of nation states. In 1866 an official named Binchun headed a fact-finding delegation to the capitals of Europe. Two years later Anson Burlingame, the retiring American minister in China, led a mission to the United

States and to the capitals of Europe, its purpose being to ask the Western powers to restrain demands for improved commercial access to China. In the meantime Sir Rutherford Alcock, the British minister to China, was discussing the revision of the Treaty of Tianjin, which was scheduled for 1868. The result was an agreement known as the Alcock Convention, which was not an unequal treaty, in that it was negotiated on a basis of equality and included reciprocal concessions.

It was at this juncture that the co-operative policy collapsed. Anti-foreign activity in China, directed particularly at missionaries, had already led to a number of incidents, notably an attack on the new China Inland Mission station at Yangzhou in 1868, in response to which Alcock had authorized the dispatch of British warships. The Alcock Convention brought forth a storm of criticism from British commercial interests and was not ratified. Then in 1870 an anti-missionary riot at Tianjin left nineteen Europeans dead, including ten French nuns. Five years later Augustus Margary, a British official, was killed near the Burmese frontier. For this China was forced to accept the Zhefu Convention of 1876, an unequal treaty which required China to send an apology mission to Britain. Ironically this led to the establishment of the first Chinese embassy abroad, thereby acknowledging the end of the traditional Chinese world order. The final addition to the unequal treaties was the Boxer Protocol of 1901. This imposed a variety of punishments on the officials held to have colluded with the Boxers, and conferred various military advantages on the West. It also required China to pay an indemnity of 450 million taels plus accumulated interest, the payment being secured on the customs duties. To enable China to pay more readily it was also agreed that import duties might be raised to a uniform 5 per cent.[2]

Imperial Encroachment on China's Periphery

In the years following 1870 China experienced a series of encroachments on territories which she regarded as part of China or in a tributary relationship with China. Some of these advances were checked, but the general outcome was the detachment of the cordon of buffer states which had surrounded China in the past.

The first incident arose over the Chinese position in Taiwan and in particular over her claim to the Liuqiu islands, which lie between Taiwan and Japan. In 1871 China and Japan had signed a commercial treaty, and this suggested that the two countries might find common ground in opposing the 'eastern advance of Western power'.[3] However, an incident later in the same year, in which fifty-four shipwrecked sailors from the Liuqiu islands were massacred by Taiwanese aborigines, was used by Japan as a pretext for sending a punitive expedition to Taiwan. The expedition provided a convenient diversion of samurai energies, pent up because of Japan's decision not to send an expedition to Korea in the previous year. In the ensuing negotiations China was unable to assert her claim over the Liuqiu islands and in 1879 these were annexed by Japan, and later became Okinawa prefecture.[4]

The next incident was a consequence of the decline of Qing power in Central Asia. In 1871 Russia had occupied the Ili valley in the north-west of Chinese

Turkestan on the pretext of securing her interests threatened by the Muslim rebellion which had broken out in the region. After the suppression of the rebellion, China sought to negotiate a Russian withdrawal from Ili. The first attempt at a settlement, the Treaty of Livadia, was angrily rejected by Chinese hardliners and both countries threatened war. A settlement was finally reached in the Treaty of St Petersburg, 1881, with China recovering Ili.

The third major threat concerned the area now known as Vietnam, which the Chinese referred to as Annam and regarded as a tributary state. French interests in the area went back to the seventeenth century, but it was only with the accession of Louis Napoleon that France began to challenge the anti-foreign and anti-Christian policies of the Nguyen, the ruling dynasty. In 1862 France forced the signing of a treaty which ceded to her the southern part of Vietnam known as Cochin China. In the 1870s France began to encroach on Tongking in the north and in 1874 forced the ruler of Vietnam to sign a treaty in which he declared his country to be independent of all foreign powers and willing to accept the protection of France. China was slow to respond and it has been suggested that she did not appreciate that in French eyes this treaty ended the tributary status of Annam.[5] Such a misunderstanding was not surprising. In 1877 Annam, in apparent contradiction of the French treaty, sent a tributary mission to China. At that time domestic political issues discouraged further French colonial expansion. However, in 1880 Jules Ferry became premier and in the following year an attempt was made to bring Tongking under French control. The situation there was confused because the upper Red river, the main commercial artery of Tongking, was controlled by the Black Flags, Chinese remnants of the Taiping rebellion, who now supported the Annamese government. In 1882 Commandant Henri Rivière, a French naval officer, in a remarkable act of derring-do, seized Hanoi. The French government felt compelled to support him and in turn the Chinese government lent its support to the Black Flags.

Between 1883 and 1885 France and China fought a sporadic campaign for the control of Tongking. In the first phase of the conflict there were a number of inconclusive engagements, in which the Black Flags fought bravely. Then in May 1884 Li Hongzhang, who had been a consistent advocate of a cautious foreign policy, signed an agreement known as the Li-Fournier Convention. This offered a compromise, with China recognizing the French treaties with Vietnam and withdrawing her troops from Tongking, while France agreed to waive an indemnity and not invade China. This agreement was repudiated indignantly by hardliners on both sides and was left subject to further negotiation.

There now occurred a minor incident which was to be accorded great significance by the two countries. The Li-Fournier Convention had referred in vague terms to the withdrawal of Chinese troops from Vietnam. In mid-June 1884 a French contingent encountered a Chinese force defending an outpost at Bac Le, some 50 miles south of the Chinese frontier. The Chinese commander refused to abandon his post pending instructions and a three-day fight ensued. Although Chinese casualties were much higher than those of the French, the fact that it was the latter who were forced to withdraw was hailed as a signal victory in China. France demanded that the terms of the Li-Fournier Convention be implemented and that France should receive a large indemnity for the 'ambush' at Bac Le. When China temporized French ships bombarded Jilong on Taiwan (although French troops failed to occupy the city) and then, on 23 August, attacked the Fuzhou shipyard, destroying all but two ships of the Fujian fleet.

This incident marked the beginning of the Sino-French War, although war as such was not declared. French ships imposed a limited blockade on the south coast of China and Chinese land forces achieved some minor successes against French troops in Tongking. In the meantime desultory negotiations took place, with France demanding an indemnity or economic rights on Taiwan, while the Chinese negotiators struggled to arrive at a peace settlement while being attacked as traitors to their country. By March 1885 a draft agreement, negotiated with the assistance of Robert Hart on the basis of the Li-Fournier Convention, was on the point of acceptance. At that moment Chinese troops recaptured Lang Son, a surprising victory which precipitated the fall of the French government. Soon afterwards an armistice was concluded and in June 1885 the two countries signed the Treaty of Tianjin, which reaffirmed the French protectorate over Vietnam and gave France economic opportunities in south-west China.[6]

The loss of Annam as a tributary state marked a further step in the collapse of China's world order. Already in 1855 Britain had imposed an unequal treaty on Thailand and by 1862 had consolidated her hold on Lower Burma. In 1886 Upper Burma was made a British protectorate, and in 1893 France completed her Indo-Chinese empire with the absorption of Laos.

The Sino-Japanese War, 1894—5

The prime reason for the outbreak of the Sino-Japanese War was rivalry between the two countries over Korea. Korea was the country which had most regularly maintained tributary relations with China – between 1637 and 1881 a total of 435 special embassies and missions were sent as part of a complex ritual of exchange between the two countries. The relationship, which was described as analogous to that between father and son, or between elder and younger brother, implied moral obligations but did not require any direct Chinese involvement in Korean affairs. Korea maintained limited contact with Japan, but otherwise was diplomatically isolated, hence her Western epithet, the 'hermit kingdom'.[7]

After the Opium Wars in China and the 'opening' of Japan by the United States in 1853, Korea came under increasing pressure to admit Western commercial and religious activity. In 1866 a persecution of Christians led to the murder of several French missionaries. In response France sent a naval squadron which captured Kanghwa island and threatened Seoul. Later the same year the *General Sherman*, an American merchant ship which had demanded the opportunity to trade at Pyongyang, was burned and its crew killed. In response to these threats the Korean court began to develop factions which adopted positions on the issues of seclusion, reform, and relationships with China and Japan.

From 1867 the Zongli Yamen began to advise the Korean court to reach an accommodation with the West. The situation became more urgent in 1873 when, in response to supposed insults by the Korean regent, Japan threatened to send a punitive expedition. This expedition was called off after those Japanese leaders who had visited the West warned of the dangers if Japan, in her unmodernized state, should take such a rash action. However, from that point onwards, it has been claimed, a Japanese intervention in Korea was only a matter of time.[8]

In 1876 Korea, with the concurrence of the Zongli Yamen, signed the Treaty of Kanghwa with Japan. This was an unequal treaty, which opened three Korean ports to trade. In it Korea was described as an 'independent state'. China did not challenge this summary ending of Korea's tributary status, but after the Japanese seizure of the Liuqiu islands in 1879, Li Hongzhang was placed in charge of relations with Korea. One of his earliest actions was to arrange for the signing of the Shufeldt Treaty with the United States, the first of a number of treaties with the Western powers which were designed to deny Japan exclusive control of the peninsula. Li also took steps to strengthen China's position in Korea by signing a commercial treaty and by appointing a young officer named Yuan Shikai to train a corps of 500 Korean troops in modern warfare. In 1884, when China was preoccupied with war with France, a pro-Japanese Korean faction headed by Kim Ok-kyun attempted a coup against the Korean king. Yuan Shikai's forces defeated this, but China was forced to make an agreement with Japan known as the Tianjin Convention of 1885. Both countries agreed to withdraw their forces from Korea and made stipulations relating to future intervention, so leaving Korea a 'co-protectorate' of China and Japan.

After 1885 it appeared that the Chinese position in Korea, nurtured by Yuan Shikai, was generally improving, but in retrospect it is apparent that this was not the case. Through the 1880s the efficiency of the Japanese armed forces had been greatly increased and new strategic objectives had been recognized. Major Jacob Meckel, the German adviser to the Japanese armed forces, likened Korea to 'a dagger pointed at the heart of Japan'. Yamagata Aritomo, the creator of Japan's modern armed forces, defined Japan's 'line of sovereignty', that is Japanese territory, and her 'line of interest', that is territory strategically necessary to maintain Japan's integrity, and the latter included Korea.[9] In 1891 Russia, which for thirty years had been quiescent with regard to her Asian interests, began to build the Trans-Siberian railway. At the same time Japanese interest in Korea as a market for textiles began to increase sharply.

This was the background to two incidents which occurred in 1894. The first was the murder of the Korean nationalist Kim Ok-kyun by another Korean in Shanghai. His death, and the treatment of his body, aroused sharp feelings in Japan, where Kim was portrayed as a martyr to Chinese backwardness. The second was the rise of an anti-foreign movement known as the Tonghak rebellion. This provided the pretext for China and Japan to send troops to Korea and for both countries then to refuse to withdraw them. By now the Japanese government was under domestic pressure to take a strong line, which it did by demanding that the Korean government institute a reform programme. The Korean failure to agree to this was taken as evidence of Chinese obstruction and Japan declared war on China on 1 August 1894.

This was a war which China was expected to win. It proved to be a war which exposed the weaknesses and limitations of the self-strengthening programme. On land, units from Li Hongzhang's Anhui army were defeated at Pyongyang. Reference has already been made to the other major reverse, the disastrous naval defeat off the Yalu river in September 1894.

To end the war China, represented by Li Hongzhang, was forced to accept the humiliating terms of the Treaty of Shimonoseki, 1895. Under it China recognized the independence of Korea and accepted the ending of tribute missions. Taiwan and the Penghu (Pescadores) islands were ceded to Japan, as was the Liaodong peninsula in southern Manchuria. China initially was required to pay an indemnity of 300 million taels, but this was reduced by one-third after Li Hongzhang had been injured by a shot fired by a Japanese fanatic. Finally, Japan acquired the rights accorded to the Western powers under the unequal treaties and added to them another significant privilege: that of engaging in industry in the treaty ports. Under the most-favoured-nation clause this right automatically accrued to the other unequal-treaty powers.

The Scramble for China

China's defeat in the Sino-Japanese War and the gains made by Japan under the Treaty of Shimonoseki precipitated the heightened demand for privileges which has been called the 'scramble for China'. The first indication that this was impending was the notorious diplomatic incident, which occurred within six days of the publication of the treaty, known as the Triple Intervention. Russia, alarmed at the prospect of Japan acquiring a foothold in Manchuria, on which Russia had designs, obtained the support of France and Germany in demanding the retrocession of the Liaodong peninsula to China. Japan, faced with the threat of a Russian bombardment of her ports, had no choice but to agree, and accept instead a larger indemnity. The memory of this public humiliation was to contribute to the coming of war between the two countries ten years later.

In return for this favour, and for assistance in paying the indemnity, China, represented by Li Hongzhang, concluded a secret treaty with Russia. China permitted Russia to build a railway (the Chinese Eastern railway) across Manchuria to Vladivostok and the two powers agreed to aid each other in the event of a Japanese attack on Korea or on their possessions. It was widely rumoured that Li had been promised a bribe of US $1.5 million for his assistance in this matter.[10]

The next move was made by Germany. At the time of the first treaty settlements, German interest in China had been slight, although Prussia had obtained an unequal treaty in 1861. After the unification of Germany, German commercial interest in China grew steadily and by the 1890s its share of foreign economic activity in China was second only to that of Britain. By the time of the Sino-Japanese War, German foreign policy was committed to a drive to world power and it was in this context that it sought a naval base and a sphere of influence in China. Its choice of base was Qingdao, situated on Jiaozhou bay, which was reputed to be the best harbour in the north of China, and which had as its hinterland the province of Shandong, with a population of 30 million people and important coal reserves. A request for a concession on Jiaozhou bay was initially refused and Germany had to find a pretext to justify seizing it by force. This came in November 1897 when two German Catholic missionaries were killed in Shandong. German troops landed near Qingdao, a German occupation was declared and the Zongli Yamen was forced to conclude a convention which gave Germany a ninety-nine year lease of Jiaozhou bay and concessions to build three railway lines and to operate mines 10 miles on each side of their tracks.[11]

The other powers now felt justified in demanding further compensation. Russia obtained a twenty-five year lease for the southern part of the Liaodong peninsula, which included the naval base of Lüshun (Port Arthur) and the port of Dalian, so obtaining control of part of the territory she had denied to Japan three years previously. She also gained the right to construct a railway (the South Manchurian railway) from Lüshun northwards to intersect with the Chinese Eastern railway at Harbin.

France's imperial interests were concentrated in south-west China. The conquest of Tongking had been undertaken mainly to enable the opening of an overland route to the province of Yunnan, which was reputed to be extremely wealthy. Already before the Sino-Japanese War France had been pressing China for improved access and after the signing of the Treaty of Shimonoseki she obtained a commercial convention which included a provision for the extension of Vietnamese railways into China. This provoked a British demand that future railways in Yunnan should connect with lines in Burma. France was also anxious to obtain a coaling station on the south-China coast, and in 1898 China agreed to a lease on Guangzhouwan on the mainland opposite the island of Hainan.[12]

There remained the case of Britain, still holding by far the largest share of foreign trade and investment in China, albeit this was only a minor part of her overseas interests. Britain's predominant concern in China was commercial and her acquisition of concessions had been to protect those interests. After the Sino-Japanese War she attempted to prevent the formation of exclusive spheres of influence, but in the face of the scramble by other European powers she revised her policy. To counter the Russian position in Manchuria, and to sustain her influence in Beijing, in July 1898 Britain obtained from China a lease of Weihaiwei on the north of the Shandong peninsula. At the same time, partly in response to the French occupation of Guangzhouwan, Britain secured a ninety-nine year lease of an area of the mainland opposite Xianggang, to be known as the New Territories.[13]

In summarizing the scramble for China the emphasis has been on the political gains made by Japan and the Western powers. As a consequence of these gains each of the powers had defined a part of China in which it exercised special, though not exclusive, privileges, an area described as a sphere of influence. The most important of these were those of Russia in Manchuria, Germany in Shandong, Britain in the Yangzi valley and in the area around Xianggang and Guangzhou, France in south-west China and Japan on the mainland opposite Taiwan.

However, much of the competition between the powers was directed at acquiring economic advantages which extended beyond their spheres of influence.

Imperialism in the Late Qing Period

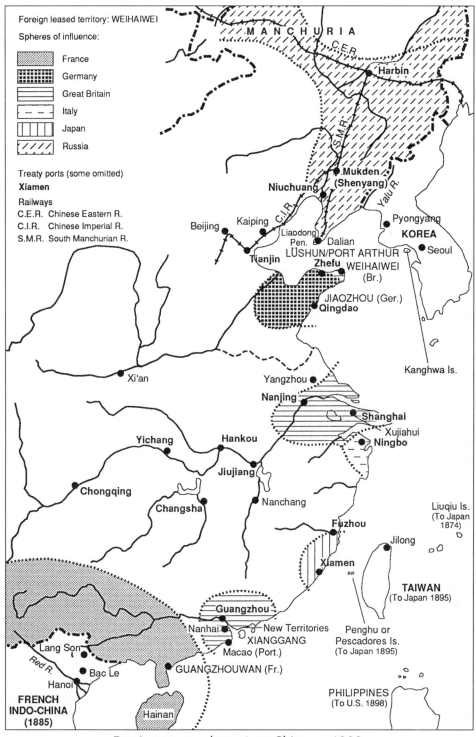

Foreign encroachment on China, *c.* 1900.

These took a number of forms, including railway and mining concessions, investments in treaty port industries and financial activities. France held a large share in the Russo-Chinese bank which provided much of the finance for the Chinese Eastern railway, and France and Belgium played leading roles in the construction of the Beijing–Hankou railway, which was completed in 1905.[14] Under the terms of the Treaty of Shimonoseki the establishment of foreign industry in treaty ports was permitted and between 1895 and 1913 at least 136 foreign-owned manufacturing and mining enterprises were established.[15] A notorious example of the extension of foreign control in mining was the surreptitious acquisition by a British company of the Kaiping coal mines.

Finally, there was the matter of foreign loans. Until 1894 the Chinese government had largely avoided foreign borrowing, but the cost of the Sino-Japanese War and the imposition of a large indemnity in the peace settlement meant that it had no choice but to seek credit. Between 1894 and 1898 China borrowed over 350 million taels on the international money market, the loans being secured on the customs duties. This burden of debt was greatly increased by the indemnity imposed by the Boxer Protocol. It was in this context that Britain's involvement in China began to shift from commerce to investments and financial services, much of these being supplied by the Hongkong and Shanghai Bank. To secure these interests it became increasingly important that Britain should exercise influence over the Chinese government and should ensure its political stability.[16]

Economic Imperialism

Perhaps the most sharply contested issue in modern Chinese history is the economic effects of Western imperialism on the country.[17] The issue may be summarized briefly: China in the eighteenth century, as presented for example by the Jesuit writer Jean-Baptiste du Halde, was an extremely prosperous country, which in many respects bore comparison with Europe[18] – but by the middle of the twentieth century she appeared to be poor and underdeveloped. Critics of the role of the West have argued that the reason for this change was the economic effects of imperialism, which damaged the economy, denied economic development and discredited the government. In response, defenders of the Western role in China have argued that the intervention of the West provided the essential shock which forced China to transform her economy. A third view argues that the impact of Western economic imperialism has been much overstated and that in truth its effect was only marginal.

The view that Western imperialism had a deleterious effect on China's economy was expressed by Karl Marx in the *New York Daily Tribune* in 1853. Referring to the origins of the Taiping rebellion he wrote:

> . . . the occasion of this outbreak has unquestionably been afforded by the English cannon forcing upon China that soporific drug called opium. Before the British arms the authority of the Manchu dynasty fell to pieces; the superstitious faith in the eternity of the Celestial Empire broke down; the barbarous and

hermetic isolation from the civilized world was infringed; and an opening was made for that intercourse which has since proceeded so rapidly under the golden attractions of California and Australia. At the same time the silver coin of the Empire, its lifeblood, began to be drained away to the British East Indies.[19]

This argument has been developed by identifying the unequal treaty system as the framework for exploitation and by finding evidence of damage to the Chinese economy. China was required to open about ninety treaty ports, some on the coast, others on navigable rivers and on frontier crossings. In the most important of these there were foreign settlements or concessions. The treaty ports existed for the convenience of Western businessmen, who enjoyed the protection of extraterritoriality. The unequal treaties had given the foreign powers control over China's external tariffs and this control prevented China from levying high duties on foreign imports to protect Chinese industries and to raise revenue. Under the provisions of the treaties China had to pay large indemnities, the one which was part of the Boxer Protocol amounting to $330 million, which was secured on customs duties.

The Chinese economy, it has been alleged, suffered from three main disadvantages. The first, described as the 'disruptive effect', concerned the impact of foreign trade on the production of iron and porcelain, but above all on the handicraft textile industry. The second, the 'drain effect', referred to the siphoning away of wealth, first by the drain of silver to pay for opium and subsequently by capital payments for indemnities and by losses from the application of unfair terms of trade. Finally, there was the 'oppression effect', which claimed that Western enterprises established in China were so efficient, and enjoyed so many advantages, that Chinese-owned modern industries were hopelessly oppressed and unable to establish themselves and obtain a share of the market.[20]

Marx noted the disruptive effect of the increased importation of English cottons after the first treaty settlement. He claimed:

> This introduction of foreign manufactures has had a similar effect on the native industry to that which it formerly had on Asia Minor, Persia and India. In China the spinners and weavers have suffered greatly under this foreign competition, and the community has become unsettled in proportion.[21]

Undoubtedly it was important for Britain to expand the market for British cotton textiles and some early success was achieved in China: by 1871 about one-third of the country's imports by value was in the form of cotton yarn and piece goods. Then, in the period between 1871 and 1910, yarn imports increased in quantity by a further twenty-four times and cotton piece goods imports doubled in quantity. Various reasons accounted for this rise, including the opening of the Suez Canal in 1869 and the introduction of the cheaper yarn produced by Bombay spinning mills.[22]

The case that these imports had a catastrophic effect on the Chinese cotton textile industry was made out by Marianne Bastid. She claimed that:

Textile manufacturing, by far the most important of the handicraft industries, was the earliest victim. First, foreign yarns replaced local yarns and thus broke the link between the crafts of spinning and weaving. Then foreign cotton fabrics supplanted locally made fabrics, breaking the connection between weaving and agriculture.[23]

In response Albert Feuerwerker argued that the 'simplistic indictment' of foreign capitalism for having progressively crushed or exploited domestic handicraft industry from the mid-nineteenth century onwards, was belied by the fact that even in the 1930s the handicraft cotton textile industry, the industry which allegedly had suffered most severely from the incursion of foreign capitalism, still produced 61 per cent of the cotton cloth made in China. Significant structural changes did take place in the textile industry, and these undoubtedly caused strain and dislocation for the population affected. For example, the importation of relatively cheap foreign yarn led to the dispersal of the handicraft weaving industry away from the traditional textile areas to areas which had not hitherto produced cloth. In the traditional areas marginal handicraft spinning, which had provided a supplementary income for peasant households, declined and the yarn required now came from the cotton mills of Shanghai.[24]

In 1870 China's principal exports were tea, which amounted to nearly one half of the total value of exports, and silk, which accounted for nearly 40 per cent of the value. Forty years later tea had fallen to less than 10 per cent of the value of exports and silk to just over 25 per cent of the value. During the same period the value of China's exports had increased by about seven times, and within this figure the value of tea exports had risen by about one-third and that of silk by more than four times.

What do these figures indicate about the performance of these two industries? Tea production was a handicraft industry which initially had adapted well to the export trade and until the 1880s Chinese exports of tea had risen sharply. Fuzhou became a major outlet for the export of black tea to Europe, carried on the famous tea clippers, and of brick tea to Russia. A number of small tea-processing plants were opened to service this trade. But the secrets of China's tea production were investigated by Robert Fortune, on behalf of the East India Company, and tea-plants were taken to India and Sri Lanka.[25] There they were cultivated on large plantations using cheap Indian field labour. Machines were used in the processing to obtain uniform quality, but the main advantage of Indian tea was that it was cheap. In 1888 British consumption of tea from India and Ceylon overtook that of tea from China. In that year Robert Hart advised the Zongli Yamen on the changes necessary in the organization of China's tea industry if it was to retain its world market, but his advice was not followed up, and the decline of the industry continued.[26]

Before the signing of the unequal treaties substantial quantities of silk were exported either as raw silk or as silk products. After the opening of Shanghai much of the export of raw silk went from there and the trade grew sharply after 1854 when the European production of silk was decimated by a silkworm disease. To produce raw silk of a uniform quality more acceptable to world markets, it was necessary to introduce steam filatures. The first steam filature was established at Shanghai in 1862 by Jardine, Matheson and Company, but this failed, allegedly because Chinese officials and merchants, anxious to protect traditional interests, prevented it from obtaining an adequate supply of cocoons.[27] The Guangzhou area was to prove more successful in developing a mechanized silk industry. In 1872 Chen Qiyuan established in his home district of Nanhai what was probably the first Chinese-run modern factory. The initial success of this venture may in part be explained by its rural location, free from bureaucratic intervention from Guangzhou. The factory also profited from a supply of cheap and reliable labour, an important source of workers in the Zhu river delta being women who followed the unusual practice of resisting marriage. However, the factory also encountered resistance from local silk weavers who used hand-reeled silk. In 1881 they smashed one of the filatures, one of the few examples of Luddism which occurred in China. The industry survived, the use of steam filatures spread, and the export of silk products continued to expand until 1929.[28]

What does the case of the silk industry suggest about the impact of economic imperialism? The obvious point is that any detailed examination of an industry reveals a complicated set of factors influencing the pattern of development. Lillian Li concluded that the slow progress of the silk industry, when compared with that of Japan, had little to do with imperialism. Instead it was due to the instability of the domestic and international markets, the inertia of government, the shortage of capital and the lack (rather than excess) of direct foreign investment.[29] In response Robert Eng argued that the silk industry was the victim of the indirect effects of imperialism, which defined China's role as a producer of raw silk. The growth of exports starved the Chinese silk industry of raw materials, the export market was controlled by foreigners and reliance on exports left silk producers vulnerable to fluctuations on the world market.[30]

The 'drain' effect has been identified, in the first instance, in the loss of silver caused by importation of opium, which until 1890 remained the most valuable single Chinese import. After the Treaty of Shimonoseki, foreign investment increased sharply and China was forced to borrow on the international money market. As a consequence a further drain occurred through the repatriation of profits and the charging of high rates of interest on loans. For example, to pay the 1895 indemnity of £30 million China took loans which would cost £100 million to redeem. The Boxer indemnity of $330 million would have cost China $739 million if it had ever been paid in full.[31] Another form of drain occurred through the application of unfair terms of trade. Between 1867 and 1936 the relative prices of imports increased by 40 per cent, so that by the end of the period a given quantity of exports could only pay for 71 per cent of the quantity of imports it could have bought at the beginning.[32]

The general response to this charge is that whatever the terms of trade which applied between China and the outside world, the economy gained some absolute benefits from participating in foreign trade, through inward investment and through the introduction of technology. Although a drain in terms of repatriation of profits is alleged, the figures suggest that at least until 1902 China enjoyed a net inflow of capital from foreign investments.[33] The argument that China was forced to pay an unfairly high rate of interest on foreign loans would appear to be unfounded as the rate usually reflected that which applied in the Chinese money market and would in any case have carried some premium for additional risk. The largest field for foreign investment was railways. Chinese railways in the first instance were rarely profitable and their returns were scarcely sufficient to pay interest charges, but other benefits accrued to China in terms of improved communications, paid employment and stimulus to industry.[34] In the calculation of the 'drain' effect mention should also be made of the remittances sent back to China by overseas Chinese, many of whom were working in the European colonies of south-east Asia.

The alleged 'oppression' effect occurred because Western enterprises were so much more efficient, and enjoyed so many advantages under the unequal treaties, that Chinese-owned modern enterprises were hopelessly oppressed. Evidence to support this view was found in cases where Chinese investment was attracted to foreign industry, rather than supporting indigenous enterprises. It was remarked that although China developed modern industries in some sectors, the heavy industrial sector was dominated by foreigners, for example by 1911 foreign capital controlled 93 per cent of China's railways. A particular argument used to confirm the 'oppression' effect was that the first significant growth period of China's modern industry came at the time of the First World War, when the competition from Western industry was temporarily reduced. For example, in Tianjin during the war years there was a sharp increase in investment in textile mills and in the production of textile piece goods which were superior to European imports.[35]

However, the 'oppression' effect argument is vulnerable to two criticisms. In the discussion of the self-strengthening *guandu shangban* enterprises it was shown that a wide variety of reasons have been adduced for their failure – if that is the right term – and if these are valid it would be unfair to concentrate the blame on the effects of imperialism. Secondly, there is the argument developed below that Western economic activity was in some respects beneficial to China.

A number of writers, among them Mark Elvin, have argued that the Chinese economy at the beginning of the modern age had reached the stage described as a 'high-level equilibrium trap'. This meant that in terms of technology, business organization and entrepreneurship, the traditional Chinese economy had reached the limit of what it could achieve. The growth of the population and the shortage of land meant that output per capita could not be increased significantly. The only way in which this situation could be changed was by the administration of an 'exogenous shock', which involved the painful process of entering world markets and accepting the products of an industrial-scientific revolution.[36]

If one accepts this view, it is then possible to view the effects of Western economic imperialism in a positive light. For example, much handicraft industry was the product of the high-level equilibrium trap. Because of the land shortage, peasant households had surplus labour which could only be used to produce handicrafts for their own consumption or to supplement the family's income. This cottage industry, if not protected by distance from the treaty ports, was vulnerable to imports of Western industrial goods, and this could cause real hardship. But foreign imports were also the catalyst for the emergence of a modern Chinese textile industry, which at first occupied a place between the more capital-intensive Western-owned treaty port mills and the smaller, more labour-intensive Chinese-owned mills of the hinterland. Nor was the positive contribution of the foreigner limited to this role. The opening of China to foreign trade led to some absolute gains from trade and a transfer of productive capital and technology. Indeed it has been claimed that 'foreign capital played a significant role in bringing about whatever economic modernization existed in China before 1937'.[37]

Mention should also be made of a third interpretation of the effect of Western economic imperialism: that its impact was marginal and has usually been exaggerated. Albert Feuerwerker, a prominent exponent of this view, responded to the claim that foreign capitalism crushed the handicraft industry with the remark:

> Anyone who would claim that the Hunan or Sichuan peasant in the 1930s dressed in Naigaiwata cottons, smoked BAT cigarettes, and used Meiji sugar has a big case to prove.[38]

To support this view Feuerwerker pointed out that the cost of transportation, internal transit taxes and the conservatism of the Chinese market, offered substantial barriers to the penetration of Western goods. China's foreign trade, although growing in the late imperial period, was in 1913 the lowest in terms of trade per head of population of the eighty-three countries for which League of Nations data were compiled. Western merchants were almost entirely excluded from China's internal marketing system and were only dominant in the import-export trade. And, as Hou Chi-ming pointed out, the amount of foreign investment in China was really very small, even by 1936 amounting to less than US $8 per capita, well below that in other underdeveloped countries.[39] Although foreign investment was small, it might be argued that it was still important, but the narrow geographical location of Western influence and the restricted favourable forward and backward linkages between the foreign sector and the domestic economy both served to limit the impact of such investment.[40]

The argument of marginality can be extended by reference to the role of the treaty ports as interpreted by Rhoads Murphey. In Asian colonies, and indeed in countries which were not colonized, treaty ports and other coastal cities became 'points of entry into Asia of an alien Western order', which were to have a devastating effect on the recipient country, remaking not only the economic landscape, but also cultural and national perceptions. But in China this did not happen – the Chinese economy was too large and too complex to be captured by Western merchants. Chinese culture was too sophisticated and the Chinese sense of identity too strong to be overwhelmed by the Western presence. Instead, the effect of the treaty ports was to create a 'new negative' which reinforced Sinocentric pride.[41] Such a view, although it underplays the role of the treaty ports, is a corrective to the common assumption that Western influence was the absolute determinant of China's modern development. A similar conclusion was reached by William T. Rowe in his study of Hankou, the major emporium of central China which became a treaty port in 1861. Although the technology of industrialization was introduced from the West, and although it was initially sponsored by Chinese officials, it was not foreign influence but conditions indigenous to the city which made it a candidate for national leadership in China's industrial and political revolutions.[42]

On the Political Consequences of Imperialism

In recent years some writers, aware that the indictment of economic imperialism has been challenged, have turned their attention to the effects of imperialism on political structures. Joseph Esherick argued that war had demonstrated China's military and political weakness and that weakness was perpetuated by the continued presence of the imperial powers under the unequal treaties which infringed China's sovereignty. After 1860 the West found it to its advantage to prop up a conservative dynasty and hinder the cause of progressive politics. By the beginning of the twentieth century, the Qing dynasty was 'reduced to little more than a despised tax-collecting agency for the foreign powers' and was quite incapable of offering the leadership and performing the roles required of an effective government.[43]

Christian Missions in China

In 1927 Tang Liangli, a Guomindang politician, wrote:

> The right of extraterritoriality and the deprivation of China's tariff autonomy, then, are the most noticeable devices for securing the humiliation and subjugation of China. The most sinister instrument of foreign imperialism, however, is to be found in Article VII of the Sino-British Treaty, which concluded the first Missionary and second Opium War. . . .[44]

Article VII provided for the protection, by the Chinese government, of persons teaching or professing Christianity. Tang Liangli justified his statement by arguing that no group of foreigners had done greater harm to China than foreign missionaries, whose activities had served to denationalize hundreds of thousands of Chinese converts and whose misrepresentations had led to China being grievously misunderstood in the West.

Christian activity in China can be traced back to the Tang period, when a Nestorian Christian church was established in Xi'an. In the late Ming period Jesuit missionaries had been permitted to reside in Beijing and had achieved some success in making conversions at court. Jesuit missionaries brought with them skills in the arts and sciences, they studied Chinese and allowed their converts to perform the Confucian rites. The Jesuit mission survived the Manchu conquest and in 1692 the Qianlong emperor granted Christianity a degree of tolerance. However, Christianity, as a foreign religion and one which relied on revelation, was vulnerable to intellectual criticism and this was encouraged by the Yongzheng emperor whose amplification of the *Sacred Edict* adjured people to 'Destroy heterodox doctrines in order to render honor to orthodox learning'.[45] Moreover, the accommodation over rites had been criticized by other missionary orders and in 1742 was condemned by the Pope. Thereafter, although Christianity did not disappear, it was subjected to restriction and persecution.

In the nineteenth century Christian missionary activity was transformed, first by the arrival of Protestant missionaries and then by the effects of the unequal treaties. Robert Morrison, sent by the London Missionary Society, reached China in 1807. Only seven years later did he make his first convert, but in the meantime he had started work on compiling the first Chinese-English dictionary. In the 1830s the first American missionaries arrived, among them Elijah Coleman Bridgman and Samuel Wells Williams, who jointly edited the *Chinese Repository*, which appeared between 1832 and 1851, in which they published scholarly articles on topics relating to China.[46] Soon afterwards Peter Parker, the first medical missionary, established a hospital in Guangzhou. Many of these early Protestant missionaries felt that their priority was the saving of souls, not the education of their flock, but by the 1840s all Protestant mission stations in China provided some education for children.[47]

Under the unequal treaties missionaries could reside and establish churches in the treaty ports and for a number of Protestant missions Xianggang became the secure base. In 1844 and 1846 France obtained two edicts which provided limited toleration for Catholicism and enabled the Jesuits to re-establish themselves at Xujiahui on the outskirts of Shanghai. France also assumed a protectorate of Catholic missions, so attaching her national prestige to the well-being of missionaries. Under the French Treaty of Tianjin, 1858, Catholic priests were accorded the right to preach their religion anywhere in the empire and Chinese subjects were given the right to practise Christianity. Two years later, in the French text of the Convention of Beijing, a clause which had been inserted duplicitously gave Catholic missionaries the right to rent and buy land in the interior for the purpose of building churches. By virtue of the most-favoured-nation clause, these provisions also applied to Protestant missions.

Under this protection Christian missionary activity expanded rapidly. By the end of the imperial period there were more than 5,000 foreign missionaries in China, over 70 per cent of them being Protestant. The largest national groupings were British and American missions, followed by those of Germany. At the same date the estimated number of Chinese converts was 1,360,000 Catholics and up to 200,000 Protestants – the latter always insisted that they were more rigorous than the Catholics in determining conversions.[48] At first Protestant activity was largely centred on the treaty ports. However, in 1865 James Hudson Taylor, prompted by the thought that 'A million a month in China are dying without God',[49] formed the China Inland Mission, which was committed to establishing a non-denominational Protestant Christian mission in every province of China. Alongside the preaching of the Gospel, missionaries became increasingly involved in philanthropic, medical and educational activities. Catholic missionaries, believing that unbaptized children were damned, established orphanages at many mission stations. The number of medical missionaries rose sharply and by 1906 it was claimed that 250 mission hospitals and dispensaries were treating some two million patients annually.

Medical missionaries pioneered the training of Chinese doctors in Western medicine, and they also translated medical works and advised on matters of public health.[50] Education became an increasingly important element in missionary activity, for it was recognized that the Chinese desire for literacy could be used to establish contact. By 1899 over 30,000 pupils were attending 1,766 Protestant schools.[51] A number of these schools, for example St John's in Shanghai, later introduced secondary level education, and the early development of universities offering a Western curriculum owed much to missionary endeavour. Missionaries also pioneered the teaching of girls in schools, and Ginling College, China's first women's institute of higher education, which opened in Nanjing in 1915, was a Protestant mission foundation.[52]

The above account may be described as the positive aspect of Christian missionary activity in China. Undoubtedly the vast majority of Western missionaries, although blinkered in their cultural outlook, were honest believers in the value of their mission and were prepared to lay down their lives for what they believed was God's work. China, with its long history and sophisticated culture, was seen as the greatest prize, but was also regarded as the toughest of all the missionary fields, because of the language problem, because of the high mortality rate among missionaries – an early American missionary in Fuzhou once commented 'missionaries in China are made to feel how near they are to eternity'[53] – and because of the overt hostility which many missionaries faced.

Why was there this hostility? It is clear that an intellectual rejection of Christianity existed well before the signing of the unequal treaties. As early as 1640 there had appeared a collection of essays compiled by a scholar from Zhejiang entitled *An Anthology of Writings Exposing Heterodoxy*, which dealt sceptically with Christian beliefs.[54] In the early years of the Qing dynasty the Jesuit Father Adam Schall, who had prepared a calendar based on Western mathematical calculations, suffered a fierce attack from an official named Yang Guangxian, who in a collection entitled *I Could Not Do Otherwise*, 1665, charged him with plotting against the state and indoctrinating the people with false ideas.[55] As mentioned above, the Yongzheng emperor had added his own condemnation of Christianity as a heterodox sect. In short, by the beginning of the nineteenth century there already existed a body of literature which provided an articulate condemnation of Christianity as a religion.

The Taiping rebellion provided a new reason for opposing Christianity. The Christian element in the Taiping ideology was not at first regarded as significant – the early imperial rescripts concerning the rebellion mentioned it only once.[56] However, Zeng Guofan was alert to the danger and in an eloquent proclamation he inveighed against the Taiping version of Christianity, which he said was plagiarized from the foreign barbarians. It deprived peasants of their land, merchants of their trade and scholars of their Confucian studies. This was an unprecedented crisis in the history of traditional Confucian moral principles and he called upon the educated classes to rouse themselves against the rebels.[57] Fifty years later the well-known missionary Timothy Richard noted that the loss of life brought about by the rebellion had left 'a legacy of hatred against Christianity, a hatred which has scarcely yet melted away'.[58]

However, it was not until the 1860s, as a consequence of the new conditions established by the second treaty settlement, that a widespread hostility towards missionaries and their activities became apparent. To explain why this occurred, Paul Cohen cited the significance of a pamphlet which first appeared in 1861 entitled Bixie jishi, A Record of Facts to Ward Off Heterodoxy, written by someone using the pseudonym 'the most heartbroken man in the world'. It is probable that the author came from Hunan and had some connection with the militia raised to oppose the Taiping rebels. The work itself was a clever admixture of true and false statements about Christian religious practices. For example, it noted that Westerners made free, not arranged, marriages and it then added that the bride must spend the night with the pastor before being married. It remarked on the higher position accorded to women in Western society and attributed it to the value set by Western men on women's menstrual flow which they drank and which accounted for their unbearable stench. It gave a detailed account of how Christians in their orphanages operated on children to facilitate anal intercourse. Another part of the book gave examples of how individuals who had embraced Christianity then committed acts of sexual perversion and suffered dire consequences. At the end of the book there was an extensive bibliography of anti-Christian works.[59]

Cohen identified the gentry as the main opponents of Christian missionaries. Missionaries posed a threat to their cultural hegemony and at the same time challenged their role in the political, economic and legal structures of rural society. Missionaries, particularly Catholics and members of the China Inland Mission, often wore the garb of a Confucian scholar. Mission schools challenged the gentry's dominance of literacy and education, missionary intervention in litigation trespassed on the gentry's relationship with the magistrate, and mission orphanages and mission work to provide relief in times of famine and flood encroached on their charitable activities.

In response the gentry read and circulated anti-Christian literature and played an important role in anti-missionary incidents. Typical of these incidents was an attack made in March 1862 on the Catholic orphanage in Nanchang in Jiangxi. Two months earlier a French missionary had arrived in Nanchang to reopen the Lazarist mission there. His arrival, and a dispute over the style in which the local official should receive him – he claimed the status of a foreign consul – gave rise to a spate of anti-missionary publications, which can be traced to two local members of the upper gentry. Two circumstances added to the tension: Nanchang was the provincial capital and examinations were being held there at the time of the incident; also the city was only 125 miles from Taiping-held territory and Christian missionary activity was seen as an encouragement to the rebels. The missionaries attempted to communicate their fears to the acting governor, but he and the local officials were unable to choose between their duty of enforcing the treaty provisions and their need to retain the confidence of the gentry and so took no action. As a result crowds collected and the orphanage and a church were destroyed, together with several tens of shops and homes owned by Chinese Catholics.[60]

More serious incidents followed and their resolution led to foreign reprisals. In 1868 Hudson Taylor of the China Inland Mission opened the first Protestant mission at Yangzhou on the Grand Canal, a city which had been captured by the Taiping rebels. As at Nanchang, anti-missionary literature appeared, but the local prefect did not take action. On 22 August a large crowd gathered, the mission buildings were plundered and the missionaries treated roughly. Because of delays in obtaining a settlement satisfactory to Britain, Rutherford Alcock, the British minister sent four gunboats to Nanjing and coerced Zeng Guofan, the governor-general, into dismissing the official held responsible for the incident. Two years later a far more violent incident occurred. A crowd, incensed by rumours of the kidnapping of children and of malpractices in an orphanage, attacked the Catholic mission in Tianjin and killed nineteen foreigners, including the French Consul, two priests and ten sisters of charity. Zeng Guofan was again required to mediate and he earned the hatred of the anti-foreign wing at court because of his willingness to reach an accommodation with France. In the event, France's involvement in the Franco-Prussian war invalidated any threat of hostilities. Nevertheless, the price to be paid in restitution was a severe one. The Tianjin prefect and magistrate were sentenced to life-long exile, eighteen Chinese were beheaded and an indemnity of 280,000 taels was paid for foreign lives lost.[61]

The settlement of incidents such as these further undermined the prestige of the Chinese government. The Western powers insisted that local officials be held responsible for allowing the attacks on missionaries to occur and demanded that they be punished. Incidents were used as a pretext to demand financial compensation and to obtain further privileges. At the end of the century anti-missionary activity became entangled with anti-dynastic agitation. In the 1890s anti-Christian riots in the Yangzi valley were at least in part fomented by secret society members, their intention being to bring down the dynasty. Anti-missionary agitation in the early stages of the Boxer uprising created a dilemma for the court. At first it sanctioned the punishment of officials who had not taken effective action to suppress the Boxers and then, as the movement grew, it made the disastrous choice of offering the movement its support.[62]

18
Nationalism and Reform in Late Imperial China

This chapter first considers the development of nationalism in China. It then examines three controversial episodes in the closing years of the Qing dynasty: the Hundred Days' reforms of 1898, the Boxer uprising of 1900–1 and the late Qing reforms of 1901–11, all of which contributed to the further development of nationalist feeling.

Nationalism

It is often suggested that nationalism, meaning identification with China as a nation state and concern for its survival and well-being, was unknown in China until the end of the nineteenth century. Until that time, politically aware Chinese identified their concerns with the integrity of Confucian culture, not with the survival of the Chinese state.

Nevertheless, it is possible to identify components of the nationalist feeling which was to develop at an earlier date. One such component was anti-Manchuism. In the seventeenth century Manchu rule had been preferred by many Chinese to a dynasty which claimed popular support. However, there was some heroic opposition to the conquest and anti-Manchu feeling was expressed by some Ming loyalist scholars, including Wang Fuzhi (1619–92), a reclusive writer from Hunan, who argued that each race should be controlled by its own ruler and should not allow encroachment by an alien race. Although the Manchus came to identify themselves closely with Confucian culture, and thus neutralize much of this feeling, this tradition of anti-Manchuism did not disappear entirely.[1]

Another component was 'anti-foreignism', which has been defined as attitudes and activities hostile to foreigners in defence of the values and institutions of the Confucian world.[2] Anti-foreignism was in evidence at the time of the Opium Wars and Lin Zexu's moral stance against the opium trade may be taken as an example of it. The war also produced new anti-foreign responses, partly because its main theatre was around Guangzhou and the people of Guangzhou were commonly regarded as exceptionally bellicose. These included xenophobia and racism. Westerners were regarded as lewd and their behaviour was seen as a threat to morality. A particular cause of outrage was the British use of Indian troops and the suspicion that they were molesting Chinese women. The war also produced a sentiment which might be described as 'proto-nationalism', the reference being to the Sanyuanli incident of 1841 referred to earlier.[3] The Guangzhou gentry who organized the resistance were xenophobic and their allegiance to the Manchus was conditional. The 'victory' at Sanyuanli seemed to indicate that the united resistance of the Chinese people could defeat the foreigner. But they remained committed to preserving the cultural *status quo*, and they identified themselves with the province and not yet with the nation.[4]

A third component of nationalism emerged from the debate over whether, and to what degree, China should change to meet the threat from the outside world. At a number of crisis points in Chinese history a dichotomy appeared between the supporters of pragmatic change and those who insisted on remaining true to Confucian values. The latter sentiment was often expressed by low- and middle-ranking officials and gentry not holding office. It was referred to as qingyi, literally 'pure discussion', which also implied a righteous attitude. In the nineteenth century this dichotomy appeared between the pragmatic actions of the self-strengthening reformers and the principled criticism levelled against them by some conservatives, the best-known example being the protest made by Woren against the inclusion of mathematics and science in the syllabus of the Tongwenguan.

The most forceful expression of qingyi opinion was directed against what was regarded as pusillanimity in foreign relations. Zeng Guofan was subjected to a barrage of criticism for his cautious handling of the settlement after the Tianjin massacre. Five years later, in 1875, the murder of the British Vice-Consul Augustus Margary incited another outburst of qingyi sentiment. One of the provisions of the Zhefu Convention was that China should send an apology mission to Britain. Guo Songtao, the official chosen to head it, had to endure humiliating comments when he was leaving his home province of Hunan.

> He stands out among his contemporaries,
> He is raised above his peers.
> Yet the nation of Yao and Shun
> Cold-shoulders him.
> He cannot serve human beings,
> So how can he serve demons?
> What is the point of abandoning
> His native land?[5]

The first settlement of the Ili crisis brought forth another storm of criticism. The strongest condemnation came from Zhang Zhidong (1837–1909), at that time a tutor in the Imperial Academy, who called for the repudiation of the treaty and the execution of the official who had signed it. Zhang was a member of a small coterie of officials known as the Qingliu, the 'party of the purists', which was renowned for its outspoken expression of qingyi views, and which was to exert considerable influence over China's foreign policy over the next decade. Zhang did not get his way over the Ili settlement, and the more moderate policies of Li Hongzhang prevailed. Nevertheless, shortly afterwards Zhang was appointed Governor of

Shanxi and then to the Governor-Generalship of Guangdong and Guangxi. It was during his tenure of that post that the most notable example of Qingliu pressure occurred. Li Hongzhang's attempts to negotiate a settlement with France over Vietnam were ridiculed and he was compared to Qin Gui, the great traitor in Chinese history who allegedly betrayed the Song dynasty. Officials who knew that China had no choice but to find an accommodation with the French were intimidated and the Empress Dowager, always careful of her position, gave her tacit support to the qingyi view, although she was astute enough to capitalize on the victory at Lang Son to make peace.

The catastrophic defeat of the Sino-Japanese War, and the scramble for concessions which followed, dealt a devastating blow to those who had advocated the moderate adjustments called for in the policy of self-strengthening. It also raised very awkward questions for those who rejected all change inspired by the West. In this vacuum a much more radical proposal began to gain support: to break from tradition in order to preserve China as a country. An early expression of this attitude, which has been described as incipient nationalism, can be found in the writings of Wang Tao (1828–97), a journalist and long-time associate of James Legge, the missionary who translated the Chinese classics. In 1880 Wang Tao wrote:

The fact that nowadays powerful neighbors and ruthless enemies continually eye us from all sides is actually a blessing for China and not a misfortune. This is just the thing we need to stimulate our determination to forge ahead. . . . For if we can become ashamed at not being as good as the Western nations it may yet be possible for us to do something about it.

Sixteen years later, after the Sino-Japanese War, Wang Tao voiced the hope that the disastrous defeat would awaken China to the need for fundamental change, and in particular to forge ahead by promoting economic reforms.[6]

A further stage in the emergence of nationalist feeling derived from the rights recovery movement, a response to the scramble for concessions. According to John E. Schrecker this brought together the traditional mainstream approach to foreign affairs and the militant qingyi response which had emerged at the time of the Sino-French War. Schrecker noted that the use of the term 'sovereignty' in foreign policy documents only became common after 1902. He took this as proof of the emphasis placed, in the last years of the Qing dynasty, on the recovery of lost sovereign rights. It prompted a variety of schemes, often with commercial or industrial implications, which received support from the local gentry and merchants.[7] These changes gave an impetus to the development of nationalism, which has been described as the 'moving force' behind the 1911 revolution.[8]

The Hundred Days' Reforms of 1898

It has been remarked that nineteenth-century Confucianism was by no means merely, nor even primarily, a reactionary and defensive response to ideas from the West.[9] The main intellectual debate of the day concerned the authenticity of the

Confucian texts. In the seventeenth century new standards had been set in *kaozheng* or textual analysis. This led to a reinterpretation of the classics which became known as the 'Han learning'. Further scholarly activity revealed that a number of the classic texts had been tampered with and new texts were established. In 1891 Kang Youwei (1858–1927), a young scholar from Guangdong, published a study entitled *An Enquiry into the Classics Forged during the Xin Period*, which challenged the orthodox views based on the Han learning and gained him instant notoriety.

China's defeat in the Sino-Japanese War forced Chinese intellectuals for the first time to give serious consideration to the challenge of Western culture. At the moment when the humiliating peace terms were made public, candidates for the *jinshi* examination had assembled in Beijing. Among them was the above-mentioned Kang Youwei, who organized a petition, supposedly signed by 1,200 degree candidates, which called for a rejection of the peace treaty, the removal of the capital and the institution of reforms, including radical changes in the operation of the bureaucracy and the introduction of a wide programme of Westernizing measures. These proposals did not get past the Censorate, but a version of the petition, which had been printed in Shanghai, was circulated widely.[10]

The defeat also had a profound effect on members of the bureaucracy and stimulated a wave of practical reforms. The most notable example of this was supported by Zhang Zhidong, the former *qingyi* critic of the conduct of the Sino-Japanese War who was now the Governor-General of Hunan and Hubei. Chen Baozhen, the Governor of Hunan, initiated a range of reforms which included the establishment of a mining bureau to exploit the province's mineral resources, the construction of a telegraph line between Hankou and Changsha and the introduction of electric lighting in Changsha. Jiang Biao, the educational commissioner, added important educational reforms. He encouraged the circulation of Western literature and added geography and mathematics to the syllabus for the *shengyuan* degree. These reforms initially received the support of senior Hunanese gentry, who accepted them as within the tradition of the pragmatic conservatism epitomized by the self-strengthening projects of Zeng Guofan.[11]

In 1895 Kang Youwei's urgent call for action had had little impact on the court, so Kang and his principal assistant Liang Qichao turned to new methods of gaining support for their ideas. Their instruments were the study society and the newspaper. In 1895 Kang organized the 'Self-Strengthening Study Society' in Beijing which recruited its membership among reform-minded officials in the capital and in the provinces – including such important figures as Zhang Zhidong, and which also numbered among its supporters Western missionaries and diplomats. The first newspaper was the *Chinese and Foreign News*, which contained essays on current affairs, for the most part written by Liang Qichao. These activities challenged a fundamental principle of Qing government, that officials should not form associations to discuss political issues, and these were suppressed.[12]

The urgent need for radical reform became increasingly apparent after the German seizure of Jiaozhou bay in November 1897. Kang Youwei's response was once again to submit a memorial to the throne calling for reform. He recommended in particular that China should follow the precedents set by Peter the Great in Russia and by the leaders of Meiji Japan. He went on to suggest that the protocol prescribing which officials had the right to advise the throne should be modified and that provincial officials should be given greater discretion in implementing reforms.[13] It seemed that this memorial had likewise gone unnoticed, and Kang continued with his scholarly research which culminated in the publication, in December 1897, of Confucius as an Institutional Reformer. In this Kang, following up his earlier work on the 'new texts', argued that Confucius, under the guise of reviving the past, had in fact been a reformer. He went on to liken Confucius' role to that of Buddha, Christ and Mohammed, as the founder of a religion. In these writings he hinted at a mystical or utopian world view which was to be elaborated further in his major work, the Book of the Great Unity.

In the meantime events had moved in Kang Youwei's favour. Since 1889 the Empress Dowager had officially been in retirement. The young Guangxu emperor was still much influenced by his former tutor Weng Tonghe, a man who had some sympathy for the cause of reform. It was Weng Tonghe who drafted the edict issued on 11 June 1898 which committed the dynasty to reform and he is usually credited with having brought Kang Youwei to the emperor's attention, and to have thus provided the opportunity for Kang to obtain the celebrated audience with the emperor five days later. During that conversation Kang remarked:

> The prerequisites of reform are that all the laws and the political and social systems be changed and decided anew, before it can be called a reform. Now those who talk about reform only change some specific affairs, and do not reform the institutions.[14]

Kang's words suggest a 'revolution from above', similar in kind to that which the Meiji government of Japan had instituted thirty years previously. What followed was certainly an extensive programme of reform. In the hundred days between 11 June and 21 September 1898 the emperor, with the assistance of Kang Youwei, Liang Qichao and Tan Sitong, the last-named being the youngest and most radical of the reformers, promulgated about forty reform edicts. These may be grouped under four headings. The most important reforms dealt with education and included the abolition of the 'eight-legged essay', the formal literary exercise required of examination candidates, and the establishment of new colleges and schools. Another group applied to the economy, with provisions for the encouragement of trade, the creation of a ministry of agriculture and the establishment of bureaus for mines and railways. A third group related to the military, with edicts proposing the abolition of the Army of the Green Standard and the creation of a new navy and a national conscript army. A fourth group abolished a variety of sinecure posts.

The only political reform introduced was to grant to all subjects the right to memorialize the throne in closed memorials – a seemingly innocuous measure which ended the exclusive privilege of memorializing held only by senior officials. It has often been assumed that the reformers intended to transform China into a constitutional monarchy, but the evidence that this was Kang's intention is not very strong.[15] Liang Qichao, Tan Sitong and other radical reformers advocated the cause of 'people's rights'. This did not imply popular participation in the political process, but the fuller participation of the gentry in politics, which might lead to a form of constitutional government.[16]

The Failure of the Hundred Days' Reforms

In Hunan the reforms previously introduced by Chen Baozhen and Jiang Biao had been widely accepted. In late 1897, with the appointment of Liang Qichao as dean of Chinese studies at the newly opened School of Current Affairs at Changsha, and the advocacy of Kang Youwei's ideas, the reform movement entered a radical phase. Members of the upper gentry who had previously supported reform became alarmed about the extensive programme of Westernization which was now being proposed. They believed it amounted to a fundamental attack on the values and institutions of the social order. Their criticisms were supported by Zhang Zhidong, the governor-general, who secured the denunciation of Kang Youwei's theories and the demotion of his supporters. In May 1898 Zhang began publication of *An Exhortation to Study*, a treatise extolling the value of moderate reform, which has been taken as a response to Kang Youwei's *Confucius as an Institutional Reformer* and which was used to combat his ideas.[17]

In Beijing the reform programme was still in full flood. However, Kang's position was precarious, for the only official appointment he held was as secretary to the Zongli Yamen, a post which he regarded as insufficiently prestigious. Attempts to strengthen the reformers' position by having four of their number, including Tan Sitong, appointed as additional Grand Council secretaries with a special responsibility for reform measures, antagonized senior officials. Behind the scenes opposition was gathering and on 21 September the Empress Dowager acted. With the support of Rong Lu, the recently appointed Governor-General of Zhili, who also commanded the armed forces of north China, the emperor was placed under house arrest and six of the leading reformers, including Tan Sitong, were arrested and speedily executed. Kang Youwei, with British assistance, found refuge in Xianggang and Liang Qichao sought asylum in the Japanese legation and later fled to Japan.

Why did the reform programme collapse so dramatically? Perhaps one should begin by referring to the alleged conspiracy to take the Empress Dowager captive. According to this version of events, which was only made public after the six reformers had been executed, Kang Youwei and his followers had conspired to use the armed forces to take over the Summer Palace. The person they asked to assist them was Yuan Shikai, who after his activities in Korea had been given the task of forming a modern army for the metropolitan province of Zhili, which became known as the Newly-Established Army. The reformers believed Yuan was sympathetic to the cause of reform and on the evening of 18 September Tan Sitong asked him to execute Rong Lu and send his troops to seize the palace. Instead, Yuan reported the conspiracy to Rong Lu and the Empress Dowager carried out her coup.[18]

Although the conspiracy theory may be dismissed as a *post facto* justification of the Empress Dowager's action, the case remains that the main reason why the reformers failed was because of her opposition. It is often assumed that Cixi was opposed to reform in principle, but it has been shown that she was in favour of moderate reform. Although the edict issued on 26 September nullified the Hundred Days' reforms, it also contained a commitment to policies to bring 'wealth and power' to the country.[19] It has been argued that her opposition was 'conditioned by a mixture of ignorance, fear, and indignation', and by some apprehension that the reformers were prepared to countenance foreign interference in Chinese affairs.[20]

Other explanations of the failure of the reformers focus on the feebleness of support for the movement and the strength of opposition to it. It was headed by two men, Kang Youwei and the emperor, 'a visionary enthusiast and an inexperienced weakling', who could only claim the active support of people from Guangzhou and the 'Platonic approval' of Zhang Zhidong. Against them were arrayed, actively or passively, 'all the forces of the empire': peasants who would have welcomed tax reductions but who otherwise asked only to be left alone, traders who feared disorder, gentry who resented the modification of customs, officials who were dismayed by loss of privileges, statesmen such as Li Hongzhang who believed that there was no alternative to the established regime, the Army of the Green Standard which resisted annihilation, ordinary Manchus who were threatened with having to work, Manchu nobles who saw the Manchu ascendancy threatened, Manchu princes of the blood who saw the Manchu throne endangered, and the Empress Dowager herself who saw her achievements over forty years being reversed.[21]

Recent views have tended to amplify that opinion. The poor judgement of the reformers was revealed in Hunan. One young reformer published an article in which he suggested that China should merge her laws and social teaching with Western counterparts, give political power equally to the people and to the sovereign and promote intermarriage with the white race. Tan Sitong himself criticized Zeng Guofan, whose role in the suppression of the Taiping rebellion had earned him enduring respect, by saying that the Hunan army had committed more atrocities than had the Taiping rebels.[22]

The suggestion that the reformers tried to push through too many radical reforms in too short a time has been challenged on the grounds that many of these modernizing reforms had already been initiated in Hunan without meeting with opposition. The educational reforms, which threatened the status of those who had succeeded in the examination system, were in fact quite modest and were not opposed by students. Instead the real reason for opposition has been found in particular threats to vested interests in terms of communication and patronage. Kang Youwei had supported permitting direct communication between the government and the people which thereby deprived senior officials of the privilege of submitting memorials. He had also encouraged the emperor to exercise his power of appointment in a way which threatened the Empress Dowager's use of patronage.[23]

Although the reformers were executed or dispersed and the Hundred Days' reform programme was abandoned, the reform period had an enduring significance. The more practical reforms were retained, among them the decision to found Beijing University. The intellectual ferment which it had stimulated did not die down. There was a rapid expansion of newspaper publication to areas away from the treaty ports, which has been seen as promoting the beginning of elite nationalism, that is nationalism as an intellectual movement.[24] In exile in Japan, Liang Qichao wrote influential essays in which he rejected the Chinese tradition and developed his ideas on nationalism.[25]

The Boxer Uprising

The Boxer uprising is both a colourful and a controversial episode in China's history. For a long time in the West it was termed a rebellion, thus maintaining the fiction that the Boxers were an anti-dynastic force. Western accounts of the uprising have often trivialized it as a negative explosion of resentment on the part of superstitious and misled peasants, and have concentrated on the European experience. On the other hand, modern Chinese studies, which assume that peasant uprisings have been the motive force of historical development in Chinese feudal society,[26] have stressed the positive aspects and have claimed that the Boxer movement proved that 'the peasants were the principal force in opposing Imperialist aggression' and the 'carving up of China'.[27] This view was echoed in Joseph W. Esherick's study of the uprising, which investigated the popular culture out of which the movement grew. Of the Boxers he said, 'they stood as a dramatic example of ordinary Chinese peasants rising up to rid China of the hated foreign presence'. As such, he added, 'they were an important episode in the emergence of mass nationalism in China'.[28]

The more detailed controversies concerning the movement refer to the origin of the Boxers and the roles of the Empress Dowager, the Manchu princes and some senior officials. With reference to their origin, it has often been stated that the Boxers can be traced to the White Lotus religion, or to the Eight Trigrams rebellion which had arisen in Shandong and Zhili in 1813. This has been categorically denied by Joseph Esherick, on the grounds that the Boxers in their day were regarded as a new phenomenon, having no connection with White Lotus organizations and not sharing the White Lotus cult of the Eternal Venerable Mother.[29] The other point of origin lies in the martial arts activities for which Shandong was particularly famous. A censor's memorial of 1808 had listed some of the martial arts groups to be found on the borders of Shandong, Jiangsu, Anhui and Henan, including the Obedient Swords, Tiger-tail Whip, the Eight Trigrams and the 'Yihe', or 'United in Righteousness' group. These groups were said to encourage gambling in markets and so cause disturbances.[30] Some writers have traced a connection between the last named group and the Boxers, but Esherick has argued that there was no direct link. The relationship between sectarian and martial arts groups is difficult to pin down: some sects had no connections with the martial arts, but quite commonly the martial arts were used by sects to recruit young males into the sectarian network.

The Boxer movement arose in the provinces of Zhili and Shandong, an area of high population density and one very vulnerable to drought and flooding. In the middle of the nineteenth century this area had suffered from the Yellow river's change to its northern course. A drought in 1876 had caused a severe famine, said to have cost two million lives. In 1898 the Yellow river burst its banks and caused extensive flooding, and two years later a prolonged drought led to further loss of life.

This area had escaped the first effects of Western imperialism, but by the late nineteenth century Western activity was becoming apparent and a potential cause of popular resentment. The import of machine-spun yarn affected the cotton-growing region of west Shandong. More obviously disruptive was the reckless activity of some missionary organizations, notably the Steyl Society, a German Catholic mission which had established itself in Shandong. It was led by Bishop Johann Anzer, an ardent advocate of the expansion of German power in China. It was the death of two missionaries from the Steyl Society, perhaps at the hands of the Big Sword society, a forerunner of the Boxers, which served as a pretext for the German seizure of Jiaozhou bay in 1897.[31]

Banditry was an endemic problem on the Shandong–Jiangsu border and in 1895 was causing sufficient concern for news of it to reach the emperor. The response of Li Bingheng, the Governor of Shandong, was on the one hand to encourage the formation of militia and on the other to use the Big Swords against the bandits. However, the Big Swords also became involved in increasingly serious anti-Christian incidents. It was this situation which lent credence to the view that the Boxers were originally militia raised by xenophobic officials, a view now discredited.[32]

More plausibly, the origins of the Boxer movement have been traced to Guan county, on the Shandong–Zhili boundary, and to the activities of a martial arts group known as the Plum Flower Boxers, which clashed with missionaries there in 1898. The Boxer slogan, 'Support the Qing, destroy the foreign [religion]' appeared in that district. But the two characteristic features of the Boxer movement in the form which was to sweep across north China – spirit possession and the invulnerability rituals which gave protection from foreign bullets – had not yet been incorporated. These features were adopted by a group calling itself the Spirit Boxers which appeared in north-west Shandong in 1896. Any young man with a pure heart, who went through a simple ritual, could become possessed by his particular deity and would then become invulnerable. Spirit Boxers were at first associated with healing, but from late 1898 the movement began to spread rapidly and Spirit Boxers began to threaten Christians. By mid-1899 the name 'Spirit Boxers' was being replaced by 'Boxers United in Righteousness'. The movement was diffused by demonstrations of boxing and the establishment of boxing grounds in villages. Clashes with Christian converts, who also used the market-place to attract converts, became increasingly frequent.[33]

The court's response to these developments was at first very uncertain. It had been unable to resist foreign demands for the dismissal of Li Bingheng after the German seizure of Jiaozhou bay. During the Hundred Days' reforms the spread of Boxer activities had received little attention from the government. After the September 1898 coup, the Empress Dowager issued two edicts which stressed the need to protect missionaries and to prevent untoward incidents. In Shandong Li

Bingheng had been replaced Yu Xian, a Manchu official, and it was he who dealt with the rising tide of Boxer activism in 1899, which as a popular movement might become a threat to the dynasty. It has been suggested that the Spirit Boxers were originally anti-Qing Ming loyalists and that Yu Xian converted their anti-dynastic sentiment to one which was pro-dynastic while still aimed at foreigners. This suggestion has been dismissed, not least because Yu Xian had previously acted firmly to suppress militant groups.[34] As Boxer disturbances multiplied in late 1899, Yu Xian tried to control events by arresting the leaders but foreigners, suspecting that he was sympathetic to the movement, protested to the Zongli Yamen and in December he was dismissed and replaced by Yuan Shikai, who was to carry out a bloody suppression of the Boxers.

It was at this point that court policy towards the Boxers began to change. In January 1900 the court issued an edict which enjoined officials to distinguish between outlaws and 'law-abiding citizens who practice various arts to protect themselves and their families'.[35] A conflict developed between the supporters of the Empress Dowager and supporters of the emperor. The former 'became dominated by a small and bitterly anti-foreign clique of Manchu princes'.[36] The issue which divided the factions was whether the policy towards Boxers should be of pacification or of annihilation. For several months the court was paralysed because of indecision on this matter.

In early 1900 Boxer activity spread across Zhili. Accusations were made that Christians had caused the drought affecting the province and increasingly severe clashes occurred between Boxers and Christian converts. In May Boxer groups were on the outskirts of Beijing and foreign alarm reached such a pitch that reinforcements for the legation guards were summoned and twenty-four warships stood offshore at Tianjin. The Boxers now began a more general attack on foreigners and this led to further foreign intervention. On 10 June Admiral Seymour and two thousand men set out from Tianjin to protect the Beijing legations. The Tianjin–Beijing railway line was cut by the Boxers and Seymour's force had to retire to Tianjin – a victory which raised the Boxers' reputation and increased fears of a foreign reprisal. These fears were justified when on 17 June the Western powers seized the Dagu forts which controlled access to Tianjin.

The court was now in an acute dilemma. Responsible officials were well aware of the danger of confronting the Western powers. On the other hand, acceding to foreign demands and attempting to suppress the Boxers would leave the dynasty facing a popular rebellion. On 21 June the court issued an edict, referred to as a 'declaration of war', which blamed the hostilities on foreigners and called for resistance. In some parts of north China attacks on foreigners reached a crescendo, the most notorious example occurring in Shanxi where Yu Xian was now governor. He personally supervised the execution of forty-four missionaries and their families. But in Shandong Yuan Shikai continued to suppress the Boxers and he and other senior provincial officials, including Li Hongzhang at Guangzhou, Zhang Zhidong at Wuchang and Liu Kunyi at Nanjing, refused to recognize the legitimacy of the declaration.[37]

From the European viewpoint the most dramatic episode in the uprising was the siege of the Beijing legations, which began on 20 June and lasted for fifty-five days. The many accounts of the siege describe an heroic resistance, but in truth the attack was never pushed home vigorously. This may have been because of the restraint exercised by Rong Lu, the Commander-in-Chief of the Beiyang forces.[38] The Boxers also besieged the Roman Catholic cathedral in Beijing where many Chinese Christians, including 850 schoolgirls, had taken refuge. The Boxers ascribed their failure to capture the cathedral to the polluting influence of the women inside. To counter this they attempted to use a Boxer unit composed of young women, known as the Red Lantern Shining, which claimed to be able to ride upon the clouds and bring down destruction on those prescribed.

The siege of the legations and the cathedral was brought to an end on 14 August when a much larger international force reached Beijing. The Empress Dowager and the emperor retired to Xi'an. The troops of the foreign powers, including those of Japan, looted Beijing and carried out punitive expeditions in the surrounding area, and Russia took the opportunity to occupy Manchuria. In September 1901 China agreed to the Boxer protocol, which required the execution of ten officials, including Yu Xian, and the punishment of one hundred others, the suspension of the examinations in forty-five cities, the destruction of the forts barring access to Beijing and the payment of an indemnity of 450 million taels, a sum so large that China was allowed to increase import duties to 5 per cent to raise revenue to pay it.

Why was China not Partitioned?

In 1900 Beijing was under foreign occupation. The emperor and the Empress Dowager had fled and the future of the dynasty was uncertain. The country had already been divided into spheres of influence and now Manchuria had been occupied by Russia. In the light of this situation, the question has often been posed: why was the country not partitioned?

Through much of the nineteenth century Britain as the dominant foreign power had assumed that her commercial interests were best served by preserving the Manchu dynasty. That policy had been undermined by China's defeat in the Sino-Japanese War and the subsequent scramble for concessions. But, although the scramble had intensified foreign encroachment, it had also shown that international rivalry made agreement over a partition very unlikely. The friction caused between Britain and France and Russia over the construction of the Beijing–Hankou railway was a good example of this.

Another explanation also refers to the actions of the Western powers as the reason for restraint. In 1899 and again in 1900 the United States, in the person of John Hay, the Secretary of State, issued diplomatic notes concerning the future of China. In the note of 1900 there was a statement of support for the preservation of China's 'territorial and administrative entity' – the word 'entity' was later changed to 'integrity'. This has sometimes been presented as merely an idealistic statement, but it also conformed with the United States' interest in securing open access to China.[39]

After the Boxer uprising, Sir Robert Hart, Inspector-General of the Imperial Maritime Customs, identified the options available to Britain.

There would seem to be a choice between three courses – partition, change of dynasty, or patching up the Manchoo rule. As regards partition – that plan, like every other, has its good and its bad sides; but, with such an enormous population, it could never be expected to be a final settlement. . . . That the future will have a 'yellow' question – perhaps a yellow 'peril' – to deal with, is as certain as that the sun will shine tomorrow. . . . As to setting up a new dynasty – there is no man of mark all China would accept; the plan would plunge the country into years of anarchy. . . . Remains, then, the third plan – to accept the existing dynasty as a going concern, and, in a word, make the best of it.[40]

All these explanations assume that China was at the mercy of Western imperialism. To accept this view implies disregarding the evidence of the emergence of a stronger and more coherent Chinese resistance in the years after the defeat by Japan.

The urgent need for China to defend itself was expressed forcefully by Kang Youwei and was a prelude to the Hundred Days' reforms.

The Russians are spying on us in the north and the English are peeping at us on the west; the French are staring at us in the south and the Japanese are watching us in the east. Living in the midst of these four strong neighbors, and being the Middle Kingdom, China is in imminent peril.[41]

From this perspective the Boxer uprising should be seen not as a catastrophe, but as 'a warning to the foreigner not to attempt the partition of China'.[42] This warning came not from the court, which had recklessly manipulated the Boxers, nor from the senior provincial officials who had kept out of the conflict, but from the people themselves.[43]

John E. Schrecker identified a more coherent form of resistance in the Chinese response to German imperialism in Shandong. Section II of the Treaty of Jiaozhou had granted Germany a concession to build three railway lines across the province and to operate mines within 10 miles of the roadbeds on either side. These concessions were to be exploited by 'Sino-German' companies, although this provision was regarded by Germany at the time as insignificant. However, it provided a loophole for one of the most successful instances of the 'rights recovery movement', an informal campaign in which merchant and gentry groups, with the support of officials, redeemed or countered economic concessions granted to foreign powers. The best example of this in Shandong was Chinese encroachment on German mining concessions, but there were other important campaigns, for example for the recovery of the Guangzhou–Hankou railway rights.[44] According to Schrecker this was a response not only to German economic imperialism, but also to China's loss of national sovereignty. This led to the emergence of a nationalist foreign policy committed to the preservation and recovery of that sovereignty.[45]

The Late Qing Reforms

After the Boxer uprising it became apparent that there was no longer a consensus on how China should be saved from internal and external threats. From about 1895, small groups emerged which were committed to the overthrow of the Manchus by force. The survivors of the reform movement, in the persons of Kang Youwei and Liang Qichao, called for the introduction of a constitutional monarchy. Meanwhile, the Manchu monarchy, to save itself, gave its support to a programme of conservative reform.

On 29 January 1901, while still in Xi'an, the Empress Dowager issued an edict in which she attributed China's problems to the shortcomings of the emperor and the failures of officials and procedures. The edict then called for the adoption of the strong points of foreign countries to make up for China's shortcomings. It criticized self-strengthening as being limited to 'the skin and hair of Western technology, but not the fundamental source of Western government'. Finally it called for senior officials to submit memorials making suggestions for reform.[46]

In the event the most important suggestions, and the ones which were to be followed, were made by Zhang Zhidong and Liu Kunyi. Their proposals included the establishment of modern schools, the reform of the examination system, the sending of students abroad, military reforms, improvements to industry and agriculture, legal and financial reforms and the replacement of the Six Boards of government with twelve ministries. Their suggestions were accepted and formed the basis of the reform programme which was thereupon instituted.

The main elements of the reform programme, and the main significance attached to these reforms, may be summarized under four headings: education, military, administrative (including fiscal and legal) and constitutional. The educational reforms began immediately with the abolition of the eight-legged essay and the revision of the classical examination syllabus to include reference to Western knowledge. In Hunan Zhang Zhidong had already initiated a reform replacing the shuyuan, the traditional Confucian academies, with schools based on Western or Japanese models. An edict issued in September 1901 announced that all academies were to be converted into colleges, all prefectures were to establish middle schools and all districts were to establish primary schools. These schools were to have a Sino-Western curriculum. In another edict approval was given to sending students overseas. On their return they would be entitled to sit the civil service examinations and be awarded either juren or jinshi degrees. There remained the matter of the examination system itself. In their original submissions Zhang Zhidong and Liu Kunyi had recommended that it should be replaced in stages and that at some time in the future the bureaucracy should be recruited from graduates of the new schools. After Japan's victory in the Russo-Japanese War, the need for rapid progress was apparent and Zhang Zhidong and Yuan Shikai petitioned for the immediate abolition of the examination system. On 2 September 1905 the Empress Dowager responded by issuing an edict to that effect.[47] As a consequence of these reforms, by 1909, according to official statistics, China had 52,348 schools and 1,560,270 students attending them.[48] In December of the same year a Ministry of Education was established to co-ordinate the educational programme.

The need for military reform had been apparent since the Sino-Japanese War had demonstrated the incompetence of the banner forces and the Army of the Green Standard and the incapacity of the regional armies which had come into being at the time of the mid-century rebellions. In 1896 two new armies were established. At Nanjing, Zhang Zhidong organized the Self-Strengthening Army and recruited German instructors to the Nanjing Military Academy which he had founded.[49] In the north Yuan Shikai took command of the Newly-Established Army, which was to be equipped with Mauser rifles and Maxim machine-guns. Both armies had minimum physical standards for their recruits and at least in theory did not accept opium addicts and men with criminal records.

In 1901 the Qing government began its own programme of military reform. The traditional military examinations were abolished and the Army of the Green Standard was reduced in size. The main objective was to create a national army which would be under the control of central government. This New Army was to comprise thirty-six divisions or 450,000 men and would be supported by a reserve. It was to be a volunteer force and its officers were to be sent to Japan for training. In 1906 an Army Ministry was created which was to control all land forces in the empire. One of its first measures was to take control of four of the six divisions commanded by Yuan Shikai. This degree of central government control over the armed forces was unprecedented and the break with the past was widened when Yuan Shikai and Zhang Zhidong were removed from their governor-generalships and the command of their military forces was transferred to Beijing. The involvement of the court in military affairs became even more apparent after the death of the Guangxu emperor in 1908. Prince Chun, the father of the infant emperor, became regent and then appointed imperial clansmen to positions of military responsibility, a policy which alarmed even senior Manchu military leaders.[50]

The range of the late Qing reforms was remarkable. The court lent its support to a campaign against foot-binding, a practice which had already been condemned by Westerners and which had been attacked by Kang Youwei. A decree against foot-binding was promulgated in February 1902 which at first was only effective in the cities and among the higher classes. In 1906 another edict prohibited the use of opium and orders were issued to restrict its cultivation and importation. By 1911, according to a Western observer, poppy cultivation had been completely eradicated in large areas of China.[51] Important legal reforms were initiated. A reason given by Western powers for the inclusion of extraterritoriality in the unequal treaties was the cruelty of the punishments prescribed under the Qing penal code. These punishments were now deleted, a new criminal code was drafted and work began on producing civil and commercial codes.

The work on a commercial code indicated that the Qing government was now prepared to take an interest in economic affairs. Until the end of the nineteenth century both the government and potential Chinese investors had been suspicious of railway construction. However, for two reasons the Boxer uprising brought about a distinct change of attitude. When Admiral Seymour attempted to relieve the Beijing legations he found that a section of track had been dismantled and he was unable to rebuild it under battlefield conditions. However, the Chinese troops sent to oppose him were able to use the railway. Two months later, when the allied armies marched to relieve Beijing, they had to march in the heat along the line of the railway because the track had been torn up. On this occasion the existence of a railway proved to be of greater help to the defenders than to the invaders.[52]

The second reason concerned the growth of nationalist feeling in China and the effect that this had on railway investment. China's first railways had largely been financed by foreign loans, but after the Boxer uprising a demand grew for 'self-built railroads'. As the government was unable to raise the capital required for railway construction it agreed to autonomous local railroad construction, that is to say the construction of provincial railway lines using capital raised locally from merchant and gentry groups. By 1907 at least nineteen such local railways had been authorized. However, the central government became increasingly uneasy about this development, which increased provincial separatism, which denied the government a potential source of revenue and which encouraged a Han nationalism critical of the Manchu court. In 1910 it decided to solicit foreign loans for railway construction. In May of the following year it announced a policy of government ownership of the trunk railway lines and the takeover of the 'self-built railroads', a policy which triggered off the crisis which led to the revolution.

The other major area of reform concerned constitutional change. This had not been part of the original programme, and the Empress Dowager's decision to permit reform in this area is usually attributed to the outcome of the Russo-Japanese War of 1904–5. Japan had introduced a constitutional form of government in 1890 and the victory over Russia was perceived as the triumph of constitutionalism over autocracy. In July 1905 the Empress Dowager announced her commitment to constitutional change. The first move was to send missions abroad, in particular to Germany and Japan, to study forms of constitutional government. In the meantime Liang Qichao, from outside China, argued for the urgent transformation of China into a genuine constitutional monarchy. The case was taken up by the Shanghai press, one newspaper asking 'Can we solve China's problems?' and answering its own question, 'That depends upon whether we get a constitution. Let us not forget that a constitution is the foundation of politics'.[53]

In August 1908 the government announced a programme which would lead to the establishment of a constitutional monarchy in nine years' time, a rate of progress which greatly disappointed the advocates of constitutionalism. Nevertheless, the first stage of that programme, the election of provincial assemblies in 1909, was an important advance. The franchise was restricted to holders of degrees, former officials and those who had a business valued at over 5,000 yuan, resulting in only 0.42 per cent of the population having the vote. Most of those who were elected were holders of civil degrees.[54] The provincial assemblies had very limited powers and these could only be exercised with the consent of the provincial governor and the governor-general. Nevertheless, when the assemblies met it was apparent that they would not be without influence. For the first time in China's history elected bodies could discuss matters of public interest, although these matters were restricted to provincial affairs. The debates often led to conflict with the provincial governor, who had the power of veto over assembly decisions. This in turn prompted demands for the immediate election of a national assembly which would have genuine power.

The first National Assembly was also elected in 1909. Half of its membership consisted of imperial nominees, the other half was elected from the membership of the provincial assemblies. As with the provincial assemblies, the intended function of the National Assembly was consultative. This role was to continue until 1917 when a parliament with legislative powers would be elected. When the National Assembly convened in October 1910 the pressure on the regency for more rapid constitutional progress was already strong and the date for the introduction of a parliament was advanced to 1913.

The Significance of the Reforms

Alexis de Tocqueville once remarked,

> . . . it is not always when things are going from bad to worse that revolutions break out. On the contrary, it oftener happens that when a people which has put up with an oppressive rule over a long period without protest suddenly finds the government relaxing the pressure, it takes up arms against it.[55]

Most evaluations of the significance of the late Qing reforms have shared this view. M.E. Cameron, the first Western writer to deal with the subject at length, concluded that the Empress Dowager was sincere in her commitment to reform and the programme she initiated had significant achievements. However, she argued that even more significant were the reforms which she did not attempt, notably financial reform and the elimination of corruption. This was not because of a disregard for China's chief needs, but because of the weakness of the court, which could not overcome the vested interests involved.[56] Mary Wright suggested that the reforms contributed positively to the coming of the revolution, by setting new forces in motion, and by generating resistance, not to the goals of the reforms but to the means the imperial government had adopted to achieve them.[57] Frederic Wakeman went further, arguing that the reforms accelerated the formation of new elites, which were to play a larger role in the fall of the dynasty than were radicals such as Sun Zhongshan (Sun Yatsen).[58] Ichiko Chuzo argued that the reforms weakened the government's position because they were contradictory in their effect. The government allowed a wider expression of public opinion but repressed individual expressions of thought. The reforms were supported or opposed by factional interests. For example, after the deaths of the Guangxu emperor and the Empress Dowager in 1908, Prince Chun gained the ascendancy and he forced Yuan Shikai, the most prominent of the military reformers, to retire. To pay for the reforms provincial governments levied extra taxes, which caused popular unrest, and the central government raised foreign loans, which affronted nationalist feeling. Finally the reforms were undertaken for a selfish purpose rather than in the national interest: 'it was reform for the sake of preserving the Qing dynasty'.[59]

19

The 1911 Revolution

On 10 October 1911 (the 'Double Tenth') a mutiny headed by officers from New Army units stationed at Wuchang led to the seizure of the triple city known as Wuhan. The rebels obtained the support of the gentry leaders of the Hubei provincial assembly, which declared the province independent from the empire and the establishment of a republic. Before the end of the month six other provinces had followed suit and by the beginning of December all the provinces of southern and central China had seceded. Sun Zhongshan (Sun Yatsen) was elected provisional President of the new republic. Shortly after the Wuhan uprising the court appealed to Yuan Shikai for support. Instead he negotiated the abdication of the Manchus and in March 1912 he was elected President of the Republic of China.

Social Changes

Despite J.G. von Herder's claim that China was an 'embalmed mummy',[1] Chinese society has never been unchanging. However, in last decades of the Qing dynasty the pace of change did accelerate rapidly. All classes in society were affected, but the most significant changes were those which concerned the traditional elite and those which led to the emergence of new social groups.

The size and composition of the traditional elite, the gentry, had altered as a consequence of the mid-nineteenth-century rebellions. The increase in numbers and change in composition upset the careful balance which had been struck between aspirants to office and those who became officials, and between those who had gone through the examination system and those who had not. In the late nineteenth century the gentry began to move away from their traditional functions and to assume roles which had hitherto been denied to them. Some gentry became involved in military affairs, others undertook to collect taxes or to involve themselves in legal disputes. Frederic Wakeman has suggested that in the past the difference in status and function between the upper and lower gentry had been so great that the court had been able to exploit it. However, after the mid-nineteenth-century rebellions the upper and lower gentry – or the gentry-commoners as he prefers to describe the latter – began to form a mutually advantageous alliance:

[T]he upper gentry now relied upon gentry-commoners to manage the administrative infrastructure of tax collection offices, famine relief bureaus, rent control agencies, and quartermaster depots that were needed to restore law and order to the countryside.[2]

Another important change related to the distinction made between the gentry and the merchants. In theory Confucianists extolled scholarship and deprecated commerce, but in practice many gentry families supported themselves in part through commercial activities. In the late nineteenth century the gap between the two groups narrowed further. The status of merchants rose and gentry became more involved in, and contributed more to, projects relating to mining, railways and other industries. This resulted in what has been described as a 'merchant-gentry alliance'.[3]

Another group which had traditionally been held in low esteem was the military class. A popular proverb stated: 'good iron is not used to make nails, and good men are not used to make soldiers'. This overstated the lowliness of their position in society. Alongside the civil examination system there were examinations for military degrees, which were contested with some seriousness. Successful candidates acquired gentry status and could then advance into the upper gentry. A more general rise in the status of professional soldiers began with the formation of the regional armies to combat the rebellions. It continued with the raising of new armies after the Sino-Japanese War and with the military reforms initiated by the Qing in the last decade of the dynasty. The officers in these forces formed a new social elite, although partly derived from the traditional gentry, who were now encouraging their sons to pursue military careers. The educational qualifications required of new recruits were higher and professional training was available through the provincial military academies, which also provided instruction in the sciences and in foreign languages.[4] In addition promising cadets were sent to military schools abroad, particularly in Japan. There many of them came into contact with revolutionary ideas and revolutionary organizations. More generally sections of the New Army became imbued with a sense of nationalism, which revealed itself in a determination to achieve military self-sufficiency for their country. Another expression of this was the movement to cut off the queue, the symbol of subservience to the Manchus, the wearing of which was regarded as incongruous for a modern soldier.[5]

The improvement in the status of merchants was also notable. In the past Chinese merchants had on occasions accumulated very large fortunes, but as a class they were socially isolated and politically weak. In the nineteenth century it became easier for merchants to acquire status and to obtain privileges through the purchase of degrees. In Hankou, in the latter half of the nineteenth century at least half of the wholesale merchants and large brokers held purchased titles.[6] At the same time new types of merchant began to appear. The term 'compradore', derived from the Portuguese word for a buyer, was first used to describe the 'licensed head servant' of a foreign household. In time compradores came to occupy a pivotal position in the operation of Western firms in China. They handled all aspects of the Chinese side of the business, and some grew wealthy and became partners or creditors in foreign firms. An outstanding example of such a person was Tang Tingshu (Tong King-sing), who began his career with Jardine, Matheson and Company in 1861. Twelve years later Li Hongzhang appointed him to run the China Merchants' Steam Navigation Company and from 1876 he was involved in the opening of the Kaiping mines. Notwithstanding his successful career as a manager, Tang Tingshu, like many other compradores, also joined the traditional elite by purchasing an official title.[7]

Another newly emerged merchant group was that of the overseas Chinese capitalists. By 1911 as many as ten million Chinese lived abroad. The vast majority of them were labourers working on the rubber plantations and tin mines of South-East Asia. They hoped that one day they would return to China and in the meantime they sent home remittances to support their families. A few became rich and invested part of their fortunes in China and some played an influential role in late-Qing plans for the development of their native country. Outstanding among these was Zhang Bishi (1840–1916), who had emigrated at the age of seventeen and who had built up a wide range of business interests including a major shipping line which dominated the coastal trade of Sumatra. After 1895 he began to invest in China, promoting a wide variety of enterprises including railways, textile mills and the Imperial Bank of China.[8]

Merchants were traditionally allowed to form guilds, associations based on the provision of specific products or services. Those from outside the community also formed that typically Chinese organization the *huiguan*, the association for people of a common geographical origin. Between 1895 and 1911 merchants in China began to develop new types of association and for the first time began to involve themselves in politics. In response to the scramble for concessions and the threat of further Western encroachment, merchants in cities such as Shanghai and Guangzhou organized unofficial commercial associations to protect their interests. Concerned about this development, and anxious to keep the merchants on their side in resisting imperialist encroachment, from 1904 the court began to encourage the establishment of chambers of commerce, which would be run by the merchants in an officially approved framework.[9]

All the above changes were undoubtedly important in creating the society which by the early years of the twentieth century was being described as 'Young China'. However, the most important element has yet to be discussed: the effects of changes in education and in particular the inclusion of Western studies in the curriculum. Some aspects of this have already been referred to, including the measures taken as part of the self-strengthening programme and the development of missionary education. However, it was only after 1895 that leading officials such as Zhang Zhidong made educational reform a priority, and only after 1901 that the government committed itself to extensive reform. Once reform had begun, progress towards creating a new school system was rapid. By 1902, in Zhejiang alone, at least thirty-six new schools had been established, for the most part on the initiative of merchant-gentry groups.[10] In 1909, in the country as a whole, there were 50,000 primary schools with an enrolment of nearly one and a half million pupils.

The main political significance of these new schools does not lie in the increase in their enrolment, nor in any difference in the class background of the pupils admitted, nor even in any major alteration to the curriculum, for none of these changes was as great a break with the past as might be supposed. The reforms were conservative in spirit and this was shown clearly in the provision for the education of girls. Zhang Zhidong had specifically forbidden the establishment of girls' schools in his 1904 school regulations. In his view if girls were to be educated this should be done at home and he demonstrated his commitment to this principle by establishing the Revere Chastity School in Hubei, which trained governesses for rich families. Nevertheless, after 1904 the number of both missionary and Chinese girls' schools continued to grow. Schooling for women was recognized and regulated from 1907, but it remained a controversial subject. Only between 1 and 2 per cent of the students in the new schools were girls.[11]

Despite these intentions the reforms had a significant impact. The ideology projected by the new school system – that it was part of Young China – raised the expectations of students, but they were then frustrated by the poor teaching and petty restrictions which they commonly encountered.[12] An important influence was exerted by students who had studied abroad. This movement, which has been described as 'probably the largest mass movement of students overseas in world history up to this point',[13] reached its peak in 1905–6, when between six and twenty thousand Chinese students were studying in Japan. When abroad students were exposed to a wide variety of influences and often rejected aspects of Chinese customs and culture. To avoid comment about their appearance many adopted Western dress and had their queues cut. When they had graduated and had returned to China, they were re-examined and awarded Chinese degrees, in the hope that they would be re-absorbed into the educational system or into appropriate employment. However, few students who had spent time abroad escaped a sense of 'cultural ambivalence', of uncertainty on how far they should proclaim their Westernization or retain their Chineseness.[14]

In the period 1895–1911 many other aspects of Chinese urban society appeared to change irreversibly. Under the terms of the Treaty of Shimonoseki industries could be established in the treaty ports. The number of workers employed in such industries – the new industrial proletariat – grew from 100,000 to 660,000. The biggest concentration of labour was in Shanghai, and it was there that the first industrial strikes took place. Factory conditions were often extremely poor, but workers found it difficult to combine their protests as their primary allegiance was usually to workers from their native district rather than to the workforce as a whole.[15]

During this period the population of some cities, in particular the treaty ports, grew very rapidly. Between 1880 and 1900 the population of Shanghai rose from 107,000 to 345,000 and by 1911 it had risen to 1,250,000. The population of these cities was dominated by young adult male immigrants, many of whom could not find permanent employment. However, during the same period other cities declined and there is no conclusive evidence to show that between 1840 and 1950 the proportion of the population living in large settlements increased. A figure of 6 per cent of the population living in conurbations of 50,000 or more is quoted for the 1930s and this may indicate the situation which prevailed in the late Qing.[16]

The movement of peasants to cities was only one of the changes affecting the mass of the population. A notable feature of late nineteenth-century China was the continued internal migration, the most dramatic example of which was migration to Manchuria. In 1858 and again in 1860 China had agreed to cede to Russia enormous tracts of territory north of the Amur and east of the Ussuri rivers, which exposed Manchuria to Russian encroachment. To counter this the Qing government relaxed restrictions on movement into the Manchu homeland and encouraged Chinese colonization of the region. Much of this migration was by displaced peasants and was prompted by a combination of factors including population growth, rebellion, unemployment brought about by new industries and natural causes. It has been suggested that this migration, and the evidence of urban drift, was an indication of rural decline characterized by very high levels of rural unemployment or underemployment.[17] This pessimistic view emphasizes the growth of a sub-proletariat, of a section of the population which was completely destitute, which had no regular employment or fixed abode and which was exceptionally vulnerable to the effects of famine and epidemics.[18] Taken together with previous remarks about the break-up of the traditional social elite and the emergence of new groups in Chinese society, the picture presented is that of a traditional social system which had reached the point of terminal decline.

There may be some truth in this view, but it has not gone unchallenged. Albert Feuerwerker pointed out that, in the absence of reliable statistics, statements about economic trends in the agrarian sector in this period are speculative. He argued that there was no conclusive evidence of a 'drastic secular fall in the peasant standard of living' in the period 1870–1911.[19] Arthur Smith, an American missionary who had spent twenty-two years in China, observed not rural decline but rural stagnation. In 1899 he wrote:

A Chinese village is physically and intellectually a fixture. Could one gaze backward through a vista of five hundred years at the panorama which that vast stretch of modern history would present, he would probably see little more and little less than he sees to-day. The buildings now standing are not indeed five hundred years old, but they are just such houses as half a millennium ago occupied the same sites, 'similar and similarly situated.' Some families that then lived in adobe dwellings now flourish under roofs of tile in houses of brick. Other families have become extinct. Now and then a new one may have appeared, but this is irregular and exceptional. Those who now subsist in this collection of earth-built abodes are the lineal descendants of those who lived there when Columbus discovered America. The descendants are doing just what their ancestors did, no more, no less, no other. They cultivate the same fields in the same way (albeit a few of the crops are modern); they go to the same markets in the same invariable order; buy, sell, and wear the same articles; marry and are given in marriage according to the same pattern.[20]

The Revolutionary Movement

According to the well-established Nationalist version of Chinese history, the 1911 revolution was largely the work of a revolutionary movement headed by Sun Zhongshan and motivated primarily by anti-Manchu feeling. Most recent interpretations of the revolution have qualified the importance of the revolutionary movement, judging it to be 'important less for what it contributed to the events of 1900–13 than for the revolutionary tradition it created'.[21] It would nevertheless be perverse to write about the revolution without mentioning some of the revolutionaries involved and without assessing the contribution of the movement to the revolution they sought to bring about.

Certainly a large share of the credit for initiating the revolutionary movement should go to Sun Zhongshan. Born near Guangzhou in 1866, Sun then spent part of his childhood in Hawaii. He was mission educated and became a Christian before he qualified as a doctor in Xianggang. At an early age he became interested in how China might be reformed and he offered his ideas to several reform-minded officials, including Li Hongzhang, who ignored his suggestions. At that point Sun abandoned reform and while in Honolulu in 1894 he formed a revolutionary group, the Society to Restore China's Prosperity. The hundred-odd members of the society were mainly from Zhongshan, Sun's native district near Guangzhou. In the following year he organized another branch of the society in Xianggang and in March 1895, as the disastrous war with Japan was coming to its end, Sun and his close supporters formulated a plan to capture Guangzhou in October. The plan assumed that China was ripe for revolution and that the secret societies and bandit gangs would rise in rebellion as soon as the rebels had struck the initial spark.[22] The plot was discovered and Sun fled to Japan with a price on his head. He was not to return to the Chinese mainland, apart from the briefest of forays, for more than sixteen years.

Over the next few years Sun travelled widely seeking support for his plans. While he was in Japan he cut off his queue and took on the appearance of a Japanese. When he was in London in 1896 he was seized by the staff of the Chinese legation and would have been returned to China for trial and execution if he had not managed to smuggle out a note in a laundry basket to a former teacher, a Dr Cantlie, who alerted the authorities and obtained Sun's release. This incident convinced Sun of his destiny and raised his hopes that Britain would support the revolutionary movement. Sun also made contact with Kang Youwei and Liang Qichao, the reformers of 1898, but failed to establish any common front with them. In 1900 he attempted another uprising, this time at Huizhou, east of Guangzhou. This did receive some popular support, but it was also crushed easily, demonstrating that a popular movement had little chance of succeeding against the forces commanded by the Qing.

In the meantime other revolutionary figures had emerged and other revolutionary groups had been formed. Among the revolutionaries was Zou Rong (1885–1905), who had been inspired by Tan Sitong, the martyr of the Hundred Days' reforms of 1898. Zou Rong was in Japan in 1903 when Japan failed to withdraw the troops which had occupied Manchuria since the Boxer uprising, an omission which infuriated Chinese students who suspected Manchu collusion. Zou Rong's response was to write an outspoken pamphlet in which he referred to 'the maladministration of the ambitious, tribal, rapacious Manchus'. He argued that the cruelty of the Manchu conquest – he recalled the infamous ten-day massacre in Yangzhou – and their enslavement of the Chinese, justified revolution. The pamphlet was published in Shanghai under the title *The Revolutionary Army* and led to Zou Rong being tried and imprisoned by the Mixed Court, the tribunal which heard cases brought against Chinese in the International Settlement. He died before he had completed his sentence.[23]

Another notable figure was Qiu Jin (1875–1907). She came from a gentry family from Zhejiang, had received a good education and had entered an arranged marriage. She was in Beijing with her husband in 1900 when the city was occupied by the international relief force, an incident which convinced her that China was on the brink of disaster. By the end of 1903 she had decided to leave her husband, to unbind her feet and to go to Japan to study. By so doing she was consciously striking a blow for women's rights while at the same time uniting that cause with nationalism. While in Tokyo she became acquainted with a leading member of the Zhejiang Restoration society. She became a well-known figure, dressing in men's clothes, carrying a short sword and frequently railing at other students for their apathy. After returning to China she began teaching in Zhejiang, while at the same time involving herself in plotting revolution with the Restoration society. Among her heroes was Sofia Perovskaya, who was hanged for her part in the assassination of Tsar Alexander II. From her and others Qiu Jin learned how an heroic elite could waken a sleeping populace and how a hero should be willing to die for the cause. So, when the Restoration society plot was discovered, she made no attempt to escape. She refused to confess under torture and was summarily executed.[24]

An important group among the revolutionaries came from Hunan. The gentry from this province had led the resistance to the Taiping rebellion and the reassertion of Confucian orthodoxy. Hunan had also witnessed the most substantial outbreaks of popular anti-foreignism expressed in the forms of anti-missionary incidents and secret society activity. Yet it was also this province which in the 1890s was at the forefront of the adoption of Westernizing reforms. The revolutionary movement was born out of this situation. Its leaders broke with the conservative reform movement in 1898. For a time they associated with the Gelaohui, the Elder Brothers society, the largest secret society organization in central China, which from the 1890s had been expressing anti-Qing sentiments. This culminated in December 1906 with the Pingliuli uprising, which was led by the Gelaohui but put down rather easily by the troops sent by Zhang Zhidong. From this incident the revolutionaries learned of the limitations of the secret societies and they switched their efforts to the conversion of members of the New Armies to the revolutionary cause.

Representative of this evolution was Huang Xing (1874–1916), who came from Changsha, the provincial capital of Hunan. When a student in Japan he had been outraged by the continued Russian occupation of Manchuria and when he returned to Hunan he organized the Huaxinghui, the Society for China's Revival. Among the society's founder members was Song Jiaoren, who was to play a prominent role in the 1911 revolution.[25]

It was in Tokyo in July 1905 that the next phase in the development of the revolutionary movement began. Russia's defeat at the hands of Japan and the events in Russia which followed, the mistreatment of Chinese immigrants to the United States, controversy over railway rights in China, all combined to increase national consciousness and revolutionary agitation, particularly among Chinese students in Japan.[26] It was at this point that Sun Zhongshan returned from Europe and had discussions with Huang Xing which resulted in the formation of the Tongmenghui, the Revolutionary Alliance. Sun was chosen as leader, but this was less because of his success as a revolutionary, or his ideological contribution, and more because of his experience of dealing with the Western powers and the support he could claim from some prominent Japanese individuals.[27]

The Revolutionary Alliance adopted Sun's political objectives which were expressed in a manifesto. This announced a four-point programme: drive out the Manchus, restore China, establish the republic and equalize landownership. Only the first of these points was clear and unequivocal. The call to restore China claimed 'China is the China of the Chinese', but it made no reference to Western imperialism and offered no suggestion on how China might be freed from it. The commitment to establish a republic referred to an elected president and an elected assembly, but did not elaborate on the constitutional arrangements which would apply. The fourth point, the equalization of landownership, offered a vague commitment to tax reform on the lines advocated by Henry George and John Stuart Mill, which had little relevance to the condition of the Chinese peasantry. Also included in the manifesto was an outline of a three-stage progression to democratic government. Immediately after the revolution the country would be placed under military law, while the evil practices of the past were being suppressed. Then would follow a period in which the military government would govern according to a provisional constitution – the arrangement to be referred to as political tutelage. Six years later the final stage would begin, with the introduction of a democratic constitution.[28]

The Revolutionary Alliance brought together all earlier revolutionary organizations apart from the Zhejiang Restoration society and under its aegis a lively debate took place about China's political future, although the problems of rural society were largely ignored. There was little contact between the alliance and the promoters of nationalist protest in the cities, for example those involved in demonstrations in Shanghai and Guangzhou against the Exclusion Act of 1904 which forbade Chinese immigration into the United States. The revolutionary strategy remained much as before, to use the secret societies to foment an uprising which would then spread to other provinces. In 1907 and 1908 six more abortive attempts took place. It was only in 1910 that a more determined attempt was made to subvert the army, with Huang Xing making contact with New Army units in Guangzhou. By then the Revolutionary Alliance had become riven by internal differences and the Qing government had persuaded foreign governments to restrict its activities.[29]

The 1911 Revolution

In 1910 it did not appear probable that China was on the verge of a revolution. The revolutionary movement had been unable to mount an effective challenge to the Qing dynasty. The dynasty itself appeared committed to a programme of reform which was beginning to produce results – by now Beijing had street lights and motor cars and no less than three railway stations.

However, at this point the dynasty's own actions precipitated a series of events which temporarily united the forces of opposition.[30] The sequence began with the Hankou–Sichuan railway crisis. It will be remembered that in response to the granting of extensive railway rights to foreign interests a rights recovery movement had arisen. Merchant and gentry consortia had raised capital and in some cases had built and begun to operate 'self-built' railways, occasionally very profitably. However, in Sichuan and in a number of other provinces, although railway companies had been chartered, insufficient capital had been raised (and some of what had been raised had been embezzled) and no construction had taken place. It was this situation which persuaded the government that it should assume the initiative and take over the construction of a national railway system using foreign loans for capital. In December 1908 Zhang Zhidong was appointed administrator of the Hankou–Sichuan line. By June 1909 he had reached a preliminary agreement with a consortium of English, French and German bankers for what became known as the Huguang loan of £6 million. Zhang died in October of that year and the negotiations were carried forward by Sheng Xuanhuai, by reputation the most venal and unscrupulous of senior officials.[31] In May 1911 it was announced that the 'self-built' railways were to be nationalized. A month later it was revealed that Sichuan investors would receive only partial compensation.[32]

The response in Sichuan was immediate. The Huguang loan had been denounced as 'a contract to sell the country'. Now a Sichuan Railway Protection League was established, which was led by Pu Dianjun, the Chairman of the Sichuan provincial assembly and a member of the upper gentry. The league 'functioned like a powerful shadow provincial government'.[33] It organized mass meetings, and its actions led to shops closing, to students boycotting classes and to talk of withholding payment of taxes. On 7 September the governor-general ordered the arrest of Pu Dianjun and other leaders of the league. At a violent protest in Chengdu government troops opened fire and about forty people were killed. The disturbances, perhaps fomented by secret society members, spread rapidly to other parts of the province, and the situation ran out of control. The government attempted to regain the initiative by transferring troops from Hubei, but it was unable to suppress the disorder.[34]

The neighbouring province of Hubei had its own record of revolutionary activities and some of these had involved soldiers of the New Army. From 1908 more serious attempts were made to organize a revolutionary movement in the armed forces. Early in 1911 a group of army revolutionaries, which called itself the Literary Institute, began to operate from an address in the Russian concession in Hankou. It had a loose connection with the Progressive Association, itself an offshoot of the Revolutionary Alliance. When news was received of the disastrous outcome of the April uprising in Guangzhou, the Progressive Association resolved that the provinces of Hubei and Hunan should become the focus of a new effort and that it would depend on the New Army in Wuchang to start an uprising in Hubei.

* Outbreak of revolution 10 October 1911, Wuhan
(Wuhan comprises the three cities
Hankou, Hanyang and Wuchang)

Provinces declaring for the revolution

by the end of October 1911

by early December 1911

RUSSIA

Amur R.

MANCHURIA

HEILONGJIANG

JILIN

OUTER MONGOLIA

MONGOLIA

INNER

ZHILI

Shenyang

FENGTIAN

Beijing

Tianjin

Dalian
(Japanese)

KOREA (Japanese)

Taiyuan

Wei Xian

SHANXI

Jinan

Qingdao
(German)

QINGHAI

GANSU

SHANDONG

Lanzhou

Xi'an

Kaifeng

JIANGXI

SHAANXI

HENAN

ANHUI

Nanjing

Shanghai

Yichang

Wuhan

Anqing

Hangzhou

Chengdu

ZHEJIANG

SICHUAN

Chongqing

Changsha

Nanchang

Pingliuli

HUNAN

JIANGSU

GUIZHOU

Guiyang

FUJIAN

Fuzhou

Kunming

Guilin

TAIWAN
(Japanese)

YUNNAN

GUANGXI

GUANGDONG

Guangzhou

Huizhou

Xianggang
(British)

INDOCHINA
(French)

Zhongshan

The 1911 Revolution and the dictatorship of Yuan Shikai.

Most interpretations of the events which followed stress that the success of the Wuchang military uprising was fortuitous. However, Edmund S.K. Fung has argued that to regard it in that way is 'to ignore the strength of the Hubei revolutionaries and the extent of the subversion already achieved in the Hubei New Army'.[35] Undoubtedly chance did play its part. The first plans were dislocated by the transfer of New Army units to deal with the crisis in Sichuan. The date of the uprising was then put back to allow revolutionary leaders including Song Jiaoren to arrive and assume the political leadership. Then an accidental bomb explosion led to the police discovering the plot and precipitated the decision to act. Even so the seizure of Wuchang was only achieved because of the pusillanimity of the Manchu Governor-General who fled from his yamen.

The revolutionaries who had gained control of the city included no senior military officers or important revolutionary leaders. Sun Zhongshan himself was in the United States and read about the Wuchang uprising in a newspaper. Unwilling to claim the leadership for themselves, the Wuchang rebels forced Li Yuanhong, the commander of the New Army's Twenty-first brigade, to accompany them to the provincial assembly. The assembly proclaimed the establishment of a republic of which the reluctant brigade commander was to be the military governor and the chairman of the assembly was to head the civil government. In effect power was immediately handed over to men who had never belonged to the revolutionary camp.[36] Messages were sent to the foreign consuls in Hankou promising that foreign interests would not be harmed and assurances were received that the powers would not aid the Manchus. Messages were also sent to other provincial assemblies and New Army units relating what had happened in Hubei and this led to declarations of independence by provinces throughout central and south China.

The dynasty, however, was not yet overthrown and its fate rested largely in the hands of Yuan Shikai. His role in subsequent events has been subject to a sharp difference in interpretation. Hostile views have remarked on Yuan's Machiavellian mind and his propensity to manipulate events which led him to deceive the revolutionaries and then to betray the republic. Alternatively, it has been suggested that Yuan's rise owed more to factors outside his control than to his own manoeuvres.[37]

Although Yuan had officially been in retirement since 1909, on the grounds that he had suffered an 'ailment of the foot', his influence with the commanders of the Beiyang army and more generally his national reputation remained strong, and this led both imperial and republican sides to ask him to assume a leadership role. The first overtures came from the court and his alleged reply was that he had not yet recovered from the 'ailment' to his foot which had forced his retirement. It seems unlikely that he ever considered saving the dynasty by crushing the revolution. The task of defeating the revolutionary army was too great and his command of the Beiyang army was by no means complete. It was therefore not surprising that he was prepared to deal with the revolutionaries, who regarded him as the one man who could achieve a Manchu abdication while preserving national unity and fending off the foreign powers.[38] As early as November Sun Zhongshan was supporting a proposal to offer Yuan the presidency of the new republic on the condition that he should abandon the dynasty. Negotiations on this matter were protracted and it was for this reason that in December Sun was elected provisional president. Further delays were then caused by a dispute over the location of the capital of the republic, whether it should be Nanjing, as Sun wished, or whether it should be Beijing, which was Yuan's power base. The decision in favour of Beijing has been seen as confirming Yuan's determination to protect his position. In March Yuan was inaugurated as provisional president and Sun stepped down the following month.

In the meantime Yuan had negotiated the end of the Manchu dynasty. The terms, entitled 'Articles of favourable treatment', were extremely generous. The emperor was to be allowed to live in the Summer Palace and would receive an annual subsidy of 4 million taels, which would be altered to $4 million when the currency reform had been completed. The Manchu princes and nobles would retain their titles and property and members of the banner forces would continue to receive their allowances pending reorganization.[39] The fate of the Manchu minority as a whole was less certain. According to Mary Wright, by the end of the Qing dynasty, the Manchu rank and file were almost completely sinicised. Despite the violence of the anti-Manchu language which had been used by the revolutionaries, only exceptionally did massacres of Manchus occur. More often it proved impossible to distinguish Manchu from Chinese and the Manchus disappeared into the population at large.[40] More recently Pamela Kyle Crossley has challenged the view of Manchu sinicisation, arguing that the Manchus in China continued to live in garrisons where they had developed a distinctive garrison culture. The garrisons in several cities were attacked. At Wuchang the Manchu 30th Regiment, which guarded the governor-general's yamen, was wiped out in something resembling 'racial slaughter'. At Yichang on the Upper Yangzi seventeen Manchu women and children were killed and their blood smeared on the doors of the yamen. The largest massacre occurred at Xi'an, three weeks after the outbreak of the revolution, where perhaps 20,000 Manchus were killed.[41]

Views on the 1911 Revolution

In recent times it has become common to treat the 1911 revolution not as a discrete event but as part of a much longer transformation. Mary Wright described the years 1900 to 1913 as the 'first phase' in a revolutionary process that was to extend to 1949 and beyond.[42] Jerome Grieder suggested that 1919, the year of the May Fourth incident, was a more significant year than 1911. Much of the 'old' China had survived the shock of the 1911 revolution, but in 1919 a new alliance of social forces attacked and subverted the very basis of the old culture.[43] Such views echoed Mao Zedong's observation in 'The Chinese Revolution and the Chinese Communist Party', published in 1940, that the bourgeois-democratic revolution began in China in 1919.[44]

Some of the more specific issues relating to the fall of the Qing dynasty have already been alluded to: the importance of the late Qing reforms in accelerating social change and encouraging the spread of nationalist ideas; the controversy over the relative importance of the revolutionary movement and the part played by Sun Zhongshan and other revolutionary leaders in bringing about the revolution; and the arguments relating to Yuan Shikai's advance to the presidency in 1912.

Did the events of 1911 to 1912 constitute a genuine revolution? Michael Gasster, commenting on a review of current writing on the topic, remarked wryly:

> The dialectic of writing on 1911 has made it first the revolution, then 'no revolution,' then 'something of a revolution,' and now back to 'not much of a revolution'. . . .

In his view 1911 was 'not so trifling a revolution' and he supported this by emphasizing the significance of the abolition of the imperial system.[45] This stress on the negative aspect of the event is evident in another influential interpretation, that of James Sheridan, who presented the 1911 revolution as an important stage in the disintegration of the traditional Chinese state.[46] This disintegration was shown most clearly by the declarations of provincial independence after the Wuchang revolt. The centrifugal movement which this implied may be related to the growth of provincialism. The crisis had been precipitated by the government's attempt to centralize control of the railways, which was part of its effort to augment its power. This ran counter to the growing identification with the interests of the province, shared to an extent by gentry, merchants and students.

The most interesting part of the discussion about the revolution concerns the roles played by various social groups, in particular those of the gentry, the bourgeoisie and the peasants. In the past the fate of a dynasty had been sealed when the gentry changed its allegiance. The fall of the Ming became inevitable when the Manchu invaders convinced the gentry that they would remain the social elite. In 1911 the decision of the gentry, as represented by the provincial assemblies, to secede from the empire, was a mortal blow to the Qing dynasty. But why did the gentry act as they did? According to Chang P'eng-yüan, the gentry of the provincial assemblies were constitutionalists, that is to say their main political objective was constitutional reform and the establishment of a parliament. They were therefore frustrated by the slowness of political reform and when the National Assembly, half of the members of which were drawn from the provincial assemblies, met in 1910 and was told that a parliament would not be elected immediately, their frustration turned to hostility. According to Chang, this was why the gentry abandoned the dynasty and supported the revolution.[47] A less favourable view of gentry motivation was put forward by Ichiko Chuzo. He argued that the position of the gentry had been undermined in the nineteenth century by the introduction of Western culture which had challenged the Confucian education which was the basis of the gentry's position. They had, therefore, resisted the Hundred Days' reforms, which sought to adopt the political and economic institutions of the West. However, when the court committed itself to a programme of constitutional reform, the gentry and rich merchants, and the many members of the lower gentry who were under their influence, reversed their position for 'they now saw in the assemblies an even more effective means than the examinations for assuring their own status and power'. Their objective was 'our native province governed by ourselves'. This they largely achieved, for according to Ichiko the gentry maintained their influence until the Communist victory of 1949.[48] Since these articles were written other writers have suggested that social and geographical divisions among the gentry may explain why some acted progressively and others in a selfish defence of their interests. Mark Elvin drew attention to the progressive activities of those with a gentry background in the treaty ports and Philip Kuhn distinguished between the conservatism of the local elite and the progressive attitudes of the national and provincial elites.[49]

The debates concerning the bourgeoisie and the masses may be dealt with more briefly. At the turn of the century a Chinese bourgeoisie was emerging. In the treaty ports the bourgeoisie had interests which were distinct from those of the gentry, whereas in rural areas a composite group, the merchant-gentry or *shen-shang*, with shared interests, was more typical. In the years before 1911 a 'bourgeois ideology' of nationalism and constitutionalism gained currency and the bourgeoisie played an important part in the boycotts of foreign goods. However, it is difficult to identify a distinct role for the bourgeoisie in the 1911 revolution. Overseas Chinese merchants gave financial support to the Revolutionary Alliance; Sichuan merchants played a prominent part in the campaign against the nationalization of the railways; in Guangzhou commercial organizations were quick to proclaim the establishment of a republic and it has even been suggested that merchants played a pivotal role in the city's decision to support the revolution.[50] But in general merchants did not take the initiative and if they did their motivation was sometimes self-interest – in Guangzhou fear of the spread of banditry and piracy prompted the merchants' decision to support the republic. In short, 'China's October Revolution was not made by the merchants, but it aroused their liveliest sympathy'.[51]

The 1911 revolution is commonly presented as an elite revolution. This view was challenged by John Lust, who drew attention to the part played by 'movements from below' in the revolutionary period. He stressed the serious decline in the living standards of the peasants in the years before the revolution, which was exacerbated by the effects of the late Qing reforms. These added to the tax burden and gave the gentry new opportunities to oppress the peasants. In 1909 and 1910 peasant discontent led to a wave of riots and protests. The main outlet for peasant resentment was the secret society and Lust noted that the revolutionaries looked to the societies for support in the various revolutionary attempts. He argued that in this relationship the societies were not the tools of the revolutionaries, but partners in a radical-popular alliance. However, doubts have been raised about the existence of any such alliance or of any basis of common interest between the peasants and the revolutionaries. If popular movements did influence the course of the 1911 revolution, it seems probable that the effects were negative, for the movements were seen as a threat to the social order, and so their activities encouraged elite groups to reach a quick political settlement.[52]

20
The Early Republic, 1912–28

The early years of the republic were dominated by the figure of Yuan Shikai, who broke with the revolutionary groups in 1913, established himself as a dictator and tried but failed to make himself emperor. From his death in March 1916 until 1928 China had no effective central government and this period is commonly referred to as the era of the warlords. During these years several important developments occurred. The outburst of nationalist feeling which erupted on 4 May 1919 has given its name to a cultural revolution which was characterized by an attack on Confucianism and by a wave of new thought. In its wake came the founding of the Chinese Communist Party (CCP) and the revival of the Guomindang (the Nationalist Party), the successor to the Revolutionary Alliance. These two parties formed a united front and in 1926 they initiated the Northern Expedition to reunite China. Within a year their alliance had collapsed and the Communists had been driven underground in the cities or had fled to the countryside. Meanwhile, the Guomindang had captured Beijing and had completed what has been termed the Nationalist revolution.

The Presidency of Yuan Shikai

Yuan Shikai's role in the events of the 1911 revolution has provoked a sharp difference of opinion and this controversy extends to the part he played as President. Nationalist historians have denounced him for betraying the revolution, and for rejecting democracy in favour of a selfish pursuit of personal power. A more dispassionate view has stressed the continuities between his regime and that of the late Qing, citing in particular his attempt to centralize power at the expense of provincial autonomy.[1]

Under the provisions of the constitution of the republic, the President exercised very considerable power. However, he was required to share that power with the provisional parliament, composed of provincial representatives, and with the Prime Minister and his cabinet. The inherent instability of this arrangement was soon apparent. The first Prime Minister was Tang Shaoyi, nephew of Tang Tingshu, the famous entrepreneur who had established the Kaiping coal mines, who was a close associate of Yuan Shikai. But Tang Shaoyi also had some sympathy for the revolutionaries and in March 1912 he joined the Tongmenghui, the Revolutionary Alliance, which had reconstituted itself as an open political party. The cabinet contained four other members of the Tongmenghui, although this representation probably overstated the influence of the revolutionary group, which held only about one-third of the seats in the provisional parliament. The weakness of Tang Shaoyi's position was revealed when Yuan Shikai overruled him on a matter relating to a foreign loan. Tang Shaoyi resigned and shortly afterwards the Tongmenghui members left the cabinet.

In August 1912 Yuan Shikai, in accordance with the provisions of the new constitution, authorized China's first elections for a Senate and a House of Representatives. The vote was given to males over twenty-one years of age who had either received elementary schooling or who paid a prescribed sum in direct taxation. This enfranchised between 4 and 6 per cent of the population. In response to this opportunity the Tongmenghui amalgamated with four other parties and renamed itself the Guomindang, the Nationalist Party, with Song Jiaoren as its effective leader.[2]

The elections took place in December and January and the Guomindang gained a majority of the seats in both houses. Song Jiaoren now began to criticize Yuan and his government for its willingness to borrow from the Western powers, and its failure to deal with the question of Outer Mongolia, which had used the opportunity of the revolution to declare its independence of China and to accept the protection of Russia. The Guomindang also began to demand that the powers of parliament be increased at the expense of the presidency and that an agreement should be reached over the division of power between central and provincial government. The situation became intolerable for Yuan. On 20 March 1913 his agents shot and fatally wounded Song Jiaoren in Shanghai railway station.

Apart from the political challenge, the other immediate threat to new government was a financial crisis. Under the early republic the Qing fiscal system continued to apply, but the government became less able to collect the revenue due to it. Only a fraction of the land tax reached the central government, the rest being retained at provincial level. Maritime customs revenue was a major source of finance, but this was almost entirely committed to servicing foreign debts. Only the salt gabelle, the revenue from the government monopoly in the production and sale of salt, was available.[3] The net revenue was inadequate to support the government or to pay Yuan's troops and it was this which forced him to contract the 'Reorganization Loan', a loan of £25 million offered by a consortium of British, French and German financial interests. This loan, the largest foreign loan yet contracted by China, was officially represented as being taken to pay for a reorganization of China's administrative system. It aroused widespread criticism, for example the Guangdong provincial government condemned Yuan's failure to submit the loan to parliament for prior approval and objected to the hypothecation of the salt revenue as security for the loan.[4]

It was widely believed that Yuan intended to use the loan to suppress opposition, and when in June he began to move against the military governors of the provinces of central and south China, who supported the Guomindang and who formed a loose anti-Yuan coalition, this expectation appeared justified. His first victim was Li Liejun, the military governor of Jiangxi, who in the following month declared Jiangxi independent, so sparking off the 'second revolution'. Six other provinces declared their independence and Yuan's opponents seized Nanjing and came close to capturing Shanghai. But by September the revolution was crushed and Yuan was more firmly entrenched in power than before.

Various reasons have been put forward to explain the rapid collapse of the Second Revolution. Certainly Yuan anticipated the threat from the revolutionaries, used the military forces under his command effectively and profited from the lack of agreement among his opponents. The foreign powers, and Great Britain in particular, believed that Yuan was better able to maintain order in China and thus to protect their interests. British help was of some significance in securing for Yuan the loyalty of the navy. On the other hand the revolutionaries received assistance from Japan, including the aid of Japanese military advisers. It is often claimed that merchants opposed the revolution, and it is true that in the major cities the chambers of commerce withheld financial support.[5] In Guangdong the revolutionary government objected to Yuan's plan to use part of the Reorganization Loan to redeem the Guangdong currency, but its failure to maintain a stable money market alienated local merchants.[6] But perhaps the main reason for Yuan's success was the political choice ostensibly on offer at the time of the Second Revolution. The revolutionaries were committed to creating a federal China, whereas Yuan represented his leadership as China's best chance of preserving unity in the face of foreign encroachment.[7]

Having crushed the Second Revolution, Yuan Shikai then took steps to centralize power, to establish a dictatorship and subsequently to make himself emperor. This implied an assault on the institutions of representative government and on provincial autonomy. He began with 'an orgy of repression and bloodletting' aimed at destroying the power of the Guomindang. Martial law was declared, secret police proliferated, members of parliament were arrested, newspapers were closed down, and thousands of people were executed. One of the worst-hit provinces was Henan, where it was reported that twenty-two thousand people had been killed. Some of the deaths occurred in the course of the suppression of the bandit group headed by the 'White Wolf', with whom Sun Zhongshan was supposed to have forged links, but in many cases the killings were at random.

Yuan also seized the political initiative. In October 1913 he browbeat the national assembly into formally electing him as president. He thereupon expelled the Guomindang members of the assembly and dissolved the party. He also set about recovering the central government's control over the provinces. Representative bodies, including the provincial assemblies, were dissolved, and Yuan worked to regain control of provincial administrations. By mid-1915 central government had effective control of twelve of the eighteen provinces of China Proper and significant influence in the remaining six. However, Yuan was unable to revive the power exercised by the Qing in Inner Mongolia, Manchuria and Tibet.[8]

Having established an effective dictatorship, Yuan embarked upon a programme of conservative reform. Some progress was made in the development of a modern judiciary and the construction of modern prisons. A number of educational reforms were promoted, including the introduction of an alphabet to facilitate the extension of literacy – reforms which had as their ultimate goal the provision of universal education, at least for the male half of the population. Some useful economic measures were introduced, including official support for programmes of livestock breeding, sugar production and cotton growing. A start was made on a geological survey of China. Programmes to reduce opium production and to achieve monetary stabilization achieved a degree of success. But Yuan's government failed to take advantage of the opportunity offered to Chinese industry and commerce by the outbreak of war in Europe. For the most part the scope and effectiveness of reforms was limited by the stress on retrenchment and by Yuan's natural caution.

The most powerful card that Yuan had held in his hand at the time of the Second Revolution was that of national unity. He had projected his model of centralized government as the only means of countering foreign encroachment. When he set about establishing the dictatorship he was soon called upon to justify that claim. At first his presumption of China's weakness led him to pursue a conciliatory policy with some degree of success. However, in 1915 he was forced into a confrontation and his handling of this crisis can be seen as either evidence of his adroitness as a politician or further proof of his preoccupation with his own interests.

The circumstances were as follows. In April 1914 Kato Takaaki became Foreign Minister of Japan and immediately began to advance Japan's interests in China. At the outbreak of war Japan entered on the allied side and demanded that Germany should surrender to her the leasehold of Jiaozhou bay. A Chinese protest was brushed aside and Japanese troops not only occupied the German leasehold, but also the cities of Wei Xian and Jinan, on the grounds that they commanded the railway line which was part of the German concession. Then in January 1915 the Japanese ambassador to China presented to Yuan personally the notorious document known as the Twenty-one Demands. The demands were divided into five groups, the first of which required China to accept Japan's claims to German interests in Shandong and to make further concessions turning the province into a Japanese sphere of influence. The second group strengthened Japan's position in Manchuria and Inner Mongolia. The third required that the Hanyeping company, China's largest coal and steel works, situated at Hanyang in the British sphere of influence on the Yangzi, should become a joint Sino-Japanese venture. The fourth group contained the apparently innocuous requirement that China, in the interests of preserving her territorial integrity, should not cede or lease any harbour or bay to any other power. Finally, the last group of demands included requirements that China should employ Japanese political, financial and military advisers, that she should agree to joint Japanese and Chinese policing of some localities, and that she should agree to purchase arms from Japan and establish a joint Sino-Japanese arsenal in China.[9]

Over the next four months these demands were leaked to the press and the British and United States governments made representations to Japan calling for their moderation. In the end most of the demands contained in the first four groups were conceded, but China succeeded in rejecting the fifth group, which if granted would have reduced her to the position of a Japanese dependency. Some of the credit for this achievement might be accorded to Britain and the United States, as both countries viewed with self-interested concern the advance of Japanese interests. Sir John Jordan, the British Ambassador to China, was firm in his condemnation, declaring 'There is no reasoning with a highwayman well armed, and Japan's action towards China is worse than that of Germany in the case of Belgium'.[10] The United States' Secretary of State, William Jennings, asserted that his country would not recognize any gains made by Japan to the fifth group of demands and this may have caused Japan to hold back.[11] Some credit should go to the Chinese diplomatic team which handled the negotiations astutely and tenaciously. Whether Yuan Shikai should receive a large share of the credit is less certain. His initial opposition to the Japanese threat may have been tempered by his need for Japanese support for his plan to become emperor.[12] His opportune leaking of the contents of the demands provoked a powerful outburst of anti-Japanese feeling and an organized boycott of Japanese goods, but Yuan was not prepared to risk his political future by placing himself at the head of a popular nationalist movement.[13]

In August 1915 a movement calling itself the Society to Plan for Peace was inaugurated to establish Yuan as the emperor of a constitutional monarchy. This step confirmed the fear long expressed by Yuan's opponents that he intended to betray the republic. His motives may have been personal aggrandizement, as his enemies alleged. He may have been lured along this path by the Japanese and then deliberately abandoned, although the evidence for this is not forthcoming.[14] He may have been encouraged to make the attempt by the arguments presented by Dr F.J. Goodnow, his American political adviser, who stressed that the Chinese were habituated to autocratic government. Most probably he was prompted by a belief that the republic had not won popular support and that a monarchy would better suit the stage of political development that China had reached. The new monarchy was not intended to be a revival of the old empire. The traditional dynastic name, the use of the kotow and the service of eunuchs were all rejected. Yuan's decision was legitimized by a body which called itself the National Congress of Representatives, which in November voted unanimously for Yuan to become emperor. The following month Yuan accepted his election and on 1 January 1916 his reign began.

Serious opposition to the monarchical change was already apparent. The intellectual criticism was headed by Liang Qichao, despite the fact that before the revolution he had been the leading advocate of a constitutional monarchy and had served in Yuan Shikai's cabinet. In a statement published in August 1915, Liang argued that the mystique of the monarchy had been destroyed by the revolution and could never be revived. Other former supporters of Yuan, both military and political figures, were also unconvinced of the sense of the monarchical attempt. For them, it has been suggested, it was easier to attack the monarchical change than admit that the policies of the dictatorship had been wrong.[15] Among the gentry a more general dissatisfaction was apparent, derived from Yuan's decision to abolish the local and provincial assemblies and from his neglect of elite education.

The catalyst which brought this opposition together in a partial and temporary alliance was a military uprising in Yunnan. The leading figure in this was Cai E, a former student of Liang Qichao, who had received his military training in Japan and who had become military governor of Yunnan after the 1911 revolution. He had supported Yuan Shikai at the time of the Second Revolution and had subsequently held appointments under the dictatorship. Cai E shared Liang Qichao's doubts about the revival of the monarchy and when he returned to Yunnan in December 1915 he became the leader of a group of military men who were disillusioned with Yuan Shikai. On 23 December they sent an ultimatum to Yuan demanding that he abandon the idea of the monarchy. Two days later, not having received a reply, they declared Yunnan independent. Early in the following year Cai E, commanding a force of about three thousand men of the Yunnanese New Army, which now called itself the National Protection Army, invaded Sichuan. This small force should have been defeated easily by the combined strength of the native Sichuanese troops, the units of the Beiyang army and the reinforcements sent by Yuan Shikai. However, a combination of brilliant generalship, failing support for Yuan and secret society assistance turned the tables and within two months the National Protection Army was in the ascendancy. This success was followed by the rapid collapse of Yuan's position. Some of his most faithful supporters, including Feng Guozhang, the senior general of the Beiyang army who was in command at Nanjing, abandoned him. Even the Japanese government withdrew its support and gave financial assistance to his opponents.

The outcome was inevitable and in March Yuan abandoned his monarchical attempt. In the following month Duan Qirui, another of Yuan's long-serving supporters, took over as Prime Minister. Preparations were in hand for Yuan's retirement from the political scene when on 6 June 1916 he died. The editor of the *Beijing Gazette* commented coolly, 'Thus Yuan himself has found the best solution of the crisis'.[16]

The Warlord Era, 1916–28

Any detailed account of this turbulent period, in which political authority fragmented and incessant wars occurred, soon becomes confusing and sterile. What follows is a summary treatment which begins with an outline of the main political developments and then discusses the survival of the central government and the characteristics of the warlord regimes.

After Yuan Shikai's death his deputy Li Yuanhong succeeded him as President and the provisional constitution of 1912 was revived. This permitted a reconciliation with the southern provinces which had seceded and a brief return to national unity. However, tension soon arose over the actions of Duan Qirui, who attempted to coerce parliament into agreeing to China's entry into the war against Germany. In response parliament voted to dismiss Duan and its recommendation was supported by the president. Duan Qirui turned for support to those military governors who were in favour of a declaration of war. One of them, Zhang Xun, known as the 'pig-tailed general' because his troops wore queues to signify his persistent loyalty to the Manchus, marched into Beijing and on 1 July 1917 declared an imperial restoration. It appeared that this was a popular move,[17] and one which was supported by the military governors, but within twelve days Zhang Xun had been driven out and Duan Qirui had regained control. Li Yuanhong was forced to resign the presidency and his place was taken by Feng Guozhang.[18]

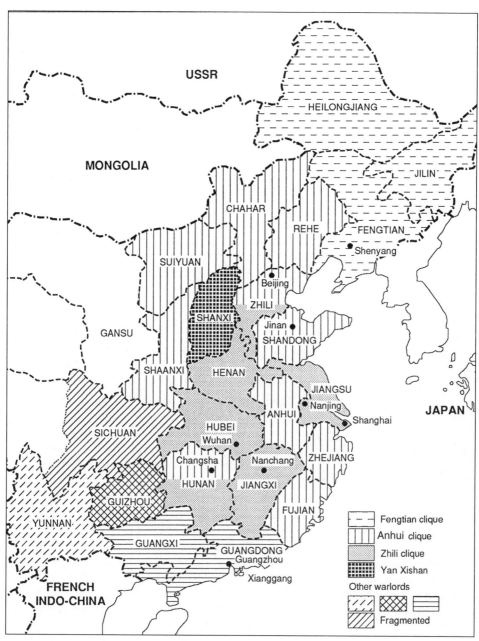

Warlord Regimes, 1920.

The combined influence of Feng Guozhang and Duan Qirui might have stabilized the situation, but for two developments. In the south, in response to Duan Qirui's return to power, Sun Zhongshan declared the establishment of an alternative government based in Guangzhou. In reply Duan Qirui launched a campaign to seize Hunan. He also negotiated the Nishihara loans from Japan and accepted Japanese military instructors. These developments sharpened the incipient factionalism among the commanders of the Beiyang army which now developed into open conflict. Duan Qirui's supporters formed the Anhui or Anfu (Anhui-Fujian) clique, while those who supported Feng Guozhang were described as the Zhili clique.

At first the Anfu clique was dominant, but in 1920 further developments led to a fragmentation of political power. In the south Sun Zhongshan, with the assistance of the local warlord, formed a new government. In the north the Zhili clique (with the support of the Fengtian or south Manchurian clique) defeated the Anhui clique. Two years later the Zhili and Fengtian cliques fought an inconclusive war, but a second war in 1924 led to the fall of the Zhili clique. This year was perhaps the extreme point of political disintegration. Thereafter rather more stable warlord regimes emerged: in Manchuria and the north-east that of the Fengtian clique headed by Zhang Zuolin, known as the 'Old Marshal'; in the poor and backward province of Shanxi, that of the 'Model Governor', Yan Xishan; in the lower Yangzi provinces that of Sun Chuanfang, formerly a member of the Zhili clique; in the middle Yangzi that of Wu Peifu, the 'Philosopher Marshal'. In the south a major warlord grouping known as the Guangxi clique gained control of that province and began to extend its influence over a wider area. Finally, a large part of the north-west was under the less stable influence of Feng Yuxiang, the 'Christian General'.

For most of this period a government in Beijing continued to operate. Its claim to legitimacy depended on the provisional constitution of 1912 which remained in force throughout most of the warlord era. Its survival indicated a persistent, if fading, hope that China might yet make the transition to a liberal democracy. The government itself remained 'the symbol of China's national sovereignty and hoped-for unity'.[19] Foreign powers recognized it as the legitimate government of the country. This enabled it to supplement its limited revenue from domestic sources with borrowing from abroad, most notoriously in the case of the Nishihara loans obtained from Japan in 1917–18. Much of this revenue went to reward its supporters, but some was applied to maintaining some of the functions of a national government. The ministry of foreign affairs made a persistent effort at rights recovery and achieved a degree of success. Having declared war in 1917, China was able to cancel the extraterritorial rights and annul the Boxer indemnity payments due to Germany and Austria-Hungary. China was also able to participate in the Paris Peace Conference of 1919 and in the Washington Conference of 1921–2. At the latter meeting Japan agreed to withdraw from Shandong and Britain relinquished her lease on Weihaiwei. In a treaty signed with the Soviet Union in 1924 China recovered rights and privileges which had been granted to the tsarist government. Other ministries could also claim some achievements. The ministry of education continued to issue directives and to encourage increased enrolment and an improvement in school educational standards. The ministry of justice made some progress in law codification and prison administration. But this did not amount to effective government – before the end of the decade the idea of a constitutional system had become exhausted and the way forward rested in the hands of regimes based on military strength.[20]

What may be said in general about the warlord regimes which emerged during this period?[21] One issue concerns their origin. Jerome Ch'en argued that warlordism was a consequence of the actions of Yuan Shikai and that Yuan's most important legacy was the creation of a large number of warlords.[22] This opinion was based on a negative judgement on Yuan's career and on the observation that many of the commanders of the Beiyang army, which was largely Yuan's creation, became warlords. Ch'en's view was attacked by Stephen R. MacKinnon, who argued that the Beiyang army was less regional and private than the regional armies of the nineteenth century, and that the personal connection between Yuan and his senior officers was not as strong as Ch'en had suggested.[23] It was also criticized by Ernest P. Young, who argued that Yuan's intentions were the opposite of warlordism, for he hoped to create a state in which the army would be an instrument of national power under central control, and civil authority would prevail over that of the military leadership.[24]

If the blame for warlordism cannot be heaped on Yuan, where should the responsibility for it rest? An influential explanation of its development was put forward by Franz Michael, who pointed out that throughout Chinese history there has been a recurrent pattern of decline in the authority of central government and the emergence of regionalist power centres. The most recent example of this decline, the warlord era of the 1920s, should be traced back to the mid-nineteenth-century rebellions, and in particular to the Taiping rebellion. In its efforts to defeat those rebellions the Qing dynasty had been forced to make fatal concessions to the gentry group and to permit the raising of regional armies by influential provincial officials. This had led to the development of what Michael called 'regionalism'.[25] This view was echoed by James E. Sheridan, who saw regional militarism as 'the culmination of a process that had begun about a century earlier'.[26]

Sheridan defined a warlord as

one who commanded a personal army, controlled or sought to control territory, and acted more or less independently.

He noted that the term was pejorative and that some writers had preferred the title dujun, on the grounds that most warlords were military governors, or had used the more neutral term 'regional militarist'.[27]

Much of the historical writing on warlords has been in the form of biographies and these provide a lively insight into their personalities and deeds. From them one can obtain interesting perspectives on the period, and curious details of their practices: how Wu Peifu's subordinates used an opium suppression bureau as a tax-collection centre,[28] and how Zhang Zuolin travelled around Shenyang (Mukden) in a large bulletproof Packard twin-six with specially mounted machine guns.[29] From their background and careers one can form an impression of the types of warlord. James Sheridan suggested that they might be divided into four groups. There were the Beiyang army leaders, the 'first-generation' warlords Feng Guozhang and Duan Qirui, to whom reference has already been made. Then there were the conservative warlords, the most notable of them being Wu Peifu, whose soubriquet, the Philosopher Marshal, was a reference to his commitment to Confucian values. A third group comprised those described by Sheridan as reactionaries, among whom he included Zhang Xun, who had restored the Manchus in 1917, and the notorious Zhang Zongchang, known as the 'Dog-meat General', who was patriotic, ruthlessly honest and very fond of eating dog meat.[30] Finally, there were some reformist warlords, a category which included Feng Yuxiang and Yan Xishan. Feng Yuxiang, the Christian General, applied his moralistic concern to the training of his troops, who were not allowed to drink, gamble or swear. In a somewhat unmethodical way he attempted a variety of social welfare reforms, including the suppression of opium smoking and the rehabilitation of addicts. He also put his men to work on road building and flood control projects. Yan Xishan was the 'Model Governor' of a Shanxi province for most of the time from the 1911 revolution to 1949. He made a sustained effort to raise literacy levels in the province and initiated campaigns against foot-binding and prostitution.[31]

A wider perspective on warlordism was provided by C. Martin Wilbur in his 'anatomy of the regional militarist system', which he analysed under four headings.[32] The first of these was that the regional militarist, or warlord, should command a territorial base. The most suitable base was one which was readily defended, which had access to the sea and which contained substantial cities. According to these criteria the most-favoured base was Manchuria and indeed the warlords of Manchuria, first Zhang Zuolin and then, after his murder in 1928 by Japanese soldiers, his son Zhang Xueliang, were never defeated on their own territory. A less suitable base was the lower Yangzi, for although it was the most prosperous region, it lacked natural defences and was a tempting prize. Some warlords, the obvious example being Feng Yuxiang, were 'mobile warlords', surviving precariously without a permanent base.

A second requirement was a source of finance sufficient to pay the warlord's troops and to buy arms and ammunition. Warlords met this need in two ways. The first method was to arrogate to themselves taxes which should have accrued to a national government. It has been estimated that in Yunnan the local warlord regularly diverted at least three-quarters of the provincial budget to military purposes.[33] The second method was to raise special taxes and surcharges. Railways were an important source of warlord income. Wu Peifu not only laid claim to the profits of the Beijing–Hankou railway, but also levied a surcharge on the goods transported, mortgaged the lands along the line and raised a bank loan by pledging railway property as a security.[34] Many warlords made large sums from growing and taxing opium. Most engaged in imaginative schemes for levying taxes, for example Feng Yuxiang collected entrance fees on the tourist attractions in Beijing.[35]

Another matter which affected the fortunes of some warlords was relations with foreign powers. Because warlordism is so frequently regarded as having had a disastrous effect on China's ability to resist foreign penetration, it is surprising to note that many prominent warlords were committed to nationalism. Many of them, including the warlords of Sichuan and Yunnan, as well as those of the Guangxi clique, although supporting provincial separatism, nevertheless expressed the desire to see China reunified. Many warlords, including Feng Yuxiang, lectured their troops on patriotic themes. Often warlords cloaked their own selfish designs with claims that they sought to destroy imperialism. Nevertheless, many warlords established mutually advantageous relationships with foreign powers. Zhang Zuolin, the warlord of Manchuria, accepted Japanese military assistance in the Fengtian-Zhili War of 1924.[36] Wu Peifu looked upon Britain and the United States as his allies and in return for a variety of favours he was able to obtain loans and arms, although these came through private rather than governmental channels.[37]

Most judgements on the warlord period emphasize the negative impact of warlordism. C.P. Fitzgerald, who lived in China during the warlord years, wrote:

> The Chinese Revolution had become an incomprehensible confusion. No principles appeared to be in conflict; no contest between democracy and tyranny was visible, no climax and no conclusion.

He noted how the civil service collapsed, the scholar class withdrew from government and the rich fled from the countryside, where banditry prevailed and where military exactions destroyed the balanced economy. Irrigation and drainage works went uncared for and disastrous floods and famines occurred.[38]

Some writers, having emphasized the negative effects of warlordism, have also noted the paradox that during the warlord era a number of positive changes were occurring. Reference has already been made to the persistence and growth of nationalism. Notwithstanding the damage that warlordism caused to the rural economy, between 1916 and 1928 the index of industrial production rose by 300 per cent.[39] In the absence of any firm political authority or of any strong ideological control, an unprecedented degree of intellectual freedom existed, and it is to the effects of this that the discussion will now turn.

The May Fourth Movement

On 4 May 1919 three thousand college students demonstrated in front of the Tianan gate in Beijing to protest against the decision made at the Paris Peace Conference that the former German interests in Shandong should be transferred to Japan. Later on the same day the house of Cao Rulin, the Minister of Communications in Duan Qirui's cabinet, was burned down and another minister was badly beaten. Both men were targeted because they were regarded as pro-Japanese and because they had been involved in the humiliating response to the Twenty-one Demands and the negotiation of the Nishihara loans. Some thirty students were arrested and one died from injuries sustained during the incident. In the days that followed, the students transformed the incident into a national protest. They sought support from other cities and initiated a boycott of Japanese goods and a campaign for the purchase of Chinese products.[40] Protests occurred in some two hundred other cities, most notably in Shanghai, where student activism brought about a general strike which closed the shops and some factories.[41]

The Beijing government's response to these events was indecisive and confused. Having allowed the incident to escalate, it then tried to clamp down and by early June over one thousand students had been arrested. When the protests continued it capitulated and released the students. On 10 June Cao Rulin and two other ministers left the government and three days later the government itself resigned. The outstanding issue was the signing of the Treaty of Versailles, which the Beijing government was prepared to do but which the Chinese delegation, under pressure from students and workers in Paris, refused to condone.[42]

The May Fourth incident, a nationalist reaction to the perceived threat to the integrity of China, gained more popular support than any previous incident. Nationalist protests in the form of demonstrations, boycotts and strikes had first appeared in the cities at the beginning of the century. In 1905 a boycott was organized to protest against the restriction of Chinese immigration into the United States. In 1908 a Japanese ship, the *Tatsu Maru*, was seized by Chinese authorities when carrying contraband and the Japanese flag was hauled down. The Japanese government demanded and received an apology and compensation. This sparked off a sharp protest, with Japanese goods being burned and workers refusing to unload Japanese ships. In Guangzhou many students, including some women, went on strike and formed a National Humiliation Society.[43] In 1915, in response to the leaked news of the Japanese Twenty-one Demands, an even more extensive agitation broke out, with patriotic plays being staged and an economic boycott being organized. After the demands had been accepted, the 7 and 9 May were designated as days of national humiliation. The May Fourth demonstrations of 1919 coincided with the annual commemoration of these days.[44] The appearance of this form of protest has been connected with the emergence of a nationalist bourgeoisie. Chinese merchants were doubly involved in the consequences of foreign intervention, 'as citizens anxious to save their country and as entrepreneurs faced with competition'.[45] They were joined in their protest by students, many of whom were their sons and daughters, whose educational environment was becoming a hotbed of nationalist agitation.

The May Fourth Movement is the term used to denote the intellectual revolution which swept China between approximately 1917 and 1921. The nationalist agitation of 1919 was an important part of this, but the movement had other origins and wider implications. It combined a fierce criticism of the past, in the form of an attack on Confucianism, with a willingness to look to the West for a solution for China's difficulties. Spanning the rejection of the past and a commitment to the future was a literary revolution which abandoned the classical written language and replaced it with a vernacular form.

Such a movement was only possible within the context of the social and economic changes of the late imperial and early republican years: the appearance of a new intelligentsia – by 1919 numbering about five million – whose education had been partly or wholly in Western-style schools,[46] the growth of great coastal cities, most notably Shanghai, and the emergence of a bourgeoisie as a political force.[47] It needed an intellectual preparation, which can be traced back to the Hundred Days' reforms of 1898, if not earlier.[48] It also required the fear engendered by the threat to China's territorial integrity and the sense of national humiliation arising out of foreign encroachment.

Two influences were of particular importance to the development of the May Fourth Movement. The first was the part played by Beijing National University in the intellectual transformation, and the second the role of the magazine *New Youth* in identifying and popularizing the issues of the day. Beijing University, or 'Beida' as it became known, had been founded in 1898, but in the first years of its existence it had served mainly as a training ground for officials and its educational standards were regarded as low. It had gained the nickname of 'The Gamblers' Den' and its staff and students were known collectively as 'The Brothel Brigade'.[49] It was to be transformed by Cai Yuanpei (1868–1940), who had been Minister of Education for a short time in the early years of the republic, but had been forced to resign after he had called for intellectual freedom. After spending some years in Europe he returned to China in 1916, and in the freer atmosphere after Yuan's death took up the post of Chancellor of Beijing University. Cai was an unusual figure, 'a classical scholar turned revolutionary'.[50] He immediately declared that the university should be a place dedicated to scholarship and gathered around him a group of distinguished scholars with iconoclastic ideas. They included Chen Duxiu (1879–1942), the dean of the school of letters and Li Dazhao (1888–1927) the librarian – the two men who became joint founders of the CCP. Also on the staff was Hu Shi (1891–1962), who had worked on a doctorate at Columbia University, his dissertation being an exposition of classical Chinese philosophy.

The second important influence was that exerted by the magazine *Xin qingnian*, also known as *New Youth* and *La Jeunesse*, which had been founded by Chen Duxiu in Shanghai in 1915. It became 'the focal point for an all-out assault on the entire system of Confucian values'.[51] In the editorial for its first number Chen had announced an 'Appeal to Youth'.

> The Chinese compliment others by saying, 'He acts like an old man although still young.' Englishmen and Americans encourage one another by saying, 'Keep young while growing old.' Such is one respect in which the different ways of thought of the East and West are manifested. Youth is like early spring, like the rising sun, like trees and grass in bud, like a newly sharpened blade. It is the most valuable period of life. The function of youth in society is the same as that of a fresh and vital cell in a human body. In the processes of metabolism, the old and rotten are incessantly eliminated to be replaced by the fresh and living.[52]

The reference to the old and new cells in an organism was characteristic of Chen Duxiu's thought. He, like many other Chinese intellectuals, had embraced Social Darwinism and believed that states must struggle for their existence and that only the fittest would survive. Whereas earlier reformers such as Kang Youwei had hoped to reform the Confucian tradition, Chen Duxiu regarded that tradition as the fundamental cause of China's weakness. He therefore advocated cultural iconoclasm, a wholesale attack on Confucian culture. This was the message which dominated the pages of *New Youth*.[53]

The best-known exposition of that attack was in the article 'The Way of Confucius and Modern Life', which Chen Duxiu published in *New Youth* in December 1916. He began by asserting that the pulse of modern life was economic and that its fundamental principle was individual independence. He then argued that Confucianism denied sons and wives personal individuality or personal property and prevented them from expressing their independent political opinions. He denounced the restrictions which Confucianism imposed on women, in particular the disapproval of the remarriage of widows. The article concluded with a powerful dismissal of Confucius who, he said, lived in a feudal age, and whose ethics, social mores and political institutions reflected the interests of a few rulers and aristocrats and had nothing to do with the happiness of the masses.[54]

Another aspect of the rejection of the past concerned language reform. The idea that the condensed and allusive style of classical Chinese (*wenyan*) should be replaced by a written form which represented the vernacular (*baihua*) can be traced back to the end of the nineteenth century. Liang Qichao experimented in writing in *baihua* and there are some examples of the use of the vernacular in magazines and in tracts produced by missionaries to be read by less-educated social groups. Late Qing fiction continued to use *wenyan*, but from about 1910 there had been an immense outpouring of urban popular fiction, referred to as the 'mandarin duck and butterfly school' because of its sentimental themes. Another innovation concerned the development of a phonetic form of written Chinese. In 1912 the ministry of education had established a committee for the standardization of Chinese pronunciation and a model system for literacy classes using an alphabet which had been approved by Yuan Shikai.[55]

These were the preparatory stages for a literary revolution in which the key figure was Hu Shi. While still a student in the United States he had written:

> China's literature has long been withered and feeble;
> In the last century no robust men have arisen.
> The coming of the new tide cannot be stayed:
> The time is at hand for a literary revolution.[56]

In January 1917 Hu Shi published an article entitled 'Some tentative suggestions for the reform of Chinese literature' in *New Youth*. The reference to 'reform' rather than 'revolution' was significant, for Hu Shi knew that many of his fellow students were opposed to his ideas. However, in the following month Chen Duxiu declared the need for a literary revolution to 'overthrow the painted, powdered, and obsequious literature of the aristocratic few, and to create the plain, simple, and expressive literature of the people'.[57]

The first and greatest exponent of this new form of literature was Lu Xun (1881–1936). Lu Xun had been a medical student in Japan at the time of the Russo-Japanese War and had been appalled by the apathy of his fellow countrymen. He decided to abandon medicine and to use literature to awaken the Chinese people, whom he described as trapped in an iron house and doomed to die of suffocation. Despite the apparent inevitability of that fate, he felt it his duty to expose the failings of Chinese culture. In a short story entitled 'A Madman's Diary', which was written in the vernacular and published in *New Youth* in April 1918, he described the China of the past, in which the morality of Confucianism had prevailed, as a cannibalistic society.[58]

The literary movement gathered momentum in 1919, and much of the student literature produced at the time of the May Fourth incident was written in the vernacular. Within a year the ministry of education had ordered a change to *baihua* in the first years of primary schools and the abandonment of textbooks in *wenyan*.[59] By now *baihua* was described as *guoyu*, that is to say the national language.

Another aspect of the May Fourth Movement was the prevalence of new thought over traditional ideas. Once again the leading figure was Chen Duxiu. *New Youth* had been charged with setting out to destroy Confucianism, a charge to which Chen responded in January 1919. He claimed that the magazine had only committed the alleged crimes because it supported two gentlemen, 'Mr Democracy' and 'Mr Science'.[60] Of course *New Youth* had not pioneered the introduction and popularization of new ideas in China. An important role in this had been played by Yan Fu (1853–1921), who from 1895 onwards had translated many of the key works of Western philosophy. It was Yan Fu who had introduced Social Darwinism to a Chinese audience. In addition Liang Qichao had discussed the ideas of the French Revolution and liberal concepts of individual freedom had been circulating since the beginning of the century. The writings of Marx were known in China before the 1911 revolution, but the political ideologies which had proved most attractive to a small but influential group of Chinese were socialism and anarchism.[61]

Nevertheless *New Youth* and other May Fourth magazines were to play an important role in introducing new ideas to a wider audience. In November 1918 Li Dazhao contributed an article to *New Youth* entitled 'The Victory of Bolshevism', which celebrated the defeat of Germany, vanquished, he claimed, not by Allied military power, but by German socialism. He then attempted a summary of the main tenets of Bolshevism and concluded with a ringing prophecy: 'The dawn of freedom has arrived! See the world of tomorrow; it assuredly will belong to the red flag!'.[62] In May 1919 a special issue of *New Youth* on Marxism appeared, edited by Li Dazhao. His article, 'My Marxist Views', provided one of the first lengthy discussions of Marxist theory in Chinese.[63] Three months later, in July and August, the magazine *Weekly Critic* carried an article by Hu Shi entitled 'More study of problems, less talk of "isms"'. Hu Shi was reacting against what he saw as the drift of Chen Duxiu and Li Dazhao into the Communist camp. He accused them of embracing a totalistic 'ism', which they imagined would provide a complete solution to China's problems. Instead Hu Shi argued for pragmatism, a methodological approach to problems which he had derived from the American philosopher and educationalist John Dewey.[64] His pragmatism cast doubt on his commitment to a total rejection of Confucian culture. He observed that New Thought could not work instantly:

What is the sole aim of the New Thought? It is to recreate civilization. Civilization was not created in *toto*, but by inches and drops. Evolution was not accomplished overnight, but by inches and drops.[65]

What views have been expressed about the character and significance of the May Fourth Movement? One issue which has received attention is whether the cultural aspects of the movement should be regarded as distinct from the incident which occurred in May 1919 and the political consequences which flowed from it. Chow Tse-tsung argued that the 'May Fourth Movement was actually a combined intellectual and sociopolitical movement. . . .'.[66] J.T. Chen disagreed, pointing out that the significant elements of cultural change were occurring before May 1919, whereas the political consequences came after the May Fourth incident. He added that there was an essential difference between the two: the cultural movement concerned thought, while the political movement concerned action, which made them complementary rather than synonymous.[67]

Another issue concerns the relationship between the May Fourth Movement and the embracing of Marxism-Leninism. The orthodox view is that the catalyst for this was the Russian Revolution which demonstrated that Marxism could precipitate a revolution. This perception struck Li Dazhao, who found in Marxism the key to China's problems. He communicated his views through the pages of *New Youth*, and then went on to found the CCP. However, there were many other ideologies circulating at the time of the May Fourth Movement and the acceptance of Marxism-Leninism and its subsequent progress may owe more to conditions within Chinese society than to the impact of the Russian Revolution and the power of Marxist-Leninist thought.[68]

Finally, what role does the May Fourth Movement occupy in China's modern history? In Guomindang accounts a sharp distinction is made between the movement as a manifestation of nationalism, which only receives praise, and the movement as a cultural phenomenon, which is treated more critically.[69] Jiang Jieshi was to deplore aspects of the intellectual and youth movements: 'the overthrow of the old ethics and the rejection of national history', 'the demand for individual emancipation and an ignorance of state and society', and 'the blind worship of foreign countries and indiscriminate introduction and acceptance of foreign civilization'.[70]

Communist writers, on the other hand, have defined the May Fourth Movement as the starting point of modern Chinese history. Mao Zedong himself was a member of the May Fourth generation and had contributed an article to *New Youth* in April 1917.[71] Many years later, in 'On New Democracy', he was to argue that the May Fourth era marked the dividing line between the 'old democracy' and the 'new democracy', the distinction being that in the 'old democracy' – a period which began at the time of the Opium Wars – 'the political guiding force of the Chinese bourgeois-democratic revolution was the Chinese petty bourgeois and bourgeois classes (the intelligentsia of both)', whereas in the 'new democracy' the political guiding force 'no longer rested solely upon the bourgeois class, but upon the proletariat'.[72]

The Founding of the CCP and the Reorganization of the Guomindang

After the Second Revolution of 1913 Sun Zhongshan abandoned parliamentary democracy and established a clandestine organization, the Chinese Revolutionary Party. In 1917, after the failure of the attempt to restore the Manchus and the ascendancy of Duan Qirui, for a few months Sun headed the 'Constitution Protection Movement' in Guangzhou, a government based on a rump of the Beijing parliament. By 1918 he had been forced to retire to Shanghai, where he planned the reorganization of the Guomindang. Two years later he was back in Guangzhou heading a Chinese Republic, but within months he had been forced to flee by the Guangdong warlord Chen Jiongming.

In the meantime the steps leading to the founding of the CCP had been taken. The sequence of events is an oft-told tale, although the details of it are incomplete and contradictory. By 1920 a scattering of people, usually living in major cities and near universities, had become converts to Marxism. They included Chen Duxiu and Li Dazhao at Beijing University and Mao Zedong in Changsha.[73] In April 1920 Grigori Voitinsky, representing the Far Eastern Secretariat of the Third Communist International, or Comintern, arrived in China with the objective of organizing a disciplined Leninist party. The result of his efforts was the establishment of a provisional central committee and the beginning of propaganda work directed at workers and young people. Marxist study groups were organized, including one started by Mao Zedong in Changsha. In July 1921 what was to be known as the First Congress of the CCP was held in Shanghai, at least one of its sessions taking place at a girls' school in the French concession. Delegates from six Marxist groups attended, although neither Chen Duxiu nor Li Dazhao was present. The Comintern was represented by a Dutchman known as Maring (alias Sneevliet). Little is certain about the decisions taken on that occasion other than that Chen Duxiu was to act as the secretary and the party was to remain in close contact with the Comintern. From later events it appears that the party also decided to concentrate its efforts on promoting a labour movement and rejected co-operation with other political parties, a stance which adumbrated a future schism within the party.

Early Communist activity was concerned with establishing its proletarian base, which involved the organization of labour centres and workers' schools and the organization of strikes. Mao Zedong was closely involved in the development of the Hunan labour movement and the organization of four strikes between 1920 and 1923.[74] The most successful instance of the party's involvement in the labour movement was the Chinese Seamen's Union strike, which began in Xianggang in January 1922 and then spread to Guangzhou and Shanghai, with some 100,000 workers taking part. The strike focused on the differential rates paid to Chinese and foreign seamen. When it was settled in March it had achieved union recognition and a significant increase in seamen's pay. In May the Communist-supported Labour Secretariat held a congress at Guangzhou which was attended by delegates claiming to represent between 200,000 and 300,000 workers. Further strikes were organized, but then the labour movement suffered a severe setback. Until January 1923 the warlord Wu Peifu had permitted industrial workers, including railway workers on the Beijing–Hankou railway line, to take industrial action. However, he became increasingly concerned about the political and financial implications of Communist activities and on 7 February a strike which had paralysed the Beijing–Hankou line was suppressed by force. The bloodiest clash occurred at Jiangan station, Hankou, where thirty-seven strikers were killed and the chairman of the Jiangan union was beheaded in front of the union headquarters for refusing to order workers back to work.[75]

In February 1923 Sun Zhongshan had been able to return to Guangzhou, but his position there remained very weak. The Guomindang had only a few thousand members and it was apparent that its ideology, based on Sun's Three Principles of nationalism, democracy and the people's livelihood, did not arouse much popular enthusiasm. His military support consisted of a motley collection of ill-equipped, poorly trained troops under no centralized command. His financial position was dire, for he had run out of credit from his Western and Chinese backers and he could not hope to collect taxes without a firm grip on a territorial base.[76]

It was at this point that the Guomindang, with Russian assistance, embarked on a major reorganization. Russia wanted to consolidate its strategic interests in Manchuria and hoped that by giving covert assistance to the Guomindang it could put pressure on the Beijing government. Russia also hoped to promote world revolution and in 1920 Lenin had announced his two-stage revolutionary policy. In the first stage Communist parties in European colonies – and Sun Zhongshan had once famously described China's condition as worse than that of a colony – should concentrate on getting rid of the colonial power. This implied forming a united front with the national bourgeoisie in a struggle for national liberation. Only after this had been achieved should Communist parties begin the struggle to overthrow capitalism and establish socialism. It was to implement this policy that in June 1923 Maring persuaded the CCP to enter into an alliance with the Guomindang, the agreement allowing CCP members to join the Guomindang on an individual basis.[77]

In October 1923 Mikhail Borodin, a senior Comintern agent, arrived in Guangzhou and with his advice the reorganization of the party began. Over the next few months he drafted a new constitution which modelled the structure of the Guomindang on that of the Russian Communist Party. Some Russian financial assistance went towards setting up party bureaux to create mass organizations among workers, peasants, youth and women. An incident concerning Sun's access to the revenues of the foreign-controlled maritime customs led to a hardening of the Guomindang's anti-imperialist line. Most importantly Russian military advisers arrived with the task of creating an effective military force. In May 1924 a military academy was opened at Huangpu (Whampoa), south of Guangzhou, with the objective of creating an officer corps indoctrinated with Guomindang ideology. Its first commandant was Jiang Jieshi (Chiang Kaishek)(1887–1975), who had recently returned from Moscow. A unified military command was created and the nucleus of a national revolutionary army was formed.[78]

Whereas Guomindang influence clearly prevailed in the party structure and in the armed forces, Communist activity was most apparent in the development of the mass movements. The Socialist Youth League, which had originally been founded by Chen Duxiu in 1920, expanded in size and became active in many schools. The labour movement was revived and a number of economic strikes were launched. More significant was the incident which occurred in June 1924 on Shamian island, the site of the French and British concessions in Guangzhou. A Vietnamese nationalist assassinated the Governor-General of French Indo-China who was visiting Guangzhou. The Western powers thereupon introduced strict regulations covering the movements of all Chinese employed on the island. In retaliation Chinese employees, with Communist encouragement, went on strike to promote 'a struggle against imperialism'. Two months later the consuls agreed to suspend the regulations and reinstate the strikers.[79]

Another interesting development was an early attempt to start a mass movement among the peasantry. The key figure was Peng Pai (1896–1929), who came from a landlord family living in Haifeng, in the east of Guangdong province. The population of this district included a large number of Hakka Chinese, the dialect group which had played a major role in the Taiping rebellion. When he had been a student in Japan, Peng Pai had been active in left-wing politics and had become involved in the peasant movement there. He returned to Haifeng in 1921 and joined the Socialist Youth League. In deference to his high educational qualifications, and perhaps because of a connection with the warlord Chen Jiongming, he was appointed district director of education – but was dismissed when local gentry complained of his radical ideas. He then decided to try to organize a peasant movement. His first sorties were not very successful. He visited villages wearing a student-style white Western suit and stiffened cap, which led him to be mistaken for an official, an army officer, or even a debt collector. When he attempted to talk to peasants about their hardships he was told 'It is fate that our life is hard'. Later he adopted peasant dress and took a gramophone to the villages to draw a crowd. In a dramatic gesture he burnt the title deeds to his own land in front of his tenants. Gradually he gained the peasants' confidence and encouraged them to propose the formation of a peasant association which would promote their interests against those of their landlords. Once launched, the association movement spread rapidly. By the end of 1922 all ten sub-districts of Haifeng county had peasant associations and six months later the Guangdong Peasant Association covered six counties and claimed a membership of 130,000. But then the association overreached itself, demanding that landlords should reduce rents to peasants whose crops had been devastated by a hurricane. The landlords' case was supported by Chen Jiongming and the peasant associations collapsed. Nevertheless, the effort was not entirely wasted. In 1923 Peng Pai had joined the CCP and after the failure in Haifeng he became the leading figure in the Guomindang Farmers' Bureau, which organized peasants in the Guangzhou region.[80]

Despite these initiatives, at the beginning of 1924 the Guomindang still seemed far from accomplishing its objective of reunifying China. However, the two wars fought in that year between the Fengtian (Manchuria) and Zhili (Beijing) cliques, wars fought on a far larger scale than any of the previous conflicts in China, bankrupted the Beijing government and destroyed the military capacity of Wu Peifu, its most able general. This, it has been argued, left not only a military weakness, but also a political and ideological vacuum that was to be filled by the Guomindang.[81]

In March 1925 Sun Zhongshan died of cancer, leaving no clear successor and raising doubts about the future of the Guomindang. But then in May a strike in a Japanese-owned factory in Shanghai was harshly suppressed by Japanese guards at the cost of one of the strikers' lives. On 30 May Shanghai students staged a demonstration in the Nanjing Road to protest about the striker's death and against the unequal treaties. The British officer in command ordered his men to fire and twelve Chinese were killed. This incident sparked off a wave of nationalist feeling which dwarfed the May Fourth Movement. Anti-foreign riots broke out in many cities. On 23 June a massive demonstration of striking workers was planned in Guangzhou, but the marchers were fired on by British and French troops and at least fifty-two Chinese were killed. There followed the bitter Guangzhou-Xianggang strike which was to last for sixteen months, paralysing the trade and amenities of the two cities.[82]

In the wake of these events the membership of the Guomindang and the CCP rose rapidly. The same was true of the Socialist Youth League, now renamed the Communist Youth League, the trade unions and the peasant associations. The National Revolutionary Army had mounted an eastern campaign which had brought much of Guangdong province under its control. Although strains had become apparent between the Guomindang and the Communists, the stage was now set for a northern expedition to reunify China.

21
The Rise of the Guomindang and the Nanjing Decade

This chapter begins with a reference to the economy and considers whether China faced an agrarian crisis in these years. It then traces the rise of the Guomindang, commencing with the Northern Expedition which set out in 1926, discusses the split in the United Front and the 'reunification' of China in 1928, and concludes with an assessment of the record of the Nanjing government for the decade from 1928–37. The final topic is the 'peasant stage' of the CCP and the heroic sequence of the Long March.[1]

An Agrarian Crisis?

In the 1920s and the 1930s the first detailed surveys of China's rural economy were carried out. The dominant picture which emerged was one of peasant immiseration and of a deepening agrarian crisis. For example, Chen Han-seng, in a study of agrarian conditions in Guangdong province made in the early 1930s, emphasized the increased concentration of landownership, the rise of rents and the price of land, increasing taxation and declining wages. At the end of his study he referred to the surplus of cheap labour and the frequency at which peasant fathers were reduced to selling their daughters. 'We close our survey, then,' he wrote, 'upon a note of misery beyond which human experience can hardly go except in times of catastrophe.'[1]

Other writers presented a more optimistic view. John Lossing Buck, whose studies of the Chinese farm economy were based on surveys conducted between 1929 and 1933, noted that 80 per cent of his informants believed that their circumstances had improved in recent years, and he cited the increased consumption of cloth as a good indicator of a rise in peasant living standards.[2] More recently Albert Feuerwerker has claimed that 'Until 1937 the total output of agriculture approximately kept pace with the growth of population', and he described this as 'a creditable performance for an agricultural sector which experienced no significant technological improvements before 1949'.[3] Ramon Myers drew attention to the unevenness of the performance, but pointed out that in Liaodong and on Taiwan, both areas then under Japanese rule, farm production outpaced population growth and per capita availability of grain increased.[4] Thomas G. Rawski, while stressing the lack of reliable statistical evidence, concluded that there was 'a variety of quantitative evidence that is consistent with the hypothesis of rising prewar real income and output per person in China's farm sector . . .'.[5]

Some of the disparity between these two views may be explained by the contrast between conditions in the 1920s and in the 1930s. In the earlier decade, although the government was ineffective and internal turmoil was the order of the day, no new crisis affected the rural economy. But in the 1930s a series of adverse circumstances occurred, beginning in 1931 with disastrous floods in the Yangzi valley and the Japanese invasion of Manchuria. From 1932 the effects of the world depression reached China, causing a severe reduction in the demand for silk and tea and a sharp decline in the manufacturing sector of the economy. The situation was exacerbated by the outflow of silver in 1934–5, in response to the United States Silver Purchase Act of 1934. This further reduced farm prices and deepened the depression of the Chinese economy.[6]

The most extensive debate has not been about the depth of the agrarian crisis, but about its cause. Two main theories have emerged. The first, known as the 'distributionist' theory, argues that the main causes of peasant immiseration were exploitation by a landlord class and the effects of Western imperialism. More specifically it asserts that the distribution of landownership became more uneven, landlord-tenant relationships became increasingly harsh, peasants fell deeper into debt and peasant living standards were further eroded. At the same time Western imperialism, which had already undermined the rural economy, continued to exert a baleful influence. One manifestation of this was the emigration of destitute peasants. In some districts around Guangzhou 10 per cent of the population had emigrated to work in the European colonies of South-east Asia, from whence they sent home remittances to support their families.

The opposing viewpoint has been called the 'eclectic' theory. It rejects the argument of rural exploitation as the main cause of rural poverty and suggests instead that the root of the problem was technological backwardness. It implies that if China had had an effective government, committed to achieving a technical transformation of agriculture and able to raise the capital to achieve that goal, then the problem of peasant immiseration would have been solved. In short, it saw as the solution to the problems of China's rural poverty a more efficient capitalist system making use of modern technology. On the other hand the 'distributionist' theory called for an attack on rural exploitation and an end to economic imperialism.

The modern debate began in 1970 with Ramon H. Myers' study of the peasant economy of Hebei and Shandong. Myers argued in favour of the eclectic view, producing evidence to show that in the provinces studied peasants' living standards were rising and that they did not suffer unduly from landlord exploitation. The key problem, he found, 'was the absence of any system generating rapid technological progress in agriculture'.[7] His study was criticized for its reliance on John Lossing Buck's survey data (which had been described as unsystematic) and on the Japanese South Manchurian Railway surveys (which were conducted among a hostile population).[8] The distributionist view was given some support by Robert

Ash who investigated the conditions of land tenure in Jiangsu in the 1920s and the 1930s. He quoted a Jiangsu folk-song:

> Two knives are at a peasant's back:
> The grain is heavy, the interest high.
> Three ways before him stand:
> To drown, to hang or to languish in gaol.

He found that lack of security of tenure, high rents and a one-sided relationship between landlord and tenant ensured that the tenant had no incentive to invest.[9] Philip Huang countered an important objection to the argument that China was experiencing an agrarian crisis in the 1920s and 1930s – that the evidence for it is largely based on surveys conducted in those decades – by extending his survey of North China back to the eighteenth century. He noted that the combined pressures of population growth and social stratification had produced a sharply divided society, which pressed most harshly on the poor peasant *before* the intrusion of the world economy, although that factor may have accelerated the process of change. For him the agrarian crisis was not a new phenomenon, but one which had long existed. But by the 1930s immiseration was so severe that 'a poor peasant . . . was like a man already standing neck-deep in water, so that even small ripples threaten to drown him'. Those who had no land and who subsisted as agricultural labourers earned wages that were so low that they could not afford to marry and they tended to become terminal members of their family.[10] Some support for the 'eclectic' theory has come from a recent study of Jiangsu and Guangdong which argued that the rural economy of these provinces, especially those parts which produced export crops, experienced considerable prosperity in the 1920s, but this was arrested when the world depression hit China.[11]

The Northern Expedition and the End of the First United Front

The Guomindang expedition to reunify China was eventually launched in July 1926 in the face of 'staggering odds' and against Russian advice.[12] Jiang Jieshi was appointed Commander-in-Chief of the National Revolutionary Army, which by now may have numbered 150,000 men, although only 65,000 were available for the expedition. The Nationalist forces were opposed by three major confederations of opponents: one headed by Wu Peifu in Hubei, Henan and northern Hunan; one by Sun Chuanfang in east China; and one headed by Zhang Zuolin in northern China. The Nationalist forces followed two major lines of advance. The western line, which crossed Hunan, encountered little opposition, but the eastern line, which crossed Jiangxi, was vigorously opposed by Wu Peifu and Nanchang was only captured after a prolonged siege. Nevertheless, by the end of 1926 the Nationalists had gained control of the seven provinces of south and central China.

How had such rapid success been achieved? Undoubtedly the commitment of the National Revolutionary Army and the benefit of Russian strategic advice were important factors. Although there was some serious fighting, there were also major defections from the Nationalists' opponents, persuaded on occasion by the attraction of 'silver bullets'. A more contentious issue is the role of popular movements in facilitating the Nationalists' progress. Harold Isaacs, a left-wing American journalist, observed that 'the masses rose in a tidal wave which swept the expeditionary armies to the banks of the Yangzi'.[13] The facts of the matter are more complicated. Before the arrival of the Nationalist forces the workers' and peasants' movements in warlord areas were largely suppressed. Propaganda teams were sent ahead of the National Revolutionary Army, and they did obtain a positive response from some organizations. For example, at a battle near Changsha a unit calling itself the Common People's National Salvation Corps, composed of some three hundred workers, students and peasants, carried out a suicide attack which cleared the way for the advancing Nationalist forces.[14] But the incidents in which the 'masses' participated were peripheral to the war and only after the arrival of the National Revolutionary Army were the unions and peasant associations revived and then able to expand rapidly. Even Isaacs' claim that it was the 'ordinary people' who supplied the dynamic has not been left unchallenged, for Angus McDonald has shown the extent to which, at this stage of the Chinese revolution, the leadership of the mass movement was still in the hands of the urban elite.[15]

From September 1926 until July of the following year a 'revolutionary spirit' was abroad in the Yangzi cities of Hankou, Hanyang and Wuchang, which jointly comprise Wuhan.[16] Communist labour organizers, including Li Lisan and Liu Shaoqi, and Mikhail Borodin on the part of the Comintern, revived the labour movement. In November a wave of strikes took place which achieved wage increases but also frightened employers into seeking reassurance from the Guomindang. In January the Guomindang moved its capital to Wuhan and immediately found itself at the centre of an anti-imperialist campaign. Western missionaries had already been under attack and now, after a series of demonstrations, a crowd seized the British concession in Hankou. The Wuhan government used the incident to gain de facto recognition from Britain and the surrender of the concession, but the event further alarmed the business community.

Meanwhile, in the countryside the sharp rise in the membership of peasant associations continued. The most dramatic example of this was in Hunan and Hubei provinces. In October 1926 Hunan claimed an association membership of 138,150; a month later the figure exceeded a million and by May 1927 the two provinces recorded a combined peasant association membership of over seven million.[17] Part of this expansion may be explained by the fact that in Hunan clandestine peasant associations had been growing before the Northern Expedition crossed the province. After the Guomindang conquest positive steps were taken to encourage this growth, with the provincial party calling for a guaranteed income for tenant farmers and a 2 per cent limit on interest rates.

It was the consequence of these events which led Mao Zedong in January 1927 to investigate the peasant movement in Hunan and to publish his famous report in the following month. In it he wrote:

> In a very short time, several hundred million peasants in China's central, southern, and northern provinces, will rise like a tornado or tempest – a force so extraordinarily swift and violent that no power, however great, will be able to suppress it.

He described the peasant movement as well organized and noted with approval the violence which had been meted out to local bullies and evil gentry. Using language that was later to be cited as evidence of 'Maoism' – that is to say of a doctrinal break with orthodox Marxism-Leninism – he referred to the poor peasants as the 'vanguard' of the revolution, placing them in the key role hitherto reserved for an industrial proletariat.[18]

These developments in the cities and in the countryside precipitated a split in the Guomindang and the subsequent collapse of the United Front with the CCP. Some members of the CCP had opposed the alliance from the start, but until 1926 its advantages appeared to outweigh its dangers. Alarm bells were rung by the *Zhongshan* incident of 20 March 1926, a pre-emptive strike carried out by Jiang Jieshi against Russian advisers and Communist Party members who he believed were plotting against him. However, the incident was smoothed over by Borodin, and Comintern policy remained firmly committed to the United Front.

The *Zhongshan* incident was symptomatic of tensions within the Guomindang which surfaced during the Northern Expedition and grew deeper with the subsequent surge of the mass movements. While the westward branch of the Northern Expedition had moved rapidly to capture Wuhan and had established a Guomindang government there, Jiang Jieshi, pursuing the eastern route, had halted at Nanchang and had made it the headquarters of the National Revolutionary Army. Whereas the Wuhan government was dominated by Communist and left-wing elements, Nanchang became the focus of right-wing Guomindang supporters.

Tension increased sharply when Jiang Jieshi and the National Revolutionary Army approached Shanghai. In February 1927 an uprising in Shanghai was brutally crushed by Sun Chuanfang's troops, but not before it had revealed the strength of Communist influence in the labour unions and had alarmed foreign interests. By contrast, Jiang Jieshi prepared for the capture of the city by more subtle means, through contacts with the progressive elements in Shanghai's bourgeoisie and with gang leaders.[19] He also strengthened his position by negotiating with Japanese interests and with the northern warlord Zhang Zuolin.

On 21 March, as National Revolutionary Army troops were entering the city, another uprising took place. The Shanghai trade unions, organized as a General Labour Union and headed by Zhou Enlai and other Communist leaders, staged a strike and followed this up by establishing a temporary town council, in effect a provisional government. While this was taking place an extremely volatile situation had arisen in Nanjing. Nationalist troops entered the city on 24 March, attacked and looted the British, American and Japanese consulates and killed several foreigners. It is not clear whether the violence occurred because of ill-discipline or whether it was politically motivated. British ships laid down a barrage to protect the foreign community. Jiang Jieshi accused the Communists of having incited the attack and assured the foreign powers that he had no intention of tolerating anti-foreign incidents. He then turned his attention to Shanghai. Between 10 and 12 April he authorized an extensive purge in which several hundred people died and the left-wing mass organizations were destroyed. National Revolutionary Army commanders loyal to Jiang certainly played an important part in this coup, but he was also assisted by gangsters belonging to the Qingbang, the Green Gang.[20]

The Shanghai April coup and the events which followed it have been taken as the key to the Nanjing decade. One view sees the coup as consummating an alliance between Jiang's military power and the wealthy capitalists of Shanghai. Another notes the ensuing wave of strong-arm tactics and extortion of funds levelled against the Shanghai merchants and sees this as a payoff for the suppression of the workers. A third argument proposes that any alliance between Jiang and the merchants was short lived and the characteristic relationship between the two parties during the Nanjing decade left the merchant class exploited and deprived of any political influence. Recently, Joseph Fewsmith has suggested that the exploitation of the merchants was not incidental, that is to say occasioned by the Nanjing government's chronic shortage of funds, but was part of the transformation of the Nanjing government from a revolutionary movement to a conservative authoritarian regime.[21]

After the Shanghai coup, the focus of attention shifted to Wuhan, where the left wing of the Guomindang continued to co-operate with the Communists. There the revolutionary spirit had been diluted by a crisis of confidence which affected every aspect of the government's activities. In the cities, class warfare had triggered an economic recession which left thousands of workers idle and business stagnant. In the countryside around, the Wuhan government had lost control of the rural revolution, which had turned to violence. In continuance of the Northern Expedition the Wuhan government sent its best armies north into Henan, but this left it unable to defend itself effectively. As a consequence, Changsha, the provincial capital of Hunan, was seized by dissident soldiers in a counter-revolutionary coup. Finally, there was the matter of the advice which the CCP was receiving from Moscow. In essence this was that notwithstanding all indications to the contrary, it should continue to co-operate with the Guomindang. In May the Comintern had debated the appropriate policy towards the agrarian revolution. Leon Trotsky had urged support for it but Stalin, whose opinion prevailed, insisted on the preservation of the United Front. On 1 June 1927 the CCP received new and contradictory instructions: the agrarian revolution should continue but peasant excesses should be curbed; unreliable generals and politicians who had remained in contact with Jiang Jieshi should be replaced. The evidence of an impending Communist takeover left Wang Jingwei, the leader of the left-wing Guomindang, little choice but to act. In July the Russian military advisers departed, Borodin was ordered back to Russia and Communist members of the Guomindang were required to renounce their Communist affiliation. By the end of the month the Communist leadership had gone underground and many members of the Communist rank-and-file had been killed.[22]

It was at this point that the Chinese Communists made their first serious, albeit ill-planned, attempts at insurrection. The first plot involved the Fourth Army, which was known to contain Communist sympathizers, in the seizure of Nanchang. The plot was launched on 1 August, the date subsequently commemorated as the birthday of the Red Army, and at first was very successful. The city was captured and a government claiming to be acting in the name of the Guomindang was installed. But the leadership was divided, no clear policies were announced, and there was no mass support. The soldiers themselves wanted to return to Guangdong, whence many of them came, and by 3 August the rebels had left the city and were marching south. They succeeded in capturing the port of Shantou in September, but by then their forces were scattered and soon defeated, although one unit headed by Zhu De survived to play a notable role in history.[23]

In the meantime Mao Zedong had been involved in the Autumn Harvest uprising, an abortive attempt to capitalize on the peasant militancy which he had described in his famous Report, and which he had later restrained in response to Comintern policy. The uprising was proposed by the Politburo, with the support of Lominadze, the Comintern representative, at a conference held on 7 August which had committed the party to the pursuit of an armed struggle which would lead from the countryside to the city. It was later celebrated as evidence of Mao's inspired identification of a new rural strategy based on a peasant insurrection. In fact Mao opposed the party leadership on strategy, arguing that to rely solely on the peasants would lead to disaster. He put his trust in such regular soldiers and militia as were available.[24] The uprising itself was a fiasco, being largely restricted to eastern Hunan, where the soldiers available were unable to capture key towns. Mao Zedong himself was taken prisoner by militia working with the Guomindang, but managed to escape and to lead survivors of the abortive uprising to the remote region on the Hunan–Jiangxi border called Jinggangshan, later to be known as the Sacred Mountain of the Revolution. There the lessons of the Autumn Harvest insurrection were to be absorbed and a new revolutionary strategy was to emerge.[25]

The third uprising, the Guangzhou Commune of December 1927, was even more badly conceived and executed. In November the Politburo adopted a policy of insurrection and decided to implement it in Guangdong to take advantage of an anticipated clash between the two leading militarists in the province. The uprising began on 11 December and at first went well, the insurgents capturing the key points in Guangzhou and establishing a soviet government. This announced a political programme calling for the confiscation of all land and the expropriation of the property of all capitalists. But there had been little preparation of the workers and the programme attracted scant popular support. Widespread looting and killing occurred. Zhang Fakui, one of the local military leaders, recaptured the city and a brutal suppression followed with more than two hundred Communists and two thousand Red Guards and Red Army men being killed. Trotsky was later to accuse Stalin of having precipitated this debacle for his own political advantage. More probably responsibility for the miscalculation lay with local Communists and Comintern agents on the spot.

Early in 1928 the Northern Expedition was renewed. By now Jiang Jieshi had consolidated his position in the Guomindang at the expense of Wang Jingwei.

Before moving north he reached a working arrangement with two important warlords: Feng Yuxiang, the 'Christian General' and Yan Xishan, the 'Model Governor' of Shanxi. Having defeated the warlord Sun Chuanfang, the expedition's forces moved on to Jinan, the capital of Shandong province and an important railway junction. The Japanese government, apprehensive that the advancing Guomindang troops might precipitate an attack on the large Japanese community there, sent in a detachment of Japanese marines. This inflamed Chinese nationalist sensibilities, and when a clash did occur and the Japanese officer commanding imposed humiliating terms on the Chinese forces, a major international incident seemed inevitable. However, Jiang Jieshi prevaricated and pressed on with the Northern Expedition. Nevertheless, the incident attracted patriotic support for the deeds of the National Revolutionary Army and helped Jiang Jieshi to achieve the final objective of the campaign, the capture of Beijing.[26] His principal remaining opponent was Zhang Zuolin, the warlord of Manchuria. As the Nationalist forces pushed north, Japan intervened and persuaded Zhang to withdraw to Manchuria, assuming that he would remain compliant with the protection of Japanese interests in that region. Zhang agreed, but as the train carrying him from Beijing approached Shenyang, it was wrecked by a bomb planted by officers of the Japanese Guandong army who hoped thereby to bring about a Japanese occupation of Manchuria. However, Zhang Zuolin's place was taken by his son, Zhang Xueliang, the 'Young Marshal'. In the meantime Nationalist forces entered Beijing and the Northern Expedition was formally concluded.[27]

The Nanjing Decade

The years from 1928 to 1937, from the conclusion of the Northern Expedition to the outbreak of war with Japan, are known as the Nanjing decade. The Guomindang made Nanjing its capital on the grounds that the city was central to its main power base, the lower Yangzi. Beijing was accordingly re-named Beiping, meaning 'Northern Peace'. From Nanjing the Guomindang, acting as a national government, aspired to rule a reunified China – apart from Outer Mongolia, Tibet, Xinjiang and Manchuria – and to create a modern nation state.

The record of the Guomindang during these years has been accorded widely varying assessments. Non-Marxist writers have emphasized the difficulties which the Nanjing government faced, and have selectively praised its achievements, noting how the Japanese invasion curtailed any long-term progress. To quote a recent example, Richard T. Phillips suggested that,

> although it is easy to point to Nanjing's failures and possible to seek to excuse them because of the difficult circumstances, some attention must be paid to what was achieved, particularly in the economic and diplomatic sphere. . . .[28]

James Sheridan defined the situation in different terms:

> Under Jiang's government, there were two Chinas: one was the modern, semi-Westernized cities of the eastern coastal provinces, inhabited by an urban elite of

Westernized intellectuals, businessmen, merchants, professionals, and officials who had little contact with life in the countryside; the other was rural China, unchanged in its poverty, ignorance, and hardship, the helpless prey of local officials, warlords, and the conservative local gentry.[29]

The most positive view of the record was put forward by Robert E. Bedeski. He argued that 'the major achievement of the Guomindang . . . was the establishment of the modern sovereign Chinese state'. He supported that view by stressing that the collapse of the imperial state system made it necessary for China to find a new political form. During the Nanjing decade its state-building efforts included the expansion of its sovereignty, the creation of national institutions and the rise in China's international stature. These achievements were to be inherited by the Communists when they came to power in 1949.[30]

Far more hostile assessments have been made by left-wing and Marxist writers. Jean Chesneaux argued that

the power of the Guomindang of Nanjing was built on a coalition between conservative social groups from the countryside and the modern business-oriented bourgeoisie from the cities, which were defending their interests against the popular forces whose militancy had become apparent in 1926 to 1927 and whose struggle continued in the red bases of Jiangxi. These interests essentially coincided with those of the [imperialist] powers. . . . The 'unification' brought about by Nanjing was limited by its necessary compromise with provincial militarists. . . . the Nanjing government made no provision for the popular masses in the decision-making process, which was under its total control, and it did not serve their economic interests.[31]

The official Chinese Communist verdict was that it was a 'comprador-feudal dictatorship', the rule of the Four Big Families, a reference to Jiang's own family, to the Song family into which he had married, and to the prominent Gong and Chen families with which he had personal and political connections.[32]

The political stance of the Nanjing government was based on Sun Zhongshan's programme, which anticipated a period of political tutelage before the introduction of democracy. Under the Organic Law of October 1928 the Guomindang established a one-party dictatorship. The party structure was pyramidal, the lowest functioning unit being the ward, above that the district and the province, and at the apex the National Congress. A similar structure existed in the armed forces. In theory the most significant organ of the party was the Central Executive Committee, but in practice its power always depended on the party leader. In deference to the role played by Sun Zhongshan in the creation of the Guomindang, even after his death Sun remained President of the party. Although Jiang Jieshi alone commanded the influence which entitled him to be party leader, his lack of seniority ensured that only in 1938 was he given the special title of General Director.

In 1931 a provisional constitution was introduced which defined the organization of the national government. It remained in force, in theory, until 1948. It provided for a five-yuan or five-branch system of government, the five *yuan* being responsible for the legislative, executive, judicial, examination and control branches of the government. The Examination *yuan* conducted the civil service examinations, and the Control *yuan* supervised the policies and morals of civil servants – both functions reminiscent of the old imperial system of government. The Examination *yuan* did indeed hold examinations, but the successful candidates supplied less than 1 per cent of the bureaucracy, the rest obtaining their position through personal connections with powerful figures. The Control *yuan* supposedly fought corruption, which was endemic in the years of the Nanjing government, but most of its victims were very junior officials.[33]

Throughout the Nanjing period Jiang Jieshi maintained a position of dominance. He achieved this by manipulating factions within the army, the party and the government. Within the army, a group known as the Huangpu clique, composed of officers from the Huangpu Military Academy of which Jiang had been the first commandant, was directly loyal to Jiang. In 1931 another group of Huangpu officers formed the highly disciplined elitist organization known as the Blue Shirts, the name referring to their wearing of Chinese cotton-cloth uniforms. The Blue Shirts was a political rather than a military movement, its purpose being to revive the Guomindang and to elevate Jiang to the position of dictator. Within the party an important clandestine faction supporting Jiang was known as the Organization Group, or the CC clique, after the brothers Chen Guofu and Chen Lifu. The CC clique, which was violently anti-Communist, expanded its influence through its control of the Guomindang's confidential records. The Political Study Group was a more loosely organized faction, which received support from businessmen and provincial leaders.

Although the Northern Expedition had nominally achieved the reunification of China, and had ushered in the period of political tutelage, the military character of the regime remained very apparent. Jiang Jieshi continued as commander-in-chief until he was temporarily forced from power in December 1931. Early in 1932 he recovered his political authority and also became chairman of the Military Affairs Commission, which gave him complete control of the armed forces.[34] Plans for the reduction in size of the National Revolutionary Army were postponed and eventually discarded. Throughout the Nanjing decade military expenditure never fell below 40 per cent of total government expenditure.[35] Such a reliance on the military was not surprising, for the army was involved in military campaigns in every year of the Nanjing decade. Some of these derived from the persistence of warlordism throughout the period. In 1929, as a protest against the planned reduction of the National Revolutionary Army, the Guangxi leaders of the Fourth Army Group rebelled but were defeated. In the following year Feng Yuxiang and Yan Xishan headed an anti-Jiang coalition and precipitated a major conflict, which was only settled in the Nanjing government's favour when Zhang Xueliang committed his Manchurian forces on Jiang's side. From 1931 the Guomindang forces prosecuted a series of campaigns against the Communist rural bases. In 1933 disaffected soldiers and Guomindang leaders headed a revolt in Fujian and announced a policy of resistance to Japan and democracy for the people. And while these internal threats were being negated, the need to resist Japanese encroachment in Manchuria and north China became ever more pressing.

The Rise of the Guomindang and the Nanjing Decade

It was against this background that the Nanjing government sought to implement its economic policies. Its achievement in this field has earned it the greatest credit. The leading lights of these reforms were Song Ziwen (T.V. Soong), a Harvard graduate whose sister married Jiang Jieshi, and Kong Xiangxi (H.H. Kung), a graduate of Oberlin, who was Mme Jiang's brother-in-law. An early reform concerned the monetary system, China having 'unquestionably the worst currency to be found in any important country'.[36] The unit of account known as the tael, which was not a coin but the equivalent of 500–600 grains of silver, was abolished and in its place a silver dollar bearing the head of Sun Zhongshan was introduced. The fact that the currency was based on the silver standard was advantageous during the world depression, but from 1933 an American silver-buying programme severely depressed the rural economy. A second area of achievement concerned banking. When Song was the Guomindang Finance Minister in Guangzhou, he had established the Central Bank of China. A new Central Bank was now established in Shanghai, with branches in major cities, and this became the institution which regulated currency and credit. Other specialist banks were established or revived: the Bank of China to deal with foreign exchange, the Bank of Communications to promote transportation and the Farmers' Bank to provide farm credit.

These reforms gave China a framework of modern financial institutions, an essential preliminary to economic development. However, their effectiveness has been criticized sharply and some of their consequences regretted. A major reason for creating a central banking group was to make available cheap credit for investment. In practice little credit was provided where it was most needed, that is in the rural sector of the economy. A more important use for the banks, from the point of view of the Nanjing government, was to sell government bonds. This was absolutely necessary as throughout the decade the budget was never balanced and government had to rely on loans to cover a deficit of approximately 20 per cent of its annual expenditure. Government bonds were sold to the banks at sharp discounts from their face value, which was very advantageous to the banks and their investors, but which diverted savings from investment to speculation.[37] Another important change which occurred during this period concerned control of the banking industry. In 1932 the twenty-six member banks of the Shanghai Bankers Association held three-quarters of the total resources of all modern Chinese banks. While Song Ziwen was finance minister he attempted to co-operate with the Shanghai bankers, allowing them a measure of independence in return for their supporting the regime with funds. But when he was replaced in 1933 by Kong Xiangxi a different relationship developed, characterized by the banking coup of 1935. Facing a financial crisis precipitated by the American silver-buying policy, Kong forced the Bank of China and the Bank of Communications to create new shares and then to exchange these for government bonds. By the end of 1936 the government holding of the assets of Chinese banks had risen from less than 20 per cent to over 70 per cent.[38]

The second area of economic achievement concerned improvements in transportation. At the end of 1927 China had about 8,150 miles of railway track,[39] but warlords had seized many railways, the railway companies were frequently in default on debt, much of the track was in a poor condition and there was a shortage of rolling stock. The whole of China could boast only about 18,000 miles of road passable to motor traffic and there were only some 20,000 motor vehicles to use them. There were no functioning airlines.[40] By 1937 a further 5,000 miles of railway track had been laid, including the completion of the Guangzhou–Hankou line, constructed by Chinese engineers and financed by remitted funds from the British Boxer indemnity. In 1929 a National Highway Planning Commission was established and the first steps were taken towards creating a modern road network. By 1936 there were 69,000 miles of road with a further 10,000 miles under construction. In the same period the Chinese National Aviation Corporation was established and scheduled passenger services were introduced.[41]

Undoubtedly these were significant improvements, but their limits should be admitted. The figures quoted for railway and road construction included the statistics for Manchuria, which from 1931 was under Japanese control. The railway system still did not extend to the wealthy province of Sichuan, let alone to the distant regions of Gansu, Xinjiang and Tibet. Much of the labour used for construction of railways and roads had been provided by conscripted peasants who received no pay for their work and little compensation for the loss of their land. Many of the new roads were constructed for military purposes and peasants were not allowed to use them.[42]

The third most-commonly quoted example of economic achievement concerns the modern industrial sector. One estimate suggested that between 1926 and 1936 the rate of industrial expansion in China Proper was running at 6 per cent per annum, and that that figure would have been higher if Manchuria had been included.[43] Statistics relating to particular industries showed impressive increases, for example, between 1927 and 1936 the generation of electricity increased from 772 to 1,724 million Kwh, an annual growth rate of 9.4 per cent; the production of coal rose from 14.2 million to 26.2 million tonnes, an annual growth rate of 7 per cent; and the output of cement rose from 498,000 to 1,243,000 tonnes, an annual growth rate of 9.6 per cent.[44] By 1937 the import of foreign coal was virtually negligible and Chinese coal exports had begun to play an important role in Japanese industry.[45]

However, this achievement should be put into perspective. In 1933 the whole of China's modern industrial sector, including transportation, contributed only 7.4 per cent to gross domestic production.[46] Modern industry was heavily concentrated in the treaty ports and was almost entirely unknown in the interior provinces. Major industries were dominated by foreign capital. In 1936 65.7 per cent of China's coal output came from mines under foreign ownership or foreign control, and the same foreign dominance was apparent in the modern cotton textile industry. Factory industry in China was predominantly consumer goods industry. Chinese-owned factories were generally small, their organization remained traditional, few managers or technicians had received adequate training and the labour force was largely unskilled.[47] Nevertheless, it has been asserted that 'During this decade, the necessary foundation was being laid for modern economic transformation'.[48]

During the Nanjing decade the Chinese economy remained overwhelmingly agricultural and farming methods remained largely traditional. Sun Zhongshan had called for agricultural improvement and during the decade attempts were made to promote change. In 1930 a land law was passed which outlined a broad programme of agricultural reforms, including the limitation of rent to 37.5 per cent of the main produce from the land. A National Agricultural Research Bureau was created in 1932 to collect statistics on crop production, and in the following year a Rural Rehabilitation Commission was set up to make studies of marketing, land tenure and rural credit. In the meantime agricultural research stations had been established and progress had been made on pest control, crop improvement and the dissemination of good farming practice. The government also supported the agricultural co-operative movement, which was intended to supply cheap credit to peasants. Perhaps these changes 'promised much for the future',[49] but the more common assessment is that the Guomindang government merely scratched the surface of the problem. In 1934 the rural co-operative movement supplied only 2.4 per cent of the loans made to peasants, the vast bulk of the credit coming from pawnbrokers, landlords, rich farmers and merchants. Much of what was borrowed went into consumption and very little went into agricultural improvement. In short, little occurred to alter the pattern of a landlord-dominated rural society.[50]

The economic record of the Nanjing government has been the subject of sharply differing interpretations. In 1957 Douglas S. Paauw, having surveyed the record relating to the agricultural and industrial sectors, and having considered the government stance with reference to investment and institutional change, concluded that 'the Guomindang was not prepared on either the conceptual level or policy level to cope with the problem of economic stagnation'. The trend towards bureaucratic capitalism, the object of which was control by the few rather than the expansion of output, did not provide the preconditions for economic growth – on the contrary the government had 'less capacity to promote economic development in 1937 than a decade earlier'.[51] Arthur N. Young attributed Paauw's damning verdict to ignorance of major parts of the record and to anti-Nationalist bias.[52] Albert Feuerwerker, however, pointed out that between 1931 and 1936 central government expenditure averaged a mere 3.5 per cent of the gross national product, and much of this was spent on the military or on servicing debt. Government policies, although they might have profound influences on the economy, 'were never realistically capable of pushing the Chinese economy forward on the path of modern economic growth'.[53] Recently Thomas G. Rawski has argued that China's economic performance was far more impressive than previously suggested, his preferred measures indicating that

China's annual rate of per capita output growth surpassed 1 percent during the interwar decades, a rate that approached comparable Japanese figures for the period 1897–1931.

This growth was rooted in the expansion of foreign trade and it was most marked in the treaty ports and Manchuria. It owed much to private enterprise, but the role of government was not inconsiderable.[54]

The Nationalist government regarded its educational policy as a key element in the creation of a modern nation state. A National Education Conference, held in May 1928, identified the aims of its educational policies to be the promotion of nationalism, the maintenance of old cultural traditions, the raising of moral and physical standards, the attainment of democracy, and the realization of social justice. It added that there should be equality of education between the sexes and that education should be compulsory when children reached school age.[55] In 1932 laws relating to primary and secondary schools were promulgated. Regulation was also applied to universities, with the designation of national universities and the issue of rules governing the award of degrees. The nationalist tone in education was exemplified by the requirements that all foreign-founded Christian colleges should register with the Ministry of Education and should appoint Chinese nationals as their heads.[56]

The educational record certainly fell short of the rhetoric. The objective of compulsory education at primary school level was not achieved. In Yunnan, in 1933, over 27 per cent of the children of relevant age were in school, but this was an exceptionally high figure. At secondary level, education was available to 213 out of every 10,000 children in Shanghai, but the figure fell to 4 out of every 10,000 in provinces such as Shaanxi, Guizhou and Gansu.[57] According to government sources, in 1932 girls only accounted for 15.1 per cent of the enrolment in primary schools. The low enrolment figures were not surprising, for the financing of primary schools was left to districts and that of secondary schools to provincial governments. Few families could afford the cost of education and only a minority of those would consider spending money on educating their daughters.

The situation with regard to higher education was no more satisfactory. The number of students enrolled in universities and colleges in 1934, amounting to less than 1 per 10,000 population, placed China at the bottom of a list of twenty-six countries compiled by the Ministry of Education. The universities were concentrated in the coastal cities, the subjects studied were disproportionately weighted towards literature and law, with science and technical subjects being less popular (although there was improvement during the decade), and much of the teaching was in the hands of staff who had trained abroad, or who based their teaching on foreign textbooks and studies. There were some notable achievements, for example the founding of the Academia Sinica as a central research academy, and the promotion of geological surveys and archaeological investigations.[58] But the concept of academic freedom was vitiated by a political regime which imposed mandatory student political training and which controlled student political expression. The consequence has been described as the 'alienated academy', with students no longer identifying with the nationalism of the Guomindang, and dissident intellectuals being forced out of their university posts.[59]

This alienation, which was a surprising feature of the Nanjing decade, arose from a marked change in the ideology projected by the Guomindang. In the 1920s it had appeared as a revolutionary party, committed to anti-imperialism and anti-warlordism. The students who had figured largely in its support were of the May Fourth generation, which had rejected Confucianism. While in alliance with the CCP, members of its left wing had promoted ideas of political, social and economic reform. But no sooner had the Nanjing government established itself than a major shift in ideology took place. Sun Zhongshan's Three Principles of the People – nationalism, democracy and the people's livelihood – remained at its centre, but the progressive implications of these ideas were balanced by conservative themes endorsed by Jiang Jieshi. He took his ideas from the neo-Confucian teachings of Zhu Xi, who emphasized the virtues of self-discipline and deference to hierarchy. Jiang rejected the cultural iconoclasm of the May Fourth period, which had manifested itself in an attack on the Confucian family and the obligations of filial piety. He reinstated the study of the Four Books, the Confucian classics, and in 1931 Confucius's birthday was made a public holiday. Even the lessons of history were revised – whereas Sun Zhongshan had found his revolutionary inspiration in Hong Xiuquan and the Taiping rebels, Jiang Jieshi admired Zeng Guofan and praised the conservative achievements of the Tongzhi restoration.[60]

However, it became apparent that it would not be simple to create a strong, independent and unified China – indeed in 1931, when China was hit by disastrous floods, the world depression and the Japanese seizure of Manchuria, it seemed that far from the Guomindang achieving a restoration, the decline was continuing. It was in this atmosphere that the Blue Shirt organization was formed and a new ideological theme was introduced. The Blue Shirts regarded the Guomindang as compromised, and would have abolished the party if that had been possible. Instead they aimed to transform its ideology by stressing dictatorship, exaltation of the nation and the total abnegation of self. In this they found their inspiration in Nazi Germany and more specifically in Mussolini's Italy. This connection and similarities in outlook and methods led Lloyd Eastman to assert that 'Fascism provided the core of the Blue Shirt ideology' and to add that Jiang Jieshi himself was intrigued by the fascist phenomenon.[61] This view was hotly contested by Maria Hsia Chang, who argued that there was no qualitative change in ideology from that inspired by Sun Zhongshan to a belief-system that was fascist. Jiang himself was only interested in fascism as a tool, as a means of mobilizing the nation. Other similarities were superficial or misleading, for example the term Blue Shirts was not a borrowing from Mussolini's blackshirts, but a reference to the type of jacket worn by the Blue Shirts. This was made from cotton cloth manufactured in China which had been popularized by Sun Zhongshan. It symbolized identification with Chinese nationalism and loyalty to the doctrines of Sun Zhongshan.[62]

The practical expression of the new ideology was the New Life Movement, launched by Jiang Jieshi in 1934, and later led by Mme Jiang. The movement called for the revival of Confucianism and in particular of the four virtues of li-yi-lian-chi, that is propriety, justice, honesty and self-respect. It began by declaring zero tolerance of minor breaches of social decorum: failing to button up one's clothes or spitting in the streets. According to Jiang:

If we are to have a new life that accords with li-yi-lian-chi, then we must start by not spitting heedlessly . . . If we are to restore the nation and gain revenge for our humiliations, then we need not talk about guns and cannon, but must first talk about washing our faces in cold water.[63]

The final aspect of the Nanjing government's record which requires evaluation is foreign policy. The Blue Shirt demand for an independent China implied an end to the unequal treaties. Wang Zhengting, who became foreign minister in 1928, proposed that foreign rights and privileges be abolished in the following order: tariff control; extraterritoriality; navigation in Chinese waters; leased territories, concessions and settlements; and the presence of foreign troops on Chinese soil (the clash with Japanese troops at Jinan in May 1928 had inflamed feelings on this issue). Whereas in its earlier days the Guomindang had threatened to use mass support to press the case for the immediate revocation of the unequal treaties, now the methods employed were strictly diplomatic. Certainly some progress was made: in 1928 the United States granted China tariff autonomy and by 1930 the other powers had followed suit. Between 1929 and 1931 China recovered the British concessions in Hankou, Jiujiang, Zhenjiang and Xiamen and the leased territory of Weihaiwei. The attempt to end extraterritoriality was less successful as the foreign powers were unwilling to make concessions until China's administration of justice and maintenance of public order reached a standard which satisfied them. It might be argued that in the 1930s China, threatened by Japan, had good reason not to alienate the Western powers and that was a sufficient excuse for the slow progress on treaty revision. The alternative argument is that internal weaknesses and divisions prevented the Nationalist government from promoting China's interests in the area of foreign relations effectively.[64]

The Chinese Communist Party: from the Guangzhou Commune to the Long March

As a consequence of the disasters of 1927 the organizational structure of the CCP was shattered and the links between the Central Committee and the developing rural bases became tenuous.[65] Until 1931, when the Central Committee relocated in Jiangxi and the Chinese Soviet Republic was established, it is justifiable to treat the two strands of the party's history as if they were largely separate.

In June 1928 the Sixth Congress of the CCP was held in Moscow; the location, chosen for security reasons, indicated the Party's increased reliance on Russia. At the Congress a post-mortem was held on recent events and decisions were taken on personnel and policies. Qu Qiubai, who had taken over from Chen Duxiu as Secretary-General in August of the previous year, was in turn replaced for committing what was later described as the 'first leftist opportunist deviation'.[66] The effective leadership of the Party was assumed by Li Lisan, a former labour leader from Hunan, who was the head of the Propaganda Department. There is a dispute over what policies were agreed at the Congress and, by implication, supported by the Comintern. One view is that the Congress took an unreasonably optimistic view of the situation in China, which led to the attempt at the rapid overthrow of the Nationalist regime, later to be condemned as the 'Li Lisan line'. Alternatively, it has been argued that the Comintern consistently urged the CCP to anticipate a protracted struggle in which it would work to weaken the

Guomindang and to build up its own strength by concentrating on three things: the creation of a Red Army, the establishment of an effective soviet government, and the continuation of mass work among peasants and workers.[67]

Back in China, Li Lisan had to deal with a situation over which he had little control, especially in terms of influence in the rural bases and command of the Red Army. The insecurity of his own position, coupled with ambiguity in the Comintern stance, may have contributed to the events which followed. In July 1929 the second plenary session of the Sixth Congress took note of the revival of the workers' struggle and the existence of soviet areas under the control of Mao Zedong and Zhu De. It accepted the Comintern view that 'the whole revolutionary movement is on the upswing', but it added opaquely that 'it is equally incorrect to maintain that the surge of the revolutionary wave is very remote or that it is imminent'.[68] A year later Li Lisan abandoned caution. A Central Committee resolution passed on 11 June drew attention to China's internal difficulties (the Nanjing government was at war with the warlords Feng Yuxiang and Yan Xishan), and to the world crisis, and asserted that 'China is the weakest link in the chain of world imperialism'.[69]

In the summer of 1930 the Communists went on the offensive. Red Army units were deployed to attack Changsha, Wuhan and Nanchang, and trade union and youth movements were ordered to foment strikes and demonstrations in those cities. The result was a disaster. Changsha was captured and held for ten days, but elsewhere the plans failed miserably. The Red Army units, which numbered 70–80,000 men, were quite inadequate for the task and the popular response was weak and unco-ordinated. Furthermore, the Red Army and rural base leaders gave only half-hearted support, Mao Zedong himself disobeying orders and calling off the second attack on Changsha.

The political resolution of the failure came at the fourth plenum of the Sixth Central Committee, held in January 1931. By this time Pavel Mif, the new Comintern representative, had arrived in China. He secured the condemnation of Li Lisan for following 'an adventurous policy of putschism' and he also obtained the appointment to the Politburo of a number of his protégés, the group of Moscow-trained Chinese students known as the Twenty-eight Bolsheviks. Later that year the Central Committee decided to relocate from Shanghai to the central soviet area in Jiangxi.

It is now time to turn to that other aspect of the CCP's history in the period 1927–31, the development of rural bases. The emphasis will be on Mao Zedong and the development of the Jiangxi central base, later to become the Jiangxi Soviet and then the central area of the Chinese Soviet Republic. It should not be forgotten, however, that there were up to fifteen Communist rural bases in south central China in the early 1930s.

After the defeat of the Autumn Harvest uprising, Mao Zedong and other survivors fled to Jinggangshan. In April 1928 he was joined by Zhu De and several hundred soldiers, deserters from the Nationalist forces which had mutinied at Nanchang in the previous year. In the months that followed, what was to be known as the Fourth Red Army took shape, and the first experiments were made in revolutionary land reform, that is the confiscation and redistribution of landlords' land. Almost immediately the base came under Nationalist attack and in December, on orders from the Central Committee, Mao and Zhu De moved 150 miles east, to the area around Ruijin on the Jiangxi–Fujian border. There work continued on improving the Red Army. Mao was now joined by Peng Dehuai, the leader of the Fifth Army, and a new programme of land reform was initiated. As experience of operating rural base areas increased, Mao's view of their importance grew. They bore, he said, the same relation to the army as did the buttocks to a person – without them a person was obliged to run about until exhausted.[70] The remoteness of the rural base areas, and the contrast between the practical problems of survival and the theoretical arguments which engaged the Central Committee, ensured that Mao would distance himself from Li Lisan's direction of the Party. However, the evidence suggests that Mao, who tended to take an optimistic view about revolutionary prospects, did not oppose the armed uprisings of the summer of 1930, although he later disclaimed responsibility, alleging that he and Zhu De had had no choice but to accept the Central Committee's decision.[71] After the failure of the uprising, Mao was implicated in the obscure Futian incident, the first major Communist purge in which Mao showed his ruthless determination by eliminating some two or three thousand officers and men of the Twentieth Red Army. They were accused of belonging to the Anti-Bolshevik group, allegedly a Guomindang organization, but the more probable explanation is that the incident was part of a power struggle directed against Li Lisan.

On 7 November 1931, the anniversary of the Russian Revolution, the Chinese Soviet Republic was established at Ruijin. Its first Congress was attended by some 600 representatives of the soviet areas, the Red Army and the labour movement. A constitution was adopted which declared that this was a 'democratic dictatorship of the workers and peasants in the soviet districts' and a programme outlined which referred to labour legislation, a land law, the abolition of foreign privileges, the emancipation of women, and the right of national minorities to secede from the state. Mao Zedong was elected President, but it is clear that his influence was to be eroded by the presence in Jiangxi of the Central Committee and in particular of the Twenty-eight Bolsheviks.

Three of the policy issues tackled by the Soviet Republic are of particular interest, those relating to the Red Army, to women and to land. With reference to the Red Army, much progress had already been made in creating a disciplined and politically aware force. It was a regular army, supported by voluntary organizations representing the mobilization of the entire population. In early 1930 its estimated strength was 100,000 men, the majority of whom were of peasant background. The army was placed under close political control, one soldier in three being a member of the CCP or the Communist Youth League, and political commissars were attached to each regiment and Party representatives organized a cell in each squad.

The Red Army's mission far exceeded that of a normal fighting force, for it had been described by Mao Zedong as 'an armed group for carrying out political tasks of a class nature'.[72] The army and its soldiers served as role models, and all regardless of rank received the same pay and enjoyed the same conditions of service. Soldiers were required to learn by heart and practise the 'three major disciplines' and the 'eight-point rules', codes of conduct for dealing with the masses. The former went as follows:

1. Obey orders in all your actions.
2. Do not take a single needle or piece of thread from the masses.
3. Turn in everything captured.

A second policy issue concerned the position of women in Chinese society and their role in the revolution. During the period of the first United Front, the Communists and Nationalists had cooperated in developing a women's movement with some degree of success, the emphasis being on the struggle for equal rights. In his 'Report of an investigation into the peasant movement in Hunan', Mao Zedong had struck a revolutionary note. He observed that men in China – he implied peasants – were subjected to three systems of authority, those of the state, the clan and religion, but women were further dominated by men. These four types of authority, he said, represented the ideology of feudalism and patriarchy. Mao continued:

> Lately, with the rise of the peasant movement, women have begun to organize rural women's associations in many places; they have been given the opportunity to lift up their heads, and the authority of the husband is tottering more and more with every passing day.[73]

In 1930 Mao carried out an investigation in the county of Xunwu in south-east Jiangxi. This provided him with recent evidence of the effect of a marriage policy which permitted freedom of marriage and divorce. In his report Mao argued that male peasants only opposed the liberation of women because they were unsure of the outcome of the land struggle. Once that struggle had been developed, their attitudes to marriage would change greatly.[74] In the following year the Jiangxi Soviet, having passed a land law, also passed a marriage law based on the marriage law of the Soviet Union. It defined marriage as 'a free association between a man and a woman to be entered into without interference from other parties and ended at the wish of either'. It offered divorced women some economic protection and they were to be favoured when awarding the custody of their children. It is unlikely that this law was implemented fully in these early years. However, the CCP did seek to involve women in its activities and they were used quite extensively in the defence forces, for intelligence and sabotage, and above all in productive labour.[75]

The third and most controversial issue concerned land reform, that is to say the confiscation and redistribution of land. Land reform was preceded by a classification of the rural population into four main groups: landlords, that is those who owned land but did not work it themselves, either hiring labour or living on rents; rich peasants who worked their own land but also hired labour and collected rents; middle peasants who either owned or rented land, which they worked themselves; and poor peasants who owned little or no land and lived by hiring out their labour. Revolutionary land reform had been initiated briefly in 1928 by Peng

Pai in the Haifeng soviet and confiscation and redistribution of land was started at the Sacred Mountain base in 1928 and in Xunwu in the following year. Mao Zedong at first favoured a radical law, which confiscated all land rather than that of the landlords alone, which placed the confiscated land in the hands of the state rather than those of the peasants, and which prohibited the sale and purchase of land. He later modified this to permit rich peasants to retain their good land and the principles of state ownership and the prohibition of land dealings were dropped. In 1930 the National Conference of Delegates from the Soviet Areas adopted what is sometimes known as the Li Lisan land policy. This announced the confiscation of landlords' land and that part of the land owned by rich peasants which they rented. The sale and purchase of land was prohibited and large holdings were not to be split up but organized as collective farms. This law was denounced by the Comintern as deviant: to the right because it permitted rich peasants to retain land and to the left because it proceeded directly to the collective stage. In 1931 the Central Committee, then dominated by Pavel Mif and the Twenty-eight Bolsheviks, promulgated a draft land law. This provided for the confiscation of landlords' land without compensation. The land of rich peasants was also to be confiscated and at the redistribution they were only to be given land of poorer quality to cultivate with their own labour.[76]

The application of this policy went through a number of phases. In the first phase landlords' and rich peasants' land was confiscated and redistributed and several thousands may have died in acts of vengeance.[77] However, it became apparent that many landlords and rich peasants had concealed the true extent of their holdings and had retained their local influence. In 1933 a Land Investigation Movement was launched to identify such cases and more generally to promote a mass movement to arouse the class struggle. Mao Zedong, whose position had been much weakened by the presence of the Central Committee in Jiangxi, may have taken the initiative on this. However, in early 1934 Mao's implementation was criticized as too moderate and the Land Investigation Movement, under the direction of Zhang Wentian, one of the Twenty-eight Bolsheviks, became more radical. He called for a reign of terror against class enemies, that is landlords and rich peasants, who were now required to do forced labour. This led to the large-scale killing and starving of those defined as reactionary elements and to the alienation of the middle peasants, who were classified as friends of the regime.[78]

At first the Nanjing government had largely ignored the existence of the rural bases and had concentrated on its struggle with warlord regimes. In December 1930 it ordered the suppression of the Communists 'within three or six months at most'. However, the Nationalist forces failed to appreciate the strength and mobility of the Red Army and the degree of popular support for the Communists. In 1931 Jiang Jieshi himself took over the direction of the campaign and committed 300,000 troops to bringing it to a speedy conclusion. Once again the swift movement of the Red Army deprived the Nationalist forces of a decisive engagement and the campaign was cut short by the news of the Shenyang Incident in September and the Japanese seizure of Manchuria. Despite the threat to the nation, Jiang chose first to pacify the country, then to oppose the foreign invader.

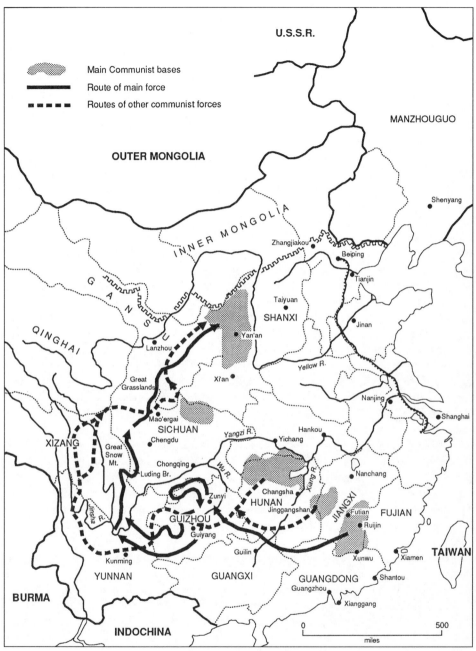

The Long March, 1934–5.

In the following year an attack was made on all the red bases, but with little success against the bases in Jiangxi.

The fifth 'bandit-suppression campaign' began in October 1933. Jiang Jieshi now employed both political and military measures. Local populations were forced to move into strategic hamlets and the *baojia*, the security system of imperial times, was revived. With advice from German military experts, he introduced a strategy of encirclement and blockade. A ring of blockhouses was constructed and the Communist supply routes were interrupted. While this campaign was still taking shape, a mutiny occurred in the ranks of the Nationalist Nineteenth Route Army, the leaders of the revolt being dissatisfied with Jiang Jieshi's failure to oppose Japan. This incident, known as the Fujian revolt, divided the Communist leadership on the question of whether to support the rebels. Whereas Zhou Enlai and some other members of the Central Committee favoured sending a force to assist them, Mao Zedong took a more cautious line, arguing that the rebels were not revolutionaries and suggesting that they should make their own way to the Jiangxi base. While the wrangling continued, Jiang Jieshi struck hard and the rebellion was crushed. Mao was later to admit that this was an error, but denied personal responsibility for the loss of the opportunity created by the revolt.[79]

The decision to abandon the Jiangxi base and to set out on what became known as the Long March was probably taken as early as May 1934, although the main evacuation did not take place until October. The most obvious reason for the decision was the deteriorating military situation. Mao Zedong later attributed this to the adoption of the erroneous strategy of simple defence, abandoning the former tactics of manoeuvre.[80] Otto Braun, the Comintern agent, claimed that the march began as an orderly strategic retreat.[81] An underlying reason for abandoning the base may have been the loss of popular support following the decision to radicalize the land investigation movement.[82]

Perhaps 120,000 people began the Long March from the Jiangxi base. This figure included about 30,000 civilians, some thirty-five women including the wives of some senior officials, and Otto Braun, the solitary European to follow the entire march. Left behind were some 20,000 casualties and the sick, including Qu Qiubai who had tuberculosis, a rearguard of 6,000 soldiers, and virtually all children, including two of Mao Zedong's.[83] The Jiangxi contingent was later joined by the Second Front Army headed by He Long from its base in Hunan, and the Fourth Front Army led by Zhang Guotao from the base established on the Sichuan–Shaanxi border.

The march began with a dramatic break-out to the south-west. The first Guomindang defensive perimeters were penetrated with some ease, but the Xiang river was only crossed after a fierce battle. The direction of the march was unclear. Mao later claimed that the intention was to move northwards to combat the Japanese, against whom the Soviet Republic had declared war in 1932, but the more likely objective was to link up with Zhang Guotao. However, Jiang Jieshi anticipated this move and the marchers were compelled to fight their way to the west, suffering very heavy losses in the process.

Early in January 1935 Communist troops crossed the Wu river and captured the important city of Zunyi in northern Guizhou. There a conference was held at which, it has been claimed, the policies of the Twenty-eight Bolsheviks were repudiated and Mao Zedong was installed as effective leader of the Party. A recent assessment has played down the factional conflict and has suggested that 'Mao was not so powerless before the Conference, nor did he become so powerful after it'.[84]

After the conference the marchers continued yet further west, eventually managing to cross the upper Yangzi, here known as the Jinsha or Golden Sands river, and then turning north through Sichuan. The route now lay through territory inhabited by minority groups. According to the account of the march given by Mao Zedong to Edgar Snow, good relations were established between the Communists and the Yi, but later on in the march other minority groups gave them a hostile reception and denied them supplies.[85] The next obstacle was the Dadu river, the crossing of which was the most famous single episode of the march. At this spot in 1863 the Taiping leader Shi Dakai had been trapped and his army destroyed. The only crossing point was the Luding bridge, an ancient chain bridge over a gorge, which was protected by machine-guns and mortars. The chains had been stripped of their planking, but Red Army volunteers swarmed over and seized the fortifications on the opposite bank. Moving on through Sichuan, the next task was to cross the Great Snow mountain, seven mountain ranges, reaching 16,000 feet. Many died of exposure and two-thirds of the pack animals were lost.

In June, at Mao'ergai in northern Sichuan, the forces under Mao Zedong met up with the better-equipped Fourth Front Army led by Zhang Guotao. The encounter was followed by a disagreement over policy and the direction the march should take. Whereas Mao Zedong favoured pressing on northwards and opposing the Japanese, Zhang Guotao was determined to proceed to Xizang with the objective of establishing a rural base there. This he did and persuaded or coerced Zhu De to accompany him. Zhu De later rejoined Mao, but the rupture with Zhang Guotao proved irreparable.

The last stage of the march lay through Gansu province, first crossing the notorious Great Grasslands, a vast and trackless swamp, where many more men died. In October 1935, just over a year from the start of the march, the First Front Army reached the north Shaanxi base area and joined up with other Red Army units. The march had extended over 5,000 miles, and less than 20,000 of those who had set out reached Shaanxi.

Assessments of the march have commonly dealt in superlatives. Edgar Snow described it as 'the biggest armed propaganda tour in history'.[86] Dick Wilson wrote of the march's four legacies: discipline and group loyalty; the guerrilla ethic – the achievement of victory over tremendous odds; independence from Russia; and the supremacy of Mao.[87] When old, Mao Zedong spoke sadly of the tremendous burden of surviving an ordeal in which so many comrades had died, and of the obligation he felt to preserve the revolution for which they had struggled – an impulse which contributed to the Cultural Revolution.[88]

22

The Sino-Japanese War
and the Civil War

Prelude to War: Japanese Aggression
and the Chinese Response

The International Military Tribunal for the Far East, sitting in Tokyo between May 1946 and November 1948, convicted twenty-two Japanese leaders of conspiracy to wage aggressive war against China. By so doing it confirmed the opinion held widely outside Japan, and subsequently reiterated in standard histories, that the Sino-Japanese War was the outcome of Japanese aggression. This pattern of aggression could be traced back to the First World War and to the Twenty-one Demands. After a period of relative calm in the 1920s, marked by the moderate policies associated with the Japanese Foreign Minister Shidehara Kijuro, aggression resumed in 1931 with the Manchurian Incident. Having created the puppet state of Manzhouguo (Manchukuo), Japan then infiltrated North China and Inner Mongolia. In July 1937, after the Marco Polo Bridge Incident, full-scale war broke out and Japan seized the main coastal cities and the most important economic areas of China and held them until defeat in 1945.

That Japanese aggression was the main cause of these events will not be disputed, but the role of Chinese nationalism in precipitating the conflict should not be discounted. Anxiety over the future status of Korea led Japan to fight wars with China and Russia and in 1910 to annex Korea as a colony. That step, intended as a final solution to threats to Japan's position in the region, encouraged the growth of Korean nationalism. As Manchuria and China Proper became increasingly important areas for Japanese investment, Chinese nationalism assumed an even more threatening aspect. The confrontation at Jinan in May 1928 nearly precipitated a major clash. In June soldiers from the Japanese Guandong army assassinated Zhang Zuolin, the Old Marshall of Manchuria, intending thereby to destabilize the region and provide the grounds for a Japanese occupation. This was a miscalculation for Zhang Xueliang, the Old Marshall's son, took control and proved to be more committed to the cause of Chinese nationalism than his father. In September 1931 officers of the Guandong army, believing that Japan's interests in Manchuria were threatened by Chinese interference, and convinced that the Japanese government was too weak-kneed to assert Japan's rights, precipitated another incident. A short section of the Japanese-owned South Manchurian railway south of Shenyang was sabotaged, and the incident was used as a pretext for attacks on Chinese forces in the area. The Japanese government tried ineffectually to curb the military, and the League of Nations, prompted by the United States, attempted to negotiate an agreement. In January, the Japanese navy bombarded the Zhabei district of Shanghai, which was defended heroically by the Nineteenth Route Army. Despite this evidence of Chinese determination to resist Japanese encroachment, Jiang Jieshi remained convinced that the interests of the Guomindang and of China would be served best by avoiding full-scale war. In March the independence of Manchuria, under the name of Manzhouguo, was proclaimed, and Puyi, the last Qing emperor, was appointed its nominal head. In May a truce was arranged in Shanghai, which provided for the withdrawal of the Nineteenth Route Army and the demilitarization of greater Shanghai.[1]

These arrangements neither contained Japanese aggression nor placated Chinese nationalism. In response to the attack on Shanghai, the Communist Chinese Soviet Republic declared war on Japan. Jiang Jieshi could not prevent the Japanese occupation of Jehe in February 1933 and in May of the same year officers of the Guandong army and Chinese officials agreed the so-called Tanggu Truce, which extended Manzhouguo to the Great Wall and demilitarized north-east Hebei, leaving Beiping and Tianjin defenceless. This temporarily halted Japan's advance into North China, but in 1935 the Guandong army resumed encroachment, forcing the establishment of autonomous governments in Hebei and Inner Mongolia.

These moves prompted a wave of Chinese protests and the revival of the student movement. On 9 December 1935 thousands of students marched in Beiping to protest against the ineffectiveness of the Guomindang response to Japanese encroachment, and their actions were emulated by students in many other parts of China. Communist historians later claimed that the CCP had played a major role in arousing the student movement, and this had initiated a nationwide movement for war against Japan.[2] In the same month the Shanghai National Salvation Association, founded by the journalist Zou Taofen and other intellectuals, demanded the withdrawal of Japanese troops from eastern Hebei and Manchuria. In May a nationwide National Salvation Association was formed which called for immediate resistance to Japan, and criticized Jiang Jieshi for his continued pursuit of civil war against the Communists. It demanded a united front of all peoples and parties, including the Communists, to stop Japanese aggression and to save North China.[3]

Pressure on Jiang Jieshi to change his mind reached a climax in late 1936. In November the National Salvation Association gave its support to a series of strikes in Japanese-owned textile factories. In response Japan demanded the arrest of the leaders of the association, including Zou Taofen, and the seven people arrested became known in the Chinese press as the Seven Gentlemen.[4] One of their most prominent supporters was Zhang Xueliang, the former warlord of Manchuria, now stationed at Xi'an and engaged reluctantly in the campaign to suppress the Communists in Shaanxi. On 4 December Jiang Jieshi flew into Xi'an to urge Zhang Xueliang to take more vigorous action. Instead Zhang arrested him and issued a circular telegram to the Nanjing government and to the nation calling for the formation of a coalition government, an end to the civil war and the holding of a

National Salvation conference.[5] After two weeks in captivity, during which time he gave a verbal assurance that he would end the civil war and resist the Japanese, Jiang Jieshi was released and was flown back to Nanjing. He was accompanied by Zhang Xueliang, who took the responsibility for what had happened, a quixotic gesture which led to his court martial and lifetime imprisonment.

The Xi'an Incident was a turning point in modern Chinese history. Nationalist writers have claimed that it enabled the Communists to escape inevitable destruction, and they have blamed Zhang Xueliang for having done irreparable damage to the nation. The Communists certainly utilized the opportunities created by Japanese aggression. In 1935 the Comintern had urged Communist parties to resist the rising tide of Fascism by forming alliances with anti-Fascist groups. In March 1936 the CCP called for a suspension of the civil war and the formation of a united front to resist Japanese encroachment. Allegedly organizations such as the National Salvation Association were Communist fronts.[6] In April Zhou Enlai had put the Communist view to Zhang Xueliang, who had been responsive to the patriotic appeal. The CCP did not precipitate the incident at Xi'an, but Zhou Enlai played a crucial role in the negotiations to secure Jiang Jieshi's release, by telling Jiang that the CCP wished to support him as the leader of the nation, committed to resistance to Japan.

In the first half of 1937 the Guomindang and the CCP negotiated a second United Front with both sides offering concessions. The Communists agreed to abandon armed insurrection, to abolish the term 'Red Army' and to place the Communist troops under central government command. The Soviet Republic would become a special region of China, and the confiscation of land from landlords would stop. In return the Guomindang would end the civil war, release political prisoners and establish democratic freedoms. It would also convene a conference – with Communist representation – to discuss national salvation, to make speedy preparations to resist Japan, and to improve the livelihood of the people.[7]

The Sino-Japanese War: Military and Political Aspects, 1937–8

Full-scale war broke out between China and Japan following an incident at Lugouqiao (Marco Polo Bridge) near Beiping on 7 July 1937. Japanese soldiers stationed in the area, believing that they had been attacked by Chinese troops, themselves attacked the town of Wanping. At first neither government sought to use the incident as a pretext for war and diplomatic moves seemed close to achieving a settlement.[8] But then the expansionist faction within the Japanese army, which wanted to strike a military blow in China to break the deadlock in the north, arranged the dispatch of reinforcements to North China and the occupation of Beiping and Tianjin. Japanese troops advanced along the main railway lines and Chinese troops fell back in disorder. The lack of a strategic defensive plan for North China, the inadequacy of Chinese war preparations and the reluctance of regional militarists to contribute to the war effort, have all been blamed for this collapse.[9]

In Shanghai the Chinese response was very different. It was here that the best Chinese forces were stationed and the greatest effort had been expended on the development of defences, including the fortifications at Wuxi on the Shanghai–Nanjing railway, built in imitation of the Hindenburg Line. An attack on the large Japanese settlement in Shanghai would divert Japanese attention from the north and might lead to foreign intervention. On 13 August Chinese forces surrounded the Japanese settlement and on the following day the Chinese air force made a disastrous attack on Japanese naval ships at anchor on the Huangpu river. Four misdirected bombs fell on the International Settlement, killing and injuring over 3,000 people. A bitter three-month battle for Shanghai ensued, which cost China some 270,000 of her best troops. On 5 November Japanese troops landed at Jinshanwei, 30 miles south of Shanghai, and quickly made the Chinese defence of Shanghai untenable.

The main Chinese forces fell back towards Nanjing, but were unable to contain the rapid advance of Japanese mechanized units and failed to use the Wuxi defences. Jiang Jieshi had given orders that Nanjing itself should be defended to the last man, but the city was rapidly surrounded and subjected to heavy bombardment, falling to the Japanese on 12 December. There followed the 'rape of Nanjing' the most shameful episode of a war in which Japanese brutality towards the civilian population was a marked feature. Chinese estimates place the number of civilians massacred at 200,000 or even as high as 300,000, with at least 20,000 Chinese women being raped. By the end of 1937 China had lost between one-third and one-half of her fighting strength, 'the military machine that had taken the Guomindang a decade to build with German assistance was essentially destroyed'.[10] But China had attracted world sympathy for the heroic defence of Shanghai and Japan's international reputation had been damaged when details of events in Nanjing were published.

In November 1937 the Nationalist government announced the transfer of its capital from Nanjing to Chongqing, 1,000 miles further up the Yangzi river. This indicated the abandonment of its original policy of military confrontation and its replacement with a strategy of prolonged resistance. This did not mean the immediate end of major military campaigns and three events are worthy of examination. One of these, the first significant Chinese victory of the war, demonstrated that the Japanese forces could be defeated. It occurred at Tai'erzhuang, near Xuzhou in northern Jiangsu, between March and April 1938. Li Zongren, a former leader of the Guangxi clique and now the most successful Nationalist general, lured a Japanese force into an extended struggle, often at close quarters. About 16,000 Japanese soldiers died, the Chinese forces suffering similar casualties.[11] In June 1938 Jiang Jieshi ordered the breaching of the levees along the Yellow river in the vicinity of Kaifeng to delay the Japanese advance. Conflicting claims were made of the consequences of this act: the Nationalists asserted that it caused few Chinese casualties and delayed the Japanese advance by three months; the Japanese claimed that it cost 300,000 Chinese lives and had a negligible effect on Japanese movements.[12] The flooding was also intended to delay the Japanese advance on Wuhan, the last major industrial complex in

Nationalist hands, and the railhead for supplies from Guangzhou. Japanese forces encountered stiff Chinese resistance as they encircled Wuhan. However, in early September Jiang Jieshi and the Nationalist leadership left the city and on 21 October the Japanese took Guangzhou virtually unopposed. With the loss of the railway link to the coast, Wuhan's importance diminished and the city fell to the Japanese forces at the end of October.

Collaboration and Resistance in Occupied China

The battle for Wuhan concluded the first phase of the war. It was now apparent that although Japan could defeat Chinese forces on the battlefield, it could not compel China to surrender. It therefore became increasingly important for Japan to find a political solution to the military impasse. In December 1937, before the fall of Nanjing, Jiang Jieshi had given serious consideration to the terms offered by Japan through the mediation of the German Ambassador Oscar Trautmann, but he had broken off the negotiations when the conditions were extended to include official Chinese recognition of Manzhouguo.[13] This had encouraged Japan to pursue the alternative solution, that of promoting puppet regimes in China. In December 1937 a Provisional Government of the Republic of China was created in North China and in March 1938 another puppet regime was established at Nanjing. In December 1938 the opportunity to achieve a more permanent solution emerged with the flight of Wang Jingwei to Hanoi.

Wang Jingwei was second only to Jiang Jieshi in the Guomindang in terms of experience and standing. He had long been closely associated with Sun Zhongshan and shared his pro-Japanese sentiments. He had been premier of the Nationalist government in 1932 at the time of the undeclared war in Shanghai and had negotiated the settlement of that conflict. He later agreed to the notorious Tanggu Truce which had designated the area between the Great Wall and Beiping as a demilitarized zone. Wang was not a defeatist, but he believed that confrontation with Japan would bring disaster and humiliation to China, a view shared by Jiang Jieshi. Nevertheless, he was regarded as pro-Japanese and in November 1935 he was injured in an assassination attempt. This caused him to retire from the premiership and make a protracted tour to Europe. He was not in China at the time of the Xi'an Incident and this, it has been alleged, prevented him from using his prestige to restrain Jiang Jieshi from engaging in war with Japan.[14]

In January 1938 Prince Konoe, the Japanese Prime Minister, formally ruled out any further negotiations with the Nationalist government. In November he announced a 'New Order in East Asia', which called for co-operation between China and Japan in resisting Western imperialism and Communism. The declaration set the scene for a negotiation with Wang Jingwei, who had already put out feelers to his Japanese contacts. By the time that Wang defected terms had already been agreed, and these were announced when he reached Hanoi. They were neighbourly friendship, joint opposition to Communism and economic co-operation. Wang also agreed to head a government of collaboration. There followed a prolonged series of negotiations which eventually led to the inauguration in March 1941 of a 'national government' headed by Wang Jingwei, with its headquarters at Nanjing.

Wang Jingwei's collaborationist government lasted until 1945, although Wang himself died in November 1944. At its greatest extent it claimed authority over much of Henan, Hubei and Anhui and parts of Zhejiang, Jiangxi and Fujian, as well as southern Guangdong and Hainan island. It had diplomatic relations with Germany and Italy and Vichy France, operated its own budget and maintained its own armed forces. But any suggestion of genuine independence was illusory for its foreign policy, economy and military stance were all closely controlled by Japan. Like all collaborators Wang Jingwei has been execrated and little good has been written about the regime he headed other than to suggest it mitigated some of the harshness of Japanese military rule for those who lived within its boundaries. At the end of the war, as an anti-Communist government, it facilitated the handover of the Nanjing–Shanghai area to Jiang Jieshi.[15] In 1946 Wang Jingwei's widow was put on trial with others accused of collaboration. She defended her husband by declaring that he had not lost an inch of Chinese territory, which had been abandoned by cowardly army officers. Instead he had chosen to do something for the abandoned populace. Her pleas did not succeed and she spent the rest of her life in prison.[16]

The concentration of historical interest in the Sino-Japanese War has been on the fortunes of the Nationalists and Communists. Only recently have studies begun to appear of conditions in the parts of China which were under puppet regimes. Fu Poshek has investigated the moral and political response of Chinese writers to the Japanese occupation of Shanghai. They had chosen to remain in Shanghai rather than make their way either to Nationalist-held Chongqing or to Communist-held Yan'an. Their dilemma was similar to that which faced Chinese intellectuals at the time of the Mongol invasion: should they become passive and cease publishing, should they resist or should they collaborate?[17] Fu Poshek found examples of writers who took each of these paths, but all had found it difficult to come to terms with the situation.[18]

Nationalist China

From Chongqing, the Nationalist government ruled over an area known as the Free Zone, which contained approximately half the population of China excluding Manchuria. Its political control was very limited. Before the war the Nationalist government's main support had been located in the lower Yangzi region and it had never exercised effective authority in west China. In Chongqing it had to obtain the co-operation of the provincial authorities and this involved making compromises. In practice it presided over a loose coalition of provincial militarists, and Jiang Jieshi's political strategy amounted to a 'balance of weakness', that is to say he maintained his position and that of his government by keeping all other political forces weak. His influence was notably tenuous in Yunnan where Long Yun, the province's effective leader, did not even share all the Nationalist government's policy objectives.[19]

In the first year of the war Jiang Jieshi and the Guomindang enjoyed a remarkable burst of popularity. At an extraordinary Congress of the Guomindang held in Wuhan in March 1938 Jiang was given the title of Director-General of the party. On the same occasion two important steps were taken to broaden the basis of the party's support. A People's Political Council was established, which included representatives of all political parties including the Communists, and the Three People's Principles Youth Corps was set up to enlist the support of the nation's youth and to revitalize the Guomindang.

However, these initiatives failed to create the support needed for the effective prosecution of a people's war. The independent members of the People's Political Council soon chafed at the political repression and censorship which was part of the Guomindang's style of government. In 1942 the council was reorganized, with the Guomindang being given the majority of seats, and thereafter it enjoyed little political influence. As for the Three People's Principles Youth Corps, the hope that it might solve the problem of party factionalism was soon forgotten. Instead the corps became a vehicle for political training and for mobilizing youth into various organizations including the Boy Scout Association. Its activities included spying on fellow students and covert operations behind enemy lines and in Communist-held areas. By the end of the war it had a membership of over a million, but its influence was limited because of continued conflict between the Youth Corps and the party itself, and because it failed to attract abler or more idealistic young people to its ranks.[20]

One of the most remarkable episodes of the first year of the war had been the migration of universities away from areas threatened by Japanese invasion. A notable example of this was the movement of students and staff of Beida, Qinghua and Nankai Universities from Beiping and Tianjin, first to Changsha and then to Kunming in Yunnan, where they formed the National South-west Associated University, otherwise known as Lianda. Some 300 students and a few professors covered the thousand miles from Changsha on foot. Such patriotic commitment might suggest that the universities would be the strongest supporters of the government which headed the resistance to the Japanese. However, at Kunming and elsewhere students and staff became alienated from the Guomindang, which demanded political obedience and distrusted the liberal aspirations of the university community.[21]

By 1945 political discontent was widely evident. At the sixth Party Congress held in May of that year, criticisms were voiced of 'pervasive corruption, opportunism, inefficiency, disregard for the public welfare, and decline of morale in party, government and army'. Jiang Jieshi was accused of being increasingly dictatorial and a liability to the government. However, the political opposition to Jiang was always weak and divided and never came close to unseating him.[22]

At the beginning of the war an heroic attempt had been made to deny Chinese industrial investment to the Japanese by dismantling and removing plant. Over 600 factories were removed in this way, and some 110,000 tons of industrial machinery transported to other sites. At the same time 42,000 skilled and semi-skilled workers, and as many university students, accompanied the trek. The

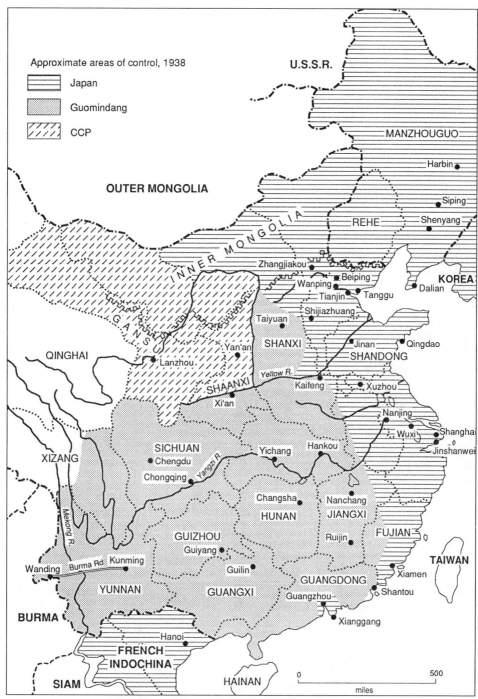

The Sino–Japanese War and the Civil War.

industrial tonnage removed was only a negligible percentage of China's existing industry, but it did form the core of Free China's industrial base.[23]

In moving from the lower Yangzi to Chongqing the Nationalists had transferred from the most developed region of China to one of the most backward and economically isolated. The government responded to the situation by attempting to establish a war economy. It took powers to nationalize industrial, mining and electrical enterprises and to mobilize labour. The main vehicle of state control was the National Resources Commission, which by 1942 controlled 40 per cent of Free China's industry and dominated the heavy and technical industries.

How successful was this war economy? There were some notable achievements but the overall picture is not very impressive. Over a thousand miles of railway track was completed, and major highways were constructed, including the 575 mile stretch of road from Kunming to Wanding on the Burmese frontier.[24] Electricity production was increased seven-fold between 1939 and 1944, but this was from a very small base. Determined efforts were made to produce liquid fuels: petroleum resources were identified and developed and quantities of industrial alcohol and petroleum from vegetable matter were also produced. But these sources supplied only a fraction of what was required and after the closing of the Burma Road in March 1942 the balance could only be obtained by airlifting in supplies. The output of coal and steel was increased, but the doubling of coal production should be compared with the record in Japanese-held territory, where coal production more than doubled. More generally, although industrial output increased sharply between 1939 and 1943, the rate of growth began to decline from 1940 and in 1943 an industrial crisis brought a sharp fall in production.

This crisis exposed the weaknesses of the Nationalist government. The main problem was inflation, which remained moderate until 1941, but between 1942 and 1945 rose at more than 230 per cent annually. The fundamental cause of this inflation was excessive government borrowing, which had been a feature of the Nanjing decade but which became much heavier after the outbreak of war. With the loss of the coastal provinces and foreign trade, the government had lost its main sources of tax revenue. At the same time the demands of war greatly increased government expenditure. Other factors which fuelled inflation were the Japanese blockade, commodity shortages, inadequate production of consumer goods and lack of confidence in the currency. These factors have been cited to demonstrate that inflation was an inevitable consequence of the war, but conversely it has been pointed out that much government expenditure was unnecessary or ill-conceived, and that inflation was not a problem in Communist-controlled areas.[25] Rampant inflation forced the Nationalist government to take drastic steps, for example to collect the land tax in kind, to make severe reductions in government expenditure on industry and communications, and to cut the real wages of officials and soldiers. Between 1937 and 1944, the nominal purchasing power of officials' salaries fell by 85 per cent and of soldiers' pay by 94 per cent, although some of this loss was offset by food and housing subsidies. Inflation brought with it attendant ills. Commodity shortages, particularly the shortage of petrol, encouraged the development of a black market. Inadequate salaries forced many officials to take second jobs and led to some becoming corrupt. For those who tried to survive honestly, the decline in living standards led to demoralization and tested their loyalty to the government.

The vast majority of the population of Free China were peasants. How did the war affect them economically and how did it influence their political attitudes? Supporters of the Nationalist government have maintained that although the war imposed a burden on the peasants, that burden did not seriously affect their economic livelihood or undermine their loyalty. In general, inflation in food prices benefits the primary producer and the evidence relating to incomes indicates that at least until 1943 farmers maintained their purchasing power. This optimistic view has been challenged by Lloyd Eastman, who has argued that in reality the war bore heavily on the peasants and that two government policies in particular added substantially to peasants' burdens. The first was conscription, which should have applied equitably to all men between the ages of 18 and 45, with certain defined exceptions. However, the selection of conscripts was often carried out by the *baojia*, the neighbourhood administrative unit, which ensured that the sons of the local elite avoided conscription, while those of the poor and weak were press-ganged into the army. After 1941 even the semblance of a system of selection was abandoned and army units abducted any available males who could not purchase their freedom. Peasants were also liable to be conscripted as labour on government projects, for example the construction of the Burma Road. Although these projects were an important part of the war effort, the demand for labour had a disastrous effect on peasant families dependent on human resources for survival.[26]

The other policy concerned taxation. It had been a measure of the limited authority of the government during the Nanjing decade that the land tax had not accrued to central government but had been administered by provincial authorities. The wartime government nationalized the land tax and then began to collect it in kind, thereby avoiding having to buy rice for the army on the open market. The new tax was supposedly equivalent to the prewar value of the land tax and related surtaxes. However, a system of compulsory purchase, and the requirement that peasants should transport their rice to government collecting stations, more than doubled the tax burden. On top of this local governments, now no longer receiving the land tax, applied a wide variety of new impositions.

How heavy was this revised tax burden? Eastman admits that even when tax collections were at their peak, in 1942 and 1943, they only amounted to about 8 per cent of the total rice and wheat output. But he has contended that variations in the incidence of tax, and corruption and tax evasion ensured that the tax burden fell more heavily on small and middle-sized landowners. Contemporary estimates suggested that they might have to hand over 30 per cent or even 50 per cent of their harvest as tax. Other evidence indicates that the gap between rich and poor families in the countryside was increasing. That many peasants did live on the verge of destitution was shown only too clearly by the Henan famine of 1942–3. Bad weather conditions had sharply reduced the harvest, but the government insisted on collecting the land tax – being faced with a choice of not feeding its troops or starving the peasants it chose the latter. The result was a man-made famine in which several million people died.[27]

What can be said of the military record of the Nationalist government? A common judgement is that after the first heroic resistance the Nationalist armies lapsed into inactivity. The quality of the military declined because of reliance on conscription, inadequate pay and training, and poor leadership.[28] Much of this is true, but it has been pointed out that the Nationalist army, although outclassed by the Japanese forces in quality, continued to resist for eight years, thus tying up a million Japanese troops and forcing Japan to expend valuable resources on the China front.[29]

The main military events of the latter part of the war may be summarized as follows. After the fall of Wuhan, Chongqing and other Nationalist-held cities came under Japanese air attack and an attempt was made to blockade the area under Nationalist control. In response the Nationalist government began to reorganize and retrain its forces, now supplemented with conscripts. In September 1939 Chinese morale was boosted when Japanese forces made a major attack on Changsha but were driven off. The Nationalist strategy now shifted to the offensive. In the winter of 1939 the entire Chinese force was committed to an attempt to drive the Japanese back to the lower Yangzi, but by April the attack had ground to a halt, exposing the limitations of the Chinese forces in terms of leadership, training and equipment.

Up to this point the united front with the Communists was still observed, although acrimonious discussions had taken place between the two sides concerning the zones in which Communist-led forces were allowed to operate. In October 1940 the Nationalist command had ordered the Communist New Fourth Army to withdraw from its base in Jiangxi to north of the Yangzi. By January it had partly complied with the instruction, but the remaining troops were attacked and severely mauled by a Nationalist force. Both sides blamed each other and claimed that the united front remained in existence, but the New Fourth Army incident effectively terminated military co-operation between the two sides.

In December 1938 the United States had offered the Nationalist government a loan of $25,000,000 for the purchase of vital supplies. This was the beginning of an increasingly important relationship between the two governments, with the United States seeking to restrain Japan by imposing economic sanctions and using economic aid to bolster Chinese resistance. Jiang Jieshi exploited the situation by offering to move against the Communists if given increased American support, but Roosevelt carefully avoided encouraging a resumption of the civil war. The attack on Pearl Harbor on 7 December 1941 converted this informal relationship into a wartime alliance. For the Nationalists the news of the Japanese attack and the inevitable American response was a cause for rejoicing. The writer Han Suyin, who was married to a Guomindang officer and who was living in Chongqing at the time, recalled:

Jiang was so happy he sang an old opera aria and played 'Ave Maria' all day. The Guomindang officials went around congratulating each other, as if a great victory had been won.[30]

It now became a United States' priority to keep China active in the war against Japan. To ensure this General Joseph W. Stilwell was appointed Chief of Staff to Jiang

Jieshi. His first task was to persuade a reluctant Jiang to commit Chinese troops to support the British campaign against the Japanese in Burma. This resulted in a severe defeat and the cutting of the Burma–Yunnan route, leaving Chongqing dependent on an airlift for its supplies from the outside world. Jiang was also resistant to Stilwell's suggestions on reducing the size of the Nationalist army and making it more effective. Because of these differences, relations between Roosevelt and Jiang Jieshi cooled and the American attitude towards the Chongqing regime became increasingly critical.

By late 1943 Japan's overall situation had deteriorated, and the Nationalist government assumed that the Japanese forces in China were no longer committed to expansion. It was at that point that Japan launched Operation Ichigo, which had as its first objective the destruction of China's main fighting units and the incapacitation of the airfields that could be used to launch air attacks against Japan. Its longer-term objective was to secure an uninterrupted overland supply line from Beiping to Hanoi, so that although Japan might lose the war against the United States, it could not be defeated in China. The campaign fell into two halves: the first inflicted a disastrous defeat on the Chinese forces in Henan; the second phase in Hunan was more evenly contested, with the Japanese suffering heavy losses before eventually capturing Changsha. The impact of Operation Ichigo on the Nationalist forces was very serious, because the Japanese deliberately targeted the elite units. As a result, 'Nationalist China was in a weaker military position on the eve of victory than at any previous point during the war.'[31]

Communist-held Areas of China

At the end of the Long March the survivors joined other Communist groups in northern Shaanxi and in December 1936 made the town of Yan'an their headquarters. Their position was extremely vulnerable and they probably would not have survived but for Zhang Xueliang's reluctance to carry out orders and eliminate them. The respite brought by the Xi'an Incident and the negotiation of the second United Front neutralized the Nationalist threat. With the outbreak of the undeclared war with Japan, the Red Army, now known as the Eighth Route Army, fought engagements in northern Shaanxi and established its credentials as an effective anti-Japanese force. In the next eight years the Communists created anti-Japanese guerrilla zones or 'liberated areas' behind the Japanese lines. Four areas in which the Communists were particularly strong were designated 'border regions', each with its own government. By the end of the war there were nineteen liberated areas, for the most part in North China, but including the area around Guangzhou and the island of Hainan.

During the war the CCP went through a political transformation. In 1937 Mao Zedong was the leader (though not without rivals) of a party with an uncertain ideology and a membership reduced to about 40,000. The leadership issue was settled at an early stage. Mao Zedong's main rivals were Zhang Guotao, whose divergence on the Long March has already been noted, and Wang Ming, one of the leaders of the Twenty-eight Bolsheviks. Zhang Guotao, who had reached Yan'an a year after Mao Zedong, had been appointed Vice-Chairman of the Shaanxi–Gansu–Ningxia border region, but was still viewed with suspicion. In April 1938 he fled to the Nationalists then at Wuhan, and was expelled from the Party. Wang Ming, who had been a critic of Mao's policies in the Jiangxi period, was in the Soviet Union during the Long March, only returning to China in October 1937. He could claim that he was supported by Stalin and the Comintern, and as the Soviet Union was supplying military aid to the Guomindang, this gave him an advantage. For a time, as Party leader in Wuhan, and prominent in the negotiations with the Guomindang and the war of resistance, Wang Ming eclipsed Mao Zedong in influence. However, unlike Mao, he lacked support within the military and after the loss of Wuhan his position weakened rapidly. At Yan'an, where Mao Zedong's relationship with the peasant masses had become increasingly important, Wang Ming ceased to be a serious rival.

At Yan'an the issue of ideological leadership was also resolved. Although Mao Zedong's early writings, in particular the 'Report of an Investigation into the Peasant Movement in Hunan' are now regarded as of major significance, when the Communists arrived at Yan'an his claim to ideological leadership had yet to be established. From 1937 he began to write theoretical works, starting with a series of lectures on dialectical materialism. He then developed two key themes which established his theoretical credentials and gave Chinese Communism its distinctive character.

The first was that of the sinification of Marxism, that is to say the assertion that Marxism, to be effective in China, had to be adapted to the Chinese context. In October 1938 he wrote:

> If a Chinese Communist, who is a part of the great Chinese people, bound to his people by his very flesh and blood, talks of Marxism apart from Chinese peculiarities, this Marxism is merely an empty abstraction. Consequently, the Sinification of Marxism – that is to say, making certain that in all of its manifestations it is imbued with Chinese peculiarities, using it according to these peculiarities – becomes a problem that must be understood and solved by the whole Party without delay. . . . We must put an end to writing eight-legged essays on foreign models. . . .[32]

The second theme concerned the postwar situation in which the Communists might emerge as the dominant force. In January 1940, in 'On New Democracy', he expanded Lenin's idea that in underdeveloped countries the revolution would be accomplished in two stages, the first a bourgeois-democratic stage, the second a socialist one. Whereas Lenin had written of a 'revolutionary-democratic dictatorship of the workers and peasants', Mao defined the participation as a 'joint revolutionary-democratic dictatorship of several revolutionary classes', a term which included – and so gave a post-revolutionary role to – the national bourgeoisie.[33]

Another important issue concerned Party organization and discipline. In 1937 Party membership included three groups: those who had followed the Long

March, local Party members, and a rapidly growing number of sympathizers who came to Yan'an from areas occupied by the Japanese. By 1940 Party membership had risen to 800,000, but many members had scant knowledge of Marxism and little respect for Party discipline. To remedy these defects and to confirm his ideological leadership, on 1 February 1942 Mao launched a training and rectification programme known as *zhengfeng* ('correcting the style of work'). In his introductory speech, entitled 'Reform in Learning, the Party, and Literature' Mao identified the main errors to be combated, beginning with 'subjectivism', which referred to the qualities required of leaders or cadres in the Party. He remarked on the lack of theoretical knowledge of those cadres who had received no formal education, but he was far more scathing about those who were educated and understood the theory, but lacked practical experience. The second error was 'sectarianism', which was a reference to divisions within the Party, an error which Mao claimed still existed but was no longer a dominant factor. Finally, there was 'Party formalism', 'the incorrect spirit in literature', in which Mao criticized the literature produced by Party members and warned them that literature and art must be for the masses.[34]

In the Yan'an period the Communists created new political institutions and established new forms of administration. Although Yan'an is often referred to as the capital of Communist-held China, in fact each border region was largely autonomous. The most developed border regions had representative governments and administrations were created at county, township and village levels. To establish their authority in rural areas the Communists had two tasks, to set aside the Guomindang administrative system and to subvert what they described as 'feudal forces' – and they had to achieve them under threat of Japanese reprisals. Their strategy was to mobilize the poor and middle peasants and then split the elite into reactionary and progressive elements, co-opting the latter to their side. Only when they had made considerable progress with this strategy did they move on to the next stage, holding rural elections. Elections at the lowest level were to choose village officials. All men and women over the age of sixteen could vote, unless they were excluded as traitors, bandits or insane. In the elections at township, county and border region levels the Communists implemented the 'three-thirds' system, whereby the posts were allotted equally between CCP members, progressives and neutral elements. If Communist candidates won more than their one-third share, they surrendered the excess posts, a policy which strengthened the Party's democratic-populist image.[35]

Communist economic policies were determined by the twin necessities of survival in a poor and isolated region and of securing the support of the rural population. There was no equivalent to the Nationalists' attempt to create a modern industrial base. However, it was important for the war effort to stimulate industrial production and this was done largely by indigenous means using available technology. Technical skills were transmitted and use was made of the one plentiful commodity, human labour. A description of a paper mill in the Shaan–Gan–Ning border region illustrated the level of technology adopted:

Large wooden water wheels drove giant grindstones set in a complicated-looking wooden superstructure, milling grass from the near-by hillsides into pulp. This factory, within a few years of its existence, has become the parent of more than a dozen other paper mills which were set up all over the Border Region with a few of its experienced hands as the nuclei of their new, farm-recruited personnel.[36]

The most urgent priority was to increase agricultural production and thereby to raise living standards above bare subsistence. In the Shaan–Gan–Ning border region the acreage of land in production was increased and some improvements were recorded in productivity. Whereas in areas under Nationalist control the tax burden on poorer peasants became heavier, in Communist-held areas a progressive tax system was introduced. To guard against famine, efforts were made to accumulate a grain reserve amounting to one year's harvest.[37]

Under the united front arrangement, the CCP had agreed to stop confiscating landlords' land and to support the Guomindang policy of rent and interest reduction – a policy which hitherto had not been enforced. This commitment has been taken as evidence that the Party had abandoned its attack on the injustices of the rural economic order. However, the Rent and Interest Reduction campaign mounted in 1942 was in reality an effective assault on rural privilege. It was accompanied by the establishment of peasant associations and the improvement of peasant security, and it involved the strict application of levels of rent and interest and the confiscation of assets from landlords who had overcharged.[38]

At the time of the Japanese invasion, the Communist forces, now constituted as the Eighth Route Army, numbered about 90,000 men. Shortly after the war began, the remnants of the Communist forces in Jiangxi and Fujian formed the nucleus of the New Fourth Army. By 1940 the two armies totalled about half a million men. At the end of the war Mao Zedong claimed that the regular forces had expanded to 910,000 men and that they were supported by a civilian militia of 2,200,000.[39]

In the early months of the war, the CCP committed its forces to opposing the Japanese advance, but more cautiously than the Nationalists. Mao Zedong allegedly suggested in September 1937 that 70 per cent of the Communists' effort should be devoted to expansion, 20 per cent to dealing with the Nationalists, and only 10 per cent directly to fighting Japan.[40] When the Nationalist forces had retreated to the south and west, Communist forces began to operate behind Japanese lines. Each of the three divisions of the Eighth Route Army was allotted a zone of military and political activity and these in time became rural bases and eventually border regions. These zones attracted Japanese punitive expeditions and the Communist forces responded with guerrilla attacks on Japanese targets, and in particular on railways.

For the most part the Communist forces avoided large-scale confrontations. However, in August 1940, in an operation known as the Hundred Regiments campaign, 400,000 troops of the Eighth Route Army simultaneously attacked Japanese positions in five provinces in north China, and caused serious damage to railways, mines and Japanese strong points. Various explanations for this sudden change in tactics have been put forward, one being that it was a response to the Japanese 'cage and silkworm' strategy. This was a reference to the Japanese use of the railway network, like the bars of a cage, to divide the resistance forces. The divisions, containing the pacified areas, were then enlarged by nibbling outwards, like the action of a silkworm on a mulberry leaf. An alternative suggestion is that the Communists, fearing that the Nationalists were close to making a deal with the Japanese, went on the offensive to contrast Nationalist defeatism with their patriotic resistance. The campaign elicited such severe reprisals from the Japanese that it might be judged a mistake. During the Cultural Revolution Peng Dehuai, who in 1940 had been Deputy Commander of the Eighth Route Army, suggested that Mao Zedong himself had had no part in its planning, which undermines the suggestion that the attack was part of a grand strategy.[41]

In response the Japanese strengthened the 'cage and silkworm' tactic, greatly increasing the number of blockhouses and strongpoints and constructing walls and ditches, including a 300 mile-long trench alongside the Beiping–Hankou railway. They also adopted a scorched earth policy, sending in 'search and destroy' missions with instructions to 'kill all, burn all, destroy all' in areas where the Communists were active, the intention being to end the close co-operation that had sprung up between the Eighth Route Army and the local populace. These policies achieved some success, for the population of the areas under Communist control declined from 44 million to 25 million and the strength of the Eighth Route Army fell from 400,000 to 300,000. They also forced the CCP to reconsider its position – thus precipitating the Party rectification programme considered above.

Explanations of the Nationalist Decline and the Communist Advance During the Sino-Japanese War

Many Westerners' descriptions of life in Chongqing emphasized the corruption of officials and the miserable state of the peasants. Those few Westerners who reached Yan'an suggested that things were very different there. Only in July 1944, when the United States sent an observer group to Yan'an – known jokingly as the 'Dixie Mission' because it went into rebel territory – did a more authoritative picture emerge. John S. Service, a United States' career diplomat, recorded his first impressions on arriving in Yan'an. He noted the veneration in which Mao was held, the contrast being with the disrespect offered to Jiang Jieshi. He commented that the 'claptrap of Chongqing officialdom' was lacking, that there were 'no beggars, nor signs of desperate poverty', that morale was high and there was no defeatism or war weariness. The impression of the group was 'we have come into a different country and are meeting a different people'.[42]

This perceived contrast between the two capitals and the two regimes was reflected in political cartoons. At the beginning of the war cartoonists had emphasized joint resistance to the common enemy and political differences had been played down. But as disillusionment grew in Chongqing and as the Communists at Yan'an developed the mass line, the contrasts between the two regimes became a subject for political comment. In this the advantage lay with the

Communists, who were willing to encourage popular culture and who used the cartoons of artists such as Hua Junwu in the *Liberation Daily*, the CCP's official newspaper at Yan'an. Their propagandists satirized the Guomindang's exploitation of the poor and emphasized the good relations which existed between the Eighth Route Army and the people in Communist-held areas.[43]

That there was a contrast between the two regimes cannot be denied, but the idealization of the Yan'an period should not go unchallenged. Among the CCP's most distinguished supporters was the writer Ding Ling. When she first arrived at Yan'an in 1937 she was impressed by the zeal and simplicity of the lifestyle and she lent her willing support to the regime. However, by 1940 she had become disillusioned by what she regarded as the double standards of the Communists in their policy towards women. In a short story entitled *When I was in Xia Village* she told of a girl who, having been abducted and raped by the Japanese, then spied for the Communists. Although a heroine, when she returned to her village she was condemned by the men for her immorality. In the rectification movement of 1942 Ding Ling was denounced for writing this type of literature.[44]

The explanation for the shift of support away from the Nationalists and towards the Communists during the war years has become one of the most extensively argued issues in modern Chinese history. In 1962 Chalmers Johnson published *Peasant Nationalism and Communist Power*. Johnson began by observing that the Communists' wartime success was in marked contrast to their experiences in the decade preceding the war, when they first undertook to organize the peasants. He suggested that the reason for this was the CCP's leadership of resistance to the Japanese army, which brought it a mass following which it subsequently used to conquer all of China. This relationship was strengthened by the Japanese response to the Hundred Regiments campaign, the notorious 'three-all' policy.

> The revolution spread and became irreversible in the years 1941–42. Instead of breaking the tie between the Eighth Route Army and the peasantry, the Japanese policy drove the two together into closer alliance. This alliance derived partly from nationalism (hatred of the invader), but to a large extent it was purely a matter of survival.[45]

This view was challenged by Donald G. Gillin, who questioned Johnson's assertion that the reason why before the war the Communists had failed to gain popular support was because most peasants did not respond to the CCP's programme of social and economic revolution. He based his argument on events in Shanxi between 1935 and 1939. When the Long March brought Communist infiltrators into Shanxi the province was still ruled by Yan Xishan, the Model Governor, an old enemy of Communism. The province was desperately poor, and Yan admitted that 70 per cent of his subjects felt sympathy for the Communists, who offered them hope of improvement. To counter that sympathy Yan himself introduced social and economic reforms. Nevertheless, when the Red Army invaded Shanxi in early 1936, the Communists received massive popular support, largely because of their advocacy of land redistribution. When the Japanese invaded the province in the following year, the Communist forces found that the elite responded to the appeal of nationalism, but the peasants were happy to work for the Japanese who paid excellent wages. It was only when the Eighth Route Army, under the guise of promoting the war effort, resumed its assault on landlords, that it gained popular support.[46]

Gillin's argument was developed by Mark Selden in The Yenan Way in Revolutionary China. Selden divided the Communist response to the threat of war, and to the situation created by war, into three parts. Prior to 1936 the CCP, at its revolutionary base in Shaanxi, implemented revolutionary land reform and ended the domination of the economy by a small landlord-commercial elite. It achieved this by mobilizing the support of the poor peasants, who were motivated by the hope of destroying the old society and implementing a new egalitarian vision. In 1936 the Party curbed the agrarian revolution in the base areas in favour of anti-Japanese resistance and a programme of moderate reform. It offered peasants security, guaranteed controls of rent and interest and an equitable tax scale, and it used the appeal of anti-Japanese nationalism to obtain the participation of the surviving elite in base-area governments. But by 1941, with Japanese pressure on the Communist bases increasing, a rectification programme was initiated to transform the party and to set new standards of commitment and new models of leadership. It became necessary to devise policies aimed at building a new society, the main task being the transformation of social and economic life at the village level. Selden called these policies the 'Yan'an Way', and described them as a bold and effective response to the war-aggravated problems of rural society.[47]

Since the appearance of Johnson's and Selden's books, much of the discussion about the growth of Communist influence has been in response to their views. Kataoka Tetsuya challenged both works for limiting the enquiry to rural areas. He adopted a sceptical attitude towards official Chinese Communist history, which stressed the importance of the rural bases, the consistency of Communist strategy, and the alleged natural community of interest between the peasants and the CCP. He argued that the Communists had failed to bring about a rural revolution in Jiangxi, and suggested that the Communist movement would have been extinguished at the end of the Long March had it not managed to secure the second united front by appealing to nationalist sentiment in the cities. The Japanese invasion was of immense benefit to the Communists, because it allowed them to claim that their expansion was a part of national resistance. It was also a disaster for the Guomindang, which lost control of the main urban areas and was coerced into remaining in the war by pressure from the United States.[48]

Chen Yung-fa studied the Communist bases in the lower Yangzi area rather than the better-established bases in the north. His main concern was how the CCP created its basis of support, and this led him to investigate how it mobilized the peasants, how it sustained their interest in mass association activities – which for them took up time better used in the struggle for survival – and how it recruited its peasant activists. He concluded that in some cases the Japanese invasion galvanized peasants to search for anti-Japanese leadership, and he accepted the centrality of the policies of mass mobilization and improvement of the peasants' economic lot which were integral to Selden's 'Yan'an Way' thesis. However, he regarded both arguments as simplistic, and stressed the complex and interactive nature of the Party's relationship with the peasant masses on whom it relied for its support.[49]

In the final year of the war with Japan two sequences of events occurred which were to influence the postwar situation. The first was the consolidation of the Communist position, indicated in part by a 40 per cent increase in CCP membership and a doubling of the Communist forces, though much of the latter was achieved by the integration of the regional and field forces. The disastrous effect of Operation Ichigo on the Guomindang's military capacity enabled the Communists to start operating in areas formerly held by the Guomindang and to introduce the mass mobilization and class struggle tactics which had been employed in the border regions.[50]

The second sequence was connected with the increasingly important role of the United States in China. Up to this point President Roosevelt had supported the Guomindang while at the same time trying to bring the Soviet Union into the war against Japan. In 1944 disillusionment with Jiang Jieshi's commitment to the war effort, and the near collapse of the Guomindang forces in the face of Operation Ichigo, encouraged Roosevelt to consider a closer relationship with the Communists. It was for this reason that the 'Dixie Mission' was sent to Yan'an in July 1944. The Communists presented themselves to the mission as agrarian reformers, committed to fighting the Japanese and anxious to avoid a renewal of the civil war. In November Patrick J. Hurley, Roosevelt's newly appointed special envoy to China, flew to Yan'an. With his encouragement a five-point agreement was drafted which offered the Communists a place alongside the Guomindang in a coalition government. When Hurley flew back to Chongqing he was accompanied by Zhou Enlai, who expected him to persuade the Nationalists to accept the agreement just made with the Communists. But instead, when Jiang Jieshi demanded that the Communists dissolve their independent armies, Hurley reneged on the agreement that he had signed.[51]

In February 1945 Roosevelt, Stalin and Churchill met at Yalta. The main subject of their negotiations was eastern Europe, but they also discussed the future of China. Stalin assured Roosevelt that he would continue to support the Guomindang, and promised that the Soviet Union would enter the war against Japan within three months of the defeat of Germany. In return he demanded and was granted important concessions in Manchuria: a lease on the naval base at Lüshun, a predominant position in Dalian, and a Sino-Soviet condominium over the South Manchurian and Chinese Eastern railways. News of this agreement strengthened Communist suspicion of the United States and this was confirmed after Roosevelt's death in April 1945, when Harry S. Truman, who was loud in his support of Jiang Jieshi and his opposition to the spread of Communism, became President. After the explosion of the first atomic bomb in July 1945, Truman anticipated being able to defeat Japan without Soviet assistance and perhaps even being able to keep the Russians out of Manchuria. In the meantime negotiations between Russia and the Nationalists, represented by Song Ziwen, had resulted in a Sino-Soviet treaty of friendship. The treaty promised Soviet support for the Nationalists and confirmed the proposals relating to Manchuria contained in the

Yalta agreement, adding the proviso that Soviet troops would withdraw from the region three months after the Japanese surrender.

Civil War and Communist Victory

The Sino-Japanese War ended in August 1945 after the dropping of atomic bombs on Japan. The response in China was astonishment, because neither the Nationalists nor the Communists were aware of the development of atomic weapons, and the Guomindang had assumed that Japan would not be defeated until 1946. Both the Guomindang and the CCP immediately made every effort to occupy the territory and to seize the arms held by the Japanese. In his General Order No. 1, General Douglas MacArthur, the Supreme Commander of the Allied Powers, ordered that the Japanese surrender to the Nationalists in China Proper and to the Russians in Manchuria. Some 60,000 United States marines were flown to north China to assist in this and up to half a million Nationalist troops were redeployed, particularly to the north, with United States' help. Meanwhile, the Communists attacked Japanese positions to compel their surrender to them, and in retaliation the Nationalists authorized Japanese forces to attack the Communists.

The immediate prize was control of Manchuria. Under the terms of the Yalta and Sino-Soviet agreements Russian troops moved into Manchuria, occupied the major cities and began removing industrial plant as reparations. In separate movements Nationalist troops and administrators arrived with American assistance, and Communist forces and cadres moved in surreptitiously by land and sea. When the November deadline for the Russian withdrawal approached, the Nationalists, aware that they had not consolidated their control over the region, negotiated an extension of the Russian occupation. At the same time Jiang Jieshi made what he later regarded as his most serious strategic error, the large-scale movement of his best troops to Manchuria.[52]

In November 1945 President Truman sent General George C. Marshall to China to try to persuade the Nationalists and Communists to accept a cease-fire and to form a coalition government. The Marshall mission was welcomed on both sides, by the Nationalists because it promised the continuation of American support, and by the Communists because it was in their interests to defer a resumption of the civil war. At first the mission appeared to be making progress, for a cease-fire began in January 1946, and all-party talks, held under the aegis of a Political Consultative Conference, reached agreement on a wide range of political and military issues. But then each side accused the other of exploiting the situation and by April the cease-fire in Manchuria had broken down. Although the Marshall mission continued until January 1947, and further negotiations took place, the chance of a settlement had been lost. Whereas Marshall's sincerity had been accepted, the contradictory nature of his position, as impartial mediator and representative of the main supporter of the Nationalists, ensured that his mission was faulted from the start. It ended with Nationalists expressing resentment of American interference and the Communists convinced that the United States remained committed to the support of their enemies.

The civil war began with the Nationalists apparently holding the advantage. Their armed forces numbered over 2.5 million men, about three times the strength of the Communists, and they were also better equipped. In addition they had some naval ships, an air force with 5,000 United States-trained pilots, and control of the transport system. Yet within three years their forces had suffered a catastrophic defeat.

The military struggle may be divided into three phases. The first, which lasted from July 1946 to June 1947, was marked by a general advance of the Nationalist troops in north China and Manchuria. Nearly all the major cities of Manchuria were occupied and even Yan'an was captured. The Communist response was to make tactical withdrawals, thus preserving their armed strength and encouraging the Nationalists to overextend their lines of communication. In Manchuria the Nationalists pressed north and came close to capturing Harbin, the high tide of their campaign. In the winter of 1946–7, Communist forces under Lin Biao, together with remnants of the forces loyal to the former warlord Zhang Xueliang, began a series of offensives and captured large quantities of Nationalist weapons and equipment. In May Lin Biao attempted but failed to capture Siping and the Communist advance was halted temporarily. However, his offensives had so weakened the Nationalist position in Manchuria that Guomindang supporters began to transfer their savings to Xianggang and Guangzhou.[53]

The second stage of the war began in June 1947, with the Communists switching to a strategy of mobile warfare, isolating Nationalist-held positions and consolidating their hold on their former base areas. Within a year they had overrun much of Manchuria and North China and had reduced the Nationalists to defending the major cities and key lines of communication. In June 1947 Communist forces crossed the Yellow river, cutting the Longhai railway and communications with Xi'an. In November they captured Shijiazhuang, an important town on the railway line between Beiping and Taiyuan. In March 1948 they at last gained control of Siping in Manchuria, leaving the Nationalists holding only three cities in the region. By April Yan'an had been recovered and this was followed by the capture of the cities of Luoyang and Kaifeng. By this time Nationalist losses and Communist recruitment had left the two sides approximately at parity.

The final stage of the war was marked by three major and dramatic campaigns. The first resulted in the capture of the three remaining Nationalist cities in Manchuria. After the fall of Siping Lin Biao had re-equipped his troops with captured American weapons. His forces now outnumbered the Nationalists and his tactics of surprise, rapid movement and concentration of firepower left them at his mercy. Nevertheless, Jiang Jieshi resisted advice to withdraw from Manchuria and consolidate his position in North China. When Shenyang was captured in November 1948, Manchuria had fallen to the Communists. Within seven weeks they had put 400,000 Nationalist troops out of action and had captured vast quantities of arms and ammunition, including 76 tanks and 150 armoured vehicles. They had also inflicted a severe psychological shock on the Nationalists, whose defeat now became conceivable.[54] Lin Biao immediately moved his forces into the Beiping–Tianjin region, where the Nationalist forces were commanded by Fu Zuoyi, one of the Nationalists' more able and honest commanders. Lin Biao successfully applied the same tactics of rapid movement, capturing Tianjin on 15 January and eight days later forcing Fu Zuoyi, who was anxious to protect Beiping from the ravages of war, to surrender with 200,000 troops, who thereupon joined the People's Liberation Army.[55]

The last and most famous campaign was that of Huai-Hai, fought between November 1948 and January 1949 near the Huai river and the Longhai railway. Both sides mustered a force of about half a million men, but the Communists had in addition a well-developed basis of civilian support. Overall command on the Nationalist side was taken by Jiang Jieshi. The Communists first attacked and destroyed the weaker Nationalist formations and then, having isolated the main Nationalist force in the area around Xuzhou, prevented its reinforcement. Nationalist morale was low, some units went over to the Communists, little use was made of air superiority and the winter was severe. On 10 January some 300,000 Nationalist troops surrendered, and the Nationalist resistance north of the Yangzi ended.

The Communists now offered peace terms but, as they branded Jiang Jieshi a war criminal and required the abolition of the Guomindang government, they were rejected. However, Jiang Jieshi resigned, his post as President being taken by Li Zongren, the former leader of the Guangxi clique, who transferred the capital to Guangzhou. In April the Communists crossed the Yangzi and occupied Nanjing, precipitating the collapse of Nationalist resistance. Shanghai fell to the Communists in May and Guangzhou in October. In December Jiang Jieshi, who had resumed the leadership of the Guomindang, transferred his government to Taiwan. He took with him China's foreign reserves and many art treasures from the mainland. He was followed by some two million Guomindang supporters, including about half a million soldiers.

In the first instance the Nationalist defeat was a military disaster, and both Nationalist and American sides explained it in those terms. Major-General David Barr, the Commander of the United States Army Advisory Group in China, writing early in 1949, gave his professional judgement on why the Nationalist army had been defeated. He stressed the strategic error of occupying and then trying to retain Manchuria, 'a task beyond its logistic capabilities'. He referred to the Communists' offensive spirit, popular support and use of 'a type of guerrilla warfare', and noted how this had encouraged a Nationalist strategy of defence and the development of what he called 'wall psychology'. He was critical about the Nationalist leadership, noting how claims of loyalty encouraged Jiang Jieshi to support inefficient generals, and he was scathing about the failure to use the air force to any effect. He suggested that one might have expected that the Nationalists' military shortcomings would be replicated on the Communist side, but he observed that this was only partly true. He concluded:

By means of total mobilization in the areas they control, propaganda, and the use of political commissars within their armed forces, they maintain loyalty to the established order. Their leaders are men of proven ability who invariably out-general the Nationalist commanders. The morale and fighting spirit of the troops is very high because they are winning.[56]

In recent years the interpretation of the Communist victory has moved away from an emphasis on military or international factors towards the view that the civil war was the armed resolution of a political struggle. How has the political decline of the Nationalist government and the rise of the Communists during this period been explained?

The first issue concerns the manner in which the Guomindang reoccupied Japanese-held territories. The inhabitants of these areas assumed that the Guomindang would punish those who had collaborated with the Japanese, but found instead that Jiang Jieshi was more concerned with strengthening his position against the Communists and other rivals. A few collaborators were executed, the most notorious being Chen Gongbo, a founder member of the CCP, who had succeeded Wang Jingwei, but many others not only escaped punishment, but were confirmed in their positions. Another complaint concerned the disposal of enemy property. Guomindang officials rapidly acquired the reputation of being carpetbaggers, intent on acquiring 'gold bars, automobiles, houses, Japanese women, and face'. Officials and army officers frequently commandeered buildings and factories for their private use. The government appointed investigation teams to probe allegations, but their efforts were dismissed as 'swatting flies'. Even more serious problems arose over the way the government managed the transition to a peacetime economy. A particular issue was the failure to compensate the patriotic industrialists and businessmen who had relocated from Shanghai and elsewhere to Chongqing and who now faced bankruptcy with the collapse of wartime industry.[57]

The above complaints were voiced in many parts of China, but they were expressed with particular bitterness in two regions, Taiwan and Manchuria. On Taiwan Chen Yi, the newly appointed governor, was accused of treating the Taiwanese more harshly than the Japanese, and his actions were seen as the cause of the uprising of February 1947, which was suppressed with great loss of life. In Manchuria Jiang Jieshi had been determined to prevent a return to the semi-autonomy of the days of Zhang Xueliang. He had therefore appointed outsiders to administrative posts and had insisted that the Guomindang forces were composed of soldiers from other parts of China. It was said sardonically that a rising similar to that on Taiwan would have occurred in Manchuria, but all who wanted to rebel had already gone over to the Communist side.[58]

Once re-established as a national government, the Guomindang continued to act in a way which excited criticism and alienated its natural supporters. Three issues may be identified: the resumption of the civil war, the alleged mismanagement of the economy, and the undemocratic and unresponsive character of the regime.

Rightly or wrongly, many Chinese believed that much of the responsibility for the resumption of the civil war lay with the Guomindang, which was consequently held to account for the consequences of that war. The most strident expression of this view was voiced by students, who demonstrated to force a response from the government. A particular issue was the support that the Guomindang was receiving from the United States, made manifest in the continued presence of American troops on Chinese soil. On Christmas Eve 1946 two American marines allegedly raped a student at Beijing University. The students responded by organizing protests which spread to Shanghai and other cities, creating the basis for a national student movement. In May 1947 the government's emergency economic reforms, which hit the students and the academic community severely, precipitated another wave of student protest. The government responded by introducing measures banning strikes and parades, which led to a series of violent confrontations, including one at Wuhan University where three students were shot dead by the police. A year later another 'student tide', in part a response to allegations of the oppression of students, served to turn the academic community further against the government and to discredit the Guomindang. The Guomindang asserted that the student movement had been fomented by the Communists, and it is probable that there was an underground student Communist organization. But this cannot explain fully the widespread student dissatisfaction, which was a response to the perceived failure of the government.[59]

Allegations of government mismanagement of the economy had been voiced during the Sino-Japanese War, and further grounds for criticism emerged during the switch to a peacetime economy. In the postwar period inflation was rampant, industrial production fell, and there were frequent strikes, the government no longer being able to control the labour movement. In February 1947 the government introduced a round of emergency reforms, including price controls and a wage freeze, but to little effect. Prices continued to soar – from late May to mid-August 1948, prices in Shanghai rose by 1,000 per cent – with disastrous consequences for government employees on salaries. In August, in a desperate gamble to control the situation, a new paper currency, the gold yuan note, was introduced to replace the *fabi*, the national currency. At the same time the government proposed dramatic increases in taxation and reductions in expenditure to cut the budget deficit, and approached the United States for a massive loan to stabilize the currency. The most contentious measure was the requirement that people should convert their gold and foreign currency into gold yuan. Within three months these measures had proved unworkable and the economy was on the verge of collapse. In November the government began to sell back its gold and silver holdings, but it was no longer possible to sustain the gold yuan currency, which became valueless. The gold yuan reform, which cost many people their savings or livelihood and destroyed their confidence in the Guomindang, has often been referred to as the immediate reason for the fall of the Nationalist government.[60]

The other major grievance concerned the lack of political progress. Sun Zhongshan had prescribed a period of political tutelage as preparation for constitutional government. The war had caused this programme to be deferred, but there now seemed no further reason for delay. At the Political Consultative Conference, a multi-party meeting held in January 1946 to discuss relations between the Guomindang and the Communists, an agreement was reached on a revision of the 1936 draft constitution and the creation of a constitutional assembly to adopt it. Both the Guomindang and later the CCP were to draw back from this agreement. In the case of the Guomindang, Jiang Jieshi wanted to implement it, but he was thwarted by the Renovationist faction, whose members were appalled by the prospect of the Guomindang giving up its monopoly of government.[61] Because there was no agreement between the Communists and Nationalists, the revision of the constitution, its promulgation on 1 January 1947, and the election of the National Assembly in November of the same year, were all measures passed unilaterally by the Guomindang. The election itself was condemned as a farce and the National Assembly ridiculed as quite incapable of upholding the principles of democracy. The Guomindang's claimed commitment to democracy was also undermined by its record on civil liberties. It used censorship and arbitrary arrest to restrict its critics. It was also implicated in political killings, the most notorious example being the murder of Wen Yiduo, a popular professor at South-west Associated University at Kunming. Wen Yiduo was a member of the Democratic League, a federation of minor opposition parties which was critical of United States' involvement in the civil war, and this may have supplied the reason for his assassination.

Explanations of the success of the CCP in attracting support and in profiting from the shortcomings of the Guomindang emphasize three main themes: victory in Manchuria, the gaining of support in the countryside, and the takeover of the cities of China Proper.

The Communist success in Manchuria derived not only from the superior tactics of the People's Liberation Army, but also because they managed to gain popular support. The way they achieved this is of considerable interest. Although Manchuria was the most industrialized region of China, in the prewar period the Communists had failed to mobilize the proletariat. It had been no more successful when it tried to promote revolution in the countryside. A possible explanation for these failures was that Manchuria was a region of recent immigration, a society which offered its people some prospect of social mobility. However, after the seizure of Manchuria by Japan, many young men joined the Communist guerrillas because they took the lead in opposing the Japanese. As this threat could not be ignored by the Japanese army, the guerrilla movement was crushed mercilessly, but it left a memory of heroic involvement which was to be vital in the civil war.[62] During the war with Japan the upper elite either fled or became compromised as collaborators, leaving a political vacuum. The Soviet occupation after the war allowed the CCP to regroup and bring in support before the Guomindang returned. The Communists now successfully applied mass mobilization techniques, and in particular promoted revolutionary land reform. What followed has been described as an 'equation of revolutionary transformation'. In return for supporting the Communists with taxation, military and labour service and food, the peasants received land and other forms of wealth confiscated from the old elite and the right to participate in the new institutions established in the countryside. This equation only balanced if those peasants who bore the burden of conflict were rewarded, and if the Communists could convince them that the revolution would not be reversed.[63]

In north China, the situation facing the CCP was rather different. At the end of the war its authority in rural areas was widespread and its techniques of mass mobilization were well established. However, it had not yet solved the problem of how to persuade peasants to commit themselves to a social revolution. During the war the CCP had renounced revolutionary land reform in favour of the more moderate policy of rent and interest reduction. Revolutionary land reform was reintroduced by the directive of 4 May 1946, which authorized the seizure of land from collaborators. The Outline Agrarian Law promulgated on 10 October 1947 went further, for it stated that all land belonging to landlords and all public land was to be taken over by the peasant association, and together with all other land in the village was to be divided equally among the total population.[64]

The reintroduction of revolutionary land reform has been described as the most important reason why the Communists obtained peasant support. This is a simplistic explanation and recently a more complex sequence of events has been identified. Although landlordism existed in north China, nevertheless tenancy in the region was relatively low, for example in Shandong and Hebei only 12 per cent of families were exclusively tenants, the rest owning at least some land. The appeal to peasants therefore had to go beyond the elimination of landlordism and embrace other grievances, including wages and taxes and the arbitrary exercise of power by the rural elite. Another important issue concerned how to develop the rural revolution. Experience had showed that the first stage should be to awaken peasants to their condition of exploitation and then at 'struggle meetings' to voice publicly their grievances against landlords and those referred to as 'local tyrants'. The second stage involved the seizure of land and goods from the landlord class, a process inevitably accompanied by violence and excess. In the third stage Communist cadres, whose task had been to steer but not to lead the mass movement, had to encourage a resolution of the struggle and the re-establishment of village unity.

Should what happened be described as a 'peasant revolution'? Since 1927, when Mao described poor peasants as the 'vanguard' of the revolution, the centrality of peasant poverty to his revolutionary strategy cannot be denied. There was a special link between the CCP and the peasants, and the Party did intend to promote a programme of radical reform in the countryside. But this was not a movement led by peasant leaders to achieve a rural revolution. The CCP had a much wider agenda, and land reform 'was an instrument of political warfare, not an end in itself'. The divergence between the CCP's aims and peasants' aspirations was to become apparent after 1949.[65]

Since the Jiangxi period, Mao Zedong had sought to engage women in the struggle by associating revolution with emancipation. Women's associations were active in the civil war and peasant women were mobilized to perform a variety of activities in support of the war effort. Women were given equal shares of confiscated land and they also benefited from the availability of divorce. The American journalist Jack Belden, an eye-witness to the struggle, wrote:

In the women of China the Communists possessed, almost ready made, one of the greatest masses of disinherited human beings the world has ever seen. And because they found the key to the heart of these women, they also found one of the keys to victory over Jiang Jieshi.[66]

The CCP's support for the emancipation of women was constrained. During the Sino-Japanese War, as the case of Ding Ling referred to above indicates, it had realized that in a patriarchal society it could not afford to alienate male peasants, and as a consequence it had dealt cautiously with women's issues. The main effort had been expended on increasing women's role in production. However, during the civil war, the reintroduction of revolutionary land reform and marriage law reform gave women a powerful incentive for supporting the Communists. As one women from a village in Shaanxi remarked, 'When I get my share [of land] I'll separate from my husband. Then he won't oppress me any more.'[67]

How large a part did these measures play in securing support for the Communists? An important factor determining the success of revolutionary land reform was the assurance that the Guomindang would not return and assist the landlords to recover their land. If this occurred the consequence could be terrible. In one village in Henan a returning landlord buried alive or shot one member of each family which had supported the Communists.[68] This meant that 'the most basic condition for the successful implementation of land reform was the military capacity to protect it against its enemies'. The armed struggle had to precede land reform, but the promise of land reform provided the motive for involvement in the armed struggle. These policies applied in combination amounted to a formula for revolution in the countryside.[69]

In the final stage of the struggle between the Guomindang and the Communists the focus of attention returned to the cities. In August 1945 the Communists captured Zhangjiakou (Kalgan), about 200 miles north-west of Beiping, and held it for about a year. They used this opportunity to demonstrate that they could run a city efficiently. Unlike the Guomindang, they dealt severely with collaborators and immediately instituted popular elections. More importantly they revived the labour unions, doubled wages and improved working conditions. At the same time Guomindang bureaucratic monopolies were abolished, private industry was encouraged and offered low interest loans, and an attempt was made to curb inflation.[70]

These policies were elaborated upon when the Communists occupied the cities of China Proper. Derk Bodde, a visiting American sinologist, recorded in his diary what happened when Beiping was 'liberated'. He commented 'there is no doubt in my mind that the Communists come here with the bulk of the people on their side'. He witnessed the victory parade in which thousands of students and workers participated, and noted the measures taken to stabilize wages by computing them in catties (1⅓ lbs) of millet. He read of the arrival of representatives of twenty anti-Guomindang political groups, including the Democratic League, and of plans to form a coalition government.

In the last few pages evidence has been presented which supports the view that the Guomindang lost its mandate to rule China in the postwar period and in direct competition with the CCP. However, it has been argued that the party's decline had set in earlier and for different reasons. Immanuel C.Y. Hsü maintained that the war with Japan 'completely exhausted the government militarily, financially, and spiritually', and it was therefore the most important near cause for the downfall of the Nationalists.[71] Ch'i Hsi-sheng has argued that the root cause of the Guomindang decline was that the party became militarized. This trend began with the succession of Jiang Jieshi to the leadership, and the compromise with the regional militarists. It was accelerated by the war and the civil war, for in each case military objectives held priority over political progress. As a consequence 'the Guomindang's political fate was probably sealed even before the civil war erupted'.[72]

23

The People's Republic of China: the Revolutionary Period to the Great Leap Forward

Between 1949 and 1976, after an initial period of consolidation, the People's Republic of China passed through three distinct stages. In each of these, while using different strategies, the political leadership attempted to translate its revolutionary vision into practice. For convenience these three stages will be referred to as the Soviet model, 1952–58, the Great Leap Forward and its aftermath, 1958–65, and the Cultural Revolution from 1966 to the death of Mao Zedong in 1976.

It is said that 'revolutions die when revolutionaries become rulers', that when new rulers grapple with the harsh realities of ruling, their revolutionary goals become increasingly indefinite and they feel obliged to compromise on their original commitments.[1] However, in China the idea of a 'continuing revolution' was embraced by its leaders and remained their most important single concern. Undoubtedly there were differences of opinion within the leadership on what policies should be pursued in continuation of the revolution – most obviously differences between Mao Zedong and Liu Shaoqi – and there were certainly other significant concerns, notably international autonomy and economic reconstruction, which at times were given priority. But until the death of Mao Zedong in 1976 the leadership remained committed to what it conceived to be its revolutionary mission. It is with the consequences of that commitment that the next two chapters are concerned.[2]

Consolidating control, 1949–52

The rapid collapse of Nationalist resistance ensured that the People's Liberation Army did not have to expend a major effort on military repression. Nevertheless, the legacies of war and civil war, the limitations of political authority, the failures of economic control and a myriad of other problems, ensured that the task which faced Mao Zedong and his supporters was truly herculean. It is a common judgement that their achievement in dealing rapidly and efficiently with these problems was remarkable, and the success of these years has been attributed to a strongly unified leadership, with a shared commitment to Marxism and a broad consensus on intentions regarding industrialization and social transformation.[3]

Although the new government declared itself to be revolutionary, it was at pains to reassure the population at large of the moderateness of its policies. In 'On people's democratic dictatorship,' published in 1949, Mao Zedong had declared that the dictatorship would be exercised by four classes: at the centre would be the working class, followed by the peasants, the bourgeoisie, and finally, on the periphery but nevertheless numbered among the people, the national bourgeoisie. Two documents, both issued in September 1949, outlined the main features of the new state. The Organic Law established the constitutional arrangements for a government in which Communists held a dominant but not exclusive position. The Common Programme guaranteed basic human rights, including freedom of speech, of movement and of religion, and promised equality for women. Other parts of the programme referred to the continuation of land reform and the development of heavy industry.[4] Policy guidelines were also laid down with respect to marriage and minority peoples.

The most pressing task was the imposition of effective control over the country. The CCP designated the wartime border regions 'old liberated areas', and those which it had gained as a result of the civil war 'new liberated areas'. The tasks of consolidating CCP control and of mobilizing support varied substantially between the two areas, but from the beginning it was important that the CCP should represent itself as the government of the whole country and of the entire population, except those elements which were defined, or who had defined themselves, as enemies of the regime. Initially the country was divided into six military regions, each directed by a commission which exercised both administrative and military authority. Party committees exercised authority at provincial, district and county levels. In the new liberated areas the day-to-day administrative order was maintained by permitting many thousands of officials who had held office under the Guomindang to remain in their posts. In the first year after the revolution salaries were often paid in kind, allowing vast amounts of paper currency to be withdrawn from circulation. Such was the importance of controlling inflation that when wage payments began again in 1950, salary points were based on the cost of living index.[5] So catastrophic had been the defeat of the Guomindang, that the new government had no cause to fear an organized opposition. Nevertheless, it was apparent that there were many who were not sympathetic towards the Communists, and this prompted various actions, including the Campaign to Suppress Counter-revolutionaries, which began in September 1950, which required that all Guomindang spies and party members register with public security officials. Those who confessed, or informed on others, were promised lenient treatment. However, arrests and executions followed. In Guangdong, a province which may not have been typical because of its propinquity to Xianggang, between October 1950 and August 1951 over 28,000 people, about one out of every thousand people in the province, were executed.[6]

At no point during its twenty-year rule had the Nationalist government exercised effective control over the whole of China Proper, let alone over the peripheral regions which were regarded as part of China. During the civil war the People's Liberation Army had recovered Manchuria and this region now became fully integrated into China under the general appellation of the north-east. Now the army had the capacity to impose direct rule over other parts of China, and by December the south-western provinces of Yunnan, Guizhou and Guangxi were firmly in Communist hands. The last remnants of Guomindang resistance in Xinjiang were crushed in March 1950, but

Outer Mongolia remained nominally an autonomous state and the whole of the northern frontier with the Soviet Union remained subject to further definition. Tibet, which had become autonomous in 1913, was 'liberated' by the People's Liberation Army in late 1950. In the following year an agreement with India recognized Chinese authority in Tibet, but left the Tibetans with substantial control over their own affairs. There remained Taiwan, now held by the Guomindang with some one million troops, which had been scheduled for 'liberation' in 1950. In October 1949 a Communist force tried but failed to capture the island of Jinmen (Quemoy). This setback, coupled with developments elsewhere, ensured that the Nationalists were able to consolidate their position on the island and with American support defy the People's Republic of China.

Another urgent priority concerned the establishment of foreign relations. Mao Zedong, when anticipating the Communist victory, had assumed that China would play an independent role in world politics. However, in 1949, in the atmosphere of the Cold War, Mao declared that China 'must lean either to the side of imperialism or to the side of socialism', and that meant leaning towards the Soviet Union. In December 1949 Mao made his first foreign visit, travelling to Moscow to negotiate with Stalin the Treaty of Alliance and Mutual Assistance, which he signed in February 1950. Two provisions of the treaty were particularly important: a declaration of military support should either country be attacked by Japan or her allies, and a promise by the Soviet Union to advance to China credits of $300 million over the next five years.[7]

In June 1950 civil war broke out in Korea. Between 1910 and 1945 Korea had been a Japanese colony, then after the war the country had been divided along the 38th parallel. In the first phase of the war North Korean troops overran South Korea, prompting a momentous United Nations' decision to send forces to assist South Korea. The United States and fifteen other nations sent troops and in addition the United States interposed its Seventh Fleet in the Taiwan Straits, thus denying China any chance of invading the island. The second phase began in September, when General Douglas MacArthur, commanding the United Nations' forces, made a dramatic amphibious landing at Inchon, behind the North Korean lines. By November the United Nations' forces were within 50 miles of the Yalu river, the frontier between North Korea and China. It was at this point that China intervened, and a very large force of the Chinese People's Volunteers (so called to allow China to deny official involvement), under the command of Peng Dehuai, pushed the United Nations' forces back to the 38th parallel.

Why should China, so soon after the revolution, risk involvement in war? The evidence weighs against suggestions that the North Korean invasion was instigated by China (although the Soviet Union may have encouraged it), or that China's entry into the war was premeditated. An American analysis of 1960, based on materials then available in the West, concluded that China's entry into the war was not dictated by Soviet policy, nor was it occasioned by a desire to assist Communist North Korea. Most probably the Chinese leadership deemed it essential to challenge the United States' alignment with Japan which was an implied threat to China's position in Asia. A recent assessment concluded that China's reasons were 'primarily security', arising from a fear of the military threat from the United States.[8]

China's involvement in the Korean War was on a large scale and at a high cost. Chinese casualties have been estimated as reaching between 700,000 and 900,000, among them Mao Anying, Mao Zedong's son by his first wife. China was forced to incur heavy debts with the Soviet Union for the purchase of arms, and was branded as an aggressor by the United Nations. In the United States, hostility arising from China's participation contributed to the McCarthy witchhunt against all who were suspected of having sympathy for the Chinese Communists. Nevertheless, involvement in the war brought some benefits to China. The war exposed serious military weaknesses, including a shortage of aircraft and inadequate logistical support, which led to a decision to modernize the People's Liberation Army. On the home front the war aroused patriotic feelings. Profiting from the situation and using the technique of the mass movement, the government set out to mobilize support, to tighten discipline and to crack down on dissidents. The Resist America, Aid Korea campaign spread themes of nationalism and anti-Americanism in schools and factories. The Three Antis movement, begun in December 1951, attacked corruption, waste and bureaucratism by cadres. The Five Antis campaign was directed against merchants and industrialists accused of failing to support the war effort. Those found guilty had their property confiscated.

Meanwhile, a major transformation was taking place in the countryside. During the civil war the CCP had endorsed the revival of revolutionary land reform, directed in the first instance against landlords who were also collaborators, and then, under the Agrarian Law of 1947, against all landlords and institutions holding land. This resulted in a violent assault on landlords as a class and led to many deaths – for example, in the village of Long Bow in Shanxi at least a dozen people were beaten to death for having been associated with the system of exploitation.[9] Many others were identified as 'feudal tails', meaning that although they were not landlords, they owned means of production which they had not earned by the sweat of their brow, so this property was also confiscated and redistributed.[10] Although the CCP condoned the revolutionary violence, it did not control it. In 1950, with the passing of the Agrarian Reform Law, which extended reform to the newly liberated areas, the government attempted to enforce a more orderly process. The purpose of the new law, as explained by Liu Shaoqi, was not only to end feudal exploitation by the landlord class, but also to preserve a rich peasant economy to enable the early recovery of agricultural production. Shortly after this more moderate line had been announced the Korean War broke out. There were alleged instances of peasants being afraid to oppose landlords, and of landlords expressing the hope that the Communist regime might be overthrown. This led to a hardening of land reform policy, with greater emphasis on establishing the class line and breaking the political power of the landlords. The implications of this were considerable, because many local cadres, and even senior party officials, came from landlord or rich peasant backgrounds, and the new line required them either to denounce their own families or to leave themselves open to denunciation. To counter this, mass mobilization techniques were employed and 'struggle meetings' were held, at which landlords were subject to criticism by poor peasants. This campaign was more controlled and more politically inspired than the earlier terror, but nevertheless resulted in many more landlords being executed or sent to forced labour camps.[11]

The revolutionary land reform programme was largely completed by 1952. It had not covered the areas occupied by national minorities, but in other respects it had been an extraordinarily extensive and thorough transformation – 'by far China's (and the world's) greatest rural movement'.[12] It was estimated that it had led to the confiscation and redistribution of about 43 per cent of China's cultivated land to about 60 per cent of the rural population – a massive transfer of property, though not as extreme as had occurred in Cuba, where 75 per cent of the cultivated land was confiscated and redistributed. The class of landlords and rural powerholders had been devastated, with estimates of the numbers who were killed ranging from 200,000 to 800,000 to a million, two million or even more.[13] The complicity of the mass of the rural population in these events assured the CCP that there could be no unmaking of the revolution.

Changes in Landholding by Class

Long Bow Village, Shanxi, 1944–8[14]

Before liberation

	Families	Persons	Land in mou	mou per capita
Landlord	7	39	680	17.4
Rich peasant	5	27	303	11.2
Middle peasant	81	395	2,533	6.4
Poor peasant	138	462	1,386	3.0
Labourer	20	64	–	–
Institutional	–	–	686	–
Totals	251	987	5,588	–

After land reform

	Families	Persons	Land in mou	mou per capita
Landlord	1	2	13	6.5
Rich peasant	4	12	55	4.6
Old middle peasant	76	341	2,057	6.0
New middle peasant	140	523	3,048	5.8
Poor peasant	29	82	416	5.1
Institutional	–	–	36	–
Totals	250	960	5,626	–

Liu Shaoqi's hope of increasing production was less easy to satisfy. By and large the landlords had not been cultivators and their disappearance from the rural scene, to put it in neutral terms, had not harmed production. In villages where landlordism had been an important feature, the relief from the burden of rent may have encouraged peasants to raise production. But the 'fruits' of land reform were very limited and their redistribution at most transformed a poor peasant into a middle peasant. The effect of reform on the village of Long Bow in Shanxi is shown in the table above. This may be compared with the average distribution per entitled peasant in the areas studied by John Wong, which amounted to 1.7 mou of land (about 0.27 of an acre), 53 catties of grain (26.5 kilograms), a little less than a quarter of a tool and about one-sixtieth of an animal. Official estimates of grain production between 1949 and 1952 indicate that it rose by 12.6 per cent, but part of this must be attributed to postwar recovery.[15] Land reform itself was incapable of producing any substantial increase in output – what was needed was collectivization and increased inputs.[16]

Closely associated with the assault on the position of the rural landlords was the determined effort made to undermine the extended family or lineage system. In the Jiangxi period the CCP had promulgated a decree which condemned the prevailing system of arranged marriages as barbaric. In 1950 a Marriage Law was passed which declared that the feudal marriage system was now replaced by the 'New Democratic Marriage' system, which required the free choice of partners and monogamy. Women were given equal rights with men over property and equal opportunities for divorce. Like the legislation on land reform, this was not simply a law but 'an instrument to transform society'. Its promulgation was accompanied by a mass campaign in which women's associations played a major role. Extensive use was made of radio and newspapers, and cadres were educated to enforce the new law. Its introduction led to a spate of divorces – one set of figures indicated that 1.3 million petitions were filed in 1953. However, in that same year it was thought necessary to launch a second mass campaign in areas where the legislation had had little impact. This measure may have hastened the decline of the extended family, which often had been more an ideal than a reality. But other features of the modified traditional family system survived in the countryside.

By 1949, it has been said, all CCP leaders had accepted the proposition that 'while only a peasant revolution could bring the Party to power, only an urban industrial revolution could lay the basis for an independent socialist society'.[17] The cities were in a desperate condition, with industrial and commercial activity at a standstill and public utilities out of commission. Social evils – gang warfare, armed robbery, drug dealing and prostitution – were commonplace. The first task was to impose order and this was achieved by declaring martial law and allocating the limited supply of experienced cadres to supervise key facilities. The Communists then had to decide how to bring about the revolutionary transformation of a culture with which they had little sympathy and of which they had limited experience. In the early stages of occupation cadres had pursued radical strategies, encouraging workers to demand higher wages and paralysing the operation of municipal bodies. A more moderate strategy was spelled out by Liu Shaoqi in

Tianjin in April 1949: the traditional sector of the economy would be left alone, and the CCP cadres would concentrate their efforts on the modern economic sector, the educational sphere and the civil service.

During these early years remarkable improvements were achieved. Prostitution, which had been commonplace in the cities and notorious in Shanghai, was virtually wiped out. Opium smoking was tackled with determination and imagination. In Guangzhou, on the 112th anniversary of Lin Zexu's destruction of the foreign opium, a campaign was launched in which opium which had been seized was destroyed, and registered opium addicts were urged to free themselves of the habit. The implication was that the new regime would succeed where Lin Zexu and his successors had failed.[18]

The dislocation caused by war and revolution was compounded by the departure of two key groups from the cities. Industrialists and owners of commercial enterprises, who had had close connections with the Guomindang, had already fled. Their enterprises were immediately confiscated and nationalized without compensation. The other group consisted of foreigners, who in the former treaty ports occupied key roles in industry and commerce, and also in education. Some foreigners chose to go immediately, and foreign businesses were thereupon confiscated. However, others, including many missionaries, educators and welfare workers, chose to stay. During the Korean War they were the target of mass campaigns to criticize foreigners, and at the same time the foreign assets of foreign firms were frozen. In April 1951 the confiscation of foreign businesses began with the requisition of the property of Shell Oil.

These events left the government in control of a wide variety of enterprises. It was not yet its intention to establish state control or ownership of the property of that group which had been defined as the 'national bourgeoisie', meaning the many thousands of owners of small businesses. By holding back it allowed industrial production to revive and it consolidated its influence among those with managerial and technical skills. However, from the time of the Korean War, the regulation of private enterprises increased and many members of the national bourgeoisie became victims of the Five Antis campaign. So important was this change of emphasis that, for the inhabitants of Tianjin, 'the revolution came not in 1949 but in early 1952'. It was a revolution which took a variety of forms. In pre-revolutionary Tianjin, as elsewhere in China's cities and towns, guanxi, that is personal relationships or connections, based on family, locality, school and friendship, had determined who would be employed by an enterprise and with which other institutions the enterprise would do business. The Five Antis campaign, which involved staff denouncing their employers for improper activities, an event known as 'tiger-beating', was also an attack on the system of personal relationships. In this way the regime penetrated the small-business community in a manner never before achieved by a Chinese government.[19] Further consolidation was achieved by the establishment of residents' committees. These committees, which first appeared in Tianjin and Shanghai in 1951 and were later introduced generally, had a wide variety of tasks, including acting as a mouthpiece for government policies and a source of information on popular responses, and promoting various programmes, including public security, literacy and sanitation.[20]

424

After taking power the Chinese Communists had relied on the statistical information, and in particular the population data, which they had inherited from the Guomindang. Only in the autumn of 1952, when the State Statistical Bureau was established, was the decision taken to hold a census on 30 June 1953. Because of the shortage of time – six months was quite inadequate to prepare for a modern census – the information sought was merely name, date of birth, sex and nationality. The census was only completed in November 1954, whereupon the State Statistical Bureau announced that on census day the population of the Chinese mainland, that is excluding the population of Taiwan and overseas Chinese, had amounted to 582,603,417 persons. The unlikely precision of this figure, and the many limitations of method in what was not a proper census, merely a registration of population, has raised doubts about the validity of the statistics obtained. However, because there are no other figures available, and because there is no plausible reason why the CCP should have manipulated the information, the results of the 1953 census are usually taken as the best available evidence on China's population at that date.

Some other figures derived from the 1953 census and from subsequent calculations are of interest. Nearly 40 per cent of the population was under fifteen years of age. Of the grand total enumerated, 51.82 per cent were men and 48.18 were women. As the number of women over the age of sixty greatly exceeded the number of men, the suspicion is that some of this imbalance must have been caused by female infanticide. Some fifty non-Han national minorities were identified and their total population put at over 35 million. Figures released in 1957 indicated that in 1953 the population had increased by 2.29 per cent and that the rate of increase remained at well over 2 per cent per annum. Immediately after the revolution the conventional Marxist view that 'in a socialist country there cannot be too many people' had been accepted. By 1957 the official line was to encourage birth control, although this was not supported by an adequate supply of contraceptives.[21]

The Soviet Model

A frequently quoted slogan of the early revolutionary years predicted: 'Three years of recovery, then ten years of development'. In 1953, now that the country had largely recovered from war and an armistice had been signed in Korea, a moderate but important policy shift took place. In August Mao Zedong announced the general line for the transition to socialism, which he said would be accomplished 'over a fairly long period of time'. By now a State Planning Commission was in existence, an indication that the transition would come about through centralized planning. In September the People's Republic of China, following the course taken by the Soviet Union under Stalin, initiated its First Five-Year Plan.

Various reasons may explain why China adopted a Stalinist strategy for economic development. Put in the baldest terms, there seemed little choice. The Soviet model was regarded as a blueprint for the creation of a socialist economy. Lenin's dictum was quoted: 'There is only one real foundation for a socialist society, and it is large industry'.[22] It was anticipated that China would receive economic and technical assistance from the Soviet Union. Finally, the Soviet Union was China's only major ally, towards whom China looked for security. Nevertheless, to embark on an economic strategy which involved such heavy reliance on a foreign power was ironic. At Yan'an Mao Zedong had written: 'We must put an end to writing eight-legged essays on foreign models.'[23] Later he was to reflect bitterly on the acceptance of the Russian model without adequately investigating its appropriateness to the Chinese situation and without incorporating any of the elements of self-reliance and innovation which had been a feature of the economy during the Yan'an period.

The economic strategy adopted in 1953 was intended to achieve the following objectives: a high rate of economic growth through a concentration on industrial progress and a particular emphasis on heavy industry; a high rate of saving and investment to serve the previous objective; and the construction of large-scale, capital-intensive industrial plants using advanced technology. The strategy also assumed the institutional transformation of agriculture, from whence much of the capital for industrialization would come.[24]

Soviet assistance was essential to enable this plan to get started. This took the form of aid in the construction, or reconstruction, of 156 major industrial enterprises, including 7 iron and steel plants, 24 electric power stations and 63 machinery plants. The aid given was comprehensive, meaning that it extended from making the original surveys to the design of the plant, its construction, the installation of the machinery and the training of personnel. In 1958–9 a further 125 projects were added to the list. The combined cost of the first 156 projects was 12.8 billion yuan, 48 per cent of the total investment allocated to the First Five-Year Plan. Soviet assistance often came in the form of the delivery of complete plants, for example the oil refinery constructed at Lanzhou was planned in the Soviet Union and 85 per cent of its equipment was Soviet in origin. The Soviet Union also sent 11,000 specialists to China and 28,000 Chinese went to the Soviet Union for training.

Some other features of the economic strategy of the First Five-Year Plan deserve attention. A decision was taken to shift the concentration of modern industrial development away from the coastal cities and the north-east. So, for example, the two major steel complexes were established at Wuhan on the middle Yangzi and in Inner Mongolia. This decision implied improvements in communications and 8.5 per cent of the total investment of the First Five-Year Plan went on railway construction, including the construction of lines from Xi'an to the Xinjiang oilfields and from Chongqing to Chengdu, increasing the railway mileage by over 20 per cent.

Another aspect of the First Five-Year Plan concerned industrial management. In the years immediately after the revolution a form of management had emerged which has been called the 'East China system', under which a committee, composed of technicians, cadres and representatives of the work force, exercised collective leadership, while the factory manager organized the productive operations.[25] At the time of the First Five-Year Plan a Soviet model of 'one-man management' was introduced, which has been described as 'a coldly rational arrangement of individual workers commanded by an authoritarian manager'. This model of 'scientific management' was associated with centralized planning and detailed production targets.[26] During the Yan'an period ideological incentives had been used to some effect – in 1943 the Party had developed a successful 'labour hero' campaign, and had honoured, but not materially rewarded, 180 labour heroes. Now the rewards were to be exclusively material, with the widespread use of piecework systems and steeply graded wage and salary scales.

What did the First Five-Year Plan achieve in terms of raising output? The table below gives a statistical measure of the performance of some industries, but these figures need to be set in a broader context. The obvious comparison is with the Soviet Union and with the Five-Year Plans initiated by Stalin. However, China launched its First Five-Year Plan when its level of economic development was still far behind that of the Soviet Union as it had been in 1928. China's output of grain per capita was less than half that of the Soviet Union and its output of steel was less than one-third. During the Five-Year Plan period, China's industrial output doubled, the most spectacular increases being achieved in the output of producer goods, notably steel and chemicals. The increase in the output of consumer goods was more modest and that of agricultural products, specifically food grains, only reached 3.7 per cent per annum. The rates of growth in the industrial sector were probably more rapid than those achieved by the Soviet Union at the time of its First Five-Year Plan. Although the Soviet contribution to the achievements of the Chinese First Five-Year Plan was considerable, only about 30 per cent of industrial output came from new or reconstructed plants, and inherited factories and mines provided over two-thirds of the increased production. Moreover, the rapid growth of producer output 'was to a large degree a continuation of a development process begun decades earlier'.[27]

Industrial output in China, by product, 1952–7[28]

	1952	1957	% increase
Pig iron ('000 tons)	1,900	5,936	212
Steel ('000 tons)	1,348	5,350	297
Electricity (m. kw. hrs)	7,260	19,340	166
Coal ('000 tons)	66,490	130,000	96
Crude petroleum ('000 tons)	436	1,438	234
Cement ('000 tons)	2,860	6,860	140
Chemical fertilizer ('000 tons)	181	631	249
Cotton cloth (m. metres)	3,829	5,050	31

Despite this record of success, the First Five-Year Plan exposed a range of economic and political difficulties. The assumption that these could not be handled within the context of rational planning led to the abandonment of the Soviet model. The most fundamental economic problem was unbalanced development, with the industrial sector racing ahead and the agricultural sector lagging behind, barely feeding the expanding population, let alone supplying industry with the raw materials needed to raise the production of consumer goods. The reference to political difficulties can best be explained by citing the case of Gao Gang, the head of the State Planning Commission and chief of the First Five-Year Plan programme. He had been identified with the rapid industrialization of the north-east and heavy reliance on Soviet aid in that region. He was also associated with the 'one-man management' system referred to above. In 1953, perhaps encouraged by remarks made by Mao Zedong, he began to intrigue against Liu Shaoqi, Mao's recognized successor. When these manoeuvres were exposed, he was accused in the Politburo of having planned to set up an 'independent kingdom' in the north-east – implying that he condoned Soviet influence in the area. Gao Gang was purged in 1954, and later committed suicide. This was the first political purge of the new regime, an indication of political rivalries within the leadership and of reservations about the role of the Soviet Union in China.[29]

Soviet influence was to be particularly apparent in education. In 1949 the CCP had inherited from the Guomindang a system which provided education for 25 per cent of the children of the primary school age group, secondary schooling for a mere 3 per cent and higher education for only 0.3 per cent of the age group. Teachers came from politically suspect backgrounds and their support for the regime was not certain. In contrast, in the former border regions, the CCP had pioneered a form of mass education which emphasized relevant knowledge and user control of schools.

After the revolution, the CCP had moved quickly to reorganize and expand education. By 1952 primary school enrolment had reached 60 per cent and there were impressive gains in middle school and technical school enrolments. Over four million adults had been declared newly literate. Religious schools and colleges had been nationalized and most Western missionary educators had departed. Following the same logic which had led to the emulation of the Soviet industrial model, the Chinese leadership turned to the Soviet Union for guidance in educational development. The effects were most apparent in higher education, the entire sector being reorganized on Russian lines. Between 1952 and 1958, six hundred Russians taught in Chinese colleges and universities, and by 1959 36,000 Chinese students had been trained in Russian universities. In the first year after reorganization one-third of the total enrolment comprised engineering students, the next largest group being teacher trainees. Courses were planned with the assistance of Russian advisers and translations of Russian textbooks were used widely. Teaching methods were formal and students were expected to memorize much of their work. Soviet influence also became substantial in secondary and primary schools, not only through the use of Soviet teaching materials and teaching methods, but also with the introduction of Soviet practices, for example the idea of 'children's palaces', a term used to describe after-school activities such as drama, sport and music.[30]

Alongside the industrial expansion of the First Five-Year Plan came the collectivization of agriculture. From what was said earlier about the effects of land reform, it will be apparent that a land system, in which the standard unit was the middle peasant farming a small and often very dispersed smallholding, could not produce the sustained growth in agricultural production required to feed the rising population and provide the raw materials required by industry. Other arguments supporting the case for moving away from individual farming included the inability of most peasant farmers to invest substantially in agricultural development, and the necessity of stemming migration to the cities by finding employment for the surplus labour in the countryside.

There were also political reasons for pressing along the road to collectivization. The Soviet Union had followed this road in the 1930s and that example remained the sole model to emulate. Another motive concerned the perceived consequences of land reform. After the reform landowners retained what were called the 'four freedoms' – the freedoms to purchase, sell and rent land; to hire agricultural labourers; to lend money; and to trade in the private market. Soon after land reform the more equal distribution of wealth began to be eroded. Within three years 20–25 per cent of the population of some areas had sold land, most of the sales being from poor peasant households to those of rich peasants.[31] In a speech given on 31 July 1955 Mao Zedong observed:

> Everyone has noticed that in recent years there has been a spontaneous and constant growth of capitalist elements in the countryside and that new rich peasants have sprung up everywhere. . . . If this tendency goes unchecked, the separation into two extremes in the countryside will get worse day by day.[32]

The solution proposed by Mao Zedong was 'the socialist transformation of agriculture as a whole through co-operation'.

Having encouraged peasants to join the revolution by offering them the ownership of land, it was an extraordinary reversal to start, within four years, the process of depriving them of that individual ownership. Both the economic and political arguments cited above assume that the decision for collectivization derived from observations of the effects of land reform. It has, however, been suggested that the Communist leadership always intended to collectivize land. Land reform was never seen as an end in itself, but as a necessary intermediate step, creating the conditions in which collectivization would become possible.[33]

The road which led from private ownership to co-operation and then to collectivization passed through several stages, the first being the mutual aid team. Such teams had been part of traditional farming practice and had also been used at Yan'an. After land reform, mutual aid teams of six or more households were set up to assist each other and to allocate scarce resources, such as draught animals and labour. At first they operated at seasons of peak demand but later they became year-round organizations. The next stage, initiated in 1954, was the combining of several mutual aid teams into Lower Agricultural Producers' Cooperatives. In these, land was pooled and farmed co-operatively, but each family retained the private ownership of its land. Crops were divided partly in accordance with the amount of labour contributed, and partly in accordance with the amount of land pooled.

In 1955 the decision was taken to move from co-operatives to collective farms, or Advanced Producers' Cooperatives. These were formed by the amalgamation of four or five of the Lower Agricultural Producers' Cooperatives, and comprised on average 158 households. In the Advanced Producers' Cooperatives private land-ownership was abolished and members were remunerated solely on the basis of their labour. By the end of 1956 the vast majority of localities had taken this step and the socialist transformation of the agricultural sector had been completed.

China's experience of collectivizing agriculture is often compared favourably with that of the Soviet Union. In the Soviet Union agricultural collectivization took place after industrial development had provided inputs in the form of agricultural machinery and chemical fertilizers. In China the sequence was collectivization first, although this was a staged process rather than an abrupt change. Whereas in the Soviet Union collectivization had been accompanied by widespread sabotage of agricultural production, and had cost the lives of up to 10,000,000 kulaks or rich peasants, in China collectivization was supposedly achieved with comparatively little opposition. A number of reasons have been given to explain the contrast, for example that China's rich peasants were neither so large a group nor so well established a feature of rural society as were the kulaks. Whereas kulaks had enough land to farm efficiently, Chinese peasant landholdings of less than 2 acres per family were too small to achieve this. Another suggestion is that the procedures adopted in China were more suitable, that the mutual aid team stage – of which there was no equivalent in the Soviet Union – was a valuable first experience of co-operation. Also, that in China the timing was correct – implying that in the short interval which had elapsed since land reform capitalist tendencies had not become established, whereas in the Soviet Union the passage of twelve years had allowed that development to take place. Thirdly it has been suggested that the fact that the CCP had its roots among the peasantry was important. The socialization of the Chinese countryside was led by 1.2 million local cadres, not forced upon a reluctant peasantry by outsiders – a feature which later gave rise to a serious underestimation of the problems which had arisen.[34]

This positive assessment of the Chinese experience has been reinforced by evidence which suggests that each advance towards collectivization was endorsed at village level and that the rapidity of the change owed something to popular support. One of the best-known Western accounts of China's collectivization endorsing this view is Jan Myrdal's *Report from a Chinese Village*, which was based on interviews conducted in 1962 with villagers from Liu Ling, Shanxi. One of Myrdal's informants, a former day labourer, told him that the Liu Ling Lower Agricultural Producers' Co-operative had been formed in 1954 with the enthusiastic support of the poor peasants and the grudging acceptance of the former wealthy members of the village.

. . . in the end, everyone was agreed and understood that with a farmers' cooperative there was no question of one gaining at the expense of another, but that all should achieve prosperity together.

He added that in the following year the majority of the village had also favoured the next step, the formation of the East Shines Red Higher Agricultural Co-operative. A minority had opposed it because it would do away with the dividend on land, but as he had no land this had been of no significance to him.[35]

This positive view was endorsed strongly by Vivienne Shue, who claimed that by appealing to the rational self-interest of the peasants, by applying a well-thought-out policy flexibly, by acting promptly, using local cadres and managing the class struggle, the CCP achieved 'several major economic and social transformations of the countryside while sustaining popular support and avoiding serious losses in agricultural production'.[36]

A very different picture of collectivization emerged from an investigation conducted in 1978 by the first group of American social scientists permitted to conduct systematic research in the Chinese countryside after the revolution. Villagers from Raoyang, 120 miles south of Beijing, looked back at the years immediately after land reform as a happy time, but recalled the progress from the small co-operatives to the large ones as having led to widespread discontent. They had opposed the drive to dig more wells, they had resented having to grow more low-priced cotton, having to abandon lucrative sideline enterprises, and having to defer consumption while expanding sales of grain to the state at low prices. They claimed that the case for collectivization had been based on falsified statistics of grain yield, that for many people collectivization was theft, that they were forced into collectives which they thought unworkable and they only acquiesced for fear of being branded as rightists. Expansive promises had been made about the rise in production that collectivization would bring, but these promises had proved empty.[37]

Criticism has also been levelled at the Chinese leadership for failing to organize the move to co-operatives and then to collectives more efficiently. On several occasions the change to co-operatives was accelerated and then slowed down and this has been seen as a reflection of disagreement within the leadership over the appropriate speed of change. There were also 'problems of disorganization and planned confusion, harsh cadre methods, and the alienation of better-off peasants that resulted from hasty implementation of the program'.[38] The commitment to collectivization was made despite opposition in the State Council when Mao Zedong announced a 'socialist high tide'. It was a policy decision which owed more to political than to economic considerations, as his speech of 31 July 1955 indicated. In it he declared, 'some of our comrades are tottering along like a woman with bound feet, always complaining, "You're going too fast"'. Those who criticized the decision were liable to be labelled as rightists. In the short term collectivization did not increase agricultural growth, and state procurement, the principal means whereby capital was transferred from agriculture to industry, had to be cut back.[39]

The reference to the danger of being branded as a rightist leads to that other instance of the radicalization of policy, the Hundred Flowers campaign of 1956 and its aftermath. This campaign was directed at the 'intellectuals', that is the educated elite. In 1949 the great majority of intellectuals had accepted the

Communist victory and had been made welcome for what they could offer to the new state. At first the only pressure exerted on them was that they should eradicate what the critic Mao Dun called 'compradore culture', 'the notion that "the moon shines brighter abroad than here at home"'.[40] In 1955, in the context of the collectivization of agriculture, a harder line was adopted towards intellectuals who persisted in claiming the right to express their own views. A principal target was the poet Hu Feng, at first criticized for harbouring bourgeois ideas, and then arrested and gaoled in 1955 for alleged counter-revolutionary activities. The mass campaign waged to attack Hu Feng alarmed intellectuals at the very moment that the CCP was seeking their endorsement of collectivization.

In January 1956 Zhou Enlai promised intellectuals an improvement in their standard of living and a reduction in their political study. In May Mao Zedong went further, announcing a relaxation of the policy towards intellectuals, declaring 'Let a hundred flowers bloom, a hundred schools of thought contend'. This encouraged artists to disregard social realism and scientists to be more active in challenging scientific theories. At first, to Mao Zedong's disappointment, the intellectuals' response was very cautious. Meanwhile, a Party rectification campaign, similar to that launched at Yan'an, had been launched. In October 1956 news of the Hungarian uprising was received with contradictory responses in China. For the Party hierarchy it implied a threat to its grip on power, but Mao Zedong interpreted it as the result of the isolation of the Hungarian Communist Party from the masses and its repression of intellectuals. His response came in his famous speech 'On the Correct Handling of Contradictions Among the People', which he gave in February 1957. In it he identified 'contradictions between ourselves and our enemies', which he described as 'antagonistic' and those 'within the ranks of the people' which could either be 'antagonistic' or 'non-antagonistic'. The resolution of non-antagonistic contradictions, through discussion and criticism, would speed up the development of socialist society.[41]

This speech, and other assurances, led intellectuals to believe that the open expression of their views would be welcomed. In April and May 1957 an unprecedented quantity of material appeared criticizing the Party, its manner of governing and the policies it pursued. Some of the criticism came from the 'democratic parties', the non-Communist parties which had been permitted to remain in existence. Chu Anping, the editor-in-chief of the *Guangming Daily*, the intellectuals' newspaper, criticized the 'old bonzes' of the Party, claiming that in the past few years the relations between the Party and the masses had not been good.

> Where is the key to the problem? In my opinion the key lies in the idea that 'the world belongs to the Party.' I think a party leading a nation is not the same thing as a party owning a nation.[42]

In the universities, the first burst of criticism came from academics who complained 'there is a tendency for political qualifications to override cultural and technical qualifications'. On 20 May 'blooming and contending' began among the students at Beijing University. They displayed large-character newspapers on a 'democratic wall' on the campus. At first the complaints were limited to criticizing the university authorities, but they soon turned to broader political issues. The first publication in China of extracts from Khrushchev's 'secret speech' denouncing Stalin appeared on Beijing University noticeboards. One hostile report claimed that a small group of students, calling themselves the 'Hundred Flowers Society' had declared 'Marxism is out of date' and had called for a 'movement for freedom and democracy.' Lin Xiling, a law student at Beijing University, made outspoken speeches on the campus. She allegedly asserted that most members of the CCP were 'rotten eggs', intellectually stagnant and useless, with very few Bolsheviks among them.[43]

On 25 May Mao Zedong warned delegates to the Youth League Congress that 'all words and actions that deviate from socialism are completely mistaken'. On 8 June the CCP launched a counterattack against its critics, whom it termed 'rightists'. Some of those who had been most prominent in the expression of their views, including Chu Anping and Lin Xiling, were singled out for particular anathema. The Anti-Rightist campaign, which extended into 1958, resulted in between 400,000 and 700,000 intellectuals being sent to the countryside or to factories for reform through labour. Among these thousands of victims, one whose fate deserved particular notice was Ding Ling. She, who had had the temerity to imply criticism of the CCP in the Yan'an days, had later been reinstated and had played a leading part in the rectification of artists and writers after 1949. Now she was accused of being a bourgeois individualist, stripped of all her positions and sent to work in the countryside.[44]

Why did this volte-face occur? Views hostile to Mao Zedong accuse him of persuading intellectuals to reveal their true opinions in order to entrap them. A less extreme interpretation is that the criticisms they voiced were far more outspoken than Mao had anticipated, for he had supposed that the intellectuals had been fully indoctrinated. Unwilling to see Party control weakened, and aware of pressing economic problems, he supported the decision to divert criticism away from the Party and on to the intellectuals. For Mao this shift was to prove decisive, for thereafter he abandoned the intellectuals as the key to economic development and looked to the next generation of educated youth to carry the revolution forward.[45]

The Great Leap Forward and the Sino–Soviet Split

The origins of the Great Leap Forward were both economic and ideological. It is difficult to resolve the relative importance and priority of the two motivations.

The First Five-Year Plan had brought major achievements, but as an economic strategy it had serious shortcomings. The concentration of investment on capital-intensive heavy industry had led to industry growing five times more rapidly than agriculture. However, the industrial sector had provided few new jobs and a Second Five-Year Plan would have to create millions of additional jobs just to accommodate labour force growth and existing unemployment in urban areas.[46]

Many of these new jobs would be in the consumer goods industries, but shortages of raw materials were impeding expansion, notably in the cotton textile industry. The fundamental problem was the relatively poor performance of the agricultural sector. Output had grown, but the increase did no more than feed the growing population and allow a very modest rise in per capita consumption. Although collectivization had increased state control over production, even in 1956 the state procurement system, which bought prescribed quantities of grain and other commodities at fixed prices, was running into difficulties. The fulfilment of procurement targets became even more difficult when private markets were reopened later that year.[47]

The need to achieve a better balance between capital-intensive projects using advanced technology and medium and small-scale projects which made better use of China's resources had been recognized from 1955. In April 1956, in a speech entitled 'On the Ten Great Relationships', Mao Zedong had expounded a theory of contradictions inherent in economic development, for example the contradiction which existed between centralized development and industrial decentralization. The outcome was the slogan 'walking on two legs' which implied that agriculture would develop alongside industry, and small-scale industry would be developed alongside large enterprises.

A wider dissatisfaction with the implications of the First Five-Year Plan strategy had also emerged. The emphasis on centralized planning and bureaucratic control, the achievement of production targets, the reliance on technical expertise, the application of 'one-man management', all contributed to a mounting criticism of the direction that the revolution was taking. Concern was expressed about excessive Soviet influence in other fields, for example in higher education. A report published in 1956 in the *People's Education* declared:

College students are really too busy. We have no Sunday: it is merely the 'seventh day of the week'. Many students spend their weekends in the library. Others carry books or Russian language-cards with them in the toilet and in the streetcar or bus. The period of reviewing for the examination is even worse. Due to excessive tension, the students constantly suffer from headaches, fatigue, insomnia and neurasthenia. . . .[48]

Another explanation of the origins of the Great Leap Forward referred to tensions within the Party leadership and the widening gap between Mao Zedong and some other CCP leaders over the direction the revolution should take. A hint of this tension had been given in 1955 when Mao overrode his more cautious colleagues on the issue of the speed of collectivization. In the Hundred Flowers campaign Mao Zedong had encouraged criticism of the Party, and then had supported the Anti-Rightist campaign which had targeted intellectuals and, by implication, the experts who had been prominent in the execution of the First Five-Year Plan.

The extent of Mao Zedong's alienation was apparent in the speech which he gave at the Supreme State Conference on 28 January 1958. This contained two key passages, the first of which emphasized Mao's faith in the potential of the masses, a faith which he had asserted so strongly at Yan'an and which he now reaffirmed:

> Our country is both poor and blank. Those who are poor have nothing to call their own. Those who are blank are like a sheet of white paper. To be poor is fine because it makes you inclined to be revolutionary. With blank paper many things can be done. You can write on it or draw designs. Blank paper is best for writing on.[49]

The second passage concerned Mao Zedong's concept of permanent revolution, which amounted to a claim that in China the revolution could advance in an uninterrupted manner from the transition to socialism, which had been basically completed with the collectivization of agriculture, to the passage from socialism to communism. Through the power of human consciousness and the strength of the human will – in which Mao had a profound faith – China could advance immediately to the next stage and become a country which was 'economically modern and socially communist'.[50]

Indications that the Five-Year Plan strategy was to be superseded by a 'great leap' multiplied in late 1957. In October the slogan 'more, faster, better, cheaper' was adopted to urge an increase in both industrial and agricultural output. In factories 'one-man management' was rejected in favour of workers' congresses and many cadres in middle-sector management were 'sent down' to participate in labour on the shop floor. Ideological exhortation increasingly replaced material incentives as the means to encourage workers to redouble their efforts. In 1958 production targets were raised dramatically and state investment greatly increased. Within three years, from 1957 to 1960, the numbers employed in state industrial enterprises doubled to over 50 million, placing an immense strain on the system of procurement of food from the countryside.

The most dramatic development was in the countryside. In April 1958 twenty-seven Advanced Producers' Co-operatives in Suiping county, Henan province, led by the Sputnik Co-operative,[51] decided to pool their resources and form a commune, to be run by a committee chosen democratically by the people. This move received official blessing in August and was followed by an extraordinary rush which, before the end of 1958, had led to 700,000 Agricultural Producers' Co-operatives being reorganized into 24,000 People's Communes, the average commune comprising about 5,000 families. The communes were hailed as the solution to the imbalance within the economy. To expand agricultural production a massive investment was to be made in land improvement and water conservancy projects. As large amounts of capital investment were not available, the improvement would be achieved by the mobilization of labour on a vast scale, a mobilization which could only be achieved by creating the much larger agricultural communes. The communes would also achieve a high level of self-sufficiency as they would have the resources to develop rural industry. In these respects the move to communes was justified on economic grounds. In addition communes would assume other functions, including the provision of educational and medical facilities and the running of the militia.

The organization of the communes also had ideological implications. Mao Zedong declared that they contained 'sprouts of communism' and this appeared justified by some features of the first communes. Private plots, which peasants had been allowed to retain in the Advanced Producers' Co-operatives, were now subsumed into the commune and cadres campaigned for the collectivization of virtually all private property. In some villages burial mounds were removed to increase the stock of agricultural land. Periodic markets and fairs were largely prohibited – further stifling the development of rural capitalism.[52] Collective kitchens were set up and a free-food policy was instituted. Crèches and nurseries were introduced to allow women with small children to participate in productive labour. These developments were hailed as an important step towards emancipating women from the double burden of work and domesticity. Income distribution, which in the Agricultural Producers' Co-operatives had been on the basis of the amount of labour contributed, was now determined by a system of work points which made allowance for need.

An equally ambitious experiment in social organization took place in the cities with the formation of urban communes. Since the revolution there had been an enormous increase in the urban population, partly as a result of urban drift, and by 1958 it approached 100 million. Prompted partly by the need to provide employment and food for these numbers, and partly by ideological commitment, urban communes, which combined industrial, agricultural, commercial, cultural and security functions, were established from autumn 1958. Many of these were centred on a factory, but they also diversified into food production and provided the range of social services to be found in rural communes. The model for this type of development was the Zhengzhou Spinning and Weaving Machine Plant commune in Henan, which had a population of some ten thousand people and provided employment in the main factory, in the subsidiary factories which recycled waste, and on the 700 mou of land farmed by the commune.[53]

The establishment of the communes coincided with a period of heightened tension in foreign affairs. The revival of the militia, through the establishment of the communes, was in part a response to this, for it was meant to secure the 'permanent mobilization' of the Chinese population. So too was the setting of a very high target for steel production in the Second Five-Year Plan, a target which could only be achieved with a contribution from rural industry, in effect from 'walking on two legs'. This was the background to the extraordinary backyard steel furnace drive of 1958. Responding to reports of an abundant harvest many communes constructed blast furnaces and, using locally mined iron ore and any scrap iron available, set out to produce steel.

For a few months in 1958 all seemed to be going well. A peasant technician from Long Bow, the Shanxi village studied by William Hinton, recalled the excitement and sense of achievement:

Those were the days. Whenever I sit at home and think about it I feel happy again. I was only twenty-one at the time. What was so great? The fact that so many people came together. Their discipline was marvelous. Everyone came to work on time and all joined in with a will. No line divided village from village, people from here and people from there! We'd never even seen iron made before, but here we were making it ourselves.[54]

The Great Leap Forward strategy also extended to educational policy. In 1958 a series of important changes was introduced, beginning with an ideological campaign aimed at suppressing bourgeois influence in education. The 'masses', including the students, were now to participate in school management. Schools would run farms and factories and students and staff would engage in productive labour. At the same time a massive increase in enrolment in educational establishments began. A large number of new primary schools were opened and an attack was made on illiteracy. An important innovation was the extension of the *minban* 'run-by-the-people' principle to secondary schools. Agricultural middle schools were established which offered a vocational syllabus. Students divided their time between study and productive labour and many staff were peasants, so enabling the schools to be largely self-supporting. Similar principles were applied in higher education, with the Jiangxi Communist Labour University, where the students built their own accommodation and then worked at reclaiming land, being cited as a national model. Entry to the university was determined in part by political criteria and many graduates became cadres, often employed as commune Party secretaries.[55]

The year 1958 saw both the high point and the beginning of the decline of the Great Leap Forward. The commune experiment in mass mobilization quickly ran into difficulties. The backyard furnaces, widely ridiculed in the West, only produced expensive and useless steel and were soon abandoned. The diversion of labour away from agricultural to industrial projects and to vast schemes of irrigation and afforestation severely disrupted the harvest. In the industrial sector the attempt 'to reconcile socialist revolutionary principles with industrial development', as it was grandiosely described,[56] resulted in conflict and uncertainty. The commitment to unrealistic production targets encouraged misuse of plant and the lowering of quality standards.

In 1959, as reports of economic problems proliferated and political criticisms began to surface, a number of modifications were made to the communes. The most important of these was to decentralize the level of ownership, decision-making and accounting from the commune to the production brigade, which in the countryside usually equated with the former Advanced Producers' Co-operative, which had been based on the village unit. This decision was announced after a meeting of Party leaders at Wuhan, the occasion also being used to reveal that Mao Zedong had relinquished the post of Head of State in favour of Liu Shaoqi, while retaining the more important post of Party Chairman.

The political conflict came into the open at the important conference held at Lushan in July 1959. Before the conference Mao Zedong had received a letter from Peng Dehuai, the distinguished People's Liberation Army commander, who was now Minister of Defence. In the previous year Peng had visited his home province of Hunan and had recorded his concern about the well-being of the peasants in a poem:

> Grain scattered on the ground, potato leaves withered,
> Strong young people have left to smelt iron,
> Only children and old women reaped the crops;
> How can they pass the coming year?[57]

In his letter Peng acknowledged the achievements of the Great Leap Forward, but went on to criticize the avoidable errors, the exaggerations of output, and the 'petty bourgeois fanaticism' which supposed that one could 'enter into communism at one step'. Mao replied to these criticisms at the Lushan conference, taking on himself some blame for the mistakes of the backyard furnaces, but his response to the more general criticism was to attack Peng Dehuai:

> We have done some good things and our backbones are strong. The majority of comrades need to strengthen their backbones. Why are they not all strong? Just because for a time there were too few vegetables, too few hair-grips, no soap, a lack of balance in the economy and tension in the market, everyone became tense. . . .[58]

For his attack, Peng Dehuai was deprived of his army command and replaced as Minister of Defence by Lin Biao, a firm supporter of Mao Zedong. This action ended the convention, which had survived from the Yan'an days, that any leader could express his opinions openly at a Party gathering.[59] Criticism of the Great Leap Forward strategy was stifled and in the spring of 1959 a second Great Leap was initiated, with even more disastrous consequences than those which attended the first.

Issues Relating to the Great Leap Forward

The Great Leap Forward and its consequences have inspired a great deal of controversy. Four issues have received particular consideration: the appropriateness of the economic strategy, the emergence of the 'two roads', the demographic disaster and the onset of the Sino-Soviet split.

The Great Leap Forward strategy was based on the perception that China's vast population could be mobilized to supplement capital investment, principally in agriculture. This would enable China to sustain a high rate of economic growth and catch up with Britain, not within fifteen years as had been the target before the Leap, but within four years. Such a strategy was later described as 'magnificent madness', bound to lead to disaster.[60] It may have cost China a decade of economic growth after 1958.[61] Nevertheless, some Western economists, writing before the full extent of the demographic disaster which followed the Leap had been exposed, gave the strategy itself a guarded endorsement. Alexander Eckstein, after referring to the exaggerated and unrealistic expectations associated with the Leap, commented,

> judicious application of underemployed labor to agricultural investment projects using preponderantly labor-intensive methods, coupled with expansion of small-

scale labor-intensive industries and the reliance on technological dualism . . . can
. . . represent crucial elements of a development plan in a densely populated
underdeveloped country.[62]

The alternative view is that the reason why the Leap failed was not because of a
faulty strategy, but because of gross failures in its implementation, the withdrawal
of the Soviet technicians and an element of misfortune, bad weather leading to
three poor harvests. Thomas Rawski argued that the Great Leap Forward years saw
experimentation which was later to prove highly fruitful, and he cited the
attempts to build rural industries with close ties to agriculture, training and
consulting programmes linking enterprises at different technical levels, and the
effort to familiarize the Chinese population with the products and techniques of
industry.[63] Victor Lippitt suggested that China had no choice but to seek a
development model suited to her needs, not one imported from the Soviet Union.
The Great Leap Forward, he claimed, 'represents a development strategy upon
which rational people might have chosen to embark'. It should be represented not
as the loss of a decade of development, but as 'the one chance to realize a decade
of development among the policy alternatives from which China could choose'.[64]

The Great Leap Forward is said to have exposed an ideological split within the
leadership, a 'two-line struggle', which dated back at least to 1949, and which was
personified in the characters of Mao Zedong and Liu Shaoqi. It has been described as

romantic revolution against organized development, mass campaigns versus
bureaucracy, slogans as opposed to plans, zeal vying with structure, purity
struggling with pragmatism.[65]

Another formulation of the same idea has been to contrast an 'engineering'
approach to making revolution, which is sequential, elitist and planned, and a
'storming' approach, which is simultaneous, egalitarian and spontaneous. The
former was adopted by the managerial types, including Liu Shaoqi, Deng Xiaoping
and Zhou Enlai, and the latter by Mao Zedong.

Allegedly this struggle became overt in the clash between Mao and Peng Dehuai
at the Lushan conference, and intensified during the Cultural Revolution, when
Mao Zedong defined the two lines as the 'bourgeois reactionary line' and the
'proletarian revolutionary line'. For some writers the concept of a 'two-line
struggle' has served as a framework for the interpretation of this stage in Chinese
history. For others the distinction between the two lines is either indistinct – for
example during his career Mao Zedong was both an 'engineer' and a 'stormer',
though perhaps more inclined to the latter in his later years – or it may represent
nothing more than 'two roads': support for or criticism of Mao Zedong.[66]

In 1960 the Western press carried reports that China was experiencing an
agricultural disaster. These reports were denied by the Chinese government and by
some Western observers in China.[67] As the allegations were linked to Peng Dehuai's
protest, most Chinese found it politic to remain silent. Official denials of a disaster
were effective and Western economists limited their judgement on the

consequences of the Great Leap to 'very severe food shortages, bordering in some areas on famine'.[68] However, in the early 1980s the release of population data enabled demographers to reconstruct the effect of the Great Leap Forward on the population. Their conclusion was dramatic: the decline in food production and the breakdown of the distribution system had set off a famine of proportions unprecedented in the twentieth century. The cumulative increase in mortality was estimated as falling between 16 and 27 million deaths. By comparison the loss of life in the Soviet Union at the time of collectivization has been estimated at approximately 5 million. The situation had been exacerbated by the Chinese government's refusal to recognize the gravity of the situation, and by its continued export of large quantities of grain.[69]

The origins of the Sino-Soviet split long precede the Great Leap Forward, although it was that campaign which led to its open acknowledgement. At Yan'an Mao Zedong had found himself free of Comintern influence and had taken the opportunity to achieve a sinification of Marxism, ensuring that the texts to be studied in the Party school were of his own composition. The Treaty of Alliance and Mutual Assistance, which Stalin and Mao had signed in February 1950, had announced common bonds of ideology and opposition to the imperialist camp. However, as Mao revealed later with some resentment, the treaty had only been agreed after two months of hard negotiation on issues such as the return to China of the Chinese Eastern railway. He had returned from Moscow suspecting that Stalin had no wish to see the People's Republic of China emerge as an independent Communist power. During the Korean War China had depended upon the Soviet Union for military equipment, but this had to be purchased. After Stalin's death in March 1953 the relationship between the two countries improved, although dependency continued, with heavy reliance on Soviet aid and technical assistance for the First Five-Year Plan. In October 1954 Khrushchev and Bulganin had visited China and had heaped fulsome praise on the achievements of China's revolution, while at the same time offering to settle a number of outstanding issues. During these years China changed its role from 'dependent ally' to 'independent equal ally', and after the Bandung conference in 1955 had also begun to play an increasingly important role in third-world affairs.[70]

Then in February 1956, at the twentieth Congress of the Communist Party of the Soviet Union, came the event which the Chinese leadership later insisted initiated the split: Khrushchev's secret speech denouncing Stalin. From the Chinese point of view this was seen as negating important aspects of Marxism-Leninism and so was liable to cause confusion within the Communist world. On a personal level Mao objected to the lack of notice about the speech and may have suspected that Khrushchev's repudiation of Stalin's personality cult might be applied to him. However, although the ideological origin of the Sino-Soviet split has been traced back to the speech, after it China and the Soviet Union still remained close allies. When Mao Zedong visited Moscow for the second time in November 1957 to celebrate the fortieth anniversary of the October Revolution, he recognized Soviet leadership of the Communist bloc, saying that the CCP was not worthy of that distinction, 'China has not even a quarter of a sputnik, whereas the Soviet Union has two' – it was on the day that Mao had arrived in Moscow that the Soviet Union had launched the second sputnik with a dog on board. Negotiations relating to military and scientific support for China took place and Khrushchev allegedly offered to supply China with a sample of an atomic bomb. However, in his speech marking the occasion Mao implied criticism of the Soviet policy towards the United States, urging that the Communist bloc should adopt a more dynamic approach in international affairs, and asserting that 'the East wind is prevailing over the West wind', and that the Eastern bloc should not be intimidated by the threat of nuclear war because 'imperialists are all paper tigers'.[71]

The Sino-Soviet split became imminent in 1958 when China abandoned Soviet economic methods and launched the Great Leap Forward. When announcements were made about phenomenal achievements in raising industrial output and when the communes were hailed as a short cut to Communism, these seemed to invalidate the Soviet model. Sino-Soviet disagreement about the appropriate response to the Lebanon crisis led to Khrushchev visiting China in August to reaffirm co-operation between the two countries. But Khrushchev also made adverse comments about the Great Leap Forward. The announcement in early 1958 of a second Leap led to explicit Soviet criticism and in July 1960 to the withdrawal of Soviet experts, a decision which the Chinese were to hold partially responsible for the failure of the Great Leap Forward.

Some explanations of the origins of the Sino-Soviet split have traced it to a fracture line in CCP leadership, that is to the ideological differences referred to above as the 'two lines'. Others have personalized it, tracing it to Mao Zedong's past resentments and aspirations for the future of the People's Republic of China. It is unlikely that a single factor could explain so complex a dispute and it is apparent that other issues also contributed to the split. One of the most potent of these was the Taiwan issue which had been reactivated in May 1957 when the United States deployed nuclear missiles on the island. In July 1958, when the Soviet Union was seeking a solution to the crisis precipitated by the American landings in the Lebanon, China condemned this as a compromise with imperialism. Shortly afterwards China announced her intention of 'liberating' Taiwan and in the following month started shelling Jinmen. The Soviet Union eventually offered its verbal support, but it was apparent that it did so reluctantly. In March 1959 Peng Dehuai, in his role as Minister of Defence, visited the Soviet Union and had conversations with Khrushchev. On his return he voiced the criticism of the Great Leap Forward which has been noted above. Here both the internal and ideological considerations contributed to the split, for Mao assumed that Peng was repeating Soviet criticisms of the communes. The next development, however, demonstrated that international relations alone could increase the tension. In the spring of 1959 the Dalai Lama had fled from Tibet and had found sanctuary in India. That summer a series of border incidents occurred involving Chinese and Indian security forces. The incidents themselves were minor, but the Russian response to them demonstrated that the Soviet Union was transferring its support from China to India.

In 1960 the split became open. The *Red Flag*, the CCP's theoretical paper, published a series of articles entitled 'Long Live Leninism', which denounced the Soviet Union's commitment to peaceful co-existence. The shock withdrawal of Soviet technicians in July may have been intended to force the abandonment of Maoist economic policies. If so, it was misjudged and the dispute widened at the Moscow conference in November 1960. Deng Xiaoping, who led the Chinese delegation, was able to secure the support of a significant minority of the delegates, the most vociferous endorsement of the Chinese position coming from Albania. This conference, it has been said, 'virtually ended the Sino-Soviet Alliance as a working relationship'.[72]

After the Great Leap Forward

In the years immediately after the Great Leap Forward China went through a period of economic recovery and political adjustment. Beneath the apparently calmer surface, tensions arose which were to provide the impetus for the Cultural Revolution.

The first task was to restore agricultural output. From 1959 the production brigade was again made the basic unit of ownership and commune facilities such as the communal dining halls were abandoned. At the same time a small proportion of the collectivized land was returned to peasants to be farmed as private plots. These plots, it was estimated, produced on average twice as much as community-owned land.[73] With the shutdown of many urban industrial enterprises and the sharp reduction in construction projects, some twenty million workers were moved to the countryside. This allowed a sharp reduction in state procurement of cereals and reversed the disastrous decline in rural consumption. At the same time state prices for agricultural products were raised. In 1962 the communes were subdivided into smaller units, each corresponding approximately to the natural marketing area. Meanwhile the production of agricultural machinery and of chemical fertilizers, which had only begun during the Great Leap Forward, was expanded rapidly. As a result of these changes, by 1965 agricultural output had nearly recovered to its pre-Great Leap Forward levels in gross, but not in per capita, terms, for the population had increased by about 80 million.[74]

Major adjustments were made in the industrial sector, which after the initial Leap had also suffered a catastrophic decline in output. Centralized planning was resumed and a strategy for recovery devised by Chen Yun, the Party's leading economist whose views had been ignored at the time of the Great Leap Forward. Large numbers of urban workers were returned to the countryside and urban communes were disbanded. A partial return was made to the management practices of the First Five-Year Plan and to the primacy of technicians. Worker involvement in planning declined and material incentives and wage differentials were restored. These measures enabled a rapid recovery of output and from 1963 a period of sustained growth began. This was marked by the development of important new industries. During the First Five-Year Plan the Soviet Union had provided expertise and plant to develop a petrochemical industry. Despite the withdrawal of Russian technicians, the output of crude oil continued to rise and by 1963 China had achieved self-sufficiency in petroleum products.

Sharp modifications were also made to the egalitarian educational policies which had been adopted at the time of the Great Leap Forward. Many schools in poorer areas were forced to close, the time allocated to productive labour in the curriculum was reduced, and greater stress was placed on educational standards, on admission requirements to middle schools and universities, and on the use of examinations to assess students. Further encouragement was given to two policies which had been endorsed at the time of the Great Leap Forward though apparently incompatible with its egalitarian thrust. One of these was a 'two-track system', which distinguished between the quality education provided in urban schools and colleges and the vocational training in work-study institutions. The other was the increased use of 'keypoint schools', developed at all levels from kindergarten to university as a means of improving standards in education. As a consequence of these changes, in the early 1960s the educational system was probably more elitist than it had been a decade earlier.[75]

The political adjustments of the post-Great Leap Forward period resulted in Mao Zedong withdrawing from the day-to-day management of affairs in favour of spending time in Shanghai and on the shores of the West Lake at Hangzhou. From time to time he intervened in the policy-making process and was usually able to make his view prevail, only to find that the policies were often amended by Liu Shaoqi, who had taken over as Chairman of the People's Republic of China in April 1959.[76] In this, Liu Shaoqi was supported by Deng Xiaoping, the General Secretary of the CCP, who had initially backed the Great Leap Forward, and by Peng Zhen, the 'mayor' of Beijing. Remaining loyal to Mao Zedong were Lin Biao, the Minister of Defence, now engaged in reviving the political commitment of the People's Liberation Army, and Mao's wife Jiang Qing, a former actress, who from 1959 had begun a campaign to bring about a revolution in cultural affairs. Zhou Enlai, the premier, balanced skilfully between the two factions.

24
From the Cultural Revolution to the Death of Mao

In the early 1960s, in response to the pragmatic, and in some eyes, revisionary policies pursued in the wake of the Great Leap Forward, a radical group emerged which supported Mao Zedong in his ambition to rekindle the revolution. The consequence was the Great Proletarian Cultural Revolution, which officially lasted for ten years from 1966. The active phase was concluded in 1969, but until Mao Zedong's death in September 1976, and the overthrow of the Gang of Four in the following month, the issues raised by the Cultural Revolution remained the dominant theme in Chinese politics.

When looking back at the Cultural Revolution after thirty years, one is struck by the discrepancy between the weighty significance accorded to it at the time, and the cool indifference or outright hostility with which it has been treated in more recent years. For example, the distinguished economist Joan Robinson, who visited China in November 1967, said of the Cultural Revolution:

To the historian of the future it will appear as the first example of a new kind of class war – a revolt of the proletariat of workers in socialist enterprises and peasants turned commune members against the incipient new class of organization men in the Communist Party.[1]

On the other hand Jonathan Spence, writing twenty years later, remarked witheringly:

The Great Leap Forward had at least had a meaningful economic and social vision at its heart. The Great Proletarian Cultural Revolution showed that neither Mao nor the CCP seemed to know how or where the nation should be heading.[2]

On the Origins of the Cultural Revolution

A number of interpretations have been advanced of the origins of the Cultural Revolution. The simplest of these is to regard it as a power struggle between Mao Zedong and his critics which dated back to the Great Leap Forward and the collapse of the collective leadership at the Lushan conference. According to this interpretation, Mao Zedong was deeply shocked and angered by Peng Dehuai's criticism of him for the failure of the Great Leap Forward, and by his subsequent loss of control which led Mao to refer to himself as a 'dead ancestor'. He responded by looking for support to Lin Biao, who in turn promoted Mao's personality cult, particularly in the People's Liberation Army, as a psychological compensation for Mao's loss of power. Until 1962 Mao was resigned to this situation, but he then began to plot a comeback using the Socialist Education movement to arouse fears of revisionism. Counting on the support of the People's Liberation Army and of 'revolutionary successors' among the younger generation, he launched what was termed a cultural revolution, although its true target was not revisionism but his political opponents. His principal opponents were Liu Shaoqi and Deng Xiaoping, although in truth they were not revisionists, but hard-line leftists.[3]

A second line of interpretation accepts the reality of the ideological differences between Mao Zedong and his opponents, and relies on the 'two-line' analysis referred to earlier. According to this interpretation a two-line struggle broke out between Mao Zedong's promotion of socialism and his opponents' lapse into revisionism. The designation of Liu Shaoqi as the 'number one person in authority taking the capitalist road' was not rhetoric but an assertion that consensus had broken down over a wide variety of issues. These included the economy, and in particular the 'spontaneous developments towards capitalism' in the countryside; the Party, which was accused of having become 'divorced from the masses'; education, where 'bourgeois individualism' thrived; foreign policy, with the Soviet Union accused of ideological revisionism and capitalist restoration; and culture, where the principle that Mao Zedong had enunciated at Yan'an – that art should serve the people – had been ignored. The Cultural Revolution was therefore launched as a last-ditch attempt to stem revisionism and preserve the revolution.[4]

Some writers have found the origins of the Cultural Revolution in the development of Mao Zedong's thought. In February 1957, at the time of the Hundred Flowers campaign, Mao had delivered his speech 'On the Correct Handling of Contradictions Among the People'. In it he had referred to the continuation of contradictions in a socialist society, and had suggested that the resolution of these contradictions would even accelerate the development of socialism. Surprisingly, he had included among the contradictions those 'between the government and the masses', and even contradictions 'between those in positions of leadership and the led'.[5] The implication was that the Party was not infallible and was not immune to bourgeois revisionism. This conclusion, it has been claimed, freed Mao Zedong from the Leninist discipline of the Party and enabled him, as a representative of the people, to criticize the Party from without.[6] At the '7,000 cadres' conference held in 1962, he demonstrated his willingness to represent the interests of the people against the Party by using racy language to attack arrogant Party bureaucrats.

> Those of you who . . . do not allow people to speak, who think you are tigers, and that nobody will dare to touch your arse . . . will fail. People will talk anyway. You think that nobody will really dare to touch the arse of tigers like you? They damn well will![7]

A fourth, psychological, interpretation may be mentioned. According to Robert Jay Lifton, the Cultural Revolution was launched by Mao Zedong to achieve revolutionary immortality. He began by noting that in 1965 Mao Zedong was seventy-four years old and was preoccupied with dying. He was acutely aware that many members of his family and many of his companions on the Long March had predeceased him, but he had survived, and this imposed a heavy obligation on him to ensure that their deaths had not been in vain. Fearing that the revolution was about to be destroyed by revisionism, he concluded that to save it he must inspire 'revolutionary successors'. These successors were the youth of the next generation, the Red Guards, whose task was to destroy the old to enable a national rebirth.[8]

Several developments in the period 1962 to 1966 contributed directly to the decision to launch the Cultural Revolution. The Socialist Education movement, launched by Mao Zedong in 1963, is often regarded as its first salvo. The movement began as a general investigation into rural conditions, then became a rectification campaign directed at rural Party cadres, and finally developed into a mass campaign directed at cadre corruption, the decline of the communes and collective farming, and the growth of capitalist tendencies in the countryside. The campaign against cadre corruption, known as the 'four cleanups', involved the dispatch of outside cadres to the countryside. Among these was Liu Shaoqi's wife, Wang Guangmei, who spent six months incognito investigating cadres in Taoyuan district, Hebei, and then sharply accused those she had investigated of corruption and counter-revolutionary tendencies. The outcome of the investigation revealed the contrast in political styles between Mao Zedong, who invoked the participation of poor peasants in the criticism of cadres, and Liu Shaoqi, who preferred to dispatch large workteams of outside cadres to the countryside to rectify the situation. In 1965 Mao countered Liu's tactics by obtaining support for a document known as the Twenty-three Articles, which played down the attack on corruption and the investigation of rural cadres, and instead emphasized the importance of the class struggle, hinting darkly that the key point of the movement was 'to rectify those people in positions of authority within the Party who take the capitalist road'. On the eve of the Cultural Revolution, the campaign had produced no clear victors, although it had heightened the tension between Mao and his opponents.

In the meantime Mao Zedong had voiced his approval of the Dazhai production brigade. This brigade, which farmed a poor area in Shanxi, was hailed as a model because in 1963, after its painfully constructed hillside terraces had been destroyed by a storm, it had not requested state help, but had rebuilt the terraces with its own labour, and then had achieved astonishingly high yields. Its peasants had been motivated not by profit but by a commitment to the collective good. Dazhai was used by Jiang Qing, Mao Zedong's wife, as a symbol of the commune ideal as it had appeared at the height of the Great Leap Forward, and as a reproach to the capitalist tendencies which had crept in since that time.

Another event significant for the start of the Cultural Revolution was the remodelling of the People's Liberation Army by Lin Biao. Peng Dehuai, the Minister of Defence until September 1959, had concentrated on transforming the army into a modern and professional force. Lin Biao, who had played a leading role in the Korean War, continued that task and the army acquitted itself well in the border clash with India in 1962. He also pressed ahead with the nuclear programme which resulted in China exploding an atomic bomb in 1964. However, Lin Biao also had political ambitions, and he set out to revive the army's revolutionary and egalitarian tradition and to enhance its reputation at the expense of that of the Party. He represented the People's Liberation Army as a model for emulation by the entire population. Campaigns to arouse political awareness centred on model heroes, such as the selfless soldier Lei Feng, who in 1958 had used his own clothes and bedding to cover up bags of cement left outside in the rain at the Anshan Iron and Steel Works. Lei Feng joined the People's Liberation Army in 1960, and the Party later the same year, but died at the age of twenty in an accident when trying to help a comrade. In 1963 Mao Zedong endorsed a campaign which used as its slogan 'Learn from the People's Liberation Army'. In return Lin Biao encouraged the development of the cult of Mao Zedong by urging that the army should become a 'great school of Mao Zedong thought'. In 1965 army ranks were abolished, reinforcing the army's claim to be the pace-setter for the revolution.[9] In October 1965 Lin Biao put his name to an article entitled 'Long Live the Victory of the People's War!'. This trumpeted the importance of Mao Zedong's contribution to the war of resistance against Japan, a war which had been 'a genuine people's war' in which the Party had relied on the masses. Although the tone of the article was bellicose, and it spoke of waging people's wars in Asia, Africa and Latin America, by the time that it was published the danger of conflict with the United States over Vietnam had receded. Despite its tone 'it indicated that China would put increasing proportions of its energy not into exporting the people's war but in assuring revolutionary continuity inside the country'.[10]

The Great Leap Forward had led to an enormous expansion of basic education. In 1965 some 116 million children, 85 per cent of those eligible, were enrolled in primary schools. However, only 14.3 per cent attended secondary school and a mere 674,000 had gone on to higher education. After the Leap, in an attempt to raise quality in education, the 'keypoint' system was adopted widely. Keypoint schools received additional resources and in effect served as a college preparatory stream. Very few students from lower category schools, which included *minban*, 'run-by-the-people' and agricultural schools, went on to higher education. Keypoint schools competed aggressively to ensure that their best students passed the college entrance examination, for this enhanced the reputation of the school. And who attended the keypoint schools and passed these examinations? Few came from a worker-peasant background, the largest group being the children of 'revolutionary cadres', that is Party bureaucrats, who had joined the revolution before 1949. This tendency was questioned by the Socialist Education movement which stressed the importance of class background for admission to senior middle schools and colleges. The movement had also emphasized the value of students going to the countryside and engaging in manual work, and their duty to continue the revolution.[11]

Mao Zedong had viewed these developments askance, and at the Spring Festival forum, held in February 1964, he expressed his criticisms of the educational system. He argued that the length of studies was excessive and there were too many subjects on the curriculum, too many old teachers had remained in their posts and too much emphasis was placed on examinations. He likened the method of conducting examinations to a 'surprise attack' and added, 'I am in favour of publishing the questions in advance and letting the students study them and answer them with the aid of books'.[12]

Another significant development concerned cultural affairs and the activities of Mao's wife, Jiang Qing. Her part in the launching of the Cultural Revolution has been subjected to an analysis similar to that applied to her husband: was she motivated by ideology, or did she nurse a personal hatred of the male-dominated cultural establishment which had denied her a significant cultural role since Yan'an days? The Party's policy line on culture had been expounded by Mao Zedong in 1942 in 'Talks at the Yan'an Forum on Literature and Art'. He asserted that the arts should serve the revolution and that they should do so by endorsing popular and proletarian values. This commitment, it was alleged, had been disregarded after the Great Leap Forward in favour of 'a more cautious, more elitist, and relatively more liberal approach'.[13] The arts were used to express covert political criticism, a notorious example being the opera written in 1960 by the historian Wu Han entitled *Hai Rui Dismissed from Office*. Hai Rui, an upright Ming official, had been dismissed by the emperor because he had protested against the confiscation of land from peasants. During the Cultural Revolution the opera was interpreted as an attack on Mao Zedong's handling of the Great Leap Forward and the dismissal of Peng Dehuai.

From the autumn of 1962 Jiang Qing began to gather allies for a campaign to revolutionize culture. The gist of their message was that the arts should be used as a weapon in the class struggle, literature and art should portray modern revolutionary heroes drawn from the ranks of the people and artists and writers should come from the proletariat. Among those who agreed with her were two Shanghai radicals, the Party chief Zhang Chunqiao and the critic Yao Wenyuan. Both later achieved notoriety as members of the Gang of Four. In 1964 their efforts seemed to have borne fruit when the 'Group of Five', headed by Peng Zhen, the first Party Secretary of the Beijing municipality, was formed to launch a cultural rectification movement. However, those in charge of the rectification were later accused of 'waving the red flag to oppose the red flag', that is to say of having been insincere in their commitment to the class struggle. In November 1965, with the publication in the *Liberation Army Daily* of an article by Yao Wenyuan attacking Wu Han's *Hai Rui Dismissed from Office*, the cultural issue became overtly political. Wu Han was forced to make a self-criticism, but the attack on writers accused of bourgeois tendencies continued and began to threaten important political figures, notably Peng Zhen himself, who had defended Wu Han who was a deputy mayor of Beijing and his subordinate.

The Cultural Revolution

The Great Proletarian Cultural Revolution officially began in early 1966 and ended with the death of Mao Zedong in 1976. Its active phase, from 1966 to 1969, may be divided into four periods: until August 1966, a period of manoeuvring; from the Eleventh Plenum until the end of the year, a period of confrontation; from January 1967 until mid-1968, seizures of power; and from mid-1968 until the ninth Party Congress in April 1969, the reconstruction of the political system.[14]

In the first months of 1966 Mao Zedong and his allies were manoeuvring for position. Lin Biao was engaged in a struggle with his Chief-of-Staff, Luo Ruiqing, who had argued that if the Vietnam conflict extended to China, the People's Liberation Army should be prepared to fight a sophisticated war with the United States, thus contradicting Lin Biao's thesis on 'people's war'. In March Luo Ruiqing was forced to make a self-criticism, which was found inadequate. He attempted suicide, but was then stripped of all his posts. In the meantime Peng Zhen and the Group of Five had tried to counter the attack on Wu Han by admitting that 'bourgeois tendencies' had appeared in culture, but this should be treated as an academic rather than as a political matter. Their position was endorsed by Liu Shaoqi as Chairman of the standing committee of the Politburo, but he thereupon left on an ill-timed visit to Pakistan and Afghanistan. Mao Zedong responded by encouraging the publication of a flood of articles critical of Wu Han and other Beijing intellectuals. In May, at a Politburo meeting, Lin Biao accused Luo Ruiqing and Peng Zhen of being involved in a military plot against Mao and his supporters. The meeting issued the 'May 16 circular', which announced the dissolution of the Group of Five and the appointment of a new Cultural Revolution Group. The group was led by Chen Boda, a close ally of Mao and formerly his political secretary, and its membership included Jiang Qing and Kang Sheng, who had been Mao's adviser on matters concerning the Soviet Union. The May 16 circular also warned:

Those representatives of the bourgeoisie who have sneaked into the Party, the government, the army, and various cultural circles are a bunch of counterrevolutionary revisionists. Once conditions are ripe, they will seize political power and turn the dictatorship into a dictatorship of the bourgeoisie. Some of them we have already seen through, others we have not. Some are still trusted by us and are being trained as our successors; persons like Khrushchev, who are still nestling beside us.

This quotation appears to imply that Liu Shaoqi was already the principal target of the Cultural Revolution. However, the evidence linking the attack on Wu Han and Peng Zhen, with that made subsequently on Liu Shaoqi, has been found wanting, and it has been suggested that it was only at a later stage that Liu Shaoqi was identified as the chief victim.[15]

The period from 16 May to 5 August was later known as the 'fifty days'. It was marked by two contradictory developments. The first occurred on 25 May when Nie Yuanzi, a young philosophy teacher at Beijing University, put up a large character poster attacking the university administration for preventing discussion of *Hai Rui Dismissed from Office*. Her action was praised by Mao Zedong and this sparked off protests at Qinghua University in Beijing, and in other universities and middle schools, in which attacks were made on persons in authority suspected of revisionist tendencies. In response Liu Shaoqi suspended university enrolment for a semester and sent in workteams to bring the student agitation under control. At first the workteams were greeted by student radicals as allies in the cause of denouncing the 'capitalist-roaders'. Later this stage was referred to as the 'white terror', when workteams had tried to suppress the student rebels.

On 16 July the seventy-three-year-old Mao Zedong made his famous swim in the Yangzi river. He then began to intervene openly in the struggle which had developed between the Cultural Revolution Group and those it accused of revisionism. Early in August a plenum of the Party's Central Committee, from which some of Mao's opponents had been excluded, agreed to a document to be known as the 'Sixteen Points'. This claimed that the Great Proletarian Cultural Revolution 'is a great revolution that touches people to their very souls and constitutes a new stage in the development of the socialist revolution in our country'. It declared that although the bourgeoisie had been overthrown 'it is still trying to use the old ideas, culture, customs and habits of the exploiting classes to corrupt the masses, capture their minds and endeavour to stage a comeback'. It then set out the objective of the Cultural Revolution

> to struggle against and overthrow those persons in authority who are taking the capitalist road, to criticize and repudiate the reactionary bourgeois academic 'authorities' and the ideology of the bourgeoisie and all other exploiting classes and to transform education, literature and art and all other parts of the superstructure . . . so as to facilitate the consolidation and development of the socialist system.[16]

The student organizations which had opposed the 'white terror' were the precursors of the Red Guards. The term 'Red Guard' was first used by students at the middle school attached to Qinghua University, and its use was acknowledged by Mao Zedong on 1 August. On 5 August Mao Zedong issued his own 'big-character poster', entitled 'Bombard the Headquarters', in which he encouraged an attack on those who had supported the workteams. In the next few days Red Guard groups proliferated in schools and colleges and on 18 August Mao Zedong reviewed a vast concourse of them in Tiananmen Square, and put on a red armband to symbolize his support for their activities. This rally was the beginning of the 'revolutionary tourism' which in the next three months brought thirteen million Red Guards to Beijing.

Immediately after the first rally Red Guard units were formed in schools and colleges throughout the country. Dai Hsiao-ai, a Red Guard from an upper middle school near Guangzhou later gave a vivid account of what happened at his school. In response to news of Mao Zedong's acceptance of a red armband, a Red Guard unit was formed to 'protect' Mao Zedong and to emulate the People's Liberation Army as 'Little Red Soldiers'. This first unit was open to all students with a good record, irrespective of class background. Soon afterwards a delegate from the Qinghua Red Guards arrived from Beijing and advised that the qualification should be the 'five kinds of red', that is to say Red Guards had to be the offspring of workers, poor peasants, revolutionary martyrs, revolutionary cadres and revolutionary soldiers – a qualification which became known as the 'blood line'. On 23 August Dai and his fellow Red Guards had gone into the city to carry out the injunction to 'destroy the four olds', the 'four olds' being old ideas, old culture, old customs and old habits. With the help of the police in identifying targets, they went into houses and destroyed or carried away anything suggestive of bourgeois culture. Unacceptable street names were changed to revolutionary slogans such as 'East is Red Road'. On 25 September Dai and ninety other students from the school went to Beijing and paraded before Mao Zedong at the Tianan gate with many thousands of Red Guards. Dai later revisited Beijing and again saw Mao, whom he described as looking 'less like a human being than like one of the proud emperors of China's past'. He also saw a dispirited-looking Liu Shaoqi. His group of Red Guards then travelled free to Tianjin, Jinan and Shanghai before returning home.[17]

From an early stage the Red Guard movement was split by factionalism. The main division lay between those who belonged to one of the 'five kinds of red' and those from a 'bourgeois' background. The former group, which included the children of revolutionary cadres who had benefited most from the Party's educational policies, wished to see the Red Guard movement remain under Party leadership and therefore concentrated their attack on cultural targets; the latter which had been discriminated against by the educational policy was more critical of the Party. The former might therefore be called 'loyalist' and the latter 'rebel'. This was ironic, for it placed Mao Zedong, who supported the rebels, on the side of the Red Guard organizations which did not represent the proletariat.[18]

In the last months of 1966 the struggle intensified. The 'five red' qualification for Red Guard membership was relaxed, enabling a much larger proportion of the student population to organize, and encouraging the emergence of rival Red Guard factions. Red Guards were allowed to contact workers in factories and communes. This allowed them to challenge Party leaders in those organizations and to form a relationship with the many workers who had grievances not dissimilar to those felt by students: the privileges of those who were of 'good status' and the cleavages of 'young versus old, temporary versus permanent employees, and mental versus manual workers'.[19] The Cultural Revolution Group, with Mao's encouragement, had gone on the offensive and from October a powerful attack was mounted against the 'persons in authority taking the capitalist road', implying Liu Shaoqi and Deng Xiaoping. In cities such as Guangzhou, senior Party leaders were criticized in wall posters and forced to make self-examinations.[20]

The 'seizures of power' stage of the Cultural Revolution began in January 1967 with the 'Shanghai storm'. In November 1966 Zhang Chunqiao, the former Secretary of the Shanghai Party Committee, and now a member of the Cultural Revolution Group, gave his support to the Workers' Headquarters, a Shanghai rebel workers' organization. This precipitated a rapid proliferation of rebel and conservative workers' organizations and led to serious clashes between the various groups. In an attempt to placate the workers the mayor of Shanghai offered them wage rises – a move later condemned as 'economism', an attempt to bribe the workers to support the conservative faction. Instead it caused an economic collapse.

In the ensuing chaos the radical groups seized power from the local Party organization in the name of the 'revolutionary masses', and declared that they would 'repudiate the bourgeois reactionary line implemented by a handful of people in the Shanghai area'. On 9 January 1967 Mao Zedong hailed their achievement as a 'seizure of power from below'. He told Lin Biao that the People's Liberation Army should support 'true revolutionary leftists' if they asked for army assistance.[21] Zhang Chunqiao returned to the city, to what was now termed the 'Shanghai Commune' in memory of the Paris Commune of 1871.

At this point it became apparent that Mao Zedong was advocating a more moderate line and the revolutionary momentum stalled. In the restoration of order in Shanghai, the People's Liberation Army played an important role, and the same was true of 'seizures of power' in other cities. The Shanghai Commune was replaced by a revolutionary committee, and a similar pattern was imposed on other cities. Revolutionary committees comprised a 'three-way alliance' of representatives of the mass organizations, party cadres who supported Mao and representatives of the People's Liberation Army. The replacement of Party committees was met with resistance and took a long time. Although the People's Liberation Army usually behaved with restraint, in several cities clashes occurred between the army and radical groups, with considerable loss of life.

In the summer of 1967 a further radical stage of the Cultural Revolution began. A particularly dangerous situation arose in Wuhan in July 1967, when the local army commander refused to obey orders from the Cultural Revolution Group, but was then compelled to surrender to a superior military force. In Beijing, increased radicalism led to the imprisonment of the Reuters correspondent Anthony Grey, to the burning down of the British legation, and to the seizure by Red Guards of the Ministry of Foreign Affairs. Even the People's Liberation Army was losing its reputation as a revolutionary model, for Jiang Qing had hinted that there were revisionists in the armed forces.

By the end of August China was on the verge of civil war and it was at that point that a more determined effort was made at restraint. This was rationalized as the transition from the first stage of the Cultural Revolution, the destruction of the old order, to the second stage, the creation of a new one. The process of forming revolutionary committees was speeded up and completed in September 1968. Jiang Qing was forced to repudiate Red Guard excesses and from September 1967 they were no longer allowed to travel the country fomenting revolutionary activities and were ordered to return to their schools and colleges. The People's Liberation Army was called upon to play a more prominent role, although still under strict instructions to avoid the use of force. But Red Guard violence continued on university campuses, in particular at Qinghua University, until August. There, in an incident known as the 'gift of mangoes', Mao Zedong himself intervened to obtain the restoration of order and the disbanding of the Red Guard organizations. At the Twelfth Plenum of the Party's Central Committee, held in October 1968, Liu Shaoqi was officially expelled from the Party. Finally, at the Ninth Party Congress held in April 1969, a new Party leadership was established, with Lin Biao nominated as Mao's successor.

What had been the upshot of the active stage of the Cultural Revolution? It is commonly agreed that it fell far short of Mao Zedong's intentions, and that the principal reason for this was that he grossly underestimated the conflicts of interest which existed among students and workers. Certainly the attack on Mao's opponents in the Party at the highest level and at regional level had led to extensive purges of officials, but the struggle had been messy and protracted, and it had produced a political order which differed little from that which existed on the eve of the Cultural Revolution.[22] Even this had only been achieved after the intervention of the People's Liberation Army in the political field.

In some other respects the impact of the Cultural Revolution was slight. Disturbances in rural communities were mainly confined to the hinterland of large cities.[23] Other rural areas largely escaped its effects, although the presence of young men and women who had volunteered or who had been sent down to the countryside contributed to the vehemence of political debates. These frequently invoked the cult of Mao Zedong.[24]

For the most part the economic effects of the Cultural Revolution were quite limited. Agricultural output was only affected marginally and by 1970 was surpassing previous levels. All important indices of industrial output fell in 1967, but by 1970 output exceeded 1966 levels. On these criteria the disruption of the Cultural Revolution 'had cost China two years of reduced output but little more, at least in the short run'.[25] Moreover, neither in agriculture nor in industry did the Cultural Revolution lead to a change of strategy, merely to greater caution as inexperienced officials succeeded those who had lost their jobs. At the time, the changes which occurred on the factory shop floor were hailed as of great significance. 'Seizures of power' took place and revolutionary committees were formed. Material incentives were condemned, cadres were expected to participate in labour and workers to share in management. In all these matters workers sought inspiration and guidance from the 'little red book', the *Quotations from Chairman Mao Zedong*. It was suggested that these changes would eliminate the division between manual labour and intellectual labour and achieve a major advance along the road to socialism.[26] However, by 1972 many of the Cultural Revolution innovations had been abandoned and material rewards and punishments were being reintroduced. Only in terms of management styles was a change perceptible. This did not amount to a rejection of the Western or Soviet impersonal management style in favour of Mao's concept of management by the masses led by the ideal cadre. Instead a balance was being struck between technical efficiency and political acceptability.[27]

However, the Cultural Revolution did have an important indirect effect on industrial strategy. In the 1960s, preoccupied with the importance of protecting China not only from its internal enemies, but also from threats from the Soviet Union and the United States, the decision was taken to build heavy industrial complexes in the interior provinces, away from the vulnerable coastal areas. This became known as the 'third front'. Between 1964 and 1971 the third front received over half of China's national investment. Thereafter the level of investment fell, many projects were left incomplete, and after 1978 more pragmatic policies were pursued.[28]

The most obvious effects of the Cultural Revolution were the disruption and humiliation it brought to many millions of people. It also directly caused about half a million deaths.[29] The most prominent victim was Liu Shaoqi, who after a period of house arrest and maltreatment, died in 1969. Deng Xiaoping was imprisoned and his son Deng Pufang was severely injured when Red Guards forced him out of a window at Beijing University. Some three million Party cadres were labelled as revisionist, and many others were required to undergo re-education at May 7 cadre schools, where they were expected to live and work like peasants. Many intellectuals also suffered. The novelist Lao She, author of Rickshaw, was made to attend study sessions and to wear a dunce's hat. Shortly afterwards he was found drowned in a lake. Ding Ling, who had been purged at the time of the Hundred Flowers movement, was forced to attend 'struggle sessions', made to stand for long periods with her arms in the 'airplane' position, and required to sleep in a stable.[30]

The dislocation of schools and colleges was very extensive. From the summer of 1966, after the arrival of the workteams, regular classes were suspended. School authorities and teachers were subjected to criticism, some being made to wear dunces' caps with inscriptions stating that they were monsters and ghosts.[31] In March 1967 Mao Zedong issued the first order for a return to the classroom, but because of the open warfare between Red Guard factions this was difficult to enforce. A second order followed in September 1967, but some schools still remained closed. Universities were even more severely disrupted, with formal teaching and admission of new students being suspended for four years. Many teachers and lecturers were subjected to various forms of abuse. For example, Zheng Peidi, a teacher of English at Beijing University, who had been found guilty of having made critical remarks about Jiang Qing, was tortured and then confined with her young baby in a building on the campus known as the 'cowshed'. She and many other members of the academic staff were required to do hard labour until she was released in an exchange of prisoners between Red Guard factions.[32] Perhaps four million students, many of whom had been Red Guards, were sent down to the countryside, to remain there for several years.

Consolidating the Cultural Revolution

In the years from 1969 until Mao Zedong's death in 1976 some of the policies initiated during the Cultural Revolution were implemented, some of the mistakes reversed and some of the excesses moderated.

A notable consequence of the Cultural Revolution had been the intervention of the People's Liberation Army into politics. Twenty-one of the twenty-nine provincial revolutionary committees set up from 1967 were headed by People's Liberation Army officers. In April 1969, at the Ninth Party Congress, Lin Biao's position as Mao's successor had been confirmed and new appointments to the Politburo were dominated by the military. However, Mao Zedong had not intended that China should become a military dictatorship, and even before the end of the active stage of the Cultural Revolution he had initiated moves to reconstruct the Party from the bottom upwards. New criteria were established for Party membership, a fresh emphasis was placed on the relationship between the Party member and the masses, and steps were taken to reduce the danger of cleavages developing within the Party, for example between new cadres and old cadres who had been re-admitted after re-education. While these measures were being introduced, the People's Liberation Army and its Party committees continued to carry out many administrative tasks. But in late 1969 the army was instructed to pay greater attention to military training, an indication that it was about to be relieved of its political role.[33]

Events took a more personal and dramatic turn at the Second Plenum of the Ninth Congress of the Party, which was held at Lushan in September 1970. There Chen Boda, former editor of the *Red Flag* and Chairman of the Cultural Revolution Group, proposed that Mao Zedong should be re-appointed Chairman of the People's Republic. As Mao had already made it clear he did not want the post, he interpreted this move as a ploy by Lin Biao to secure it for himself. Thereafter, Mao Zedong set out to undermine Lin Biao's position and they became further estranged over the question of rapprochement with the United States. In September 1971 Lin Biao disappeared and was later reported to have been killed in a plane crash when fleeing to the Soviet Union after attempting a coup against Mao Zedong. This incident, known as the '571 plot', involved an attack on Mao Zedong's special train. Lin's death provided Mao Zedong and Zhou Enlai with an excuse to purge his allies in the Politburo. This reduced but did not eradicate the political influence of the People's Liberation Army.[34]

After Lin Biao's death, the succession to Mao, who was seventy-seven years old at the time, became the dominant political issue. His stance was to maintain a balance between two groupings. One comprised the more pragmatic senior Party members, including Zhou Enlai and Deng Xiaoping, the latter having survived disgrace at the time of the Cultural Revolution to be rehabilitated in October 1974. The other group, the Cultural Revolution radicals, Jiang Qing, Zhang Chunqiao and Yao Wenyuan, had been joined by Wang Hongwen, a former worker in a Shanghai cotton mill and an activist at the time of the 'Shanghai storm', who in 1973 had been promoted to the number three position in the Party hierarchy. This group was to be known as the Gang of Four. In 1975 Deng Xiaoping was in the ascendancy and to the radicals' chagrin he pressed ahead with a number of urgent reforms, including reducing the size of the People's Liberation Army. However, when Zhou Enlai died in January 1976, Mao decided against appointing Deng Xiaoping as Premier in favour of Hua Guofeng, the former First Secretary of the Hunan Party, the person he considered most likely to consolidate the Cultural Revolution.

During the Cultural Revolution China's foreign policy had been marked by a shrill denunciation of imperialism, leading to the encouragement of anti-British riots in Xianggang, and a sharp deterioration in relations with the Soviet Union. By 1968 China, apart from her friendship with Albania, was almost entirely isolated from the outside world. Then in 1969 a sequence of events began which brought about a dramatic realignment in China's foreign relations. In March Chinese troops attacked a Russian patrol on Zhenbao (Damansky) island on the Wusuli (Ussuri) river, which marks the frontier between Heilongjiang province and the Soviet

Union. The immediate cause was a dispute over the ownership of the island, and the incident came after an increase in tension along the length of the Sino-Russian frontier. Chinese aggression may have been engineered by Lin Biao to strengthen his position. The incident was used by the Chinese leadership to dramatize the Russian nuclear threat and the build-up of Russian forces along the frontier. The population was urged by Mao Zedong to 'dig tunnels deep, store grain everywhere and be prepared for war and natural disasters.' Subsequent negotiations reduced the number of border incidents, but the tension between the two countries remained high.[35]

It was this situation, and the continuing rivalry between the two superpowers in the Middle East, that led China to arrive at an accommodation with the United States after twenty years of hostility. The first moves have been traced back to 1968, in response to indications that the United States might withdraw from Vietnam. After the clash on Zhenbao island more direct contacts were made and in October 1970, in a symbolic gesture, Edgar Snow was invited to stand alongside Mao Zedong at the National Day celebrations. In July 1971 Henry Kissinger, the United States' National Security Advisor, made a secret trip to China to prepare the way for President Nixon to visit in the following year. From the Chinese point of view Nixon's visit was a great success: it was presented as having been arranged at the request of the United States, and the communiqué which concluded it promised peaceful co-existence without making any stipulation about the People's Republic's 'one China' policy and claim to Taiwan. This amicable atmosphere did not survive Nixon's resignation in August 1974, but at least Sino-American relations had achieved a degree of normalcy.[36]

The most enduring influence of the Cultural Revolution was on education, and the new education of the period to Mao's death has been described as 'the most sustained effort at transforming a modern school system the world has known'.[37] Many of Mao Zedong's criticisms of the educational system were now translated into practice. The curriculum was shortened and from 1972 the standard arrangement was for students to spend five years at primary school, four or five years at middle school and three years at university, shortening the cycle of schooling by up to one-third. More time was spent on political education, with lessons on how peasants and workers had been exploited in the past. Primary school children were taught the 'five loves': 'love our great socialist motherland; love our great Chinese people; love our great CCP; love our great People's Liberation Army; and love our great leader Chairman Mao.' Great emphasis was placed on self-reliance, and even primary school pupils were expected to participate in productive labour. Middle schools ran factory complexes with advice from workers organized into Mao Zedong Thought Propaganda Teams, and these enterprises made a substantial contribution towards the cost of running the school. The Marxist idea of the integration of theory and practice was followed up, with peasants advising on the contents of study material and less use being made of books. Admission procedures for entry to post-elementary education were revised, the criteria for university entry being a minimum of two years' work experience, selection by the masses and completion of junior middle school.

As with all the changes wrought by the Cultural Revolution, much was temporary and much was soon modified by realism. By 1972 some examinations were reintroduced under the euphemism 'cultural testing', and in universities basic theoretical courses replaced some applied courses. Nevertheless, other Cultural Revolution policies remained in force. Publicity was given to students whose supposed actions endorsed Mao Zedong's educational philosophy. One case was that of Zhang Tiesheng, who in 1973, when taking the cultural test for entry to a provincial college, handed in a blank examination paper, alleging that unlike other entrants he had been unable to study because he had been working. Another example was that of Huang Shuai, a girl attending a Beijing primary school, who accused her teacher of being harshly critical of the pupils and threatening them with punishment, instead of encouraging them to express their own views or helping them to produce their own school rules. A typical development of this period was the opening of 'July 21 worker's universities', the model for which was the Shanghai Machine Tools Plant, where the students were chosen from workers and peasants with practical experience. After a shortened course, which emphasized practical applications and 'proletarian politics', the students returned to their place of work.[38]

The Death of Mao Zedong and the Succession Crisis

Between 1976 and 1978 a complex struggle took place between the contenders for the succession to Mao, the protagonists being the Gang of Four and Deng Xiaoping and his supporters. Mao's elevation of the moderate Hua Guofeng after Zhou Enlai's death in January 1976 had infuriated the Gang of Four, and they began to undermine his authority and also to criticize the memory of Zhou Enlai. In April 1976, in a spontaneous demonstration of popular affection for the late Premier, thousands of people began laying wreaths and cards at the foot of the Heroes' Monument in Tiananmen Square. Some of these carried inscriptions critical of the Gang of Four. The demonstration was attributed to Deng Xiaoping's influence and on 5 April it was suppressed violently. Two days later Deng Xiaoping was removed from all his offices.

In July 1976, while Mao Zedong lay dying, China experienced one of its worst recorded earthquakes, which destroyed the coal-mining city of Tangshan, 160 miles south-east of Beijing. It was in this area that in the nineteenth century Li Hongzhang had established China's modern coal industry. The official death toll was placed at 242,000 people. Typical of the mood of the time, China rejected offers of international assistance.

Mao Zedong died on 9 September 1976. Hua Guofeng delivered the funeral oration flanked by the Gang of Four, who appeared to assume that the succession was now within their grasp. However, in the following month, without giving any warning, Hua Guofeng had them arrested. Implying that he was Mao Zedong's chosen successor, he accused them of having plotted to usurp power. Over the next few months, as Hua Guofeng assumed all the significant positions in the Party and state, it appeared that he might establish his authority firmly. However, he soon found himself faced with demands that Deng Xiaoping should be reinstated, and this was conceded in July 1977, although Hua continued to hold the senior positions. For the next three years an uneasy compromise existed between the two men, but by 1980 Deng Xiaoping had manoeuvred his supporters into key positions and Hua Guofeng had been relieved of all significant posts. His claim to be Mao Zedong's chosen successor, and his association with the Cultural Revolution, which in 1976 had appeared to be his strongest qualifications, had proved to be a political death certificate.

25

From the Death of Mao to the Death of Deng

This final chapter considers political developments in China from the death of Mao Zedong in September 1976 to the Tiananmen Square massacre of 4 June 1989, and to the death of Deng Xiaoping in February 1997. It then looks at some of the broader themes of this period, notably the economic policies pursued and the results achieved, and a number of social themes: the 'one-child family' policy, the condition of women in Chinese society, and the position of ethnic minorities with particular reference to Tibet. Finally it turns to the theme of Greater China, with reference to the reunification of Xianggang and China and the recent history of the Republic of China on Taiwan.

Political Developments

By 1981 Deng Xiaoping had successfully undermined Hua Guofeng's position and had established his own nominees within the Party leadership. These included Zhao Ziyang, like Deng Xiaoping from Sichuan, who was appointed Premier in September 1980, and Hu Yaobang, who became Chairman of the Party's Central Committee.

The decisiveness of the political change which had taken place was confirmed in November 1980 with the opening of the trial of the Gang of Four. They were accused of having plotted against the state and having persecuted to death many thousands of people during the Cultural Revolution. The defendants included five military commanders accused of complicity in Lin Biao's attempted coup. Most of the defendants had little to say, but Jiang Qing defended herself vigorously, claiming that her actions were taken on Mao Zedong's behalf. This defence was rejected on the grounds that although Mao had committed mistakes, the crimes of the Gang of Four were entirely different in nature. Jiang Qing and Zhang Chunqiao were sentenced to death, but the sentences were deferred for two years to allow repentance. All the other defendants received long terms of imprisonment. The sentences on Jiang Qing and Zhang Chunqiao were later commuted to life imprisonment. In 1991 it was reported that Jiang Qing, by then seriously ill, had committed suicide.

The trial of the Gang of Four was an indirect indictment of Mao Zedong. At the Sixth Plenum of the Eleventh Central Committee, held in June 1981, a

459

document entitled 'The Resolution of the Central Committee on some Historical Problems since 1949' was approved. This praised Mao's contribution to the Party's victory in 1949 and the policies he had pursued until 1956; it criticized his departure from the Party's correct position and his rejection of the advice of Liu Shaoqi and Deng Xiaoping at the time of the Great Leap Forward; finally it castigated him for his mistaken allegations of revisionism which had led to the 'ten years of horror' of the Cultural Revolution. Nevertheless, it concluded that Mao's positive contribution to the revolution far outweighed his mistakes, and that Mao Zedong Thought should continue to guide the Party.[1]

In August 1977 the Party had committed itself to the Four Modernizations:[2] the modernization of agriculture, industry, science and technology, and national defence – the intention being that China would be transformed into a modern state by the year 2000. The political context in which economic development would take place was defined by Deng Xiaoping in March 1979 as the 'four cardinal principles', the principles being: the socialist road, the democratic dictatorship of the people, the leadership of the Communist Party, and adherence to Marxism-Leninism and Mao Zedong Thought. Later that year a change was made in the electoral law to allow for contested elections to people's congresses operating at county and urban district level. The National People's Congress, an indirectly elected body in existence since 1954, which hitherto had acted merely as a rubber stamp for Party decisions, was permitted to make modifications to draft legislation. In the 1980s some other modest political reforms were introduced on the grounds that they would enable the economy to develop. One change concerned the distinction between the Party and the state which, during the Cultural Revolution, had become confused. In the early 1980s new constitutions for both Party and state were adopted and efforts were made to ensure that the Party restricted its activities to policy matters while the organs of the state acted as the executive. However, an attempt to separate the functions of the Party and the People's Liberation Army failed. Another political development concerned the domination of the Party by elderly veterans. Deng Xiaoping himself refused to accept the Chairmanship of the Central Committee and favoured a collective leadership, appointing younger and better-educated people to senior positions. In September 1985 a special Party conference was held which obtained the resignation of 131 senior veterans.

These measures fell far short of genuine political participation, or what in the West would be termed democracy. Nevertheless, they raised hopes among student and worker activists that they might be the prelude to developments such as had occurred in Yugoslavia and Poland. In 1978, encouraged by the re-emergence of Deng Xiaoping, and the reversal of the official condemnation of the Tiananmen Square incident of April 1976, a small democratic movement appeared. Its first manifestation was the pasting of posters on a wall on Chang'an Avenue, the main east–west street in Beijing. The posters on 'democracy wall', as it came to be called, asserted the right to 'freedom of assembly and expression', and initiated a political debate on a wide range of issues. A notable contribution was a poster headed 'The Fifth Modernization', that is democracy, which had been written by Wei Jingsheng, a student at Beijing University who also worked as an electrician at Beijing Zoo. He later became the most famous victim of government repression, although he was not a typical representative of the movement because of his anti-Marxist views. At first this activity was tolerated by the authorities, and Deng Xiaoping, who welcomed the criticisms of Mao which were being expressed, even told a foreign journalist that it was a good thing. But from February 1979, after the Chinese invasion of Vietnam, Deng asserted the 'four cardinal principles' and repression began. In March Wei Jingsheng and other activists were arrested and political activity was curbed. In April 1981 a nationwide swoop led to the arrest of all other activists.[3]

In the early 1980s Deng Xiaoping's government promoted economic modernization, which entailed major social disruption, and an open-door policy which greatly increased contacts between China and the outside world. The circulation of liberal ideas was welcomed cautiously by Hu Yaobang, the Secretary-General of the Party, but the more conservative Party leaders condemned such influences as 'spiritual pollution'. Tension between progressive forces and Party reactionaries became acute in December 1986 when a student movement began on the campus of the Chinese University of Science and Technology at Hefei in Anhui province, where Fang Lizhi, a prominent intellectual who sympathized with the students' views, was Vice-President. The origins of the movement lay in students' concern over increasing Japanese investment in China. They had intended to demonstrate on the fiftieth anniversary of the 9 December 1935 protests against Japanese encroachment, but the demonstrations were scotched by the government. In December 1986, following allegations that the elections to the people's congresses had been tampered with, protest marches took place at Hefei and demonstrations spread to university campuses in Shanghai, Beijing and other cities. After some hesitation the Party hardliners reacted, dismissing Fang Lizhi and arresting dissidents. It then became apparent that Deng Xiaoping, who earlier had appeared to be in sympathy with the students, had sided with the hardliners and had dismissed Hu Yaobang for failing to deal effectively with the protesters.

In 1987 Deng Xiaoping resigned from the Party's Central Committee, although he retained the Chairmanship of the Military Affairs Commission, and consequent control of the People's Liberation Army. Zhao Ziyang became Secretary-General of the CCP and Li Peng, a protégé of Zhou Enlai, took over as Premier. The general direction of policy, the energetic pursuit of the Four Modernizations, remained unchanged. Although political reform was not approved, the campaign against dissidence was moderate. At the National People's Congress held in April 1988 some expressions of opinion were permitted. But many important issues – Party corruption and the one-child family policy, to name but two – were not open to discussion.

In April 1989 Hu Yaobang died, and his death, like that of Zhou Enlai, provided the occasion for demonstrations and demands for his posthumous rehabilitation, which implied a reconsideration of the suppression of the democracy movement. Hu Yaobang's funeral, which was held on 22 April, became the occasion for a massive student demonstration in Beijing and in the weeks that followed Tiananmen Square was the scene for daily rallies. The seventieth anniversary of 4 May 1919, with its reference to democratic freedoms, was commemorated with massive unofficial parades in Beijing and in many other cities. It became increasingly apparent that the Party leadership was divided on how to respond. Zhao Ziyang, who had been abroad when the demonstrations began, offered some sympathy for the ideas expressed by the demonstrators. On the other hand Li Peng, the Premier, concluded that the challenge to the Party's authority resembled that of the Solidarity labour union in Poland and had to be crushed. When Mikhail Gorbachev visited China in the middle of May, such was the scale of the demonstrations in Tiananmen Square, where a thousand students had started a hunger strike, that his official reception had to be shifted to the airport, a humiliating admission of the Chinese leadership's weakness. On 19 May Zhao Ziyang visited the hunger strikers, giving the impression that a positive response to the student demands might be forthcoming, but in truth the chance of a compromise had already passed, if indeed it had ever existed. On the same day Deng Xiaoping had confirmed the reliability of the People's Liberation Army. The following day martial law was proclaimed and the army was given the task of clearing the demonstrators from Tiananmen Square. It still seemed possible that bloodshed might be avoided, for the events in Beijing were the subject of international attention and the white statue of the Goddess of Democracy, erected in the square on the night of 29 May, associated the students' struggle with democratic movements throughout the world. The first army units to arrive in Beijing appeared unwilling to use force and there were some signs that the students were growing tired and the demonstrations were losing momentum. Such hopes disregarded the determination of Deng Xiaoping to assert his authority. In the evening of 3 June troops broke down the barricades erected by the protesters and opened fire. Many of the casualties were shot in the streets around Tiananmen Square rather than on the square itself. By the early hours of 4 June all resistance had been crushed and the evidence that a massacre had occurred was being removed.

There are wide discrepancies between the estimates of the casualties inflicted on the demonstrators. Official sources initially denied that any deaths had occurred, but later disclosed that twenty-three students had been killed accidentally. The first Western reports estimated the casualties at 3,000 dead and 10,000 wounded, but these figures were later amended to between 400 and 800 dead.[4]

There are also widely differing explanations of why the Chinese government acted in the way that it did. The official version claimed that what had occurred was not a student demonstration, but a counter-revolutionary movement, which had foreign support and had been given encouragement by elements within the leadership who planned to carry out a coup. This was an implied accusation against Zhao Ziyang, who had failed to condemn the students, and who was therefore dismissed. Western explanations have regarded the student protests as genuine and have interpreted the resort to violence as the conclusion of a power struggle within the leadership. Both Zhao Ziyang and Li Peng hoped to succeed Deng Xiaoping, and each used the rise of discontent to discredit the other. Li Peng won because he anticipated correctly that Deng Xiaoping would eventually use force to resolve the situation.

In political terms the years from the Tiananmen Square massacre to Deng Xiaoping's death in February 1997 saw little change. The student leaders of the demonstrations were hunted down and many who had participated were arrested. Jiang Zemin, the Secretary of the Party's Shanghai branch, became Secretary-General, but Deng Xiaoping's influence remained paramount. The collapse of the Soviet Union served as a further reminder of the danger to the Party of political compromise. At the Fourteenth Party Congress, held in October 1992, the Party dictatorship was reaffirmed, the reference to Marxism-Leninism and Mao Zedong Thought was repeated and the need to suppress political 'turmoil' – the term used for the 1989 demonstrations – was reiterated. From 1994 Deng Xiaoping ceased to appear in public, but until his death – and thereafter – the essence of his programme, the maintenance of a political dictatorship while transforming China into a 'socialist market economy', prevailed.

Economic Transformation

Deng Xiaoping's political reputation will always be clouded by his responsibility for the Tiananmen Square massacre, but his achievement in transforming the Chinese economy will secure him a high position among the creators of modern China.

The transformation of agriculture began in 1978. The modified commune system, introduced in 1963 after the Great Leap Forward, had preserved the principle of the public ownership of land and had also continued the bureaucratic administrative system and restrictions on private enterprise which had discouraged initiative. The growth in agricultural output, which was recorded at 3.1 per cent per annum between 1966 and 1978, although sufficient to meet the needs of a rising population, provided only a slow improvement to rural living standards. The model of agricultural development, the Dazhai brigade, had represented the belief that the key to raising output was the application of collective human endeavour. However, Dazhai's claims had been shown to be fraudulent, and the collective model no longer appeared to be relevant.

The first agricultural reforms encouraged peasants to produce more on their private plots for sale on the free market. The next step was to introduce the 'household responsibility system'. Under this system, the ownership of the land remained collective, but individual families contracted to cultivate specific plots with nominated crops and to hand over a proportion of the harvest to the production team. The family could retain the surplus or sell it as it wished. This system spread rapidly and led to a sharp increase in output, a diversification of production and a rapid growth in rural marketing. At first responsibility contracts only lasted for a year, but they were later extended to up to fifteen years, so that the concept of public ownership of land effectively disappeared. A new slogan appeared, 'To get Rich is Glorious'. A new entrepreneurial class of peasants emerged, a new term was popularized, the 'ten thousand yuan' household, unashamed of its material success.[5]

The few years after 1978 were a golden era for agriculture. In 1984 grain output for the first time topped 400 million tonnes, and this was also a record year for

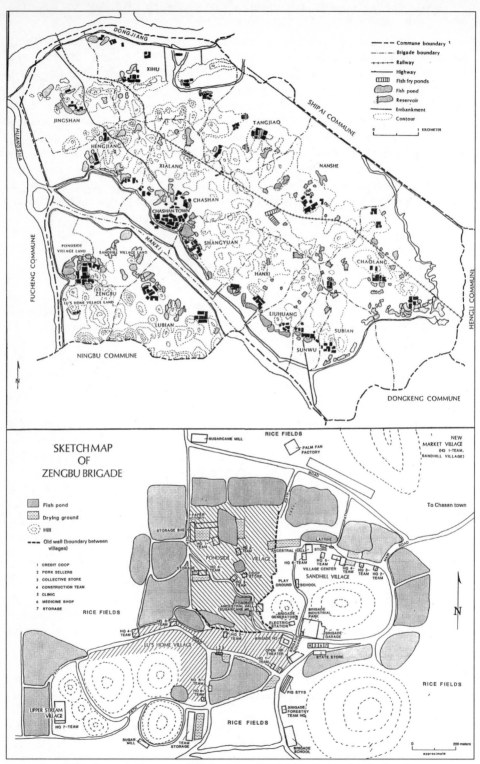

Chashan commune (above) and Zengbu brigade (below).

cotton production. Much of this increase was achieved by raising the yield per unit area, an achievement explained partly by the greater independence and stronger profit motive of farmers, and partly by the increased application of modern inputs, particularly chemical fertilizers. But from 1984, from the peasants' viewpoint, things began to change for the worse. In that year the state monopoly of the trade in grain was ended and the price paid for grain bought under the official grain purchase system was reduced. The reduction in grain prices, coupled with an increase in the cost of inputs, cut farm income. This short-term squeeze on farmers was accompanied by the resurgence of longer-term and more intractable problems. In the mid-1990s China had 22 per cent of the world's population and 7 per cent of its arable land. China's population was rising and its stock of arable land was falling – from 112 million hectares in 1957 to 96 million hectares in 1989 – because of the demands of development. Farm output could be increased by investment, but that had fallen sharply, or by diversification, but small-scale production, for example the raising of pigs, was not very profitable. In short the break-up of collective farming and the institution of the responsibility system had not solved the structural problems of Chinese agriculture.[6]

At the same time major changes were taking place in the organization of industry. Up to this point, although the Cultural Revolution had affected the use of incentives and management practices, much of industry retained the characteristics of the Soviet period. It was state-owned and state-supported, no attempt was made to ascertain profitability, prices were fixed arbitrarily, and workers generally held their posts for life irrespective of their efficiency. From 1978 an industrial version of the responsibility system was introduced. Enterprises, which previously had been required to pass all their profits on to the state, were now allowed to retain a proportion of their surplus and distribute it as incentives. In some enterprises new management techniques were introduced, allowing managers much greater freedom of operation. Price controls were removed from many products, leading to moderate inflation. The development of private industrial and commercial enterprises was permitted. A stock market opened in Shanghai in 1986.

Perhaps the most significant change affecting the economy was the opening in 1979 of four 'Special Economic Zones' at Zhuhai, north of Aomen (Macao), Shenzhen, just north of Xianggang, Shantou and Xiamen. The introduction of these zones flew in the face of the tradition of self-sufficiency, for they were designed to attract foreign capital to China. Foreign firms were offered advantageous terms for investments, suitable sites for the construction of factories and plentiful and presumably cheap labour. At the same time other inducements were given to encourage foreign trade and tourism. Two centuries previously the Qianlong emperor had informed the King of England 'there is nothing we lack . . . We have never set much store on strange or ingenious objects, nor do we need any more of your country's manufactures . . .'.[7] Between 1978 and 1993 China's external trade increased from $20.64 billion to $195.8 billion and she 'moved away from autarky to become increasingly dependent on international commerce'.[8] In 1992, in recognition of Guangdong's outstanding contribution to this achievement – through the 1980s the province had recorded 12.4 per cent growth per annum – Deng Xiaoping made a celebrated southern tour which included a visit to Shenzhen. He predicted that Guangdong province might join the 'four little dragons', the economies of Xianggang, Singapore, Taiwan and South Korea, as a 'fifth little dragon'.

Western appraisals of the results of Deng Xiaoping's economic policies have been largely favourable, but they have also contained warnings of danger ahead. The extraordinarily rapid growth of the economy – from 1980 to 1993 China's real gross national product grew at an average annual rate of 9.36 per cent per annum – has been acknowledged, but the risk of overheating has been stressed, and indeed there have been severe bottlenecks and a worrying rise in inflation.[9] The disastrous implications of the deteriorating land/population ratio have already been mentioned. A major problem concerns the future of state-owned industrial enterprises which in 1995 employed 100 million workers and supplied half the nation's industrial output. Such is the unprofitability of many of these enterprises that in 1994 the cost of propping up the state sector came close to half the total national budget for the year.[10] Economic growth has been very uneven and it has produced wide discrepancies of wealth, both individually and regionally. It has also brought with it corruption and other social evils which in its early years as the government of China the CCP declared it had abolished. The early performance of the Special Economic Zones led to comments that they had been set up hastily and had failed to attract the foreign capital needed to make them viable. It was suggested that China's late conversion to free market economics has left her at a disadvantage compared with the established economy of Japan and the rapid growth of the 'four little dragons'. These warnings remain relevant, but the momentum of China's economic advance still remains very impressive after more than twenty years of unprecedented growth.

Social Issues

Any consideration of China's future involves a reference to population and to the effectiveness of the one-child family policy which was initiated in 1979. After the Great Leap Forward a birth control campaign was introduced which urged late marriage and family limitation. During the Cultural Revolution the campaign was abandoned and high fertility rates were recorded for some years, although the general trend was probably downwards. In 1971 a new family planning policy was launched, which used the slogan 'late, spaced, few' and recommended that in the cities a family should have a maximum of two children, although three were allowed in the countryside. After Mao Zedong's death, the commitment to economic expansion forced an urgent consideration of the implications of population growth. Demographers, estimating the current average birth rate to be 2.3 children per couple, predicted that by the year 2000 China's population would be 1.282 billion people. The cost of feeding and educating that number of people would impose an enormous burden on the economy – the amount of grain required in the year 2000 would be 50 per cent higher than the total output for 1980. It was for this reason that the decision was taken to impose the draconian 'one-child family' policy. Some exceptions were allowed, for example if the first child was born with congenital defects. The most important exemption was that most minority groups in China were not subject to the 'one-child family' policy. The policy was launched with massive publicity and powerful material incentives and disincentives were applied to ensure compliance. In 1984 it was acknowledged that the campaign had been so coercive that it had become self-defeating and some modifications were made to the range of exemptions.[11]

Many questions arise about the effectiveness of the policy and about the methods which have been used to enforce it. Undoubtedly there has been a dramatic decline in fertility rates, reinforcing a trend already observable in the early 1970s. The policy has been more effective in urban areas, where the system of surveillance and the issue of 'single-child family' certificates has been applied rigorously, than in rural areas. At most it has slowed the rate of growth of China's population, which continues to rise. Recent predictions indicate the population will reach 1.5 billion by the year 2025. Much of this growth is due to longer life expectancy and the changing age structure of the population – by 2008 one-quarter of all the world's elderly people will live in China.[12]

The implementation of the policy has aroused strong criticism, with particular reference to the encouragement of abortion, sterilization and female infanticide. Abortion is officially referred to as a 'back-up' method of birth control, but allegations have been made of the widespread use of late and compulsory abortion, although the typicality of this evidence has been questioned.[13] Cases of compulsory sterilization, which carries a strong social stigma, have also been reported. In China the assumption that only sons can continue the family line and perform the ancestral rites has meant that traditionally the birth of a daughter has been greeted with disappointment. There is extensive, albeit patchy, evidence that in the past deliberate discrimination against girls, either in terms of withholding food and health care or through female infanticide, was commonplace. A recent study suggests that in the nineteenth century, in rural Liaoning, infanticide accounted for between 20 and 25 per cent of female infant mortality.[14] Female infanticide and the neglect of girls may have diminished in the early Communist period. However, an analysis of the demographic data for the 1980s concluded that the introduction of the one-child family policy had led to a disturbing increase in the practice. The official response to allegations of infanticide was to point out that it was illegal and that it therefore did not occur. However, Western reporters operating clandestinely in China have alleged that the abandonment of girls and their neglect to the point of death was done with official connivance.[15]

The issue of female infanticide is related to the broader question of the status accorded to women in modern Chinese society. In the 1930s the Communists and the Nationalists produced competitive versions of the role that women might occupy in modern China. The Communists implied that only through their victory could the goals of female emancipation and equality be achieved. At the Jiangxi soviet they had introduced laws relating to marriage and land which offered women equality, but the implementation of those provisions which were liable to alienate male peasant support was deferred through the Yan'an period.

After the Communist victory the 'woman question', a term which encompassed reference to the family, marriage and divorce, as well as women's economic role, was addressed by the passage of the Land and Marriage Laws, which transformed the economic and legal position of women. Both pieces of legislation were promoted by mass movements and in both cases extensive propaganda campaigns were mounted to overcome opposition. Substantial efforts were made to raise women's educational standards and to increase their role in production. The Great Leap Forward period witnessed a major, although ill-fated, attempt to free women for employment by relieving them of domestic tasks. The Cultural Revolution, if seen as an attack on inequalities in Chinese society, may also be regarded as a step towards the resolution of the 'woman question'. The Marriage Law of 1980 reaffirmed and strengthened the equality of women within marriage. The change in women's legal status, the evidence of widespread changes in their material condition, their improved access to education and to political activity, can scarcely be contested. Nevertheless, the extent of women's emancipation in China remains the subject of debate. The matter of female infanticide has already been mentioned, and other examples of abusive behaviour towards women, for example tolerance of wife-beating, can also be documented. Although women have come to occupy many responsible positions they have scarcely penetrated the most senior ranks of the Party or government. In the countryside many features of the traditional marriage system have survived, including the payment of bride-price and dowries.[16] This led Judith Stacey to conclude:

> In rural China, the communist revolution appears to have had the somewhat ironic effect of strengthening a reformed version of traditional peasant family structure. . . . Patrilocality, a semiarranged marriage system, and even a form of bride-price appear to be durable survivals in postrevolutionary rural China.[17]

China's Minorities

Histories of China inevitably focus attention on the activities of the 92 per cent of the population which is Han Chinese, and neglect the 8 per cent of the population which belongs to fifty-five recognized minority nationalities. The largest group, the Zhuang, who for the most part inhabit Guangxi, number over 15 million. Other large groups include the Hui – Chinese-speaking Muslims – and the Uighur of the north-west, the Miao in the south and west, and some four million Tibetans. The minority nationalities occupy about five-eighths of China's total land area, predominantly in the less populated parts of western China, which are also China's border regions.

Over the last two millennia Han Chinese have encroached on the territory of minority groups. For most of that time imperial policy allowed minorities to administer themselves through a tribal headman system. On occasions, for example during the reign of Yongzheng (1722–35), an interventionist policy was pursued, and minorities such as the Miao were brought under closer imperial control. During the republican period Sun Zhongshan favoured minority self-determination, but Jiang Jieshi generally supported a policy of closer integration. The constitution of 1954 declared that China was a 'multinational unitary state', that is to say the People's Republic of China was a single republic with numerous nationalities. This formula recognized the minority nationalities but did not allow them to secede. In the early years of Communist rule minority culture was encouraged and a degree of local economic autonomy accepted. However, during the Great Leap Forward minority nationalities were forced to accept the introduction of communes, with attendant changes to their economic practices. The Cultural Revolution, which reduced all political issues to the class struggle, brought additional pressures on minority groups to become assimilated. The 1982 constitution reaffirmed the 'multinational state' policy, and warnings were issued against 'great Han chauvinism'. However, the absolute prohibition on secession remained and assimilatory activities continued, most insidiously through Han migration. The most dramatic example of this occurred in Xinjiang, where in 1953 only about 6 to 10 per cent of the population was Han Chinese, but by 1982 this figure had risen to over 40 per cent.[18]

The gravest challenge to China's minorities policy has come from Tibet. Tibet had fallen under Chinese political control in the eighteenth century, and Qing suzerainty had later been recognized internationally, for example by the Anglo-Chinese agreement of 1906. However, after the 1911 revolution Chinese troops were withdrawn and in 1913 the Dalai Lama declared Tibet independent, although this was not accepted by China. In 1950 the People's Liberation Army 'liberated' Tibet, which then became an autonomous region within the People's Republic of China, running its own internal affairs with an assurance that its social system would be left intact. However, from 1954 Chinese influence in eastern Tibet began to increase. Units of the People's Liberation Army used Tibetan labour to construct roads and airfields, allegedly to facilitate a second Chinese invasion. In 1959 a revolt broke out at Lhasa and after Chinese intervention the Dalai Lama and some 80,000 Tibetans fled to India. The revolt was suppressed and Tibet was occupied by the Chinese army and rising numbers of Han Chinese settlers. There now began a sustained attack on Tibetan culture which has been described as an act of vandalism and conversely as the destruction of an oppressive feudal system. During the Cultural Revolution the cultural assault was intensified and many religious buildings, including Ganden, Tibet's third largest monastery, were destroyed. Much of this destruction was carried out by young Tibetan Red Guards, with Chinese encouragement.[19] In the constitution of 1982 explicit statements were made that the autonomy of minority areas should extend to economic and cultural matters. No concession, however, was made on the matter of secession and when demonstrations in favour of independence occurred in Tibet in 1989 these were put down severely. As long as the Dalai Lama is an exile he will remain the focus of demands for religious freedom and for freedom from Chinese oppression.[20]

Muslim groups in Xinjiang have also been strongly resistant to assimilation. Since the collapse of the Soviet Union and the independence of the republics of Kazakhstan, Kirgizstan, Tajikistan and Uzbekistan, Kazakh, Kirgiz, Tajik and Uzbek minorities in China have been able to observe the autonomy and higher living standards of their relations over the border. The Uighur, the largest minority nationality in this group, with a population in 1982 of over 6 million in China and some 200,000 in the former Soviet Union, have been particularly resentful of Chinese interference. The Uighur identify very strongly with Islam and there is a close relationship between resurgent Islam and the rise of Uighur nationalism. The Uighur participated in a rebellion at the time of the Cultural Revolution, and in 1980–1 there were violent demonstrations in Xinjiang accompanied by demands for Uighur self-rule. In 1997 bomb explosions in Beijing were attributed to an Uighur nationalist organization.

Aomen, Xianggang and Taiwan

The return of Xianggang to China on 30 June 1997, and that of Aomen in December 1999, will formally conclude the colonial history of the two territories. In modern times Aomen has been in a backwater of history. As a Portuguese possession, it was treated as neutral during the Second World War, and the Portuguese position remained unchallenged at the time of the Communist victory. Only during the Cultural Revolution, when violent demonstrations took place, did the status of the enclave receive international notice. The withdrawal of Portugal from her overseas commitments in the 1970s left China in effective control of the territory. In 1987 it was agreed that Aomen would return to China in 1999, but it would be allowed to retain its capitalist structure for a further fifty years. This situation is illustrated by the dominating presence of the Bank of China building on the Aomen waterfront.

The modern history of Xianggang has been more controversial. In the nineteenth century Xianggang was the centre of British imperialist interest in East Asia, but by the interwar years it had been eclipsed by Shanghai. During the republican period the British presence was attacked by Chinese nationalists, but anti-British sentiment subsided when Xianggang was occupied by the Japanese during the Second World War. The fall of Shanghai to the Communists aided the economic resurgence of Xianggang. Many refugees with useful skills found sanctuary there and the territory achieved a new economic importance at the time of the Korean War, when it began to develop as a manufacturing centre. At the time of the Great Leap Forward the flow of refugees from China soared and threatened to destabilize the colony. Relations between Britain and China became critical during the Cultural Revolution when Red Guards attacked the colonial government offices. However, it became apparent that for the time being the Chinese government wanted Xianggang to retain its separate status. In the 1970s and 1980s the economy boomed and the territory became the major conduit for economic activity between China and the outside world. By now Britain had relinquished virtually all its imperial possessions and Xianggang had become a political anomaly. When Margaret Thatcher, the British Prime Minister, visited China in 1982, discussions began on the future of Xianggang, which resulted in the Sino-British Joint Declaration of September 1984. In this Britain agreed to return the entire territory to China in 1997, when the ninety-nine-year lease on the New Territories expired. In return China guaranteed that Xianggang would become a 'special administrative region', with its own laws and would be allowed to retain its political freedoms and the capitalist system. This was the arrangement which Deng

Xiaoping referred to as 'one country, two systems'. The negotiations then turned to the drafting of the Basic Law which would serve as the constitution of Xianggang after 1997, but progress was interrupted by the events of 1989, with the Chinese authorities accusing subversive elements in Xianggang of fomenting the democracy movement, and Xianggang residents drawing pessimistic conclusions about the future of the territory after the events in Tiananmen Square. A brain-drain, the emigration of well-educated and wealthy Chinese from Xianggang, to overseas destinations, in particular to Canada, accelerated. However, Xianggang's continuing prosperity, now closely linked with the meteoric rise of Shenzhen, served to reassure the majority of the Chinese population that the transfer of power would not affect their livelihood adversely. Those who were concerned about their political future were forced to adopt an attitude of fatalism.[21]

The future political relationship between the People's Republic of China and the Republic of China on Taiwan, which over the last half century has been characterized by confrontation, is less easy to predict. After the Nationalist defeat on the mainland, Taiwan became the centre of Nationalist resistance. That resistance might have been cut short but for the Korean War and the United States' decision to incorporate Taiwan into its strategy for containing Communism. Until 1972, that is to say until Nixon's visit to mainland China, Taiwan's security was closely linked to the United States, and her relationship with the People's Republic was largely determined by that relationship.

The Republic of China continued the political tradition of the Nationalist period on the mainland and Jiang Jieshi remained as President until his death in April 1975. After a short break he was succeeded by his son Jiang Jingguo, who died in office in 1988. Whereas Jiang Jieshi had ruled in an authoritarian style and had relied on mainland Chinese for his support, his son pursued a policy of cautious liberalization and increasingly incorporated Taiwanese Chinese into his administration. Before his death the monopoly of political power enjoyed by the Guomindang had ended, open elections had been held and opposition parties had taken their seats in the National Assembly. In 1996 the first direct presidential elections were held, with Li Denghui, the Guomindang candidate, gaining a landslide victory.

In the meantime Taiwan had made extraordinary economic progress. This can be attributed to various factors, beginning with the legacy of the Japanese colonial period, during which Taiwanese agriculture had been developed systematically to supply sugar and rice to Japan, and subsequently an industrial base had been constructed to support Japan's aim of self-sufficiency. Other parts of the colonial legacy were an extensive railway network and a relatively well-educated population. Despite these advantages, Taiwan's economic prospects in the immediate postwar period could not be described as good. The island was deficient in mineral resources, she participated in the rampant inflation of the closing years of the Nationalist era on the mainland, and the arrival of some two-million Nationalist supporters and refugees had created an extremely unstable political situation.

The first step towards creating a sound economy was land reform. Land rents were reduced from over 50 per cent of the main crop to 37.5 per cent; land formerly held by Japanese settlers was sold to Chinese smallholders on easy terms;

and Chinese landlords were required to sell any land they held in excess of 3 hectares of paddy fields and 6 hectares of other land. The inspiration for the reform is often traced to Sun Zhongshan's policy of 'land to the tiller'. Its implementation owed much to the Chinese-American Joint Commission on Rural Reconstruction, and to substantial economic aid received from the United States. The reform had several beneficial effects: it broke the economic power of the landlords, stimulated a steady rise in agricultural output, and provided the government with capital for investment in economic development.

The next step the government took was to develop an infrastructure conducive to the development of small-scale consumer industry. These industries, once they had supplied the domestic market, exported an increasing proportion of their output. In the 1960s the Taiwanese economy began to grow rapidly. Agriculture continued to perform well, but the dramatic change was in industrial production, which in the 1960s rose by 20 per cent annually. The expansion came first in the output of textiles and in industries processing wood, leather and paper. Before the end of the decade, the electronics industry had begun to grow and through the 1980s Taiwanese industry produced increasing quantities of technologically advanced goods. Taiwanese living standards rose sharply, and much of the industrial output continued to be absorbed by the domestic market. At the same time exports boomed and by 1994 Taiwan's foreign currency reserves were the second highest of any country in the world.[22]

Epilogue

Few historians can resist concluding a history without making some predictions about the future. Here conjecture will be limited to speculation concerning 'Greater China', a phrase used to convey various meanings, but here referring to the provinces of Guangdong and Fujian – the former including Shenzhen and Hainan island, the latter including Xiamen – and Xianggang and Taiwan. This region, with a population of over 120 million, has become increasingly integrated economically over the past few years through trade and investment. It is also linked by a lively popular culture, personified by Deng Lijun, Taiwan's famous singer. Xianggang is the entrepôt for much of the trade within the region and for a large share of the trade between China and the outside world. A marked feature of the integration is the relocation of labour-intensive manufacturing industry from Xianggang and Taiwan to the mainland, to take advantage of lower labour costs in the People's Republic of China. In 1993 it was estimated that 80 to 90 per cent of Xianggang's manufacturing industries had been relocated to Guangdong, creating employment for three million people. In 1987 Taiwan relaxed its foreign exchange controls and removed its ban on travel to the mainland. Four years later it permitted investment on the mainland. Since then Taiwanese investment in China has soared, much of it going to Guangdong, but recently a good deal has also gone to Xiamen, on the mainland opposite Taiwan. Inward investment into the mainland has raised living standards to such an extent that by 1991 the per capita income of the population of Shenzhen was five times higher than the national average. Much of this investment came from Chinese living in Xianggang or Taiwan, but a considerable amount came from overseas Chinese living in South-east Asia. Overseas Chinese, estimated at 55 million in the early 1990s, already play a very important role in the economies of Indonesia, the Philippines, Malaysia and Thailand. There are concentrations of Chinese wealth in the United States, Canada and many other countries. Overseas Chinese, for sentimental as well as sound economic reasons, are disposed to invest in mainland China. The rise of 'Greater China' is a testimony to the dynamism of their contribution to date. The political, economic and cultural consequences of the emergence of 'Greater China' may have a dramatic effect on the future of China as a whole, and may lead to the emergence of China as the world's next superpower.[23]

Notes

Introduction

1. Quoted in John Meskill, *The Pattern of Chinese History: Cycles, Development, Stagnation?* (Lexington, D.C., Heath, 1968), pp. 2–3.
2. Edwin O. Reischauer and John K. Fairbank, *East Asia: The Great Tradition* (Boston, Houghton Mifflin, 1960), pp. 115–18.
3. Gungwu Wang, *The Structure of Power in North China During the Five Dynasties* (Kuala Lumpur, University of Malaya Press, 1963), pp. 1–6.
4. Wolfram Eberhard, *A History of China*, fourth edition (London, Routledge and Kegan Paul, 1977).
5. John K. Fairbank, Edwin O. Reischauer and Albert M. Craig, *East Asia: The Modern Transformation* (Boston, Houghton Mifflin, 1965).
6. Hisayuki Miyakawa, 'An outline of the Naito hypothesis and its effects on Japanese studies of China', *Far Eastern Quarterly*, 14.4, 1955, pp. 533-52.
7. Basil Guy, *The French Image of China Before and After Voltaire* (Geneva, 1963).
8. Hélène Carrère d'Encausse and Stuart Schram, *Marxism and Asia: An Introduction with Readings* (London, Allen Lane, 1969), pp. 7–8.
9. Karl A. Wittfogel, *Oriental Despotism: A Comparative Study of Total Power* (New Haven, Yale University Press, 1957, 1970). See also Wittfogel, 'Chinese society: An historical survey', *Journal of Asian Studies*, 16.3, May 1957, pp. 343–64.
10. Étienne Balazs, 'China as a permanently bureaucratic society', in Étienne Balazs, *Chinese Civilization and Bureaucracy* (New Haven, Yale University Press, 1964, 1967), p. 21.
11. Peter C. Perdue, *Exhausting the Earth: State and Peasant in Hunan 1500–1850* (Cambridge, Massachusetts, Harvard University Press, 1987).
12. Richard von Glahn, *The Country of Streams and Grottoes: Expansion, Settlement, and the Civilizing of the Sichuan Frontier in Song Times* (Cambridge, Massachusetts, Harvard University Press, 1987); Hugh R. Clark, *Community, Trade, and Networks: Southern Fujian Province from the Third to the Thirteenth Century* (Cambridge, Cambridge University Press, 1991).
13. G. William Skinner, *The City in Late Imperial China* (Stanford, Stanford University Press, 1977).
14. Susan Naquin and Evelyn S. Rawski, *Chinese Society in the Eighteenth Century* (New Haven, Yale University Press, 1987), pp. 138–216.
15. Ssu-Yü Teng, *Historiography of the Taiping Rebellion* (Cambridge, Massachusetts, Harvard University Press, 1962).
16. Colin Mackerras, *Western Images of China*, (Hong Kong, Oxford University Press, 1989), pp. 262–75.
17. Paul A. Cohen, *Discovering History in China: American Historical Writing on the Recent Chinese Past* (New York, Columbia University Press, 1984).
18. Michael Oksenberg, 'Politics takes command: An essay on the study of post-1949 China', CHC (15), pp. 543–90.
19. Norma Diamond, 'Rural collectivization and decollectivization in China – A review article', *Journal of Asian Studies*, 44.4, August 1985, pp. 785–92.
20. Michael Loewe and Edward L. Shaughnessy eds, *The Cambridge History of Ancient China: From the Origins of Civilization to 221 BC* (Cambridge, Cambridge University Press, 1999).
21. Edward L. Davis, *Society and the Supernatural in Song China* (Honolulu, University of Hawai'i, 2001).
22. Mark Elliott, review of Herbert Franke and Denis Twitchett eds, *The Cambridge History of China*, vol. 6. *Alien Regimes and Border States, 907–1368* (Cambridge, Cambridge University Press, 1994) in *Journal of Asian Studies* 55.1, February 1996, pp. 146–9.
23. Evelyn S. Rawski, 'Reenvisioning the Qing: The significance of the Qing period in Chinese history,' *Journal of Asian Studies* 55.4, November 1996, pp. 829–50.

Notes

24. Ping-ti Ho, 'In defense of sinicization: A rebuttal of Evelyn Rawski's "Reenvisioning the Qing"', *Journal of Asian Studies*, 57.1, February 1998, pp. 123–55.
25. James A. Millward, *Beyond the Pass: Economy, Ethnicity, and Empire in Qing Central Asia, 1759–1864* (Stanford, Stanford University Press, 1998), p. 251.
26. Edward J. M. Rhoads, *Manchus & Han: Ethnic Relations and Political Power in Late Qing and Early Republican China, 1861–1928* (Seattle, University of Washington Press, 2000).
27. D. Twitchett ed., *The Cambridge History of China, vol. 8. The Ming Dynasty* (Cambridge, Cambridge University Press, 1998).
28. Richard Von Glahn, *Fountain of Fortune: Money and Monetary Policy in China, 1000–1700* (Berkeley, University of California Press, 1996).
29. Roy Bin Wong, *China Transformed: Historical Change and the Limits of European Experience* (Ithaca, Cornell University Press, 1997).
30. Kenneth Pomeranz, *The Great Divergence: China, Europe, and the Making of the Modern World Economy* (Princeton, Princeton University Press, 2000).
31. Dorothy Ko, *Teachers of the Inner Chambers: Women and Culture in Seventeenth-Century China*, (Stanford, Stanford University Press, 1994).
32. Susan Mann, *Precious Records: Women in China's Long Eighteenth Century* (Stanford, Stanford University Press, 1997), p. 8.
33. Jonathan Spence, *Treason by the Book* (London, Allen Lane, 2001).
34. Jane Kate Leonard, *Controlling from Afar: The Daoguang Emperor's Management of the Grand Canal Crisis, 1824–1826* (Ann Arbor, University of Michigan Center for Chinese Studies, 1996).
35. Barry C. Keenan, *Imperial China's Last Classical Academies: Social Change in the Lower Yangzi, 1864–1911* (Berkeley, University of California, Institute of East Asian Studies, 1994).
36. John Fitzgerald, *Awakening China: Politics, Culture, and Class in the Nationalist Revolution* (Stanford, Stanford University Press, 1996), p. 348.
37. Frederic Wakeman, Jr, 'A revisionist view of the Nanjing decade: Confucian Fascism,' in Frederic Wakeman, Jr and Richard Louis Edmonds eds, *Reappraising Republican China* (Oxford, Oxford University Press, 2000), pp. 141–78.
38. Odoric Y.K. Wou, *Mobilizing the Masses: Building Revolution in Henan* (Stanford, Stanford University Press, 1994), 379.
39. Ralph A. Thaxton Jr, *Salt of the Earth: The Political Origins of Peasant Protest and Communist Revolution in China* (Berkeley, University of California Press, 1997), p. 319.
40. Pauline B. Keating, *Two Revolutions: Village Reconstruction and the Cooperative Movement in Northern Shaanxi, 1934–1945* (Stanford, Stanford University Press, 1997).
41. Peter J. Seybolt, *Throwing the Emperor from His Horse: Portrait of a Village Leader in China, 1923–1995* (Boulder, Colorado, Westview Press, 1996).

Chapter One

1. Louisa G. Fitzgerald Huber, 'The relationship of the Painted Pottery and the Lung-shan cultures', in David N. Keightley ed., *The Origins of Chinese Civilization* (Berkeley, University of California Press, 1983), pp. 177–216.
2. K.C. Chang, 'Sandai archaeology and the formation of states in ancient China: processual aspects of the origin of Chinese civilization', in Keightley ed., *The Origins of Chinese Civilization*, pp. 495–521.
3. Paul Wheatley, *The Pivot of the Four Quarters: A Preliminary Enquiry into the Origins and Character of the Ancient Chinese City* (Edinburgh, Edinburgh University Press, 1971) p. 58.
4. Noel Barnard, 'Further evidence to support the hypothesis of indigenous origins of metallurgy in ancient China' and Ursula Martius Franklin, 'On bronzes and other metals in early China', both in Keightley ed., *The Origins of Chinese Civilization*, pp. 237–77.
5. Kwong-yue Cheung, 'Recent archaeological evidence relating to the origin of Chinese characters', in Keightley ed., *The Origins of Chinese Civilization*, pp. 323–91.
6. David N. Keightley, *Sources of Shang History: The Oracle-Bone Inscriptions of Shang China* (Berkeley, University of California Press, 1978), pp. 57, 59.
7. Wheatley, pp. 52–63.

8. David N. Keightley, 'The Late Shang state: when, where, and what?' in Keightley ed., *The Origins of Chinese Civilization*, pp. 523–64.
9. Ping-ti Ho, *The Cradle of the East* (Hong Kong, The Chinese University of Hong Kong, 1975), pp. 354–7.

Chapter Two
1. At least twenty different dates have been proposed for the conquest of the Shang by the Zhou, ranging from 1122–1018 BC.
2. Herrlee G. Creel, *The Origins of Statecraft in China*, Vol. I, *The Western Chou Empire* (Chicago, University of Chicago Press, 1970), pp. 42–3.
3. D.C. Lau trans. and ed., *Mencius* (Harmondsworth, Penguin, 1970), p. 128.
4. Wolfram Eberhard, *A History of China*, fourth edition (London, Routledge & Kegan Paul, 1977), p. 23.
5. Edward L. Shaughnessy, 'Historical perspectives on the introduction of the chariot into China', *Harvard Journal of Asiatic Studies*, 48.1, June 1988, pp. 189–237.
6. Franz Michael, *China Through the Ages* (Boulder, Westview Press, 1986), p. 27.
7. Jacques Gernet, *A History of Chinese Civilization* (Cambridge, Cambridge University Press, 1985), p. 53.
8. Kwang-chih Chang, *The Archaeology of Ancient China*, third edition (New Haven, Yale University Press, 1977), pp. 346–76.
9. Henri Maspero, *La Chine antique* (Paris, Boccard, 1927), p. 66.
10. Derk Bodde, 'Feudalism in China', in Rushton Coulborn ed., *Feudalism in History* (Hamden, Connecticut, Archon Books, 1965), pp. 49–92.
11. Quoted in Bodde, p. 58.
12. Charles O. Hucker, *China's Imperial Past* (London, Duckworth, 1975), p. 33.
13. Cho-yun Hsu and Katheryn M. Linduff, *Western Chou Civilization* (New Haven, Yale University Press, 1988), p. 147.
14. Lau, *Mencius*, p. 177.
15. Cho-yun Hsu, *Ancient China in Transition* (Stanford, Stanford University Press, 1965), p. 118.
16. Gernet, p. 62.
17. Hsu, *Ancient China*, p. 35.
18. Xueqin Li, *Eastern Zhou and Qin Civilizations* (New Haven, Yale University Press, 1985), pp. 315–29.
19. Li, pp. 371–98.
20. Hsu, *Ancient China*, p. 56.
21. Derk Bodde, 'The state and empire of Ch'in', in CHC, 1, p. 24.
22. Hsu, *Ancient China*, p. 13.
23. Bodde, 'The state and empire of Ch'in', pp. 99–100.
24. Hsu, *Ancient China*, p. 71.
25. Hsu, *Ancient China*, p. 1.
26. Lau, *Mencius*, p. 101.
27. Hsu, *Ancient China*, p. 121.
28. D.C. Lau trans. and ed., *Confucius: The Analects* (Harmondsworth, Penguin, 1979), p. 10.
29. R. Dawson, *Confucius* (Oxford, Oxford University Press, 1981), p. 11.
30. Lau, *Confucius: The Analects*, p. 114.
31. Lau, *Confucius: The Analects*, p. 121.
32. W.T. de Bary et al. eds., *Sources of Chinese Tradition*, I (New York, Columbia University Press, 1960), p. 40.
33. D.C. Lau trans. and ed., *Lao Tzu: Tao Te Ching* (Harmondsworth, Penguin, 1975), p. 11.
34. Lau, *Lao Tzu*, p. 57.
35. Lau, *Lao Tzu*, p. 121.
36. From the *Chuang Tzu* trans. by Arthur Waley, in Cyril Birch ed., *Anthology of Chinese Literature* (New York, Grove Press, 1965), p. 82.
37. Lau, *Confucius: The Analects*, p. 143.
38. Lau, *Mencius*, p. 82.
39. Lau, *Mencius*, p. 49.
40. Quoted in de Bary, *Sources of Chinese Tradition*, I, p. 127.
41. De Bary, *Sources of Chinese Tradition*, I, p. 133.

Notes

Chapter Three

1. Derk Bodde, 'The state and empire of Ch'in', in CHC, 1, p. 20.
2. Charles O. Hucker, *China's Imperial Past* (London, Duckworth, 1975), p 43.
3. Bodde, 'The state and empire of Ch'in', p. 20.
4. *Shiji*, quoted in Bodde, 'The state and empire of Ch'in', pp. 31–2.
5. J.J.L. Duyvendak, *The Book of Lord Shang* (London, Arthur Probsthain, 1928), p. 2.
6. Duyvendak, p. 159.
7. Yu-ning Li ed., *Shang Yang's Reforms and State Control in China* (White Plains, New York, M.E. Sharpe, 1977), pp. lxxvii–lxxx.
8. Xueqin Li, *Eastern Zhou and Qin Civilizations* (New Haven, Yale University Press, 1985), p. 429.
9. Li ed., *Shang Yang's Reforms*, p. 78.
10. Derk Bodde, *China's First Unifier: A Study of the Ch'in Dynasty as Seen in the Life of Li Ssu 280?–208 BC* (Leiden, 1938, reprinted Hong Kong, Hong Kong University Press, 1967), p. 129.
11. Bodde, 'State and empire of Ch'in', p. 47.
12. Li Ssu, 'Memorial on annexation of feudal states', in T. de Bary et al eds., *Sources of Chinese Tradition*, I (New York, Columbia University Press, 1960), pp. 139–40.
13. Bodde, *China's First Unifier*, pp. 178–9.
14. Bodde, *China's First Unifier*, pp. 168–9.
15. Li, *Eastern Zhou and Qin Civilizations*, pp. 240–6.
16. Arthur Waldron, *The Great Wall of China* (Cambridge, Cambridge University Press, 1992).
17. Herold J. Wiens, *Han Chinese Expansion in South China* (Shoe String Press, n.p., 1967), pp. 130–3.
18. De Bary, *Sources of Chinese Tradition*, I, p. 141.
19. Ulrich Neininger, 'Burying the scholars alive: On the origins of a Confucian martyr's legend', in Wolfram Eberhard, Krzysztof Gawlikowski and Carl-Albrecht Seyschab eds., *East Asian Civilizations: New Attempts at Understanding Traditions, 2: Nation and Mythology* (Munich, Simon and Magiera, 1983).
20. Bodde, *China's First Unifier*, p. 121.
21. Quoted in Wen Fong ed., *The Great Bronze Age of China: An Exhibition from the People's Republic of China* (London, Thames and Hudson, 1980), pp. 356–7.
22. J.P. Harrison, *The Communists and Chinese Peasant Rebellions* (London, Gollancz, 1970), p. 279.
23. De Bary, *Sources of Chinese Tradition*, I, pp. 150–6.
24. Harrison, p. 220.
25. Xueqin Li ed., *The First Emperor of China* (White Plains, New York, International Arts and Sciences Press, 1975), p. lxiv.
26. Bodde, 'The state and empire of Ch'in', pp. 89–90.

Chapter Four

1. Cho-yun Hsü, *Han Agriculture: The Formation of Early Chinese Agrarian Economy (206 BC–AD 220)* (Seattle, University of Washington Press, 1980), p. 3.
2. Michael Loewe, *Chinese Ideas of Life and Death: Faith, Myth and Reason in the Han Period (202 BC–AD 220)* (London, George Allen & Unwin, 1982), p. 3.
3. Loewe, *Chinese Ideas of Life and Death*, p. 116. See also Michael Loewe, *Ways to Paradise: The Chinese Quest for Immortality* (London, George Allen & Unwin, 1979), pp. 17–59.
4. Loewe, *Ways to Paradise*, pp. 60–85.
5. De Bary, *Sources of Chinese Tradition*, I, pp. 154–5.
6. The Empress Lü was said to have been bitterly jealous of a concubine of Liu Bang, the Lady Qi. After Liu Bang's death, she poisoned the concubine's son and caused the lady herself to be seized, and had her hands and feet cut off and her organs of speech and hearing destroyed. She was then thrown on a dunghill. The empress invited her own son, the emperor, to go and see the 'human sow'. The sight drove the emperor mad. See W.F. Mayers, *The Chinese Reader's Manual* (Shanghai, American Presbyterian Press, 1874; Taipei, Literature House Ltd, 1964), p. 144.
7. Hans Bielenstein, *The Bureaucracy of Han Times* (Cambridge, Cambridge University Press, 1980), pp. 125–31.
8. Michael Loewe, 'The concept of sovereignty', in CHC, 1, p. 732.
9. A.F.P. Hulsewé, 'Ch'in and Han law', CHC, 1, pp. 520–44.

10. Nancy Lee Swann, *Food and Money in Ancient China: The Earliest Economic History of China to AD 25* (Princeton, Princeton University Press, 1950), pp. 174–5.

11. Michael Loewe, *Everyday Life in Early Imperial China During the Han Period 202 BC–AD 220* (London, Carousel, 1973), pp. 128–36.

12. Ying-shih Yü, 'Han foreign relations', CHC, 1, pp. 377–462.

13. Michael Loewe, *Crisis and Conflict in Han China 104 BC–AD 9* (London, George Allen & Unwin, 1974), pp. 11–13.

14. Burton Watson trans., *Courtier and Commoner in Ancient China: Selections from the* History of the Former Han *by Pan Ku* (New York, Columbia University Press, 1974), p. 56.

15. De Bary, *Sources of Chinese Tradition*, I, pp. 162–3.

16. Ch'i-yün Ch'en, 'Confucian, Legalist, and Taoist thought in Later Han', CHC, 1, p. 769.

17. De Bary, *Sources of Chinese Tradition*, I, p. 189.

18. Hulsewé, 'Ch'in and Han law', CHC, 1, p. 534.

19. Loewe, *Crisis and Conflict in Han China*, pp. 37–90.

20. Loewe, *Crisis and Conflict in Han China*, p. 114.

21. Loewe, *Crisis and Conflict in Han China*, pp. 139–40.

22. Hu Shih, 'Wang Mang, the socialist emperor of nineteen centuries ago', *Journal of the North China Branch of the Royal Asiatic Society*, 59, 1928, pp. 218–30.

23. Charles O. Hucker, *China's Imperial Past* (London, Duckworth, 1975), p. 129.

24. Hans Bielenstein, 'Wang Mang, the restoration of the Han dynasty and Later Han' CHC, 1, p. 239.

25. De Bary, *Sources of Chinese Tradition*, I, pp. 180–2.

26. Ban Gu, *Hanshu*, de Bary, *Sources of Chinese Tradition*, I, p. 226.

27. Sadao Nishijima, 'The economic and social history of Former Han', CHC, 1, p. 589.

28. Hucker, *China's Imperial Past*, p. 130.

29. Franz Michael, *China Through the Ages* (Boulder, Westview Press, 1986), pp. 80–1.

30. Bielenstein, 'Wang Mang', p. 239.

31. James P. Harrison, *The Communists and Chinese Peasant Rebellions* (London, Gollancz, 1970), p. 281.

32. Bielenstein, 'Wang Mang', p. 275.

33. Patricia Ebrey, 'The economic and social history of Later Han', CHC, 1, p. 614.

34. Etienne Balazs, 'Political philosophy and social crisis at the end of the Han dynasty', in Etienne Balazs, *Chinese Civilization and Bureaucracy* (New Haven, Yale University Press, 1967), pp. 198–205.

35. Zhongshu Wang, *Han Civilization* (New Haven, Yale University Press, 1982), p. 207.

36. Balazs, 'Political philosophy', p. 192.

37. Rafe de Crespigny, *Northern Frontier: The Policies and Strategy of the Later Han Empire* (Canberra, Australian National University, 1984), pp. xiii, 417–25.

38. Balazs, 'Political philosophy', pp. 192–3.

39. Bielenstein, 'Wang Mang', pp. 289–90.

Chapter Five

1. For example, L. Carrington Goodrich, *A Short History of the Chinese People*, third edition (London, Harper Torchbooks, 1959), p. 84.

2. Mark Elvin, *The Pattern of the Chinese Past* (London, Eyre, Methuen, 1973), p. 20.

3. E.O. Reischauer and John K. Fairbank, *East Asia: The Great Tradition* (Boston, Houghton Mifflin Company, 1960), pp. 128–9.

4. Wolfram Eberhard, *A History of China*, fourth edition (London, Routledge and Kegan Paul, 1977), p. 114.

5. Patricia Buckley Ebrey, *The Aristocratic Families of Early Imperial China: A Case Study of the Po-ling Ts'ui Family* (Cambridge, Cambridge University Press, 1978), pp. 16–19.

6. Eberhard, p. 119.

7. Eberhard, p. 143.

8. W.J.F. Jenner, *Memories of Loyang: Yang Hsüan-chih and the Lost Capital (493–534)*, (Oxford, Clarendon Press, 1981), p. 28.

9. Eberhard, p. 144.

10. Charles O. Hucker, *China's Imperial Past* (London, Duckworth, 1975), p. 183.

478

11. Reischauer and Fairbank, p. 158.
12. Jenner, p. 38.
13. Jenner, Appendix III.
14. Guo Xiang, *Commentary on the Zhuangzi*, quoted in de Bary, *Sources of Chinese Tradition*, I, p. 243.
15. Zong Bing, *Introduction to Landscape Painting*, quoted in de Bary, *Sources of Chinese Tradition*, I, p. 254.
16. Kenneth K.S. Chen, *Buddhism in China: A Historical Survey* (Princeton, Princeton University Press, 1964), pp. 124–8.
17. Jenner, p. 148.

Chapter Six
1. Arthur F. Wright, 'The Sui dynasty (581–617)', in CHC, 3 pp. 57–61.
2. Arthur F. Wright, *The Sui Dynasty* (New York, Knopf, 1978), p. 84.
3. Wright, 'The Sui dynasty', p. 106.
4. Wright, quoting Xiao Yu's reply to the Tang Emperor Taizong in 621, *The Sui Dynasty*, p. 71.
5. Wright, *The Sui Dynasty*, p. 173.
6. Howard J. Wechsler, *Mirror to the Son of Heaven: Wei Cheng at the Court of T'ang T'ai-tsung* (New Haven, Yale University Press, 1974), p. 16.
7. Howard J. Wechsler, 'The founding of the T'ang dynasty: Kao-tsu (reign 618–26),' CHC, 3, p. 161.
8. William Frederick Mayers, *The Chinese Reader's Manual* (Shanghai, American Presbyterian Mission Press, 1874; Taipei, Literature House, 1964), p. 122.
9. Arthur F. Wright, 'T'ang T'ai-tsung: The man and the persona', in John C. Perry and Bardwell L. Smith eds., *Essays on T'ang Society: The Interplay of Social, Political and Economic Forces* (Leiden, E.J. Brill, 1976), pp. 17–32.
10. Wright, 'T'ang T'ai-tsung', p. 26.
11. Wright, 'T'ang T'ai-tsung', p. 29.
12. Quoted in Wechsler, *Mirror to the Son of Heaven*, p. 84.
13. Wei Zheng's posthumous reputation led to him being transformed into a Daoist adept and a door god. In the Cultural Revolution he was praised by Mao Zedong's opponents as an example of someone who dared to criticise the emperor, by implication who would have dared to criticise Mao. See Wechsler, *Mirror to the Son of Heaven*.
14. D.C. Twitchett, *Financial Administration under the T'ang Dynasty*, second edition (Cambridge, Cambridge University Press, 1970), pp. 1–16.
15. David G. Johnson, *The Medieval Chinese Oligarchy* (Boulder, Westview Press, 1977), pp. 28–30, 48–50.
16. Ichisada Miyazaki, *China's Examination Hell: The Civil Service Examinations in China* (New Haven, Yale University Press, 1981), p. 113.
17. Stanley Weinstein, *Buddhism under the T'ang* (Cambridge, Cambridge University Press, 1987), p. 12.
18. D.C. Twitchett and Howard J. Wechsler, 'Kao-tsung (reign 649–83) and the empress Wu: the inheritor and the usurper' in CHC 3, p. 244.
19. Twitchett and Wechsler, p. 258.
20. Twitchett and Wechsler, p. 251.
21. C.P. FitzGerald, *The Empress Wu* (London, Cresset Press, 1956), p. 31.
22. Twitchett and Wechsler, p. 273.
23. Johnson, pp. 128–9.
24. Twitchett, *Financial Administration*, p. 75.
25. FitzGerald, p. 116.
26. FitzGerald, p. 163.
27. FitzGerald, pp. vii, 197–8.
28. Richard W.L. Guisso, 'The reigns of the empress Wu, Chung-tsung and Jui-tsung (684–712)' in CHC, 3, and R.W.L. Guisso, *Wu Tse-t'ien and the Politics of Legitimation in T'ang China* (Washington, Western Washington, 1978).
29. D.C. Twitchett, 'Hsüan-tsung (reign 712–56),' CHC, 3, pp. 462–3.
30. Edwin G. Pulleyblank, *The Background of the Rebellion of An Lu-shan* (Oxford, Oxford University Press, 1955), pp. 47–8, 192–5.
31. Pulleyblank, *Background of the Rebellion*, pp. 30–2.

32. Twitchett, *Financial Administration*, pp. 87–9.
33. Pulleyblank, *Background of the Rebellion*, p. 59.
34. Mayers, p. 6.
35. Pulleyblank, *Background of the Rebellion*, p. 59.
36. Twitchett, 'Hsüan-tsung', p. 402.
37. Edwin G. Pulleyblank, 'The An Lu-shan Rebellion and the origins of chronic militarism in Late T'ang China', in Perry and Smith, pp. 39–40.
38. Translated by Witter Bynner in Cyril Birch, compiler and editor, *Anthology of Chinese Literature: From Early Times to the Fourteenth Century* (Harmondsworth, Penguin Books, 1967), p. 282.
39. Pulleyblank, *Background of the Rebellion*, p. 1.
40. Pulleyblank, *Background of the Rebellion*, p. 27.
41. C.A. Peterson, 'Court and province in mid- and late T'ang', in CHC, 3, pp. 471–2.
42. Peterson, pp. 485–6.
43. Twitchett, *Financial Administration*, pp. 39–40.
44. C. A. Peterson, 'The Restoration completed: Emperor Hsien-tsung and the provinces', in Wright and Twitchett, *Perspectives on the T'ang* (New Haven, Yale University Press, 1973), pp. 151–91.
45. Edwin O. Reischauer, *Ennin's Travels in T'ang China* (New York, Ronald Press, 1955), p. 7.
46. Reigned 846–59, to be distinguished from his famous predecessor who reigned 712–56.
47. Robert M. Somers, 'The end of the T'ang', CHC, 3, 682–789.

Chapter Seven
1. Denis Twitchett, 'Introduction', CHC, 3, p. 33.
2. Arthur F. Wright, 'Changan', in Arnold Toynbee ed., *Cities of Destiny* (London, Thames and Hudson, 1967), p. 143.
3. Edward H. Schafer, *The Golden Peaches of Samarkand: A Study of T'ang Exotics* (Berkeley, University of California Press, 1963), p. 142.
4. Edward H. Schafer, *The Vermilion Bird: T'ang Images of the South* (Berkeley, University of California Press, 1967), p. 230.
5. For an account of his journey see Arthur Waley, *The Real Tripitaka and Other Pieces* (London, George Allen and Unwin, 1952). Waley called Xuan Zang 'Tripitaka', a Sanskrit word meaning 'three baskets', referring to the triple canon of Buddhist scriptures.
6. Waley, p. 39.
7. René Grousset, *In the Footsteps of the Buddha* (London, George Routledge and Sons, 1932), pp. 270–84.
8. C.P. FitzGerald, *The Southern Expansion of the Chinese People* (London, Barrie and Jenkins, 1972), p. 2.
9. Schafer, *The Vermilion Bird*, pp. 45–7.
10. Mark Elvin, *The Pattern of the Chinese Past* (London, Eyre Methuen, 1973), pp. 204–9.
11. Herold J. Wiens, *Han Chinese Expansion in South China*, (Hamden, Connecticut, Shoe String Press, 1967), pp. 272–4.
12. Hugh R. Clark, *Community, Trade, and Networks: Southern Fujian Province from the Third to the Thirteenth Century* (Cambridge, Cambridge University Press, 1991), pp. 19–37.
13. FitzGerald, p. 77.
14. FitzGerald, pp. 60–6.
15. Thomas J. Barfield, *The Perilous Frontier: Nomadic Empires and China* (Oxford, Basil Blackwell, 1989), pp. 9, 131.
16. Barfield, p. 49.
17. Barfield, p. 145.
18. Quoted in René Grousset, *The Empire of the Steppes: A History of Central Asia* (New Brunswick, Rutgers University Press, 1970), p. 102.
19. Quoted in Barfield, pp. 146-7.
20. Howard J. Wechsler, 'T'ai-tsung (reign 626–49) the consolidator', in CHC, 3, p. 230.
21. Richard W.L. Guisso, 'The reigns of the empress Wu, Chung-tsung and Jui-tsung 684–712', in CHC 3, p. 285.
22. Michael T. Dalby, 'Court politics in late T'ang times', in CHC, 3, p. 677.
23. Barfield, p. 155.

24. Quoted in Grousset, *The Empire of the Steppes*, p. 122.

25. Barfield, p. 12.

26. From the *Liao Shih*, quoted in Barfield, p. 172.

27. John Whitney Hall, *Japan from Prehistory to Modern Times* (Tokyo, Charles E. Tuttle, 1971), p. 40.

28. Ryusaku Tsunoda, W.T. de Bary and Donald Keene compilers, *Sources of Japanese Tradition* (New York, Columbia University Press, 1964), I, p. 47.

29. Mikiso Hane, *Premodern Japan: A Historical Survey* (Boulder, Westview Press, 1991), p. 34.

30. Edwin O. Reischauer, *Ennin's Travels in T'ang China* (New York, The Ronald Press, 1955), pp. 272–94.

31. Gungwu Wang, 'Ming relations with Southeast Asia: A background essay' in J.K. Fairbank ed., *The Chinese World Order: Traditional China's Foreign Relations* (Cambridge, Massachusetts, Harvard University Press, 1968), pp. 34–62.

32. Sechin Jagchid and Van Jay Symons, *Peace, War, and Trade along the Great Wall: Nomadic-Chinese Interaction through Two Millennia* (Bloomington, Indiana University Press, 1989), pp. 1–23.

Chapter Eight

1. From Jacques Gernet, *Les aspects économiques du Bouddhisme dans la société chinoise du Ve au Xe siècle* (Saigon, 1956), as summarised in Arthur F. Wright, 'T'ang T'ai-tsung and Buddhism', in Arthur F. Wright and Denis Twitchett eds., *Perspectives on the T'ang* (New Haven, 1973), p. 241.

2. Kenneth K.S. Chen, *Buddhism in China: A Historical Survey* (Princeton, Princeton University Press, 1964), p. 204.

3. Chen, p. 204.

4. De Bary, *Sources of Chinese Tradition*, I, p. 292.

5. Stanley Weinstein, *Buddhism under the T'ang* (Cambridge University Press, Cambridge, 1987), p. 4.

6. Weinstein, p. 26.

7. Weinstein, pp. 60–1.

8. Weinstein, p. 84.

9. Weinstein, p. 91.

10. De Bary, *Sources of Chinese Tradition*, I, p. 373.

11. Edwin O. Reischauer trans., *Ennin's Diary: The Record of a Pilgrimage to China in Search of the Law* (New York, The Ronald Press), 1955, p. 361.

12. De Bary, *Sources of Chinese Tradition*, I, pp. 380–2.

13. John T. Meskill ed., *An Introduction to Chinese Civilization* (Lexington, Columbia University Press, 1973), pp. 110–11.

14. Charles O. Hucker, *China's Imperial Past* (London, Duckworth, 1975), p. 219.

15. A.C. Moule, *Christians in China Before the Year 1550* (London, Society for Promoting Christian Knowledge, 1930), pp. 38–9.

16. F.S. Drake, 'Mohammedanism in the T'ang dynasty', *Monumenta Serica*, VIII, 1943, pp. 1–40.

17. De Bary, *Sources of Chinese Tradition*, I, p. 370.

18. David McMullen, *State and Scholars in T'ang China* (Cambridge, Cambridge University Press, 1988).

19. Charles Hartman, *Han Yü and the T'ang Search for Unity* (Princeton, Princeton University Press, 1986), pp. 1–3.

20. De Bary, *Sources of Chinese Tradition*, I, p. 375.

21. David McMullen, 'Han Yü: An alternative picture', *Harvard Journal of Asiatic Studies*, 49.2, Dec. 1989, pp. 603–57.

22. Wu-chi Liu, *An Introduction to Chinese Literature* (Bloomington, Indiana University Press, 1966), p. 69.

23. Tao Qian, 'Two poems on returning to dwell in the country', translated by William Acker, in Cyril Birch, compiler and editor, *Anthology of Chinese Literature: From the Earliest Times to the Fourteenth Century* (New York, Grove Press 1965), p. 183.

24. Stephen Owen, *The Great Age of Chinese Poetry: The High T'ang* (New Haven, Yale University Press, 1981), pp. 3–6.

25. Owen, p. 39.

26. Owen, p. 109.

27. Translated by William Acker, Birch, p. 232.

28. Arthur Cooper, *Li Po and Tu Fu* (Harmondsworth, Penguin Books, 1973), p. 109.

29. Cooper, pp. 18–19.
30. Owen, pp. 197–8.
31. Arthur Waley, *The Life and Times of Po Chü-i, 772–846 AD* (London, George Allen and Unwin, 1949), p. 163.
32. Liu, p. 92.
33. Trans. by Waley, Birch, p. 277.
34. A.C. Graham, *Poems of the Late T'ang* (Harmondsworth, Penguin Books, 1981), p. 117.
35. Birch, pp. 258–9.
36. Edward H. Schafer, *The Vermilion Bird: T'ang Images of the South* (Berkeley, University of California Press, 1967), p. 143.
37. For a translation by Waley of 'The Story of Miss Li', see Birch, pp. 300–13.
38. William Dolby, *A History of Chinese Drama* (London, Paul Elek, 1976), pp. 5–8.
39. Arthur F. Wright, 'Changan', in Arnold Toynbee, *Cities of Destiny* (London, Thames and Hudson, 1967), p. 146.
40. Michael Sullivan, *The Arts of China* (London, Sphere Books, 1973), p. 127.
41. Sullivan, p. 134.
42. Michael Sullivan, 'The heritage of Chinese art', in Raymond Dawson ed., *The Legacy of China* (Oxford, Oxford University Press, 1964), p. 226.
43. Dong You (active 1119–26), quoted in Arthur Waley, *An Introduction to the Study of Chinese Painting* (London, 1923), p. 117.
44. Max Loehr, *The Great Paintings of China* (Oxford, Phaidon, 1980), pp. 41–6.
45. William Watson, *Style in the Art of China* (Harmondsworth, Penguin Books, 1974), Plates 101 a, b.
46. Jessica Rawson ed., *The British Museum Book of Chinese Art* (London, British Museum Press, 1992), pp. 232–4.
47. Rawson, p. 145.

Chapter Nine

1. E.O. Reischauer and J.K. Fairbank, *East Asia: The Great Tradition* (Boston, Houghton Mifflin Company, 1960), p. 194.
2. Winston W. Lo, *An Introduction to the Civil Service of Sung China* (Honolulu, University of Hawaii Press, 1987), p. 56.
3. Gungwu Wang, *The Structure of Power in North China during the Five Dynasties* (Kuala Lumpur, University of Malaya Press, 1963).
4. E.A. Kracke, Jr., *Civil Service in Early Sung China, 960–1067* (Massachusetts, Harvard University Press, Cambridge, 1953, 1968), p. 1.
5. John W. Chaffee, *The Thorny Gates of Learning in Sung China: A Social History of Examinations* (Cambridge, Cambridge University Press, 1985), pp. 47–65.
6. Thomas H.C. Lee, *Government Education and Examinations in Sung China* (Hong Kong, The Chinese University Press, 1985), pp. 22–3, 62–3.
7. Kracke, pp. 194–5.
8. Chaffee, p. 182.
9. Figures from a study by Sun Kuo-tung, quoted in Lee, pp. 211–15.
10. Etienne Balazs, 'A forerunner of Wang An-shih', in Etienne Balazs, *Chinese Civilization and Bureaucracy: Variations on a Theme* (New Haven, Yale University Press, 1967).
11. James T.C. Liu, *Ou-yang Hsiu: An Eleventh-Century Neo-Confucianist* (Stanford, Stanford University Press, 1967), pp. 52–64.
12. De Bary, *Sources of Chinese Tradition*, I, p. 414.
13. Quoted in James T.C. Liu, *Reform in Sung China: Wang An-shih (1021–1086) and his New Policies* (Massachusetts, Harvard University Press, Cambridge, 1959), p. 49.
14. Quoted in John Meskill ed., *Wang An-shih: Practical Reformer?* (Boston, D.C. Heath and Company, 1963), p. 21.
15. Quoted in Meskill, p. 25.
16. Meskill, p. 39.
17. Liu, *Reform in Sung China*, p. 13.

18. Meskill, pp. 77-81.
19. Meskill, pp. 82–90.
20. Liu, *Reform in Sung China*, pp. 114–16.
21. Ray Huang, *China: A Macro History* (New York, M.E. Sharpe Inc., 1989), pp. 118–21.
22. Kao Yu-kung, 'A study of the Fang La rebellion', *Harvard Journal of Asiatic Studies*, 24, 1962–3, pp. 17–63.
23. See chapter 7.
24. Otherwise 'Jürched'.
25. Jing-shen Tao, *The Jurchen in Twelfth-Century China: A Study of Sinicization* (Seattle, University of Washington Press, 1976), pp. 3–13.
26. Tao, p. 34.
27. Herbert Franke, 'The Jin dynasty', in CHC, 6, pp. 215–320.
28. Tao, pp. 92–4.
29. Hellmut Wilhelm, 'From myth to myth: The case of Yüeh Fei's biography', in Arthur F. Wright and Denis Twitchett eds., *Confucian Personalities* (Stanford, Stanford University Press, 1962), pp. 146–61, and James T.C. Liu, 'Yüeh Fei (1103–1141) and China's heritage of loyalty', *Journal of Asian Studies*, 31.2, Feb. 1972, pp. 291–7.
30. James T.C. Liu, *China Turning Inward: Intellectual-Political Changes in the Early Twelfth Century* (Cambridge, Massachusetts, Harvard University Press, 1988), p. 83.
31. Richard L. Davis, *Court and Family in Sung China, 960–1279: Bureaucratic Success and Kinship Fortunes for the Shih of Ming-chou* (Durham, Duke University Press, 1986), p. 85.
32. Davis, p. 86.
33. Herbert Franke, 'Chia Ssu-tao (1213–1275): A "bad last minister"?', Wright and Twitchett, *Confucian Personalities*, pp. 217–34.
34. Franke, 'Chia Ssu-tao', pp. 226–9.
35. Mark Elvin, *The Pattern of the Chinese Past* (London, Methuen, 1973), pp. 111–99.
36. Elvin, p. 179.
37. Etienne Balazs, 'The birth of capitalism in China', in Balazs, *Chinese Civilization and Bureaucracy*, pp. 34–54.
38. Peter J. Golas, 'Rural China in the Song', *Journal of Asian Studies*, 39.2, 1980, pp. 291–325.
39. Robert Hartwell, 'A revolution in the Chinese iron and coal industries during the northern Sung, 960–1126 AD', *Journal of Asian Studies*, 21, 1961–2, pp. 153–162.
40. Robert P. Hymes, *Statesmen and Gentlemen: The Elite of Fu-chou, Chiang-hsi, in Northern and Southern Sung* (Cambridge, Cambridge University Press, 1986).
41. Davis, p. xv.
42. Golas, p. 302.
43. Etienne Balazs, 'Chinese towns' in Etienne Balazs, *Chinese Civilization and Bureaucracy*, pp. 66–78. See also Jacques Gernet, *Daily Life in China on the Eve of the Mongol Invasion 1250–1276* (London, George Allen & Unwin, 1962).
44. Patricia Buckley Ebrey, *The Inner Quarters: Marriage and the Lives of Chinese Women in the Sung period* (Berkeley, University of California Press, 1993), pp. 4–6.
45. Ebrey, pp. 261–71.
46. Liu, *China Turning Inward*, pp. 55–80.
47. De Bary, *Sources of Chinese Tradition*, I, pp. 457–60, 465–70.
48. Wei-ming, Tu 'The Confucian tradition in Chinese history', in Paul S. Ropp ed., *Heritage of China: Contemporary Perspectives on Chinese Civilization* (Berkeley, University of California Press, 1990), pp. 112–37.
49. Michael Sullivan, *The Arts of China* (London, Sphere Books, 1973), p. 159.
50. Quoted in Joseph Levenson, *Modern China and its Confucian Past* (New York, Anchor Books, 1964), p. 29.
51. Peter C. Swann, *Art of China Korea and Japan* (London, Thames and Hudson, 1963), p. 137.

Chapter Ten
1. Jacques Gernet, *A History of Chinese Civilization* (Cambridge, Cambridge University Press, 1985), pp. 360–84.
2. Ray Huang, *China: A Macro History* (New York, M.E. Sharpe Inc., 1989), p. 147.
3. F.W. Mote, 'The growth of Chinese despotism: A critique of Wittfogel's theory of oriental despotism as applied to China', *Oriens Extremus*, 8.1, August 1961, pp. 1–41.

4. John D. Langlois Jr ed., *China under Mongol Rule* (Princeton, Princeton University Press, 1981), pp. 3–21.
5. F.W. Mote, 'Chinese society under Mongol rule, 1215–1368', in CHC, 6, pp. 618–22.
6. Thomas Allsen, 'The rise of the Mongolian empire and Mongolian rule in north China', in CHC, 6, pp. 321–413.
7. Igor de Rachewiltz, 'Yeh-lü Ch'u-ts'ai (1189–1243): Buddhist idealist and Confucian statesman', in Arthur F. Wright and Denis Twitchett eds., *Confucian Personalities* (Stanford, Stanford University Press, 1962), pp. 189–216.
8. Herbert Franke, *From Tribal Chieftain to Universal Emperor and God: The Legitimation of the Yüan dynasty* (Verlag der Bayerischen Akademie der Wissenschaften, Munich, 1978), p. 38.
9. De Rachelwiltz, p. 214.
10. Hok-lam Chan, 'Chinese official historiography at the Yüan court: The composition of the Liao, Chin, and Sung histories', in Langlois, *China Under Mongol Rule*, pp. 56–106.
11. Mote, 'Chinese society under Mongol rule', pp. 651–3.
12. Paul Heng-chao Ch'en, *Chinese Legal Tradition under the Mongols: The Code of 1291 as Reconstructed* (Princeton, Princeton University Press, 1979), p. xvi.
13. Ch'i-ing Hsiao, 'Mid-Yüan politics', in CHC, 6, pp. 490–560.
14. Ch'en, pp. 80–8.
15. Elizabeth Endicott-West, 'The Yüan government and society', in CHC, 6, p. 613.
16. Witold Rodzinski, *A History of China*, I, (Oxford, Pergamon Press, 1979), pp. 184–5.
17. Endicott-West, 'The Yüan government and society', p. 613.
18. Elizabeth Endicott-West, 'Merchant associations in Yüan China: The Ortoy', *Acta Asiatica*, 2.2, 1989, pp. 127–54.
19. H.H. Lamb, *Climate: Past and Future* (London, Methuen, 1977), II, pp. 447, 456.
20. de Rachewiltz, pp. 195–8.
21. Yün-hua Jan, 'Chinese Buddhism in Ta-tu: The new situation and new problems', in Hok-lam Chan and Wm. Theodore de Bary eds., *Yüan Thought: Chinese Thought and Religion Under the Mongols* (New York, Columbia University Press, 1982), pp. 390–3.
22. Herbert Franke, 'Tibetans in Yüan China', in Langlois ed., p. 306.
23. Wing-tsit Chan, 'Chu Hsi and Yüan Neo-Confucianism', in Chan and de Bary, pp. 197–231.
24. Wei-ming Tu, 'Towards an understanding of Liu Yin's Confucian eremitism', in Chan and de Bary, pp. 233–77.
25. *Six Yüan Plays* translated with an introduction by Liu Jung-en, (Harmonsdworth, Penguin Books, 1972), p. 10.
26. Stephen H. West, 'Mongol influence on the development of Northern Drama', in Langlois ed., pp. 434–65.
27. Morris Rossabi, 'The Muslims in the early Yüan dynasty', in Langlois ed., pp. 257–95.
28. *The Travels of Marco Polo*, translated and with an introduction by Ronald Latham (Harmondsworth, Penguin Books, 1958), p. 36.
29. John W. Haeger, 'Marco Polo in China? Problems with internal evidence', *Bulletin of Sung and Yuan Studies*, 14, 1978, pp. 22–30.
30. Morris Rossabi, *Voyager from Xanadu: Rabban Sauma and the First Journey from China to the West* (New York, Kodansha International, 1992).
31. Ch'i-ch'ing Hsiao, *The Military Establishment of the Yüan Dynasty* (Cambridge, Massachusetts, Harvard University Press, 1978), pp. 3–32.
32. Hsiao, pp. 32, 62–3.
33. John W. Dardess, 'The transformations of messianic revolt and the founding of the Ming dynasty', *Journal of Asian Studies*, 29.3, 1970, pp. 539–58.
34. Charles O. Hucker, *The Ming Dynasty: Its Origins and Evolving Institutions* (Ann Arbor, The University of Michigan Center for Chinese Studies, 1978), p. 24.
35. Hsiao, pp. 3–8.
36. Ch'en, pp. 41–67.

Notes

Chapter Eleven

1. Edward L. Dreyer, *Early Ming China: A Political History* 1355–1435 (Stanford, Stanford University Press, 1982), p. 237.
2. John W. Dardess, 'The transformations of Messianic revolt and the founding of the Ming dynasty', *Journal of Asian Studies*, 29.3, 1970, pp. 539–58.
3. Frederick W. Mote, 'The rise of the Ming dynasty' in CHC, 7, pp. 11–57.
4. The term is used anachronistically to denote Zhu Yuanzhang's regime.
5. Edward L. Dreyer, 'Military origins of Ming China', CHC, 7, pp. 58–106.
6. Dreyer, *Early Ming China*, pp. 69–70, 155–6.
7. Dreyer, *Early Ming China*, pp. 76–87; Romeyn Taylor, 'Yüan origins of the *wei-so* system', in Charles O. Hucker ed., *Chinese Government in Ming Times: Seven Studies* (New York, Columbia University Press, 1969), pp. 23–40.
8. Charles O. Hucker, *The Ming Dynasty: Its Origins and Evolving Institutions* (Ann Arbor, Center for Chinese Studies, University of Michigan, 1978), p. 43.
9. Ray Huang, *Taxation and Governmental Finance in Sixteenth-Century Ming China* (Cambridge, Cambridge University Press, 1974), p. 42.
10. Ray Huang, 'Fiscal administration during the Ming dynasty', in Hucker ed., *Chinese Government in Ming Times*, pp. 73–128.
11. Edward L. Farmer, *Early Ming Government: The Evolution of Dual Capitals* (Cambridge, Massachusetts, Harvard University Press, 1976), pp. 114–28.
12. Hok-lam Chan, 'The Chien-wen, Yung-lo, Hung-hsi, and Hsüan-te reigns, 1399–1435', in CHC, 7, pp. 182–304.
13. J.V.G. Mills trans. and ed., *Ma Huan, Ying-yai sheng-lan: The Overall Survey of the Ocean's Shores* [1433] (Cambridge, Cambridge University Press, 1970), p. 10.
14. Hok-lam Chan, p. 278.
15. Farmer, p. 133.
16. Dreyer, *Early Ming China*, p. 252.
17. Frederick W. Mote, 'The T'u-mu incident of 1449' in Frank A. Kierman and John K. Fairbank eds., *Chinese Ways in Warfare* (Cambridge, Massachusetts, Harvard University Press, 1974), pp. 243–72.
18. Arthur Waldron, *The Great Wall of China: From History to Myth* (Cambridge, Cambridge University Press, 1992), pp. 91–107.
19. Frederick W. Mote, 'The growth of Chinese despotism: A critique of Wittfogel's theory of Oriental Despotism as applied to China, *Oriens Extremus*, 8.1, 1961, pp. 1–41.
20. Albert Chan, *The Glory and Fall of the Ming Dynasty* (Norman, University of Oklahoma Press, 1982), pp. 18, 32.
21. Hok-lam Chan, p. 287.
22. Charles O. Hucker, *The Censorial System of Ming China* (Stanford, Stanford University Press, 1966), pp. 147–51; 232–4.
23. Jung-pang Lo, 'Policy formulation and decision-making on issues respecting peace and war', in Hucker ed., *Chinese Government in Ming Times*, pp. 41–72.
24. Ping-ti Ho, *Studies on the Population of China, 1368–1953* (Cambridge, Massachusetts, Harvard University Press, 1974), pp. 258–65.
25. Dwight H. Perkins, *Agricultural Development in China, 1368–1968* (Edinburgh, Edinburgh University Press, 1969), pp. 5–78.
26. Peter C. Perdue, *Exhausting the Earth: State and Peasant in Hunan, 1500–1850* (Cambridge, Massachusetts, Harvard University Press, 1987), p. 49.
27. Sadao Nishijima, 'The formation of the early Chinese cotton industry', in Linda Grove and Christian Daniels eds., *State and Society in China: Japanese Perspectives on Ming-Qing Social and Economic History* (Tokyo, University of Tokyo Press, 1984), pp. 17–77. See also Ramon H. Myers, *The Chinese Economy: Past and Present* (Belmont, Wadsworth Inc., 1980), pp. 96–8.
28. Mark Elvin, *The Pattern of the Chinese Past* (London, Methuen, 1973), pp. 268–76.
29. Huang, *Taxation and Governmental Finance*, pp. 182–9.
30. Fang-chung Liang, *The Single-Whip Method of Taxation in China* (Cambridge, Massachusetts, Harvard University Press, 1970), p. 1.

31. Lloyd E. Eastman, *Family, Fields, and Ancestors: Constancy and Change in China's Social and Economic History,* 1550–1949 (Oxford, Oxford University Press, 1988), p. 139.
32. Huang, *Taxation and Governmental Finance,* pp. 130, 313–23.
33. Hucker, *The Ming Dynasty,* pp. 55–6.
34. Huang, *China: A Macro History* (New York, M.E. Sharpe, 1989), p. 161.
35. Hilary J. Beattie, *Land and Lineage in China: A Study of T'ung-ch'eng County, Anhwei, in the Ming and Ch'ing Dynasties* (Cambridge, Cambridge University Press, 1979).
36. Chung-li Chang, *The Chinese Gentry: Studies on Their Role in Nineteenth-Century Chinese Society* (Seattle, University of Washington Press, 1967), p. xvii.
37. Ping-ti Ho, *The Ladder of Success in Imperial China: Aspects of Social Mobility, 1368–1911* (New York, Columbia University Press, 1967), pp. 92–105, 256.
38. Cyril Birch, *Stories from a Ming Collection: Translations of Chinese Short Stories Published in the Seventeenth Century* (New York, Grove Press, Inc., 1958), pp. 37–96.
39. Katherine Carlitz, 'Desire, danger, and the body: stories of women's virtue in late Ming China', in Christina K. Gilmartin et al eds. *Engendering China: Women, Culture, and the State* (Cambridge, Massachusetts, Harvard University Press, 1994), pp. 101–24.
40. Wu-chi Liu, *An Introduction to Chinese Literature* (Bloomington, Indiana University Press, 1966), pp. 195-237.
41. Charles O. Hucker, *China's Imperial Past: An Introduction to Chinese History and Culture* (London, Duckworth, 1975), p. 406.
42. Waldron, *The Great Wall,* pp. 122–39.
43. Ray Huang, *1587, A Year of No Significance: The Ming Dynasty in Decline* (New Haven, Yale University Press, 1981), pp. 156–74.
44. Quoted in Jonathan Spence, *The China Helpers: Western Advisers in China 1620–1960* (London, The Bodley Head, 1969), pp. 6–7.
45. Ray Huang, 'The Lung-ch'ing and Wan-li reigns, 1567-1620', in CHC, 7, p. 522.
46. Edwin O. Reischauer and John K. Fairbank, *East Asia: The Great Tradition* (Boston, Houghton Mifflin, 1960), p. 341.
47. Charles O. Hucker, 'The Tung-lin movement of the late Ming period' in Fairbank ed., *Chinese Thought and Institutions* (Chicago, University of Chicago Press, 1957), pp. 132–62.
48. Frederic E. Wakeman, 'China and the seventeenth-century crisis', *Late Imperial China,* 7.1, June 1986, pp. 1–26.
49. James Bunyan Parsons, *The Peasant Rebellions of the Late Ming Dynasty* (Tucson, University of Arizona Press), 1970.

Chapter Twelve
1. Frederic Wakeman, *The Great Enterprise: The Manchu Reconstruction of Imperial Order in Seventeenth-Century China,* two volumes (Berkeley, University of California Press, 1985).
2. Quoted in J. Mason Gentzler ed., *Changing China: Readings in the History of China from the Opium War to the Present* (New York, Praeger Publishers, 1977), p. 135.
3. Franz Michael, *The Origin of Manchu Rule in China* (John Hopkins Press, 1942, reprinted New York, Octagon Press, 1972), pp. 39–47; Wakeman, *The Great Enterprise,* I, pp. 23–66.
4. Michael, p. 79.
5. Robert B. Oxnam, *Ruling from Horseback: Manchu Politics in the Oboi Regency 1661–1669* (Chicago, University of Chicago Press, 1975), pp. 5–6.
6. Angela Hsi, 'Wu San-kuei in 1644: A reappraisal', *Journal of Asian Studies* 34.2, Feb. 1975, pp. 443–53.
7. Quoted in Wakeman, *The Great Enterprise,* I, pp. 316-17.
8. Wakeman, *The Great Enterprise,* I, pp. 556–69.
9. Frederic Wakeman, 'Localism and loyalism during the Ch'ing conquest of Kiangnan: The tragedy of Chiang-yin', in Frederic Wakeman and Carolyn Grant eds., *Conflict and Control in Late Imperial China* (Berkeley, University of California Press, 1975), pp. 43–85.
10. Ralph C. Croizier, *Koxinga and Chinese Nationalism: History, Myth and the Hero* (Cambridge, Massachusetts, Harvard University Press, 1977). See also John E. Wills, 'Maritime China from Wang Chih to Shih Lang: themes in peripheral history', in Jonathan D. Spence and John E. Wills eds., *From Ming to Ch'ing:*

Conquest, Region, and Continuity in Seventeenth-Century China (New Haven, Yale University Press, 1979), pp. 201–38.

11. Charles O. Hucker, *China's Imperial Past: An Introduction to Chinese History and Culture* (London, Duckworth, 1975), p. 295.

12. Wakeman, *The Great Enterprise*, II, pp. 886–9.

13. Wakeman, *The Great Enterprise*, I, pp. 458–61.

14. Oxnam, pp. 41–3.

15. Wakeman, *The Great Enterprise*, II, pp. 909–11.

16. Wakeman, *The Great Enterprise*, II, pp. 1013–5, 1058–9.

17. Oxnam, pp. 50–63.

18. Oxnam, pp. 64–89.

19. Oxnam, pp. 90–117; Lawrence D. Kessler, *K'ang-hsi and the Consolidation of Ch'ing Rule 1661–1684* (Chicago, University of Chicago Press, 1976), pp. 30–9.

20. Kessler, pp. 39–46.

21. Wakeman, *The Great Enterprise*, II, pp. 1099–102.

22. Kessler, pp. 85–6.

23. Wakeman, *The Great Enterprise*, II, pp. 1110–12.

24. Kessler, pp. 97–103.

25. Hucker, p. 297.

26. Jonathan D. Spence, *Emperor of China: Self-Portrait of K'ang-hsi* (London, Jonathan Cape, 1974), p. 46.

27. Kessler, pp. 105–11.

28. Spence, *Emperor of China*, p. 22.

29. Morris Rossabi, *China and Inner Asia: From 1368 to the Present Day* (London, Thames and Hudson, 1975), p. 141.

30. Preston M. Torbert, *The Ch'ing Imperial Household Department: A Study of Its Organization and Principal Functions, 1662–1796* (Cambridge, Massachusetts, Harvard University Press, 1977), pp. 14–39.

31. Jonathan D. Spence, *Ts'ao Yin and the K'ang-hsi Emperor: Bondservant and Master* (New Haven, Yale University Press, 1966, 1988).

32. Silas H.L. Wu, *Communication and Imperial Control in China: Evolution of the Palace Memorial System 1693–1735* (Cambridge, Massachusetts, Harvard University Press, 1970).

33. Spence, *Emperor of China*, p. 79.

34. Madeleine Zelin, *The Magistrate's Tael: Rationalizing Fiscal Reform in Eighteenth-Century Ch'ing China* (Berkeley, University of California Press, 1984), pp. 1–24.

35. Pei Huang, *Autocracy at Work: A Study of the Yung-cheng Period, 1723–1735* (Bloomington, Indiana University Press, 1974), p. 27 and n. 2.

36. Silas H.L. Wu, *Passage to Power: K'ang-hsi and His Heir Apparent, 1661–1722* (Cambridge, Massachusetts, Harvard University Press, 1979), p. 23.

37. Wu, *Passage to Power*, p. 95.

38. Spence, *Emperor of China*, p. 145.

39. Huang, p. 21.

40. Huang, pp. 78–80; Wu, *Passage to Power*, pp. 179–83.

41. Quoted in Beatrice S. Bartlett, *Monarchs and Ministers: The Grand Council in Mid-Ch'ing China, 1723–1820* (Berkeley, University of California Press, 1991), p. 104.

42. Zelin, pp. 29–32.

43. Huang, p. 272.

44. Zelin, pp. 303–8.

45. Susan Naquin and Evelyn S. Rawski, *Chinese Society in the Eighteenth Century* (New Haven, Yale University Press, 1987), p. 219.

46. See chapter 7.

47. Harold L. Kahn, *Monarchy in the Emperor's Eyes: Image and Reality in the Ch'ien-lung Reign* (Cambridge, Massachusetts, Harvard University Press, 1971), p. 181.

48. Bartlett, pp. 180, 266–7, 278.

49. Lawrence D. Kessler, 'Ethnic composition of provincial leadership during the Ch'ing dynasty', *Journal of Asian Studies*, 28.3, May, 1969, pp. 489–511.

50. Kahn, p. 136.
51. L. Carrington Goodrich, *The Literary Inquisition of Ch'ien-lung* (1935, New York, Paragon Book Reprint, 1966).
52. R. Kent Guy, *The Emperor's Four Treasuries: Scholars and the State in the Late Ch'ien-lung Era* (Cambridge, Massachusetts, Harvard University Press, 1987).
53. Benjamin A. Elman, *From Philosophy to Philology: Intellectual and Social Aspects of Change in Late Imperial China* (Cambridge, Massachusetts, Harvard University Press, 1984).
54. Joseph Fletcher, 'Ch'ing Inner Asia c. 1800' in CHC, 10, pp. 35–106.
55. John K. Fairbank and Ssü-yu Teng, 'On the Ch'ing tributary system,' in John K. Fairbank and Ssü-yu Teng, *Ch'ing Administration: Three Studies* (Cambridge, Massachusetts, Harvard University Press, 1968), p. 112–13.
56. Wang Tseng-tsai, 'The Macartney Mission: a bicentennial review', in Robert A. Bickers ed., *Ritual and Diplomacy: The Macartney Mission to China 1792–1794* (London, The British Association for Chinese Studies and Wellsweep, 1993), pp. 43–56.
57. Lloyd E. Eastman, *Family, Fields, and Ancestors: Constancy and Change in China's Social and Economic History, 1550–1949* (Oxford, Oxford University Press, 1988), pp. 3–14.
58. Ping-ti Ho, *Studies on the Population of China, 1368–1953* (Cambridge, Massachusetts, Harvard University Press, 1967), p. 270.
59. Mark Elvin, *The Pattern of the Chinese Past* (London, Eyre Methuen, 1973), pp. 298–315.
60. Paul S. Ropp, *Dissent in Early Modern China: Ju-lin wai-shih and Ch'ing Social Criticism* (Ann Arbor, University of Michigan Press, 1981), p. 60.
61. Paul S. Ropp, 'The seeds of change: reflections on the condition of women in the early and mid-Ch'ing', *Signs: Journal of Women in Culture and Society*, 2.1, Autumn 1976, pp. 5–23.
62. Arthur W. Hummel ed., *Eminent Chinese of the Ch'ing Period (1644–1912)* (Washington, United States Government Printing Office, 1943–4; Taipei, Literature House, 1964), p. 956.
63. Susan Mann, 'Learned women in the eighteenth century,' in Christina K. Gilmartin, Gail Hershatter, Lisa Rofel and Tyrene White eds., *Engendering China: Women, Culture and the State* (Cambridge, Massachusetts, Harvard University Press, 1994), pp. 27–46.
64. Philip Kuhn, *Soulstealers: The Chinese Sorcery Scare of 1768* (Cambridge, Massachusetts, Harvard University Press, 1990), p. 1.
65. Kuhn, pp. 30–48, 223.
66. Susan Naquin, *Shantung Rebellion: The Wang Lun Uprising of 1774* (New Haven, Yale University Press, 1981), p. 101.
67. Naquin, pp. 148–64.
68. David S. Nivison, 'Ho-shen and his accusers: ideology and political behavior in the eighteenth century,' in David S. Nivison and Arthur F. Wright eds, *Confucianism in Action* (Stanford, Stanford University Press, 1959), pp. 209–43.
69. Albert Feuerwerker, *State and Society in Eighteenth-Century China: The Ch'ing Empire in Its Glory* (Ann Arbor, Center for Chinese Studies, University of Michigan, 1976), pp. 73–5.

Chapter Thirteen
1. J.L. Cranmer-Byng (ed.), *An Embassy to China: Being the Journal Kept by Lord Macartney During His Embassy to the Emperor Ch'ien-lung 1793–1794* (London, Longmans, 1962), pp. 212–13.
2. Susan Naquin and Evelyn S. Rawski, *Chinese Society in the Eighteenth Century* (New Haven, Yale University Press, 1987), p. x.
3. Madeleine Zelin, *The Magistrate's Tael: Rationalizing Fiscal Reform in Eighteenth-Century Ch'ing China* (Berkeley, University of California Press, 1984), pp. 303–8.
4. Yi Wan, Shuqing Wang and Yanzhen Lu (compilers) *Daily Life in the Forbidden City* (Hong Kong, Viking, 1988), pp. 172–8.
5. Lawrence D. Kessler, 'Ethnic composition of provincial leadership during the Ch'ing dynasty', *Journal of Asian Studies* 33.3, May 1969, pp. 489–511.
6. For fuller accounts of the operation of central government see Richard J. Smith, *China's Cultural Heritage: The Ch'ing Dynasty, 1644–1912* (Boulder, Colorado, Westview Press, 1983), pp. 36–43 and I.C.Y. Hsü, *The Rise of Modern China*, fifth edition (Oxford, Oxford University Press, 1995), pp. 45–59.

Notes

7. T'ung-tsu Ch'ü, *Local Government in China under the Ch'ing* (Stanford, Stanford University Press, 1969), p. 14.
8. Chung-li Chang, *The Chinese Gentry: Studies on Their Role in Nineteenth-Century Chinese Society* (Seattle, University of Washington Press, 1967), pp. 8–32 and Table 27.
9. Chang, p. 116.
10. Quoted in Chang, p. 115.
11. Ping-ti Ho, *Studies on the Population of China, 1368–1953* (Cambridge, Massachusetts, Harvard University Press, 1959), p. 270.
12. Dwight H. Perkins, *Agricultural Development in China 1368–1968* (Edinburgh, Edinburgh University Press, 1969), p. 24.
13. Wolfram Eberhard, *China's Minorities: Yesterday and Today* (Belmont, California, Wadsworth, 1982).
14. Quoted in Ho, p. 148.
15. Ho, p. 152.
16. Johanna Menzel Meskill, *A Chinese Pioneer Family: The Lins of Wu-feng, Taiwan 1729–1895* (Princeton, Princeton University Press, 1979).
17. Ho, p. 270.
18. 1 mou is approximately one-sixth of an acre.
19. Albert Feuerwerker, *State and Society in Eighteenth-Century China: The Ch'ing Empire in Its Glory*, Michigan Papers in Chinese Studies (Ann Arbor, University of Michigan, 1976), pp. 81–2.
20. Robert Fortune, *A Journey to the Tea Countries of China* (London, John Murray, 1852, reprint London, Mildmay Books, 1987), pp. 92–5.
21. Mark Elvin, *The Pattern of the Chinese Past* (London, Eyre Methuen, 1973), p. 306.
22. Ramon H. Myers, *The Chinese Economy: Past and Present* (Belmont, California, Wadsworth, 1980), pp. 26–7, 61–90.
23. Lloyd E. Eastman, *Family, Fields, and Ancestors: Constancy and Change in China's Social and Economic History, 1550–1949* (Oxford, Oxford University Press, 1988), pp. 149–57.
24. *Shen* literally means a sash and implies the holder of a higher degree or an official; *shi* indicates a scholar. See Chang, p. xviii, n. 6.
25. Chang, p. 1.
26. Chang, p. 173.
27. See Franz Michael's introduction 'Regionalism in nineteenth-century China', in Stanley Spector, *Li Hung-chang and the Huai Army: A Study in Nineteenth-Century Chinese Regionalism* (Seattle, University of Washington Press, 1964), pp. xxi–xliii.
28. Nora Waln, *The House of Exile* (Harmondsworth, Penguin Books, 1938), pp. 37–9.
29. Smith, pp. 149–53.
30. Évariste Huc, *The Chinese Empire: Forming a Sequel to the Work Entitled 'Recollections of a Journey Through Tartary and Thibet'* (2 vols, 1855, New York, Kennikat Press, 1970), I, p. 248.
31. Paul S. Ropp, 'Women in Late Imperial China: A review of recent English language scholarship', *Women's History Review* ,3.3,, 1994, pp. 347–83.
32. Susan Mann, 'Learned women in the eighteenth century', in Christina K. Gilmartin, Gail Hershatter, Lisa Rofel and Tyrene White (eds), *Engendering China: Women, Culture, and the State* (Cambridge, Massachusetts, Harvard University Press, 1994), pp. 27–46.
33. Quoted in Raymond Dawson, *Confucius* (Oxford, Oxford University Press, 1981), p. 53. Yao and Shun were legendary sage-emperors.
34. Naquin and Rawski, pp. 64–6.
35. Smith, pp. 10–11.
36. Cao Xueqin, translated by David Hawkes, *The Story of the Stone* (5 vols, Harmondsworth, Penguin Books, 1973–)
37. Translated by Arthur Waley in Cyril Birch (ed.), *Anthology of Chinese Literature* (2 vols, New York, Grove Press Inc., 1972), II, p. 198.
38. Mann, pp. 28–9.
39. Peter Swann, *Art of China, Korea and Japan* (London, Thames & Hudson, 1963), p. 232.
40. Smith, p. 189.
41. Smith, pp. 168–9.

42. Jessica Rawson (ed.), *The British Museum Book of Chinese Art* (London, British Museum Press, 1992), pp. 279–80.

43. Hae-jong Chun, 'Sino-Korean tributary relations in the Ch'ing period', in John King Fairbank (ed.), *The Chinese World Order* (Cambridge, Massachusetts, Harvard University Press, 1968), pp. 90–111.

44. Ta-tuan Ch'en, 'Investiture of Liu-ch'iu kings in the Ch'ing period', in Fairbank (ed.), *The Chinese World Order*, pp. 135–64.

45. Joseph Fletcher, 'Ch'ing Inner Asia *c.* 1800', CHC ,10, pp. 35–106.

46. R.K.I. Quested, *Sino-Russian Relations: A Short History* (Hemel Hempstead, George Allen & Unwin, 1984), pp. 28–61.

47. John King Fairbank, *Trade and Diplomacy on the China Coast: The Opening of the Treaty Ports, 1842–1854* (Stanford, Stanford University Press, 1969), pp. 39–53.

48. Shunhong Zhang, 'Historical anachronism: The Qing court's perception of and reaction to the Macartney Embassy', in Robert A. Bickers (ed.), *Ritual & Diplomacy: The Macartney Mission to China 1792–1794* (London, The British Association for Chinese Studies and Wellsweep, 1993), pp. 31–42.

49. J. Mason Gentzler (ed.), *Changing China: Readings in the History of China from the Opium War to the Present* (New York, Praeger Publishers, 1977), pp. 23–5.

50. James L. Hevia, 'The Macartney Embassy in the history of Sino-Western relations', in Bickers (ed.), pp. 57–79.

Chapter Fourteen

1. Jane Kate Leonard, *Wei Yuan and China's Rediscovery of the Maritime World* (Cambridge, Massachusetts, Harvard University Press, 1984), pp. 63–77.

2. Frederic Wakeman, 'The Canton trade and the Opium War', CHC ,10,, pp. 163–212, at pp. 163–4.

3. Wakeman, 'The Canton trade', p. 172.

4. Michael Greenberg, *British Trade and the Opening of China 1800–42* (Cambridge, Cambridge University Press, 1951; New York, Monthly Review Press, 1979), pp. 139–41.

5. Harley Farnsworth McNair, *Modern Chinese History: Selected Readings* (New York, 1923; Paragon Book Reprint Corporation, 1967), pp. 67–8.

6. Jack Beeching, *The Chinese Opium Wars* (London, Hutchinson, 1975), pp. 44–56.

7. Quoted in McNair, pp. 99–101.

8. James M. Polachek, *The Inner Opium War* (Cambridge, Massachusetts, Harvard University Press, 1992), pp. 126–8.

9. Wakeman, 'The Canton trade', p. 185.

10. Arthur Waley, *The Opium War Through Chinese Eyes* (London, George Allen & Unwin Ltd, 1960), pp. 28–31.

11. China had no national currency at this time. The basic coin circulating for foreign commerce at Guangzhou was the Spanish dollar which in sterling was worth between £0.20 and £0.25.

12. Frederic Wakeman jr, *Strangers at the Gate: Social Disorder in South China, 1839–1861* (Berkeley, University of California Press, 1966), pp. 11–21.

13. John Morley, *The Life of William Ewart Gladstone* (2 vols, London, Edward Lloyd, 1908), I, p. 168.

14. Quoted in Tyler Dennett, *Americans in Eastern Asia: A Critical Study of the Policy of the United States with Reference to China, Japan and Korea in the 19th Century* (New York, Macmillan, 1922), p. 107.

15. Karl Marx, *New York Daily Tribune*, 20 September 1858, reprinted in Dona Torr (ed.), *Marx on China 1853–1860: Articles from the New York Daily Tribune* (London, Lawrence & Wishart, 1968), p. 55.

16. P.C. Kuo, *A Critical Study of the First Anglo-Chinese War with Documents* (Shanghai, 1935, reprinted Taipei, Ch'eng Wen Publishing Co., 1970), pp. 1–2.

17. John King Fairbank, *Trade and Diplomacy on the China Coast: The Opening of the Treaty Ports 1842–1854* (Harvard University Press, 1953, revised edition Stanford, Stanford University Press, 1969), p. 74.

18. Greenberg, p. 212.

19. Hsin-pao Chang, *Commissioner Lin and the Opium War* (Cambridge, Massachusetts, Harvard University Press, 1964), p. x.

20. D.K. Fieldhouse, *Economics and Empire 1830–1914* (London, Weidenfeld and Nicolson, 1973), p. 212.

21. Polachek, pp. 63–135.

22. Fairbank, *Trade and Diplomacy*, pp. 226–47.

23. Kuo, p. 199.
24. John King Fairbank, 'Synarchy under the treaties', in John King Fairbank (ed.), *Chinese Thought and Institutions* (Chicago, University of Chicago Press, 1957), pp. 204–31.
25. Quoted in Beeching, p. 164.
26. British Parliamentary Papers, *Report of the Select Committee on Commercial Relations with China*, 12 July 1847.
27. Fairbank, *Trade and Diplomacy*, pp. 200–1.
28. Wakeman, *Strangers at the Gate*, pp. 90–2.
29. Quoted in W.C. Costin, *Great Britain and China 1833–1860* (Oxford, Oxford University Press, 1937, 1968), pp. 149–50.
30. Fairbank, *Trade and Diplomacy*, pp. 84–5.
31. Quoted in Polachek, p. 215.
32. Polachek, p. 21.
33. Wakeman, *Strangers at the Gate*, p. 94.
34. J.Y. Wong, *Yeh Ming-ch'en:Viceroy of Liang Kuang 1852–8* (Cambridge, Cambridge University Press, 1976), p. xix.
35. Te-kong Tong, *United States Diplomacy in China, 1844–60* (Seattle, University of Washington Press, 1964), p. 263.

Chapter Fifteen
1. Stuart Schram, *The Political Thought of Mao Tse-tung*, revised and enlarged edition (London, Praeger, 1969), p. 262.
2. Frederick Wakeman, 'Rebellion and revolution: The study of popular movements in Chinese history', *Journal of Asian Studies* ,36.2,, February 1977, pp. 201–37 and Kwang-ching Liu, 'World view and peasant rebellion: Reflections on post-Mao historiography', *Journal of Asian Studies* ,40.2,, February 1981, pp. 295–326.
3. Ping-ti Ho, *Studies on the Population of China, 1368–1953* (Cambridge, Massachusetts, Harvard University Press, 1959), p. 270.
4. Philip A. Kuhn, *Rebellion and Its Enemies in Late Imperial China: Militarization and Social Structure, 1796–1864* (Cambridge, Massachusetts, Harvard University Press, 1970), p. 39.
5. Susan Mann Jones and Philip A. Kuhn, 'Dynastic decline and the roots of rebellion', CHC ,10,, pp. 107–62, at p. 111.
6. Mann and Jones, pp. 119–28.
7. Franz Michael, 'Military organization and power structure of China during the Taiping Rebellion', *Pacific Historical Review* ,18,, 1949, pp. 469–83.
8. Susan Naquin, *Millenarian Rebellion in China: The Eight Trigrams Uprising of 1813* (New Haven, Yale University Press, 1976), pp. 7–60.
9. Kuhn, pp. 37–50.
10. Naquin, p. 267.
11. Jonathan D. Spence, *The Search for Modern China* (London, Hutchinson, 1990), p. 169.
12. Mann and Jones, pp. 134–6; Frederic Wakeman jr, *Strangers at the Gate: Social Disorder in South China, 1839–1861* (Berkeley, University of California, 1966), pp. 117–25, 139–48. See also Jean Chesneaux (ed.), *Popular Movements and Secret Societies in China 1840–1950* (Stanford, Stanford University Press, 1972).
13. Theodore Hamberg, *The Visions of Hung Siu-Tshuen, and Origin of the Kwang-si Insurrection* (Hong Kong, China Mail Office, 1854; New York, Praeger Publishers, 1969), pp. 9–12.
14. Robert P. Weller, *Resistance, Chaos and Control in China: Taiping Rebels, Taiwanese Ghosts and Tiananmen* (Seattle, University of Washington Press, 1994), pp. 69–85.
15. On the importance of millenarian expectations to the development of mass movements see Jonathan Spence, *God's Chinese Son: The Taiping Heavenly Kingdom of Hong Xiuquan* (London, HarperCollins, 1996) and the present author's '"Golden bricks and golden houses await you": Prophecy and millenarianism in the Taiping rebellion', in Bertrand Taithe and Tim Thornton (eds), *Prophecy: The Power of Inspired Language in History 1300–2000* (Stroud, Sutton Publishing, 1997), pp. 143–60.
16. Franz Michael and Chung-li Chang, *The Taiping Rebellion: History and Documents* (3 vols, Seattle, University of Washington Press, 1966–71), II, pp. 131–9.

17. Yu-wen Jen, *The Taiping Revolutionary Movement* (New Haven, Yale University Press, 1973), pp. 81–2.
18. Michael II, p. 109.
19. Michael, II, pp. 309–20.
20. Michael, II, pp. 561–4.
21. Jen, p. 145.
22. Liu, p. 311 and n. 62.
23. Mary Clabaugh Wright, *The Last Stand of Chinese Conservatism: The T'ung-Chih Restoration, 1862–1874*, second edition (Stanford, Stanford University Press, 1962), p. 198.
24. Quoted in J.S. Gregory, *Great Britain and the Taipings* (London, Routledge & Kegan Paul, 1969), p. 79.
25. Michael, III, pp. 748–76.
26. Kathryn Bernhardt, *Rents, Taxes, and Peasant Resistance: The Lower Yangzi Region, 1840–1950* (Stanford, Stanford University Press, 1992), p. 86.
27. Michael, I, p. 169.
28. James H. Cole, *The People Versus the Taipings: Bao Lisheng's "Righteous Army of Dongan"* (Berkeley, University of California Center for Chinese Studies, 1981).
29. Elizabeth J. Perry, *Rebels and Revolutionaries in North China, 1845–1945* (Stanford, Stanford University Press, 1980), pp. 10–47.
30. Ch'ang-hua Ma, 'An explanation of the term Nien', in Elizabeth J. Perry (ed.), *Chinese Perspectives on the Nien Rebellion* (New York, M.E. Sharpe, 1981), pp. 72–5.
31. Ch'ang-hua Ma, 'The relationship between the Nien Army and the White Lotus Society', in Perry (ed.), pp. 59–69.
32. Perry, pp. 113–17.
33. Quoted in Siang-tseh Chiang, *The Nien Rebellion* (Seattle, University of Washington Press, 1954, 1967), p. 34.
34. Perry, p. 130.
35. Michael, I, p. 125.
36. Kwang-ching Liu, 'The Ch'ing Restoration', CHC ,10,, pp. 409–90 at pp. 468–70.
37. C.A. Curwen, *Taiping Rebel: The Deposition of Li Hsiu-ch'eng* (Cambridge, Cambridge University Press, 1977), p. 25.
38. Liu, 'The Ch'ing Restoration', pp. 469–77.
39. Kwang-ching Liu, 'The military challenge: the north-west and the coast', CHC ,11,, pp. 202–73.
40. Wright, p. 110.
41. Kwang-ching Liu, 'The military challenge', pp. 225–35.
42. Immanuel C.Y. Hsü, 'The great policy debate in China, 1874: maritime defense vs. frontier defense', *Harvard Journal of Asiatic Studies* ,25,, 1965, pp. 212–28, reprinted in I.C.Y. Hsü (ed.), *Readings in Modern Chinese History* (New York, Oxford University Press, 1971), pp. 258–70.
43. Liu, 'The military challenge', pp. 235–43.
44. Curwen, p. 37.
45. Ho, pp. 236–48, 275–8.
46. Chung-li Chang, *The Chinese Gentry: Studies on Their Role in Nineteenth-Century Chinese Society* (Seattle, University of Washington Press, 1967), pp. 94–115, 138–41.
47. Kuhn, pp. 189–225.
48. Franz Michael, Introduction 'Regionalism in nineteenth-century China', in Stanley Spector, *Li Hung-chang and the Huai Army: A Study in Nineteenth-Century Chinese Regionalism* (Seattle, University of Washington Press, 1964), pp. xxi–xliii.
49. Wright, pp. 57–8.
50. Kwang-ching Liu, 'The limits of regional power in the late Ch'ing period: a reappraisal', *Ch'ing-hua hsüeh-pao*, NS ,10.2,, July 1974, pp. 207–23.
51. Bernhardt, p. 120.

Chapter Sixteen
1. Mary Clabaugh Wright, *The Last Stand of Chinese Conservatism: The T'ung-Chih Restoration, 1862–1874*, second edition (Stanford, Stanford University Press, 1962), p. 50.
2. Wright, pp. 43–67.

3. Wright, pp. 79–84.
4. Kwang-ching Liu, 'The Ch'ing Restoration', CHC ,10,, pp. 409–90.
5. Wright, p. ix.
6. James Polachek, 'Gentry hegemony: Soochow in the T'ung-chih Restoration', in Frederic Wakeman jr and Carolyn Grant (eds), *Conflict and Control in Late Imperial China* (Berkeley, University of California Press, 1975), pp. 211–56.
7. Jonathan K. Ocko, *Bureaucratic Reform in Provincial China: Ting Jih-ch'ang in Restoration Kiangsu, 1867–1870* (Cambridge, Massachusetts, Harvard University Press, 1983), pp. 10–11, 59–61, 171–8.
8. Feng Guifen, 'On the Adoption of Western Knowledge', in Ssu-yu Teng and John King Fairbank (eds), *China's Response to the West: A Documentary Survey 1839–1923* (New York, Atheneum, 1963), pp. 51–2.
9. Ting-yee Kuo and Liu Kwang-ching, 'Self-strengthening: the pursuit of Western technology', CHC ,10,, pp. 491–542, 504–11.
10. Knight Biggerstaff, *The Earliest Modern Government Schools in China* (New York, Kennikat Press, 1961, 1972), pp. 94–153.
11. Teng and Fairbank, p. 64.
12. Kuo and Liu, p. 519.
13. Arthur W. Hummel (ed.), *Eminent Chinese of the Ch'ing Period (1644–1912)* (Washington, United States Government Printing Office, 1943–4; reprinted Taipei, Literature House, 1964), pp. 402–5.
14. Kuo and Liu, p. 431. See also John L. Rawlinson, *China's Struggle for Naval Development 1839–1895* (Cambridge, Massachusetts, Harvard University Press, 1967), pp. 34–7.
15. Thomas L. Kennedy, *The Arms of Kiangnan: Modernization in the Chinese Ordnance Industry, 1860–1895* (Boulder, Westview Press, 1978), pp. 64, 74, 109–10.
16. Teng and Fairbank, p. 82.
17. Steven A. Leibo, *Transferring Technology to China: Prosper Giquel and the Self-strengthening Movement* (Berkeley, University of California Institute of East Asian Studies, China Research Monograph 28, 1985), pp. 74–6.
18. Teng and Fairbank, p. 110.
19. Albert Feuerwerker, *China's Early Industrialization: Sheng Hsüan-huai (1844–1916) and Mandarin Enterprise* (Cambridge, Massachusetts, Harvard University Press, 1958, reprinted New York, Atheneum, 1970), p. 98.
20. Chi-kong Lai, 'The Qing state and merchant enterprise: The China Merchants' Company, 1872–1902', in Jane Kate Leonard and John R. Watt (eds), *To Achieve Security and Wealth: The Qing Imperial State and the Economy, 1644–1911* (Ithaca, Cornell University Press, 1992), pp. 139–55.
21. Chi-kong Lai, 'Li Hung-chang and modern enterprise: The China Merchants' Com-pany, 1872–1885', in Samuel C. Chu and Kwang-ching Liu (eds), *Li Hung-chang and China's Early Modernization* (New York, M.E. Sharpe Inc., 1994), pp. 216–47.
22. Ellsworth C. Carlson, *The Kaiping Mines, 1877–1912*, second edition (Cambridge, Massachusetts, Harvard University Press, 1971), p. 7.
23. Carlson, p. 12.
24. Gideon Chen, *Tso Tsung-t'ang: Pioneer Promoter of the Modern Dockyard and the Woollen Mill in China* (Beijing, Yenching University, 1938; reprinted New York, Paragon Book Reprint Corporation, 1968), pp. 57–72.
25. Stephen C. Thomas, *Foreign Intervention and China's Industrial Development, 1870–1911* (Boulder, Westview, 1984), pp. 91–4.
26. Albert Feuerwerker, *The Chinese Economy ca. 1870–1911* (Ann Arbor, University of Michigan, 1969), p. 21.
27. Feuerwerker, *China's Early Industrialization*, pp. 216–17.
28. Wright, pp. 9–10, 312.
29. Joseph R. Levenson, *Modern China and Its Confucian Past: The Problem of Intellectual Continuity* (New York, Anchor Books, 1964), pp. 81–9.
30. Biggerstaff, p. 19.
31. The term employed by Mongols to refer to themselves when addressing the emperor.
32. Teng and Fairbank, p. 76.
33. Raphael Pumpelly, 'A journey in northern China', *Galaxy* ,8,, 1869, pp. 467–76, quoted in J.A.G. Roberts, *China Through Western Eyes: The Nineteenth Century* (Stroud, Alan Sutton, 1991), pp. 97–8.

34. David Pong, *Shen Pao-chen and China's Modernization in the Nineteenth Century* (Cambridge, Cambridge University Press, 1994).

35. David Pong, 'Confucian patriotism and the destruction of the Woosung railway, 1877', *Modern Asian Studies* ,7.4,, 1973, pp. 647–76.

36. W.J. Macpherson, *The Economic Development of Japan c. 1868–1941* (Basingstoke, Macmillan Education Ltd, 1987), p. 77.

37. Feuerwerker, *The Chinese Economy*, p. 61.

38. Dwight H. Perkins, 'Government as an obstacle to industrialization: The case of nineteenth-century China', *Journal of Economic History* ,27.4,, 1967, pp. 478–92.

39. Rawlinson, pp. 174–85.

40. Rawlinson, pp. 140–5.

41. Thomas L. Kennedy, 'Self-Strengthening: An analysis based on some recent writings', *Ch'ing-shi wen-t'i* ,3.1,, November 1974, pp. 3–35.

42. Feuerwerker, *China's Early Industrialization*, pp. 13–14.

43. Wellington K.K. Chan, 'Government, merchants and industry', CHC ,11,, pp. 416–62.

44. Jonathan Spence, *The China Helpers: Western Advisers in China 1620–1960* (London, The Bodley Head, 1969), p. 152.

45. Yen-p'ing Hao and Erh-min Wang, 'Changing Chinese views of Western relations, 1840–1895', CHC ,11,, pp. 142–201.

46. Biggerstaff, pp. 21–2.

47. Frances V. Moulder, *Japan, China, and the Modern World Economy: Toward a Reinterpretation of East Asian Development ca. 1600 to ca. 1918* (Cambridge, Cambridge University Press, 1977), pp. 189–97.

48. Wright, p. 300.

49. Between 1868 and 1880 the Japanese government established a number of industrial enterprises, among them the Tomioka silk-reeling mill. This was intended to facilitate the introduction of foreign technology, to demonstrate its profitability and to upgrade the quality of Japanese reeled silk for the export market. In fact Tomioka was poorly sited, was closed to visitors, did not make a profit and the French machinery which it introduced was not that adopted in the private sector of the silk industry. Kozo Yamamura, *A Study of Samurai Income and Entrepreneurship* (Cambridge, Massachusetts, Harvard University Press, 1974), pp. 178–9.

50. Kennedy, p. 152.

51. Thomas, pp. 81–108.

52. Leonard and Watt, pp. 1–6 and Chi-kong Lai, 'The Qing state', pp. 139–56.

Chapter Seventeen

1. A 'concession' was an area leased from the Chinese government by a foreign power and then sublet to foreign nationals; a 'settlement' was an area set aside by the Chinese government for foreign residence, where foreigners leased plots from Chinese landholders. See P.D. Coates, *The China Consuls: British Consular Officers, 1843–1943* (Hong Kong, Oxford University Press, 1988), p. 161.

2. Immanuel C.Y. Hsu, 'Late Ch'ing foreign relations, 1866–1905', CHC ,11,, pp. 70–141.

3. Yoshitake Oka, 'National independence and the reason for the state's existence', 1961, quoted in Marlene J. Mayo (ed.), *The Emergence of Imperial Japan: Self-Defense or Calculated Aggression?* (Lexington, D.C., Heath and Company, 1970), pp. 1–12.

4. Hsu, pp. 102–3.

5. Lloyd E. Eastman, *Throne and Mandarins: China's Search for a Policy during the Sino-French Controversy 1880–1885* (Cambridge, Massachusetts, Harvard University Press, 1967), pp. 41–3.

6. Eastman, pp. 174–205.

7. Key-hiuk Kim, *The Last Phase of the East Asian World Order: Korea, Japan, and the Chinese Empire, 1860–1882* (Berkeley, University of California Press, 1980), pp. 4–38.

8. William G. Beasley, 'A question of timing and not of goals', in Mayo, pp. 25–30.

9. Peter Duus, *The Rise of Modern Japan* (Boston, Houghton Mifflin Company, 1976), p. 125.

10. Hsu, p. 112.

11. John E. Schrecker, *Imperialism and Chinese Nationalism: Germany in Shantung* (Cambridge, Massachusetts, Harvard University Press, 1971), pp. 1–42.

Notes

12. Robert Lee, *France and the Exploitation of China 1885–1901* (Hong Kong, Oxford University Press, 1989).
13. L.K. Young, *British Policy in China 1895–1902* (Oxford, Clarendon Press, 1970), pp. 43–91.
14. Lee, pp. 56–109.
15. Albert Feuerwerker, 'Economic trends in the late Ch'ing empire, 1870–1911', CHC ,11,, pp. 1–69.
16. P.J. Cain and A.G. Hopkins, *British Imperialism: Innovation and Expansion 1688–1914* (London, Longman, 1993), pp. 422–46.
17. See for example Andrew J. Nathan, 'Imperialism's effects on China', *Bulletin of Concerned Asian Scholars* ,4.4,, Dec. 1972, pp. 3–8; Joseph Esherick, 'Harvard on China: The apologetics of imperialism', *Bulletin of Concerned Asian Scholars* ,4.4,, Dec. 1972, pp. 9–16; John King Fairbank, 'Imperialism in China: An exchange', *Bulletin of Concerned Asian Scholars* ,5.2,, 1973, pp. 32–3.
18. Colin Mackerras, *Western Images of China* (Hong Kong, Oxford University Press, 1989), pp. 35–6.
19. Karl Marx, 'Revolution in China and Europe', *New York Daily Tribune*, 14 June 1853, in Dona Torr (ed.), *Marx on China 1853–1860: Articles from the New York Daily Tribune* (London, Lawrence & Wishart, 1968), pp. 1–2.
20. Chi-ming Hou, *Foreign Investment and Economic Development in China 1840–1937* (Cambridge, Massachusetts, Harvard University Press, 1965, 1973), pp. 91–6.
21. Torr, p. 3.
22. Feuerwerker, p. 19.
23. Jean Chesneaux, Marianne Bastid and Marie-Claire Bergère, *China from the Opium Wars to the 1911 Revolution* (New York, Pantheon Books, 1976), p. 214.
24. Feuerwerker, pp. 15–28.
25. Robert Fortune, *A Journey to the Tea Countries of China; Including Sung-lo and the Bohea Hills; with a Short Notice of the East India Company's Tea Plantations in the Himalaya Mountains* (London, John Murray, 1852, reprinted London, Mildmay Books, 1987).
26. Robert P. Gardella, 'Reform and the tea industry and trade in late Ch'ing China: The Fukien case', in Paul A. Cohen and John E. Schrecker (eds), *Reform in Nineteenth-Century China* (Cambridge, Massachusetts, Harvard University Press, 1976), pp. 71–9.
27. Lilian M. Li, *China's Silk Trade: Traditional Industry in the Modern World 1842–1937* (Cambridge, Massachusetts, Harvard University Press, 1981), p. 164.
28. Robert Y. Eng, *Economic Imperialism in China: Silk Production and Exports, 1861–1932* (Berkeley, University of California Press, 1986).
29. Li, pp. 197–206.
30. Eng, pp. 181–96.
31. Nathan, p. 4.
32. Hou, p. 197.
33. Hou, pp. 194–210.
34. Hou, pp. 39–42.
35. O.D. Rasmussen, *Tientsin: An Illustrated Outline History* (Tientsin, Tientsin Press, 1925), quoted in J.A.G. Roberts, *China Through Western Eyes: The Twentieth Century* (Stroud, Alan Sutton, 1992), pp. 51–2.
36. Mark Elvin, *The Pattern of the Chinese Past* (London, Eyre Methuen, 1973), pp. 285–316.
37. Robert F. Dernberger, 'The role of the foreigner in China's economic development', in Dwight H. Perkins (ed.), *China's Modern Economy in Historical Perspective* (Stanford, Stanford University Press, 1975), pp. 19–47.
38. Feuerwerker, p. 16.
39. Hou, p. 214.
40. Dernberger, pp. 28–30, 39.
41. Rhoads Murphey, 'The treaty ports and China's modernization', in Mark Elvin and G. William Skinner (eds), *The Chinese City Between Two Worlds* (Stanford, Stanford University Press, 1974), pp. 17–71.
42. William T. Rowe, *Hankow: Commerce and Society in a Chinese City, 1796–1889* (Stanford, Stanford University Press, 1984), p. 13.
43. Esherick, pp. 13–14.
44. Liang-li T'ang, *China in Revolt. How a Civilization Became a Nation*, quoted in Jessie G. Lutz (ed.), *Christian Missions in China: Evangelists of What?* (Boston, D.C. Heath and Company, 1965), p. 51.

45. Paul A. Cohen, *China and Christianity: The Missionary Movement and the Growth of Chinese Antiforeignism 1860–1870* (Cambridge, Massachusetts, Harvard University Press, 1963, 1967), p. 11.
46. Paul A. Cohen, 'Christian missions and their impact to 1900', CHC ,10,, pp. 543–90.
47. Evelyn S. Rawski, 'Elementary education in the mission enterprise', in Suzanne Wilson Barnett and John King Fairbank (eds), *Christianity in China: Early Protestant Missionary Writings* (Cambridge, Massachusetts, Harvard University Press, 1985), pp. 135–51.
48. K.S. Latourette, *A History of Christian Missions in China* (London, Society for Promoting Christian Knowledge, 1929), pp. 537, 680.
49. Pat Barr, *To China with Love: The Lives and Times of Protestant Missionaries in China 1860–1900* (Newton Abbot, Victorian & Modern History Book Club, 1973), p. 11.
50. Cohen, 'Christian Missions', pp. 574–6.
51. Rawski, pp. 136–7.
52. John King Fairbank, E.O. Reischauer and Albert M. Craig, *East Asia: The Modern Transformation* (Boston, Houghton Mifflin Company, 1965), pp. 333, 660.
53. Ellsworth C. Carlson, *The Foochow Missionaries, 1847–1880* (Cambridge, Massachusetts, Harvard University Press, 1974), p. 11.
54. Cohen, *China and Christianity*, p. 21.
55. Arthur W. Hummel (ed.), *Eminent Chinese of the Ch'ing Period (1644–1912)* (United States Government Printing Office, Washington, 1943–4; Taipei, Literature House Ltd, 1964), pp. 889–92.
56. J.C. Cheng, *Chinese Sources for the Taiping Rebellion 1850–1864* (Hong Kong, Hong Kong University Press, 1963), pp. 13–38.
57. Vincent Y.C. Shih, *The Taiping Ideology: Its Sources, Interpretations, and Influences* (Seattle, University of Washington Press, 1967, 1972), pp. 397–8.
58. Shih, p. 423.
59. Cohen, *China and Christianity*, pp. 34–60.
60. Cohen, *China and Christianity*, pp. 88–109.
61. Cohen, *China and Christianity*, pp. 229–47.
62. Cohen, 'Christian missions', p. 573.

Chapter Eighteen
1. Jerome B. Grieder, *Intellectuals and the State in Modern China: A Narrative History* (New York, The Free Press, 1983), pp. 36–47.
2. Charlton M. Lewis, *Prologue to the Chinese Revolution: The Transformation of Ideas and Institutions in Hunan Province, 1891–1907* (Cambridge, Massachusetts, Harvard University Press, 1976), p. 4.
3. See above p. 30–1.
4. Frederic Wakeman, jr, *Strangers at the Gate: Social Disorder in South China, 1839–1861* (Berkeley, University of California Press, 1966), pp. 11–58.
5. J.D. Frodsham, *The First Chinese Embassy to the West: The Journals of Kuo Sung-t'ao, Liu Hsi-hung and Chang Te-yi* (Oxford, Clarendon Press, 1974), p. xxxvii. The 'nation of Yao and Shun' is a reference to China.
6. Paul A. Cohen, *Between Tradition and Modernity: Wang T'ao and Reform in Late Ch'ing China* (Cambridge, Massachusetts, Harvard University Press, 1974), p. 232.
7. John E. Schrecker, *Imperialism and Chinese Nationalism: Germany in Shantung* (Cambridge, Massachusetts, Harvard University Press, 1971), pp. 249–59.
8. Mary Clabaugh Wright, 'Introduction: The rising tide of change', in Mary Clabaugh Wright (ed.), *China in Revolution: The First Phase 1900–1913* (New Haven, Yale University Press, 1973), p. 3.
9. Grieder, p. 52.
10. Luke S.K. Kwong, *A Mosaic of the Hundred Days: Personalities, Politics, and Ideas of 1898* (Cambridge, Massachusetts, Harvard University Press, 1984), pp. 87–90.
11. Lewis, pp. 41–5. See also Joseph W. Esherick, *Reform and Revolution in China: The 1911 Revolution in Hunan and Hubei* (Berkeley, University of California Press, 1976), pp. 13–16.
12. Hao Chang, 'Intellectual change and the reform movement, 1890–8', CHC ,11,, pp. 274–338.
13. Kwong, pp. 129–30.
14. Ssu-yu Teng and John King Fairbank (eds), *China's Response to the West: A Documentary Survey 1839–1923* (New York, Atheneum, 1963), pp. 177–9.

Notes

15. Kwong, p. 197.
16. Daniel H. Bays, *China Enters the Twentieth Century: Chang Chih-tung and the Issues of a New Age, 1895–1909* (Ann Arbor, University of Michigan Press, 1978), pp. 30, 40–1.
17. Lewis, pp. 42–3, 54–68.
18. Kwong, pp. 213–24. See also Jerome Ch'en, *Yuan Shih-k'ai 1859–1916: Brutus Assumes the Purple*, second edition (London, George Allen & Unwin Ltd, 1972), pp. 38–43.
19. Sue Fawn Chung, 'The image of the Empress Dowager Tz'u-hsi', in Paul A. Cohen and John E. Schrecker (eds), *Reform in Nineteenth-Century China* (Cambridge, Massachusetts, Harvard University Press, 1976), pp. 101–10.
20. Kwong, p. 223.
21. Hosea Ballou Morse, *International Relations of the Chinese Empire* (3 vols, Shanghai, 1910; Paragon Reprint, New York), III, pp. 158–9.
22. Lewis, p. 59.
23. Jack Gray, *Rebellions and Revolutions: China from the 1800s to the 1980s* (Oxford, Oxford University Press, 1990), pp. 132–5.
24. Chang, pp. 329–38.
25. Joseph R. Levenson, *Liang Ch'i-ch'ao and the Mind of Modern China*, second revised edition (London, Thames and Hudson, 1965).
26. David D. Buck (ed.), *Recent Chinese Studies of the Boxer Movement* (New York, M.E. Sharpe, 1987), p. 3.
27. James P. Harrison, *The Communists and Chinese Peasant Rebellions: A Study in the Rewriting of Chinese History* (London, Victor Gollancz Ltd, 1970), p. 233.
28. Joseph W. Esherick, *The Origins of the Boxer Uprising* (Berkeley, University of California Press, 1987), p. xiii.
29. Esherick, *Boxer Uprising*, pp. 219–21.
30. Esherick, *Boxer Uprising*, p. 46.
31. Schrecker, pp. 11–14, 33.
32. Buck, pp. 18–20.
33. Esherick, *Boxer Uprising*, pp. 206–23.
34. Victor Purcell, *The Boxer Uprising: A Background Study* (Cambridge, Cambridge University Press, 1963), pp. 213–14 and Esherick, *Boxer Uprising*, p. 226 and note 86.
35. Esherick, *Boxer Uprising*, p. 272.
36. Esherick, *Boxer Uprising*, p. 273.
37. Immanuel C.Y. Hsu, 'Late Ch'ing foreign relations, 1866–1905', CHC ,11,, pp. 70–141, at p. 123.
38. The view that Rong Lu acted as a restraining force during the siege was supported by a document known as 'The diary of His Excellency Ching Shan', a translation of which appeared in J.O.P. Bland and E. Backhouse, *China Under the Empress Dowager* (London, Heinemann, 1910), pp. 251–306. It is now clear that this was a forgery perpetrated by Edmund Backhouse. See Hugh Trevor-Roper, *Hermit of Peking: The Hidden Life of Sir Edmund Backhouse* (Harmondsworth, Penguin Books, 1978).
39. John King Fairbank, *The United States and China*, fourth edition (Cambridge, Massachusetts, Harvard University Press, 1983), pp. 320–2.
40. Sir Robert Hart, *'These From the Land of Sinim'* (London, Chapman & Hall, 1901), p. 50.
41. Kang Youwei, 'Statement for the "Society for the Study of Self-Strengthening" ', 1895, quoted in Teng and Fairbank, p. 152.
42. Purcell, p. 271.
43. Mingnan Ding, 'Some questions concerning the appraisal of the Boxer movement', in Buck, pp. 24–41.
44. Bays, pp. 163–84.
45. Schrecker, pp. 171–91, 249–59.
46. Teng and Fairbank, p. 196.
47. William Ayers, *Chang Chih-tung and Educational Reform in China* (Cambridge, Massachusetts, Harvard University Press, 1971), pp. 215–16, 239–44.
48. Chuzo Ichiko, 'Political and institutional reform, 1901–11', CHC ,11,, pp. 375–415.
49. Ayers, pp. 113–21.
50. Ichiko, pp. 412–13.

51. Sir Alexander Hosie, *On the Trail of the Opium Poppy* (2 vols, London, George Philip & Son, 1914), II, pp. 287–8.
52. Ralph William Huenemann, *The Dragon and the Iron Horse: The Economics of Railroads in China 1876–1937* (Cambridge, Massachusetts, Harvard University Press, 1984), p. 61.
53. Quoted in P'eng-yüan Chang, 'The Constitutionalists', in Wright (ed.), *China in Revolution*, p. 160.
54. P'eng, pp. 145–53.
55. A. de Tocqueville and S. Gilbert (trs.), *The Ancien Régime and the French Revolution* (London, Fontana, 1976), p. 196.
56. Meribeth E. Cameron, *The Reform Movement in China 1898–1912* (Stanford, Stanford University Press, 1931), pp. 199–200.
57. Mary Clabaugh Wright, 'Introduction' to Wright (ed.), *China in Revolution*, pp. 29–30.
58. Frederic Wakeman, jr, *The Fall of Imperial China* (New York, The Free Press, 1975), p. 228.
59. Ichiko, pp. 411–15.

Chapter Nineteen
1. Colin Mackerras, *Western Images of China* (Hong Kong, Oxford University Press, 1989), p. 110.
2. Frederic Wakeman jr, *The Fall of Imperial China* (New York, The Free Press, 1975), p. 166.
3. Wakeman, pp. 234–5.
4. Lloyd E. Eastman, *Family, Fields, and Ancestors: Constancy and Change in China's Social and Economic History, 1550–1949* (Oxford, Oxford University Press, 1988), pp. 203–4.
5. Edmund S.K. Fung, *The Military Dimension of the Chinese Revolution: The New Army and Its Role in the Revolution of 1911* (Canberra, Australian National University Press, 1980), pp. 62–86.
6. Eastman, p. 194.
7. Jerome Ch'en, *China and the West: Society and Culture 1815–1937* (London, Hutchinson, 1979), pp. 220–4.
8. Michael R. Godley, *The Mandarin-capitalists from Nanyang: Overseas Chinese Enterprise in the Modernization of China 1893–1911* (Cambridge, Cambridge University Press, 1981), pp. 1–4.
9. Edward J.M. Rhoads, 'Merchant associations in Canton, 1895–1911', in Mark Elvin and G. William Skinner (eds), *The Chinese City Between Two Worlds* (Stanford, Stanford University Press, 1974), pp. 97–118.
10. Mary Backus Rankin, *Elite Activism and Political Transformation in China: Zhejiang Province, 1865–1911* (Stanford, Stanford University Press, 1986), p. 175.
11. Sally Borthwick, *Education and Social Change in China: The Beginnings of the Modern Era* (Stanford, Hoover Institution Press, 1983), pp. 128–45.
12. Borthwick, pp. 114–18.
13. Marius Jansen, 'Japan and the Chinese revolution of 1911', CHC ,11,, pp. 339–74, at pp. 348–53.
14. Ch'en, pp. 158–9.
15. Marianne Bastid-Bruguière, 'Currents of social change', CHC ,11,, pp. 535–602, at pp. 571–6.
16. Mark Elvin, 'Introduction', Elvin and Skinner, *The Chinese City*, pp. 1–15.
17. See Kung-chuan Hsiao, *Rural China: Imperial Control in the Nineteenth Century* (Seattle, University of Washington Press, 1967), pp. 396–407 and Albert Feuerwerker, 'Economic trends in the late Ch'ing empire, 1870–1911', CHC ,11,, pp. 2–15.
18. Bastid-Bruguière, pp. 586–9.
19. Feuerwerker, p. 6.
20. Arthur H. Smith, *Village Life in China: A Study in Sociology* (New York, Fleming H. Revell Company, 1899), p. 312.
21. Michael Gasster, 'The republican re-volutionary movement', CHC ,11,, pp. 463–534, at p. 463. See also Mary Clabaugh Wright (ed.), *China in Revolution: The First Phase, 1900–1913* (New Haven, Yale University Press, 1973), pp. 45–8.
22. Harold Z. Schiffrin, 'The enigma of Sun Yat-sen', in Wright (ed.), *China in Revolution*, pp. 443–74.
23. Chün-tu Hsüeh and Geraldine R. Schiff, 'The life and writings of Tsou Jung', in Chün-tu Hsüeh (ed.), *Revolutionary Leaders of Modern China* (London, Oxford University Press, 1971), pp. 153–209.
24. Mary Backus Rankin, 'The emergence of women at the end of the Ch'ing: The case of Ch'iu Chin', in M. Wolf and R. Witke (eds), *Women in Chinese Society* (Stanford, Stanford University Press, 1975), pp. 39–66.

25. Charlton M. Lewis, *Prologue to the Chinese Revolution: The Transformation of Ideas and Institutions in Hunan Province, 1891–1907* (Cambridge, Massachusetts, Harvard University Press, 1976), pp. 163–6, 185–96, 197–201.

26. Lewis, p. 177.

27. Schiffrin, pp. 462–3.

28. Ssu-yu Teng and John King Fairbank (eds), *China's Response to the West: A Documentary Survey 1839–1923* (New York, Atheneum, 1963), pp. 227–9.

29. Gasster, pp. 505–6.

30. Gasster, p. 515.

31. Albert Feuerwerker, *China's Early Industrialization: Sheng Hsuan-huai (1844–1916) and Mandarin Enterprise* (New York, Atheneum, 1970), pp. 81–2.

32. Ralph William Huenemann, *The Dragon and the Iron Horse: The Economics of Railroads in China 1876–1937* (Cambridge, Massachusetts, Harvard University Press, 1984), pp. 72–80.

33. John Fincher, 'Political provincialism and the national revolution', in Wright (ed.), *China in Revolution*, pp.185–226, at pp. 205, 216.

34. Gasster, pp. 520–4.

35. Fung, pp. 202–3.

36. Vidya Prakash Dutt, 'The first week of revolution: The Wuchang uprising', in Wright (ed.), *China in Revolution*, pp. 383–416.

37. See for example Immanuel C.Y. Hsü, *The Rise of Modern China*, fifth edition (Oxford, Oxford University Press, 1995), pp. 470–82 and Ernest P. Young, 'Yuan Shih-k'ai's rise to the Presidency', in Wright (ed.), *China in Revolution*, pp. 419–42.

38. Young, pp. 423, 425.

39. Reginald F. Johnston, *Twilight in the Forbidden City* (Victor Gollancz, 1934; Oxford, Oxford University Press, 1989), pp. 95–7.

40. Wright, *China in Revolution*, p. 23.

41. Pamela Kyle Crossley, *Orphan Warriors: Three Manchu Generations and the End of the Qing World* (Princeton, Princeton University Press, 1990), pp. 197, 224–8.

42. Wright, *China in Revolution*, pp. 62–3.

43. Jerome B. Grieder, 'Communism, nationalism, and democracy: The Chinese intelligentsia and the Chinese revolution in the 1920s and 1930s', in James B. Crowley (ed.), *Modern East Asia: Essays in Interpretation* (New York, Harcourt, Brace & World, Inc., 1970), pp. 207–34.

44. Stuart R. Schram, *The Political Thought of Mao Tse-tung*, revised edition (New York, Frederick A. Praeger, 1969), p. 230.

45. Michael Gasster, 'Comments from authors reviewed', *Modern China* ,2.2,, April 1976, p. 205.

46. James E. Sheridan, *China in Disintegration: The Republican Era in Chinese History, 1912–1949* (New York, The Free Press, 1975), pp. 18–21.

47. P'eng-yüan Chang, 'The Constitutionalists', in Wright (ed.), *China in Revolution*, pp. 143–83.

48. Chuzo Ichiko, 'The role of the gentry: An hypothesis', in Wright (ed.), *China in Revolution*, pp. 297–317.

49. Joseph W. Esherick, '1911: A review', *Modern China* ,2.2,, April 1976, pp. 141–82, at pp. 162–8.

50. Edward J.M. Rhoads, *China's Republican Revolution: The Case of Kwangtung, 1895–1913* (Cambridge, Massachusetts, Harvard University Press, 1975), pp. 222–9.

51. Marie-Claire Bergère, 'The role of the bourgeoisie', in Wright (ed.), *China in Revolution*, pp. 229–95.

52. John Lust, 'Secret societies, popular movements, and the 1911 revolution', in Jean Chesneaux (ed.), *Popular Movements and Secret Societies in China 1840–1950* (Stanford, Stanford University Press, 1972), pp. 165–200. See also, Esherick, '1911', pp. 173–8.

Chapter Twenty

1. Ernest P. Young, *The Presidency of Yuan Shih-k'ai: Liberalism and Dictatorship in Early Republican China* (Ann Arbor, University of Michigan Press, 1977) and 'Politics in the aftermath of revolution: The era of Yuan Shih-k'ai, 1912–16', CHC ,12,, pp. 209–55.

2. K.S. Liew, *Struggle for Democracy: Sung Chiao-jen and the 1911 Chinese Revolution* (Berkeley, University of California Press, 1971), pp. 172–84.

3. Albert Feuerwerker, 'Economic trends, 1912–1949', CHC ,12,, pp. 28–127 at pp. 100–1.
4. Edward J.M. Rhoads, China's Republican Revolution: The Case of Kwangtung, 1895–1913 (Cambridge, Massachusetts, Harvard University Press, 1975), pp. 260–1.
5. Marie-Claire Bergère, 'The Chinese bourgeoisie, 1911–37', CHC ,12,, pp. 721–825 at pp. 741–2.
6. Rhoads, pp. 261–2.
7. Young, 'The era of Yuan Shih-k'ai', p. 234.
8. Young, Yuan Shih-k'ai, pp. 141–2.
9. For the text see David John Lu, Sources of Japanese History (2 vols, New York, McGraw-Hill Book Company, 1974), II, pp. 106–9.
10. Quoted in Jerome Ch'en, Yuan Shih-k'ai, 1859–1916: Brutus Assumes the Purple, second edition (London, George Allen & Unwin, 1972), p. 156.
11. Ikuhiko Hata, 'Continental expansion, 1905–1941', in Peter Duus (ed.), The Cambridge History of Japan, Volume 6: The Twentieth Century (Cambridge, Cambridge University Press, 1988), pp. 271–314 at pp. 280–1.
12. Ch'en, p. 152.
13. Young, Yuan Shih-k'ai, pp. 189–90.
14. Young, Yuan Shih-k'ai, p. 219.
15. Young, Yuan Shih-k'ai, p. 231.
16. Young, Yuan Shih-k'ai, p. 238.
17. Reginald F. Johnston, Twilight in the Forbidden City (London, Victor Gollancz Ltd, 1934; Oxford, Oxford University Press, 1987), pp. 138–9.
18. James E. Sheridan, 'The warlord era: Politics and militarism under the Peking government, 1916–28', CHC ,12,, pp. 284–321 at pp. 308–9.
19. Andrew J. Nathan, 'A constitutional republic: The Peking government, 1916–28', CHC ,12,, pp. 256–83 at p. 256.
20. Nathan, pp. 267, 283.
21. For a summary of the literature see J.A.G. Roberts, 'Warlordism in China', Review of African Political Economy ,45/6,, 1989, pp. 26–33.
22. Ch'en, p. 214.
23. Stephen R. MacKinnon, 'The Peiyang army, Yüan Shih-k'ai, and the origins of modern Chinese warlordism', Journal of Asian Studies ,32.3,, 1973, pp. 405–23.
24. Young, Yuan Shih-k'ai, p. 242.
25. Franz Michael, 'Introduction', in Stanley Spector, Li Hung-chang and the Huai Army: A Study in Nineteenth-Century Chinese Regionalism (Seattle, University of Washington Press, 1964), pp. xxi–xliii.
26. James E. Sheridan, Chinese Warlord: The Career of Feng Yü-hsiang (Stanford, Stanford University Press, 1966), p. 1.
27. Sheridan, 'The warlord era', p. 284.
28. Odoric Y.K. Wou, Militarism in Modern China: The Career of Wu P'ei-fu, 1916–39 (Canberra, Australian National University Press, 1978), p. 76.
29. Gavan McCormack, Chang Tso-lin in Northeast China, 1911–1928: China, Japan, and the Manchurian Idea (Folkestone, Dawson, 1977), p. 201.
30. Yü-t'ang Lin, 'The Dog-meat general', in Edgar Snow (ed.), Living China: Modern Chinese Short Stories (London, George C. Harrap & Co. Ltd, 1936), pp. 222–5.
31. Donald G. Gillin, 'Portrait of a warlord: Yen Hsi-shan in Shansi province, 1911–1930', Journal of Asian Studies ,19.3,, May 1960, pp. 289–306.
32. C. Martin Wilbur, 'Military separatism and the process of reunification under the Nationalist regime, 1922–1937', in Ping-ti Hou and Tang Tsou (eds), China in Crisis (Chicago, University of Chicago Press, 1968), volume I, Part 1, pp. 203–63.
33. Donald S. Sutton, Provincial Militarism and the Chinese Republic: The Yunnan Army, 1905–1925 (Ann Arbor, University of Michigan Press, 1980), pp. 259–60.
34. Wou, pp. 71–2.
35. Sheridan, Chinese Warlord, p. 157.
36. McCormack, p. 134.
37. Wou, pp. 151–97.

38. C.P. Fitzgerald, *The Birth of Communist China* (Harmondsworth, Penguin Books, 1964), p. 52.
39. John K. Chang, *Industrial Development in Pre-Communist China: A Quantitative Analysis* (Edinburgh, Edinburgh University Press, 1969), pp. 60–1.
40. Tse-tsung Chow, *The May Fourth Movement: Intellectual Revolution in Modern China* (Cambridge, Massachusetts, Harvard University Press, 1960, 1967), pp. 84–144.
41. Joseph T. Chen, *The May Fourth Movement in Shanghai: The Making of a Social Movement in Modern China* (Leiden, E.J. Brill, 1971).
42. Chow, pp. 145–67.
43. Mary Clabaugh Wright, *China in Revolution: The First Phase, 1900–1913* (New Haven, Yale University Press, 1968) pp. 10, 33.
44. Chow, pp. 22, 130–1.
45. Marie-Claire Bergère, *The Golden Age of the Chinese Bourgeoisie 1911–1937* (Cambridge, Cambridge University Press, 1989), p. 50.
46. Chow, p. 379.
47. Bergère, *The Golden Age*, pp. 207–17.
48. Charlotte Furth, 'May Fourth in history', in Benjamin I. Schwartz (ed.), *Reflections on the May Fourth Movement: A Symposium* (Cambridge, Massachusetts, Harvard University Press, 1972), pp. 59–68.
49. Jerome B. Grieder, *Intellectuals and the State in Modern China: A Narrative History* (New York, The Free Press, 1981), p. 217.
50. Jerome B. Grieder, *Hu Shih and the Chinese Renaissance: Liberalism in the Chinese Revolution, 1917–1937* (Cambridge, Massachusetts, Harvard University Press, 1970), p. 78.
51. Jonathan D. Spence, *The Gate of Heavenly Peace: The Chinese and Their Revolution, 1895–1980* (London, Faber and Faber, 1982), p. 107.
52. Ssu-yu Teng and John King Fairbank (eds), *China's Response to the West: A Documentary Survey 1839–1923* (New York, Atheneum, 1963), p. 240.
53. Yü-sheng Lin, *The Crisis of Chinese Consciousness: Radical Anti-traditionalism in the May Fourth Era* (Madison, University of Wisconsin Press, 1979), pp. 56–81.
54. W.T. de Bary et al. (eds), *Sources of Chinese Tradition* (2 vols, New York, Columbia University Press, 1964), II, pp. 153–6.
55. Young, *Yuan Shih-k'ai*, p. 198.
56. Grieder, *Hu Shih*, p. 80.
57. Chow, p. 276.
58. Spence, pp. 109–10. 'A Madman's Diary' is included in Gladys Yang (ed. and tr.), *Silent China: Selected Writings of Lu Xun* (Oxford, Oxford University Press, 1973), pp. 3–13.
59. Chow, p. 279.
60. Chow, p. 59.
61. Martin Bernal, 'Chinese Socialism before 1913', in Jack Gray (ed.), *Modern China's Search for a Political Form* (London, Oxford University Press, 1969), pp. 66–95.
62. Teng and Fairbank, pp. 246–9.
63. Arif Dirlik, *The Origins of Chinese Communism* (Oxford, Oxford University Press, 1989), p. 46.
64. Grieder, *Hu Shih*, pp. 45–51.
65. Teng and Fairbank, pp. 252–5.
66. Chow, p. 358.
67. Chen, pp. 6–7, 18–19.
68. Dirlik, pp. 3–15.
69. Yü-sun Chou, 'The May 4th Movement and the modernization of China', in Yu-ming Shaw (ed.), *Chinese Modernization* (San Francisco, Chinese Materials Center Publications, 1985), pp. 91–110.
70. Chow, pp. 342–7.
71. Stuart Schram, 'Mao Tse-tung's thought to 1949', CHC ,13,, pp. 789–870, at pp. 789–90.
72. Chow, pp. 350–1.
73. Jerome Ch'en, 'The Chinese Communist movement to 1927', CHC ,12,, pp. 505–26, at p. 507.
74. Lynda Shaffer, *Mao and the Workers: The Hunan Labor Movement, 1920–1923* (New York, M.E. Sharpe, 1982).
75. Wou, pp. 219–25.

76. C. Martin Wilbur, *The Nationalist Revolution in China, 1923–1928* (Cambridge, Cambridge University Press, 1983), pp. 2–5.
77. Ch'en, 'The Chinese Communist movement', p. 519.
78. Wilbur, pp. 8–14.
79. Jean Chesneaux, *The Chinese Labor Movement 1919–1927* (Stanford, Stanford University Press, 1968), pp. 247–8.
80. Roy Hofheinz jr, *The Broken Wave: The Chinese Communist Peasant Movement, 1922–1928* (Cambridge, Massachusetts, Harvard University Press, 1977), pp. 139–78; Fernando Galbiati, *P'eng P'ai and the Hai-Lu-feng Soviet* (Stanford, Stanford University Press, 1985), pp. 100–59.
81. Arthur Waldron, *From War to Nationalism: China's Turning Point, 1924–1925* (Cambridge, Cambridge University Press, 1995), pp. 1–10, 241–80.
82. Chesneaux, pp. 290–318.

Chapter Twenty-one
1. Han-seng Chen, *Landlord and Peasant in China: A Study of the Agrarian Crisis in South China* (New York, International Publishers, 1936; Westport, Hyperion Press Inc., 1973), p. 112.
2. John Lossing Buck, *Land Utilization in China* (Nanjing, University of Nanjing, 1937; New York, Paragon Book Reprint Corp., 1968), pp. 458–60.
3. Albert Feuerwerker, 'Economic trends, 1912–1949', CHC ,12,, pp. 28–127, at pp. 64, 67.
4. Ramon H. Myers, *The Chinese Economy: Past and Present* (Belmont, Wadsworth Inc., 1980), p. 181.
5. Thomas G. Rawski, *Economic Growth in Prewar China* (Berkeley, University of California Press, 1989), p. 321.
6. Lloyd E. Eastman, *Family, Fields, and Ancestors: Constancy and Change in China's Social and Economic History, 1550–1949* (New York, Oxford University Press, 1988), pp. 96–8.
7. Ramon H. Myers, *The Chinese Peasant Economy: Agricultural Development in Hopei and Shantung, 1890–1949* (Cambridge, Massachusetts, Harvard University Press, 1970).
8. Thomas B. Wiens, Review of Myers, *The Chinese Peasant Economy, Modern Asian Studies* ,9.2,, April 1975, pp. 279–88.
9. Robert Ash, *Land Tenure in Pre-Revolutionary China: Kiangsu Province in the 1920s and 1930s* (London, Contemporary China Institute, School of Oriental and African Studies, University of London, 1976), pp. xi, 50.
10. Philip C.C. Huang, *The Peasant Economy and Social Change in North China* (Stanford, Stanford University Press, 1985), p. 299. The quotation is from R.H. Tawney, *Land and Labour in China* (London, Allen and Unwin, 1932).
11. David Faure, *The Rural Economy of Pre-Liberation China: Trade Expansion and Peasant Livelihood in Jiangsu and Guangdong, 1870–1930* (Hong Kong, Oxford University Press, 1989), p. 202.
12. Donald A. Jordan, *The Northern Expedition: China's National Revolution of 1926–1928* (Honolulu, University Press of Hawaii, 1976), p. 67.
13. Harold R. Isaacs, *The Tragedy of the Chinese Revolution* (London, Secker & Warburg, 1938), p. 126.
14. Roy Hofheinz jr, *The Broken Wave: The Chinese Communist Peasant Movement, 1922–1928* (Cambridge, Massachusetts, Harvard University Press, 1977), p. 130.
15. James E. Sheridan, *China in Disintegration: The Republican Era in Chinese History, 1912–1949* (New York, The Free Press, 1977), pp. 167–8 and Angus W. McDonald, *The Urban Origins of Rural Revolution: Elites and the Masses in Hunan Province, China, 1911–1927* (Berkeley, University of California Press, 1978), pp. 264–80.
16. Vincent Sheean, *Personal History* (New York, Literary Guild, 1934), p. 226.
17. Hofheinz, p. 104.
18. Stuart Schram, *The Political Thought of Mao Tse-tung*, revised and enlarged edition (New York, Frederick A. Praeger, 1969), pp. 250–9. The reference to the poor peasants being the 'vanguard' of the revolution was deleted from the revised editions of Mao Zedong's works.
19. Marie-Claire Bergère, *The Golden Age of the Chinese Bourgeoisie 1911–1937* (Cambridge, Cambridge University Press, 1989), pp. 235–9.

Notes

20. C. Martin Wilbur, *The Nationalist Revolution in China, 1923–1928* (Cambridge, Cambridge University Press, 1984), pp. 88–113.
21. Joseph Fewsmith, *Party, State, and Local Elites in Republican China: Merchant Organizations and Politics in Shanghai, 1890–1930* (Honolulu, University of Hawaii Press, 1985), pp. 1–14, 197–203.
22. Wilbur, pp. 135–46.
23. Tso-liang Hsiao, *Chinese Communism in 1927: City vs Countryside* (Hong Kong, The Chinese University of Hong Kong, 1970), pp. 81–104.
24. Hofheinz, pp. 53–7.
25. Roy Hofheinz, 'The Autumn Harvest insurrection', *China Quarterly* ,32,, October 1967, pp. 37–87.
26. Jordan, p. 160.
27. Wilbur, pp. 180–5.
28. Richard T. Phillips, *China Since 1911* (London, Macmillan, 1996), p. 84.
29. Sheridan, p. 23.
30. Robert E. Bedeski, 'China's wartime state', in James C. Hsiung and Steven I. Levine (eds), *China's Bitter Victory: The War with Japan 1937–1945* (New York, M.E. Sharpe Inc., 1992), pp. 33–49.
31. Jean Chesneaux, Françoise Le Barbier and Marie-Claire Bergère, *China from the 1911 Revolution to Liberation* (Hassocks, The Harvester Press, 1977), p. 198.
32. (Anonymous) *An Outline History of China* (Beijing, Foreign Languages Press, 1958), p. 371.
33. Lloyd E. Eastman, *The Abortive Revolution: China under Nationalist Rule, 1927–1937* (Cambridge, Massachusetts, Harvard University Press, 1974), pp. 10–11, 18–19.
34. Tuan-sheng Ch'ien, *The Government and Politics of China, 1912–1949* (Stanford, Stanford University Press, 1970), pp. 177–90.
35. Feuerwerker, p. 106.
36. Arthur N. Young, *China's Nation-Building Effort, 1927–1937: The Financial and Economic Record* (Stanford, Stanford University, Hoover Institution Press, 1971), p. 163.
37. Douglas S. Paauw, 'The Kuomintang and economic stagnation 1928–1937', in Albert Feuerwerker (ed.), *Modern China* (Englewood Cliffs, Prentice-Hall Inc., 1964), pp. 126–35.
38. Parks M. Coble, *The Shanghai Capitalists and the Nationalist Government, 1927–1937* (Cambridge, Massachusetts, Harvard University Press, 1986), pp. 18, 197–9.
39. Feuerwerker, p. 93.
40. Young, p. 29.
41. Young, pp. 314–25.
42. Eastman, *The Abortive Revolution*, pp. 210–12.
43. John K. Chang, *Industrial Development in Pre-Communist China: A Quantitative Analysis* (Edinburgh, Edinburgh University Press, 1969), pp. 60, 99.
44. Young, pp. 396–7.
45. Tim Wright, *Coal Mining in China's Economy and Society 1895–1937* (Cambridge, Cambridge University Press, 1984), pp. 70–1, 194.
46. Wright, p. 13, quoting Dwight H. Perkins, 'Growth and changing structure of China's twentieth-century economy', in Dwight H. Perkins (ed.), *China's Modern Economy in Historical Perspective* (Stanford, Stanford University Press, 1975), pp. 115–65, at p. 119.
47. Feuerwerker, pp. 57–63.
48. Chang, p. 115.
49. Young, p. 306.
50. Feuerwerker, p. 88.
51. Paauw, p. 135.
52. Young, p. 395.
53. Feuerwerker, p. 99.
54. Rawski, pp. xxi–xxii, 332, 344.
55. Colin Mackerras, 'Education in the Guomindang period, 1928–1949', in David Pong and Edmund S.K. Fung (eds), *Ideal and Reality: Social and Political Change in Modern China 1860–1949* (New York, University Press of America, 1985), pp. 153–83.
56. E-tu Zen Sun, 'The growth of the academic community 1912–1949', CHC ,13,, pp. 361–420.
57. Sheridan, p. 231.

58. Sun, pp. 391–6.

59. Wen-hsin Yeh, *The Alienated Academy: Culture and Politics in Republican China, 1919–1937* (Cambridge, Massachusetts, Harvard University Press, 1990).

60. Mary C. Wright, 'From revolution to restoration: The transformation of Kuomintang ideology', *Far Eastern Quarterly* ,14.4,, August 1955, pp. 515–32, reprinted in Joseph R. Levenson, *Modern China: An Interpretative Anthology* (London, Macmillan, 1971), pp. 99–113.

61. Lloyd E. Eastman, 'The Kuomintang in the 1930s', in Charlotte Furth (ed.), *The Limits of Change: Essays on Conservative Alternatives in Republican China* (Cambridge, Massachusetts, Harvard University Press, 1976), pp. 191–210. A similar view was expressed in Hung-mao Tien, *Government and Politics in Kuomintang China 1927–1937* (Stanford, Stanford University Press, 1972), p. 64.

62. Maria Hsia Chang, ' "Fascism" and modern China', *China Quarterly* ,79,, September 1979, pp. 553–67.

63. Quoted in Eastman, *The Abortive Revolution*, p. 67.

64. Young, p. 426; Edmund S.K. Fung, 'Nationalist foreign policy, 1928–1937', in Pong and Fung, pp. 185–217.

65. Jerome Ch'en, 'The Communist movement 1927–1937', CHC ,13,, pp. 168–229 at p. 171.

66. Jacques Guillermaz, *A History of the Chinese Communist Party 1921–1949* (London, Methuen and Co. Ltd, 1972), p. 179.

67. Richard C. Thornton, *The Comintern and the Chinese Communists 1928–1931* (Seattle, University of Washington Press, 1969).

68. Benjamin I. Schwartz, *Chinese Communism and the Rise of Mao* (Cambridge, Massachusetts, Harvard University Press, 1951, 1968), p. 133.

69. Guillermaz, pp. 196–201.

70. Stuart Schram, *Mao Tse-tung* (Harmondsworth, Penguin Books, 1967), p. 136.

71. Jerome Ch'en, *Mao and the Chinese Revolution* (London, Oxford University Press, 1967), p. 157.

72. Schram, *Political Thought of Mao Tse-tung*, p. 272.

73. Schram, *Political Thought of Mao Tse-tung*, p. 258.

74. Mao Zedong, *Report from Xunwu*, translated with an introduction and notes by Roger R. Thompson (Stanford, Stanford University Press, 1990), pp. 212–17.

75. Delia Davin, 'Women in the Liberated Areas', in Marilyn B. Young (ed.), *Women in China: Studies in Social Change and Feminism* (Ann Arbor, Center for Chinese Studies, University of Michigan, 1973), pp. 73–91.

76. Tso-liang Hsiao, *The Land Revolution in China, 1930–1934: A Study of Documents* (Seattle, University of Washington Press, 1969), pp. 3–77.

77. Guillermaz, p. 213.

78. Trygve Lötveit, *Chinese Communism 1931–1934: Experience in Civil Government*, second edition (Copenhagen, Curzon Press, 1978), pp. 154–84.

79. Guillermaz, pp. 224–6.

80. Edgar Snow, *Red Star Over China* (London, Victor Gollancz Ltd, 1937), p. 179.

81. Otto Braun, *A Comintern Agent in China 1932–1939* (London, Hurst, 1982), pp. 81–4.

82. Lötveit, pp. 210–11.

83. The subsequent history of the Jiangxi base and of the dozen other bases in south China – a record which challenges the Mao-centred explanation of Communist success – is investigated in Gregor Benton, *Mountain Fires: The Red Army's Three-Year War in South China, 1934–1938* (Berkeley, University of California Press, 1992).

84. Benjamin Yang, 'The Zunyi conference as one step in Mao's rise to power: A survey of historical studies of the Chinese Communist Party', *China Quarterly* ,106,, 1986, pp. 235–71.

85. Dick Wilson, *The Long March: The Epic of Chinese Communism's Survival* (Harmondsworth, Penguin Books, 1971, 1977), pp. 292–318; Snow, pp. 194–6, 204–5; Schram, *Mao Tse-tung*, pp. 187–8.

86. Snow, p. 207.

87. Wilson, pp. 292–318.

88. Robert J. Lifton, 'The death of the leader', in Richard Baum and Louise B. Bennett (eds), *China in Ferment: Perspectives on the Cultural Revolution* (Englewood Cliffs, Prentice-Hall Inc., 1971), pp. 88–94.

Notes

Chapter Twenty-two

1. Akira Iriye, 'Japanese aggression and China's international position 1931–1949', CHC ,13,, pp. 492–546.

2. John Israel, *Student Nationalism in China 1927–1937* (Stanford, Stanford University Press, 1966), pp. 111–56.

3. Parks M. Coble, 'Chiang Kai-shek and the Anti-Japanese movement in China: Zou Tao-fen and the National Salvation Association, 1931–1937', *Journal of Asian Studies* ,44.2,, February 1985, pp. 293–310.

4. One of the Seven Gentlemen was a woman lawyer. See Tien-wei Wu, *The Sian Incident: A Pivotal Point in Modern Chinese History* (Ann Arbor, University of Michigan Center for Chinese Studies, 1976), p. 223, n. 24.

5. Wu, p. 82.

6. Coble, p. 303.

7. Lyman Van Slyke, 'The Chinese Communist movement during the Sino-Japanese War 1937–1945', CHC ,13,, pp. 609–722.

8. Ikuhiko Hata, 'Continental expansion, 1905–1941', in Peter Duus (ed.), *The Cambridge History of Japan,Volume 6:The Twentieth Century* (Cambridge, Cambridge University Press, 1988), pp. 271–314.

9. Marvin Williamsen, 'The military dimension, 1937–1941', in James C. Hsiung and Steven I. Levine (eds), *China's BitterVictory:TheWar with Japan 1937–1945* (NewYork, M.E. Sharpe Inc., 1992), pp. 135–56, at p. 137.

10. Hsi-sheng Ch'i, *Nationalist China at War: Military Defeats and Political Collapse, 1937–1945* (Ann Arbor, University of Michigan Press, 1982), p. 43.

11. Ch'i, pp. 49–51.

12. Frank Oliver, *Special UndeclaredWar* (London, Cape, 1939), pp. 208–10.

13. John Hunter Boyle, *China and Japan at War, 1937–1945: The Politics of Collaboration* (Stanford, Stanford University Press, 1972), pp. 69–72.

14. Han-sheng Lin, 'A new look at Chinese Nationalist "appeasers" ', in Alvin D. Coox and Hilary Conroy (eds), *China and Japan: A Search for Balance since World War I* (Santa Barbara, ABC-Clio, Inc., 1978), pp. 211–41.

15. T'ien-wei Wu, 'Contending political forces during the war of resistance', in Hsiung and Levine, pp. 51–78.

16. Boyle, p. 362.

17. See pp. 162–3, above.

18. Poshek Fu, *Passivity, Resistance, and Collaboration: Intellectual Choices in Occupied Shanghai, 1937–1945* (Stanford, Stanford University Press, 1993).

19. Lloyd E. Eastman, *Seeds of Destruction: Nationalist China in War and Revolution 1937–1949* (Stanford, Stanford University Press, 1984), pp. 10–44.

20. Eastman, pp. 89–107.

21. E-tu Zen Sun, 'The growth of the academic community 1912–1949', CHC ,13,, pp. 361–420.

22. Lloyd E. Eastman, 'Nationalist China during the Sino-Japanese War 1937–1945', CHC ,13,, pp. 547–608.

23. William C. Kirby, 'The Chinese war economy', in Hsiung and Levine, pp. 185–212.

24. Hung-hsun Ling, 'China's epic struggle in developing its overland transportation system during the Sino-Japanese War', in Paul K.T. Sih (ed.), *Nationalist China During the Sino-Japanese War, 1937–1945* (New York, Exposition Press, 1977), pp. 243–71.

25. Arthur N. Young, *China and the Helping Hand 1937–1945* (Cambridge, Massachusetts, Harvard University Press, 1963), pp. 41–2; Eastman, *Seeds of Destruction*, p. 220.

26. Eastman, *Seeds of Destruction*, pp. 146–52.

27. Eastman, *Seeds of Destruction*, pp. 45–70.

28. Edmund Clubb, *Twentieth Century China*, second edition (New York, Columbia University Press, 1972), pp. 232–4.

29. Young, pp. 417–19.

30. Quoted in Michael Schaller, *The United States and China in the Twentieth Century* (New York, Oxford University Press, 1979), p. 70.

31. Ch'i, p. 82.
32. Stuart Schram, *The Political Thought of Mao Tse-tung*, revised and enlarged edition (London, Frederick A. Praeger, 1969), pp. 172–3.
33. Schram, p. 230.
34. Boyd Compton, *Mao's China: Party Reform Documents, 1942–44* (Seattle, University of Washington Press, 1952), pp. 9–53.
35. Yung-fa Chen, *Making Revolution: The Communist Movement in Eastern and Central China, 1937–1945* (Berkeley, University of California Press, 1986), pp. 223–58.
36. Quoted in Peter Schran, *Guerrilla Economy: The Development of the Shensi-Kansu-Ninghsia Border Region, 1937–1945* (Albany, State University of New York Press, 1976), p. 143.
37. Schran, pp. 186, 200.
38. Lee Ngok, 'Mass mobilization and revolutionary war in China, 1937–1945: The emergence of the "Yenan Way"', *Journal of Oriental Studies* ,11.2,, 1973, pp. 246–56.
39. Van Slyke, p. 621.
40. James Pinckney Harrison, *The Long March to Power: A History of the Chinese Communist Party, 1921–1972* (London, Macmillan, 1972), p. 284.
41. Chalmers A. Johnson, *Peasant Nationalism and Communist Power: The Emergence of Revolutionary China 1937–1945* (Stanford, Stanford University Press, 1962), pp. 56–8; Van Slyke, pp. 676–8.
42. John S. Service, *Lost Chance in China: The World War II Despatches of John S. Service*, edited by Joseph W. Esherick (New York, Random House, 1974), pp. 178–81.
43. Chang-tai Hung, *War and Popular Culture: Resistance in Modern China, 1937–1945* (Berkeley, University of California Press, 1994), pp. 221–69.
44. Jonathan D. Spence, *The Gate of Heavenly Peace: The Chinese and Their Revolution, 1895–1980* (London, Faber and Faber, 1982), pp. 285–95.
45. Johnson, p. 59.
46. Donald G. Gillin, ' "Peasant nationalism" in the history of Chinese Communism', *Journal of Asian Studies* ,23.2,, February 1964, pp. 269–89.
47. Mark Selden, *The Yenan Way in Revolutionary China* (Cambridge, Massachusetts, Harvard University Press, 1971, 1974), pp. 79–83, 208–9, 277.
48. Tetsuya Kataoka, *Resistance and Revolution in China: The Communists and the Second United Front* (Berkeley, University of California Press, 1974).
49. Chen, pp. 499–521.
50. Van Slyke, pp. 708–11.
51. Schaller, pp. 99–103.
52. Suzanne Pepper, 'The KMT-CCP conflict 1945–1949', CHC ,13,, pp. 723–88, at pp. 728–9.
53. Steven I. Levine, *Anvil of Victory: The Communist Revolution in Manchuria, 1945–1948* (New York, Columbia University Press, 1987), pp. 131–2.
54. Levine, p. 136.
55. The name adopted by the Communist forces in July 1946.
56. Major-General David Barr, 'Report of operational advice given to the Generalissimo . . . submitted early in 1949', in *United States Relations with China with Special Reference to the Period 1944–1949* (Washington, D.C., Government Printing Office, 1949), in Immanuel C.Y. Hsü (ed.), *Readings in Modern Chinese History* (New York, Oxford University Press, 1971), pp. 546–54.
57. Suzanne Pepper, *Civil War in China: The Political Struggle, 1945–1949* (Berkeley, University of California Press, 1978, 1980), pp. 9–35.
58. Pepper, *Civil War*, p. 204.
59. Pepper, *Civil War*, pp. 42–93.
60. Eastman, *Seeds of Destruction*, pp. 172–202.
61. Eastman, *Seeds of Destruction*, pp. 108–29.
62. Chong-sik Lee, *Revolutionary Struggle in Manchuria: Chinese Communism and Soviet Interest, 1922–1945* (Berkeley, University of California Press, 1983), pp. 307–21.
63. Levine, pp. 229–35.
64. Pepper, *Civil War*, p. 288.
65. Levine, p. 243.

Notes

66. Quoted in William Hinton, *Fanshen: A Documentary of Revolution in a Chinese Village* (Harmondsworth, Pelican Books, 1972), p. 469.
67. Delia Davin, 'Women in the Liberated Areas', in Marilyn B. Young (ed.), *Women in China: Studies in Social Change and Feminism* (Ann Arbor, University of Michigan Center for Chinese Studies, 1973), pp. 73–87.
68. Jack Belden, *China Shakes the World* (Harmondsworth, Penguin, 1973), pp. 300–1.
69. Pepper, *Civil War*, p. 329.
70. Pepper, *Civil War*, pp. 333–50.
71. Immanuel C.Y. Hsü, *The Rise of Modern China*, fifth edition (Oxford, Oxford University Press, 1995), p. 639.
72. Ch'i, p. 240.

Chapter Twenty-three
1. Maurice Meisner, *Mao's China: A History of the People's Republic* (New York, The Free Press, 1977), pp. 55–7.
2. Lowell Dittmer, *China's Continuous Revolution: The Post-Liberation Epoch 1949–1981* (Berkeley, University of California Press, 1987), pp. 1–2.
3. Frederick C. Teiwes, 'Establishment and consolidation of the new regime', CHC ,14,, pp. 51–143.
4. Mark Selden (ed.), *The People's Republic of China: A Documentary History of Social Change* (New York, Monthly Review Press, 1979), pp. 186–93.
5. Ezra F. Vogel, *Canton Under Communism: Programs and Politics in a Provincial Capital, 1949–1968* (Cambridge, Massachusetts, Harvard University Press, 1969), pp. 80–1.
6. Vogel, pp. 63–4.
7. Michael B. Yahuda, *China's Role in World Affairs* (London, Croom Helm, 1978), pp. 51–3.
8. Allen S. Whiting, *China Crosses the Yalu: The Decision to Enter the Korean War* (Stanford, Stanford University Press, 1960); Mineo Nakajima, 'Foreign relations: From the Korean War to the Bandung Line', CHC ,14,, pp. 259–89; Yufan Hao and Zhihai Zhai, 'China's decision to enter the Korean War: History revisited', *China Quarterly* (121), March 1990, pp. 94–115.
9. William Hinton, *Fanshen: A Documentary of Revolution in a Chinese Village* (Harmondsworth, Penguin Books, 1972), p. xvii.
10. Isabel and David Crook, *Revolution in a Chinese Village: Ten Mile Inn* (London, Routledge & Kegan Paul, 1959, 1979), pp. 130–7.
11. Meisner, pp. 100–12.
12. John Wong, *Land Reform in the People's Republic of China: Institutional Transformation in Agriculture* (New York, Praeger, 1973), p. xvi.
13. Teiwes, p. 87.
14. Adapted from Hinton, p. 699.
15. Wong, pp. 164, 246.
16. Victor D. Lippit, *Land Reform and Economic Development in China: A Study of Institutional Change and Development Finance* (New York, International Arts and Sciences Press Inc., 1974), pp. 141–6.
17. Kenneth G. Lieberthal, *Revolution and Tradition in Tientsin, 1949–1952* (Stanford, Stanford University Press, 1980), p. 2.
18. Vogel, pp. 65–6.
19. Lieberthal, pp. 125, 173.
20. Franz Schurmann, *Ideology and Organization in Communist China*, second edition (Berkeley, University of California Press, 1968), pp. 374–7.
21. Leo A. Orleans, *Every Fifth Child: The Population of China* (London, Eyre Methuen, 1972).
22. Chi Yun, 'How China Proceeds with the Task of Industrialization', 1953, quoted in Selden, pp. 290–4.
23. Stuart R. Schram, *The Political Thought of Mao Tse-tung*, revised edition, (London, Frederick A. Praeger, 1969), p. 72.
24. Alexander Eckstein, *China's Economic Revolution* (Cambridge, Cambridge University Press, 1977), pp. 50–4.
25. Stephen Andors, *China's Industrial Revolution: Politics, Planning, and Management, 1949 to the Present* (London, Martin Robertson, 1977), pp. 50–2.
26. Schurmann, pp. 253–62.

27. Thomas G. Rawski, *China's Transition to Industrialism: Producer Goods and Economic Development in the Twentieth Century* (Ann Arbor, University of Michigan Press, 1980), pp. 29, 40.

28. Adapted from Nai-ruenn Chen and Walter Galenson, *The Chinese Economy Under Communism* (Edinburgh, University of Edinburgh Press, 1969), pp. 62–3.

29. Teiwes, pp. 97–103.

30. John Cleverley, *The Schooling of China*, second edition (London, Allen & Unwin, 1991), pp. 127–35.

31. Wong, p. 188.

32. Mao Zedong, 'The question of agricultural cooperation', 31 July 1955, in J. Mason Gentzler, *Changing China: Readings in the History of China from the Opium War to the Present* (New York, Praeger, 1977), pp. 277–83.

33. Edwin E. Moise, *Land Reform in China and North Vietnam* (Chapel Hill, University of North Carolina Press, 1983), pp. 13, 269.

34. Kang Chao, *Agricultural Production in Communist China, 1949–1965* (Madison, University of Wisconsin Press, 1977), p. 55; Meisner, pp. 155–7; Teiwes, pp. 117–19.

35. Jan Myrdal, *Report from a Chinese Village* (Harmondsworth, Penguin Books, 1967), pp. 154–5.

36. Vivienne Shue, *Peasant China in Transition: The Dynamics of Development Toward Socialism, 1949–1956* (Berkeley, University of California Press, 1980), pp. 321–33.

37. Edward Friedman, Paul G. Pickowicz and Mark Selden, with Kay Ann Johnson, *Chinese Village, Socialist State* (New Haven, Yale University Press, 1991), pp. 181–2, 185–7.

38. Teiwes, p. 111.

39. Nicholas R. Lardy, 'Economic recovery and the 1st Five-Year Plan', CHC ,14,, pp. 144–84.

40. Jonathan D. Spence, *The Gate of Heavenly Peace: The Chinese and Their Revolution, 1895–1980* (London, Faber and Faber, 1982), p. 322.

41. Schram, pp. 304–12.

42. Roderick MacFarquhar (ed.), *The Hundred Flowers* (London, Stevens and Son Limited, 1960), p. 51.

43. MacFarquhar, pp. 130–41.

44. Merle Goldman, 'The Party and the intellectuals', CHC ,14,, pp. 218–58.

45. Goldman, p. 254.

46. Chen and Galenson, pp. 43–5.

47. Nicholas R. Lardy, 'The Chinese economy under stress, 1958–1965', CHC ,14,, pp. 360–97.

48. Quoted in P. Mauger et al., *Education in China* (London, Anglo-Chinese Educational Institute, 1974), p. 12.

49. Stuart Schram (ed.), *Mao Tse-tung Unrehearsed: Talks and Letters, 1956–1971* (Harmondsworth, Penguin Books, 1974), pp. 91–5.

50. Meisner, pp. 204–16.

51. Sputnik, the first satellite to orbit the earth, was launched by the Soviet Union in October 1957.

52. Friedman, Pickowicz and Selden (eds), pp. 235–8.

53. Selden, pp. 454–9.

54. William Hinton, *Shenfan* (London, Secker & Warburg, 1983), p. 205.

55. Suzanne Pepper, 'New directions in education', CHC ,14,, pp. 398–431.

56. Andors, p. 89.

57. Friedman, Pickowicz and Selden (eds), p. 233.

58. Selden, pp. 474–82.

59. Kenneth Lieberthal, 'The Great Leap Forward and the split in the Yenan leadership', CHC ,14,, pp. 293–359, at p. 316.

60. Franz Schurmann and Orville Schell (eds), *Communist China* (Harmondsworth, Penguin Books, 1968), p. 397.

61. Alexander Eckstein, Walter Galenson and Ta-chung Liu eds, *Economic Trends in Communist China* (Edinburgh, Edinburgh University Press, 1968), p. 7.

62. Eckstein, p. 59.

63. Rawski, p. 53.

64. Victor D. Lippitt, 'The Great Leap Forward reconsidered', *Modern China* ,1.1,, January 1975, pp. 92–115.

65. Craig Dietrich, *People's China: A Brief History* (Oxford, Oxford University Press, 1986), pp. 5–6.

66. James Peck, 'Revolution versus modernization and revisionism: A two-front struggle', in Victor Nee and James Peck (eds), *China's Uninterrupted Revolution: From 1840 to the Present* (New York, Pantheon Books, 1975), pp. 57–217; Dittmer, pp. 6–7.
67. Felix Greene, *The Wall Has Two Sides: A Portrait of China Today* (London, Jonathan Cape, 1962), pp. 352–3.
68. Eckstein, p. 203.
69. Jasper Becker, *Hungry Ghosts: China's Secret Famine* (London, John Murray, 1996).
70. Yahuda, pp. 51–101.
71. John Gittings, *Survey of the Sino-Soviet Dispute: A Commentary and Extracts from Recent Polemics 1963–1967* (London, Oxford University Press, 1968), pp. 73, 79–84.
72. Allen S. Whiting, 'The Sino-Soviet split', CHC ,14,, pp. 478–538, at p. 519.
73. Shahid Javed Burki, *A Study of Chinese Communes, 1965* (Cambridge, Massachusetts, Harvard University Press, 1970), pp. 35–42.
74. Lardy, 'Chinese economy under stress', pp. 391–2.
75. Meisner, p. 285. See also Suzanne Pepper.
76. Lowell Dittmer, *Liu Shao-ch'i and the Chinese Cultural Revolution: The Politics of Mass Criticism* (Berkeley, University of California Press, 1974), pp. 50–1.

Chapter Twenty-four
1. Joan Robinson, *The Cultural Revolution in China* (Harmondsworth, Penguin Books, 1969), p. 28. On the use of the term 'new class' to describe the elite of a bureaucratic Communist Party, see Milovan Djilas, *The New Class* (London, Thames and Hudson, 1957).
2. Jonathan D. Spence, *The Search for Modern China* (London, Hutchinson, 1990), p. 617.
3. Philip Bridgman, 'Mao's "Cultural Revolution": Origin and Development', in Richard Baum and Louise B. Bennett (eds), *China in Ferment: Perspectives on the Cultural Revolution* (Englewood Cliffs, Prentice-Hall Inc., 1971), pp. 17–30.
4. Gerald Tannenbaum, 'China's Cultural Revolution: Why it had to happen', and Richard Baum, 'Ideology redivivus', in Baum and Bennett (eds), pp. 60–66, 67–77.
5. Stuart Schram, *The Political Thought of Mao Tse-tung*, revised edition (New York, Frederick A. Praeger, 1969), pp. 305–6.
6. Maurice Meisner, *Mao's China: A History of the People's Republic* (New York, The Free Press, 1977), pp. 182–5.
7. Stuart Schram (ed.), *Mao Tse-tung Unrehearsed: Talks and Letters, 1956–71* (Harmondsworth, Penguin Books, 1974), p. 14.
8. Robert Jay Lifton, 'The death of the leader', in Baum and Bennett (eds), pp. 88–94.
9. Kenneth Lieberthal, 'The Great Leap Forward and the split in the Yenan leadership', CHC ,14,, pp. 293–359, at pp. 335–42; Meisner, pp. 293–5.
10. Thomas Robinson, 'China confronts the Soviet Union: Warfare and diplomacy on China's Inner Asian frontiers', CHC ,15,, pp. 218–301.
11. Suzanne Pepper, 'New directions in education', CHC ,14,, pp. 398–431.
12. Schram, *Mao Tse-tung Unrehearsed*, pp. 197–211.
13. Jack Gray and Patrick Cavendish, *Chinese Communism in Crisis: Maoism and the Cultural Revolution* (London, Pall Mall Press, 1968), p. 83.
14. Harry Harding, 'The Chinese state in crisis', CHC ,15,, pp. 107–217.
15. Lowell Dittmer, *Liu Shao-ch'i and the Chinese Cultural Revolution: The Politics of Mass Criticism* (Berkeley, University of California Press, 1974), pp. 67–118.
16. David Milton, Nancy Milton and Franz Schurmann (eds), *People's China: Social Experimentation, Politics, Entry on to the World Scene 1966–72* (Harmondsworth, Penguin Books, 1977), pp. 269–81.
17. Gordon A. Bennett and Ronald N. Montaperto, *Red Guard: The Political Biography of Dai Hsiao-ai* (London, George Allen & Unwin Ltd, 1971).
18. Harding, pp. 145–6.
19. Martin King Whyte, 'Urban life in the People's Republic', CHC ,15,), pp. 682–742, at p. 718.
20. Ezra F. Vogel, *Canton Under Communism: Programs and Politics in a Provincial Capital, 1949–1968* (Cambridge, Massachusetts, Harvard University Press, 1969), p. 328.
21. Milton et al., pp. 287–96.
22. Harding, p. 189.

23. Richard Madsen, 'The countryside under communism', CHC ,15,, pp. 619–81, at pp. 660–1.

24. Anita Chan, Richard Madsen and Jonathan Unger, *Chen Village: The Recent History of a Peasant Community in Mao's China* (Berkeley, University of California Press, 1984), pp. 169–71.

25. Dwight H. Perkins, 'China's economic policy and performance', CHC ,15,, pp. 475–539, at p. 482.

26. Charles Bettelheim, *Cultural Revolution and Industrial Organization in China: Changes in Management and the Division of Labor* (New York, Monthly Review Press, 1974), pp. 78–80.

27. Andrew Watson, 'Industrial management – experiments in mass participation', in Bill Brugger (ed.), *China: The Impact of the Cultural Revolution* (London, Croom Helm, 1978), pp. 171–202.

28. Barry Naughton, 'Industrial policy during the Cultural Revolution: Military preparation, decentralization, and leaps forward', in William A. Joseph, Christine P.W. Wong and David Zweig (eds), *New Perspectives on the Cultural Revolution* (Cambridge, Massachusetts, Harvard University Press, 1991), pp. 153–81.

29. Harding, p. 214.

30. Jonathan D. Spence, *The Gate of Heavenly Peace: The Chinese and Their Revolution, 1895–1980* (London, Faber and Faber, 1982), pp. 344–50.

31. Bennett and Montaperto, pp. 40–4.

32. Peidi Zhang, 'My days in the cowshed', *London Review of Books* , 4.20,, November 1982, pp. 13–14.

33. Dennis Woodward, 'Political power and gun barrels – the role of the PLA', in Brugger ed., pp. 71–94.

34. Roderick MacFarquhar, 'The succession to Mao and the end of Maoism', CHC ,15,, pp. 305–401.

35. Michael B. Yahuda, *China's Role in World Affairs* (London, Croom Helm, 1978), pp. 225–6.

36. Jonathan D. Pollack, 'The opening to America', CHC ,15,, pp. 402–72.

37. John Cleverley, *The Schooling of China*, second edition (London, Allen & Unwin, 1991), p. 180.

38. Cleverley, pp. 180–214.

Chapter Twenty-five

1. David Wen-wei Chang, *China Under Deng Xiaoping: Political and Economic Reform* (London, Macmillan, 1988), pp. 34–7.

2. Liu Shaoqi had first identified the 'Four Modernizations' in 1956.

3. Andrew J. Nathan, *Chinese Democracy: The Individual and the State in Twentieth Century China* (London, I.B. Tauris & Co. Ltd., 1986).

4. I.C.Y. Hsü, *The Rise of Modern China*, fifth edition (Oxford, Oxford University Press, 1995), p. 937.

5. Xinxin Zhang and Sang Ye, *Chinese Lives: An Oral History of Contemporary China* (London, Penguin Books, 1989), pp. 8–13.

6. Frank Leeming, 'Necessity, policy and opportunity in the Chinese countryside', in Denis Dwyer (ed.), *China: The Next Decades* (Harlow, Longman, 1994), pp. 77–94.

7. Ssu-yu Teng and John King Fairbank (eds), *China's Response to the West: A Documentary Survey 1839–1923* (New York, Atheneum, 1963), p. 19.

8. Maria Hsia Chang, 'Greater China and the Chinese "global tribe"', *Asian Survey* ,35.10,, October 1995, pp. 955–67.

9. Inflation fell from 25 per cent in 1994 to 7 per cent in 1996, see Avery Goldstein, 'China in 1996: Achievement, Assertiveness, Anxiety?', *Asian Survey* ,37,, January 1997, pp. 29–42.

10. John Bryan Starr, 'China in 1995: Mounting problems, waning capacity', *Asian Survey* ,36.1,, January 1996, pp. 13–24.

11. Elisabeth Croll, Delia Davin and Penny Kane (eds), *China's One-Child Family Policy* (London, Macmillan, 1985).

12. Sarah Harper, 'China's population: Prospects and policies', in Dwyer (ed.), pp. 54–76.

13. Stephen W. Mosher, *Broken Earth: The Rural Chinese* (London, Robert Hale, 1984), pp. 224–61; Norma Diamond, 'Rural collectivization and decollectivization in China – A review article', *Journal of Asian Studies* ,44.4,, August 1985, pp. 785–92.

14. James Z. Lee and Cameron D. Campbell, *Fate and Fortune in Rural China: Social Organization and Population Behavior in Liaoning 1774–1873* (Cambridge, Cambridge University Press, 1997), pp. 58–70.

15. Judith Banister, *China's Changing Population* (Stanford, Stanford University Press, 1987), pp. 220–1.

16. Sulamith Heins Potter and Jack M. Potter, *China's Peasants: The Anthropology of a Revolution* (Cambridge, Cambridge University Press, 1990), p. 207–10.

Notes

17. Judith Stacey, 'Toward a theory of family and revolution: Reflections on the Chinese case', *Social Problems* ,26.5,, June 1979, pp. 499–506.
18. Banister, p. 326.
19. Chris Mullin and Phuntsog Wangyal, *The Tibetans: Two Perspectives on Tibetan-Chinese Relations* (London, Minority Rights Group, 1983).
20. Colin Mackerras, *China's Minority Cultures: Identities and Integration since 1912* (New York, Longman, 1995).
21. Brian Hook, 'The continuity of Hong Kong: Key factors in retrospect and prospect', in Dwyer (ed.), pp. 203–21.
22. Ralph Clough, 'Taiwan under Nationalist rule, 1949–1982', CHC ,15,, pp. 815–74; Hsü, pp. 904–25.
23. David Shambaugh, 'Introduction: The emergence of "Greater China"', *China Quarterly*, 136, December 1993, pp. 653–9 and other articles in that issue.

Select Bibliography

GENERAL WORKS

Adshead, S.A.M. China in World History (London, Macmillan, 1988).

Barfield, Thomas J. The Perilous Frontier: Nomadic Empires and China (Oxford, Basil Blackwell, 1979).

Ch'en, Kenneth K.S. Buddhism in China: A Historical Survey (Princeton, Princeton University Press, 1964).

Creel, H.G. Chinese Thought: From Confucius to Mao Tse-tung (London, Methuen, 1962).

Crespigny, Rafe de. China This Century, Hong Kong, Oxford University Press, 1992

de Bary, W.T. Wing-tsit Chan and Burton Watson, Sources of Chinese Tradition, two volumes (New York, Columbia University Press, 1960).

Eastman, Lloyd E. Family, Fields, and Ancestors: Constancy and Change in China's Social and Economic History, 1550–1949, Oxford, Oxford University Press, 1988

Eastman, Lloyd E. Family, Fields and Ancestors (Oxford, Oxford University Press, 1988).

Eberhard, Wolfram A History of China, fourth edition (London, Routledge & Kegan Paul, 1977).

Eberhard, Wolfram China's Minorities: Yesterday and Today, Belmont, California, Wadsworth, 1982

Elvin, Mark The Pattern of the Chinese Past (London, Eyre, Methuen, 1973).

Fairbank, J.K. ed., The Chinese World Order (Cambridge, Massachusetts, Harvard University Press, 1968).

——. The Great Chinese Revolution, 1800–1985, New York, Harper & Row, 1986

——. China: A New History, Cambridge, Massachusetts, The Belknap Press of Harvard University Press, 1994

Gray, Jack Rebellions and Revolutions: China from the 1800s to the 1980s, Oxford, Oxford University Press, 1990

Gernet, Jacques trans. J.R. Foster, A History of Chinese Civilization (Cambridge, Cambridge University Press, 1985).

Grieder, Jerome B. Intellectuals and the State in Modern China: A Narrative History, New York, The Free Press, 1981

Harrison, James P. The Communists and Chinese Peasant Rebellions: A Study in the Rewriting of Chinese History (London, Gollancz, 1970).

Ho, Ping-ti Studies on the Population of China, 1368-1953 (Cambridge, Massachusetts, Harvard University Press, 1959, 1967).

Hucker, Charles O. China's Imperial Past: An Introduction to Chinese History and Culture (London, Duckworth, 1975).

Hsü, Immanuel C.Y. The Rise of Modern China, fifth edition, Oxford, Oxford University Press, 1995

Jagchid, Sechin and Symons, Van Jay Peace, War and Trade along the Great Wall: Nomadic Chinese Interactions through Two Millennia (Bloomington, Indiana University Press, 1989).

Liu, Wu-chi An Introduction to Chinese Literature (Bloomington, Indiana University Press, 1966).

Loewe, Michael Imperial China: The Historical Background to the Modern Age (London, George Allen and Unwin, 1966).

Mackerras, Colin Western Images of China, Hong Kong, Oxford University Press, 1989

Meskill, John T. An Introduction to Chinese Civilization (Lexington, D.C. Heath, 1973).

Michael, Franz China Through the Ages: History of a Civilization (Boulder, Westview Press, 1986).

Miyazaki, Ichisada trans. Conrad Schirokauer, China's Examination Hell: The Civil Service Examinations of Imperial China (New Haven, Yale University Press, 1981).

Myers, Ramon H. The Chinese Economy: Past and Present (Belmont, Wadsworth, 1980).

Perkins, Dwight H. Agricultural Development in China, 1368–1968 (Chicago, Aldine, 1969).

Reischauer, E.O. and Fairbank, John K. East Asia: The Great Tradition (Boston, Houghton Mifflin, 1960).

Phillips, Richard T. China since 1911, London, Macmillan, 1996

Ropp, Paul S. ed., Heritage of China: Contemporary Perspectives on Chinese Civilization (Berkeley, University of California Press, 1990).

Rossabi, Morris China and Inner Asia from 1368 to the Present Day (New York, Pica, 1975).

Select Bibliography

Sheridan, James E. *China in Disintegration: The Republican Era in Chinese History, 1912–1949*, New York, The Free Press, 1977

Smith, Richard J. *China's Cultural Heritage: The Ch'ing Dynasty, 1644–1912*, Boulder, Colorado, Westview Press, 1983

Spence, Jonathan D. *The Search for Modern China* (London, Hutchinson, 1990).

Teng, Ssu-yu and Fairbank, John King (eds). *China's Response to the West: A Documentary Survey 1839–1923*, New York, Atheneum, 1963

Wakeman, Frederic jr. *The Fall of Imperial China*, New York, The Free Press, 1975

Waldron, Arthur *The Great Wall of China: From History to Myth* (Cambridge, Cambridge University Press, 1990).

Waldron, Arthur F. x*Buddhism in Chinese History* (Stanford, Stanford University Press, 1959, 1970).

THE CAMBRIDGE HISTORY OF CHINA

Abbreviated as CHC (1), etc. General editors Denis Twitchett and John K. Fairbank, Cambridge, Cambridge University Press, 1978–

Volume 1: *The Ch'in and Han Empires, 221 BC–AD 220*, edited by Denis Twitchett and Michael Loewe, 1987, CHC (1).

Volume 3: *Sui and T'ang China, 589–906, Part I*, edited by Denis Twitchett, 1979, CHC (3).

Volume 6: *Alien Regimes and Border States, 710–1368*, edited by Denis Twitchett, 1994, CHC (6).

Volume 7: *The Ming Dynasty 1368–1644, Part 1*, edited by Frederick W. Mote and Denis Twitchett, 1988, CHC (7).

Volume 10: *Late Ch'ing, 1800–1911, Part 1*, edited by John King Fairbank, 1978, CHC (10).

Volume 11: *Late Ch'ing, 1800–1911, Part 2*, edited by John King Fairbank and Kwang-ching Liu, 1980, CHC (11).

Volume 12: *Republican China 1912–1949, Part 1*, edited by John King Fairbank, 1983, CHC (12).

Volume 13: *Republican China 1912–1949, Part 2*, edited by John King Fairbank and Albert Feuerwerker, 1986, CHC (13).

Volume 14: *The People's Republic, Part 1: The Emergence of Revolutionary China 1949–1965*, edited by Roderick MacFarquhar and John King Fairbank, 1987, CHC (14).

Volume 15: *The People's Republic, Part 2: Revolutions within the Chinese Revolution 1966–1982*, edited by Roderick MacFarquhar and John King Fairbank, CHC (156).

WORKS BY CHAPTER

Meskill, John *The Pattern of Chinese History: Cycles, Development, or Stagnation?* (Lexington, D.C. Heath, 1968).

Chapter One

Chang, Kwang-chih *The Archaeology of Ancient China*, third edition (New Haven, Yale University Press, 1977).

Ho, Ping-ti *The Cradle of the East: An Inquiry into the Indigenous Origins of Techniques and Ideas of Neolithic and Early Historic China, 5000–1000 BC* (Hong Kong, The Chinese University of Hong Kong, 1975).

Keightley, David N. ed., *The Origins of Chinese Civilization* (Berkeley, University of California Press, 1983).

Watson, William *Early Civilization in China* (London, Thames and Hudson, 1966).

Wheatley, Paul *The Pivot of the Four Corners: A Preliminary Enquiry into the Origins and Character of the Ancient Chinese City* (Edinburgh, Edinburgh University Press, 1971).

Chapter Two

Coulborn, Rushton ed., *Feudalism in History* (Hamden, Connecticut, Archon, 1965).

Creel, Herrlee G. *The Origins of Statecraft in China: Vol 1, The Western Chou Empire* (Chicago, University of Chicago Press, 1970).

Dawson, Raymond *Confucius* (Oxford, Oxford University Press, 1981).

Hsu, Cho-yun *Ancient China in Transition: An Analysis of Social Mobility, 722–222 BC* (Stanford, Stanford University Press, 1965).

Hsu, Cho-yun and Linduff, Katheryn M. *Western Chou Civilization* (New Haven, Yale University Press, 1988).

Lau, D.C. trans. and ed., *Mencius* (Harmondsworth, Penguin, 1970).

Lau, D.C. trans. and ed., *Lao Tzu: Tao Te Ching* (Harmondsworth, Penguin, 1975).
Lau, D.C. trans. and ed., *Confucius: The Analects* Harmondsworth, Penguin, 1979).
Li, Xueqin trans. K.C. Chang, *Eastern Zhou and Qin Civilizations* (New Haven, Yale University Press, 1985).

Chapter Three
Bodde, Derk *China's First Unifier: A Study of the Ch'in Dynasty as Seen in the Life of Li Ssu 280?–208 BC* (Leiden, 1938; Hong Kong, Hong Kong University Press, 1967).
Duyvendak, J.J.L. *The Book of Lord Shang: A Classic of the Chinese School of Law* (London, Probsthain, 1928).
Fong, Wen *The Great Bronze Age of China: An Exhibition from The People's Republic of China* (London, Thames and Hudson, 1980).
Li, Yu-ning *The First Emperor of China* (White Plains, New York, International Arts and Sciences Press, 1975).
Li, Yu-ning ed., *Shang Yang's Reforms and State Control in China* (White Plains, New York, M.E. Sharpe, 1977).

Chapter Four
Bielenstein, Hans *The Bureaucracy of Han Times*, (Cambridge Cambridge University Press, 1980).
Ch'ü, T'ung-tsu ed. Dull, Jack L. *Han Social Structure* (Seattle, University of Washington Press, 1972).
Crespigny, Rafe de *Northern Frontier: The Policies and Strategy of the Later Han Empire* (Canberra, Australian National University, 1984).
Hsü, Cho-yun ed. Dull, Jack L. *Han Agriculture: The Formation of Early Chinese Agrarian Economy* (206 BC–AD 220) (Seattle, University of Washington Press, 1980).
Loewe, Michael *Everyday Life in Early Imperial China During the Han Period 202 BC–AD 220* (London, Carousel, 1973).
Loewe, Michael *Crisis and Conflict in Han China 104 BC–AD 9* (London, George Allen and Unwin, 1974).
Loewe, Michael *Ways to Paradise: The Chinese Quest for Immortality* (London, George Allen and Unwin, 1979).
Loewe, Michael *Chinese Ideas of Life and Death: Faith, Myth and Reason in the Han Period* (202 BC–AD 220) (London, George Allen and Unwin, 1982).
Wang, Zhongshu trans. K.C. Chang et al, *Han Civilization* (New Haven, Yale University Press, 1982).

Chapter Five
Ebrey, Patricia Buckley *The Aristocratic Families of Early Imperial China: A Case Study of the Po-ling Ts'ui Family* (Cambridge, Cambridge University Press, 1978).
Jenner, W.J.F. *Memories of Loyang: Yang Hsüan-chih and the Lost Capital* (493–534) (Oxford, Clarendon Press, 1981).

Chapters Six to Eight
Cooper, Arthur *Li Po and Tu Fu* (Harmondsworth, Penguin, 1973).
Drake, F.S. 'Mohammedanism in the T'ang Dynasty', *Monumenta Serica*, 8, 1943, 1–40.
Ecsedy, Hilda 'Cultivators and barbarians in ancient China', *Acta Orientalia Hungaricae* (Budapest), 27, 1974, 327–49.
FitzGerald, C.P. *The Empress Wu* (London, The Cresset Press, 1956).
FitzGerald, C.P. *The Southern Expansion of the Chinese People* (London, Barrie and Jenkins, 1972).
Graham, A.C. *Poems of the Late T'ang* (Harmondsworth, Penguin, 1981).
Guisso, R.W.L. *Wu Tse-t'ien and the Politics of Legitimation in T'ang China* (Washington, Western Washington Press, 1978).
Hartman, Charles *Han Yü and the T'ang Search for Unity* (Princeton, Princeton University Press, 1986).
Hartwell, Robert M. 'Demographic, political and social transformations of China, 750–1550', *Harvard Journal of Asiatic Studies*, 42.2, December 1982, 365–442.
Hawkes, David *A Little Primer of Tu Fu* (Oxford, Clarendon Press, 1969).
Johnson, David G. *The Medieval Chinese Oligarchy* (Boulder, Westview, 1977).
Mackerras, Colin *The Uighur Empire* (744–840): *According to the T'ang Dynastic Histories* (Canberra, Australian National University, 1968).
McMullen, David *State and Scholars in T'ang China* (Cambridge, Cambridge University Press, 1988).
Owen, Stephen *The Great Age of Chinese Poetry: The High T'ang* (New Haven, Yale University Press, 1981).
Perry, John C. and Smith, Bardwell L. eds., *Essays on T'ang Society: The Interplay of Social, Political and Economic Forces* (Leiden, E.J. Brill, 1976).
Pulleyblank, Edwin G. *The Background of the Rebellion of An Lu-shan* (London, Oxford University Press, 1955).

Select Bibliography

Pulleyblank, Edwin G. 'The An Lu-shan Rebellion and the origins of chronic militarism in late Tang China', in John Curtis Perry and Bardwell L. Smith eds, *Essays on T'ang Society* (Leiden, E.J. Brill, 1976).

Reischauer, Edwin O. *Ennin's Travels in T'ang China* (New York, Ronald Press, 1955).

Reischauer, Edwin O. *Ennin's Diary: The Record of a Pilgrimage to China in Search of the Law* (New York, Ronald Press, 1955).

Robinson, G.W. *The Poems of Wang Wei* (Harmondsworth, Penguin, 1973).

Schafer, Edward H. *The Golden Peaches of Samarkand: A Study of T'ang Exotics* (Berkeley, University of California, 1963).

Schafer, Edward H. *The Vermilion Bird: T'ang Images of the South* (Berkeley, University of California, 1967).

Twitchett, Denis C. *Financial Administration under the T'ang Dynasty*, second edition (Cambridge, Cambridge University Press, 1970).

Waley, Arthur *The Life and Times of Po Chü-i 772–846 AD* (London, George Allen and Unwin, 1949).

Waley, Arthur *The Poetry and Career of Li Po, 701–762 AD* (London, George Allen and Unwin, 1950).

Waley, Arthur *The Real Tripitaka and Other Pieces* (London, George Allen and Unwin, 1952).

Waley, Arthur *Ballads and Stories from Tun-huang: An Anthology* (New York, Macmillan, 1960).

Wechsler, Howard J. *Mirror to the Son of Heaven: Wei Cheng at the Court of T'ang T'ai-tsung* (New Haven, Yale University Press, 1974).

Weinstein, Stanley *Buddhism under the T'ang* (Cambridge, Cambridge University Press, 1987).

Wiens, Herold J. *Han Chinese Expansion in South China* (Hamden, Connecticut, Shoestring, 1967).

Wright, Arthur F. 'Symbolism and function: Reflections on Ch'ang-an and other great cities', *Journal of Asian Studies* 14.4, 1965, 667–79.

Wright, Arthur F. *The Sui Dynasty* (New York, Knopf, 1978).

Wright, Arthur F. and Twitchett, Denis eds, *Perspectives on the T'ang* (New Haven, Yale University Press, 1973).

Chapter Nine

Bol, Peter K. *"This Culture of Ours": Intellectual Transitions in T'ang and Sung China* (Stanford, Stanford University Press, 1992).

Chaffee, John C. *The Thorny Gates of Learning in Sung China* (Cambridge, Cambridge University Press, 1985).

Davis, Richard L. *Court and Family in Sung China, 960–1279: Bureaucratic Success and Kinship Fortunes for the Shih of Ming-chou* (Durham, Duke University Press, 1986).

Ebrey, Patricia P. *Family and Property in Sung China: Yüan Tsai's Precepts for Social Life* (Princeton, Princeton University Press, 1984).

Gernet, Jacques trans. H.M. Wright, *Daily Life in China on the Eve of the Mongol Invasion, 1250–1276* (London, George Allen and Unwin, 1962).

Glahn, Richard von *The Country of Streams and Grottoes: Expansion and Settlement, and the Civilizing of the Sichuan Frontier in Song Times* (Cambridge, Massachusetts, Harvard University Press, 1987).

Hymes, Robert P. *Statesmen and Gentlemen: The Elite of Fu-chou, Chiang-si, in Northern and Southern Sung* (Cambridge, Cambridge University Press, 1986).

Kracke, E.A. *Civil Service in Early Sung China, 960–1067* (Cambridge, Massachusetts, Harvard University Press, 1953).

Lee, Thomas H.C. *Government, Education and Examinations in Sung China* (Hong Kong, The Chinese University Press, 1985).

Liu, James T.C. *Reform in Sung China, Wang An-shih, 1021–1086 and His New Policies* (Cambridge, Massachusetts, Harvard University Press, 1959).

Liu, James T.C. *Ou-yang Hsiu, An Eleventh Century Neo-Confucianist* (Stanford, Stanford University Press, 1967).

Liu, James T.C. *China Turning Inward: Intellectual-Political Changes in the Early Twelfth Century* (Cambridge, Massachusetts, Harvard University Press, 1988).

Liu, James T.C. and Golas, Peter J. eds., *Change in Sung China: Innovation or Renovation?* (Lexington, Massachusetts, 1969).

Lo, Winston W. *An Introduction to the Civil Service of Sung China, with Emphasis on Its Personnel Administration* (Honolulu, University of Hawaii Press, 1987).

McKnight, Brian E. *Village and Bureaucracy in Southern Sung China* (Chicago, University of Chicago Press, 1971).

Meskill, John *Wang An-shih: Practical Reformer?* (Boston, D.C. Heath, 1963).

515

Metzger, Thomas A. *Escape from Predicament: Neo-Confucianism and China's Evolving Political Culture* (New York, Columbia University Press, 1977).

Rossabi, Morris *China among Equals: The Middle Kingdom and Its Neighbors* (Berkeley, University of California Press, 1983).

Shiba, Yoshinobu trans. Mark Elvin, *Commerce and Society in Sung China* (Ann Arbor, University of Michigan, 1970).

Tao, Jing-shen *The Jurchen in Twelfth-Century China: A Study of Sinicization* (Seattle, University of Washington Press, 1976).

Wang, Gungwu *The Structure of Power in North China during the Five Dynasties* (Stanford, Stanford University Press, 1967).

Chapter Ten

Ch'en, Paul Heng-chao *Chinese Legal Tradition under the Mongols* (Princeton, Princeton University Press, 1975).

Dardess, John W. *Conquerors and Confucians: Aspects of Political Change in Late Yüan China* (New York, Columbia University Press, 1973).

Hsiao, Ch'i-ch'ing *The Military Establishment of the Yüan Dynasty* (Cambridge, Massachusetts, Harvard University Press, 1978).

Langlois, John D. ed., *China under Mongol Rule* (Princeton, Princeton University Press, 1981).

Chapter Eleven

Atwell, William 'International bullion flows and the Chinese economy circa 1530–1650', *Past and Present*, 95, May 1982, 68–90.

Atwell, William 'Some observations on the "Seventeenth-Century Crisis" in China and Japan', *Journal of Asian Studies*, 45.2, February 1986, 223–44.

Croizier, Ralph C. *Koxinga and Chinese Nationalism: History, Myth and the Hero* (Cambridge, Massachusetts, Harvard University Press, 1977).

Dardess, John *Confucianism and Autocracy: Professional Elites and the Founding of the Ming Dynasty* (Berkeley, University of California Press, 1983).

Dreyer, Edward *Early Ming China: A Political History, 1355–1435* (Stanford, Stanford University Press, 1982).

Dunstan, Helen 'The late Ming epidemics: A preliminary survey', *Ch'ing-shih wen-t'i*, 3, 1975, 1–59.

Esherick, Joseph and Rankin, Mary eds., *Chinese Local Elites and Patterns of Dominance* (Berkeley, University of California Press, 1990).

Farmer, Edward L. *Early Ming Government: The Evolution of Dual Capitals* (Cambridge, Massachusetts, Harvard University Press, 1976).

Grove, Linda and Daniels, Christian eds, *State and Society in China: Japanese Perspectives on Ming-Qing Social and Economic History* (Tokyo, University of Tokyo Press, 1984).

Huang, Philip C.C. *The Peasant Family and Rural Development in the Yangzi Delta, 1350–1988* (Stanford, Stanford University Press, 1990).

Huang, Ray *Taxation and Governmental Finance in Sixteenth-Century Ming China* (Cambridge, Cambridge University Press, 1974).

Huang, Ray *1587, A Year of No Significance: The Ming Dynasty in Decline* (New Haven, Yale University Press, 1981).

Hucker, Charles O. *The Censorial System of Ming China* (Stanford, Stanford University Press, 1966).

Hucker, C.O. ed., *Chinese Government in Ming Times: Seven Studies* (New York, Columbia University Press, 1969).

Hucker, Charles O. *The Ming Dynasty: Its Origins and Evolving Institutions* (Ann Arbor, University of Michigan Press, 1978).

Mills, J.V.G. *Ma Huan: Ying-yai sheng-lan, "The Overall Survey of the Ocean's Shores"* 1433] (Cambridge, Cambridge University Press, 1970).

Mori, Masao 'The gentry in the Ming', *Acta Asiatica*, 38, 1980, 31–53.

Parsons, James B. *The Peasant Rebellions of the Late Ming Dynasty* (Tucson, University of Arizona Press, 1970).

Struve, Lynn A. *The Southern Ming, 1644–1662* (New Haven, Yale University Press, 1984).

Wakeman, Frederic 'China and the seventeenth-century crisis', *Late Imperial China*, 7.1, June, 1986, 1–26.

Chapter Twelve

Bartlett, Beatrice S. *Monarchs and Ministers: The Grand Council in Mid-Ch'ing China* (1723–1820) (Berkeley, University of California Press, 1991).

Select Bibliography

Dennerline, Jerry *The Chia-ting Loyalists: Confucian Leadership and Social Change in Seventeenth-Century China* (New Haven, Yale University Press, 1981).

Fairbank, J.K. and Teng, S.Y. *Ch'ing Administration: Three Studies* (Cambridge, Massachusetts, Harvard University Press, 1960).

Feuerwerker, Albert *State and Society in Eighteenth-Century China: The Ch'ing Empire in its Glory* (Ann Arbor, University of Michigan Press, 1976).

Goodrich, L. Carrington *The Literary Inquisition of Ch'ien-lung* (1935, New York, Paragon Book Reprint, 1966).

Guy, R. Kent *The Emperor's Four Treasuries: Scholars and the State in the Late Ch'ien-lung Era* (Cambridge, Massachusetts, Harvard University Press, 1987).

Ho, Ping-ti 'The significance of the Ch'ing period in Chinese history', *Journal of Asian Studies*, 26.2, February 1967, 189–95.

Huang, Pei *Autocracy at Work: A Study of the Yung-cheng Period, 1723–35* (Bloomington, Indiana University Press, 1974).

Kahn, Harold L. *Monarchy in the Emperor's Eyes: Image and Reality in the Ch'ien-lung Reign* (Cambridge, Massachusetts, Harvard University Press, 1971).

Kessler, Lawrence D. 'Ethnic composition of provincial leadership during the Ch'ing dynasty, *Journal of Asian Studies*, 28.3, May 1969, 489–511.

Kessler, Lawrence D. *K'ang-hsi and the Consolidation of Ch'ing Rule, 1661–1684* (Chicago, University of Chicago Press, 1978).

Kuhn, P.A. *Soulstealers: The Chinese Sorcery Scare of 1768* (Cambridge, Cambridge University Press, 1990).

Naquin, Susan *Shantung Rebellion: The Wang Lun Uprising of 1774* (New Haven, Yale University Press, 1981).

Naquin, Susan and Rawski, E.S. *Chinese Society in the Eighteenth Century* (New Haven, Yale University Press, 1987).

Nivison, D.S. 'Ho-shen and his accusers: ideology and political behavior in the eighteenth century', in Nivison, David S. and Wright, A.F. eds., *Confucianism in Action* (Stanford, Stanford University Press, 1959).

Ropp, Paul S. *Dissent in Early Modern China: Ju-lin wai-shih and Ch'ing Social Criticism* (Ann Arbor, University of Michigan Press, 1981).

Spence, J.D. *Ts'ao Yin and the K'ang-hsi Emperor: Bondservant and Master* (New Haven, Yale University Press, 1966).

Spence, J.D. *Emperor of China: Self-Portrait of K'ang-hsi* (London, Jonathan Cape, 1974).

Spence, Jonathan and Wills, John eds., *From Ming to Ch'ing: Conquest, Region, and Continuity in Seventeenth-Century China* (New Haven, Yale University Press, 1979).

Torbert, Preston M. *The Ch'ing Imperial Household Department* (Cambridge, Massachusetts, Harvard University Press, 1978).

Wakeman, Frederic *The Great Enterprise: The Manchu Reconstruction of the Imperial Order in Seventeenth-Century China*, two volumes (Berkeley, University of California, 1985).

Wu, Silas H.L. *Communication and Imperial Control in China: Evolution of the Palace Memorial System 1693–1735* (Cambridge, Massachusetts, Harvard University Press, 1970).

Wu, Silas H.L. *Passage to Power: K'ang-hsi and His Heir Apparent, 1661–1722* (Cambridge, Massachusetts, Harvard University Press, 1979).

Zelin, Madeleine *The Magistrate's Tael: Rationalizing Fiscal Reform in Eighteenth-Century Ch'ing China* (Berkeley, University of California, 1984).

Chapter Thirteen

Bickers, Robert A. (ed.). *Ritual & Diplomacy: The Macartney Mission to China 1792–1794*, London, The British Association for Chinese Studies and Wellsweep, 1993

Chang, Chung-li. *The Chinese Gentry: Studies on Their Role in Nineteenth-Century Chinese Society*, Seattle, University of Washington Press, 1967

Ch'ü, T'ung-tsu. *Local Government in China under the Ch'ing*, Stanford, Stanford University Press, 1969

Cranmer-Byng, J.L. (ed.). *An Embassy to China: Being the Journal Kept by Lord Macartney During His Embassy to the Emperor Ch'ien-lung 1793–1794*, London, Longmans, 1962

Naquin, Susan and Rawski, Evelyn S. *Chinese Society in the Eighteenth Century*, New Haven, Yale University Press, 1987

Perdue, Peter. *Exhausting the Earth: State and Peasant in Hunan, 1500–1850*, Cambridge, Massachusetts, Harvard University Press, 1987

Watt, John. *The District Magistrate in Late Imperial China*, New York, Columbia University Press, 1972

Chapter Fourteen

Chang, Hsin-pao. *Commissioner Lin and the Opium War*, Cambridge, Massachusetts, Harvard University Press, 1964

Fairbank, John King. 'Synarchy under the Treaties', in John King Fairbank (ed.), *Chinese Thought and Institutions*, Chicago, University of Chicago Press, 1957, pp. 204–31

——. *Trade and Diplomacy on the China Coast: The Opening of the Treaty Ports 1842–1854*, revised edition, Stanford, Stanford University Press, 1969

Greenberg, Michael. *British Trade and the Opening of China 1800–42*, Cambridge, Cambridge University Press, 1951

Kuo, P.C. *A Critical Study of the First Anglo-Chinese War with Documents*, Shanghai, 1935, reprinted Taipei, Ch'eng Wen Publishing Co., 1970

Polachek, James M. *The Inner Opium War*, Cambridge, Massachusetts, Harvard University Press, 1992

Tong, Te-kong. *United States Diplomacy in China, 1844–60*, Seattle, University of Washington Press, 1964

Wakeman, Frederic jr. *Strangers at the Gate: Social Disorder in South China, 1839–1861*, Berkeley, University of California Press, 1966

——. 'The Canton Trade and the Opium War', CHC (10), pp. 163–212

Wong, J.Y. *Yeh Ming-ch'en:Viceroy of Liang Kuang 1852–8*, Cambridge, Cambridge University Press, 1976

Chapter Fifteen

Cole, James H. *The People Versus the Taipings: Bao Lisheng's 'Righteous Army of Dongan'*, Berkeley, University of California Center for Chinese Studies, 1981

Hamberg, Theodore. *The Visions of Hung Siu-Tshuen, and Origin of the Kwang-si Insurrection*, Hong Kong, China Mail Office, 1854; New York, Praeger Publishers, 1969

Jones, Susan Mann and Kuhn, Philip A. 'Dynastic decline and the roots of rebellion', CHC (10), pp. 107–62

Kuhn, Philip A. *Rebellion and Its Enemies in Late Imperial China: Militarization and Social Structure, 1794–1864*, Cambridge, Massachusetts, Harvard University Press, 1970

——. 'The Taiping rebellion', CHC (10), pp. 264–317

Michael, Franz and Chang, Chung-li. *The Taiping Rebellion: History and Documents*, 3 vols, Seattle, University of Washington Press, 1966–71

Naquin, Susan. *Millenarian Rebellion in China: The Eight Trigrams Uprising of 1813*, New Haven, Yale University Press, 1976

Perry, Elizabeth J. *Rebels and Revolutionaries in North China, 1845–1945*, Stanford, Stanford University Press, 1980

Shih, Vincent Y.C. *The Taiping Ideology: Its Sources, Interpretations, and Influences*, Seattle, University of Washington Press, 1967, 1972

Spector, Stanley. *Li Hung-chang and the Huai Army: A Study in Nineteenth-Century Chinese Regionalism*, Seattle, University of Washington Press, 1964

Spence, Jonathan. *God's Chinese Son: The Taiping Heavenly Kingdom of Hong Xiuquan*, London, Harper Collins, 1996

Wakeman, Frederic jr. *Strangers at the Gate: Social Disorder in South China, 1839–1861*, Berkeley, University of California Press, 1966

Chapter Sixteen

Bernhardt, Kathryn. *Rents, Taxes, and Peasant Resistance: The Lower Yangzi Region, 1840–1950*, Stanford, Stanford University Press, 1992

Chan, Wellington K.K. 'Government, merchants and industry', CHC (11), pp. 416–62

Chu, Samuel C. and Liu, Kwang-ching (eds). *Li Hung-chang and China's Early Modernization*, New York, M.E. Sharpe Inc., 1994

Select Bibliography

Feuerwerker, Albert. *China's Early Industrialization: Sheng Hsuan-huai (1844–1916) and Mandarin Enterprise*, Cambridge, Massachusetts, Harvard University Press, 1958, reprinted New York, Athenaeum, 1970

Frodsham, J.D. *The First Chinese Embassy to the West: The Journals of Kuo Sung-t'ao, Liu Hsi-hung and Chang Te-yi*, Oxford, Clarendon Press, 1974

Kennedy, Thomas L. *The Arms of Kiangnan: Modernization in the Chinese Ordnance Industry, 1860–1895*, Boulder, Westview Press, 1978

Kuo, Ting-yee and Liu, Kwang-ching. 'Self-strengthening: the pursuit of Western technology', CHC (10), pp. 491–542

Leonard, Jane Kate and Watt, John R. (eds). *To Achieve Security and Wealth: The Qing Imperial State and the Economy, 1644–1911*, Ithaca, Cornell University Press, 1992

Liu, Kwang-ching. 'The Ch'ing Restoration', CHC (10), pp. 409–90

Ocko, Jonathan. *Bureaucratic Reform in Provincial China: Ting Jih-ch'ang in Restoration Kiangsu, 1867–1870*, Cambridge, Massachusetts, Harvard University Press, 1983

Polachek, James. 'Gentry hegemony: Soochow in the T'ung-chih Restoration', in Frederic Wakeman jr and Carolyn Grant (eds), *Conflict and Control in Late Imperial China*, Berkeley, University of California Press, 1975, pp. 211–56

Rankin, Mary Backus. *Elite Activism and Political Transformation in China: Zhejiang Province, 1865–1911*, Stanford, Stanford University Press, 1986

Wright, Mary Clabaugh. *The Last Stand of Chinese Conservatism: The T'ung-chih Restoration, 1862–1874*, second edition, Stanford, Stanford University Press, 1962

Chapter Seventeen

Barnett, Susan Wilson and Fairbank, John King (eds). *Christianity in China: Early Protestant Missionary Writings*, Cambridge, Massachusetts, Harvard University Press, 1985

Cohen, Paul A. *China and Christianity: The Missionary Movement and the Growth of Chinese Antiforeignism 1860–1870*, Cambridge, Massachusetts, Harvard University Press, 1963, 1967

——. 'Christian missions and their impact to 1900', CHC (10), pp. 543–90

Eastman, Lloyd E. *Throne and Mandarins: China's Search for a Policy during the Sino-French Controversy 1880–1885*, Cambridge, Massachusetts, Harvard University Press, 1967

Eng, Robert Y. *Economic Imperialism in China: Silk Production and Exports, 1861–1932*, Berkeley, University of California Press, 1986

Hao, Yen-p'ing. *The Comprador in Nineteenth Century China: Bridge Between East and West*, Cambridge, Massachusetts, Harvard University Press, 1970

Hou, Chi-ming. *Foreign Investment and Economic Development in China 1840–1937*, Cambridge, Massachusetts, Harvard University Press, 1965, 1973

Hsü, Immanuel C.Y. 'Late Ch'ing foreign relations, 1866–1905', CHC (11), pp. 70–141

Kim, Key-hiuk. *The Last Phase of the East Asian World Order: Korea, Japan, and the Chinese Empire, 1860–1882*, Berkeley, University of California Press, 1980

Lee, Robert. *France and the Exploitation of China 1885–1901*, Hong Kong, Oxford University Press, 1989

Lutz, Jessie G. (ed.). *Christian Missions in China: Evangelists of What?*, Boston, D.C. Heath and Company, 1965

Murphey, Rhoads. *The Treaty Ports and China's Modernization: What Went Wrong?*, Ann Arbor, University of Michigan, 1970

Thomas, Stephen C. *Foreign Intervention and China's Industrial Development, 1870–1911*, Boulder, Westview, 1984

Chapter Eighteen

Ayers, William. *Chang Chih-tung and Educational Reform in China*, Cambridge, Massachusetts, Harvard University Press, 1971

Bastid, Marianne. *Educational Reform in Early Twentieth-Century China*, Ann Arbor, University of Michigan Press, 1988

Bays, Daniel H. *China Enters the Twentieth Century: Chang Chih-tung and the Issues of a New Age, 1895–1909*, Ann Arbor, University of Michigan Press, 1978

Borthwick, Sally. *Education and Social Change in China: The Beginnings of the Modern Era*, Stanford, Hoover Institution Press, 1983

Buck, David D. (ed.). *Recent Chinese Studies of the Boxer Movement*, New York, M.E. Sharpe, 1987

Chang, Hao. 'Intellectual change and the reform movement, 1890–8', CHC (11), pp. 274–338

Cohen, Paul A. *Between Tradition and Modernity: Wang T'ao and Reform in Late Ch'ing China*, Cambridge, Massachusetts, Harvard University Press, 1974, 1987

Esherick, Joseph W. *The Origins of the Boxer Uprising*, Berkeley, University of California Press, 1987

Franke, Wolfgang. *The Reform and Abolition of the Traditional Chinese Examination System*, Cambridge, Massachusetts, Harvard University Press, 1960

Fung, Edmund S.K. *The Military Dimension of the Chinese Revolution: The New Army and Its Role in the Revolution of 1911*, Canberra, Australian National University Press, 1980

Ichiko, Chuzo. 'Political and institutional reform, 1901–1911', CHC (11), pp. 375–415

Kwong, Luke S.K. *A Mosaic of the Hundred Days: Personalities, Politics, and Ideas of 1898*, Cambridge, Massachusetts, Harvard University Press, 1984

Lewis, Charlton M. *Prologue to the Chinese Revolution: The Transformation of Ideas and Institutions in Hunan Province, 1891–1907*, Cambridge, Massachusetts, Harvard University Press, 1976

Schrecker, John E. *Imperialism and Chinese Nationalism: Germany in Shantung*, Cambridge, Massachusetts, Harvard University Press, 1971

Schwartz, Benjamin. *In Search of Wealth and Power: Yen Fu and the West*, Cambridge, Massachusetts, Harvard University Press, 1964

Chapter Nineteen

'A symposium on the 1911 revolution', *Modern China* (2.2), April 1976, pp. 139–226

Bastid-Bruguière, Marianne. 'Currents of social change', CHC (11), pp. 535–602

Bergère, Marie-Claire. *The Golden Age of the Chinese Bourgeoisie 1911–1937*, Cambridge, Cambridge University Press, 1989

Ch'en, Jerome. *Yuan Shih-k'ai, 1859–1916: Brutus Assumes the Purple*, second edition, London, George Allen & Unwin Ltd, 1972

Crossley, Pamela Kyle. *Orphan Warriors: Three Manchu Generations and the End of the Qing World*, Princeton, Princeton University Press, 1990

Esherick, Joseph W. *Reform and Revolution in China: The 1911 Revolution in Hunan and Hubei*, Berkeley, University of California Press, 1976

Eto, Shinkichi and Schiffrin, Harold Z. (eds). *The 1911 Revolution in China: Interpretative Essays*, Tokyo, University of Tokyo Press, 1984

Gasster, Michael. 'The republican revolutionary movement', CHC (11), pp. 463–534

Jansen, Marius. 'Japan and the Chinese revolution of 1911', CHC (11), pp. 339–74

Rankin, Mary Backus. *Elite Activism and Political Transformation in China: Zhejiang Province, 1865–1911*, Stanford, Stanford University Press, 1986

Rhoads, Edward J.M. *China's Republican Revolution: The Case of Kwangtung, 1895–1913*, Cambridge, Massachusetts, Harvard University Press, 1975

Schiffrin, Harold. *Sun Yat-sen and the Origins of the Chinese Revolution*, Berkeley, University of California Press, 1970

Wilbur, C. Martin. *Sun Yat-sen: Frustrated Patriot*, New York, Columbia University Press, 1976

Wright, Mary Clabaugh (ed.). *China in Revolution: The First Phase, 1900–1913*, New Haven, Yale University Press, 1973

Chapter Twenty

Ch'en, Jerome. 'The Chinese Communist movement to 1927', CHC (13), pp. 789–870

Chen, Joseph T. *The May Fourth Movement in Shanghai: The Making of a Social Movement in Modern China*, Leiden, E.J. Brill, 1971

Chesneaux, Jean. *The Chinese Labor Movement 1919–1927*, Stanford, Stanford University Press, 1968

Chow, Tse-tsung. *The May Fourth Movement: Intellectual Revolution in Modern China*, Cambridge, Massachusetts, Harvard University Press, 1960, 1967

Dirlik, Arif. *The Origins of Chinese Communism*, Oxford, Oxford University Press, 1989

Select Bibliography

Feuerwerker, Albert. 'Economic trends, 1912–1949', CHC (12), pp. 28–127

Galbiati, Fernando. P'eng P'ai and the Hai-lu-feng Soviet, Stanford, Stanford University Press, 1985

Gillin, Donald G. Warlord: Yen Hsi-shan in Shansi Province, 1911–1949, Princeton, Princeton University Press, 1967

Hofheinz, Roy jr. The Broken Wave: The Chinese Communist Peasant Movement, 1922–1928, Cambridge, Massachusetts, Harvard University Press, 1977

Kapp, Robert A. Szechwan and the Chinese Republic: Provincial Militarism and Central Power, 1911–1938, New Haven, Yale University Press, 1973

Lary, Diana. Warlord Soldiers: Chinese Common Soldiers 1911–1937, New York, Cambridge University Press, 1985

Liew, K.S. Struggle for Democracy: Sung Chiao-jen and the 1911 Chinese Revolution, Berkeley, University of California Press, 1971

Lin, Yü-sheng. The Crisis of Chinese Consciousness: Radical Anti-traditionalism in the May Fourth Era, Madison, University of Wisconsin Press, 1979

McCormack, Gavan. Chang Tso-lin in Northeast China, 1911–1928: China, Japan and the Manchurian Idea, Folkestone, Dawson, 1977

Meisner, Maurice. Li Ta-chao and the Origins of Chinese Marxism, Cambridge, Massachusetts, Harvard University Press, 1967

Schwartz, Benjamin I. (ed.). Reflections on the May Fourth Movement: A Symposium, Cambridge, Massachusetts, Harvard University Press, 1972

Sheridan, James E. Chinese Warlord: The Career of Feng Yü-hsiang, Stanford, Stanford University Press, 1966

——. 'The warlord era: Politics and militarism under the Peking government, 1916–1928', CHC (12), pp. 284–321

Sutton, Donald S. Provincial Militarism and the Chinese Republic: The Yunnan Army, 1905–1925, Ann Arbor, University of Michigan Press, 1980

Waldron, Arthur. From War to Nationalism: China's Turning Point, 1924–1925, Cambridge, Cambridge University Press, 1995

Wilbur, C. Martin. 'Military separatism and the process of unification under the Nationalist regime, 1922–1937', in Ping-ti Ho and Tang Tsou (eds), China in Crisis, Chicago, University of Chicago Press, 1968, vol. I, part 1, pp. 203–63

——. The Nationalist Revolution in China, 1923–1928 Cambridge, Cambridge University Press, 1984

Wou, Odoric Y.K. Militarism in Modern China: The Career of Wu P'ei-fu, 1916–1939, Canberra, Australian National University Press, 1978

Young, Ernest P. The Presidency of Yuan Shih-k'ai: Liberalism and Dictatorship in Early Republican China, Ann Arbor, University of Michigan Press, 1977

——. 'Politics in the aftermath of revolution: The era of Yuan Shih-k'ai, 1912–1916', CHC (12), pp. 209–55

Chapter Twenty-One

Ash, Robert. Land Tenure in Pre-Revolutionary China: Kiangsu Province in the 1920s and 1930s, London, Contemporary China Institute, School of Oriental and African Studies, University of London, 1976

Bedeski, Robert E. State Building in Modern China: The Kuomintang in the Prewar Period, Berkeley, China Research Monographs 18, Institute of East Asian Studies, University of California, 1981

Ch'en, Jerome. 'The Communist movement 1927–1937', CHC (13), pp. 168–229

Coble, Parks M. The Shanghai Capitalists and the Nationalist Government, 1927–1937, Cambridge, Massachusetts, Harvard University Press, 1986

Eastman, Lloyd E. The Abortive Revolution: China under Nationalist Rule, 1927–1937, Cambridge, Massachusetts, Harvard University Press, 1974

Fewsmith, Joseph. Party, State and Local Elites in Republican China: Merchant Organizations and Politics in Shanghai, 1890–1930, Honolulu, University of Hawaii Press, 1985

Hsiao, Tso-liang. The Land Revolution in China, 1930–1934: A Study of Documents, Seattle, University of Washington Press, 1969

Jordan, Donald A. The Northern Expedition: China's National Revolution of 1926–1928, Honolulu, University of Hawaii Press, 1976

Lötveit, Trygve. *Chinese Communism, 1931–1934: Experience in Civil Government*, second edition, Copenhagen, Curzon Press, 1978

Paauw, Douglas S. 'The Kuomintang and economic stagnation, 1928–1937', in Albert Feuerwerker (ed.), *Modern China*, Englewood Cliffs, Prentice-Hall Inc., 1964, pp. 126–35

Perry, Elizabeth J. *Shanghai on Strike: The Politics of Chinese Labor*, Cambridge, Cambridge University Press, 1995

Schram, Stuart. *Mao Tse-tung*, Harmondsworth, Penguin Books, 1967

Thompson, Roger (ed. and tr.). *Mao Zedong: Report from Xunwu*, Stanford, Stanford University Press, 1990

Wilson, Dick. *The Long March: The Epic of Chinese Communism's Survival*, Harmondsworth, Penguin Books, 1971, 1977

Young, Arthur N. *China's Nation-Building Effort, 1927–1937: The Financial and Economic Record*, Stanford, Stanford University, Hoover Institution Press, 1971

Chapter Twenty-Two

Boyle, John Hunter. *China and Japan at War, 1937–45: The Politics of Collaboration*, Stanford, Stanford University Press, 1972

Chen, Yung-fa. *Making Revolution: The Communist Movement in Eastern and Central China, 1937–1945*, Berkeley, University of California Press, 1986

Ch'i, Hsi-sheng. *Nationalist China at War: Military Defeats and Political Collapse, 1937–1945*, Ann Arbor, University of Michigan Press, 1982

Compton, Boyd. *Mao's China: Party Reform Documents, 1942–44*, Seattle, University of Washington Press, 1952

Eastman, Lloyd E. *Seeds of Destruction: Nationalist China in War and Revolution 1937–1949*, Stanford, Stanford University Press, 1984

——. 'Nationalist China during the Sino-Japanese War 1937–1945', CHC (13), pp. 547–608

Hsiung, James C. and Levine, Steven I. (eds). *China's Bitter Victory: The War with Japan 1937–1945*, New York, M.E. Sharpe Inc., 1992

Johnson, Chalmers A. *Peasant Nationalism and Communist Power: The Emergence of Revolutionary China 1937–1945*, Stanford, Stanford University Press, 1962

Levine, Steven I. *Anvil of Victory: The Communist Revolution in Manchuria, 1945–1948*, New York, Columbia University Press, 1987

Pepper, Suzanne. *Civil War in China: The Political Struggle, 1945–1949*, Berkeley, University of California Press, 1978, 1980

——. 'The KMT-CCP conflict 1945–1949', CHC (13), pp. 723–88

Schram, Stuart. 'Mao Tse-tung's thought to 1949', CHC (13), pp. 789–870

Selden, Mark. *The Yenan Way in Revolutionary China*, Cambridge, Massachusetts, Harvard University Press, 1971, 1974

Van Slyke, Lyman. 'The Chinese Communist movement during the Sino-Japanese War 1937–1945', CHC (13), pp. 609–722

Young, Arthur N. *China and the Helping Hand 1937–1945*, Cambridge, Massachusetts, Harvard University Press, 1963

Chapter Twenty-Three

Becker, Jasper. *Hungry Ghosts: China's Secret Famine*, London, John Murray, 1996

Dittmer, Lowell. *China's Continuous Revolution: The Post-Liberation Epoch 1949–1981*, Berkeley, University of California Press, 1987

Eckstein, Alexander. *China's Economic Revolution*, Cambridge, Cambridge University Press, 1977

Friedman, Edward, Pickowicz, Paul G. and Selden, Mark, with Johnson, Kay Ann. *Chinese Village, Socialist State*, New Haven, Yale University Press, 1991

Gittings, John. *Survey of the Sino-Soviet Dispute: A Commentary and Extracts from Recent Polemics 1963–1967*, London, Oxford University Press, 1968

Goldman, Merle. 'The Party and the intellectuals', CHC (14), 218–58

Hinton, William. *Fanshen: A Documentary of Revolution in a Chinese Village*, Harmondsworth, Penguin Books, 1972

Lardy, Nicholas R. 'Economic recovery and the 1st Five-Year Plan', CHC (14), pp. 144–84

——. 'The Chinese economy under stress, 1958–1965', CHC (14), pp. 360–97

Select Bibliography

Lieberthal, Kenneth G. *Revolution and Tradition in Tientsin, 1949–1952*, Stanford, Stanford University Press, 1980

Meisner, Maurice. *Mao's China: A History of the People's Republic*, New York, The Free Press, 1977

Shue, Vivienne. *Peasant China in Transition: The Dynamics of Development Toward Socialism, 1949–1956*, Berkeley, University of California Press, 1980

Teiwes, Frederick C. 'Establishment and consolidation of the new regime', CHC (14), pp. 51–143

Vogel, Ezra F. *Canton under Communism: Programs and Politics in a Provincial Capital, 1949–1968*, Cambridge, Massachusetts, Harvard University Press, 1969

Whiting, Allen S. 'The Sino-Soviet split', CHC (14), pp. 478–538

Chapter Twenty-Four

Baum, Richard and Bennett, Louise B. (eds). *China in Ferment: Perspectives on the Cultural Revolution*, Englewood Cliffs, Prentice-Hall Inc., 1971

Bennett, Gordon A. and Montaperto, Ronald N. *Red Guard: The Political Biography of Dai Hsiao-ai*, London, George Allen & Unwin Ltd, 1971

Chan, Anita, Madsen, Richard and Unger, Jonathan. *Chen Village: The Recent History of a Peasant Community in Mao's China*, Berkeley, University of California Press, 1984

Dittmer, Lowell. *Liu Shao-ch'i and the Chinese Cultural Revolution: The Politics of Mass Criticism*, Berkeley, University of California Press, 1974

Harding, Harry. 'The Chinese state in crisis,' CHC (15), pp. 107–217

Joseph, William A., Wong, Christine P.W. and Zweig, David (eds). *New Perspectives on the Cultural Revolution*, Cambridge, Massachusetts, Harvard University Press, 1991

MacFarquhar, Roderick. 'The succession to Mao and the end of Maoism', CHC (15), pp. 305–401

Schram, Stuart (ed.). *Mao Tse-tung Unrehearsed: Talks and Letters, 1956–1971*, Harmondsworth, Penguin Books, 1974

Chapter Twenty-Five

Banister, Judith. *China's Changing Population*, Stanford, Stanford University Press, 1987

Clough, Ralph. 'Taiwan under Nationalist rule, 1949–1982', CHC (15), pp. 815–74

Croll, Elizabeth, Davin, Delia and Kane, Penny (eds). *China's One Child Family Policy*, London, Macmillan, 1985

Dwyer, Denis (ed.). *China: The Next Decades*, Harlow, Longman, 1994

Mackerras, Colin. *China's Minority Cultures: Identities and Integration since 1912*, New York, Longman, 1995

Nathan, Andrew J. *Chinese Democracy: The Individual and the State in Twentieth Century China*, London, I.B. Tauris and Co. Ltd, 1986

Potter, Sulamith Heins and Potter, Jack M. *China's Peasants: The Anthropology of a Revolution*, Cambridge, Cambridge University Press, 1990

Wolf, Margery. *Revolution Postponed: Women in Contemporary China*, Stanford, Stanford University Press, 1985

Zhang, Xinxin and Sang, Ye, *Chinese Lives: An Oral History of Contemporary China*, London, Penguin Books, 1989

INDEX

Index

Index

Index

Index

Index